F.B. Eyes

F.B. Eyes

How
J. Edgar Hoover's
Ghostreaders
Framed
African American
Literature

WILLIAM J. MAXWELL

PRINCETON UNIVERSITY PRESS
Princeton and Oxford

Copyright © 2015 by Princeton University Press

Published by Princeton University Press, 41 William Street, Princeton, New Jersey 08540

In the United Kingdom: Princeton University Press, 6 Oxford Street, Woodstock, Oxfordshire OX20 1TW

press.princeton.edu

Jacket art © James Wechsler, *Freedom of Information: Paul Robeson, 3.124*, 2006. Acrylic and India ink on paper, 28″ x 20.″ Jacket design by Pamela Schnitter.

All Rights Reserved

ISBN 978–0–691–13020–0

Library of Congress Control Number: 2014933936

British Library Cataloging-in-Publication Data is available

This book has been composed in Minion Pro and Ideal Sans

Printed on acid-free paper. ∞

Printed in the United States of America

10 9 8 7 6 5 4 3 2 1

For Dad, the Third (1932–2011), and Bix, the Fifth (2004–)

The title of this book is inspired by Richard Wright's poem "The FB Eye Blues."

That old FB eye
Tied a bell to my bed stall
Said old FB eye
Tied a bell to my bed stall
Each time I love my baby, gover'ment knows it all.

Woke up this morning
FB eye under my bed
Said I woke up this morning
FB eye under my bed
Told me all I dreamed last night, every word I said.

Everywhere I look, Lord
I see FB eyes
Said every place I look, Lord
I find FB eyes
I'm getting sick and tired of gover'ment spies.

—Richard Wright, "The FB Eye Blues" (1949)

Contents

Acknowledgments   xi

Introduction   1
  The FBI against and for African American Literature   1
  The Files and the FOIA   7
  Five Theses and the Way Forward   15

Part One/Thesis One: The Birth of the Bureau, Coupled with the Birth of J. Edgar Hoover, Ensured the FBI's Attention to African American Literature   25
  The Bureau before Hoover   29
  Hoover before the Bureau   35
  Bureau of Letters: Lit.-Cop Federalism, the Hoover Raids, and the
      Harlem Renaissance   42

Part Two/Thesis Two: The FBI's Aggressive Filing and Long Study of African American Writers Was Tightly Bound to the Agency's Successful Evolution under Hoover   59
  Flatfoot Montage: The Genre of the Counterliterary FBI File   63
  The Counterliterary State and the Charismatic Bureaucracy:
      Trimming the First Amendment, Fencing the Harlem Renaissance   68
  Persons to *Racial Conditions*: Literary G-Men and FBI
      Counterliterature from the New Deal to the Second World War   76
  Afro-Loyalty and Custodial Detention: Files of World War II   85
  Total Literary Awareness: Files of the Cold War   94
  COINTELPRO Minstrelsy: Files of Black Power   107

Part Three/Thesis Three: The FBI Is Perhaps the Most Dedicated and Influential Forgotten Critic of African American Literature   127
  Reading Like a CIA Agent   131
  Reading Like an FBI Agent   141

Critics behind the Bureau Curtain: Meet Robert Adger Bowen
and William C. Sullivan   150

Ask Dr. Hoover: Model Citizen Criticism and the FBI's
Interpretive Oracle   165

**Part Four/Thesis Four: The FBI Helped to Define the
Twentieth-Century Black Atlantic, Both Blocking and Forcing
Its Flows**   175

The State in the Nation-State; the State of the Transnational Turn   180

The State of Black Transnationalism; the State in the Black Atlantic   186

Checking Diasporan ID: Hostile Translation and the Passport Office   195

State-Sponsored Transnationalism: The Stop Notice and the Travel
Bureau   205

Jazz Ambassadors versus Literary Escapees   212

**Part Five/Thesis Five: Consciousness of FBI Ghostreading Fills
a Deep and Characteristic Vein of African American Literature**   215

Reading Ghostreading in the Harlem Renaissance: New Negro
Journalists and Claude McKay   225

Invisible G-Men En Route to the Cold War: George Schuyler,
Langston Hughes, and Ralph Ellison   232

Mysteries and Antifiles of Black Paris: Richard Wright, William
Gardner Smith, and Chester Himes   243

Black Arts Antifiles and the "Hoover Poem": John A. Williams,
James Baldwin, Sam Greenlee, Melvin Van Peebles, Ishmael Reed,
Amiri Baraka, Nikki Giovanni, and Sonia Sanchez   259

Bureau Writing after Hoover: Dudley Randall, Ai, Audre Lorde,
Danzy Senna, and Gloria Naylor   269

**Appendix: FOIA Requests for FBI Files on African American Authors
Active from 1919 to 1972**   277

Notes   285
Works Cited   315
Index   343

Acknowledgments

This book was not ghostwritten. If it had been, it would not have taken so long. All the same, I have had many virtual coauthors since 2006. First among them is the FBI (the post-Hoover one, that is), which responded helpfully to scores of FOIA requests and less official questions. My thanks above all to Kirk Cromer, Dr. John F. Fox Jr., David Sobonya, and the staff of the Record/Information Dissemination Section. Other archives, academic and governmental, provided needed information and unexpected documents: the Beinecke Rare Book and Manuscript Library at Yale University; the Clemson University Special Collections Library; the Library of Congress; the Moorland-Spingarn Research Center at Howard University; the National Archives in both Washington, D.C., and College Park, Maryland; the Special Collections Department at the J. Willard Marriott Library at the University of Utah; and the home team libraries of Washington University in St. Louis and the University of Illinois, Urbana-Champaign. My visits to some of these collections were supported by two timely institutional patrons, namely, the Center for the Humanities Faculty Fellowship program at Washington University and the University Scholars program at the University of Illinois.

The good people of Princeton University Press embraced this book from the very beginning, even before the FOIA requests piled high. In particular, I've benefited from the quick and reassuring work of Brigitta van Rheinberg, Ellen Foos, Juliana Fidler, Larissa Klein, Bob Bettendorf, Jenny Wolkowicki, and Claudia Acevedo, who deserves a fireproof raise. Two supervising editors, Hanne Winarsky and Alison MacKeen, improved my prose with inspiring blue pencils (both put the edit back in editing). My editor during the production process, Anne Savarese, graciously inherited both the tome and its author. Kathleen Kageff proved that copyediting can invigorate, while Thomas Broughton-Willett's index discovered what the book actually said. The manuscript readers chosen by the press—George Hutchinson and an anonymous reader at the start, and two anonymous readers at the close—encouraged and cautioned in good measure.

Friends, coworkers, and less indulgent audiences did some editing of their own. At the University of Illinois, numerous colleagues read early drafts or made them possible, including Nina Baym, Matti Bunzl, Martin Camargo, Jed Esty, Chris Freeburg, Jim Hansen, Matt Hart, Gordon Hutner, Trish Loughran,

Justine Murison, Carol Neely, Cary Nelson, Curtis Perry, Audrey Petty, Rick Powers, Cathy Prendergast, Siobhan Somerville, Mark Thompson, and David Wright. Stephanie Foote, Bob Parker, Michael Rothberg, Cristina Stanciu, and Joe Valente were (and remain) comrades-in-arms. At Washington University in St. Louis, Gerald Early and Rafia Zafar, my senior colleagues in African American literature and African American Studies, showed me the ropes while helping me finish old jobs. A new English department seamlessly welcomed my work, with special assistance from Miriam Bailin, Mary Jo Bang, Guinn Batten, Dillon Brown, Wayne Fields, Dan Grausam, Dillon Johnston, David Lawton, Joe Loewenstein, Marina MacKay, Bill McKelvy, Ed McPherson, Steven Meyer, Bob Milder, Anca Parvulescu, Carl Phillips, Vivian Pollak, Jessica Rosenfeld, Wolfram Schmidgen, and Vince Sherry. Gerald Early, Jian Leng, Barb Liebmann, Erin McGlothlin, and Elzbieta Sklodowska made my stint at the Center for the Humanities a productive one, while Iver Bernstein taught me the ways of American Culture Studies. Jean Allman, Adrienne Davis, Garrett Duncan, Andrea Friedman, Ron Himes, Ignacio Infante, Angela Miller, Shanti Parikh, Gaylyn Studlar, and Rebecca Wanzo helped me build bridges across campus, not too large a place to begin with. Paulo Loonin, Jaydee Lee, and Digital Librarian Shannon Davis skillfully built the book's website, "The F.B. Eyes Digital Archive," with crucial sponsorship from Joe Loewenstein, Douglas Knox, and the Humanities Digital Workshop. My graduate and undergraduate students at Wash. U.—as good as advertised—reenergized me when necessary. So did Kathy Schneider, administrator and pal extraordinaire. Campuses and conferences beyond St. Louis and Urbana-Champaign asked me to present ideas and then to change them. Cheers to the organizers of sessions for the American Studies Association, the Modern Language Association, the Modernist Studies Association, and the Richard Wright Centennial Conference in Paris. I owe even more to the colleagues who invited me to deliver papers at Ohio State, Ohio University, Penn State, Smith College, Southern Illinois University, Stanford University, the University of Maryland, and the University of North Carolina.

Then there are the colleagues here and there whom I talk to less formally, but whose effects on my work are most serious. Gary Holcomb, George Hutchinson, Jim Smethurst, Alan Wald, and Mary Helen Washington have been rocks, though they may disagree with the foundations of what follows. The list of other far-flung scholars who did the book good is long. It begins with Michael Bérubé, Sara Blair, Melba Boyd, Jeremy Braddock, Caleb Crane, Claire Culleton, Brian Dolinar, Eve Dunbar, Brent Edwards, Barbara Foley, Danny Franken, Scott Herring, Robert Hill, Marty Hipsky, Caren Irr, Lawrence Jackson, Gene

Jarrett, Benjy Kahan, Betsy Klimasmith, Aaron Lecklider, Karen Leick, Robert Levine, Eric Lott, John Lowe, Kathlene McDonald, Adam McKible, Jim Miller, Joycelyn Moody, Aldon Nielson, Evie Shockley, Amrit Singh, Michelle Stephens, Michael Thurston, Priscilla Wald, Maurice Wallace, Ken Warren, Mark Whalan, and John Young. Last and hardly least, my thanks to Professor Sonia Sanchez and to the late poet-teachers Amiri Baraka and Lorenzo Thomas, veterans of the history approached in this book who opened up poems or FBI files or more reliable lines of communication.

Members of my family, the scholars included, do not appear in the index but probably should. The Walkers and the Riegers always asked how the writing was going and accepted the answers; the Maxwell-Binders generously hosted twice-a-year mellowings in the capital of Texas. Meanwhile, at home in St. Louis, Elvis is still king, Bix makes beautiful music, and Jules remains the soul of grace and intelligence. Though it pales in comparison, the best of this book comes from them.

Brief sections of this book appeared in earlier forms in the following: as "Editorial Federalism" in *Publishing Blackness: Textual Constructions of Race Since 1850*, edited by George Hutchinson and John K. Young and published by the University of Michigan Press (copyright © 2013 by the University of Michigan); as "Total Literary Awareness" in *American Literature and Culture in an Age of Cold War*, edited by Steven Belletto and Daniel Grausam and published by the University of Iowa Press (copyright © 2012 by the University of Iowa Press; used with permission); as "Wright among the G-Men" in *Richard Wright: New Readings in the Twenty-First Century*, edited by Alice Mikal Craven and William E. Dow and published by Palgrave Macmillan in 2011 (reproduced with permission of Palgrave Macmillan; available from: http://www.palgrave-connect.com/pc/doifinder/10.1057/9780230340237); as "Ghostreaders and Diaspora Writers" in *Modernism on File: Writers, Artists, and the FBI, 1920–1950*, edited by Claire A. Culleton and Karen Leick and published by Palgrave in 2008 (reproduced with permission of Palgrave Macmillan; available from: http://www.palgraveconnect.com/pc/doifinder/10.1057/9780230610392); and as "F.B. Eyes" in *Left of the Color Line: Race, Radicalism, and Twentieth-Century Literature of the United States*, edited by Bill V. Mullen and James Smethurst and published by the University of North Carolina Press (copyright © 2003 by the University of North Carolina Press; used by permission of the publisher; www.uncpress.unc.edu).

Richard Wright's poem "The FB Eye Blues" from *The Richard Wright Reader*, published in 1978 by Harper and Row, is copyright © 1978 by Ellen Wright; reprinted in part here with permission of John Hawkins & Associates, Inc., and the Estate of Richard Wright. Excerpt from "Hoover Trismegistus," copyright © 1993 by Ai, from *The Collected Poems of Ai*, is used by permission of W. W. Norton & Company, Inc. Excerpts from "A Short Essay of Affirmation Explaining Why (With Apologies to the Federal Bureau of Investigation)" from *The Collected Poetry of Nikki Giovanni, 1968–1998*, by Nikki Giovanni, are copyright © 2003 by Nikki Giovanni; chronology and notes copyright © by Virginia C. Fowler; reprinted here by permission of HarperCollins Publishers. Dudley Randall's poems "F.B.I. Memo" and "Informer" from *Roses and Revolutions: The Selected Writings of Dudley Randall* (Detroit: Wayne State University Press, 2009) are reprinted by permission of the Dudley Randall Literary Estate. Excerpts from Sonia Sanchez's poem "A Modern Song of the F.B.I." are reprinted by permission of the author.

F.B. Eyes

Introduction

The FBI against and for African American Literature

The Federal Bureau of Investigation, the most storied name in U.S. law enforcement, capped its long struggle against African American protest with a homemade imitation of black prose. Late in the evening of November 20, 1964, FBI assistant director William C. Sullivan, a former English teacher who still dreamed of a professorship at a snug New England college, fed a sheet of unwatermarked paper into a worn-down, untraceable typewriter—both items were common tools of the trade within Domestic Intelligence, the Bureau division where Sullivan held sway.[1] Then as now, the Bureau's mission was twofold, to enforce U.S. federal laws and to protect U.S. national security. Inside Sullivan's Domestic Intelligence Division, however, security trumped law. Secretive counterintelligence, the effort to mislead enemies by mimicking or otherwise hijacking their trusted sources of information, overshadowed aboveboard crime fighting. By devoting his literary ambition to the covert art of counterintelligence, the Irish American house intellectual nicknamed "Crazy Billy" had climbed to the number four spot in the FBI, overseeing all national security investigations within the United States. And his clout exceeded his rank. As J. Edgar Hoover's preferred interpreter—and impersonator—of the civil rights movement, Sullivan had become the legendary FBI director's heir apparent as a racial policeman, poised to assume command of a grimy war on so-called black hate groups. Channeling Hoover's outrage at the news that Martin Luther King Jr. had won the Nobel Peace Prize, Sullivan burned midnight oil like a journalist on deadline. By the end of the night, he had transformed his carefully anonymous sheet into a history-making poison-pen letter:

> King, look into your heart. You know you are a complete fraud and a great liability to all us Negroes. White people in this country have enough frauds of their own but I am sure they don't have one at this time that is any where [sic] near your equal. You are no clergyman and you know it. I repeat that you are a colossal fraud and an evil, vicious one at that. You could not believe in God and act as you do. Clearly you don't believe in any personal moral principles.

King, like all frauds your end is approaching. You could have been our greatest leader. . . . We will now have to depend on our older leaders like [Roy] Wilkins a man of character and thank God we have others like him. But you are done. Your "honorary" degrees, your Nobel Prize (what a grim farce) and other awards will not save you. King, I repeat you are done. . . .

The American public, the church organizations that have been helping—Protestants, Catholics and Jews will know you for what you are—an evil beast. So will others who have backed you. You are done.

King, there is only one thing left for you to do. You know what it is. You have just 34 days in which to do [it] (this exact number has been selected for a specific reason, it has definite practical significant [*sic*]). You are done. There is but one way out for you. You better take it before your filthy, abnormal fraudulent self is bared to the nation. (Sullivan to Martin Luther King Jr.)

What was the "one way out" urged in Sullivan's letter? The question was anxiously debated by the inner circle of the Southern Christian Leadership Conference (SCLC) that received it in Atlanta. Ralph Abernathy, Joseph Lowery, Andrew Young, lawyer Chauncey Eskridge, and King himself gathered to interpret the text alongside King's wife, Coretta Scott King. Uncomfortably enough, she had first opened a package containing both the letter and audio evidence of her husband's extramarital affairs, a compilation tape recorded by FBI bugs planted in hotel rooms from Los Angeles to Washington, D.C. Some in the SCLC huddle argued that Sullivan's unsigned message was meant to blackmail King into declining the Nobel, an honor that Hoover improbably considered his own due. Others interpreted the thirty-four-day deadline as a schedule for suicide. Everyone agreed that the letter sought more than an ugly divorce, and that only the FBI possessed the technical know-how (and the shrewd spite) to join the tape to the threat. Hoover's eavesdroppers "are out to break me," a depressed, unsleeping King concluded in a conversation ironically preserved by FBI phone tapping (qtd. in Garrow, *Bearing* 374). "They are out to get me, harass me, break my spirit" (374), he lamented, his case of the FBI blues a signal that Sullivan's blow had come near its mark.

Recent historians of the Bureau have suggested that King underestimated the scope of his tormentors' ambition. In the emerging consensus of post-Hoover scholarship, race matters as a pivotal theme of FBI history, and Sullivan's notorious act of epistolary counterintelligence reflects a lengthy and comprehensive campaign against African American activism, not just a jealous crusade to silence the most charismatic spokesman of the civil rights generation.[2] On this view, the nadir of FBI history reached in Sullivan's letter took decades to prepare. The vendetta against King can be said to have begun no later than August 1919, when a twenty-something Hoover first joined the Bureau's new Radical Division amid the bloody race riots of the "Red Summer." Cementing the Bureau's early wariness of the self-defending and stridently modern "New Negro," the southern-born, fast-rising Hoover paved the way to King's hounding by triggering over forty years of investigations of African American dissent. A who's who of black protest was spied on, often infiltrated, and sometimes formally indicted by Hoover's FBI: among these individuals and organizations were the National Association for the Advancement of Colored People (NAACP); Ida B. Wells-Barnett and her antilynching drives; William Monroe Trotter and the National Equal Rights League; Marcus Garvey and the Universal Negro Improvement Association (UNIA); the Christian pacifist Congress of Racial Equality (CORE); A. Philip Randolph and his World War II March on Washington movement; Elijah Muhammad and the Nation of Islam; Malcolm X and his breakaway Organization of Afro-American Unity (OAAU); King's rebellious junior partners at the Student Nonviolent Coordinating Committee (SNCC); and black socialists and communists of every phase and faction. In short, the Hoover Bureau targeted practically the whole of the African American freedom movement starting with the first signs of the Harlem Renaissance.[3] In the disillusioned judgment of Tyrone Powers, a retired black FBI agent, the Bureau's steady aim was "to weaken and unlink the unified chain" of black self-organization, frustrating any sustained "move forward by African Americans" (367). While denying that the FBI thwarted the lawful progress of African American groups, Hoover affirmed his lasting duty to probe their contact with communists and lesser subversives. Considered "from an intelligence standpoint" alone, the director informed Congress in 1964, the Bureau's concern with radical influence on black America was obvious and permanent (*J. Edgar Hoover Speaks* 54).

Given all this, the blunt malice of Sullivan's letter to King looks like an artless smoking gun, final proof of the Hoover Bureau's unswerving racism. Yet the complication of the letter's race-passing literary artifice, its involved design to police black assertion under cover of black expression, may be just as revealing. Such literary artifice, this book argues, can indeed clarify overlooked wrinkles in the FBI's influential history. When it comes to Sullivan's twisted letter, the wrinkles are several. The white Sullivan's unnamed black speaker, an embittered guardian of Christian morality who commands King to "look into [his] heart," writes on behalf of "all us Negroes," and from a location inside or sympathetic to the nonviolent civil rights movement, a place where Roy Wilkins of the NAACP is a trusted household name and the endorsement of the ecumenical spectrum assisting the movement is reckoned a strategic good. This Negro persona lectures King from sorrow as much as anger—"You could have been our greatest leader"—at least when not slinging accusations of Satanic evil, hammering out an ominous drumbeat of *you are done, you are done,* or honing the chilling rhetoric of the precisely timed but indistinct threat (no nonviolence promised here). Sullivan's insider paints himself as a biblically based movement ally called to brutality only by knowledge of a preacher's hypocrisy. "Protestants, Catholics and Jews will know you for what you are—an evil beast," he forewarns, threatening King on the home field of the King James translation, where evil beasts imperil the righteous from Genesis 37:20 to Titus 1:12. By the time that King is offered "one way out," Sullivan's letter has blessed a number of the touchstones, religious and political, of the same black-led movement it plots to decapitate.[4]

What clues do the race-crossing literary gambits of Sullivan's letter hold about the larger life of Hoover's FBI—clues, that is, beyond the awful signs of the Bureau's capacity to invite the death of Martin Luther King? For one, the letter's claim to speak for "us Negroes" unveils the link between FBI counterintelligence and "American Africanism," Toni Morrison's name for American literature's formative reliance on ventriloquized blackness (6). Although Morrison, a Nobel Prize–winning novelist, gravitates to the elevated examples of Edgar Allan Poe, Herman Melville, and Willa Cather, Sullivan's far less imaginative fiction is determined to prove her point that Africanist accents and characters loom whenever white American writers seek ways "of policing matters of class, sexual license, and repression, formations and exercises of power, and meditations on ethics and accountability" (7). Among other things, Sullivan's letter, an FBI indictment preoccupied with sex, morality, and political control, suggests that the pseudo-Africanist "policing" of all these matters could be quite literal. By the same token, the letter does its best to illuminate the FBI's part in blackface minstrelsy's literary afterlife. Beginning as a wildly popular "nineteenth-century theatrical practice, principally of the urban North, in which white men caricatured blacks for sport and profit" (Lott, *Love and Theft* 3), blackface endured into the mid-twentieth century as a symbolic resource for white authors (usually male) on the make. The letter demonstrates that Norman Mailer, William Styron, and other hiply liberal, Democratic Party–linked novelists of the 1950s and 1960s were not the only professional dissimulators then attracted to minstrelsy's "second skin" (Szalay, *Hip Figures* 4). As later pages of this book will show, the nominally Democratic Sullivan helped to transform the postwar literature of FBI counterintelligence into a liberal-bashing outpost of burnt cork.

But there is something even stranger, and more significant, than these keys to Bureau minstrelsy at work in Sullivan's experiment in black authorship. His impulse to both join and beat the field of African American letters when baiting King highlights the curious fact that FBI harassment of black political leadership was habitually tied to an excited fear of black writing. As Sullivan, a voracious race-reader, knew inside and out, Hoover's hard-line police and intelligence service also qualified as an informed consumer of African American prose, poetry, and theater. Poring over novels, stories, essays, poems, and plays as well as political commentary and intercepted correspondence, the FBI acted as a kind of half-buried readers' bureau with aboveground effects on the making of black art. The "G" in the Bureau's iconic "G-Man," this is to say, should have stood not just for "government," but also for what I call "ghostreading," a duplicitous interpretive enterprise that, like ghostwriting, might be grasped through its effects if not always caught in the act. Unlike nearly every other institution of U.S. literary study, prone to showing interest only during well-promoted black renaissances, America's ghostreading national constabulary rarely took its eyes off the latest in African American writing between 1919 and 1972. And during this more-than-fifty-year period, the whole of its Hoover era, the Bureau never dismissed this writing as an impractical vogue relevant only to blacks (or to bleeding-heart white "Negrotarians," for that matter). Count the FBI, then, among the most dedicated foes of the diverse African American literary intellectuals, here loosely labeled "Afro-modernists," who worked to modernize racial representation beginning with the Harlem Renaissance. But count it, too, among the most faithful readers ever convinced by the focal thesis of these intellectuals, the still-enticing proposition "that black cultural production is necessarily central to black politics" (Warren, *So Black* 28). For Sullivan and the rest of the Bureau's cloak-and-dagger ghostreaders, black politics and black literary production in particular were powerful bedfellows whom only the FBI could separate.

Even now, when we know perhaps too much about the FBI's many fingerprints on twentieth-century American media, these dramatic claims for its literary curiosity may appear inflated.[5] Where, exactly, is the evidence of an advanced Afro-modernist reading program among FBI agents, an apparently unsophisticated group typecast by CIA rivals as provincial and philistine "Fordham Bronx Irish"? Why has the pattern of Bureau spying on black writing, as opposed to its spying on some black writers, not been seen before?[6] Part of the evidence for the Bureau's concerted interest in African American letters is public and reasonably obvious—though previously uncompiled or misunderstood. Typified by Richard Wright's poem "The FB Eye Blues" (1949), the source of this book's title and epigraph, the work of Afro-modernist authors provided vivid testimony of their place on FBI reading lists. From the earliest journalism of the Harlem Renaissance to the performative verse of the Black

Arts movement, these authors wrote openly about the Bureau and its intimate scrutiny. James Weldon Johnson and W.E.B. Du Bois led the first wave of black Bureau-writers, followed by such resonant voices as Langston Hughes, Chester Himes, James Baldwin, Amiri Baraka, Sonia Sanchez, Nikki Giovanni, Ishmael Reed, and even the deradicalizing Ralph Ellison (late drafts of the single most canonical African American novel make the Invisible Man a G-Man too). As I suggest at greater length in the last part of this book, the worst of ghostreading was distinct from muzzling state censorship, and the peculiar modernity of Afro-modernist literature was in fact partly articulated in response to Bureau eyeballing. In *The Man Who Cried I Am* (1967), an exemplary historical novel (and chaotic antisurveillance romance) of the black 1960s, John A. Williams proposed that "the secret to converting *their* change to *your* change was *letting them know that you knew*" (386; emphasis in original). Many other Afro-modernists embraced Williams's open secret and strived to convert the burden of FBI novel-gazing into grounds for artistic and social innovation, betting on the positive change in letting the Bureau know that, like King, its black writer-targets knew of their place in the crosshairs. "The FB Eye Blues," a poem composed in classic blues stanzas, embodies this bet in miniature, moaning back at a Bureau familiar enough to repeat to Wright's confessional speaker "all [he] dreamed last night, every word [he] said" (l. 10). Laying bare the FBI's access to a writer's bed, dreams, and words, Wright wagers, could jumpstart novel fusions of the black vernacular and the modern Esperanto of national security.

Paradoxically, Wright and like-minded Afro-modernists here collaborated with Hoover's publicity-hungry FBI in at least one respect: the writers conspired with the spies to ensure that the secret of Bureau ghostreading would not fossilize into wholly privileged information, or what the vernacular of espionage dubs a "double secret" or secret secret, a confidence not widely known to exist. The FBI tipped its hand about its snooping on black writing, circulating beyond government channels virtual book reports and critical essays starting with the emphatic *Radicalism and Sedition among the Negroes as Reflected in Their Publications* (1919). Bureau ghostreaders hoped that using such disclosures to keep the secret of Bureau awareness a widely suspected "single secret" would deter potential literary outlaws and reeducate their audiences. The Afro-modernists tipped their hand in turn by circulating imaginative reactions to these Hooverite stabs at literary criticism. Their hope was that corroborating suspicions of federal spying would not quiet the outspoken but rather underscore black writing's heightened gravity. Without declaring a decisive victor in the clash between spy-critics and black Bureau-writers, this book thus relies on dueling public documents of African American literature and FBI literary commentary to help establish their surprising depth of contact.[7]

The Files and the FOIA

More important evidence for the arguments of *F.B. Eyes* lies in a less approachable archive first examined here in full: fifty-one declassified but mostly unpublished FBI files on individual authors, ranging from 3 to 1,884 pages each, that together capture the Bureau's internal deliberations on half a century of African American literary talent. In bulk, of course, these and other specimens of the Bureau's files never aimed at double secrecy. The young Hoover's Radical Division boasted of 60,000 files on assorted suspects, publications, and political parties months after its founding in 1919; two years later, it claimed an index of 450,000 names and titles (U.S., Dept. of Justice, *Annual, 1921* 129). Hoover's first book from a commercial publisher, the noirish Bureau history *Persons in Hiding* (1938), advertised the FBI's files as stepping-stones to infamy bearing the "names of the Nation's most desperate criminals who may be to-morrow's most publicized menaces to society" (49). By the early 1970s, popular tours of FBI headquarters marched awestruck visitors (I was one) past rows of filing cabinets reminding guests of the Bureau's tens of millions of records on U.S. citizens. Like the Soviet secret police dossiers analyzed by Cristina Vatulescu, the FBI's metastasizing files thus served as "a highly visible spectacle of secrecy" (2). Hoover's closest political and journalistic allies, the beneficiaries of juicy, career-building leaks, were invited to view his file-hoard from an appreciative distance. Leaks excluded, the files' abundance was flaunted as a crime-control measure before a less dependent national audience, a slice of whom, we will see, joined novelist John A. Williams in gesturing back with literary "antifiles" of their own. What Williams and the rest of the Hoover-era public could not know, though, were the specifics behind the spectacle of omniscience, the full, non-cherry-picked contents of particular FBI files. These contents, relatively accessible since Hoover's death, are precisely what this book reads to fill out its case for the FBI as an institution tightly knit to African American literature.

Yet precisely which fifty-one files does *F.B. Eyes* rely on, and from where did they come? About eight years ago, I began systematically directing U.S. Freedom of Information Act (FOIA) requests to the national offices of the FBI, hoping to enhance a small collection of Bureau documents then confined to Afro-modern "greatest hits": namely, copies of the previously released FBI files of James Baldwin, Ralph Ellison, Langston Hughes, Claude McKay, Richard Wright (who was indeed right about those prying government eyes), and Andy Razaf, the lyricist of the Invisible Man's biting theme song, "(What Did I Do to Be So) Black and Blue." The breathtaking growth of the Bureau and other branches of U.S. intelligence in the years after 9/11 and the 2001 Patriot Act inspired me to expand my collection. Altering our sense of antistatism and other hallmarks of the American past, this striking reemergence and expansion of federal surveillance power also transformed our sense of the intellectual present. To my mind, the sudden "return of the state" exposed gaps in reigning academic habits of thinking, feeling, and historicizing African American culture transnationally, beyond the borders of the U.S. nation-state. Acquiring a wide range of FBI files on twentieth-century African American writers, I imagined, would equip me to explore how earlier generations of black internationalists had wrestled with the hostile state institutions usually discounted in then-cutting-edge transnational theories. Specific revelations in the files I had already seen likewise argued for more. Letters, clippings, and photographs in the Claude McKay file I consulted for my edition of the *Complete Poems* (2004) had offered unique insight into his decade of globetrotting away from Harlem's renaissance, a bohemian adventure in fact prescribed by a transatlantic Bureau manhunt.[8] Alarming international surveillance and oddball literary-critical acumen were documented in the files on Baldwin, Ellison, and Wright as well, suggesting the value of a sweep of the genre beyond this all-male circle.

In the fall of 2006, I thus set out to learn just how many authors guilty of being black and sometimes blue had attracted files at Hoover's FBI.[9] To generate a field of telling names for FOIA requests, I turned to the second edition of *The Norton Anthology of African American Literature* (2004, edited by Henry Louis Gates Jr. and Nellie Y. McKay), then the gold standard of its kind, and created a list of every deceased writer grouped there with black literary movements between 1919 and 1972, the whole of Hoover's rule at the Bureau. (I confined my list to the dead because, for very good reasons, the FBI does not entertain third-party FOIA requests on living persons. At the time of this writing in 2013, this list had grown to forty-eight names.) I then added a nonrandom sample of fifty-eight names of my own, concentrating not merely on the likeliest suspects (e.g., headlining literary communists such as Frank Marshall Davis, President Barack Obama's Hawaiian mentor in blackness), but also on departed but up-and-coming subjects of revisionist literary history (Marita Bonner, Henry Dumas, George Wylie Henderson, Eric Walrond, etc.). With the help of an overqualified research assistant, Cristina Stanciu, I assembled the biographies and obituaries recommended by the FBI to assist its internal research, and I surface-mailed packet after packet of FOIA petitions to the Bureau's Record/Information Dissemination Section currently located in Winchester, Virginia, occasionally short-circuiting the official process thanks to generous scholars who had gotten there first.[10]

The results of my file-quest as of 2013 are interpreted throughout this book, and itemized, writer-by-writer, in its appendix. Suffice it to say here, however, that the Bureau admits to having "filed" just less than half of the names on my unscientific but indicative list of noteworthy Afro-modernists. Twenty-three of the forty-eight historically relevant authors in the *Norton Anthology*—or roughly 48 percent—were first canonized by the FBI. Twenty-eight more from my supplementary list of fifty-eight—or another 48 percent—were also certified by Bureau paperwork, raising the total to fifty-one "filees" out of 106 inquires, and an overall filing rate of 48 percent. Twelve out of the fifty-one files, or 23 percent, are devoted to women, including the poets Gwendolyn Bennett and Georgia Douglas Johnson and the playwrights Alice Childress and Lorraine Hansberry. In part 2, I present the reasons why I believe the almost identical percentages of the filed from the *Norton Anthology* and from my own supplementary list are meaningfully high—disproportionately high, moreover, in comparison to what FOIA pioneers Herbert Mitgang, Natalie Robins, and Claire Culleton have shown us of the FBI's file-stalking of white American writers.[11] In several parts of *F.B. Eyes*, I illustrate that the surveillance of a dozen black literary women did not prevent either their male peers or Hoover's virtually all-male school of ghostreaders from projecting a conclusive showdown between G-Men and black men. Whatever the full significance of these various numbers and percentages (it requires all of the pages that follow to approach it), it is certain that the FBI produced reams of formal ghostreading in response to its fifty-one filees, women included, with Hansberry, for instance, prompting a file of 1,020 pages: far longer, then, than any book ever published on *A Raisin in the Sun* (1959) and the rest of Hansberry's prematurely silenced work, an object of special Bureau obsession. The collected files of the entire set of authors comprise 13,892 pages, or the rough equivalent of forty-six 300-page PhD theses. If this seems an artificial comparison or a low blow—and, from some angles, it is both—it should be noted that the average length of the forty-five files with page numbers we can count is a healthy 309 pages. FBI ghostreaders genuinely rivaled the productivity of their academic counterparts.

Academic historians of the FBI complain about a more recent, less efficient aspect of the Bureau's institutional culture: its sometimes agonizingly (some have said criminally) slow and uncooperative response to FOIA requests, first allowed for Bureau records in 1974. Assuming the role of the scholar-detective, one of the few marketable guises left to academic authors seeking a general audience, professors frustrated by FOIA hurdles commonly flavor their narratives of FBI spies with anecdotes of their own tenacious sleuthing.[12] In my case, the scholar-detective costume has proved tempting, but ultimately unwearable. This is not to say that the Bureau's replies to my FOIA requests were uniformly quick, clarifying, or heartening to historical preservationists. At least twenty-four of the fifty-one files I stockpiled had never been requested before, and some of these previously unearthed documents took Bureau processors nearly two years to scour, line by line, for legally permitted deletions in the name of privacy, law enforcement, or national security.[13] (In addition to formalistic close reading and statistical distant reading, both applied to Bureau documents in this book, FBI files may therefore demand inconveniently delayed reading.) A cluster of files required two- or three-digit payments to cover copying costs. Others, such as the probable files on *Black Aesthetic* editor Addison Gayle Jr. and Third World Press founder Carolyn Rodgers, seem to have been lost as the Bureau evaluates inactive records for possible transfer to the National Archives. More than one irreplaceable file—those on *Jubilee* author Margaret Walker and *Dessa Rose* author Sherley Anne Williams, for example—has been pronounced historically unworthy and knowingly destroyed under the auspices of an ongoing "Records Retention Plan and Disposition Schedule," a court-ordered procedure for weighing the right to life of aging FBI documents. (More later on this misnamed plan, which could use the services of a knowledgeable African Americanist.)[14]

Much of the worst that can befall a FOIA request to the Bureau is compressed in the tale of the disappeared file of Alain Locke, the editor of the crucial *New Negro* anthology of 1925 and the headmaster of the civil-rights-through-copyright school within the Harlem Renaissance. My initial query about a potential Locke file resulted in the disturbing report that "[r]ecords which may be responsive" to my request "were destroyed on September 3, 2004" (Hardy, 19 Oct. 2006). "Since this material could not be reviewed," the head of the FBI's Record Section spelled out, thickening the mystery, "it is not known if it actually pertains to your subject" (Hardy, 19 Oct. 2006). I then appealed what seemed a late-model catch-22 to the Justice Department's Office of Information and Privacy, whose associate director conveyed the better news that "the FBI has informed a member of [her] staff that this response was in error. In fact, records responsive to [my] request were transferred to the National Archives and Records [Administration] (NARA)" (McLeod). I thus "might wish to make a new request directly to NARA," she suggested (McLeod). Taking her lead, I did wish it and learned from a frankly irritated librarian at NARA that "[w]hile it is certainly possible that the FBI transferred records concerning Mr. Locke to NARA in [*sic*] September 3, 2004, we cannot search for these records without more information from the FBI. While the FBI has transferred thousands of feet of records to NARA over the past several years, they retain custody of their central name index. As all FBI records are filed by case file number, and not by name, we would need the numbers of case files pertaining to Mr. Locke" (Mathis). Falling short of Conan Doyle's Sherlock Holmes and Chester Himes's Coffin Ed Johnson, I then let the trail grow cold. FOIA law combined with enlightening interdepartmental frictions may keep U.S. federal agencies somewhat forthright by international standards, but the withholding of the FBI's central name index is a maneuver from the shadowy Eurozone where Franz Kafka meets George Orwell. Under cover of a buck-passing tautology, FBI files of serious historical value have been buried in the National Archives (the self-described "nation's record keeper") as deeply as they were in Hoover's famed but closed cabinets ("What Is?").

Thankfully, however, the fate of the Locke file, transferred from the Bureau to the bureaucratic void, was atypical in my experience: forty-six of the fifty-one files I hunted down were untouched by the paradoxes of the Records Retention Plan. Locating usable files with the Bureau's assistance, it turned out, was easier than sorting through the thousands of pages of them sent to me in sturdy government cardboard. In the end, the majority of my file requests were answered swiftly; my contacts with the staff of the FBI Record Section were courteous under both the George W. Bush and the Obama administrations; and most released files were comparatively free from massive national security excisions, the bane of three generations of FOIA researchers.[15] (As the technology of file censorship changes with the times, unruly cross-outs in black pen have become neat rectangles of electronic "white-out" applied to scanned documents [see figures 0.1 and 0.2].)

Pragmatically speaking, a bit too much, rather than too little, finally slipped through the FBI's edits, making the scholar-as-detective persona less fitting than the role of scholarly batch processor. The sheer volume of the response to my FOIA requests indeed suggests that today is an unprecedentedly good time to study the Hoover Bureau's devotion to Afro-modernist writing. Ironically, the prolonged explosion of counterterrorist secrecy seems to be opening some of the remaining secrets of Hoover's cultural Cold War. Twentieth-century confidences are no longer protected with uniform ferocity as old informers pass away, new enemies are engaged covertly and officially, and another protracted, indefinite, and increasingly customary war—the Global War on Terror, whatever its latest official name—has become the Bureau's highest priority. On the FBI's Internet home page, "terrorism" is now the primary answer to the question of "What We Investigate," and an international rogues gallery of "Most Wanted Terrorists" threatens to eclipse the latest edition of the "Ten Most Wanted" list, a Hoover trademark dating from 1950 (FBI.gov). If the openly shredded Margaret Walker and Sherley Anne Williams files could talk, they would tell us that growing indifference to pre-9/11 swaths of the Bureau's past may pose a greater peril than stubborn concealment. The FBI's instinctive secrecy has not faded away but has moved on.

While the contents of my fifty-one files were rarely anticlimactic, the means of acquiring them thus could be. The same Cristina Vatulescu quoted above,

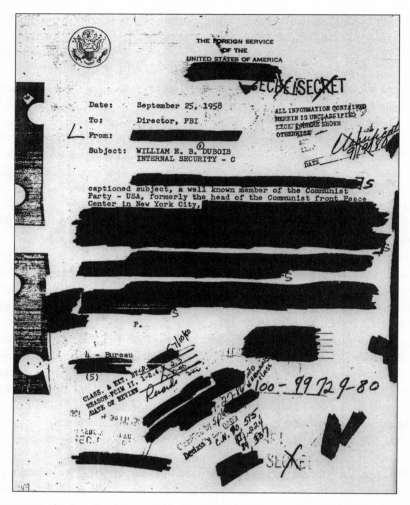

FIGURE 0.1: The classic hand-drawn, blacked-out look of FOIA censorship, sampled from the FBI's 756-page file on W.E.B. Du Bois. (Courtesy of the FBI.)

an ingenious critic of police aesthetics on the communist side of the Cold War, recounts a four-year ordeal en route to her first look at Soviet-era intelligence files from her native Romania. The moment when she sat at a desk at the headquarters of the former Securitate and finally laid eyes on "the files of some of [her] favorite Romanian writers," she confesses, was "one of the most exhilarating" of her life (11). Inspecting the files of Hoover's intelligence service no longer requires this sort of charged, belly-of-the-beast meeting with singular

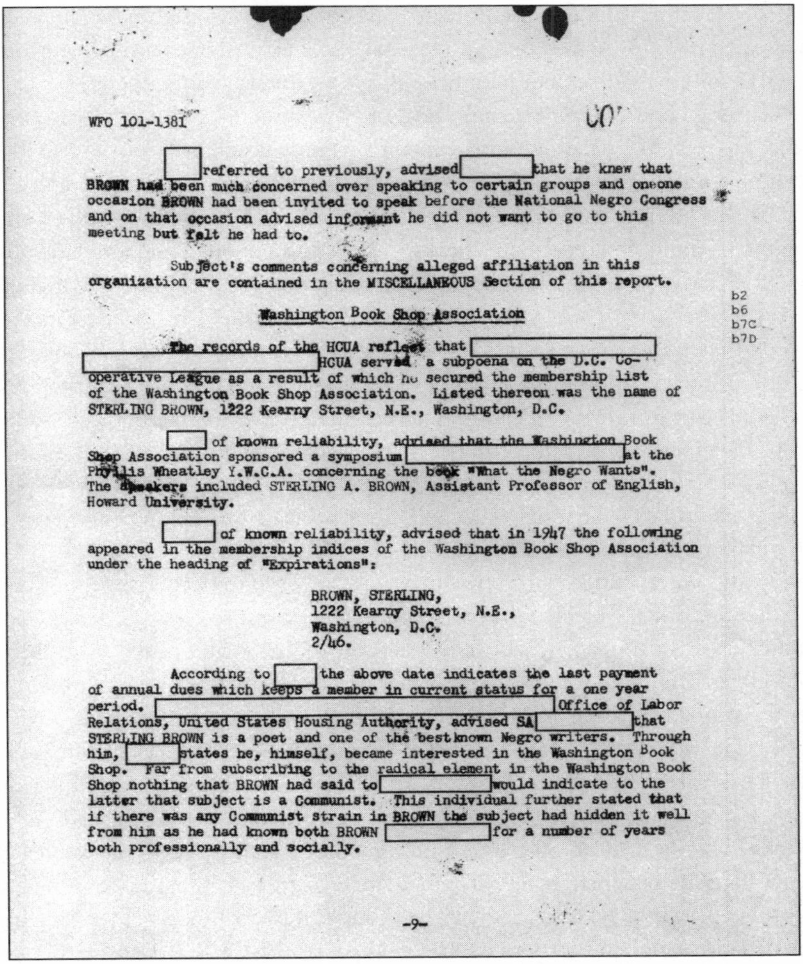

FIGURE 0.2: The look of FOIA censorship in the new millennium: Neat patches of electronic "white-out" applied to scanned documents, here taken from the newly released FBI file of poet-critic Sterling Brown. (Courtesy of the FBI.)

texts. Symptomatically, "The Vault," the contemporary FBI's busiest archive, is located nowhere and everywhere and forever open to the public, an online library of 6,700 digitized documents instantly accessible "in the comfort of your home or office" (Vault.fbi.gov). Hoping for a less comfortable encounter after years of mail-order file reading, I thus wrote to David Sobonya, the FBI's public information officer for FOIA requests, and arranged an in-person visit to the

J. Edgar Hoover Building, the Bureau's cast concrete Washington headquarters dedicated in 1975. Armed only with a legal pad, I arrived one summer morning in 2012 for an appointment with the F.B. eye on Pennsylvania Avenue.

Gaining access to the Bureau's "Seat of Government," now a high-rise Brutalist fortress, had become more difficult since my childhood tour of the FBI's former home in the Justice Department. In the wake of 9/11, group sightseeing at the Hoover Building is irregular, at best, and individual callers must penetrate multiple credentials checks, magnetic weapons detectors, and full-body scanners looking like airlocks from a science fiction film. Once through tightened security, I was welcomed by the FBI's resident historian, Dr. John F. Fox Jr., who kindly indulged my interest in seeing the building's nonvirtual Reading Room, an opposite number of Vatulescu's perch at the Securitate. No desks overflowed with original files and exhilarated scholars; that day, no one at all occupied the computer stations and swivel chairs that made the Reading Room resemble a modest commercial office. Things were more stimulating inside Fox's personal office, where a portrait of abolitionist Frederick Douglass hung on one wall (Fox's PhD was earned in American history), and bookcases were stuffed with scholarship on his employer (the seemingly unneeded title *Unlocking the Files of the FBI* occupied one space). We spoke freely about FBI historiography, which Fox is professionally committed to fostering and correcting, and agreed on the value of David Garrow's scrupulous book on the Bureau and Martin Luther King Jr. Kirk Cromer, an experienced FOIA processor, joined us to talk about the development of the Record/Information Dissemination Section. Cromer, an African American proud of his work with historians of the civil rights movement, estimated that in the mid-1970s blacks composed 40 to 50 percent of the Bureau staff hired to answer FOIA requests. This proportion has dropped since the main FOIA office moved to northern Virginia, he observed, but he thought it likely that several of my files on African American writers had been close-read first by African American processors. The conversation flowed smoothly, with the three of us, variously occupied by the FBI, agreeing to agree on much. When I asked Fox what he finally thought about the dealings between Hoover's Bureau and African Americans, however, the accord politely broke down. Hoover was a typically paternalistic racist of his day, Fox stated, but also a potent adversary of the Ku Klux Klan. The "racial culture" of Hoover's FBI was little different from the rest of the U.S. federal government, he claimed. The files I had gathered with the help of Fox and other affable Bureau employees had led me to different conclusions. Racial culture at the Hoover Bureau was hardly typical, these files instructed, not least when it came to the Hooverites' fascinated policing of black literary culture.

Five Theses and the Way Forward

While *F.B. Eyes* quotes from dozens of unknown or little-known FBI files on African American writers, it does not describe them page by page or case by case. Those interested in the often-troubling nuts and bolts of particular files can examine the electronic copies available through this book's website, accessible at http://digital.wustl.edu/fbeyes (like the files held in the FBI's "Vault," these online documents can be read in domestic tranquility). Avoiding inventories of file ingredients, *F.B. Eyes* instead mines Bureau files for traces of the uneasy intimacy of African American writing and FBI ghostreading, the latter an almost exclusively white occupation under Hoover's leadership. In the process, I dissect evidence of the criminal intent of Hoover and Sullivan's "black hate" counterintelligence program and other authentically scandalous chapters of Bureau surveillance. But my overarching aim is to read the files responsively as well as judgmentally, and to reconstruct rather than prosecute the meddling of the FBI in Afro-modernist letters, a collision of dissimilar cultural forces wrongly assumed to occupy disconnected worlds.

One danger in this approach to the files is the temptation to glamorize the abuses of state espionage by aestheticizing its texts—a temptation similar to that experienced by fans of better-written spy literature. I try to avoid this temptation here, while admitting that Hoover's FBI, a star of page and screen, schemed to glamorize most everything it touched. More to the point, I note that FBI files on Afro-modernists are peppered with ghostreaders' judgments of the true and the beautiful; like Vatulescu's craft-conscious literary files of the communist secret police, these Bureau texts were thus often "pre-aestheticized" at their moments of composition.[16] A second danger in my approach to the files is the risk of reviving an insulting and disproven vision of African American literature as an art more acted on than acting. When seen through the spyglass of FBI ghostreading, do Afro-modernist authors reappear as professional victims, objects of (white/police/government) domination whose only proper subjects are evasion or surrender? Is the old, clumsy, pre-Foucauldian "repressive model" of state sovereignty back in black?[17] As mentioned above, the last part of *F.B. Eyes* makes it plain that African American writers answered these questions in advance, and in the negative. Through novelistic antifiles and acid "Hoover Poems," they acted to elevate or transcend their terms of engagement with the FBI, exposing unsightly facts about government spying while recycling them into imaginative fictions. Earlier parts of *F.B. Eyes* do stress the daunting pressures placed on Afro-modernism by Hoover's Bureau, a feeder of racial paranoia, a seizer of U.S. passports, and by no means a simply stimulating foil for African American artists. In particular, part 4, a look at the FBI's underestimated influence across the international "Black Atlantic," emphasizes the Bureau's capacity to construct a rigid border and to incriminate those within it—in other words, its capacity to "frame" African American literature in the two most restrictive senses invoked in my subtitle, *How J. Edgar Hoover's Ghostreaders Framed African American Literature.* From start to finish, however, *F.B. Eyes* tests its sobering discoveries from FBI files against counterstatements from the Bureau's African American targets. It documents the scope of FBI interference to produce a more accurate picture of the barriers scaled by literary expressions of African American agency. During the long, uneven insurgency of Afro-modernism, the combined peaks and crashes of the Harlem Renaissance, the "Indignant Generation," and the Black Arts movement, this form of agency indeed overcame state-built obstacles we are just beginning to see.[18]

On the other side of the coin, *F.B. Eyes* spends a good number of pages charting the influence of Afro-modernist writing where it might be least expected: inside the operations of Hoover's FBI, a pacesetter in American criminology and "the global leader among national criminal detection agencies" (Jeffreys-Jones 2). Taken together, parts 1 and 2 of the book offer a revisionist history of the Bureau's Hoover era recentered on the intersection of American literature and black-white race relations, not coincidentally the home junction of African American writing. Part 1 submits that the Bureau's involvement with the literary thoroughly racialized the common analogy between the writer and the spy. Like all of the book's five parts, it devotes ample textual and historical detail to the task of proving a brash and initially counterintuitive thesis: in this case, *The birth of the Bureau, coupled with the birth of J. Edgar Hoover, ensured the FBI's attention to African American literature.* The argument begins with twin portraits: one of the Bureau before Hoover, and the other of Hoover before the Bureau. Each portrait displays how its subject was born into an atmosphere wary of the entrance of the New Negro and alert to the uses of literary self-advertisement. I then turn to Hoover's hiring by the Bureau in 1919, and his rapid upgrade of an already insistently literary agency into the citadel of what I call "lit.-cop federalism," the desire to inject a compelling federal police presence into the print public sphere. Cashing in on the antiradical Red Scare and his early work experience at the Library of Congress, Hoover combined the resources of this federalism—curatorial, editorial, and authorial—to promote the nationwide clout of the first national police force in U.S. history. The early FBI thus wrote up more than its thousands of case files: it also issued a raft of animated government reports and mass-market hype vetted, bylined, or authored by Hoover, the editor- and eventual agent-in-chief. Impressed by the page count of Bureau self-exposure, the *New Yorker* would dryly thank the head

G-Man for ensuring "that a moderately literate criminal ought to be able to avoid capture indefinitely" (Jack Alexander, "The Director—III" 25).

One thing a moderately literate criminal might have noted was the Hoover Bureau's unusual concern with African American writing. As I discuss toward the end of part 1, the FBI's first major work of literary criticism was the essay-pamphlet *Radicalism and Sedition among the Negroes as Reflected in Their Publications*. Excerpted in the *New York Times* and ratified in the *Congressional Record*, *Radicalism and Sedition* was a precocious assessment of Harlem Renaissance poetry and a valuable anthology of black journalism produced at the crossroads of Marxist and New Negro radicalisms. In its even glance at both creative and polemical literary genres—poems as well as treatises—*Radicalism and Sedition* predicts the inclusiveness of the FBI's working definition of Afro-modernist writing, a definition I adopt as my own. In its generous quotations and supporting commentary on Afro-modernism's seriousness of purpose, it reveals another, more flattering sense of the Bureau's "framing" of African American literature. In the manner of a state museum, the FBI collected, preserved, and educationally labeled works of black art, exhibiting foreign objects it intended to defang but came to emulate. Most importantly, *Radicalism and Sedition* illustrates the chief reason why the FBI ghostread African American writing in the first place. The New Negro instigators of Afro-modernism, this essay acknowledged, both threatened and drove the Bureau's custom blend of racial animus and literary aspiration, the fuel for some of the agency's earliest efforts to win national approval for federal policing.

Part 2 of *F.B. Eyes* carries my revisionist history of the FBI forward from the Harlem Renaissance to the year 1972—both the height of Afro-modernism's "Renaissance II," otherwise known as the Black Arts movement, and the year of Hoover's death in office. Along the way, part 2 pursues the thesis that *The FBI's aggressive filing and long study of African American writers was tightly bound to the agency's successful evolution under Hoover.* I begin by introducing the features that distinguish FBI author files as a genre, and I go on to identify some of the factors—ideological and bureaucratic—behind the Hoover Bureau's chronic interest in filling them. Yet the lion's share of part 2 samples dozens of individual files and related black texts to track the Bureau's evolving dialogue with Afro-modernism across several stages of FBI institutional history, those shifting contexts in which Hoover successfully maneuvered to serve and outlast nine different U.S. presidents. Following an anomalous break during the Great Depression, Hoover's ghostreaders returned with a vengeance to the scene of Afro-modernism in the early 1940s. Worried by wartime black internationalism, they placed Gwendolyn Bennett, Langston Hughes, George Schuyler, and a minimum of eight other African American authors on a dubiously legal

"Custodial Detention" list, an index of prominent dissidents subject to summary arrest and military confinement in case of national emergency (another
of the authentic scandals, then, of FBI ghostreading). Then, in the late 1940s
and 1950s, on the eve of the civil rights movement, Hoover's Bureau answered
the mainstreaming of African American writing with a program to detect cultural assimilation before it occurred. The case of *A Raisin in the Sun*, haunted
and reviewed by FBI agents before its New York premiere, is emblematic of
this Cold War stage of Bureau ghostreading, intent on advanced warning of
literary threats to state segregation. Finally, in the late 1960s and early 1970s,
FBI ghostreaders followed Hoover's lieutenant William C. Sullivan in meeting
Afro-modernism with both severity and the sincerest form of flattery. Sullivan's
blackface letter to King was the tip of a coming iceberg, since the Black Power
movement and its Black Arts sibling motivated stacks of synthetic black writing at the FBI, a wave of G-Man minstrelsy green-lighted at headquarters but
largely composed in outlying Bureau field offices. With Sullivan and Hoover's
endorsement, ghostreading came to approximate a national writer's workshop
in which the Bureau's long-standing passion for black literature married its
even older longing to create a literature of its own. This last stage of Hooverite
ghostreading inspired the unifying concept of part 2: "counterliterature," my
term for an adaptable strain of counterintelligence that attempts to convert literary challenges into criminological advantages. As employed by Hoover's FBI,
counterliterature digested and repurposed the voices of Afro-modernist authors. Propagating in-kind replies to the fifty-one filees noted above, it aspired
to police African American writing with some of its own literary medicine and
succeeded in enriching the FBI's unlikely status as a clued-in government race
expert. Fusing literary inspiration and counterintelligence technique, the idea
of counterliterature encapsulates the mixture of literary history and police and
intelligence history plied in the whole of this book.[19]

Part 3 of *F.B. Eyes* marks a break from the concept of counterliterature,
though not initially from the question of Afro-modernism's influence within
Hoover's Bureau. Its topic is the theory and practice of FBI reading, the intellectual precondition for ghostreading's enlistment in any larger criminological
project. As usual, the organizing thesis is not shy: *The FBI is perhaps the most
dedicated and influential forgotten critic of African American literature.* But
the file evidence, here especially, is plentiful. I begin by demonstrating that
the Bureau's many files on Afro-modernist authors are, among other things,
recognizably literary-critical documents, analytical encounters with black
writing that cannot always resist the pleasures of the enemy text. I move on
to illuminate the interpretive principles of these files against the backdrop of
the best-known entanglement of American espionage and American literary

criticism: the firsthand stamp of Yale University–bound New Criticism on the counterintelligence branch of the CIA. By the 1950s, the conventions of CIA-endorsed New Critical formalism had crept into FBI critical practice. Ahead of the CIA's invention in 1947, however, Bureau ghostreaders had cobbled together a separate mode of spy-reading, one sympathetic to pre–New Critical academic schools and exceptionally attuned to the political mindfulness of Afro-modernist writing. In their serious approach to African American literature, critics recruited from the "Fordham Bronx Irish" outperformed the mandarin WASPs of the CIA.

Part 3 then looks beyond G-Man stereotypes to explore the literary training of those Bureau agents tasked with criticizing Afro-modernism. Individual FBI ghostreaders have tended to disappear behind cloaks of bureaucratic anonymity and FOIA redaction; the names of living Bureau agents, for example, are usually removed from FBI files prior to public release. Nonetheless, the literary lives and opinions of two supervising critics at the FBI—William C. Sullivan and Robert Adger Bowen, the latter the lead author of *Radicalism and Sedition* and of earlier stories in Uncle Remus–level black dialect—have been aired in unconventional autobiographies and here serve to answer an inevitable question about ghostreading: whodunit? The last section of part 3 assesses the impact of Bureau ghostreaders on an interested non-Bureau audience: not, in this instance, African American writers themselves, but the self-appointed reader-patriots, black and white, who turned to Hoover as a literary-critical wise man. One Houstonite in this camp gamely wrote the FBI director with questions about the "writings and connections" of Langston Hughes, and about something fuzzier: "I seem to remember that [*A Raisin in the Sun*] was a highly controversial production written by a Leroi [*sic*] Jones and that Jones is something of a professional trouble maker and rabble rouser. If you cannot furnish information pertaining to this play and its author please advise where I might obtain such details" (U.S., Federal, Hughes, 8 July 1970). *A Raisin* was no unforgiving *Dutchman* (1964), and Jones/Baraka did not look much like Hansberry, but the Houstonite rightly supposed that Hoover's FBI knew what it took to learn differently. Despite the closed contents of FBI files, a fairly accurate impression of the Bureau's attentiveness to Afro-modernism escaped the Washington Beltway and proceeded to generate critical correspondence imagining the state apparatus as the brains of a nationwide interpretive community. The aura of FBI ghostreading was thus capable of touching nonprofessional readers outside the FBI. In its small way, it helped to ensure that impassioned common reading and ideologically honed suspicious reading were not, in fact, mutually exclusive styles of twentieth-century literary reception, the assumptions of stylish academic "surface reading" to the contrary.[20]

Part 4 maintains the spotlight on the effects of ghostreading outside FBI headquarters, a widened focus held throughout the rest of the book. In this portion of *F.B. Eyes*, the beyond-the-Beltway subject is the evidence that Bureau literary criticism encroached on the travels of African American expatriates around the "Black Atlantic," Paul Gilroy's now-standard model of the zone of transnational exchange "based on the structure of the African diaspora [in] the Western hemisphere" (*The Black Atlantic* 15). The FBI file of recurrent expatriate Langston Hughes repeatedly quotes his claim that "Negroes are growing in international consciousness" (U.S., Federal, Hughes, 3 June 1947). Hughes's file and many others, I point out, also confirm that the Bureau concluded it should grow in the same way. As early as the 1920s, the FBI exceeded its domestic authority to influence the movements of expatriate Afro-modernists—this even as it nationalized itself on the U.S. home front through its program of literary federalism. In Paris, the European capital of the Black Atlantic, and several of its satellites in Africa and Latin America, FBI informants and legal attaché agents kept tabs on a network of black literary travelers they tried to link by the vulnerabilities of statelessness alone. Hence *F.B. Eyes*'s most far-reaching thesis: *The FBI helped to define the twentieth-century Black Atlantic, both blocking and forcing its flows.*

Part 4 first accents the present-day relevance of FBI internationalism, outlining its up-to-date challenges to theories of the state in relation to the nation, the police, and transnational literature. The national security state's adventures in transnational policing, I argue, underscore the need to integrate the dynamic of state security into U.S. literary history, even—and especially—following this history's "transnational turn." Over the past two decades, high-profile attention to writers' transatlantic journeys has clarified Afro-modernism's ties to radical Pan-Africanism, to less politicized black cosmopolitanisms, and to the print-cultural practice of black diaspora. Yet the parallel history of FBI internationalism reminds us not to neglect the coercive state power lurking on the right side of the "nation-state" hyphen. For this reason, the remainder of part 4 inspects the two main means through which Hoover's state police interfered in the flows of the Black Atlantic. The first is the Bureau's translation of foreign-language texts and riffling of U.S. passport applications to track or immobilize black literary travelers. FBI files verify that in addition to the famous passport withdrawal visited on W.E.B. Du Bois, the passports of dramatist Shirley Graham Du Bois, critic Harold Cruse, novelist William Gardner Smith, and cartoonist-essayist Ollie Harrington were revoked for years at a time. The passport records of James Baldwin, Katherine Dunham, Lorraine Hansberry, Chester Himes, Langston Hughes, John O. Killens, Julian Mayfield, Claude McKay, Willard Motley, Louise Thompson Paterson, Dudley Randall, George Schuyler, Walter White, and

Richard Wright were all combed by the Bureau for travel patterns and abusable irregularities, with Alice Childress's papers checked twice after New York agents discovered her ties to a "Committee to Restore Paul Robeson's Passport" (U.S., Federal, Childress, 20 Mar. 1958). Recovered FBI files thus remind us of the steep ticket price of Black Atlantic mobility: for many of the most diaspora-minded Afro-modernists, black internationalism entailed the real prospect of global surveillance or national house arrest. The mistranslations required when thinking and writing across a multilingual African diaspora were not the only impediments and goads faced by those who best articulated twentieth-century black internationalisms.[21]

Part 4 then clarifies a second, complementary means by which the Bureau acted against traveling African American authors: the incongruous weapon I label "state-sponsored transnationalism." When not keeping prominent Afro-modernists from drifting, the U.S. state police could *encourage* them to drift, practically underwriting extended world tours. The FBI files of Baldwin, Du Bois, McKay, Motley, and Smith—all of whose passports were endangered—also contain an underbrush of "stop notices," official instructions to advise the Bureau if a traveler attempted to return through a U.S. port of entry. Considered as instruments of border policing, "stops" were less literal than their name suggests. Yet they had the power to pinpoint their targets' international crossings to the minute, sometimes before that minute arrived, and occasionally down to the airplane seat number. They provided U.S. state agencies with a ready pretext to detain and quiz literary suspects on arrival.

Most significant of all was the stop's unwritten service as a government travel advisory: if you had appreciated lands beyond the Bureau's ideological orbit, stops counseled, you should continue to do so, and stay away. Most of the African American authors troubled by stop notices understood this message, though few respected it permanently. McKay, who composed *Home to Harlem* (1928) in France, correctly assumed that U.S. officials would not "let me in . . . without special intervention" (letter to Max Eastman, [?] April 1933). He returned to black Manhattan only after James Weldon Johnson and Walter White (a cagey friend of Hoover with his own Bureau file) pulled strings with FBI skeptics at the State Department. James Baldwin, who mock-showcased a copy of the best-selling *FBI Story* (1956) while writing in Turkey, noticed that the same U.S. passport that pronounced him "a free citizen of a free country" when in Europe "underwent a sea change" when flashed at checkpoints "on the other side of the ocean" (James Baldwin, *No Name* 378). Reinterpreted at the stopped-up borders of white America, Baldwin's national ID card warned him "that I was not an African prince, but a domestic nigger and that no foreign government would be offended if my corpse were to be found clogging up the sewers" (378).

Baldwin's open disdain for the Bureau became a cause célèbre among ghostreaders during the years he talked up *The Blood Counters*, a never-completed exposé sworn to blast Hoover "to the wall" (U.S., Federal, Baldwin, 7 June 1963). Part 5 of *F.B. Eyes* surveys this and less notional examples of African American writing about the Bureau—many of them, like Baldwin's unfinished book, attempts to force a sea change in the balance of literary surveillance. As in part 4, the focus thus falls on events and histories outside FBI headquarters. Here, however, this outward focus finally involves closer encounters with Afro-modernist poems, stories, essays, and novels than with their silhouettes in FBI files. My fifth and last thesis turns the agenda fully over to such black texts and affirms that *Consciousness of FBI ghostreading fills a deep and characteristic vein of African American literature.*

The expressly literary effects of FBI ghostreading might be measured in slippery but provocative metrics of silencing: the number of novels abandoned or banned from bookstores and libraries; the number of early radical poems unreprinted or apologized for; the number of whole literary careers shortened or never started. Proof of book-killing, stop-the-presses FBI censorship of Afro-modernist literature is thin on the ground, however. Past this and the even hazier data of Bureau-inspired self-censorship lies a more definite archive of contact, the collected works of an Afro-modernism that actively grappled with Hoover's FBI across various styles, genres, and generations. The page production of many years of African American literature, in other words, is solid, surface-readable evidence that African American authors declined to suffer ghostreading in silence.

Exhaustive treatment of Afro-modernism's increasingly raw conversation with the FBI might fill another book, so part 5 highlights a handful of major episodes on the road from 1919 to 1972 and beyond. The first of these episodes is the prompt reply to FBI ghostreading in the early journalism and foundational poetry of the Harlem Renaissance. Just as James Weldon Johnson and other columnist-midwives of the renaissance publicly greeted *Radicalism and Sedition*, the Bureau's original rejoinder to Afro-modernism, Claude McKay refined the opening statements of renaissance verse in light of his vocal police readership. McKay's once-baffling preference for the traditional Shakespearian sonnet, I argue, consciously echoed the censor-burdened poetry of early modern England, a prior expression of cultural renaissance saddled and energized by state interference. In McKay's hands, the FBI's inspiration for Afro-modernism was thus first extended to the level of literary form.

The second section of part 5 charts the FBI's migrant standing in Afro-modernist prose from the mid-1930s through the early Cold War and ranges from George Schuyler's pulp fiction to Langston Hughes's beloved "Simple" stories to Ralph Ellison's drafts of *Invisible Man* (1952). In a near-final version of Ellison's Great American Novel, the transparent narrator dreams of faithful service under "a master FBI man" ("Writings" 186), an unconscious confession of blindness that also divulges repressed ties between the mask of black servility and the loyal-American disguise of the G-Man. The third section of part 5 revolves around the expatriate trio of Chester Himes, Richard Wright, and William Gardner Smith and investigates their interlocking fictions of so-called *Rive noire* Paris in the late 1950s and early 1960s. Despite their impressive differences, all three of these Bureau-hunted novelists produced black Parisian detective fictions inventively stretched in the direction of the "antifile," an emerging genre of novelized counterinvestigation that recoded known forms of FBI rhetoric. The fourth section less selectively addresses the profusion of black Bureau writing in the late 1960s and early 1970s. Briefly taking the stage are such novelists as John A. Williams, Sam Greenlee, and Ishmael Reed, each of whom published fantasies of a Black Nationalist secret service able to outfox the FBI. Also featured are Amiri Baraka, Nikki Giovanni, and Sonia Sanchez, a poetic collective joined in agreement over Hoover's place in the demonology of the Black Arts movement. "J. EDGAR HOOVER WILL / SOON BE DEAD" (ll. 13–14), Baraka promised in "Three Movements and a Coda" (1963–65), the anticipation of a string of "Hoover Poems" that dance on the FBI's looming grave and that offset the better-remembered canon of Black Arts "Coltrane Poems," elegies commemorating a jazz culture hero who died before his nation-time— exactly unlike Hoover, an aged national icon born in a bygone century.

The fifth and final section of part 5 acts as a historical coda and an epilogue to *F.B. Eyes* as a whole. It sketches African American literature's less heated and less defining skirmish with the FBI after Hoover's unpoetic death—a skirmish now led by black women including Ai, Audre Lorde, Danzy Senna, and Gloria Naylor. Naylor's Orwellian book *1996*, a "fictionalized memoir" published in 2005, pictures a Jewish American officer of the National Security Agency (NSA) who commands spy-readers to produce a "detailed synopsis" of each of her publications: "Every newspaper article, every book review, is to be read and analyzed. . . . Files from the FBI and CIA are ordered. . . . Yes, by the end of the day, Gloria Naylor's life will become, no pun intended, an open book" (33). As *F.B. Eyes* sees it, *1996* suggests that surveillance-fed paranoia can make for crude anti-Semitism, and, despite itself, for penetrating literary history. In the style of Naylor's eponymous protagonist, her life an open book to readerly spies, the national loyalty of the fifty-one African American writers filed by Hoover's FBI was in fact tested through literary evidence. Like both Naylor and her author-function, these writers plead that a shaping awareness of the national security state was not reserved for Don DeLillo, Joan Didion, and other post-1945 white postmodernists. Decades before the "post-" met the modern, or spylike epistemological uncertainty became a required sign of literary contemporaneity, or the CIA and NSA became models of state security gone virulently imaginative, Afro-modernism confidently represented the ploys and tastes of U.S. intelligence. For better and for worse, what helped to make this modernism a relatively coherent body of texts was its common knowledge of being good enough—and "BaddDDD" enough—to keep FBI ghostreaders up at night, turning its pages.[22]

All five parts of *F.B. Eyes* make hay from the similarities between ghostreaders and academic literary critics, two classes of interpreters fond of decryption, identity theft, and (often enough) hermeneutics of suspicion. But the whole of the book also benefits from a considerable difference between these two professional readerships: academic literary critics are more open to debate, and much less displeased by citation. In addition to the critics already mentioned, *F.B. Eyes* has taken inspiration and free pointers from several different sets of literary scholars. These include historians of Afro-modernism's voyages and exchanges outside the United States (Brent Hayes Edwards, Michelle Stephens); diverse chroniclers of the *longue durée* of Afro-modernism beyond the Harlem Renaissance (Lawrence Jackson, James Smethurst, Kenneth Warren); wide-ranging biographers of the radical experience of literary surveillance (Carole Boyce Davies, Barbara Foley, Gary Holcomb, Alan Wald, Mary Helen Washington); new Americanists freshly interested in old questions of literature, the state, and politics as such (Sean McCann, Michael Szalay); and, closest to home, skilled analysts of the clues linking other U.S. literatures to the covert sphere of espionage (Erin Carlston, Michael Holzman, Timothy Melley). For its part, History with a capital *H*, the kind that hurts and that refuses most academic desires, has continued to offer inspiration of its own. Begun five years after 9/11, this book was finished in the summer of 2013, a confusing season in which NSA contractor Edward Snowden first revealed quantities of electronic spy-reading that put Naylor's *1996* to shame, and then found asylum under the wings of a onetime lieutenant colonel of the Soviet KGB. Published as we enter a phase of skepticism about government spying unparalleled since the 1970s, *F.B. Eyes* hopes to contribute to the renewed case against unchecked surveillance. It also aims to offer hope in the likely event that this case fails to stem the tide. When all is said and read, the Afro-modernist writers shadowed by the FBI illustrate both the painful costs of epidemic ghostreading, and the ways in which liberating expression can exploit and withstand it.

Part One/Thesis One

The Birth of the Bureau, Coupled with the Birth of J. Edgar Hoover, Ensured the FBI's Attention to African American Literature

J. Edgar Hoover, the FBI director who added the "Federal" to the Bureau's name, managed and symbolized American state power for a longer term than any U.S. president. The photograph of this national bulwark on the jacket of *J. Edgar Hoover on Communism* (1969), one sequel to Hoover's anticommunist classic *Masters of Deceit* (1958), depicts a ruddy, graying, older man, stocky and tidy. He sits at the edge of a desk and balances an anonymous book on his right thigh, the red of the binding offsetting his neatly coordinated blue suit and tie. His face is dominated by the loose jaw, spatulate nose, and wide, baggy eyes that inspired his frequent caricature as a bulldog (see figure 1.1).

Yet for all its resonance, this familiar image of the sturdy, vigilantly literate Hoover, the Cold War icon who personified a watchful "Fourth Branch of Government," has blocked our view of the comparably significant young Hoover first hired by the Bureau's Radical Division in 1919. Then pictured as a "slender bundle of high-charged electric wire" (Vaile), this twenty-four-year-old Hoover embodied a clean-cut, streamlined, dynamically modernized shift in American police leadership. In shades of Nick Carraway, the true star of *The Great Gatsby* (1925), one Jazz Age newspaper feature cast him as a dead ringer for "an active young bond salesman" (qtd. in Hoover, Scrapbooks).[1]

While the FBI was attracting some of its first headlines by chasing African American boxer Jack Johnson, an even younger John Edgar Hoover was earning the modern nickname "Speed" by delivering groceries in his native Washington, D.C., grinding out the grades that made him valedictorian of the Central High class of 1913, and drilling Company A in his school's corps of cadets. His zealous neatness, watertight memory for written detail, gift for steering

FIGURE 1.1: The official portrait of an aging Hoover used on the back jacket of *J. Edgar Hoover on Communism* (1969). (Courtesy of and copyright © MPI/Getty Images.)

conversations and agendas, and piercing staccato speech (perfect for the debate team but too rapid for stenographers, went the story) expedited success in all these lines (Gentry 65). A family photo from the period shows a three-quarter-profile view of Hoover in his cadet uniform, a white-gloved, stern-faced teen-aged captain almost as thin as his ceremonial sword (see figure 1.2). Descended on his mother's side from Swiss mercenaries, he practiced a rapid military step even off the parade field.

Hoover's paramilitarized Bureau, its squad division designed with reference to the Central High cadets, gave no quarter to the thoughtfully hard-hitting New Negroes who followed Jack Johnson. Even so, the FBI's longest-serving director matured in thrall to parallel "martial technologies for racial becoming" (Gilroy, *Against* 233), disciplines of drill, uniform, and mass pageant suitable to rearm white American manhood for a new century of racial challenge at home and abroad. Hoover's cadet photo seems a world away from his portrait as an anticommunist heavyweight but ironically resembles the images of the young and restless New Negroes that so alarmed him at the FBI's Radical Division.

FIGURE 1.2: The spartan teenaged Hoover in the uniform of the Central High cadet corps, circa 1912. (Courtesy of the National Archives and Records Administration.)

There, pictures of dignified, soldierly, and sometimes armed black men printed in the *Crisis*, the D.C. *Bee*, and dozens of other African American papers were collected with dismay (see figure 1.3).

Supplanting the "Old Crowd Negro" *Vanity Fair* tunefully identified with "the Cotton-Picker, the Mammy Singer and the Darky Banjo-Player" ("Enter" 61), pugnacious New Crowd Negroes—the first avant-garde of the Harlem Renaissance—were urged to rehabilitate the face of the race through "education and physical action in self defense" (Randolph and Owen 74). W.E.B. Du Bois's 1919 editorial "Returning Soldiers" pushed the black veterans in the front ranks of the New Crowd to march for liberty even after leaving the killing fields of World War I. "Make way for Democracy!" Du Bois ventriloquized ("Returning

FIGURE 1.3: A decorated New Negro soldier in his U.S. Army uniform, his photograph printed in the same 1919 issue of the *Crisis* that featured Du Bois's scorching editorial "Returning Soldiers." (Courtesy of the Modernist Journals Project.)

Soldiers"). "We saved it in France, and by the Great Jehovah, we will save it in the United States of America, or know the reason why" (13). While Hoover spent the war years as a stateside employee of the Justice Department, and the Red Summer of 1919 as a foe of the African Americans who met vigilantes with bullets and invective, his highest ambition could have inhabited much the same language—language underlined, in fact, in an early FBI exposé protesting Du Bois's supposed encouragement of "radicalism and sedition" in the souls of black folk (U.S., Senate, *Radicalism* 1).

Part 1 of *F.B. Eyes* aims to add depth and detail to less-familiar portraits of Hoover as a young militant, and to establish the character of the also young law enforcement agency he joined in the wake of World War I. Starting with these two beginnings, one personal and one institutional, is not knee-jerk biog-raphism, since together they opened the FBI's appointment with black letters. Explaining why Hoover and the Bureau began to pursue African Ameri-can writing, this part of the book presents the first of its five theses: namely, *The birth of the Bureau, coupled with the birth of J. Edgar Hoover, ensured the FBI's attention to African American literature.* Section 1 recounts how the pre-Hoover Bureau emerged amid the social divisions of early twentieth-century America, and how it cultivated both literary publicity and public anti–New Negroism to whet an undivided national appetite for federal policing. Section 2 examines how the pre-Bureau Hoover managed his surprising familiarity with Afro-America—a familiarity possibly genetic as well as disciplinary in nature. Asking if Hoover was secretly blacker than Huck Finn, it turns out, promises more than idle race fiction. Section 3 establishes that with Hoover's hiring by the Bureau during the first Red Scare and the dawn of Harlem's cultural rebirth, the FBI's racial and literary preoccupations only deepened. Under Hoover's watch, the earliest Harlem Renaissance writing became the common passion of Bureau anti–New Negroism and "lit.-cop federalism," the latter defined below as the effort to inject a compelling federal police presence into the U.S. print public sphere. Among Hoover's many organizational coups, this is to say, was seizing on Afro-modernism to link the racial and literary means through which the FBI had sought nationwide public approval. Years before Hoover and his "Hoover boys" battled machine-gunning gangsters and entered the heroes' gal-lery of Depression America, they aimed to make a national public enemy of the Harlem Renaissance. In the process, they helped to modernize literary surveil-lance for the American Century.

The Bureau before Hoover

During Hoover's drawn-out administration, when the four Bureau heads that preceded him were virtually impossible to recall, the director received birthday greetings every July 26. The anniversary was not his, precisely, but the FBI's. On July 26, 1908, the year that also premiered the Model T and the Geiger coun-ter, a thirty-four-person "Special Agent Force" was established as a permanent investigative arm of the U.S. Department of Justice. Members of Congress, un-aware that the Bureau's founding would mark a permanent increase in federal police power, foresaw enough to protest the imperial aura of "a general system of spying upon and espionage of the people, such as has prevailed in Russia, in France under the Empire, and at one time in Ireland" (Walter I. Smith). But Attorney General Charles Bonaparte, a grandnephew of the French emperor, relied on a congressional recess and an executive order from President Theodore

Roosevelt to charge the proto-FBI with detecting and prosecuting a short list of federal crimes. A handful of postal, banking, and antitrust violations were placed under its watch, along with criminal acts against the national government. (By way of comparison, a full 3,300 offenses fell under Bureau jurisdiction by 2001 [Jeffreys-Jones 2].) Bonaparte and Roosevelt, the two fathers of invention in the executive branch, joined fellow Progressive reformers of their era in revering morality, efficiency, and managerial expertise, disdaining the constitutional niceties that threatened the president's reign over the national good. They pressed the Bureau's earliest bosses to reconcile the cool-headed administrative efficiency vital to President Roosevelt's Progressive reforms with a light American gloss on authoritarian Bonapartism—a synthesis perfected, with a twist, under Hoover's uniquely charismatic bureaucracy, part Progressive archetype in its standardization, professionalization, and quasi-scientific management, and part cult of anticommunist personality. Stanley W. Finch, the first head of the new force, fit Roosevelt and Bonaparte's bill by commanding his "brick agents," or street-level investigators, to wire itemized expense accounts directly to the Justice Department. Finch's successors were usually as demanding yet notably more flamboyant, supervisors of a Progressive corruption hunt not always cut out to embody Progressive standards of moral probity. Together, they cleared the way for the immersion in literature and the drive against black American dissent that stamped Hoover's tenure.

From Clemenceau to Sarkozy, French presidents and prime ministers have longed to fuse the man of government with the man of letters. Across the Atlantic, this desire more commonly infected chiefs of the federal police. Judging from library catalogs, the directors who led the Bureau through World War I and the early 1920s considered the hunt for literary fame a part of their job description. National law enforcement, they assumed, required tales of gallant crime fighting to justify itself to a relatively underpoliced country, one in which private political detectives such as the Pinkerton Agency exerted unusual influence and the hostile powers that united to defeat radical Reconstruction—southern Democrats and northern industry—greeted the twentieth century equally wary of federal investigation. Adapting the literary formula of Allan Pinkerton, whose illustrated history *The Molly Maguires and the Detectives* (1877) suspensefully advertised his labor spy business, early FBI leaders sought to transform the mutual advantages of high book sales, personal celebrity, and conservative political catechism into countrywide support for what was, in effect, America's national detective agency.

In 1919, New Yorker William J. Flynn took the reins of what was now called the "Bureau of Investigation," renamed the FBI proper in 1935. His humbly titled crime magazine, *Flynn's Weekly*, endeavored to close Pinkerton's sale of the credentialed professional detective and to polish Flynn's own reputation as America's top anarchist chaser–turned–top cop. Flynn's replacement, William J. Burns, was an ex–Secret Service operative and likeably crooked nightclub fixture whose wooden acting in the silent film *The Exposure of the Land Swindlers* (1913) did not stop the *New York Times* from reviewing him as the only detective of genius produced on American soil (Richard Gid Powers, *Broken* 123). When not playing the part of the virtuoso bloodhound, connecting with friend Sir Arthur Conan Doyle, or facilitating the Justice Department's descent into the "Department of Easy Virtue," Burns found time to produce books such as *The Masked War: The Story of a Peril That Threatened the United States by the Man Who Uncovered the Dynamite Conspirators and Sent Them to Jail* (1913). A shelf of self-promoting follow-ups made true-crime renown into Bureau-building pulp. For Burns and Flynn, literary success was also a means of low-cost crime deterrence. Why cross the government man who always gets his anarchist? their readers were coached to ask. As Richard Gid Powers suggests, Hoover's own nonfiction, initially just at home in *True Detective Mysteries* as in *Masters of Deceit*, could draw from an old Bureau recipe for turning Pinkerton-style marketing to public account (*Broken* 44).

The young FBI's attitude to non-Bureau authorship, meanwhile, was less indulgent. In February 1911, fewer than three years after its founding, the Bureau opened its first two files on civilian literary perpetrators. In one of them, the Justice Department confronted American modernism's transatlantic high in the person of Ezra Pound. "This bureau has been advised that Dr. Ezra Pound . . . left the United States in February 1911 and proceeded to Rapallo, Italy," reports the file's first entry (qtd. in Robins 32). Between Finch's directorship and Hoover's death, the documentation of Pound's geographic and political migrations swelled to a *Cantos*-sized 1,512 pages. In its other earliest literary file, the Bureau acknowledged American modernism's socialist front in the form of the *Masses*, the magazine "of outstanding liberals and radicals" founded the same month as Pound's departure for Rapallo (qtd. in Robins 34). Agents underlined the presence of John Reed in the editorial mix, zeroing in on the author of *Ten Days That Shook the World* (1919), a classic eyewitness sketch of the Russian Revolution whose notes they briefly seized in 1918. Pound and Reed, the latter an actual Soviet secret agent, were each suspected of treasonous behavior that exceeded his literary bad manners. The traffic they inspired at FBI headquarters nonetheless reveals the Bureau's concern, in advance of the formal "Publication Section" created in 1920, that radical enemies also recognized the links among law, letters, and ideas of justice. A broad-minded spectator of literary modernism under construction, the Bureau anticipated the new modernist studies of twenty-first-century English departments in regarding Pound and Reed's diverging roads as equally iconoclastic.

It was not until Hoover's employment in 1919 that the FBI acknowledged African American literary modernism as such. Yet the Bureau's encounter with New Negro combativeness, this modernism's starter fuel, can be dated from what is sometimes called the FBI's first great case. In 1912, Chicago police did what a posse of Great White Hopes could not and overcame African American boxer Jack Johnson, crowned the first black heavyweight champion of the world the year the Bureau was founded. A Texan with a patient uppercut and a "golden smile," Johnson had a talent for punishment that led African Americans to consider the physical inferiority of the Caucasian. In the opposite corner, novelist Jack London forgot the best of his socialism long enough to vow that the "White Man must be rescued" (4). For his part, Johnson was not always enchanted by his role as a racial symbol, agonizing over the near-riots that shadowed his victories over white opponents. But he lacked all hesitation when defying those who invoked white supremacy to condemn his freewheeling love life. "I am not a slave and . . . I have the right to choose who my mate shall be without the dictation of any man," he insisted (qtd. in Ward 310). Johnson's most galling social crime—enthusiastically consensual relations with an overlapping series of white wives and girlfriend "sports"—was technically not a federal offense. Chicago-based FBI agents were eager to accompany city cops in collecting evidence against him, however, once the local district attorney invoked the Mann Act, a 1910 law elevating interstate trade for the purpose of prostitution into a federal felony. As noted by intelligence historian Rhodri Jeffreys-Jones, the act's official title, the White Slave Traffic Act, "told its own story" (6), divulging a textbook case of ideological inversion, the world of American racial slavery turned upside down. "All of the horrors which have ever been urged, either truthfully or fancifully, against the black-slave traffic," pledged the law's author, Illinois representative James Mann, "pale into insignificance as compared to the horrors of the so-called 'white slave traffic' " (Mann).

With a push from Bureau director Stanley Finch, temporarily retitled commissioner for the suppression of white slave traffic, the FBI embraced the Mann Act as a summons for sprawl, a "pretext for the Progressive expansion of social regulation in the name of social health" (Diffee 413). Fanning out from the beachhead in Chicago, Bureau field offices were opened in New York, Baltimore, San Antonio, and San Francisco, all commissioned to enforce the act without compromise. (By midcentury, over fifty such offices gave the FBI entrée to most of urban America [Theoharis, "Appendix"].) A Chicago agent discovered the Mann Act charge against Johnson that stuck: violating the nation's peace and dignity in transporting Belle Schreiber, a jilted white lover eager for payback, from Pennsylvania to Illinois with intent to install her as a madam. In June 1913, Johnson was sentenced to a $1,000 fine and a term in federal prison. He would flee to Canada before serving a day and land high and dry in Paris, later a requisite stop for African American authors hoping to escape the F.B. eye. In 1920, after seven years of exile, he reentered the United States via Mexico and paid his dues with less than a year in Leavenworth prison, a favorite of his sports-loving warden but the unwilling inspiration of toughened anti-intermarriage laws.

In contrast to Jack Johnson, the Bureau did not long evade the consequences of what Richard Gid Powers, Hoover's best scholarly biographer, describes as the FBI's original "travesty of justice" (*Broken* 69). As black Americans immediately perceived, Johnson had been victimized by federal authorities because of his color. The Mann Act, ostensibly intended to punish interstate criminal enterprise, had been bent to chastise the personal conduct of a one-man insult to white supremacy. District Attorney Harry Parkin cheerfully confessed to the charge of example making, admitting that Johnson's misfortune was to be the foremost symbol "of the evil in permitting the intermarriage of whites and blacks" (qtd. in Ward 344). In Powers's analysis, the FBI's first big case therefore doubles as its original sin, a premeditated "first 'big push' *away* from the important, but difficult and sensitive, economic and political investigations" Attorney General Bonaparte had planned for it in 1908 (*Broken* 66; emphasis in original). Jack Johnson's conviction, Powers proposes, fed the Bureau's weakness for "splashy investigations with big publicity payoffs that did not annoy any important political or economic interests" (66). The Bureau's color-struck crusade against private corruption in fact rose with the boxer's fall. Marcus Garvey, too, would be considered for Mann Act prosecution, one in a string of sexualized foils who promised to consolidate white support for federal law enforcement on both sides of the Mason-Dixon line. Under Hoover's guidance, these foils were framed as tools of a fundamentally immoral communist conspiracy, threats to "every home and fireside" in the nation (U.S., House, *Attorney General* 154).

Powers is on solid ground in noting that risky FBI prosecutions of congressional corruption and antitrust violations would be few between the Jack Johnson case and the 1970s. However, insofar as the Johnson case demonstrated how Bureau interests could be served by stalking the most audacious African American voices, it opened a vein of FBI reconnaissance of "racial matters" as important, difficult, and sensitive as any. Answering the latest incarnations and pronouncements of the New Negro became big business at the Bureau even before the federal intelligence system came of age, offering an alternative to frontal assaults on more entrenched interests that nevertheless represented no harmless, purely symbolic diversion. Like the fictional Bureau agent who prowls through Howard Sackler's Jack Johnson play *The Great White Hope* (1968), true-life FBI men beat Hoover to the racial punch, resolving that Johnson and other charismatically free-traveling black moderns could not be permitted "to go on impressing and exciting" the pacesetters of the Great Migration, the black thousands voting with their feet against parochialism (Sackler 78). At times, the Bureau was tempted to criminalize the Great Migration itself, jolted by the exodus of 400,000 black southerners between 1915 and 1919 alone. In 1916, FBI special agents spent months unsuccessfully seeking evidence of a Republican plot to flood the North with reenfranchised blacks. The same year, the Bureau contemplated a mail ban of the black-owned newspaper the *Chicago Defender*, the migration's most effective advertising circular. The *Defender* would retain its postal privileges, but not before Robert Abbott, the paper's self-made editor, was pulled in for questioning (Schmidt 62–67). "Abbott in his zeal for the betterment of his people may have overstepped the bounds of propriety," an offended FBI interviewer reported back to Washington (qtd. in Washburn 17).

Such racial partisanship at the Bureau allowed *Birth of a Nation* (1915), D. W. Griffith's epic film of neo-Confederacy, to go easy on the FBI-like "Bureau of Military Justice" damned in the film's novelistic source, Thomas Dixon's *The Klansman* (1905). By the time Griffith's gift to the Klan hit American screens, the FBI's wars on white slavery and black migration had overwritten memories, fresher to Dixon, of the southern invasion of federal police during Radical Reconstruction (Jeffreys-Jones 35–36).[2] Several inclinations of the Bureau aroused this social rewhitening of federal policing, not all of them crudely instrumental. The Jack Johnson case revealed the FBI as something of a typically Progressive institution, inclined to meet the test of the New Negro with the wisdom of the redeemed white South. Like Progressive-in-chief Teddy Roosevelt, who admitted that in this rare instance he was unable to think clearly, the Bureau found the race problem genuinely baffling beyond the terms of the post-Reconstruction status quo. At the same time, however, the Bureau mounted challenges to the New Negro aware of their power to win favor across American states and regions. As W.E.B. Du Bois argued in his monumental *Black Reconstruction in America* (1935), the Reconstruction-ending Compromise of 1877 had launched a rebuilding of national unity in opposition to ex-slaves. "All hatred that the whites after the Civil War had for each other," he concluded, "gradually concentrated itself" on rising African Americans (*Black Reconstruction* 125). A North-South coalition of distaste and dominance over the black population was cultivated by the Supreme Court's *Plessy v. Ferguson* decision of 1896, by congressional inaction on spectacle lynching, and by the refusal of the executive branch to enforce the Fourteenth Amendment solidifying black citizenship (Marx 196). Touting its interstate manhunt for Jack Johnson and its scandalized suspicion of the Great Migration, the FBI did not hesitate to nationalize itself on the back of such nation-knitting betrayals. In this way, the Bureau set anti–New Negroism beside national literary publicity as a second vehicle for projecting a good name across state lines. As we will see, one of J. Edgar Hoover's earliest managerial feats was to blend these two vehicles of Bureau self-nationalization, a maneuver that drew his agents to the earliest journals of the Harlem Renaissance.

Hoover before the Bureau

The world-famous Hoover looked back on a birth fateful in setting and timing. On New Year's Day of 1895, he was delivered at home at 413 Seward Square, a two-story residence in a quiet crossroads of civil servants seven blocks from the U.S. Capitol. The lace-curtained stucco house in which he entered the world would be his home until 1938, and he left it pledged to enshrine its values forever. "As a youth I was taught basic beliefs," Hoover recalled in a 1959 address (qtd. in "Auxiliary"). "Cynics," he allowed, "may regard this with derision. For instance, I was taught that no book was ever to be placed above the Bible. Children in my youth were taught the code of the American flag and to defend it against any manner of desecration, as a symbol of life, liberty, and justice" (4). Hoover's memories are defensively calculated, decked with stars and stripes, basics and Bibles, the secondhand furniture of nativist nostalgia. Glorifying the Hoover family custom of state service, they supply a usable personal past for the straight-and-narrow code inscribed on the FBI shield: "Fidelity, Bravery, Integrity." Yet these memories also accurately render a long ago that was homesick for a fading America, a childhood captivated by visions of a purer, more homogeneous democracy. The finest thing about the director's boyhood, vouches *J. Edgar Hoover, Modern Knight Errant* (1958), a smitten youth-market biography, was its "old-fashioned leanings" (Comfort 10).

White restoration, the redemption of the antebellum order of things, was the engine of Hoover's education in sight of the U.S. Capitol. The usual explanation of Hoover's Bureau-shaping racism in relation to the "southern conservatism" (Jeffreys-Jones 8) and "virtual apartheid" (Summers 349) of his boyhood misses the crucial detail that D.C. was not so much segregated as segregat*ing* in the new century. The same capital city that sponsored a national coalition of dominance over blacks sheltered the country's largest, most prosperous, and most intricately snobbish African American metropolitan society prior to Harlem's rise. For decades after the 1877 compromise, black Washington was spared the lynching and less vicious displays of white reconsolidation common in the deeper South. "Washington wasn't South" to us, remembered one African American resident, imaginatively relocating what was then the southernmost nonsegregated city in the country (qtd. in Yellin 19). The relative freedom of the capital was reflected in its status as a harbor for black southern migrants, so-called New Cits who upped D.C.'s African American population to 94,000 by 1910 (Kerr 49). Several thousand black professionals—teachers, lawyers, dentists, ministers, physicians, civil servants, and Howard professors, such as Sterling Nelson Brown, the poet's father—catered to this growing community when not serving the nation at large (Ruble 51). In 1907, no fewer than 2,785 African Americans worked in federal offices, over 10 percent of the total federal workforce in the city, with 415 occupied as government managers, engineers, scientists, and clerks (Yellin 25). A few years later, every U.S. dollar produced by the Bureau of Engraving and Printing incorporated the signature of a black Washingtonian, the register of the Treasury Department; this symbol of Afro-Washington's place in state officialdom was circulated wherever American money talked (4). Even the *Washington Post* was moved to celebrate the dapper and degreed New Negroes of D.C.'s elite "Four Hundred," taking cues from Booker T. Washington's *A New Negro for a New Century* (1900) in an editorial boasting of "a standard of [black] culture unequaled, and in some respects impossible, in any other city" ("Lines").

Prosegregation feeling congealed after the 1912 presidential election, however, the contest that propelled Democrat Woodrow Wilson to the White House and, soon enough, to the realization that his Progressive "New Freedom" would not include black federal workers, increasingly Jim-Crowed in their capital offices. Not long after Hoover led the Central High cadet corps in Wilson's inaugural parade, the Virginia-born, Georgia-raised president dismissed all but two members of President William Howard Taft's makeshift "Black Cabinet" and consigned black civil servants to inferior tables and toilets, proclaiming an end to corrupt Republican patronage. Segregation would be federalized in Wilson's chapter of the Progressive era, the underbelly of successful antitrust and eight-hour-day legislation. Progressive ideas about industrial and governmental efficiency "did not cause Wilsonian racial discrimination," clarifies historian Eric S. Yellin; it was pre-Progressive racism that "led Wilson to exclude black people from his 'New Freedom'" (6). But Wilsonians managed to "hit upon discriminatory and discursive practices that allowed them to claim simultaneously" the virtues of white restoration and Progressive advancement: for example, the practice of battling both crooked party favoritism and wasteful "black sloth" in federal employment (6). In tune with Wilson's racially biased changes in government hiring came the "Dixification" of D.C.'s private racial climate under the first southern president since the Civil War, a friend of Thomas Dixon who praised *Birth of a Nation* as history written with lightning. Booker T. Washington observed that he had "never seen the [District's] colored people so discouraged and so bitter" as in the aftermath of Wilson's crackdown (letter to Oswald Garrison Villard 248). The city's ballooning NAACP branch, by 1916 the largest in the country and a self-constituted "national vigilance committee . . . for Negro manhood rights," was one antidote to dejection (qtd. in Green 181). Another was the earliest non-Harlem scene of the Harlem Renaissance, led by poet-hostess Georgia Douglas Johnson at the literary Saturday Nighters Club, bandleader-composer Duke Ellington at the Oriental Gardens, and philosopher-impresario Alain Locke at Howard University, all three victims of FBI snooping under Hoover's directorship. Jean Toomer's *Cane* (1923) to the contrary, the drama of belated segregation set D.C.'s Afro-modernism flowing even before "Prohibition and the War" reanimated Seventh Street, the city's downscale black Broadway (39).

Hoover's family, headed by a government man dependent on the federal bureaucracy for his income and esteem, occupied the front lines of several local campaigns for white separation. To the Hoovers' alarm, a growing population of African Americans brushed the edges of Pipetown, the neighborhood surrounding the family home on Seward Square, at the turn of the century. From his post within the U.S. Coastal and Geodetic Survey, Hoover's depressive father Dickerson nodded his approval as "Jim Crow corners" seemed to counterattack, spreading from the Bureau of Engraving and Printing, the department where black men had risen the highest (Green 166). The defeat of black plans to march through the federal institutions eased the elder Hoover's rise from platemaker to chief of the survey's print shop. J. Edgar Hoover's ascent to the top of his class and the corps of cadets was staged in a school he chose in part for its racial exclusivity. Central High meant a three-mile walk from Seward Square, but it boasted a reputation joined to its founding as the first consciously white academy in the District, the negative image of tony Dunbar High, the first public high school for African Americans in the entire United States. Hoover's early religious life was likewise racially marked, and likewise pursued with one eye to advancement in the worldly city. Along with his older brother Dick, the teenaged Hoover transferred membership to the Old First Presbyterian Church, opting for one of Washington's swankiest congregations. In 1910, he watched as the resident committee on arrangements turned colored delegates away from the sixth World Sunday School Convention (Green 165). Hoover's response to this enforcement of spiritual segregation was to volunteer as a Sunday school teacher at Old First, memorably leading classes in his cadet uniform, a Christian soldier marching to the lectern. Studying law by night at nearby George Washington University after graduating from Central High, Hoover gave his limited free time to the Kappa Alpha Order, the southern fraternity that contributed rituals to the original Ku Klux Klan. Hoover was not then, nor did he ever become, a Klansman. In time, he authorized the implosion of the third Klan through the counterintelligence program code-named "COINTELPRO—White Heat," the FBI's most successful infiltration effort of the 1960s and the ironic blueprint of the bloody COINTELPRO introduced against "black hate groups."[3] But the Washington Hoover first conquered was a whitening city in which segregation qualified as an incomplete project and a rising social asset. He did his best to complete the former in order to acquire the latter.

Inside Washington institutions beginning in the 1930s, a generation removed from segregation's local victory, explaining Hoover's pursuit of racial distinction was a common parlor game. Secure players claimed that this pursuit stemmed from Hoover's own racial impurity. Gore Vidal, the radical aristocrat raised in the upper boxes of white D.C. during the Great Depression, recollected that when "Hoover was becoming famous . . . it was always said of him—in my family and around the city—that he was mulatto. People said he came from a family that had 'passed'" (qtd. in Summers 350). Gossip about the sources of Hoover's "swarthy skin" and wavy black hair entered less lofty conversations at FBI headquarters (Tucker 158). Was Hoover the son of an African American mother secretly adopted by the Hoover family? (Ackerman, "Five Myths"). Inquiring minds at "SOG"—the Bureau's D.C. office imagined as the nation's true Seat of Government—wanted to know. Wesley Swearingen, a disaffected ex-FBI man, remembered skeptical after-hours talk of Hoover's birth certificate, witnessed only by J. Edgar's brother, and unfiled until 1938. "[F]or all the FBI agents," he clarified, "they'd go back and check everything about your family, your relatives, and everything else, to make sure they're squeaky clean. And here, Hoover's the director, and nobody really knows where he came from" (qtd. in Spannaus). Sam Noisette, Hoover's doorman and one of his Bureau's tiny cadre of African American special agents, supposed that Hoover really came from somewhere colored. At least once, this self-described "black man who knows his place" was overheard referring to the director as a "soul brother" (qtd. in Summers 123, 350). "Afrodoptions" of Hoover were less guarded within the privacy of black communities up and down the East Coast. There, the celebrity gangbuster was often recognized as a double "spook," spy and race man, a politically untouchable counterpart of Clark Gable and Rudolph Valentino, also claimed as race-passing undercover agents (Summers 350). If the word was right from Boston's Roxbury to Miami's Liberty City, the director possessed an old Negro bloodline on top of his confidential respect for New Negro militancy.

Hoover likely knew and resented the stories of his racial passing, more costly in official Washington than the accurate rumors of his emotional marriage to FBI associate director Clyde Tolson, the life partner who played the punishing assistant principal to Hoover's aloof chief executive for an impressive forty-four years. (Blandly, the suburban legend of Hoover's erotic cross-dressing is almost certainly unfounded. Despite the favorite mental image of millions of Americans, the Bureau director was no "tyrant in a tutu" [Weiner, *Enemies* xv]).[4] About Hoover, "there were two things taken for granted in my youth," confided the openly gay Vidal, "that he was a faggot and that he was black. Washington was and is a very racist town, and I can tell you that in those days the black blood part of it was very much the worst. . . . That's what many people flatly believed about Hoover, and he must have been so upset by it" (qtd. in Summers 350–51). Hoover's attacks on King and other African American activists, recent radical critics suggest, were fueled by the same brand of self-referential disgust, cultivated in the same gossipy southern city, that fed his disdain for less reputable gay men. To political theorist Thomas Dumm, for example, it is clear that racial and sexual "[h]atred and self-loathing operated in tandem for Hoover. In a sense, he resisted the compulsory heterosexuality dominant in Washington social life. If one took that argument seriously, though, one would also have to say that he was a pioneer in the movement for civil rights for African Americans. But in both cases the closeted character of his resistance had damaging effects that redounded far beyond Hoover himself" (81). Relieving his racial difference as well as his sexual otherness by lashing out at those less careful, Dumm's Hoover installs himself in the most reactionary of modern closets, an enclosure from which great power flows "in the name of exclusion and security" (88).

The fullest largely nonfictional exploration of Hoover's possible blackness takes the form of a hard-to-find small press book by Millie L. McGhee, a California teacher in search of peaceful coexistence with the director's spirit. In *Secrets Uncovered: J. Edgar Hoover—Passing for White?* (2000), McGhee details the conviction of her African American ancestors that Hoover was a self-denying chip off the family tree. McGhee's mother waited until the author was fifty years old, the book reports, to confirm that Hoover was "our cousin," the second cousin of McGhee's maternal grandfather, Big Daddy, to be exact, and the child of a slave-owning Hoover relative "so light-skinned that he was given . . . the conspicuous given name of 'Ivory'" (219). Photographs of an olive-toned J. Edgar Hoover in his thirties strike McGhee as evidence of these family ties, while the Hoovers' oddly amended Washington census records are harmonized with missing names in her own family's pedigree chart. Even so,

Secrets Uncovered self-critically sets the McGhees' oral tradition in dialogue with two opposed narratives of ancestry: an unpolished historical novel–cum– "recovered memory" of slavery authored by McGhee herself, and the cautious testimony of a professional genealogist, George Ott of Salt Lake City, whom she hired to sift through written archives from the Mormon Family History Center to rural Mississippi, come what may.

In his share of *Secrets Uncovered*, Ott maintains that the tie between Ivory and J. Edgar is fictitious. Yet he also offers courthouse evidence that several of Hoover's ancestors were Pike County, Mississippi, slave owners who lived in proximity to several of McGhee's maternal relations, opening the option that Hoover men formed relationships with a contemporaneous female slave, Emily Allen, a foremother of the modern McGhees. Tightening an incestuous knot of love and denial straight from William Faulkner's *Go Down, Moses* (1942), Ott conjectures that John T. Hoover, J. Edgar's grandfather, may have been the mulatto son of Hoover's great-grandfather William: a son who snatched the advantages of passing as white, but who was aware of his mothering by Allen, a trusted household slave who may also have slept with William's father, Christian (224). Although John Hoover died a decade before J. Edgar's birth, John's wife, Celia, survived until the future Bureau legend was fourteen. Substantiating McGhee family lore, she thus lived long enough to reveal to J. Edgar the Faulknerian secret of his unsegregated parentage—just ahead of his determination to taste the cream of segregating Washington.

Short of a posthumous DNA test, we will never know for sure if Dumm and McGhee have the edge on official history, and if Hoover should thus be added to the list of eminent African American public servants. Thus far, his sanctioned relatives, Anglo-Saxon and Swiss American, have declined the path taken by Thomas Jefferson's, who finally acknowledged the kinship of the descendants of Sally Hemmings, Jefferson's enslaved mistress, after such a test in 1998. In its own unscientific terms, however, *Secrets Uncovered* proves that Hoover belongs with Jefferson in the company of southern-born nation builders whose liaisons with blackness dramatize America's reluctantly interracial history. In the case of the McGhees' conclusion that Hoover was at least as black as Hemmings and Jefferson's grandchildren, the historical stake is not a share of the American founding, but instead a role in the emergence of the modern American security state. The Hoover-FBI complex is generously recast as an interracial Frankenstein, a hybrid monster that might atone by confessing a backdoor secret. Hoover's historically challenged vow that "there will never be a Negro Special Agent" cannot deter Millie McGhee from picturing a partly Negro director and institution, troubled by deception and needy for forgiveness (qtd. in Sullivan, *The Bureau* 268). Applying Ralph Ellisonian logic to the history of U.S. espionage, she submits that Bureau segregation was never the airtight, opaque jug Hoover's institution declared it was. The recent unmasking of William A. Bailey, Herbert Boulin, William E. Lucas, and other early black FBI informants, forgotten antiheroes of the first Red Scare, bears out McGhee's insistence (Kornweibel, *"Seeing"* xiii). As a newly minted Bolshevik chaser, Hoover was in fact willing to manage polished African American spies such as Dr. Arthur Ulysses Craig, best remembered as the country's "first black graduate electrical engineer" but also, we now know, the Bureau's first regular black undercover operative, the New Negro scholar gone anticommunist mole (Kornweibel, *"Seeing"* 61, 85). James Wormley Jones, the first black American to become a full-fledged FBI agent and another product of a patriotic black middle class, enjoyed a lifelong correspondence with the director (Kornweibel, *"Seeing"* 104, 109). Walter White, the Harlem Renaissance elder and race-passing investigator of lynching, denied an early request "to brief Hoover on the racial situation" but volunteered information designed "to protect the NAACP from guilt by association with more militant groups" (Kornweibel, *"Seeing"* 62). Decades later, pressured by civil rights critics to validate his racial evenhandedness, Hoover recalled that "Walter used to visit me any time he was in Washington. . . . I consider him a friend and a man who had a purpose and principle" (qtd. in Booker 33). The Americanist element in New Negro culture thus made for as many strange bedfellows as its racial primitivism.

To Millie McGhee, exposing the Bureau's hidden dash of color is simultaneously a means to heal her own broken spirit, to satisfy a thwarted, ghostly Hoover who "really wants this story told" (230), and to dull the ache that FBI racism has "inflicted on our Nation" (7). To McGhee's grandfather Big Daddy, quoted in *Secrets Uncovered*, exposing Hoover's mixed ancestry is a means to reveal the high costs of special black insight into "mulatto America": costs toted up, for him, in nothing less than the assassination of Martin Luther King Jr., one of whose "group of detectives found out the truth about J. Edgar's black bloodline, and threatened to expose him," with revenge taken at the Lorraine Motel in Memphis (229). Big Daddy's vision of Hoover and King as dueling intelligence chiefs—colored spy versus colored spy, one passing and one proudly black, each leading armies of racial inspectors—figures the close rivalry between FBI and African American histories as a genetic detective story.[5] While Hoover preferred to imagine this rivalry in other terms, his native city similarly advised him that clandestine watchfulness was the price of settled racial appearances, his own and the Bureau's. The semblance of racial purity required perpetual wariness, Hoover learned and relearned: first during Washington's delayed march to segregation; and later, as hearsay about his descent from black domestics jeopardized his familiarity with Noisette, James Crawford, and Worthington Smith,

African American chauffeurs and handymen whom Hoover elevated to special agent grade during World War II, the better to beat the draft without threatening his dependence (Richard Gid Powers, *Secrecy* 323). On the peculiar front where FBI literary criticism met the grammar of espionage, Hoover's drive for racial distinction meshed with the investigative procedures of his Bureau, urging on each techniques for maximizing the value of interracial traffic while camouflaging its damaging display. Close study, official reproach, grudging respect, and muted employment of African American writing became an FBI hallmark—a literary analog of Hoover's publicly deniable confidence in black intimates such as Annie Fields, his maid and solitary full-time housemate after his mother's death, the first person whom he greeted each morning for decades, and the first to discover his body after his own passing. The last person with whom Hoover ever spoke, black gardener James Crawford, quietly inherited half of the director's well-tailored suits after the state funeral.

Bureau of Letters: Lit.-Cop Federalism, the Hoover Raids, and the Harlem Renaissance

"Wanted. A servant at 413 Seward Square" (Hoover, "The Weekly Review" 20). So reads an item in Hoover's earliest surviving literary effort, a two-page neighborhood newspaper from 1906 that the eleven-year-old reported and, like Millie McGhee, published under his own steam. Apart from advertising the Hoover family's comfortable place in the federally employed D.C. middle class, "The Weekly Review" hints at several of Hoover's lasting rhetorical preferences. These include the proverbial saw ("Where there is a will, there is a way."); the prescriptive guide to better health and blameless appearance ("Eat slowly. Don't eat adulterated food. Don't eat too much. Don't eat between meals. Clean your teeth."); and the case study of disaster bravely averted ("Escaped from death. On Friday, about 12:15 o'clock, Mrs. Hoover, of 413 Seward Square, S.E. came near to losing her life. She was frying some eggs for lunch, and the blaze caught to her back") (20–21). From the standpoint of the Bureau's entanglement with Afro-modernism, the most revealing item arrives at the end of a feature on the bicentennial of Benjamin Franklin, the American thinker-tinker whose *Autobiography* (1793) shines through Hoover's maxims on the virtues of will and steady chewing. "Franklin's two-hundredth anniversary was celebrated on Wednesday last," notes the director-to-be (21). "At the Library [of Congress] there were books which he has printed, papers written by him, and the Declaration of Independence, signed by him" (21).

Both the Franklin plan of textual governance and the archival muscle that exhibited it impressed Hoover's literary education and molded the operations of his FBI. Within this document-squirreling bureaucracy, binding marginalia in Hoover's royal blue ink preceded the last word of his signature. The authority of this autograph was augmented by a torrent of books, files, leaflets, manuals, articles, index cards, press releases, top-secret reports, and mass-market hype vetted, bylined, or authored by the agent-in-chief. Bureau procedure, observes William H. Epstein, consisted "primarily of a huge catalogue of words" (77). Redrafted by Hoover, the William J. Flynn–William J. Burns model of the FBI author-director mushroomed into a thoroughgoing literarization, strategic and obsessive, of federal policing. Under J. Edgar's signature, the Bureau became a purveyor of what I call "lit.-cop federalism," state supervision pursued through a cluster of text-centered desires and activities ranging from the archival to the editorial, the interpretive to the authorial. Not just a kind of intragovernmental newspaper, a provider of crime bulletins and special investigative reports to Congress and the executive branch, Hoover's FBI grew to be a very real and very ambitious library, publisher, critic, and author-function, often aiming to catapult its words beyond the Washington Beltway.

Binding these various literary identities together was the unsecret mission of lit.-cop federalism: the mission to cross the theoretically bright line between state power and civil society, and to insert a beefed-up, well-read federal police presence into the U.S. print public sphere.[6] The results of this crossing, striking in range and page count, expressed an institutional imperative as well as a raging egotism. Unlike his peers in more deeply rooted secret police forces, up and spying in every European country by the turn of the twentieth century, Hoover was called on to build a national countersubversive force in the world capital of public relations. Print attracted him as the most potent PR instrument: for one thing, when the young lawyer came to work for the Bureau in 1919, there were no nationwide radio broadcasts. Down the road, the Bureau's sensitive antenna for publicity discovered alternatives to the print public sphere in a blossoming mass-media ecology. Beginning in the 1930s, the FBI was only too happy to lend its technical advice and improbable star image to radio and the movies, and, later in the game, to television.[7] And beginning with its very first investigation of a New Negro author, the FBI's part-time literary critics were forced to contend with the transnational public for African American writing. All the same, Hoover's Bureau never agreed to the demotion of the word, nor questioned the vitality of print within the citizens' theater of discursive exchange and political participation long involved in U.S. nation building. The FBI entered this theater with words blazing, determined to revamp a public sphere originally intent on keeping police power at a critical distance. The modern American art of state censorship, it ensured, would involve more exploration than repression of the literary marketplace.

Passionate about "making personal replies to citizens who write to him praising the F.B.I.," the mature Hoover of the 1930s officially reserved late-night hours for Romantic authorship, scribbling away "past midnight" in his Justice Department office (Jack Alexander, "The Director—I" 20). Had his day-time schedule as FBI director allowed him to administer the physical printing of the Bureau's publications, he might have leaped at this literary task as well. The preteen Hoover ran off his "Weekly Review" at first hand, most likely on the government-issued letterpress of the Steamboat Inspection Service, where his brother Dick built his own small kingdom in the state apparatus (Richard Gid Powers, *Secrecy* 20). Hoover's father, showing the way, had followed his own male parent into the print shop of the U.S. Coastal and Geodetic Survey (USCGS), preparing for a managerial job by making plates for nautical charts. Bureau scholars have relished speculating on the consequences of Hoover's up-bringing in a patriarchal culture of cartography. Literary critic William Beverly is most inventive in claiming that the scientific national land survey that oc-cupied the USCGS during the last decades of the nineteenth century provided a roadmap for the FBI's federalization of crime fighting. To Beverly's mind, the USCGS's transcontinental project ensured that "the unification and scientific refinement of *regional* representations into *national* maps [became] the family business" of Hoover men, a tradition of "suturing . . . the nation's space" passed down through three generations (33). When a male Hoover graduated from removing local cartographic tics to eradicating interstate crime, his "effort to federalize police communication and surveillance" naturally "applied the na-tionalizing and mapping principles of his forefathers' work with the USCGS laterally to another medium" (33). The notion of a lateral pass from uniform USCGS national maps to uniform FBI national crime reports is not implau-sible; in the parallel case of Soviet intelligence, the NKVD (predecessor of the KGB) thought it prudent to ingest the entire national map business (Postnikov 248). Yet the largest inheritance the USCGS left the Bureau was probably less abstract. Corroborating Franklin's self-publishing example, Hoover's print-shop legacy encouraged him to oversee Bureau representations at plate level, meddling everywhere from conception to consumption. Good press, the family business advised, belonged to those who operated one.

Guidelines for managing the publications of Bureau foes, meanwhile, emerged from another federal paper mill, the Library of Congress, where Hoover first saw Franklin's documents and worked for tuition money while studying law at George Washington University. In 1913, fresh from Central High, Hoover was hired as a junior messenger, filling the library's lowliest po-sition to the tune of $30 a month. When he left the Library of Congress in 1917, he was taking home twice this salary and tipped as a curatorial star in the making (Richard Gid Powers, *Secrecy* 39–40). "I'm sure he would be the chief librarian if he'd stayed with us," a coworker later volunteered (qtd. in Gentry 67). Over the four years in which Hoover discovered his talent for bibliography, the Library of Congress was pushed past the million-volume mark and into the front rank of American research collections by Herbert Putnam, the patrician superintendent and an "early example of the bureaucratic empire builder" eventually embodied by Hoover himself (Richard Gid Powers, *Secrecy* 39). Putnam's first imperious scheme took aim at the library's antiquated cataloging method, a tool unable to rescue the avalanche of donated paper rotting in the basement. Rejecting the Dewey decimal system as arbitrary in its division and numeration of subjects, Putnam spearheaded the development of the entirely new Library of Congress classification, envisioned as a national standard from its origin in 1900.

In Clint Eastwood's murky Hollywood biopic *J. Edgar* (2011), the young Hoover seems to invent the Library of Congress cataloguing system on his own from scratch and grit, the better to win the typing hand of his lifelong secretary, Helen Gandy. As a matter of fact, however, Hoover's job in the library required him to master Putnam's earlier creation, which replaced irregular, handwritten catalogs with mechanically reproducible printed cards, their finely differentiated subject headings bent on anatomizing the whole of human knowledge. Posted afterward to the FBI, Hoover took Putnam's cards with him. Reorganizing scattered Bureau records once dominated by Stanley Finch's mass-surveillance listing of all known prostitutes, he installed an elaborate "Editorial File System" of his own. With this import from the Library of Congress, Hoover appears to turn the Michel Foucault of *Discipline and Punish* (1975) on his famous head. Foucault's discipline-dealing nineteenth-century sociologists borrowed the epistemic machinery of the card index from the Parisian criminal records division, quietly benefiting from the discoveries of sweeping penal surveillance (Foucault, *Discipline* 281). Reversing the pattern, the FBI chief seized the card index back from the human sciences, rebalancing interdisciplinary accounts to the advantage of the police. In more homely terms of comparison, however, Hoover's file system kept Herbert Putnam of the Library of Congress right side up, embracing multidirectional cataloging in a "scientific format," each new item receiving a unique code, a generic classification, and all pertinent cross references (U.S., Dept. of Justice, *Annual, 1920* 173). According to Hoover's arrangement, crimes, actual and potential, were logged and interlogged like the library's books, and more than a few books like crimes. Possibly unlawful articles of language and literature ate up index cards as the FBI assumed the Library of Congress's national ambition, striving to become the criminological equivalent of Putnam's "bureau of information for the entire country" (Goodrum and Dalrymple 37). The novel felonies invited by the instantaneous telegraph; the rapid surface transport stoking the "migratory nature" of modern radicals—both necessitated a central police directory, Hoover reasoned, a national register able to "ascertain in a few minutes the numerous ramifications" of suspicious persons, places, and texts (U.S., House, *Attorney General* 166).

Hoover's opportunity to revise the Library of Congress classification was provided by political violence. Following an inaccurate May Day bombing campaign against senators, cabinet secretaries, and Supreme Court justices, a suicide bomb successfully demolished the facade of Attorney General A. Mitchell Palmer's Washington town house one evening in June 1919. "The outrages of last night," a shaken Palmer lectured reporters on the morning after, "indicate nothing but the lawless attempt of an anarchistic element in the population to terrorize the country and stay the hand of the government" (qtd. in "'Attempt'" 1). "Free speech has been outraged long enough," roared a more vengeful *Washington Post*, so "[l]et there be a few free treatments in the electric chair" ("'Attempt'" 1). The Red Summer best known to students of African American literature, a season of labor strikes, twenty-five or more white riots, and unprecedented black self-defense, was thus initiated by a wave of radical terrorism and untamed conservative recoil. In its own time, this wave was credited to the revolutionary contagion of the *biennio rosso*, the "Red Years" baptized by the Italian left and inaugurated by the 1917 Bolshevik coup in Petrograd (Richard Gid Powers, *Secrecy* 56). Since Al Qaeda's strikes on the Pentagon and World Trade Center in September 2001, the wave has been rediscovered as the "first 9/11," a once-again-legible precedent raising serious questions about the balance of patriotism and pluralism, civil liberty and public security (Ackerman, *Young J. Edgar*; Weiner, *Enemies* 3–55).

Like the second 9/11, the first presented a shaken federal government with the chance to secure a policeman's wish list. No later than the end of June, Palmer's snap prediction that the bombings "will only increase and extend the activities of our crime detecting force" had been fulfilled (qtd. in "'Attempt'" 1). Congress supplemented the Justice Department's $1.5 million antiradical drive by $500,000—about an extra five million in 2013 currency. The increase went to fund a new unit within the Bureau of Investigation, the Radical Division, open for business on the first of August. Within a year, this forerunner of the Martin Luther King Jr.–harassing Domestic Intelligence Division was the largest department in the FBI, boosting the number of Bureau agents from 301 to 579, occupying more than half of all headquarters' staff time, and confidently renaming itself the General Intelligence Division (Jeffreys-Jones 72; Preston 209–10; Post 269).

The overt task of the FBI Radical Division was to serve as a judicious Department of Homeland Security–style aggregator of terrorist threats, Palmer's eyes, ears, and editor in seeking "a thorough-going understanding of the situation as a whole" (U.S., Dept. of Justice, *Annual, 1919* 13). Equally weighty was the unwritten charge to consolidate the Bureau's advantage over the Secret Service and other intragovernmental police rivals while completing the federalization of political intelligence, a transfer of countersubversive power-knowledge away from autonomous urban "bomb squads" and Pinkerton-style private labor spies. This nationalizing of antiradical data collection was endorsed by the pulp literature of Bureau directors Flynn and Burns, not to mention by Allan Pinkerton himself, who came to call for "the centralization of the surveillance of anarchists and Bolsheviks in the Bureau of Investigation" (qtd. in Schmidt 54). It was given an enduring rationale by the antistatist Marxist internationalism of the Russian Revolution, and a trained constituency by World War I, the inspiration for blanket federal investigations of leftists under cover of the Espionage Act (1917), Sedition Act (1918), and Alien Act (1918). According to Frank J. Donner, the dean of civil libertarian intelligence historians, the same Great War that bred "awareness of the potential effectiveness of intelligence as a weapon against domestic enemies" also mustered a bonus army of intelligence operatives, a large class of "soldiers, ex-officers, reservists, [and] patriotic amateur detectives" schooled in espionage and "thirsting for peacetime assignments" once the firing stopped (47). The patriotic but draft-deferred Hoover did not have to wait long after the armistice to reapply the craft of intelligence he had studied at the Enemy Alien Registration unit, a wartime annex of the Justice Department. Two years out of law school and the Library of Congress, he was tapped as the first head of Palmer's fledgling Radical Division, and ordered to ensure there would be no repeat of the first 9/11.

"Modern life requires the nimble brain of youth for work like that of [the Bureau]," theorized the *Louisville Courier-Journal*, favorably spinning Hoover's tender age (qtd. in Hoover, Scrapbooks). "Courage, daring, intuition, what is known as the 'sixth sense,' boldness tempered always by prudence, are the requirements for success in intelligence work," the paper had it (qtd. in Hoover, Scrapbooks). In practice, off the feature page, the twenty-four-year-old Bureau administrator applied more boldness than prudence to the role of the New Spy, an unfriendly relative of the New Woman and the New Negro, one in a string of smartly novel modernist social types. Hoover's preventive war against "red terror" found him micromanaging an unparalleled roundup of radicals. In November 1919 and again in January 1920, agents of the Bureau burst simultaneously into meeting halls, theaters, cafés, bookstores, and a few unlucky bowling alleys, seizing upwards of 10,000 mostly noncitizen anarchists and communists in over thirty U.S. cities—altogether, the "biggest mass arrests in American history" (Weiner, *Enemies* 34). Membership in the proscribed radical parties was flexibly determined. Bureau agents arrested everyone at a session of a "Tolstoi Club," for example, enforcing their employer's tendency to confuse literary and political affiliations (David Williams 562). Hundreds of casualties of the "dragnet inquiry," guilty only of speaking against war and capitalism, were then deported in line with the extralegal procedures Hoover had rehearsed at the Enemy Alien unit: temptingly, the banishment of noncitizen revolutionaries did not qualify as a criminal proceeding under a 1918 Congressional statute. While the Harlem socialist journal the *Messenger* rationalized "that you cannot deport true ideas and principles by deporting persons" ("Deportation"), Hoover's Bureau superior William J. Flynn had grounds to brag that the raids unsurgically removed the "brains of the ultra-radical movement" (qtd. in Schmidt 275).

Years later, after the FBI's warrantless snatch-and-exile maneuver had passed unfavorably into history as the first "Red Scare," a model eruption of the paranoid style in American politics, Hoover adopted a policy of declining all responsibility. Don Whitehead's *The FBI Story* (1956), the closest thing to an authorized institutional biography, paints the roundup as a dark pre-Hooverite episode, a relatively irresponsible witch hunt in which "the Bureau's agents were not trained to protect civil liberties" (14). The anticommunism of Hoover's Cold War FBI inherited none of the excesses of "Palmer's 'Red Raids'" (46), Whitehead attests, coining a formula for Palmer's responsibility even more reductive than the commonly used "Palmer Raids." Seen clearly, however, the facts and style of the matter suggest that history might as well recall the "Hoover Raids," sweeps designed amid the regimented fervor of the newborn Radical Division, the crux of the Bureau's makeover as a countersubversive command center. No pure product of mass hysteria, the Hoover Raids mark the rise of American anticommunism as a political initiative preceding the emergence of the Soviet Union as a genuine threat to U.S. national security—and all this while the Bureau privately suspected that the 1919 bombings were the work of small anarchist cells (Schmidt 19, 149).[8]

The single major decision on the raids Hoover did not make—confining the ambush to easily expelled noncitizens—was one he could be counted on to perfect, having received the Radical Division post primarily because of his qualifications as an "alien expert" (Richard Gid Powers, *Secrecy* 66). As for the rest of the planning, Hoover took working control of the attack by the fall of 1919. With the media-coached wits of the New Spy, he isolated particular communist factions and anarchist celebrities (never sharply distinguished) to lend a face to the enemy. Emma Goldman, the feminist-anarchist and free-loving

"Queen of the Reds," became the raids' totemic target after Hoover's shocked review of "Patriotism: A Menace to Liberty" (1908) and like-minded Goldman contributions to *Mother Earth*. He personally presented the government's case at Goldman's deportation hearing, writing a long brief against the Communist Party that became a touchstone of the anticommunist imagination when reprinted during the Cold War.[9] Conceivably relying on his father's contacts, he obtained detailed maps of northern Russia to assist the navigation of the U.S.S. *Buford*, the decrepit "Soviet Ark" that delivered Goldman and 248 other deported radicals to the infant Soviet Union (U.S., House, *Attorney General* 174). Most crucial for the Bureau's management of lit.-cop federalism, he prepared for all of the above by building the FBI into one of the world's great libraries of radical writing, a collection larger than any American peer, whether private, public, or, like the Bureau's, taxpayer funded, shamelessly peddled, and aggressively off-limits.

Hoover was unembarrassed to advance the impression that the Radical Division chief should more closely resemble Herbert Putnam of the Library of Congress than Sir Edward Henry of Scotland Yard, the dashing modernizer of the London Metropolitan Police who survived an assassin's bullet in 1912, and then testified on his attacker's behalf. Like Henry's detectives, Hoover's were brain-working investigators, unlicensed to make arrests or carry guns until the gangster clashes of the Great Depression. (In FBI apocrypha, the Bureau's call to arms is commemorated in Machine Gun Kelly's panicky coinage of an undying nickname: "Don't shoot, G-Men!") Yet unlike the tenants of Scotland Yard, Hoover's earliest G-for-government men were fact finders who inspected more treatises than crime scenes. (G-Women were very few outside the secretarial pool and stayed that way during the Hoover era in part because the fighting G-Man of the 1930s was defined against sexy gun molls and overindulgent gangland "momsters," symbolic staples of the Bureau's campaign to upgrade federal firepower [Strunk 18].) Those responsible for "bomb outrages," Hoover explained through an *Annual Report of the Attorney General*, split their time between assembling explosives and arranging insurrectionary phrases (U.S., Dept. of Justice, *Annual, 1920* 171). Perhaps thinking of the pink-colored pamphlets found at the sites of all the 1919 bombings, he claimed that the ultraradicals' "sole purposes were to commit acts of terrorism and to advocate, by word of mouth and by the circulation of literature, the overthrow of the Government of the United States by force and violence" (172). To Hoover, eager for deportation-worthy verbal evidence of revolutionary intent, propaganda of the deed and word were barely distinguishable, and literary knowledge was a weapon of both terrorism and its governing foe. Gone was the Victorian insistence that labor agitators understood just one rhetoric, physical force (Jeffreys-Jones 43). In its place, Hoover's modern theory of bilingual extremism may have beaten the post-Marxist New Left to the conclusion that literary language in and of itself performed political action (McCann and Szalay 440–41). In any case, his theory demanded that the Bureau swiftly obtain the "nucleus for an excellent working library" (U.S., Dept. of Justice, *Annual, 1920* 178).

Even in the storm of the Hoover Raids, this working library was nourished by a systematic extraction of radical texts. "All literature, books, papers and anything hanging on the walls should be gathered up," the Bureau instructed agents prior to the busts (qtd. in Schmidt 285). Following the 1919 invasion of the Russian People's House in Manhattan, trucks were requisitioned to remove dangerous treasure: not crates of firearms, but reams of writing. Entire institutional libraries were swallowed by Hoover's, twenty-five tons worth in New York in January 1920 alone, commandeered "almost say by the bale," in the boast of Attorney General Palmer (U.S., House, *Attorney General* 18). Private collections were pinpointed for forced acquisition, with detectives prepared to infiltrate common hiding places for rare books: walls, ceilings, carpets, and mattresses, in addition to desks and safes. One down-and-out Italian philosopher returned home to find his unique set of anarchist theory packed as an involuntary donation (Lowenthal 88). Sonia Kaross, a Lithuanian immigrant to Philadelphia detained in the second dragnet, marveled at the attention paid to "all my books, all my letters . . . every little paper they could get hold of. They threw it all into big bags like the post office has . . . and I could never get anything back" (qtd. in Schultz and Schultz 162). Thanks to Hoover's librarian-pirates, the Radical Division's "collection of pamphlets and books" soon contained the "constitutions, programs, and platforms of practically all of the extreme radical groups" (U.S., Dept. of Justice, *Annual, 1921* 129). Every pound of the collection was "savage material," declared Palmer, "but much of it infernally well written and appealing to the thoughtless, dissatisfied crowd" (U.S., House, *Attorney General* 18). As conducted by the Bureau, the Hoover Raids were also crusades to capture the Left's devilishly attractive written artifacts.

When it came to periodical literature, evidence of a radical press apparently "backed by giant funds of stolen loot," Bureau librarians had it comparatively easy, obtaining most titles at newsstands and through filtered subscriptions (U.S., House, *Attorney General* 18). By 1920, the Radical Division received, reviewed, and "carded" 625 separate newspapers and journals in search of left-wing news (U.S., Dept. of Justice, *Annual, 1920* 179). Like Herbert Putnam's acquisitions for the Library of Congress, Hoover's were "international in scope; national in service" (Putnam, qtd. in Goodrum and Dalrymple): 236 of the publications were printed "in 25 foreign languages" and handled "by a corps of 40 multi-lingual translators" who issued daily summaries from a dedicated "Bureau of Translations and Radical Publications" operating out of New York, the FBI's mission to the U.S. capital of literary radicalism (Donner 35). Pursuing the Bureau's first methodical program of literary scholarship, hires in the D.C.-based "Radical Publications Section" prepared biographies "of all authors, publishers, editors, etc., showing any connection with an ultraradical body or movement" (U.S., Dept. of Justice, *Annual, 1920* 179). With typical haste, Hoover's depository grew beyond the nuclear stage in shelf weight and personnel and credibly flaunted "a greater mass of data upon [radicalism] than is anywhere else available" (U.S., Dept. of Justice, *Annual, 1919* 13). By late 1920, the collection overfilled its space in the Justice Department, leading Hoover to consider asking his bibliographic training ground, the Library of Congress, to take possession (Schmidt 164). No part of Hoover's archive was ever absorbed into Putnam's empire. But its acquisitive edge over its closest American rival, the Rand School's Meyer London Library in New York, only grew. In distinction to the socialist Rand School collection, shrunken after suffering its own police invasion in 1919, the Bureau's stockpile of radical documents was more likely to raid than be raided.[10]

No surprise, then, that Hoover's cataloging of the spoils called on the imperial scope of the Library of Congress classification, calculated to allow specification within great volume, and acutely attentive to literary distinctions. The largest and longest-to-construct grouping in the Library of Congress system was the Language and Literature category, what cataloging historians honor as the "monumental Class P" (LaMontagne 246). In Hoover's revision of the classification, the subjects of this grouping enjoyed comparably close attention. Already in 1921, the cabinets of the Radical Division were crammed with "approximately 450,000" index cards addressing ominous "activities and subjects," many literary-criminal (U.S., Dept. of Justice, *Annual, 1921* 129). The rhetoric of hijacked revolutionary banners, mixed with photographs of "Trotsky, Lenine [sic] and some of the other most noted Bolsheviks," decorated the walls above (Hoover, qtd. in Richard Gid Powers, *Secrecy* 107). This interior design suggested a traditional rogue's gallery refracted through the montage technique of pre-Stalinist Soviet modernism, a style echoed in the juxtaposition of text, placards, and photos in the first edition of John Reed's *Ten Days That Shook the World*, an acknowledged object of Bureau fascination. Hoover's Radical Division library mounted the enemy's advanced aesthetic signature as a trophy of archival victory.

For civil libertarians such as Louis Post, assistant secretary of labor and the most effective contemporary critic of the Hoover Raids, the Radical Division's "card-index system" was the heart of a "kaiseristic police mechanism," an appliance of the same Old World despotism the United States had only recently battled at the Marne and Belleau Wood (Post 47). For its fast-talking Bureau creator, however, this system was a welcome engine of publication as well as a signature apparatus of modern radical hunting. Archives, French theory has taught us, are generative as well as conservative instruments; true to form, Hoover's index also served as a writerly black box in which text collection modulated into text creation, and the stimulus of Putnam's Library of Congress merged with that of the USCGS print shop.[11] An exceptional state archive arose as a result, flaunted as a national treasure like its French and British relations but accessible to the public only through self-issued catalogues. Thumbing through the index for fresh affronts, the Radical Division furnished sympathetic newspapers with precomposed printing plates designed to warn "homes, religion and property" of the latest "menace of Bolshevism" (qtd. in Donner 39). Hoover edited a government-only paper of his own, the biweekly *Bulletin of Radical Activities*, its miscellaneous safety tips and atrocity exhibits recalling the recipe of his boyhood "Weekly Review". A pamphlet dubbed *The Red Radical Movement* (1920), circulated more generously to "all the magazines and newspapers in the United States" (U.S., House, *Attorney General* 208), assembled photostats of the most militant publications grabbed during the Hoover Raids, a procession of radical spoils uncertain of historical victory. "Striking passages" had been "marked for convenience," instructed the pamphlet, inviting blood-curdling headlines and editorials (qtd. in Schmidt 295). Attorney General Palmer, after the June 1919 bombing a reader experienced with nighttime terror, blurbed the finished product as "interesting, significant, and entertaining" but unsafe for "late at night, when you are at home in your own house. It gives you the creeps a little" (U.S., House, *Attorney General* 155). More literal-minded than the CIA, whose headquarters once disguised itself behind a plaque reading "Government Printing Office" (Dulles 6–7), the Bureau's Radical Division made itself an overt government publisher, its central card index, the building block of lit.-cop federalism, inspiring chilling tales. Hoover's first formal titles, the index ensured, were essays in anticommunist bibliography laced with cheap horror.

Yet every other product of the Bureau's library paled next to a publication focused where the racial and textual means of FBI self-nationalization meshed, and Hoover's literary advocacy met confrontational anti–New Negroism. Before *The Red Radical Movement* raised its eerie head, Hoover lent his archive's authorial services to *Radicalism and Sedition among the Negroes as Reflected in Their Publications*, a twenty-six-page narrative written and released in late 1919. The Bureau's first major work of book-talk, *Radicalism and Sedition* rates as the American state's earliest acknowledgment of the Harlem Renaissance and as a seminal document of African Americanist criticism produced from any quarter. As we will see, this Hooverite production, instantly denounced by the *Messenger* as "vicious, reactionary, and race prejudiced" ("A. Mitchell Palmer"), failed to introduce as much shaping pressure into the field of black letters as Langston Hughes's "The Negro Artist and the Racial Mountain" (1926), Zora Neale Hurston's "Characteristics of Negro Expression" (1934), or Richard Wright's "Blueprint for Negro Writing" (1937). All things considered, however, it prepared the Bureau to read such African American manifestos as matters of national gravity.

Radicalism and Sedition, sometimes wrongly attributed to Hoover alone, was researched, outlined, and slanted by several hands within the federal espionage community, among them lead ghost Robert Adger Bowen of the FBI's Bureau of Translations and possibly Major Arthur Loving of Army intelligence, the most valuable African American secret agent of World War I.[12] Whatever its standing as an interracial, interdepartmental collaboration, however, the text's primary inspiration lay in Hoover's anxious scrutiny of the black share of the Red Summer. The finished text's schedule of deployment, moreover, was tied to Hoover's ever-more-public role as a tract- and mind-reading congressional informant, an expert purveyor, as David Levering Lewis puts it, "of confidences about the actions, ideas, and morals of American citizens" (*W.E.B. Du Bois* 7). Starting life as a special report to the attorney general, *Radicalism and Sedition* was exposed to Congress in 1919 in the Senate-mandated publication *Investigation Activities of the Department of Justice* and then extracted in the *New York Times* and distributed widely in booklet form by Hoover in 1920. Its opening sentence speaks ill of two repeat offenders: the first, the summer 1919 "race riots in Washington, Knoxville, Chicago, Omaha, and Arkansas"; and the second, the "more radical Negro publications . . . quick to avail themselves of the situation as cause for the utterance of inflammatory statement—utterances which in some cases have reached the limit of open defiance and a counsel of retaliation" (U.S., Senate, *Radicalism* 161–62).

With their fighting words, the New Negro voices amplified by *Radicalism and Sedition* opened a fresh domestic front in the war of verbal terrorism Hoover elsewhere fought against enemy aliens—a front identified, in this case, with widespread civil disorder rather than targeted assassination. Hoover personally witnessed the first race riot on the list in the weeks before his posting to the Radical Division. Passing the worst of the Washington bloodshed on his way down Pennsylvania Avenue, the White House sidewalk a battle royal, Hoover's eyes were stung by "the Negro's pride in fighting back" (181). *Radicalism and Sedition* aptly quotes, at astonishing length, an insider's report that Washington blacks "openly declare the war here . . . the greatest event since the

Civil War. The Negro has demonstrated right in sight of the White House and Congress which refuse to protect him or reward his loyalty that he is afraid neither to kill nor to die for so sacred a thing as liberty and home" (181). Facing "bands of armed mobs," the insider continues, D.C. blacks had organized themselves into gaily disciplined ensembles "shouting jubilant war songs, as if it were a carnival and gala day" (181). Those veiled in the belated segregation of the capital had returned to light, reinvented as the opposite numbers of Central High's Company A on parade.

With New Negro militancy blurring the lines drawn during Hoover's adolescence—lines in Washington social geography, and perhaps in his own ancestry—*Radicalism and Sedition* retaliates with flights of fantastically definitive intelligence. "[T]here can no longer be any question," it pronounces, "of a well-concerted movement among a certain class of Negro leaders of thought and action to constitute themselves a determined and persistent source of a radical opposition to the Government" (U.S., Senate, *Radicalism* 162). Trumpeting signs that the "ill-governed reaction toward race rioting" of African American journals invited both an "outspoken advocacy of the Bolsheviki" and an "openly expressed demand for social equality," the Bureau publication solders together a durable conceptual chain (162). *Radicalism and Sedition* documents the birth moment when Hoover's first-wave anticommunism was fused to his defensive racism, and the Radical Division's speech-sensitive countersubversion program was bound to a Mann Act–primed New Negrophobia. The racial and literary vocabularies of Bureau self-nationalization had been joined in a single vivid public statement. The rest, as they say, is history that climaxes with the FBI's cold war on Martin Luther King.

The history of the specifically literary federalism that climaxed in the Bureau's blackface letter to King can also be traced to *Radicalism and Sedition*. Attentive to several strains of African American writing, the publication's survey of New Negro poetry, the groundwork genre of the Harlem Renaissance, is especially charged and scrupulous. Hoover and comrades cast this poetry as the distillation of the black-Red connection—the lyrical cement of the conceptual chain just mentioned—and reproduce nine poems encountered in an exhaustive survey of black periodicals. Surprised to learn that several of "the Negro magazines are expensive in manufacture, being on coated paper throughout, well-printed, and giving evidence of the possession of ample funds" (U.S., Senate, *Radicalism* 162),[13] Radical Division ghostreaders had launched a special project to monitor the "Negro Press"—the only ethnic English-language press so tracked by the Bureau's Translations department, a unit later designated the Book Review Section, as if the FBI were a true-crime magazine. The Bureau's spy-readers scanned every issue of the groundbreaking Harlem Renaissance journals, the most intellectually significant black-run institutions of the rebirth, classed by the bibliocentric Hoover among the "principal phases of the Negro movement into which inquiry should be made" (qtd. in Kornweibel, *"Seeing"* 23). A. Philip Randolph's *Messenger* struck the FBI director as the veritable "headquarters of revolutionary thought" (qtd. in Kornweibel, *"Seeing"* 85). Marcus Garvey's *Negro World* impressed him as a disloyal vehicle of Bolshevik propaganda, this despite the pages of anticommunist testimony to the contrary. The Harlem *Crusader*, Cyril Briggs's organ of the authentically Soviet-supporting African Blood Brotherhood, received the rating of "entirely radical" and unwittingly employed an undercover FBI source, Earl E. Titus, as an advertising agent (qtd. in Kornweibel, *"Seeing"* 151). All three of these journals, and fourteen more, play credited roles in *Radicalism and Sedition*, ransacked to demonstrate that "[t]he Negro is 'seeing red,' " and quoted "as fully therefrom" as space allowed (U.S., Senate, *Radicalism* 163). Catching word of all this spy-reading, W.E.B. Du Bois tartly remarked that "[w]e black folk have for some years been trying to get the United States Department of Justice to look into several matters that touch us," lynching perhaps above magazine publication ("Causes" 5).

What emerges from *Radicalism and Sedition*'s heap of citation is one of the better anthologies of early New Negro poetry, beating James Weldon Johnson's *Book of American Negro Poetry* to the punch by three years, and Locke's 1925 New Negro edition of the *Survey Graphic* by half a modernist generation. The fourteen end-rhymed lines of Claude McKay's sonnet "If We Must Die" (1919) are reprinted with care, their communal extension of *Measure for Measure*'s "If I must die" (Shakespeare 3.1.93) even then understood as a key to Harlem's renaissance:

> If we must die, let it not be like hogs
> Hunted and penned in an inglorious spot
> While 'round us bark the mad and hungry dogs
> Making their mock at our accursed lot. (ll. 1–4)

Couched as "a much-quoted poem about the negro [*sic*] with his back against the wall and fighting to the death" (U.S., Senate, *Radicalism* 163), the sonnet's viral spread through the Negro world is charted in detail. Noncanonical poems hailing martial self-sacrifice, McKay's partners in the shift from plantation dialect to elevated Standard English, are also presented in bulk. The less regular measures of Carita Owens Collins's "This Must Not Be!," for example, are transplanted intact from the Garveyite press:

And that same blood
So freely spent on Flanders fields
Shall yet redeem your race.
Be men, not cowards.
And demand your rights. (ll. 11–15)

"Don't Tread on Me," a chorus from Harlem socialist–turned–jazz lyricist Andy Razaf, is relocated from the *Crusader*:

It's time for us "to do or die,"
To play a bolder part.
For by the blood you've spilled in France
You must and will be free.
So from now on let us advance
With this: Don't tread on me! (ll. 11–16)

Brows are creased over the fully reprinted poem "Her Thirteen Black Soldiers," free verse by Archibald Grimké commemorating actual Negro troops who absorbed McKay's teaching and retaliated against white attackers in Houston:

[America] had ears, but she stuffed them with cotton
That she might not hear the murmured rage of her black soldiers.
They suffered alone, they were defenseless against insult and violence,
For she would not see them nor hear them nor protect them.
Then in desperation they smote the reptilian thing,
They smote it as they had smitten before her enemies,
For was it not her enemy, the reptilian thing, as well as their own? (ll. 9–15)

Without quite meaning to, the collected verse of *Radicalism and Sedition* argues that the literary transformation sometimes traced to McKay's "violent sonnets" alone instead stemmed from the trauma and opportunity of the Red Summer, the spark for a whole wave of prefatory renaissance verse expressing radical content in proper poetic English.

Despite its impressively catholic selections, however, *Radicalism and Sedition*'s critical glosses offered little competition for Locke's or James Weldon Johnson's. Most of these glosses are thin, steeped in a stunted interpretive code in which literary interest is measured by moral or ideological admissibility rather than by truth, beauty, or a less Romantic appetite for social action: "For certain of these publications there is not a good word to be said—all of their effort and product is bad, and intentionally bad" (U.S., Senate, *Radicalism* 87).

Questions of literary form arise as pretexts for mockery. "[D]iscriminating taste in verse structure and grammar," *Radicalism and Sedition* tells us, "was not one of the cultural effects of Harvard University upon the minds of the editors of the Messenger [*sic*]" (179). The uneasy comedy poking ivy-covered New Negroes nonetheless shades into confessed respect for black writers "of education," their brash lyrics "not to be dismissed lightly as the ignorant vaporing of untrained minds" (162). The *Negro World*'s pride in black authors equipped with "fine, pure English, with a background of scholarship behind them," was "not an idle one," Hoover and company concede (162). Reviewing *Radicalism and Sedition* for the *New York Age*, James Weldon Johnson shrewdly underscored that the honing of a "clear, intelligent, and forcible" New Negro voice "is what shocks the writer of the report more than anything else" ("Report"). "He is a man who has evidently, like many others, been asleep on the Negro," Johnson deduces, and what "astonishes him most is the fact that these articles are written by Negroes who know how to use the English language" ("Report"). Robert Adger Bowen's preliminary drafts of the report would have given Johnson deadlier ammunition, owning up to the "marked ability" of militant black authors and distinguishing their products from the "bombast and nonsense" of the "plantation negro [*sic*] preacher" ("Radicalism" 1). The New Negro "means business," Bowen confirmed, "and it would be well to take him at his word" (1).

The same publication that first blended the racial and literary vocabularies of FBI self-nationalization thus also previewed lit.-cop federalism's long-haul posture toward Afro-modernist writing. Here, as later in the Hoover years, that posture was flexibly conflicted: versed in industrious, sometimes unrivaled research; deadly serious, though inexact, about the seeming hotline between aesthetic defiance and urban restiveness; spiced up with ridicule of alleged technical deficiencies; yet shot through with nervous admiration for black erudition and sophistication of purpose, confusing blows to the cultural supports of racial hierarchy. In the end, how many refinements of "verse structure and grammar" separated McKay from Robert Service, the "Canadian Kipling" who ranked as Hoover's favorite poet? In the style of the Jamaican Kipling's "If We Must Die," Service's poems of racial regeneration through violence also advised strivers to smile and scrap when facing unbeatable, evenly metrical walls:

If you're up against a bruiser and you're getting knocked about—
Grin.
If you're feeling pretty groggy, and you're licked beyond a doubt—
Grin. ("Grin" ll. 1–4)

How comfortably distinct was Andy Razaf's "Don't Tread on Me" from the pugnacious sing-song of "The Bully Bolsheviki," a poem scrapbooked and perhaps composed by Hoover himself, disrespectfully "dedicated to 'Comrade' Louie Post," the vocal enemy of the Hoover Raids?

> The "Reds" at Ellis Island
> Are as happy as can be.
> For Comrade Post at Washington
> Is setting them all free. (ll.1–4)

Confronting early New Negro verse, as in confronting New Negro militancy, the margins of racial difference narrowed and blurred. Egged on by uncomfortable likeness, enabled by a comprehensive archive and its enticements to publication, the impulse to supervise African American writing became a constitutive inclination of Hoover's FBI, the enduring upshot of its linked investments in New Negro modernity and national literary influence. In the long run, the Bureau's observation of the darkening mirror of black literature was almost as vital to its cultural power as the "War on Crime," the deadly and glamorous Depression-era battle with John Dillinger, Bonnie and Clyde, and other heartland mobsters–cum–social bandits that ushered Hoover into the gossip columns and supposedly introduced the FBI to its classic self. When even shrewd Bureau historians defer to Hoover's promotion engine and plug the gangster era as the crucible in which a "band of amateurish agents" picked up the gun and became "the professional crime-fighting machine of yore" (Burrough, front matter), they slight evidence that the "Hoover boys" cut their teeth by professionalizing literary publicity and literary surveillance for the American Century.[14] Studious G-Men (the "G" is for ghostreading, too) transformed the Bureau into the head office of lit.-cop federalism, part library, part editorial board, part authors guild, part literary-critical tendency, all parts committed to sowing state authority in the print public sphere. For decades after defeating the first of many crime waves, they aimed this federalism at public enemies armed with book contracts and newspaper columns, dozens of them the creators of Afro-modernism.

Part Two/Thesis Two

The FBI's Aggressive Filing and Long Study of African American Writers Was Tightly Bound to the Agency's Successful Evolution under Hoover

Thanks to disclosures forced by the U.S. Freedom of Information Act (FOIA), we now can see that the FBI kept an eye peeled on the Harlem Renaissance, and that it learned to train on the builders of this movement, the laboratory of Afro-modernism, its legendary system for archiving and exploiting the results of intelligence work. Gwendolyn Bennett, Sterling Brown, W.E.B. Du Bois, Langston Hughes, Georgia Douglas Johnson, Alain Locke, Claude McKay, Louise Thompson Patterson, J. A. Rogers, George Schuyler, Walter White: all were eventually favored with FBI files, the nation's highest medal of radical honor, some thin (Douglas Johnson's is all of six sheets) and some as thick as windy literary biographies (Du Bois's scales 756 pages). While the Bureau's voguish interest in Harlem's New Negroes faded with the Great Depression, its survey of Afro-modernism persisted from World War II through the Black Arts movement formally declared in 1965. In the early 1940s, the FBI began compiling dossiers on Lloyd Brown, Frank Marshall Davis, Katherine Dunham, Ray Durem, Chester Himes, John O. Killens, Theodore Ward, and Richard Wright. In the depths of the Cold War, a busy season of FBI ghostreading, no fewer than twenty-two African American literary intellectuals were first tracked by Bureau paperwork, among them Frank London Brown, Alice Childress, Harold Cruse, Shirley Graham Du Bois, Lonne Elder III, Ralph Ellison, E. Franklin Frazier, Lorraine Hansberry, Calvin Hernton, Lance Jeffers, Charles S. Johnson, Bob Kaufman, Julian Mayfield, Willard Motley, William Pickens, Saunders Redding, and William Gardner Smith. Three Cold War files created in the 1950s—James Baldwin's, Amiri Baraka's, and Hoyt Fuller's—looked forward to the last great wave of FBI book-clubbing, an elaborate counterintelligence program to outwrite the Black Arts movement able to draw from dossiers on Lucille Clifton, St. Clair Drake, Addison Gayle Jr., Pauli Murray, Larry Neal, Dudley Randall, Iceberg Slim/Robert Beck, Sherley Anne Williams—and likely many more. As the introduction noted, FOIA rules stipulate that third-party historians may request copies of FBI files only after their subjects' deaths. Absent self-requests made public by living Black Arts veterans (Baraka, for one, deposited part of his file at the Moorland-Spingarn Research Center before his death in 2014), we can thus only guess at the existence of dossiers on Adrienne Kennedy, Ntozake Shange, Haki Madhubuti, and the rest. Sonia Sanchez has acknowledged a personal file in exchanges with nongovernmental interviewers. Like Paule Marshall before them, Ishmael Reed and A. B. Spellman have turned up on trustworthy lists of writers indexed by the FBI for high crimes of petition signing (Robins 411). When the full tally is accessible, it will shock and awe if Bureau filing of Black Arts writers did not top the currently documented high point of the Cold War.

Not everything, then, can yet be known about the FBI's half century of spying on black authorship, an institutionalized fascination stretching from the Red Summer of 1919 to Hoover's death just weeks before the Watergate break-in. Especially unhelpful in the search for knowledge is the destruction of Margaret Walker's Bureau file and other unique historical documents, casualties of the federal Records Retention Plan discussed earlier. For all this, a number of meaningful conclusions about the collision of black letters and Bureau surveillance can already be reached. Assisted by the detective work of earlier researchers, my 106 FOIA requests reveal that the Washington, D.C., national headquarters of the FBI opened a minimum of fifty-one files on individual African American authors and critics active during the Hoover years, 1919 to 1972. Measured more narrowly, nearly half (twenty-three of forty-eight) of the historically relevant writers featured in the second edition of *The Norton Anthology of African American Literature* (2004) were first consecrated by the Bureau. Encompassing 13,892 pages in all, the heft of these author files outweighs one G-Man's assurance that "there was no *conscious* effort aimed at writers" (qtd. in Robins 401; emphasis in original). Taken together, the files demonstrate that modern African American writing repeatedly and disproportionately sparked high-strung federal scrutiny, a by-product of the Harlem Renaissance that ranged into the "Renaissance II" of the Black Arts movement.

According to the Bureau's own declassified word, Hoover and many lesser FBI ghostreaders pored over scores of Afro-modernist poems, plays, stories, novels, essays, and reviews—some even before publication with the aid of bookish informers at magazines and publishing firms. Alarmingly, the files divulge that the FBI readied preventive arrests of the majority of the black authors shadowed in its archive. Twenty-seven of fifty-one were caught in the invisible dragnet of the Bureau's "Custodial Detention" index and its successors, hot lists of precaptives "whose presence at liberty in this country in time of war or national emergency," Hoover resolved, "would be dangerous to the public peace and the safety of the United States Government" (Hoover, Directive 409). By the time of the Black Panthers and Black Power, Hoover's literary-critical G-Men were versed enough to produce an Afro-modernism of their own, an eccentric style of state minstrelsy bent to counterintelligence purposes of simulation, infiltration, and plausibly deniable manipulation. The early and creative intensity of the Bureau's watch on black literature has been unknowingly minimized, the files collectively suggest, both in literary studies and in recent historical exposés harnessing FOIA requests to uncover either the Bureau's "war on words" or its "secret file on black America," parallel tracks that should acknowledge their underground crossings.[1] The backdating and thick description of FBI surveillance of legal dissent, a muckraking preoccupation since Hoover's passing, is thus due for extension into the field of African American literary history. And the Bureau's peculiar contributions to this history are due at least a moment of national self-reflection. Even now, when it takes massive NSA "data mining" to excite resistance to the surveillance of daily life, it is not just an academic matter that U.S. state intelligence essentially arranged to jail the African American literary tradition at midcentury. Well before the labeling of the prison-industrial complex, the republic of black letters joined black urban communities as an exceptional zone of police supervision.

Similarly troubling but less predictable, perhaps, the same fifty-one files suggest that Afro-modernist writing served as the unwitting muse behind some of the most audacious (and legally doubtful) policies Hoover's FBI aimed against it. The course of this writing helped to spur a series of FBI literary containment operations, assorted "counterliteratures," as I call them, evolving over five decades and five uneven phases of Bureau history. In the foreword to his Cold War best seller *Masters of Deceit* (1958), the public hero and author-effect signed J. Edgar Hoover indicated that "our time," the twentieth century's transitive but always urgent here and now, would never outmode the verdict of the Hoover Raids (vi). "My conclusions of 1919 remain the same," he professed, for "Communism is the major menace of our time" (vi). Yet the judgment of this proudly frozen thinker on how the Bureau could best fight communism and entwined threats to American integrity was subject to change in practice and was prompted to some extent by the shifting designs of black letters. In this light, it is no paradox that William C. Sullivan, one ghostwriter behind Hoover's anticommunist thunder in *Masters of Deceit*, also entered the history of secret authorship in the accent of a civil rights proponent bitterly disenchanted with

Martin Luther King—an accent translating the latest in black self-assertion into malignant counterintelligence.

Counterliterature, as I customize the term, is the application of classic counterintelligence strategy to the swamps of literary argument. When a spy service employs counterintelligence to spy on the spies spying on it, it does not rush to liquidate all traces of the enemy's agents and techniques after detecting them. Instead, it strives to maneuver or mimic these uncovered assets to turn them against their original controllers. Counterintelligence is therefore a means of recycling knowledge, a practice of resurrection and pastiche rather than of wholesale destruction and primary invention (Hawkes). The "Double-Cross system" that provided the proudest Allied espionage victory of World War II can illustrate the point: its success rested on the impersonation of blown Nazi spies, masterminded by British handlers who preserved the fingerprints of German undercover work while reversing its strategic aims (Masterman). In the case of the specifically counterliterary brand of counterintelligence, the counterfeiting and reversal of enemy knowledge is literary-critical in character. As employed by the ghostreaders of Hoover's FBI, counterliterature digested and repurposed the public voices of Afro-modernist authors. Propagating in-kind replies to the fifty-one names noted above, it endeavored to police black writing with some of its own imaginative medicine and succeeded in enriching the FBI's authority and ambition at almost every phase of the process.

Evidence of the various recycling programs of Bureau counterliterature can be found in a mixed bag of sometimes opposing sources. These include the FBI files just discussed, above all, but also Hoover's own published writing, once-secret FBI ethnography on the mood of black America, wartime black journalism, Black Arts novels, and the Bureau's out-and-out forgeries of black nationalist literature. This second part of *F.B. Eyes* explains the fluid significance of the Bureau's many dossiers on African American writers in relation to all these sources. Section 1 begins by identifying the various ingredients that composed the mixed genre of the counterliterary FBI file. Reading the Bureau's collected writing on Claude McKay, it pinpoints how these ingredients initially answered the call of the Red Summer, the anti-Red roundup, and the racial radicalism of the Harlem Renaissance. Section 2 clarifies how the filing routines of Renaissance-era Bureau counterliterature supplemented Hoover's rebranding of the FBI as both a strangely charismatic bureaucracy and a pocket of federal resistance to the First Amendment.

Retracing some of the main lines of FBI history, the rest of part 2 then demonstrates how Bureau counterliterature was stamped by four distinct phases of the institution's developing Hoover era, altogether long enough to form a kind of police Mesozoic. The glamorous and violent phase of Bureau history between the New Deal and the early 1940s is treated in section 3. Section 4 analyzes the changing shape of Bureau counterliterature during World War II. Section 5 does the same for the McCarthy period. Finally, section 6 reviews the creative upheaval in Bureau counterliterature during the Black Power 1960s and 1970s. Author files and adjoining documents disclose that Hoover's FBI, the principal custodian of lit.-cop federalism, angled during all these phases to enlarge the state's ability to determine aesthetic value, scheming and networking like some National Endowment for Artistic Gumshoes. But these documents likewise show that his Bureau pursued changeable, art-educated enhancements of police tactics, converting varying currencies of literary capital into novel forms of criminological capital. Through both types of meddling, the Bureau paved the way to this book's second thesis, of necessity its most historically sprawling: *The FBI's aggressive filing and long study of African American writers was tightly bound to the agency's successful evolution under Hoover.*

Flatfoot Montage: The Genre of the Counterliterary FBI File

Claude McKay's pride of place in 1919's *Radicalism and Sedition among the Negroes as Reflected in Their Publications* led him to another dubious Bureau breakthrough. At the risk of spreading "archive fever," the mania to master state records coupled with the homesick craving to fix beginnings, it should be known that McKay was the first black author individually scrutinized and "filed" by Hoover's ghostreaders (Derrida 1–5). Even before it was looking for Langston, the FBI was nosing around Claude, the Jamaican-born poet, novelist, and nomadic political radical whom the State Department denounced as a "notorious negro [*sic*] revolutionary" (U.S., Federal, McKay, 11 Mar. 1924). When not waiting tables, cultivating a mature Standard English idiom, or stirring Harlem's renaissance with the sonnet "If We Must Die," McKay spent his early New York years, 1914 to 1919, harmonizing the leftist styles of Harlem, Greenwich Village, and Moscow. Back in Manhattan in 1921 after a London stint, the balancing act earned him posts of honor with downtown's soft-focus Marxist journal, the *Liberator*, and uptown's confrontational left-nationalist bloc, the African Blood Brotherhood. It also reinstalled him at the spot his Bureau critics most feared, the crossroads where black resistance bargained with the devil of world communism.

The prominence of McKay's sonnets in New Negro magazines, well documented in *Radicalism and Sedition*, alone might have made him famous at the FBI's Radical Division. But his specifically political attachments also put his money where his verse was. Bureau informants witnessed him triangulating among memberships in the young Communist Party, the International

Workers of the World (IWW), and the African Blood Brotherhood. Evidence of McKay's place in the subculture where such radicalisms met queer New York sent up additional red flags. Decades before Senator Joseph McCarthy protested the resemblance of "Communists and queers," cheering on a full-blown "Lavender Scare," the closeted Hoover was learning to equate revolutionary ambition and the release of undercover sexual desire (David Johnson 3). In advance of James Baldwin, Willard Motley, and Pauli Murray, their Bureau files stocked with amateur queer theory, McKay's bisexuality exposed him to the FBI director's linkage of leftism, racial blackness, sexual irregularity, and "inflammatory statement" (U.S., Senate, *Radicalism* 161). First among all black writers, McKay ran afoul of Hoover's relatively diplomatic constellation of the keywords of right-wing antimodernism, later—and in a quite different context—the kindling for the Nazis' bonfire of racially degenerate art.

Topping the list of FBI apprehensions, however, was McKay's concentrated foreignness of address. An unnaturalized black voice skeptically embracing a cruel-fair America, he spoke on the wrong side of the post–World War I whitening of U.S. citizenship, a location where state functionaries aggravated what Du Bois diagnosed as the painful twoness of the Negro and the American. A fire-breathing West Indian voice at that, McKay baited the immigrant guilt-by-verbal-association consecrated in the Hoover Raids and magnified by the Bureau's then-frustrated pursuit of fellow Jamaican radical Marcus Garvey. ("Unfortunately," Hoover groused before the "Soviet Ark" shoved off in 1919, Garvey had "not as yet violated any federal law whereby he could be proceeded against on the grounds of being an undesirable alien, from the point of view of deportation" [U.S., Federal, Garvey, 11 Oct. 1919]. By the final chapters of Garvey's 1,407-page FBI file, now easily available courtesy of the Bureau's electronic "Vault," Hoover had gotten his man.)[2] Little wonder, then, that by late 1921 the FBI pronounced McKay the single strongest link between Harlem's race capital and Moscow's Vatican of communism. Beginning in December, a neat decade after the opening of its original Ezra Pound and John Reed files, the FBI began filling a dossier whose initial page tells of its subject's faith in communism and guilt over tardy IWW dues (U.S., Federal, McKay, 16 Dec. 1921). Jumping the gun on *Harlem Shadows* (1922), a verse collection the Bureau reckoned "a collection of radical poems," the front-running poet of New Negro modernism was classified as an official enemy of his adopted country, his friendship enough to win Harlemites their own Bureau write-ups (U.S., Federal, McKay, 3 Feb. 1923; Kornweibel, *"Seeing"* 177).

McKay's groundbreaking Bureau file, while not wholly representative, may still serve as a window onto the generic features of the FBI's many counter-literary files on Afro-modernists.[3] Compiled long before the adoption of the

Freedom of Information Act, it sees no need to disguise counterliterary techniques, plots, and fears. One strand of the file is typical in substantiating Michel Foucault's grim notion of the modern "police text," the literature "of a complex documentary organization" which, unlike the linear and synthetic "methods of judicial or administrative writing," captures sundry, proliferating traces of "attitudes, possibilities, suspicions—a permanent account of individuals' behavior" (*Discipline* 214). All manner of uncorroborated attitudes, possibilities, and suspicions cohabit with nuggets of definite biographical data in the McKay file, enough to compose a dense rather than fanatical description by the standards of Bureau spy-criticism. McKay's 193 pages of Bureau commentary are comparable to Lance Jeffers's 187 and John O. Killens's 194—weightier than Alice Childress's 27, for example, but lighter than the 309-page average among all black authors.

As with most Bureau dossiers on cultural figures, McKay's is a heterogeneous bundle. A file on an individual subject of literary interest would begin with a single index card, the Hoover-mandated seed-text of all FBI investigations. Under favorable conditions of authorial production and Bureau reception, the card would then grow into a lush hodgepodge of "investigative reports, legal forms, interviews, memorandums, petitions, letters, articles, . . . news clippings," and collected literary works, collated and "clipped together in one folder" (Robins 17). Punitive, quotidian, and conventionally literary forms of textuality mingled between cardboard covers, the interior resembling the montage modernism the Bureau disliked everywhere outside its D.C. office.

McKay's file, recounting the period from 1921 to 1940, mixes writing from many sources and discourses. There are memoranda carefully transcribing and typifying his sonnets and other Standard English poetry; field notes from Bureau spies assigned to tail him around Manhattan; accounts of his foreign political speeches compiled by U.S. legations in Europe; cautionary letters from Hoover and then Bureau director William J. Burns to State Department officials, and vice versa; summarized articles on McKay translated from Soviet newspapers; and blurry reproductions of photographs of McKay with *Liberator* editor Max Eastman and other communist company. The collaged assortment of McKay's Bureau collection is the product of group creation, Hoover and Burns sharing authorship with a pack of lower-level police-readers and informants, many anonymous. Here, as in the Soviet and Romanian cases interpreted by Cristina Vatulescu, the "poetics of the personal file" incongruously realizes "the much-extolled communist ideal of communal authorship" (14). Authoring files by committee, the Bureau stalked radical literary opponents in sympathy with one of their model working methods—not the only means by which the FBI profited from literary experiments it publicly trashed.

Unlike the obtainable files of the Black Power era, McKay's file shows little evidence of prerelease censorship (or what the Bureau's Record/Information Dissemination Section now prefers to earmark as "[e]xcisions . . . made to protect information exempt from disclosure pursuant to FOIA," or the Freedom of Information Act [Kelso]). A few names have been erased to protect personal privacy, as has one probable reference to McKay's love of men (U.S., Federal, McKay, 13 Dec. 1922). Even in its unexpurgated passages, however, the file's interest in McKay's sexuality is distinct, of a piece with its tendency to criminalize temperament along with political dissidence. As Foucault insinuates about police text in general, the file certifies the felony of an identity as much as any illegal activity, McKay's heretical being as much as his revolutionary doing. For the special benefit of Hoover, the belligerently straitlaced executive editor (though rarely the single author) of Bureau police writing, McKay's private conduct is thus confirmed to be as illicit as his political contacts. Purloined letters in which the poet complains of unsanitary Frenchmen and a bout of venereal disease are placed into the record in their entirety (29 Feb. 1924). So are breathless accounts of his cash-starved begging to friends and his ambiguously "confidential" business with a white radical woman (31 Jan. 1924; 13 Dec. 1922). Welded to McKay's Bureau reputation as a "notorious negro revolutionary" was an identity as a sexually flexible bohemian reprobate.

More of the McKay file's pages than not, however, show prurient police text yielding to what we might call "judicial text," reportage soberly combing through hints of treason and preparing overt forms of state interference. Sheets accumulate furiously as McKay undertakes a 1922–23 pilgrimage to the Soviet Union, the citadel of the Marxist revolution he later designated as "the greatest event in the history of humanity" (U.S., Federal, McKay, 26 Jan. 1924). Initially, the Bureau was led to expect modernist expatriation on the standard American plan: an unnamed, "strictly confidential source" dropped word that "the well-known radical of New York City . . . contemplates going to Europe" (21 July 1922). McKay's arrival in Moscow in late October 1922, just before the Fourth Congress of the Communist International (Comintern) opened its doors, exposed a more disciplined itinerary and corroborated his aura of alien allegiance. The Bureau's early capacity for international intelligence gathering is proven by the paper storm that followed. American diplomats in Riga, Latvia, then a nest of anti-Soviet espionage, reported on McKay's part in Comintern deliberations on the "Negro Question" and translated his several contributions to the Soviet press (7 Dec. 1922; 11 Dec. 1922). Director Burns conveyed the gist of the bad news to the State Department and asked that "MacKay" and other black Co-mintern delegates be held for "appropriate attention" on attempting to reenter the United States (12 Dec. 1922). The reach and energy of the Bureau's efforts to discover this M(a)cKay's travel schedule are staggering. Newspaper accounts of Russian-bound shipping were screened; the wife of African Blood Brother-hood leader Cyril Briggs was pressed for clues in her Harlem apartment; and the U.S. Passport Office ransacked its records, concluding that the poet and his comrades would sail as merchant seamen, just as theorists of the Black Atlantic might have it (16 Dec. 1922; 6 Jan. 1923; 11 Jan. 1923).

The Bureau's international surveillance of Afro-modernism—not confined to McKay—holds lessons for recent theories of black transnationalism, the con-cern of part 4. Its implications for lit.-cop federalism and for the Bureau school of literary criticism, leading contributors to the miscellaneous genre of the Bu-reau author file, are introduced later in part 2 and treated at length in part 3. Worth noting here is the case that the majority of the files devoted to Harlem Re-naissance figures reveal anxieties over cosmopolitan fickleness and inadequate patriotism. With the exception of McKay's younger admirer Langston Hughes, his file opened in 1925, the Bureau began gauging the national loyalty of other writers of the rebirth, all of them U.S. citizens, during a second world war. Ster-ling Brown, Gwendolyn Bennett, and Louise Thompson Patterson's files are products of 1941, the year the United States entered the global conflict. George Schuyler, J. A. Rogers, and W.E.B. Du Bois's dossiers saw the light of head-quarters in 1942. Walter White's compilation followed in 1943, with Georgia Douglas Johnson's closing the set in 1945. Alain Locke's file, acknowledged by the Bureau but currently AWOL after a transfer of early records to the National Archives, may have been opened in any of these years.[4]

The 1943 initiation date of the White file is provocative: the FBI's established interest in the NAACP officer beginning in 1919 suggests that earlier pages or perhaps entire dossiers on Harlem Renaissance figures may have gone miss-ing, either accidentally or in uncharted regions of "routine records destruction schedules," as the Justice Department euphemizes them (McLeod). In any case, the historical range of the renaissance files we now possess proves that FBI fas-cination with African American letters outlived the first edition of the Radical Division, formally closed in 1924. Following bruising congressional hearings on the Justice Department's contributions to the Red Scare, the Division's of-ficial undoing was an August summit bringing Hoover face to face with the American Civil Liberties Union (ACLU), an FBI critic born in opposition to the Hoover Raids. The sit-down was one Hoover could not refuse, since it was brokered by the new attorney general, Harlan Stone, a future Supreme Court justice more inclined than A. Mitchell Palmer to denounce the operations of secret police in a constitutional republic. In October 1924, Hoover paid the revised price of elevation to the Bureau directorship by filing a memorandum of understanding with Stone's office, a reluctant acknowledgment of the ACLU position that "activities of Communists and other ultra-radicals have not up to the present time constituted a violation of the Federal statutes, and consequently, the Department of Justice, theoretically, has no right to investigate such activities" (qtd. in Preston 243). No pure mea culpa, theoretically or otherwise, the document effectively deputized Hoover as the brake on his own excesses. By the same token, the broader agreement ensured that Hoover's antiradical archive would survive Justice Department revisionism as the Red Raids were recoded as a Red Scare. In December 1924, Hoover assumed the Bureau's highest post with the assurance that his library remained FBI property, its hundreds of thousands of cards and pages safe with him failing a special act of Congress. The "examination of radical magazines and the collection of data on radicals and radical organizations [had] been wholly discontinued by specific orders of the Attorney General," crowed the ACLU (Roger N. Baldwin 20). But the archival footing of the counterliterary file had escaped the shredder.

The Counterliterary State and the Charismatic Bureaucracy: Trimming the First Amendment, Fencing the Harlem Renaissance

The Hughes file was thus not the FBI's final counterliterary montage despite an absence of new dossiers on African American authors between 1925 and 1939, a reform era in FBI administration as well as the era of battle with gangster America. The Bureau's disproportionate attention to Afro-modernism diminished during this period, with Hoover's concentration partly diverted by the authorial facet of lit.-cop federalism, the director sanctioning a flood of G-Man-themed stories and books. Meanwhile, FBI surveillance of non-Harlem modernism, less associated with the extremes of the Hoover Raids, picked up the pace. Files on Sherwood Anderson and Erskine Caldwell were launched in 1932, with Ernest Hemingway, John Steinbeck, and Arthur Miller entering the Bureau collection in 1935, 1936, and 1938, respectively (Robins 24; Jeffreys-Jones 130). If Natalie Robins is correct, the numerical peak of Bureau investigations of U.S. authors was reached in the years between the Spanish Civil War and World War II, the prime of the Popular Front and American literary communism (16). By the early 1940s, the start of another world war and another declared national emergency, the spotlight returned to Afro-modernism per se, presumed to be a tributary of unAmericanism since 1919.

Within the Hoover-led Bureau, rationales for continued literary surveillance were plentiful. But all relied on the post–World War I rebuilding of the FBI as the shelter of a permanent state of exception within the American state. Giorgio Agamben, the Italian philosopher and semiofficial radical theorist of the George W. Bush years, has argued that the Great War and its aftermath doubled "as a laboratory for testing and honing the functional mechanisms and apparatuses of the state of exception," the unexpectedly ordinary condition of Western government marked by "a suspension of the juridical order itself," rather than by the establishment of a special variety of martial law (14). In the American case, Agamben identifies a wartime president, Woodrow Wilson, who preferred to have his suspension of juridical order delegated to him by the legislative branch. Exceptional but nonmartial laws were therefore passed by the House and Senate, sparing Wilson from a Lincoln-like declaration of the law's cancellation in a time of national emergency. "[F]rom 1917 to 1918," Agamben recalls, "Congress approved a series of acts (from the Espionage Act of June 1917 to the Overman Act of May 1918) that granted the president complete control over the administration of the country" (21). Not only did these acts prohibit sins of commission "such as collaboration with the enemy and diffusion of false reports"; they also "made it a crime to 'willfully utter, print, write, or publish any disloyal, profane, scurrilous, or abusive language about the form of government of the United States'" (21).

As Agamben sees it, the Wilson-era abandonment of legal regulation of presidential dominion has never been abandoned.[5] Realizing that the power of the executive to trump coequal branches is "essentially grounded in the emergency linked to a state of war," Wilson's successors from Franklin D. Roosevelt through Barack Obama have maintained "the metaphor of war [as] an integral part of the presidential political vocabulary" (21). The post-9/11 projection of a counterterrorist war without end has threatened to obscure such fine points, but it remains the case that Agamben's American history lesson overlooks the repeal of the worst of the 1917–18 acts in the early 1920s. Some passport restrictions continued, as we will see in part 4, yet the Sedition Act of 1918, the basis of the criminalizing of speech critical of "the form of government of the United States," was overturned by Congress in 1921. The object in recalling this hiccup in the chain of presidential sovereignty is not to minimize persistent threats to free expression. In the not-quite ancient days of October 2001, after all, the Justice Department's Office of Legal Counsel could advise that "First Amendment speech and press rights may also be subordinated to the overriding need to wage war successfully" (Yoo and Delahunty 24). Instead, the object is to highlight the special conditions of U.S. state exceptionalism following World War I. In the American instance, conserving a state of counterliterary exception—a suspension of uniform protection of constitutional guarantees of "freedom of speech, or of the press"—required another delegation of sovereign authority.

With Hoover helming the FBI's literary outreach program, this authority, once ceded to the president by a compliant Congress, was transferred from the White House to a supportive subsidiary (a "Federal Bureau") of the executive branch: informally at first, then semiofficially, as we will see, in the later 1930s. In this sense, the FBI became a nesting place for coercive power within a consensus-conscious postwar order, the protector of an exceptional state within the American state. Preserving the authoritarian air of World War I (Agamben's War to End All Non-Executive Power), the Bureau's Seat of Government safeguarded the logic of a publicly shelved struggle against treacherous expression. For almost two decades following the armistice, Hoover frankly promoted this struggle's return to daylight via legal trimming of the First Amendment. In 1926, he reported that he hoped "to find some theory of law and some statement of facts to fit it" capable of recriminalizing radical propaganda (letter to J. A. Dowd). "No one wants any legislation that abridges the freedom of the press or the freedom of speech," he assured a 1930 meeting of a House special committee, "but there should be a law" making it "a crime to advocate the overthrow of the Government through force or violence, through word of mouth, or by printed literature" (U.S., House, *Investigation* 36). Still at the task in 1937, Hoover informed the *New Yorker* that since "the Sedition Act has long . . . been repealed," he would "view with favor the passage of legislation making the advocacy of violent revolution a crime in itself" (Jack Alexander, "The Director—II" 22). The director's yearning for such legislation was largely fulfilled by the Alien Registration Act, better known as the Smith Act, "the most drastic restriction on freedom of speech," judged legal philosopher Zechariah Chafee, "ever enacted in the United States during peace" (443). Redolent of the first Red Scare, this 1940 federal statute brandished criminal sanctions and alien registration requirements at those who would "willfully advocate, abet, advise or teach the duty, necessity, desirability or propriety of overthrowing the Government of the United States or of any State by force or violence" ("18 USC § 2385"). As discussed below, lower-flying directives issued by Franklin D. Roosevelt in 1936 and 1939 even more candidly honored the Bureau's protection of the state's counterliterary prerogative.

One measure that prepared Hoover to keep the counterliterary flame in the years between the Sedition and Smith Acts was his modernization of the style of power Agamben correlates with the state of exception: namely, the style über-sociologist Max Weber termed "charismatic." From the perspective of the passionate Hooverologist, Weber's portrait of the charismatic leader in *Economy and Society* (1922) can seem an abstract translation of the heroic anticommunist chapter of the Hoover legend, both of these tales painting a champion who seizes a "task that is adequate for him and demands obedience and a following by virtue of his mission" (Weber, *Economy* 246). Yet Hoover's greatest practical successes actually flowed from integrating charismatic habits with administrative arrangements drawn from the arsenal of bureaucracy, that resource of modern officialdom that Weber describes as charisma's gravedigger. Beginning with his simultaneous organizing of the Hoover Raids and the Radical Division library, Hoover laid the foundations for a uniquely charismatic federal bureaucracy, a semi-independent department of state administration with unprecedented advantages of central planning and public brand recognition.

With one arm, the Great Director defeated institutional lethargy ("the normal state of bureaucracy," quips Richard Gid Powers [*Secrecy* 90]) through charismatic weapons of publicity-hungry moralism and relentless individual "involvement in the details of enormous enterprises" (Weber, *Economy* 196). Personally fond of luxury and family, Hoover nonetheless met the charismatic norm by publicly renouncing great wealth and marrying only the Bureau (also the employer of Clyde Tolson, his all-but-legal husband). With his other arm, however, Hoover remodeled the FBI into the most efficient office in Washington, a Progressive bureau in name and design possessing Weber's bureaucratic touchstone of "fixed and official jurisdictional areas," each staffed by nonpatronage employees with "regulated qualifications," in most cases, after 1924, university degrees in law or, more rarely, accounting (Weber, *Economy* 196). Job responsibilities at the FBI were distributed according to classical bureaucratic "principles of office hierarchy and of levels of graded authority," all ranks beholden to a prized collection of "written documents"—the headquarters files—tended by "subaltern officers and scribes of all sorts" (Weber, *Economy* 196–97). As we have seen, the centrality of file keeping to Hoover's Bureau preceded his promotion to the directorship; after his death, this centrality was eulogized in the thick concrete of the J. Edgar Hoover Building, the Bureau's moated headquarters dedicated in 1975. There, a block-square scaffolding of offices on the fourth, fifth, and sixth floors topped a mass of documents, fifty-eight million index cards strong, before computerized records claimed the day. The Hoover Building may not have been the "world's largest file cabinet" (Donner 169), exactly, but its columns were in fact specially reinforced to bear the weight of the Bureau's paper archive (Fox). For its part, the Bureau office fashioned during Hoover's own time was well suited to converting his penchants into federal policies and procedures—one reason why part 1 detailed some of the director's biographical quirks. Among these penchants was an animus against African American writing, systematized through bureaucratic routines of filing, indexing, book collecting, book reviewing, and author stalking, this last the special literary-critical language of streetwise brick agents. The state of counterliterary exception could not have dreamed up a federal agency better equipped for its long-term storage, or more sympathetic to its origins in the Wilsonian presidency, an arena of legalistic absolutism miniaturized in Hoover's charismatic-bureaucratic leadership.

None of this is to suggest that the FBI's synthesis of governing techniques allowed it to exert anything much like panoptical power over American literature. Hoover's intent to corner the market on police charisma meant that he could never occupy the all-seeing but anonymous position at the bull's-eye of Benthamite surveillance. Aside from the membership of the post-Depression U.S. Communist Party, the single population subjected to the full force of Hooverite discipline was the FBI's own employees. The self-containment of the male FBI agent's mandatory white shirt and dark suit—a chiaroscuro design of the 1930s and the inspiration for reservoir dogs and men in black—was only the half of it. The bodies of G-Men became the foils of a whole rhetoric of military honor prohibiting weight gain, wet handshakes, on-the-job coffee drinking, even changes in marital status without first notifying the home office. Forty-five minutes of daily exercise were required, at least when gym facilities were nearby (Jack Alexander, "The Director—II" 25). One Bureau water-cooler tale had Hoover drawing on a phrenological code unmentioned in the civil service regulations, and firing a survivor of agent training class for an unaesthetic skull shape: "One of them is a pinhead. Get rid of him!" (Schott 41–42). Every agent spared the director's axe was expected to be "a personal representative of Mr. Hoover," from close-cut hair to spit-shined shoes (Schrecker 204). "Often ridiculed as the personal fetish of an aging control freak," explains Ellen Schrecker, "the carefully crafted image of respectability and professionalism that these regulations reinforced contributed mightily" to the Bureau's publicity offensives (204).

Effective projections of FBI discipline beyond the Bureau's payroll normally rested on winning, less punishingly, the consent of some of the governed. For example, in the case of the Bureau's deep penetration of the Cold War Communist Party (perhaps 20 percent of party members informed for the FBI in the 1950s [Hewitt 52]), success depended on old-fashioned blackmail in combination with a popular anticommunism the FBI inflamed but did not dictate. Several of the early achievements of FBI literature hunting drew on a widespread understanding of propaganda as a menace to the American Republic—an understanding established as a nativist norm during World War I, when new technologies of tendentious persuasion, pioneered by the British, were wielded by all combatants seeking U.S. public support (Wollaeger 13–26). In both cases, the uncommon strengths of Hoover's charismatic bureaucracy did not free it from the outward-directed obligations of semiautonomy. Internal Bureau equations of directorial will and office system still had to be solved with reference to larger movements in American antiradicalism.

In one counterliterary campaign, however, the FBI consistently risked outpacing both executive branch superiors and the right wing of American public opinion. Hoover's sociology of modernist literature defined its producers as likely vehicles or butts of radical propaganda. Bucking what became academic common sense, Hoover assumed that modernism and agitprop were "less like strange bedfellows than like conjoined twins," born together to "rethink political emotion as a matter for culture" (Wollaeger 1, xiv). Thanks to their talent and weakness for sensational persuasion, modernist authors were prone to devolve into what Hoover termed "Communist thought-control relay stations" (qtd. in Robins 50).[6] Once bent to the task of political transmission, these literary relay stations were as powerful a radicalizing force as any experience of economic inequality or racial discrimination. Hoover's criminological experience equipped him with the assumption that social unrest was caused not by inequitable structures but by individual perpetrators, some of them aesthetically inclined. The Bureau director thus shared the modernist avant-garde's extravagant estimation of the artist's ability to order minds in a fallen world, though never the avant-garde's faith in its own virtuous novelty. Corrupting vanguards with access to print found an admiring audience, Hooverites believed, in the group A. Mitchell Palmer baroquely insulted as the "'parlor Bolsheviki,' the Philistines of our social period, who, enveloped in the cigarette smoke and airs of superiority, have lost the touch of just proportion in their measurements of 'the good and bad in modernism'" (U.S., House, *Attorney General* 25). Bureau-defined modernists, both good and bad, found an even readier audience in Afro-America—a readership the FBI acknowledged and respected where other state authorities saw comic half-literacy at best, but a readership the Bureau first envisioned through the prism of *Radicalism and Sedition*'s account of the Red Summer, a fever dream of "inflammatory statement" fulfilled by black-on-white violence. Given their especially "emotional nature," explained Hoover lieutenant Robert Adger Bowen, Negroes could be "widely informed and led" by radical expression ("The Radical Press"); according to the Bureau's ad hoc racial genealogy, the African ranked as both the lady and the extremist of the races. In the same 1930 House testimony in which he urged prior restraint of seditious language, Hoover consequently specified that there was little more dangerous than supplying the rhetoric of racial parity to a racially diverse public (U.S., House, *Investigation* 37).

Art-appreciative even in its reductionism, Hoover's theory of rapid conversion via literary modernism met its match in the supposed ease with which New Negro audiences danced to radical tunes. And this lesson found bureaucratic expression in the racial metrics of FBI file keeping, with McKay's dossier followed by dozens of others devoted to Afro-modernist authors, front-line salespeople of "racial enmity" to black audiences. As noted above, 51 of the 106 Freedom of Information Act (FOIA) inquiries listed in this book's appendix, or nearly 50 percent, extracted evidence of Bureau surveillance of black writers and critics with national reputations in the Hoover era. If Malcolm X, Eldridge Cleaver, and Martin Luther King Jr. are added to the list—movement martyrs with selections in *The Norton Anthology of African American Literature*—the math edges even higher. The weight of these numbers can be assessed through two measures, imperfect but expressive. The first measure is the Bureau's rate of positive responses to recent FOIA requests of any kind. Between 2005 and 2009, the whole of George W. Bush's second term and year one of the first Obama administration, the FBI discovered relevant materials in only a third of its FOIA cases ("2009 Rosemary Award"). The great bulk of my FOIA requests, dating from 2006 to 2008, the heart of this stretch, yielded records significantly more often, with almost half producing evidence of FBI files.[7] The second measure is the total of 148 files on American writers of all ethnicities and all Bureau stages disclosed in Natalie Robins's comprehensive survey *Alien Ink: The FBI's War on Freedom of Expression* (1992). Just four names in Robins's book—James Baldwin's, Amiri Baraka's, Langston Hughes's, and Richard Wright's—match those on my own list. The forty-seven other "filed" African American writers I discuss increase Robins's grand total from 148 to 195, or by about one-third. The drawn-out roll call of black writers with FBI files thus seems the work of something more concerted than chance; the Bureau acted on a tenacious suspicion, I believe, that authoring Afro-modernism and jeopardizing national security were one and the same. Judging from decades of archival practice, the FBI imagined that African American writing shattered the bonds of the slave narrative without breaking with the signs of the criminal.

Given this lasting attention to African American writing first prompted by the Red Summer, pioneering anthologists of the Harlem Renaissance can be forgiven for suggesting that the Hoover Raids inspired black Manhattan's concentration on aesthetic rebirth. For the Nathan Irvin Huggins of *Voices of the Harlem Renaissance* (1976) and the David Levering Lewis of *The Portable Harlem Renaissance Reader* (1994), Hoover's Radical Division ranked as an unknowing author of the art-first New Negro awakening, the Harlem-based movement defined as black America's authentic modernism for almost one hundred years. The repressive policing of the first American Red Scare, Huggins contends, sparked a "channeling of [New Negro] energy from political and social criticism into poetry, fiction, music, and art" in the early 1920s (9). Lewis, adopting the psychoanalytical vocabulary, describes this Red Scare re-routing as a "cultural sublimation of civil rights" (*The Portable* xxiv). The hints of Huggins and Lewis on Hoover's role as a renaissance godfather take a less-traveled road: inattention to the FBI's reckoning with Afro-modernism cannot be pinned on them. But these hints still discount the Bureau's operative thesis that New Negro poetry and fiction were themselves, early and always, arma-ments of "political and social criticism." Like literary historian Barbara Foley, Hoover and company seemed to recognize that culturalism was not so much the inhibited successor to Harlem Renaissance political radicalism as "its dia-lectical counterpart" (*Spectres* 6).

Nor do Huggins's and Lewis's hints acknowledge the Bureau's own refined cultural turn under pressure from black renaissancism. The arrival of Harlem Renaissance literature helped to stir Hoover's agency to embrace the state of counterliterary exception, and, more directly, to undertake a landmark police action against a minority modernism. As *Radicalism and Sedition* shows, Bu-reau spy-readers were motivated to inspect Harlem's rebirth years before Carl Van Vechten took the "A" train and were faced with novelties both ominous and thrilling to the engineers of the national-security state. Here was a mod-ernism welcomed by recent city migrants as well as by settled "parlor pinks," a bridge between racialist and Marxist internationalisms that fed urbane self-representation and urban self-defense. The FBI's prying into this modernism entailed its first counterliterary step to convert black literary innovation into criminological capital. Refining the nineteenth-century conception of the criminal as a "type of species, the 'dangerous individual'" (Herzog 37), the Bureau transformed the arrival of Claude McKay, Langston Hughes, and their New Negro peers into the birth of a new criminal genus, one whose deviant literacy, independent of any felony, endangered national security in place of by-gone slave codes.[8] Subjecting this new genus to modern methods of examina-tion, knowledge, and discipline, the Bureau worked to envelop the New Negro's literary witness within a networked counterliterature of its own, a fastidious archive of police texts constituted not in terms of Foucault's "bodies and days," but in terms of radical works and racial histories (Foucault, *Discipline* 189). In a pivotal wager, the FBI bet that the novel racial communication of Harlem's renaissance could be recirculated to the state's advantage, rebuilt as a tool to map, file, and out-write an entire ethnic modernism.

Persons to Racial Conditions: Literary G-Men and FBI Counterliterature from the New Deal to the Second World War

The FBI's fabrication of a new literary-criminal type demanded no break with its self-promoting mission as the 1920s crashed and the Great Depression deepened. While still supposedly advising his chauffeur to avoid left turns, the politically conservative Hoover pursued an unpredicted détente with the New Deal. Franklin D. Roosevelt's appreciation for Bureau-dug dirt jump-started the alliance, but the president's like-minded patronage of state involvement in the literary field may have sealed it. Despite the Bureau's reputation for punitive philistinism, Hoover's agency, a connoisseur of big government, was not too out of step with the New Deal's generous arts policy.[9] Looking into the Federal Writers' Project (FWP), a Works Progress Administration program for under-employed authors established in 1935, FBI lit.-cops saw both a worrisome boot camp for those "Communist thought-control relay stations" and a sympathetic peer of their own "Publications Section," founded that same year to broaden the Bureau's already substantial cultural influence. Ideological and managerial differences between the FBI and FWP were stark, of course. Bureau-collected oral histories cast suspicion rather than nobility on their folk informants, for example, and landed in sealed investigative files rather than in popular *American Guide* books. But both Hoover's FBI and Henry Alsberg's FWP qualified as publicly subsidized antennas collecting literary intelligence and transmitting striking representations of state interests in turn. To adapt literary critic Michael Szalay, both of these federal agencies lobbied the Depression public with the message "that Americans needed to consume art as surely as they needed social security" (*New Deal Modernism* 5).

During Roosevelt's make-or-break first term, the Bureau took the lead of the federal "War on Crime," fighting fire with both fire and culture. Countering the pulps' Depression-fed attraction to Ma Barker, Pretty Boy Floyd, and other would-be Robin Hoods with automatic weapons, Hoover's agency oversaw the popular reaction-fantasy of the strapping and scientific state cop. Keenly conformist while gangsters flashed unschooled resistance, the Government Man refitted the classic ratiocinative detective to return machine-gun fire and resist the bob-haired gun moll, the 1920s flapper rebuilt as a criminal Svengali (Strunk 25). Encouraged by the success of the James Cagney film *G-Men* (1935), the FBI endorsed the methodical but brawny hero at the heart of dozens of G-Man movies (*Public Hero Number One, Show Them No Mercy*), radio shows (*Radio Gangbusters, This Is Your F.B.I.*), comic strips (*Secret Agent X-9, War on Crime*), and cheap periodicals (*G-Men Magazine, The Feds*). Kids with unformed literary interests were introduced to G-Man heroism through bubble-gum cards and cardboard FBI shields on cereal boxes, the latter flashed in a wave of risky citizens' arrests. "You must agree to back the Government Men in all their activities—and to disseminate public opinion opposed to the gangster and the racketeer," members of a Junior G-Men Club were instructed ("Federal Flashes").

Combined with the Bureau's fearsome record in killing flesh-and-blood "Public Enemies," the G-Man's mass-cultural victories moved Congress to pass most points of Roosevelt's aggressive Twelve Point Crime Program and to double Bureau appropriations between 1932 and 1936 (Theoharis, "A Brief History" 38). Over the full course of the FDR years, 1933–45, the FBI's annual budget bulged from 2.7 to 45 million dollars, and its workforce of special agents grew from 266 to some 5,000 (Olmstead 9). For Hoover in particular, the G-Man's star turn was a ticket to Hollywood parties and White House signing ceremonies—both FDR and Ginger Rogers liked to be photographed by his side. By the successful conclusion of the Depression War on Crime, the Bureau director reigned as an exceedingly popular paradox, the secret policeman–cum–media celebrity–cum–New Deal poster boy. As Richard Gid Powers observes in his major study of the FBI in popular culture, Hoover and his G-Men conquered the 1930s by operating on several strata "of American culture generally considered quite distinct" (*G-Men* xii). Their achievement "depended on the hidden connections between politics and popular entertainment; the Bureau's reputation was kept aloft by the pressure of fantasy on politics and of politics on the public's fantasy life" (xii). Managing this two-way pressure with luck and energy, Hoover and the Bureau's cultural emissaries became crucial salesmen of the New Deal, marketing the fantasy of a gallant interventionist state more vividly than any social security table (Potter, *War on Crime* 3).

Such marketing success depended on group work: like the Federal Writers' Project, the FBI cultivated a large literary stable reliant on state support. Supplied with interesting case memoranda by the Publications Section, former crime reporters including Rex Collier, Courtney Ryley Cooper, Herbert Corey, and Henry Suydam lapped up raw FBI texts, molding them to attention-grabbing templates learned in daily journalism (Richard Gid Powers, *G-Men* xvi). The title of Corey's 1936 valentine to the Bureau, *Farewell, Mr. Gangster!*, neatly captures the Hoover school's join-the-posse zeal. In the more skeptical eye of Frank Donner, the staff of Hoover's alternative writers' project served "the most elaborate propaganda apparatus ever developed by a government agency" (91). The rising charisma of the director's charismatic-bureaucratic leadership was reflected in his service as "our first minister of propaganda" (91) and replicated even in the collective realm of Bureau authorship. A shelf of G-Man narratives came to bear his signature, all of them literary. (Despite the

FBI's hogging of screens and airwaves, Hoover continued to place literature at the top of the modern media pyramid.) "The warfare between crime and the forces of law and order has been the topic of narration and writing since prehistoric man," Hoover noted in a 1936 address, and he too jumped to satisfy this primitive appetite ("Patriotism").

What Donner calls "the interplay between the process of opinion formation and the Director's self-promotion" (91) was perfected in a stack of Depression-era articles by Hoover, dozens of them yearly in the mid-1930s, sixteen of them in the *American Magazine* alone between 1934 and 1936. Marveling at the page count, the *New Yorker* wryly thanked the director for ensuring that "[t]he ways of the FBI have been so exhaustively publicized . . . that a moderately literate criminal ought to be able to avoid capture indefinitely" (Jack Alexander, "The Director—III" 25). Hoover's literary New Deal came of age in his earliest commercial book, *Persons in Hiding*, published by the nongovernmental firm of Little, Brown in 1938. From one angle, *Persons* adheres to the "FBI formula" repeatedly applied by Courtney Ryley Cooper, the beneficiary of Bureau patronage anointed to write *Persons*'s foreword, and perhaps to ghostwrite an entire draft (Richard Gid Powers, *G-Men* 104). Like Cooper's *Ten Thousand Public Enemies* (1935), the very first book on the FBI, Hoover's narrative discourse is indebted to the hard-boiled style of James M. Cain and Dashiell Hammett. The director's first-person voice is pitiless, mannishly jaded, and violently snappy: "I'm going to tell the truth about these rats. . . . I'm going to tell the truth about the miserable politicians who protect them and the slimy, silly or sob-sister convict lovers who let them out on sentimental or illy-advised [*sic*] paroles" (xviii). Like *Ten Thousand Public Enemies*, *Persons*'s plot consists of a cycle of fleshed-out case files, tied together by two gimmicky lifelines: a histrionic "chain of evil" linking the famous Public Enemy cases of 1933–34, and a virtual tour of Bureau headquarters (here is the crime laboratory, there is the national fingerprint file, etc.) (Richard Gid Powers, *G-Men* 104). The criminological theory elaborated in Hoover's final chapter adopts the censorious hailing of public responsibility central to Cooper's self-aggrandizing vision of New Deal policing. Greater "than the fault of the criminal or of the parent," hypothesizes Hoover, "is the gullible and lethargic attitude which is common to practically all our citizens" (311). The passive, technically innocent public, persons in hiding from accountability, is most to blame for rising crime rates, and therefore the primary target of literary first responders.

From another, more interesting angle, *Persons in Hiding* can be read as an effort to tighten Hoover's grip on the FBI's shadow writer's project. Advertisements for the director's muscular ratiocination emphasize his crystallizing critical literacy. "[O]ften a few scribbled words in red ink, written down instantly after his reading of an investigative report," blusters the Hoover-approved foreword, "will be the starting point of a new line of investigation which will close an important case, resulting in the conviction of an offender" (ix). Specifically literary offenders, Hoover's rivals and *frères*, are tried and sentenced. In spite of its embrace of hard-boiled naturalism, for example, *Persons* wards off the related school of proletarian literature, associating its social thematics with the errors of sob-sister criminology. When Hoover indicts the position "that the bitterness of the downtrodden, ground in the mills of big corporations, or unjustly incarcerated, brings about crime as a symptom of rebellion" (300), he is unclear if radical novels or liberal defense lawyers are his primary targets. (Concerned citizens wrote Hoover after discovering that Richard Wright's *Native Son* [1940], its last third dominated by attorney Boris Max, represented both these enemies.) *Persons*'s critical outreach to New Deal modernism underlines Szalay's contention that "[l]iterary engagements with the welfare state . . . did not emerge simply as a function of traditionally liberal, centrist political convictions" (*New Deal Modernism* 3). As Hoover saw it, such engagements best emerged under the influence of a literary-federalist state that itself engaged the print public sphere, rectifying the writer's market through conservative criticism as well as liberal assistance.

Throughout the Great Depression, the Bureau's production of such criticism was not excessively devoted to Afro-modernism. Hoover's *Persons in Hiding* is again suggestive: unlike *American Agent* (1936), a competing War-on-Crime memoir by star triggerman Melvin Purvis, the G-Man who shot John Dillinger and Pretty Boy Floyd, Hoover discovers no comic darkies on the gangster front. (" 'What are they doing?' 'Dey ain't doin' nothin'; dey's dead,' " writes the South Carolina–born Purvis, shoving a poor relation of Amos and Andy into the bloody scene of the Barker gang's slaying [167].) *Persons in Hiding* instead insists that "the typical desperate criminal" is as socially white as the nation allows, "of American stock with a highly patriotic American name. He must not come from the slums of a great city . . . but from a small town, where all is supposed to be gladness and light" (93). Correspondingly, as far as the dilemma of Bureau surveillance was concerned, the Depression was the best of times for Afro-modernism. Nonblack authors from southern towns (William Faulkner, file opened 1939) and northern slums (Clifford Odets, file opened 1935) then took the brunt of Bureau reading. Richard Wright, adopting the choral voice of "us black folk" in the government-sourced photo-history *Twelve Million Black Voices* (1941), might protest the dissonant remoteness of most of the New Deal, his people "too far down at the bottom of the ditch for the fingers of government to reach us" (48). Yet there were unspoken advantages in the fact that

African American writers of the 1930s were more familiar with the light touch of the FWP than with the manipulations of Hoover's writers' bureau. Before Wright's FBI file was assembled in 1942, *Native Son* was privileged to fight its battles against censorship on the comparatively favorable terrain of the Popular Front and the Book of the Month Club.

The period of Bureau detachment from African American letters crumbled with America's entrance into World War II. Beneath the surface of the Bureau's 1930s reform era was a gradual return to the business of political investigation that escalated with the coming of war, and that reinstalled African American writing near the heart of FBI counterliterature. In August 1936, President Roosevelt summoned Hoover to the White House, absorbed his panoramic account of the radical menace, and urged wide-ranging searches of domestic enemies both communist and fascist. The Bureau director, sympathetic to the hint of another imperial presidency, worried out loud over Attorney General Stone's 1924 strictures against noncriminal investigations but proposed the solvent of a little-known 1916 statute authorizing the Bureau to probe matters raised by the State Department. The president, roping Secretary Cordell Hull into a meeting the next day, stressed the international dimension of the fascist/communist threat and pressured the State Department to issue a confidential referral. "Go ahead and investigate the cock-suckers," Hull reportedly told Hoover (qtd. in Weiner, *Enemies* 168). Hoover's authority would thus expand along with Roosevelt's even as increased federal power helped to transform American politics into "a national drama focused on the personality of the president" (McCann 7). The FBI director would cite the secret intelligence power permitted him that day for the rest of his administrative life (Weiner, *Enemies* 75).

Presuming that FDR had revalidated the Bureau's defense of the state of counterliterary exception, Hoover discreetly resumed work on the antiradical library he had mothballed but not destroyed in 1924. Bureau clerks reopened the collection's Library-of-Congress-style file classification system, compiling fresh directories of subversives. They resubscribed to radical newspapers, periodicals, and pamphlet services. These enhancements eased the president's controversial 1939 decision to vest the FBI with primary responsibility for "the investigation of all espionage, counter espionage, and sabotage matters" on the home front (qtd. in U.S., Senate, Select Committee, *Intelligence Activities* 26), a choice the Bureau interpreted as an invitation to wholesale radical watching for the rest of the Hoover era (Donner 57). The September outbreak of war in Europe propelled FDR's creation of a vigilant "FBI Front" into the public domain. Hoover made use of the crisis by inducing the president to issue a combination press release and Magna Carta, a decree of Bureau liberties urging all "law enforcement officers in the United States promptly to turn over to the nearest representative of the Federal Bureau of Investigation any information obtained by them relating to espionage, counterespionage, sabotage, subversive activities and violations of the neutrality laws" (Roosevelt). The FBI's uppermost place in the countersubversive pecking order was honored with the presidential seal.

With Roosevelt's declaration of a limited state of emergency in September 1939, Hoover felt free to broadcast the continuing state of counterliterary exception and tune up its Bureau instruments. He publicly reconstituted the General Intelligence Division, the child of the old Radical Division, waving the warrant of the proclamation of emergency and boasting of the unit's refilled file cabinets—research tools Vito Marcantonio, the progressive congressman from East Harlem, denounced as "a system of terror by index cards" (Marcantonio). Hoover informed the House Appropriations Committee of his recharged intent to investigate propaganda opposed to the American way of life. Under FDR and the coming of World War II—not McCarthyite Republicanism and Cold War panic—most practical limits on Hoover's surveillance of presumed enemies were broken in plain sight. Wiretapping, "trash covers" (garbage-can inspection), "mail covers" (mail monitoring), and "black bag jobs" (authorized break-ins) became visible within the Bureau's tool kit, however deep their results were buried in an exclusive "Do Not File" file, the absurdist height of Bureau archivism (Theoharis, *The FBI and American Democracy* 107). The political ironies of the FBI-FDR pact have been chewed over in congressional inquiries and critical intelligence scholarship; the literary repercussions far less so.[10] In effect, however, the predictable right-wing suspects were latecomers to a reading society recreated in 1939, a combination of New Deal and Hooverite literary federalisms unshackled by official emergency. Through the Smith Act of 1940, normally remembered as a catalyst of 1950s containment culture, Congress blessed this odd couple's wartime mission. As we will see, only a straight-and-narrow attorney general, Hoover's nominal superior at the Justice Department, moved to stem an open season on unwanted political expression.

On December 8, 1941, the morning after Pearl Harbor, the Bureau faced two grave assignments, each tied to the agency's elevation under Roosevelt. The first was deflecting blame for the "second 9/11" Hoover was originally appointed to the Radical Division to prevent, a severe test of the FBI's new duty to avert sabotage. "The nation's super Dick Tracy, FBI Director J. Edgar Hoover, is directly under the gun" for Pearl Harbor, claimed the *Washington Times-Herald* (qtd. in Richard Gid Powers, *Secrecy*), but Hoover's arguments for naval jurisdiction over Hawaiian waters put him back on the accustomed side of the barrel by late December. The second assignment was nearly as earthshaking: FDR placed Hoover in charge of national press censorship with ships still burning in the harbor. Arguably, this was the job for which the director had apprenticed since 1919, yet it threatened the balance of correction and contribution to national literature that the FBI's brand of lit.-cop federalism had achieved in the 1930s. Hoover thus did not look back when the chief censor's position was shifted to an editor at the Associated Press. FDR, reassured in confidential reports that Hoover found seditious writing almost everywhere he looked, gave the director room to improvise more selective restrictions.

African American journalism, personally read and scapegoated by Hoover beginning with the first Red Scare, accordingly met with inordinate Bureau criticism during World War II. In the FBI leader's handling of an unapologetic state of counterliterary exception, the best-read black writing went back to the head of the firing line. The wide influence of the wartime black press, notes journalism historian Patrick S. Washburn, set the stage for a collision with the FBI "that had its genesis more than twenty years before," deep in the New Negro era (39). In numbers far exceeding the audience for New Negro periodicals, three-and-a-half to six million of the nation's thirteen million African Americans were estimated to read race newspapers during the early 1940s, with the average total weekly print run growing from 600,000 copies in 1933 to more than 1,800,000 by 1945 (39). Relatively well-capitalized northern publications armed with relative freedom of speech became shakers of national black opinion, the *Pittsburgh Courier* stoking the famous "Double V" campaign: victory against fascism abroad and racial discrimination at home. Hoover's initial impulse against a regrouped enemy was to prosecute the lot with endangering the war effort (this despite the tiny 2 percent of conscientious objectors hailing from the black community [Jeffreys-Jones, *The FBI* 133].) Precluding the countersubversive alliance of the Palmer years, however, Hoover's partner at the Justice Department was Attorney General Francis Biddle, a stringent civil libertarian proud of the small number of sedition prosecutions compared to the last world war. No indictments of the black press went forward under his department's signature.

Hoover thus learned to direct his ominous clipping files up the White House chain of command and to propose lower-level criminal inquiries into low-profile journals such as the *Oklahoma City Black Dispatch*, rightly suspected of opposing the segregation of black troops. While few large-circulation papers were placed in backdoor legal jeopardy, Hoover ordered local FBI agents to visit and quiz their editors, house calls that were common until the peace was declared. "Edgar Hoover is busy again," wired a staff member of the *Courier* in 1942 (qtd. in Washburn 174). "We had another visit last week. They stayed an hour. The usual rah-rah" (174). It was an unusual day, publisher P. B. Young Sr. recalled, when FBI agents neglected to spend an hour with a black editor somewhere (Washburn 82). A handful of prominent papers pledged allegiance in hopes of keeping G-Men out of their offices, the *Chicago Defender*, for example, express-mailing Hoover a copy of an editorial vowing that the "Negro press will not blemish its magnificent record of sound patriotism by indulging in subversive advocacy to the impairment of the national will" ("Freedom"). John H. Johnson of *Negro Digest* risked a fawning personal letter to Hoover requesting a 1,500-word article, "Negroes in Crime," an assignment the director declined after receiving confidential word of the *Digest*'s faint likeness to the *Courier* and other "militant Negro" venues (U.S., Federal, *Negro Digest/Black World*, 22 Mar. 1945; 4 Apr. 1945). Less pragmatic voices took their visits from the Bureau public. *Atlanta Daily World* columnist Cliff MacKay lashed out in print against a pair of agent interviews, the FBI's means of communicating the return of ghostreading door-to-door. "One gathers after the conversation," he complained, "that some white people would like to read 'sedition' and 'subversive activity' into the determination of Negroes to achieve democracy here at the same time they are called upon to fight for its preservation abroad. Nothing could be further from the truth, as these FBI agents were told on both occasions of their visits" (MacKay). As documented in part 5 of *F.B. Eyes*, authors of black fiction soon joined MacKay in broadcasting the public secret of Bureau surveillance, the postwar moment marking the widespread appearance of the FBI as an overt counter in the African American novel.

Had wartime black journalists known of the FBI's best-researched challenge to their independence, they might have been even more outspoken. In September 1943, Hoover received the results of a secret *Survey of Racial Conditions in the United States* compiled by the Bureau's Internal Security Division and released in a select edition of six, one copy bound for the White House. In its raw, file-and-enclosure form, this extraordinary text, code-named *RACON*, consisted of roughly 77,000 pages, 60,000 more than even the Martin Luther King file (Robert A. Hill, *The FBI's RACON* xvii). As presented for Hoover's approval, *RACON* still ran to 730 pages, enough to recap a city-by-city mass observation of everyday black life near the end of Jim Crow.[11] The report's length was of its essence: Hoover had ordered all Bureau field offices to "ascertain the extent of agitation among the American Negroes," thus transforming station chiefs from Albany to San Juan into coauthors anxious to meet Hoover's standards of attentiveness (qtd. in Robert A. Hill, *The FBI's RACON* 15). *RACON*, like the Bureau's personal files on African American authors, was thus to be a communal composition shaped by the prospect of executive editing at the Seat of Government. Hoover's local collaborators answered their charge by mining Soviet and Japanese veins of "un-American ideology working among the Negro people," just as ordered (75). Yet they also intuited their deeper calling to solve what Ralph Ellison branded the mystery of the zoot suit, the riddle of the "profound political meaning" then animating the cool pose of young Afro-America, more than an affair of wide-brimmed hats, baggy "reet pleat" pants, and fashionable defiance of wartime cloth rationing ("Editorial" 300).

Hoover publicized his own crack at this mystery a month after *RACON* reached his desk. Writing with Frederick L. Collins, a late enrollee in the Bureau writer's program, he offered the October 1943 *Collier's* magazine "Slickers in Slacks," an article retailoring the zoot suit as a criminal vehicle.[12] "[L]oosely cut garments" hanging from "dark-skinned, slick-haired youths" defied "spruce, well-tailored" Americanism, Hoover and Collins advised (77). But such threads fit perfectly for hiding shoplifted goods, they insisted. With its deep pockets and draped caches, their zoot suit turned style into criminal revolt. The communal authors of *RACON*, by contrast, anticipated Ellison's *Invisible Man* (1952) in envisioning the zoot suit as an abstraction—angular symbol, not sharpened tool—of the increased "tempo of living" affecting all African American migrants to the industrial city, "large numbers of whom probably have never before experienced urban life" (412). The wartime speed-up of the Great Migration, *RACON*'s authors continued, "has brought about an increased congestion in the already heavily populated areas and has created a tension and new complexity in race relationship [*sic*] heretofore nonexistent in many areas" (412). With this accent on headlong black modernization, the expansion of interracial competition into virgin urban territory, and other blatantly sociological happenings, *RACON* approached the slant of *To Stem the Tide: A Survey of Racial Tension Areas of the U.S.* (1943), a contemporary pamphlet supervised by Charles S. Johnson, chair of sociology at historically black Fisk University and eventual subject of a 422-page FBI file.[13] Hoover's aversion to structural causality in the study of race did not force the deletion of such analysis from *RACON*, an assessment of "racial tension areas" that cautiously respected the kind of sweeping urban ethnography also found in St. Clair Drake and Horace Cayton's *Black Metropolis: Negro Life in a Northern City* (1945). Less guardedly, *RACON* valued the *raison d'état* behind the wartime monument then imagined as the sociological study to end all studies. Without lauding racial equality as the goal of American nationhood, the FBI's *Survey of Racial Conditions* rivaled Gunnar Myrdal's *An American Dilemma* (1944) in approaching objective interracial intelligence as a needed resource of U.S. state power, then battling in Asia, Europe, and North Africa to represent the general interests of humanity (Singh 134–36). *RACON* thus matched a distinguished sociological club in considering the world war an occasion for systematic study of the "Negro problem," once more a domestic issue of foreign dimensions.

Moving from sociological to literary judgment, the latter a trademark of the FBI director, *RACON* went deeper into the Hoover grain. A twenty-three-page appendix to the report, "The Negro Press," channels *Radicalism and Sedition among the Negroes as Reflected in Their Publications*, the 1919 document that first confessed the Bureau's interest in Afro-modernist writing. Like *Radicalism and Sedition*, *RACON*'s literary-critical appendix protests the entanglement of black journalism in a web of world war, racial violence, and imported anti-American ideology. Reinforcing Bureau unease over black loyalty, "Zoot Suit Riots" in Los Angeles had interrupted the composition of *RACON* in June 1943 and helped to kindle Harlem's explosion that August. Echoing *Radicalism and Sedition*'s objections to "the utterance of inflammatory statement" amid urban unrest (U.S., Senate, *Radicalism* 161), *RACON* seconds "the opinion that the Negro press is a strong provocator [*sic*] of discontent among Negroes" (419). As with the earlier FBI publication, *RACON*'s criticism ironically hinges on generous reading and reproduction of African American writing, again considered one of the "principal phases of the Negro movement" (Hoover, qtd. in Kornweibel, *"Seeing"* 23). With its encompassing lists, summaries, and excerpts of articles from the *Defender*, the *Pittsburgh Chronicle*, and beyond, *RACON* doubles as a scholarly index of the black press at its wartime pinnacle. Despite the Bureau's best efforts to dismiss "alleged instances of discrimination against Negroes" as sensational reporting, a grudgingly admiring *RACON* finally rates black journalism with "the outstanding agitational as well as influential forces among the Negro race" (411). This verdict flattered Hoover's impression that blacks were especially receptive to the propaganda of the word, a feature of the director's casual hermeneutic theory formed in the aftermath of a previous world war. Gauged by *RACON* alone, it thus appears that the Bureau's return to the scene of Afro-modernism in the early 1940s meant the recreation of some of the earliest weapons of FBI counterliterature. Examining the counterliterary author files of the same period, however, shows that this return also produced original forms of criminological currency.

Afro-Loyalty and Custodial Detention: Files of World War II

In spite of its echoes of the Red Summer and the Hoover Raids, *RACON*'s investigation of wartime black journalism failed to ignite legal proceedings against publishers. From the relieved outlook of 1947, P. B. Young Sr. of the *Norfolk Journal* concluded "that years of watching and distilling . . . every line, every word printed in the Negro press that could by any process of reasoning have been classified as treasonable brought not one single arrest, not one single act of suppression" (qtd. in Washburn 166). Young's pride in the "undiminished patriotism" of race journalism was justified insofar as the FBI's incitements to collective prosecution, cheered on by FDR, could not budge Attorney General Biddle (166). Outside Biddle's control, however, *RACON's* dragnet was filtered into at least sixteen separate Bureau files on Afro-modernist authors.[14] In these mostly unfamiliar documents of the FBI front, thousands of pages of lives and works are sifted. The authors inspected—often with their knowledge—include eight of the New Negro veterans mentioned above (Sterling Brown, Gwendolyn Bennett, Louise Thompson Patterson, George Schuyler, J. A. Rogers, W.E.B. Du Bois, Walter White, and Georgia Douglas Johnson) plus a postrenaissance group of the same number. Prison novelist and *New Masses* editor Lloyd Brown's file was opened in 1940, as was that of Spanish Civil War poet and Black Arts progenitor Ray Durem. Harlem Writers Guild founder John O. Killens, author of the southern antiromances *Youngblood* (1954) and *'Sippi* (1967), followed in 1941, with world-famous black naturalist Richard Wright joining him in 1942. Frank Marshall Davis, the Kansas-born poet and Hawaiian adviser of Barack Obama; Katherine Dunham, the writer-ethnographer-choreographer; Chester Himes, the Paris-dwelling architect of the Harlem *policier*; and Theodore Ward, the author of the Federal Theatre Project hit *Big White Fog* (1938), all entered Bureau consciousness in 1944.[15] With the exception of the era of state-sponsored McCarthyism, the years of U.S. involvement in World War II triggered more investigations of individual African American writers than any other phase of Bureau operations. The war's FBI front was also a scene of serious counterliterary inquiry.

This is not to say that every Afro-modernist file of the early 1940s is a document of censorious barbarism. There were no references to wayward novels when John O. Killens, then clerking at the National Labor Relations Board, was first charged with adherence to the "Communist Racial Equality Slate"; mistrust of his writing began to color his FBI "SECURITY MATTER" reports only in the 1950s (U.S., Federal, Killens, 10 Mar. 1942). The relevant sections of Katherine Dunham's file cast literature as just one of her vocations. They center instead on a 1944 Mexico City vacation and a subsequent "FOREIGN TRAVEL CONTROL" interview (U.S., Federal, Dunham, 23 Oct. 1944). "Katherine the Great" would not attract intense Bureau citation until she founded the Dunham School of Dance near Times Square in 1945, an academy recognized for its "ethno-choreological" union of movement training and anthropological narrative. G-Man enthusiast Walter Winchell, the creator of the modern gossip column, telegrammed FBI headquarters with a prurient tease about the school in 1948, its rhetoric drawn from the scandal-pushing blind item: "You'd be gee-whizzed at the after-hour orgies that take place thrice weekly at one of [New York's] most famous interpretive dance studios (Katherine Dunham's . . .)" (13 Apr. 1948). Respecting the compositional procedures that exposed Claude McKay's file to all manner of racialized "police text," Hoover approved the wire for preservation in Dunham's 229-page profile.

The Bureau's contributions to Walter White's 83-page file are also free from a will to censorship. In its place, the White collection itemizes an elaborate trading of literary favors between the FBI and an NAACP leader acquainted with Hoover even before he became Bureau chief. Among other services bartered, White asks for FBI assistance in producing the frontline journalism eventually assembled in his book *The Rising Wind* (1945). Seeking a hand with a 1943 trip "to the European and Pacific theatres of operation," White politely taps Bureau assets, hoping for Hoover's aid in "expediting . . . the FBI report to the War Department on my personal security" (U.S., Federal, White, 23 Sept. 1943). "Especially am I grateful for your willingness to send a memorandum urging that I be admitted to go right up to the battlefields," he spells out (23 Sept. 1943). The author of *The Fire in the Flint* (1924) and *Rope and Faggot* (1929) dangles a mysterious quid pro quo to repay Hoover's recommendation: "And I hope, also, that I shall be able to demonstrate my appreciation by performing the missions we discussed" (23 Sept. 1943). Later pages in the file hint at the nature of these missions, more likely to involve intelligence on African American troop morale than OSS-style skullduggery in European capitals. Adapting the banner vocabulary of *RACON*, White and Hoover then exchange a series of letters concerning White's privileged insight into "RACIAL CONDITIONS, DETROIT, MICHIGAN" (19 June 1944). "Specifically," White advises the Bureau director, "it is recommended that investigation be made of the sources of the rumors regarding the so-called 'Bumping Club' and a 'Negro D-Day,'" urban legends of black sabotage against "streetcars, buses, and crowded pedestrian traffic," all busy flashpoints of northern interracialism (22 May 1944). Too late to influence *RACON*, White's participant-observation reports managed to communicate his flirtation with the dicey role of race man/FBI informer—a peculiar mirror image of his role as light-skinned spy for darker America. Courting Bureau indulgence through inside scoops and classified texts, White provided the kernel of truth in Hoover's claim that one of his best friends was (deliberately and institutionally) Negro. White not only drove the NAACP into the arms of "the anticommunist impulse," as Manning Marable phrases it (21); he also became one of a handful of black literary intellectuals to negotiate, actively and voluntarily, with Hooverite antiradicalism (many more, we will see, used their writing to negotiate critically with Hooverite ghostreading).

Poet Georgia Douglas Johnson's FBI file, seventy-seven pages thinner than White's, shows the Bureau's interest in perhaps the pettiest of wartime literary crimes: sponsoring a "Social Letter Club," advertised in African American newspapers and magazines, for the benefit of lonely-hearted black soldiers. Unconcerned to distinguish among pen names, maiden names, married names, and criminal pseudonyms, Bureau ghostreaders here recount their investigation of "MRS. HENRY LINCOLN JOHNSON, with aliases, MARY STRONG, GEORGIA DOUGLAS JOHNSON, PAUL TREMAINE, NINA TEMPLE, NINIVA GLADSTONE, " one suspected of violating "War Department regulations regarding soliciting communications between persons in or attached to the military service and unknown individuals" (U.S., Federal, Georgia Douglas Johnson, 15 Mar. 1945). Interviewed by Bureau detectives at Halfway House, her residence in Northwest D.C. and formerly one of the feeder salons of the Harlem Renaissance, Johnson explained "that her true name is MRS. HENRY LINCOLN JOHNSON" and that her true intent was patriotic (15 Mar. 1945). It was she who had mailed a dubious letter written by two black servicemen to the Office of Censorship, hoping for clarification of the wartime laws of correspondence. Johnson's in-person assurances did the trick, leading to a dismissal of her case. But not before the Bureau created a representative scene of G-Men quizzing a suspect in a cradle of Afro-modernism, once the weekly retreat of Langston Hughes, Alain Locke, and Jean Toomer.

The Bureau's counterliterary appetite was better fed by wartime cases concerning the adoption of African Americans by the state's cultural bureaucracy. Regardless of its parallels with the Federal Writers' Project, the Bureau's patronage system distrusted the New Deal's overtures to black artists. Gwendolyn Bennett—poet, graphic artist, coconspirator behind *Fire!!*, the classically scandalous little magazine of the Harlem Renaissance—came to Bureau notice during a 1941 Works Progress Administration loyalty investigation, her position as director of a federally financed Harlem art center hanging in the balance. Accused of intimacy "with the intellectual group of the Communist Party" and of making "a false statement in submitting an affidavit . . . stating she was not a Communist" (U.S., Federal, Bennett, 23 Mar. 1944; 24 June 1941), Bennett had been dragged before a hearing at the WPA's New York office. She had won acquittal by stonewalling all guilt by literary association, denying that she "ever wrote under a pen name or that she ever read Communist literature" (23 Mar. 1944). But the Bureau was a hanging judge, interpreting the hearing as reason enough to launch its own "Internal Security" watch lasting until 1955 (23 Mar. 1944).

The guiding voice of Bennett's cooperatively authored file is insultingly skeptical, notwithstanding its description of the bearer of a "pleasant disposition [who] always appears smiling and good humoured" (23 Mar. 1944). An orienting "synopsis of facts" describes the subject as a "negress" whose birthplace and marital status cannot be taken at her word (23 Mar. 1944). She "claims to have been born at Giddings, Texas," scoffs an agent of the New York field office, and "claims to have been married" (23 Mar. 1944). Her literary associations are grounds for stacks of judicial text preparing punishment. "[T]he subject was chairman and sponsor of the Negro Playwrights Company," the home of Theodore Ward's "Communist play BIG WHITE FOG" (23 Mar. 1944). Worse, she is "very friendly with RICHARD WRIGHT" (23 Mar. 1944). The WPA's exoneration of Bennett had thus proved nothing definitively; she could no sooner bury her shady cultural alliances than enroll in the FBI's alternative writers' program. A lineup-ready photo of Bennett was therefore secured after her return to her government job, along with a copy of her signature, hijacked from the photostat of a bank check. ("Some difficulty has been experienced in obtaining sufficient handwriting specimens of the subject in view of the fact that most of her correspondence and work is done by typewriter" [22 Feb. 1945].) All mail to her apartment was scanned, and her case was added to a Bureau index of major threats to the state, Bennett being an artist never pardoned for tapping an unwary source of federal aid (23 Mar. 1944; 5 May 1944).

Sterling Brown's 105-page file charts a comparable investigation of literary loyalty, another dry run of McCarthyite procedure and cross-examination of the artist's fidelity to the state that feeds him. In the fall of 1941, just before Pearl Harbor locked down the climate of suspicion, a "[h]ighly confidential source" triggered a federal case against the FWP veteran, fresh from editing *The Negro Caravan* (1941), the most inclusive black anthology of the decade (U.S., Federal, Sterling Brown, 1 Apr. 1942). Brown, now an employee of both Howard University and the education division of the Federal Security Agency, was suspected of violating the Hatch Act, a 1940 federal law intended to prevent on-the-job politicking by New Dealers and, more relevantly, to remove government workers who belonged to "any political party or organization which advocates the overthrow of our constitutional form of government in the United States" ("Hatch Act"). Evidence had surfaced of Brown's presence "on the active indices of the American Peace Mobilization and the Washington Committee for Democratic Action" (4 Oct. 1941). Adding intrigue to imprecision, an unnamed FBI source had planted word that Brown was a covert "member of the Communist Party" (4 Oct. 1941). Purportedly too valuable to appear on the roll of Washington's party branch, he was said to work secretly and "directly out of the National Office of the Communist Party in New York" (4 Oct. 1941). Folklore collection and undercover Stalinism had rarely coexisted so peacefully in a single comrade, at least until Brown's accuser recanted in full (3 Mar. 1953).

FBI intelligence officers, appointed by Congress as Hatch Act enforcers, summoned Brown to a Bureau interview all his own. Actually well-informed informers had led the agents to expect "an outstanding negro [*sic*] poet" constitutionally unable to refuse invitations to speak on "Negro prose and poetry indiscriminately" (1 Apr. 1942). An especially knowledgeable—and cynical—source volunteered a theory of Brown's poetic trajectory, describing a shift from folk expression to proletarian realism undertaken for crossover fame and fortune: "Informant states BROWN had first concerned himself with writing poetry concerning the folk lore of the colored people. Informant stated that BROWN was advised that in order that his poetry would receive national recognition it would be necessary for him to write poetry concerning matters of a social nature" (1 Apr. 1942). Brown did not disappoint in person, speaking at length under oath of his devotion to the black vernacular, and then requesting a full transcript of the results. Tackling a string of questions anticipating the customary anticommunist formula—"are you at the present time or have you ever been" a so-and-so, agents repeatedly asked—he denied ongoing party ties, citing his alienation by Stalin's "Hitler tie-up," the hasty Nazi-Soviet pact of 1939 (31 Mar. 1942). Brown handled the ordeal more boldly in contending that a radical Negro is any who argues that "democratic rights and privileges should come to all people, regardless of race or religion" (31 Mar. 1942). "I have gotten, I suppose[,] the reputation as a radical because of my position on the race matter in America," he proudly deduces (31 Mar. 1942). Brown concludes with the claim that his political postures were expressed best in his books, the acid tests of the writer's loyalty: "I am perfectly willing for the things that I have written to be thoroughly investigated for where I stand. I think that that would be indication more than this type of membership" (31 Mar. 1942). Without taking the Fifth, or talking eccentric Brechtian rings around his accusers, Brown's replies to proto-McCarthyism compose a hidden transcript of intellectual courage. Reminding Bureau agents of the conclusive evidence of the literary word, and trusting the democratizing power of persuasion even under police investigation, his testimony deserves circulation beyond the terms of the FBI story. For one thing, this testimony allowed Brown to write another day. In August 1942, his Hatch Act case was closed, and Howard University administrators heard reassuring news of his purity (12 Aug. 1942).[16]

Brown's schooling of the Bureau may have had little to do with it, but the largest group of Afro-modernist files of the early 1940s indeed embraces the idea that thorough review of literary testimony is the key to judging Afro-loyalty. In these reading-intensive collections, the FBI file rhetorics of judicial text and literary-critical text fuse, and imaginative writing invites plans to arrest authors for thought crimes. One case in point is the George S. Schuyler file, 181 pages in length and active into his reactionary old age. Among this file's final items is an inquiry from an Auburn University graduate student, hand-addressed to

FBI headquarters in 1967. Thrown by the mentions of Hoover in Schuyler's autobiography, *Black and Conservative* (1966), the student requests the director's "commentary—unofficially of course—on . . . [Schuyler's] imprint on America and especially on his race" (U.S., Federal, Schuyler, 23 Oct. 1967). Within a week, Hoover replies with a stock denial of assistance: the director is unable to "furnish comments of the type you desire" (30 Oct. 1967). But Hoover's refusal owed nothing to ignorance of Schuyler's work and impact. The World War II portion of Schuyler's file recounts an extensive inquest into a suspect "said to be the most radical and widely read negro [*sic*] writer in the country," a one-pen hazard to "the present war efforts" (16 Feb. 1942). Schuyler's mission as the most communicative African American anticommunist got him nowhere with FBI documentarians. The *Daily Worker* could call him a police agent to its red heart's content; real federal police kept the file pages coming.

As screened by the Bureau and cooperating military spies, Schuyler's public statements were impressively dangerous, jeopardizing "Army and Navy policies relative to Negroes" and contributing "to the present low morale of same" (16 Feb. 1942). His lecture "Propaganda and Its Effects," recorded by a plainclothes federal agent in 1942, employed alarmingly "brilliant metaphors" to dissect techniques of government persuasion that the FBI had practiced since World War I (16 Feb. 1942). Schuyler's written arguments, equally distressing, were kept in "close check," investigators rummaging through libraries and newsstands for every publication on his resume (16 Feb. 1942). His first novel, *Black No More* (1931), was reviewed by several federal ghostreaders. In the FBI's most insightful crack at the text, a New York agent accurately identified an overarching "satire on inequality among the white and colored races" (22 Sept. 1942). Even Bureau ghostreaders at times recognized the joke of white supremacy.

Considering the whole of Schuyler's work, however, Army spies found little to smile about. The author was "the most dangerous Negro in the country today," concluded military intelligence, the single force most likely to "agitate a rebellion among Negro soldiers stationed in the South" (16 Feb. 1942). Hoover showed every sign of agreeing. Twice in 1944, he forwarded installments of Schuyler's *Pittsburgh Courier* column to the assistant attorney general, evading Biddle's skepticism while pressing for the conclusion that "the writing, publication and circulation of this editorial constitutes a violation of the sedition or related statutes" (? Apr. 1944; 22 May 1944). The deepest cut against Schuyler came the year before. Sometime in the spring of 1943, Hoover visited on Schuyler his harshest punishment for literary security risks: a place on the FBI's "Custodial Detention" list, the hidden validation of leftist fears of Bureau "terror by index cards" (1 Mar. 1943). Like everyone on the list, Schuyler was measured for a scarlet letter that stripped rights and regulated mobility. His classification, like Gwendolyn Bennett's, propelled street-level surveillance and regular updates of his photo and home address. It placed him on a register of enemies "whose presence at liberty in this country in time of war or national emergency would be dangerous to the public peace and the safety of the United States Government" (Hoover, Directive 409). It exposed him to summary arrest, surrender of habeas corpus, and indefinite confinement in a military stockade, should Hoover's will align with domestic crisis and presidential consent. Schuyler, imprisoned for desertion during World War I, might have spent a second war behind bars had post–Pearl Harbor sabotage given free rein to the FBI Front. "Negroes and Indians have often been run off their land and penned in virtual concentration camps," Schuyler noted, risking his *Courier* column to defend interned "citizens of Nipponese ancestry" (qtd. in U.S., Federal, Schuyler, 6 June 1942). He was closer to camp walls than he knew.

The Custodial Detention program, a mainstay of the Bureau's preventive antiradicalism until the 1970s, was not inspired by Schuyler's threat to the health of the state. Instead, the program dated to the weeks following Roosevelt's 1939 declaration of a limited state of emergency. Under the spell of catastrophe, Hoover ordered the listing of all U.S. citizens and residents suspected of "affiliation with organizations engaged in activities in behalf of a foreign nation, participation in dangerous subversive movements, advocacy of the overthrow of Government by force and violence, et cetera"—the "et cetera" allowing the widest of roundups (Hoover, Directive 410). Despite the convenient vagueness, the criteria used for listings on the basis of "advocacy" were specially attuned to counterliterary history. From the first, Hoover advised that candidates for detention should be investigated through "newspaper morgues" and "public libraries," not just through confidential informants and other human intelligence sources (Directive 410). The very notion of legible though dormant subversion may have descended from the literary-critical foundations of FBI archivism. Moreover, the reasons for adding an individual to the index eventually included the dissemination of propaganda sympathetic to foreign interests and "opposed to the American way of life," routine terms for unwelcome literary action the Bureau had premiered during the Hoover Raids (Hoover, qtd. in Richard Gid Powers, *Secrecy* 233).

Traditional Bureau recipes for criminalizing literary speech were thus baked into Custodial Detention policy. They remained intact after Attorney General Biddle declared the Custodial listing "impractical, unwise, and dangerous" in July 1943 (U.S., Federal, Lloyd Brown, 16 July 1943). In response to this censure, Hoover characteristically saluted upward but stayed the course, rechristening a substantially unchanged program as the "Security Index." Developing further antiradical indexes and reading larger populations onto their rolls in fact became a consuming task of the Bureau as the 1940s shaded into the Cold War. An abundance of deterrent programs mushroomed at the Seat of Government. G-Men subalterns and scribes hustled to fill a "Communist Index," a "Reserve Index," an "Agitator Index," a "Key Activist Index," and a nostalgically named "Rabble-Rouser Index." The comprehensive Security Index, in turn retitled the "Administrative Index," ingested 26,000 names by 1954 and survived in secret until 1976, four years beyond Hoover. Thanks to the archival prowess of his charismatic bureaucracy, Hoover's preparations to intern radical America, more discreet yet more ambitious than in the first Red Scare, outlived the Hoover era.[17]

During World War II, the granddaddy of Bureau detention indexes struck first against Afro-modernists when aiming at American writing. Or so indicates the best seized evidence. Natalie Robins's discussion of 144 nonblack U.S. authors with FBI files mentions just one clear-cut Custodial Detention case, Theodore Dreiser's, opened in 1941.[18] In comparison, a minimum of eleven African American writers who came to Bureau notice in the early 1940s received Custodial Detention cards or their renamed equal. Schuyler's early Custodial Index listing was followed by Bennett's assignment to the Security Index in 1944. Also placed on one or the other or both of these indexes were Lloyd Brown, Frank Marshall Davis, W.E.B. Du Bois, Ray Durem, Chester Himes, Langston Hughes, Louise Thompson Patterson, Theodore Ward, and Richard Wright, one viable scorecard of midcentury black writing. J. A. Rogers, too, barely avoided elevation from a "Subversive Reference" to a Custodial Detention card, a subject of Bureau interest thanks to his ties to the *Courier* and Schuyler ("[t]hese two men are the most highly paid writers in the country," claimed one easily impressed informer [U.S., Federal, Rogers, 29 Mar. 1942].) Black literary offenders of "alien allegiance" were thus disproportionately pre-targeted for arrest, this even as Hoover opposed the internment of Japanese American citizens, collective punishment the Bureau director, to his credit, ruled "a bit hysterical" (qtd. in Richard Gid Powers, *Secrecy* 249).

With the war in the rearview mirror, the director may have detected similar hysteria in a suspicious subgenre of black nationalist writing, John A. Williams's *The Man Who Cried I Am* (1967) its key text. Retelling African American literary history as a spy thriller, Williams's larger-than-life roman à clef traces the conversion of expatriate black writers into decolonized secret agents. Marked for death in Paris, *The Man*'s Harry Ames, a facsimile of Richard Wright, manages to circulate a captured copy of the "King Alfred Plan," an FBI-CIA timetable for detaining and disappearing twenty-two million African Americans. Williams's novel of cloak-and-dagger race war qualifies as more than a highbrow tribute to black paranoia. With its tale of the Wright circle detecting the Afro-concentration camps of the future, *The Man Who Cried I Am* retells the hidden history of Hoover's pre-internment of African American letters—a true story best guessed by the cohort of black writers pursued by the Bureau. Williams's retelling of the plot against black intelligence thus imaginatively turns the tables on U.S. national security, but his novel's violent intrigues, incompletely redeemed by his Wright's martyrdom, also reflect how the expansive internationalism of midcentury African American writing motivated new ferocity in Bureau counterliterature.[19] If the literary boom of the Harlem Renaissance prodded the FBI to encircle Afro-modernism with its own networked counterwriting, then the rebirth's echoes in the global theater of World War II motivated counterliterary blueprints for imprisoning Afro-modernist authors on the home front, cordoning them off from foreign ties. During the 1950s, the Security Index and related Bureau black lists made room for Frank London Brown, Alice Childress, Harold Cruse, Shirley Graham Du Bois, Lorraine Hansberry, Ollie Harrington, Lance Jeffers, Bob Kaufman, John O. Killens, Julian Mayfield, Willard Motley, and William Gardner Smith. In the 1960s, James Baldwin, Amiri Baraka, and Larry Neal joined the indexed. Adding in his 1940s listees, Hoover thus arranged to intern more than half of the black writers (twenty-seven of the fifty-one) now shown to be investigated by the FBI between 1919 and 1972. It is not too strong to say that Bureau counterliterature prepared to jail the African American literary tradition at midcentury; seen through the fog of war and Cold War, its living authors looked menacing enough to confine en masse. If the Security Index had been unleashed beyond the FBI archive, black writing in every genre could have become a type of prison literature.

Total Literary Awareness: Files of the Cold War

In the aftermath of "V-J Day," it first appeared that the Custodial Detention list's medicine for African American writers would go the way of the Soviet Ark, a relic of anticommunist emergency flushed from Bureau memory. "The world that the FBI faced in September 1945 was very different from the world of 1939 when the war began," the Bureau's self-produced online history remarks (FBI .gov). African Americans, tasting "equality during wartime labor shortages, had developed aspirations and the means of achieving these goals [they] had lacked before the war" (FBI.gov). Harry Truman of half-southern Missouri, elevated to the White House after FDR's death, was privately less sympathetic to black aspirations than the fallen president. Yet the realpolitik of a regionally fractured Democratic party and a Soviet-challenged national image pushed his administration to employ honeymoon capital to widen cracks in white su-premacy opened by wartime organizing. In 1946, Truman appointed the board of the first federal Civil Rights Commission. Inside a year, its integrated mem-bership had issued the landmark report *To Secure These Rights*, recommend-ing presidential measures to eliminate religious and racial segregation. In 1948, Truman gave southern Democrats hell by endorsing the commission's advice to desegregate the U.S. military. As viewed by the late historian Manning Marable, these overtures lured African Americans into a shortsighted, long-lasting ac-cord with Cold War liberalism (Marable 23). As viewed by the FBI, they were an immediate challenge to display egalitarian bona fides.

Marching ahead of the army, the Bureau honored its black troops in the Oc-tober 1947 edition of *Ebony*, black America's best-circulated source of positive images. The unsigned, splashily illustrated cover story "Negro FBI Agents in Action" cautioned that Bureau recruits doing secret work "cannot be publicly identified" (9), a handy dodge for an institution that employed all of fifteen black agents (as opposed to black confidential informers) between 1919 and 1956 (Jeffreys-Jones 135). Hoover's publicity-seeking Crime Records Divi-sion nonetheless permitted flattering portraits of two racial exceptions: James E. Amos, one of the Bureau's "crack agents," and Sam Noisette, the director's "personal aide" ("Negro FBI Agents" 9), a "soul brother" to Hoover introduced in part 1. Amos is painted as a hard-bitten encyclopedia of G-Man wisdom, a "[g]ray and balding" survivor of gangland battles who "has gum-shoed for the FBI for the past 26 years" (11). His assistance in writing "an unhappy finis to Marcus Garvey's dramatic 'Back to Africa' movement" suggests the inconve-nient truth of his hiring before the Hoover era (11). Hoover's younger protégé Noisette, by contrast, is cast as the trusted doorman of the national-security/publicity state, "the greeter to thousands of Americans who come to Wash-ington to see how the world's most scientific anti-crime agency works" (13). Between the heading, "Front Man for the FBI," and the handsome photo of Noisette attending to criminological relics in the director's reception room, Hoover's postwar Bureau clarifies its comfort with black window dressing, the personal aide rivaling the crack agent as the representative black F.B. eye.

Not long after the *Ebony* piece, however, the Bureau's favorite African American employees were known to work on retainer, far from headquarters. From January to October 1949, FBI spies shined in the Smith Act trial of eleven Communist Party leaders arrested for advocating the violent overthrow of the United States. All eleven were found guilty as charged under the 1940 statute, the verdict upheld by the Supreme Court's *Dennis* decision of 1951, an opinion virtually outlawing American communism. Ellen Schrecker, the prominent lib-eral chronicler of McCarthyism, suggests that the trial was a painful blend of

barricades shouting match and literary-critical seminar. Anticommunist prosecutors and communist theoreticians loudly clashed over the layers of double-
talk in "Aesopian language" in the Marxist-Leninist canon. As in the original
Red Raids, crescendos of rhetorical violence in leftist writing were presumed
guilty of the performative, and legal briefs were thick with selections from the
Bureau's library of radical publications (Schrecker 195). Yet what clinched the
jury's guilty verdict was the personal touch of well-rehearsed FBI informers—or
make that loyal "informants," in the sanitizing terminology promoted by their
Bureau handlers. African American William Cummings, a Toledo, Ohio, auto-
worker who entered the Communist Party for the FBI in 1943, was one of seven
witnesses chosen to take the stand from a casting call of sixty. According to
his testimony, vicious Marxist literature rhymed with informal party schooling,
which "taught militants that one day the streets would run with blood" (qtd. in
Marable 28).

Cummings was not the only African American infiltrator working for
Hoover. While the total number remains hazy, it is increasingly clear that a disproportionate percentage of the FBI's approximately one thousand informers in
the postwar Communist Party were black, about half of these salaried professional anticommunists for reasons of conviction or necessity (Schrecker 228).
Recruiting African American sources was preferred as the Bureau schemed to
transform the party's staunch antiracism into an existential threat. The "lingering obsession with white chauvinism protected black members from suspicion," FBI historian Kenneth O'Reilly explains, and "[w]hite communists who
accused Negro comrades of working for the FBI often found themselves accused of racism and drummed out of the party" (*"Racial Matters"* 266). Federal
Loyalty Board and McCarthy committee hearings thus often hosted the likes of
William O. Nowell, once one of the party's longest-serving African American
recruits, a graduate of Soviet cadre schools who appeared on behalf of the U.S.
government at over forty trials and hearings between 1948 and 1954. Manning
Johnson, formerly an experienced party manager, received $4,500 a year from
the Justice Department for his eagerness to lie "a thousand times" to defend
national security (qtd. in Marable 28). Lola Belle Holmes pulled in speaker's
fees from the ultraconservative John Birch Society after testifying at the Smith
Act trial of black communist Claude Lightfoot (Caute, *The Great* 547). Julia
Clarice Brown, a Clevelander who named 120 names of ex-comrades before
the House Un-American Activities Committee (HUAC), offered a race-based
defense of her double-faced cohort in *I Testify: My Years as an F.B.I. Undercover
Agent* (1966). "[T]here can be no doubt," she proclaimed, "that the real and
ultimate goal of Soviet strategists is the absolute domination of world humanity
by a Caucasian Communist elite" (115). In Brown's calculation, Soviet Premier

Nikita Khrushchev had more in common with Alabama's segregationist governor George Wallace than either could afford to admit.

Making cases and headlines, Julia Brown and similar Bureau informers helped to create an aura of undercover daring seductive enough to diminish the attractions of James Amos and other aging FBI idols of the gangster era. Shapeshifting spies starred in the breakthrough Bureau entertainments of the early 1950s, finally unseating the self-consistent gangbusters of *Persons in Hiding* and *Ten Thousand Public Enemies*. "I was a Communist for the FBI" declared the informer hero of a 1951 film, flexibly classed as a documentary for its Academy Award nomination. Hubert Philbrick, a witness at the Smith Act trial and the introducer of Julia Brown's book, penned *I Led Three Lives: Citizen, "Communist," Counterspy*, a 1952 memoir adapted for network television. By the middle of the decade, Cold War secret agents had completed the burial of perhaps the Bureau's greatest fiction, the New Deal "Public Hero" (a burial anticipated in *Ebony*'s equal praise for Amos and Noisette, the latter more Man Friday than hard-boiled G-Man). The public enemy plot had given way to an "espionage plot" feeding off the corpse of Soviet spying, a security threat largely removed, in fact, from American territory by 1951, the year Senator Joseph McCarthy first denounced an immense communist conspiracy and in turn invented "one of the most consequential conspiracy theories in U.S. history" (Olmstead 84, 85). Projected in sepia tone, the FBI's new protagonist looked oddly like the narrator of Ralph Ellison's *Invisible Man* (1952), a classic shorn of its overt Bureau references before the last draft. Ellison's talkative leading man matched the FBI's as a clever screen for clashing ideological impressions, resurrected from the party underground to speak on the frequencies of anticommunist consensus. Hoover pugnaciously shielded his rising class of spy-heroes, black and white, from "pseudoliberal" criticism. "You find reference to [informants] in the Bible," he insisted to the readers of *U.S. News and World Report* ("How U.S. Reds" 139). Along the way, he defended the African American informers who played a willful part in persecuting W.E.B. Du Bois, Amiri Baraka, and several of the other writers discussed in this book. Here, too, the story of the FBI's engagement with Afro-modernism is not always a black-and-white morality tale.

Uncovering the deepest logic behind the victory of the FBI spy-hero means inspecting the Bureau's role in the long McCarthy era, the anticommunist crusade that outlived the reign of the Wisconsin senator, polarizing American life from the late 1940s to the early 1960s. Aspects of this role followed from the micropolitics of Hoover's break with Truman, a president guilty of establishing the CIA in 1947, a detested Bureau rival from start. Hoover repaid Truman's differences from the supportive FDR with an appearance before HUAC, dramatizing the Bureau's fresh partnership with antiadministration Red-baiters dismayed by the pace of liberal anticommunism. Testifying that HUAC and the FBI shared a paramount goal, "protection of the internal security of the nation," Hoover renounced his primary alliance with executive power by blessing the congressional McCarthyite tactic of prescriptive publicity against Soviet penetration (qtd. in Richard Gid Powers, *Broken* 211). For the remainder of the Truman administration, the FBI disdained both special service to the president and the remnants of the Democratic New Deal that once fostered it. In their place, the Bureau slipped its secret file on Truman to his Republican opponents and arranged to protect state security—and the state of counterliterary exception—in concert with a grateful Republican Congress. Following the outbreak of the Korean War, this Congress bucked Truman's veto to pass the Internal Security or McCarran Act, reauthorizing the Bureau's Custodial Detention program. Its descendants on Capitol Hill approved or sweetened every yearly FBI budget request until Hoover's death.[20] Beneath the director's ostentatious nonpartisanship, the soul of FBI antiradicalism reenlisted in the GOP.

Almost at once, however, the Bureau's technical assistance to McCarthyism exceeded the requirements of Hoover's feud with the Democrats. In Ellen Schrecker's account, the FBI contrived to occupy "the bureaucratic heart of the McCarthy era" (203). "Had observers known in the 1950s what they have learned since the 1970s, when the Freedom of Information Act opened the Bureau's files," she speculates, "'McCarthyism' would probably have been called 'Hooverism'" (203). As with my coinage of the 1919–20 "Hoover Raids," Schrecker's case for Cold War Hooverism depends on a high regard for the functioning of the FBI's charismatic bureaucracy, its design, management, and marketing of a "machinery of political repression" able to install reactionary anticommunism as a touchstone of good government (203). Providing undercover informers to Smith Act prosecutors was just one part of this machinery. Under a secret "Responsibilities Program," established in 1951, the Bureau dispatched file-based, not-for-attribution memoranda to governors and other "appropriate authorities," warning of possible communists on the payroll (212). Well-honed Bureau techniques for indexing dissent directly fed the emblematic sin of the blacklist, fingering over four hundred public employees for firing, most of them school and university teachers. The names the FBI could not legally communicate to state officials it delivered to the Boy Scouts, the Red Cross, and other wholesome quasi-publics. At least until 1953, when Hoover began to fear the senator's sloppiness, the FBI supplied Joseph McCarthy's Permanent Investigations Subcommittee with everything it could: public praise; back-channel political advice; prejudicial information on enemies culled from the Bureau archives; and a former FBI agent, Don Surine, to serve as chief investigator. In the McCarthy who fell from grace, Hoover met an anticommunist more media-drunk than himself and did not enjoy the reflected glare. Even HUAC, the director wrote, seemed to care more about headlines than national security (Schrecker 215). Thanks to Hoover's relative discretion, his term as McCarthyism's comptroller-in-chief only enhanced his charismatic appeal. Buoyed by popular anticommunism, public esteem for the director reached its apex, envisioning an untouchable among law-and-order untouchables. In the appraisal of one contributor to *Kids' Letters to the F.B.I.* (1966), a little classic of youthful obedience, Jesus was indeed a "hero," but "Mr. Hoover has done more toward helping to keep down juvenile delinquency, as well as other crimes" (Adler n.p.).

Hoover was worshipped less earnestly by the minority of American liberals revolted by McCarthyism in any form, their discontent galvanizing unprecedented open criticism of the Bureau—and unprecedented Bureau pushback. The publication of Max Lowenthal's *The Federal Bureau of Investigation* (1950), the first vigorously unauthorized history of the institution, is a cautionary object lesson. Over five hundred pages and a decade in the making, released within weeks of the Bureau's first "Ten Most Wanted" list, Lowenthal's book mounts a painstaking, lawyerly case against the FBI's aura as "the infallible watchdog of American security and liberty" (front matter). The Hoover Bureau's appetite for "rumors, suspicions and gossip," Lowenthal concludes, "is the realization of the fear expressed" by the FBI's earliest skeptics, the congressmen who confronted Theodore Roosevelt and Charles Bonaparte with the fear that the Bureau "might some day adopt practices habitual to political police systems in Europe but abhorrent to a democracy" (465). Lowenthal, a former Supreme Court clerk, onetime congressional aide, and friend of President Truman, derived little comfort from the quiet approval of his indictment at the White House: word alone of his book's appearance attracted a prodigious Bureau counterattack. Wilting under fire, sales of *The Federal Bureau of Investigation* failed to break seventy-five hundred, disappointing distinguished independent publisher William Sloane (Gentry 387). Considered in relation to the history of lit.-cop federalism, however, the book thrived as an inspiration for the intensified Bureau counterliteratures of the 1950s.

Hoover, furious that his ghostreaders had failed to pick up scent of Lowenthal's history prior to an advanced notice in *Publishers Weekly*, plunged into a firing mood even before the book's release. "Mr. Hoover, if I had known this book was going to published," swore Louis Nichols, head of the Crime Records Division, "I'd have thrown my body between the presses and stopped it" (qtd. in Gentry 386). Nichols mended fences with Hoover by supervising an instant refutation. Within the Seat of Government, this "prebuttal" of Lowenthal's charges planted the seeds for the most successful Bureau self-narrations of the 1950s: Hoover's own *Masters of Deceit* (1958), two million paperbacks sold, and Don Whitehead's rose-tinted *The FBI Story* (1956), written inside a Bureau office furnished with hand-picked case summaries. Beyond FBI headquarters, Walter Winchell and other Bureau-friendly columnists immediately adopted the prebuttal's stalking points, their objections reinforced in planted editorials. Head agents at the Bureau's field offices were directed to discourage bookstores from stocking Lowenthal's title. One up-and-comer proposed that G-Men remove copies from public libraries but was shot down with the news that stolen words might be replaced, increasing sales. Lowenthal's home was kept under observation; during one of his out-of-town business trips, his wife awoke to a 3:00 a.m. call from a team of agents. Bureau allies denounced him as a treasonous New Deal relic on the floor of Congress and dragged him before an executive session of HUAC (Gentry 386–87). A *Nation* piece with an immortal title, "The FBI Reviews a Book," called attention to the mystery of the session's transcript, publicly released, without clarification, "just one day before Mr. Lowenthal's book went on sale."

All of this extraordinary literary-critical activity took place in advance of *The Federal Bureau of Investigation*'s printing. "Perhaps coincidentally, perhaps not," journalist Curt Gentry remarks, "the page proofs of the book vanished from the motorcycle sidecar of a messenger en route from the printer to the publisher" (386). Absolutely noncoincidental in the Lowenthal affair is the Cold War expansion of FBI counterliterature into an agenda I call "Total Literary Awareness." Half a century before the National Security Agency's Internet-scouring Prism system and the Pentagon's Total Information Awareness (TIA) program, an earlier effort to aggregate every electronic prediction of terrorist activity, the Bureau's "TLA" program sought precocious knowledge of all published threats to the state—especially threats to the state of the Bureau's reputation. Cold War Hooverism's hyperactive counterliterary meddling thus did not end with the bowdlerization of State Department libraries abroad, enforced by Bureau crony Roy Cohn during a 1953 tour of European capitals. Back in the United States, the impulse was to know enough of domestic publishing to screen suspicious books before they reached the shelves. Despite its inability to regulate the whole of U.S. writing, TLA equipped FBI counterliterature with newfound reach and muscle.

Some of the tentacles of Total Literary Awareness have been unraveled by literary historian Claire Culleton. Delving into the Bureau's 234-page file on commercial publisher Henry Holt, she uncovers evidence of Hoover's "custodial relationship" with the pillars of the Cold War book market ("Extorting" 237).[21] Holt employees sent the Bureau all manner of literary foreknowledge, from book proposals, to page proofs, to advance copies—so much material, in fact, that an editorial staffer wrote Hoover with the news that "I am beginning to feel like a member of the FBI myself" (qtd. in Culleton, "Extorting" 239). Predictably, Hoover and his ghostwriters were asked to provide blurbs for *The Hidden Russia* and other anticommunist titles. Just as often, however, the Bureau was granted uncommon rights of prerefusal. Holt editor Milt Hill, for example, asked for "advice as to whether we should do or not" an autobiography of Senator McCarthy, receiving a green light since it "would be a friendly book from a Bureau standpoint" (qtd. in Culleton, "Extorting" 244–45). Books less kind to the Bureau were rejected with its help at Holt and other firms. The manuscript of Fred Cook's muckraking *The FBI Nobody Knows*, eventually published in 1964, was refused at Random House (home of *The FBI Story*) after Bennett Cerf shredded professional ethics by forwarding a copy to Hoover (243). Editorial informants such as Cerf, recruited in the wake of the Lowenthal embarrassment, made it practically impossible to criticize the FBI through a major New York publisher without costly delay. With the FBI fed the minutes of editorial board meetings at *Time* and *Life*, *Fortune* and *Look*, the *Reader's Digest* and the *Daily Worker*, points along the full spectrum of U.S. print culture were opened to Bureau preawareness. To revise Louis Nichols, there was now most always a body poised to throw itself between the presses.

Critical nonfiction was the initial target of the Bureau's Cold War campaign to impose itself between unflattering portraiture and the reading public. Yet the Afro-modernist files of the period demonstrate that Total Literary Awareness also kept watch over imaginative literature. Judging from Lorraine Hansberry's file, for example, the FBI refused to believe that playwrights deserved to choose who evaluated their trial runs.[22] Just escaped from the University of Wisconsin to freelance work in New York City, Hansberry's otherwise overlooked contributions to small labor papers inspired a 1952 security check, the trigger of a 1,052-page file that closed only with copies of her obituary noting her premature death (U.S., Federal, Hansberry, 21 July 1952). Again exposing its sensitivity to young literary talent, the FBI leapt into coordinated national action when hearing of her intent to attend a Montivedeo peace conference in 1953. The "Washington field office is requested to examine the files of the Passport Division of the United States Department of State," Hansberry's Bureau file attests, "in an effort to obtain all available background material on the subject, any derogatory information contained therein, and a photograph and complete description" (30 Mar. 1953). The Milwaukee office unproductively rummaged through her Wisconsin transcripts for other crumbs of scandal, while Chicago discovered her family's prominence in the city's racially fractured real estate business (14 Mar. 1953). New York revealed her independent employment as an "instructor of a class in Literature of the Negro" at the progressive Jefferson School and traced her residence to Bleecker Street in Greenwich Village, this literature's downtown office since the Harlem Renaissance (18 Dec. 1953). For all their prescient interest, none of the Bureau's field offices predicted Hansberry's posthumous emergence as a voice of lesbian feminism, uncharacteristically missing the implication of her draft play for Sappho, *Andromeda the Thief.* Neither could they envision her dismissal by Black Power nationalists for sins of "leftwing accommodation to middle-class ideology" (Cruse 267). What historian Peniel Joseph describes as her "unusual biography—an upper-middle-class black woman who abandoned a comfortable existence for identification with the racially and politically oppressed"—struck the Bureau as a typical profile of the present danger (26–27).

By the mid-1950s, male gazers at the New York branch of the Bureau were familiar enough with Hansberry's everyday life and looks to record her adoption of an "'Italian' cut" hairstyle (11 Oct. 1956). (Some of the same F.B. eyes had officially described Louise Thompson Patterson as "130 lbs.," "Ginger"-colored, and "Good looking" [U.S., Federal, Patterson, 24 Sept. 1941].) The Bureau's premature discovery of *A Raisin in the Sun*, the play that made Hansberry famously young and gifted, was par for this course. In 1958, a year before *Raisin's* Broadway premiere, Hoover ordered New York's special agent in charge to "conduct [a] necessary investigation in an effort to establish whether the play . . . is in any way controlled or influenced by the Communist Party and whether it in any way follows the Communist line" (5 Sept. 1958). No academic lectures were required for the Bureau to expect the militancy beneath Hansberry's crossover appeal: her Security Index card was preparation enough (5 Sept. 1958). The file ingredients that follow Hoover's edict approximate the contents of a drama fanatic's scrapbook. Clipped reviews and playbills track *Raisin's* try-outs through the provinces, documenting the conquest of American theater one East Coast city at a time. Reports from the *New Haven Register* and *Journal-Courier* on the play's Connecticut run are carefully cut and pasted, but the highest aim is seeing a trial production in the flesh (23 Jan. 1959). Since the Bureau's New Haven office had failed to witness the show for itself, "Philadelphia is requested to designate an Agent to attend in order that a true picture of the play's content can be obtained and properly analyzed" (29 Jan. 1959). When the FBI's long experience in deciphering Afro-modernism met the rushed demands of Total Literary Awareness, only a Bureau-trained reviewer was thought up to the task.

The particular reviewer selected, a Philadelphia-based special agent whose name has been lost to FOIA censorship, fulfilled his assignment at the Walnut Theater with a perceptive and even-tempered four-page review. Sustaining interpretive positions while describing narrative arcs, volunteering minutely witty descriptions of characters and costumes, this talented ghostreader bids for a place in the upper echelon of FBI English heads, a pecking order explained in the next part of this book. The reviewer begins with reference to a plot summary previously published in the *Philadelphia Daily News*, the FBI file equivalent of dismissive in-text citation. What comes after, the agent's independent analysis of Hansberry's work, will not respect the obvious. Hoover's orders to measure *Raisin*'s debts to communism are dispensed with swiftly. "The play contains no comments of any nature about Communism as such," the reader certifies, "but deals essentially with negro [*sic*] aspirations, the problems inherent in their efforts to advance themselves, and varied attempts at arriving at solutions" (5 Feb. 1959). The review takes flight when party lines give way to the intersection of racial and dramatic tensions: "The contrasting proposals for solutions are set up through the character delineations of the widowed mother, her son, and her daughter. The specific bone of contention which is the central theme of the plot is the sum of $10,000 received by the widow as a result of the death of her husband" (5 Feb. 1959). Themes, plots, and bones might be conflated, but the Bureau reviewer insightfully sketches the interiors of Beneatha, the Younger family's quick-witted medical-student daughter, a character searching for an attractive partner in racial uplift "under the amused and tolerant scrutiny of the other women"; George Murchison, her assimilationist suitor captured by his "over narrow, over emphatic ivy league clothes"; and Joseph Asagai, his principled Nigerian rival, quickened by anticolonial ambition to "overthrow the rule of European nations, find political freedom, . . . and make [his] own future" (5 Feb. 1959). "Africa," continues the reviewer, "is a matter which is only dimly comprehended by the other members of the family"—this lack of understanding matching the mostly white audience at the Walnut, only a handful of whom "appeared to dwell on the propaganda messages" (5 Feb. 1959). As it happened, New York audiences were little more attuned to *Raisin*'s layers of Pan-Africanism, muted by Hansberry's South Side Chicago setting, the familiar scene of domestic naturalism's native sons. A mysterious Philadelphia FBI agent may thus have been among the first to understand the play's budding black internationalism, encouraged by TLA policy to forward his discovery to Washington prior to the Broadway opening. Communism as such was a welcome absence in *Raisin*, this ghostreader assumed, yet the play's love match between Nigeria and black Chicago required exposure to federal authorities, then prioritizing U.S.-Africa policy under the Eisenhower administration's new Bureau of African Affairs.[23]

Dozens of less thoughtful FBI agents spent workdays in the grip of TLA investigations, packing the personal files of Afro-modernists only suspected of literary intent. Again and again, Bureau critics provided emerging black writers of the Cold War with some of their earliest notices, often nit-picking and hidden from productive use, yet impressed by any sign of professional development. For example, the 1951 file of Alice Childress, Hansberry's sister playwright in the orbit of Paul Robeson's journal *Freedom*, reflects an FBI agent's study in the Billy Rose Theatre Collection of the New York Public Library. Knowing that Childress had been trained in drama "since her Junior High School days"—she was a skilled enough actress to receive a Tony Award nomination in 1944— this Bureau researcher applied the scholarly lessons of FBI archivism, sifting through Billy Rose catalogs for hints of original plays of her own (U.S., Federal, Childress, 20 Mar. 1951). The ghostreaders who assembled Lance Jeffers's file of 1949, 187 pages devoted to a poet Trudier Harris dubbed a "black nationalist without a movement" (397), prepared for his publications to come by combing every credit hour of his creative writing major. A 1950 Bureau memo reveals that Jeffers was "working toward a Bachelor of Science degree in writing" at Columbia, where his schedule required "20 points composed of English, composition, and French" (U.S., Federal, Jeffers, 26 Jan. 1950). "To date," reported an FBI agent, hovering like a tuition-paying parent, Jeffers "has earned 69 points of the necessary 124 points which are needed for graduation" (26 Jan. 1950). In the instance of Calvin Hernton's 1955 file, the Bureau confessed its interest in books with no chance of reaching the publisher. Tracking the cofounder of *Umbra* magazine even while he was an MA candidate at Fisk, Bureau prereaders took seriously the typically self-admiring efforts of a student novelist (male-bohemian subgenre) to write what he knew best. Unassumingly titled *The Recognition of Man*, Hernton's manuscript-in-progress is described as "the story of two individuals who are attending a college or university. One of these individuals is principally interested in exploitation of any persons over whom he can gain control, while the other is a poor but hard working character who is attempting to get an education, and who takes occasion throughout the book to explain to the other character the difference between right and wrong as concerns the various phases of life which the average person will encounter" (U.S., Federal, Hernton, 14 Mar. 1955). Interviewed by an FBI team despite this off-putting thumbnail, Hernton pled artistic myopia, promising he was "not interested in Communism and [advising] that his principal interest is in his writing and because of this he does not know what goes on around him" (14 Mar. 1955). Prereading even more ghostly materials occupied the agents assigned the case of Julian Mayfield in 1954, the year the actor-novelist relocated to Puerto Rico. After observing that "the subject stayed in his house most of the time and appeared to occupy much of his time by typing," the hunt was on to discover the written results (U.S., Federal, Mayfield, 30 Nov. 1955). Though it failed to learn precisely "what material the subject was typing" in Naranjito, the

FBI lingered close enough to hear literary sounds from Mayfield's rooms until 1974, his novels *The Hit* (1957), *The Long Night* (1958), and *The Grand Parade* (1961) paving the way to his service as a speechwriter for Kwame Nkrumah, Ghana's founding head of state (30 Nov. 1955). The CIA, for its part, took an interest in Mayfield sensitive enough to be censored in full even today, "pursuant to an Executive Order" (Nelson).

Better established Afro-modernists, first publications under their belts, also faced TLA prereading, the greater intensity of the chase signaling their graver threat. Critic and novelist J. Saunders Redding, investigated by the Bureau from 1953 to 1968, managed to produce *To Make a Poet Black* (1939), a landmark social history of African American literature, without Bureau preknowledge. The success of his postracial passing novel *Stranger and Alone* (1950), however, left him with several acquaintances willing to talk with the FBI, nameless cronies prone to recommending "that any writing or lecturing done by the applicant be reviewed before being presented" (U.S., Federal, Redding, 27 Feb. 1953). The need for such vigilance stemmed not from Redding's hedged attraction to communism, but rather from the ambiguous politics of his passionate intensity, the product of an artistic temperament supposedly marinated in racial grievance. Redding's tendencies to be "very emotional and high-strung" emerge in his books on "the disadvantages and handicaps of being a Negro," and thus attract interpretations "very different . . . than the author may have intended to impart" (27 Feb. 1953). Willard Motley's file, a toxic amalgam of Bureau worries over black queerness and black cosmopolitanism, nears its 1967 conclusion with news of the novelist's withering life in Mexico, stranded abroad by the homosexuality provisions of the Immigration and Nationality Act (U.S., Federal, Motley, 18 Mar. 1954). "[G]one into full retirement" and dependent on the income "from the paper-back edition of 'Let No Man Write My Epitaph,' " he is said "to keep a group of young boys about him and only spasmodically works on a new book" (7 Mar. 1961). Motley's writing in its "white life" prime attracted vigorous forms of TLA scrutiny. A confidential report accurately revealed that Motley's second book, a novel "about soldiers home from the wars and tentatively titled 'They Fished All Night' is being gestated on an Oregon ranch" (18 Mar. 1954). Surveillance of Motley's usual literary neighborhood in Chicago followed an informant's hands-on account of the making of *Knock on Any Door* (1947), the best-selling portrait of an Italian altar boy–turned–gangster: "the story contains certain passages describing in minute detail a homosexual act. . . . [I]t would be rather difficult to depict in such graphic style an act which had not been experienced by the narrator" (18 Mar. 1954). The queer milieu of Motley's work hours presented not only sexual opportunities for the author-narrator, concluded another source, but also "personality portraits for projection in his writings, much [*sic*] of which deal with socio-logical problems and adjustment" (18 Mar. 1954). In the case of the Motley file, Total Literary Awareness plunged the Bureau into the dynamism of Chicago's urban interzone, a community where type-mixing social fictions sprang from unconventional loves.

Not every Afro-modernist file initiated in the long McCarthy era—the busiest period of FBI counterliterature—opens with signs of the Bureau's post-Lowenthal resolve. Given the large number of these files, twenty-two in all, holes in the TLA blanket should be expected. Ralph Ellison's collection, opened in 1950, busied itself with the security challenges of his White House visits and American Academy in Rome fellowships. (Ellison's drafts of *Invisible Man*, dis-cussed in part 5, returned some of the Bureau's relative kindness.)[24] E. Franklin Frazier's and Charles S. Johnson's employment by UNESCO sparked manda-tory loyalty investigations in 1953 and 1952, respectively; so did William Pick-ens's work for the "Interracial Section" of the U.S. Saving Bonds program in 1947. Andy Razaf (file opened 1949), Shirley Graham Du Bois (1950), Lonne Elder III (1954), Frank London Brown (1955), and writer-cartoonist Ollie Har-rington (1951), his dossier active into the twenty-first century, were pursued as garden-variety unionists or communists before their artistic ambitions as-sumed equal billing. Black Beat Bob Kaufman (1950), a radical "of the water-front" rumored to have been "expelled from the CP for degeneracy," received much the same treatment (U.S., Federal, Kaufman, 21 June 1956). William Gardner Smith (1951), Ollie Harrington's fellow Francophile, was recognized as the author of *The Last of the Conquerors* (1948) yet was initially sought by the FBI for Socialist Workers Party membership (U.S., Federal, Smith, 5 May 1951). *The Crisis of the Negro Intellectual* (1967) was eventually added to the Bureau li-brary, but Harold Cruse (1950) was first recruited as an undercover Communist Party informant (he proved willing to name names of onetime comembers, but nothing more) (U.S., Federal, Cruse, 26 Nov. 1956). Hoyt Fuller's (1954), Amiri Baraka's (1957), and James Baldwin's (1958) files took on shape and weight in the 1960s and are most accurately measured as documents of that period.

The Afro-modernist files of the long McCarthy era nevertheless establish Total Literary Awareness as the distinctive Cold War contribution to the stock-pile of FBI counterliteratures. Showing searches high and low for word of texts scorning the Bureau's height of popular support, these files suggest that the accelerated assimilation of postwar African American writing encouraged the application of post-Lowenthal counterliterary techniques to imaginative lit-erature. Heeding the upbeat future of black drama, fiction, and poetry, three cultural "shock troops of the modern civil rights movement" (Dittmer 1), the Bureau moved to slow the racial integration of literary realms beyond its journalistic enemies list. A new strain of criminological knowledge emerged—data on the *intent* to fantasize racial equality and other un-American activities—as G-Men listened for typewriters through keyholes. By this point in the counterliterary story, the presence of TLA at the primal scene of literary invention may seem another gloomy milestone in the Bureau's serial encroachment on black authorship. In this latest installment, police power claws at the door to composition, the first and most autonomous of the social processes (writing, editing, printing, publishing) that twenty-first-century editorial theory claims are actually responsible for the authorizing of texts. If, as John K. Young argues, white "control of the means of production" of black books reveals the difference race makes for "apparently universal descriptions of the relationship between the author and the public" (19), then what is revealed by Hooverism's hurry to check black manuscripts before they reached publishers of any color? Under TLA, Addison Gayle Jr.'s figure of the "invisible censor, white power," assumed material form, incarnating the black writer's racialized self-doubt as a federal interloper, a state spook who sat beside the creative "sanctuary of [the] private room" (Gayle, Introduction xx). Synchronized with the indexing of African American authors for possible arrest, TLA thus dogged Cold War–era Afro-modernism with the prospect of cradle-to-grave supervision. This prospect was wholly realized hardly ever, of course. TLA, conceived in response to a memorable failure of Bureau preknowledge, most often conceded its imperfect origins in practice. *A Raisin in the Sun* might be preread insightfully, for example, but could not be stopped in its tracks before reintegrating Broadway. The play was stalked on its trial run, in fact, because of the Bureau's ineffectual knowledge of its prestigious destination. Here, Total Literary Awareness was incompletely totalizing, and the surrounding Cold War "containment culture" was more leaky than advertised (Nadel 5). Even so, the jarring extension of Bureau counterliterature to the point of literary production left tracks sufficiently deep to inspire Afro-modernism's next generation, black aesthetes who burned to resist state interference.

COINTELPRO Minstrelsy: Files of Black Power

When LeRoi Jones answered the assassination of Malcolm X by taking the subway to Harlem, he brought the future of black art with him. So thought Jones himself, black America's most decorated younger writer, who couched his 1965 escape from the integrated island of downtown New York bohemia as "a socially and intellectually seismically significant development" and who came to honor his new address with the Bantuized Arabic name of Amiri Baraka (Baraka, *The Autobiography* 297). So thought poet Sonia Sanchez, essayist Larry Neal, free jazz saxophonist Albert Ayler, and the rest of the band of black nationalist culture workers who helped Baraka to build the Black Arts Repertory Theatre/School (BARTS) in the shell of an abandoned brownstone off Lenox Avenue. Refurbishing run-down rooms and styles to reoccupy ground zero of the Harlem Renaissance, the core cadre of the Neal-christened Black Arts movement regarded Afro-America's immediate cultural past as something to "be radicalized or destroyed," block by inner-city block (Neal, "The Black" 63).

As revisionist historians of Black Power have come to insist, BARTS's "pioneers of the new order" did not, in truth, paint their second renaissance on an abandoned urban canvas (Baraka, *The Autobiography* 295). Despite McCarthyism's best effort, black art remained in session in Harlem before their arrival. Langston Hughes, a living spirit of the New Negro, had undertaken his own pilgrimage uptown in 1947, and was still installed in his studio-home at East 127th Street. Specifically black nationalist returns to Black Manhattan had previously been launched by the Uptown Writers circle and the Harlem Writers Group, the latter the hit-making workshop of Maya Angelou's memoir *I Know Why the Caged Bird Sings* (1970) (Smethurst, *The Black* 171, 118). Tailing Afro-modernism wherever it roamed, the FBI was already on the spot as well, in place to witness BARTS's musical overture to the Harlem community, a Garvey-style May Day parade down 125th Street paced by the Afro-futurist sounds of the Sun Ra Arkestra. A 141-page Bureau file on BARTS—40 of those pages still suppressed—reveals the presence of federal informers before the school's investiture. "On April 30, 1965, a meeting was held at the Black Arts Repertory Theatre School, 109 West 130th Street, New York City. At this meeting," the file attests, "a leaflet was handed out which announced that the Black Arts Theatre School was going to open" (U.S., Federal, Black Arts Repertory, 24 Sept. 1965). There to receive the birth announcement in the spring, the FBI stuck around to benefit from BARTS's low-cost summer education program. A pair of agency moles attended the pioneering Afro-American history classes of Harold Cruse, taking notes as he refined the arguments of *The Crisis of the Negro Intellectual* (among them criticism of Baraka's weakness for guerilla bravado) (Baraka, *The Autobiography* 213). After the school's premature folding, Baraka became convinced that the Bureau had exploited his ideological blinders to disrupt BARTS's precocious nation-time. The combined "duress of ignorance and the FBI," he reflected, broke the cradle of the Black Arts and sent the mission reeling from Harlem to Newark ("The Wailer" xi). Second-wave Black Arts theaters sprouted in abundance west of the Hudson River—BLKARTSOUTH in New Orleans; Black Arts West in San Francisco; somewhat later, Ron Himes's Black Rep in St. Louis—but their New York inspiration survived less than a year.

Why were agents of Hooverism clued-in enough to infiltrate the prototypical institution of the Black Arts movement, and canny enough, perhaps, to help close it before its time? One major reason was incubated in the Bureau world of the early 1960s. This was the Hooverites' ambivalent reaction to the momentum of the civil rights movement—a movement the Bureau, unlike Baraka, initially doubted BARTS would transcend. On the one hand, the FBI approached civil rights activism as a political and publicity challenge, motivation to expand its courtship of liberal patriots. The Bureau thus strived to complement the civil rights ethos in the pages of *Ebony*, recalling the days of outreach after Truman's integration of the military. In the 1962 feature "The Negro in the FBI," fifteen years down the road from "Negro FBI Agents in Action," Hoover once more reached for the role models James Amos and Sam Noisette, again boasting of the latter's amateur "painting of his airedale dog hanging on the walls of his home" (Booker 30). On this second *Ebony* go-round, however, the rhetoric of interracial familialism did not end with Hoover's investment in the tamest African American art. "Without hesitation or the use of notes," observed black reporter Simeon Booker, Hoover reminisced "about his great Negro FBI agents, great in the sense they have served and continue to serve unselfishly and without fanfare in his crime busting family" (29). Away from *Ebony*, on the operational ground, the Bureau was sufficiently concerned with the good name of Hoover's marginally integrated family to answer liberal suspicion with stepped-up investigations of white terrorism. Following the "Mississippi Burning" killings of Freedom Summer volunteers James Chaney, Andrew Goodman, and Michael Schwerner, the FBI indulged President Lyndon Johnson's backslapping and initiated a counterintelligence program against the Klan and eighteen other "White Hate Groups" (Cunningham 32). At the very same time, however, the Bureau continued to meet candid criticism by civil rights leaders with resentment and dirty tricks. As suggested in the introduction, King was never forgiven his opinion that Hoover's red-baiting abetted southern racists. Hence the other, punishing hand of the Bureau's response to civil rights organizing: a determination to penetrate each and every civil rights group in order to split the movement analytically and practically, to sort "irresponsible" displays of black dissent into the dustbin of treason. While John Lewis, Diane Nash, and other student demonstrators on King's left demanded to know which side the Bureau was on, the most accurate answer was both.

By 1967, however, with ghettoes burning from Newark to Detroit, the Bureau's ambivalence had flattened into solid opposition. With the urban militancy of BARTS looking less like a failed experiment than the wave of the black future, the Bureau responded with its own abrasive acronym, "COINTELPRO—Black Nationalist/Hate Groups," a project happy to undercut all sympathy (inside and outside the FBI) for African American protest. The FBI's first COINTELPRO—a condensation of the words "counterintelligence program"—had been launched against an already deflating U.S. Communist Party in 1956. The program's signature, virtuoso covert action calculated to "expose, disrupt, misdirect, discredit, or otherwise neutralize" threats, pushed the envelope beyond the aggressive hoarding of raw intelligence and cooked literature, the steadiest fixture of Bureau antiradicalism since 1919 (U.S., Federal, COINTELPRO, 25 Aug. 1967). In effect, the "counter" in this intensified class of FBI counterintelligence signified an endeavor to cripple radicalism in the bud, to unfold the preemptive ambition of Total Literary Awareness across the terrain of domestic politics. As U.S. Senate investigators later discovered, COINTELPRO techniques ranged promiscuously from "the trivial (mailing reprints of *Reader's Digest* articles to college administrators) to the degrading (sending anonymous poison-pen letters intended to break up marriages) to the dangerous (encouraging gang warfare and falsely labeling members of a violent group as police informers)" (U.S., Senate, Select Committee, *Intelligence Activities* 3). Incongruously, the inspiration for the transfer of these techniques from communist to black nationalist enemies was found in the victories of the Bureau's COINTLEPRO against "White Hate" groups, a veiled cause of the Klan's decline from 14,000 to 4,300 members between 1964 and 1971 (Jeffreys-Jones 172). Social movement analyst David Cunningham explains that the anti-Klan crackdown provided a template for domesticating labels of subversion. "No longer did a subversive group have to be controlled or intimately tied to a hostile foreign power," he clarifies (Cunningham 32). "[T]hereafter, domestic targets engaging in 'criminal conspiracy' and willing to undermine the Constitution" warranted the application of methods earlier wielded against foreign fighters and resident "enemy aliens" (32). Enabled by northern public impatience and Hoover's return to the fold of a less scrupulous Democratic presidency, secret wars against internal irritants could again be declared without congressional approval. In a bubble created with good intentions, the Bureau turned uninhibited methods sharpened against the Klan on the Klan's bitterest enemies, shifting slickly from white hate to black.

Applied against the parties of "Black Hate," COINTELPRO scaled new heights of transgression. By the fall of 1967, each FBI field office housed one to four agents who worked exclusively on recruiting informers within black communities, now assumed to rival communist cells as revolutionary flashpoints. Casual neighborhood sources, mostly older property owners, were enlisted for what the Bureau branded its "Ghetto Listening Post" plan. "Afro-American type bookstores" became one of these sources' hangouts, names there taken of the "owners, operators, and clientele" who challenged the primacy of the FBI's radical archive (qtd. in O'Reilly, *"Racial Matters"* 268).[25] The completion of a "Black Nationalist Photograph Album," 8" x 10" glossies preferred, occupied other spies. Younger, less settled informers, some military veterans, infiltrated national master targets (the Nation of Islam [NOI], the Revolutionary Action Movement [RAM], and the Student Nonviolent Coordinating Committee [SNCC]), as well as lesser political factions (Detroit's Malcolm X Society, Cleveland's New Libya, and an inoffensive democratic action committee at Mississippi's Tougaloo College). One newly declassified FBI file indicates that the New York division alone controlled 126 confidential informants able to insinuate themselves into the "Black Nationalist Movement" (U.S., Federal, Black Nationalist Movement, 8 Feb. 1968). The breadth of coverage bore resemblance to the original, anticommunist COINTELPRO, in which the FBI defined "communist association" with strict imprecision. Kenneth O'Reilly nonetheless locates the uniqueness of COINTELPRO—Black Hate in its conception of a peril elastic "enough to include, in theory, at least, every member of a particular race who happened to be a member of any organization whatsoever" (279–80). The legacy of the Great Society thus includes not only the Civil Rights and Voting Rights Acts, O'Reilly holds, but also "the emergence of surveillance as the principal element in the federal government's relationship with its black citizens" (*"Racial Matters"* 262).

The great exception to COINTELPRO—Black Hate's rule of uniform racial guilt was the Oakland-based Black Panther Party, armed opponents of police brutality and racial capitalism whom Hoover elected as the "greatest threat to the internal security of the country" in 1968, the year of Richard Nixon's successful "Law and Order" campaign for president (qtd. in U.S., Senate, Select Committee, *Hearings* 377). Their attraction as left icons boosted by Bureau hostility, Huey Newton, Bobby Seale, and their followers endured 233 of the 295 major counterintelligence actions approved for use against black "haters." As a result, the Panthers bore the brunt of COINTELPRO's comfort with black death, rationalized at the Seat of Government by Seale's call to "talk about shooting the God damned FBI" (qtd. in O'Reilly, *"Racial Matters"* 296). The legendary Japanese American radical Richard Aoki, an FBI informer as well as the source of the Panthers' first rifles, did not single-handedly "set up" his black comrades for revolutionary suicide, as investigative journalist Seth Rosenfeld has proposed (*Subversives* 424).[26] Instead, the Bureau and its informers fed and then outstripped the Panthers' romance with the gun on multiple fronts. Employing "snitch jacketing," the bogus identification of suspects as police informants, California FBI offices provoked bloody clashes between the Panther Party and Ron Karenga's US organization, then competing for influence over UCLA's fledgling black studies department.[27] The gun slayings of four Panthers over eight months of 1969 impressed the San Diego branch as a "tangible re-sult" of COINTELPRO operations (qtd. in Cunningham 33). In Chicago, Wil-liam O'Neal, a Panther bodyguard and FBI provocateur, betrayed local Panther leader Fred Hampton, shot twice through the head in his own bedroom by a police riot squad. (O'Neal received a $300 Bureau bonus for his diagram of Hampton's apartment including "the specific location of his bed and night-stand" [Bloom and Martin 238].) The gory extent of COINTELPRO—Black Hate, confirmed only in the 1970s, helped to persuade Amiri Baraka that the Bureau had executed Malcolm X (Baraka, "The Black Arts Movement" 498). It convinced James Baldwin that he and other black Americans were "all ex-pendable," an internal colony's condemned-in-waiting ("An Open Letter" 21). Hoover and his Nixonian enablers would "not hesitate for an instant," Baldwin declared, to trigger the permanent removal of African Americans that "they insist is the will of the people" (21). As with all the Afro-modernists (Richard Wright the single possible exception), Baldwin's trial-by-Bureau ended with-out a death sentence. Yet he correctly perceived that political murder was an accepted outcome of the FBI's quarrel with the nationalist phase of the black freedom movement. Such state violence was not precisely a weapon "located within the mainstream of government policy toward blacks," as O'Reilly judges, but far too easy at hand within one federal bureau's unconventional arsenal (*"Racial Matters"* 324).

Despite the unmatched bloodiness of FBI surveillance during the Black Power era, some of COINTELPRO—Black Hate's most malicious weapons were literary ones, untraceable typewriters rather than shotguns fired at sec-ond hand. A few of these weapons were tried and untrue, manufactured in the counterliterary panics of earlier decades. For example, the makeshift harass-ment of African American newspapers, a favorite of the Bureau on the World War II home front, was revised for less polite times. COINTELPRO agents, it has been confessed, conspired to douse the offices of the Black Panther Party paper with a quart of solution "capable of duplicating a scent of the most foul smelling feces available" (U.S., Senate, Select Committee, *Supplementary* 31). (The Bureau's equivalents of "Q," James Bond's supplier of spy-gadgets, never managed to fabricate what they envisioned as "a dispenser capable of squirt-ing a narrow stream for a distance of approximately three feet," so the solution failed to hit the fan [31].) Other inventions of the COINTELPRO laboratory were more successfully realized, however, not least an unprecedented type of counterliterary authorship. FBI police-readers spent the final years of the Hoover administration rearming themselves as full-blown police-writers, crafting new tools of active literacy to complement their new encouragement of active violence. Singling out the Black Power phase of Bureau counterliterature, this is to say, was a hunger to speak the foe's literary language. William C. Sullivan's blackface letter to King was the tip of a coming iceberg: Black Power and its Black Arts sibling inspired reams of synthetic black writing from the FBI, a rash of police minstrelsy green-lighted at the Bureau's Washington headquarters but largely composed in outlying Bureau field offices. With Sullivan's endorsement, COINTELPRO—Black Hate became a sort of national writer's workshop in which the FBI's long-established dedication to reading African American literature married its even older desire to spawn a literature of its own. In its wedding of literary reception and production, this COINTELPRO fostered the creative pinnacle of Bureau counterliterature, the culmination of expressive Hooverism arriving even as Hoover's own powers of expression, entering their seventies, dimmed fast.

Much effective COINTELPRO work called on aptitudes also responsible for effective imaginative writing. The informer's daily impersonation required a real-seeming imagining of the life of the targeted other. The dangerous fiction of the "snitch jacket" fabricated an informer's character in its absence. COINTELPRO—Black Hate drew on such quasi-literary standbys of intelligence tradecraft while devoting exceptional energy to the invention of less metaphorical fictions. Dozens of G-Men stole time from the turmoil of the late 1960s and early 1970s to counterfeit writing in Black Nationalist vernaculars, concocting hundreds of poems, letters, comics, political platforms, and at least one entire newspaper. Conceding the spiraling African American literacy rate (now greater than 95 percent [Beckles 64]), the FBI's overwhelmingly white agent-authors vied with the black radical voices Hoover heard "spreading their philosophy . . . through various mass communication media" (qtd. in Churchill and Vander Wall 93).

The U.S. Senate's outraged after-report on COINTELPRO samples the handiwork of these race-changing G-Men in several genres. Reading between the lines of legal footnotes, literary types can distinguish the FBI rendition of the prison conversion narrative, a critical strain of Black Power literature from Malcolm X to Eldridge Cleaver, from "Soledad Brother" George Jackson to maximum security poet Etheridge Knight, here redrafted as a kind of epistolary snitch jacketing. "Around the first part of Feb[ruary] I was locked up at the local pigpen with this dude who told me he was a Panther," wrote a supposed inmate and actual Charlotte FBI agent to Panther headquarters (qtd. in U.S., Senate, Select Committee, *Supplementary* 48). "[He] told me [his visitors] were his lawyers but they smelled like pig to me. . . . You don't know me and I'm not a Panther but I want to help with the cause when I can" (48). The Marxian flourish of the letter writer's put-on signature—"A lumpen brother" (48)—suggests a second common genre of FBI-authored Afro-modernism: the pastiched Black

Power manifesto. Take, for instance, a 1970 composition designed to alienate the Panthers from worshipful white radicals, crammed with hortatory nationalist intertexts from Malcolm X ("by all means necessary") to Stokely Carmichael ("Black Control over Black People"): "Since when do us Blacks have to swallow the dictates of the honky SDS [Students for a Democratic Society]? Doing this only hinders the Party progress in gaining Black Control over Black People. . . . The Black Panther Party theory for community control is the only answer to our problems and that is to be followed and enforced by all means necessary to insure control by Blacks over all police departments regardless of whether they are run by honkies or uncle toms" (qtd. in U.S., Senate, Select Committee, *Supplementary* 43). In the odd case of the FBI, America's national police department was run by honkies who would seize control of black speech through ersatz blacker-than-thouism.

Some of the most considered works of FBI Afro-modernism, floating in an ocean of declassified paperwork, escaped notice in the Senate's after-report on COINTELPRO. Hiding in plain sight in the Bureau's master "COINTELPRO—Black Nationalist" file, upward of 6,000 pages now available on government-issued CD-ROM, is proof that the pacesetting New York field office theorized and supplied demands for both high and low state minstrelsy. "Membership in black nationalist and hate groups consists primarily of the intelligentsia and the unintelligent," the office gauged in a 1968 memorandum (U.S., Federal, COINTELPRO, 4 Apr. 1968). For the first, intellectual group of nationalists, "who spend endless hours discussing ways and means to effect their 'revolution[,]' a subtle middle class type publication" was preferred (4 Apr. 1968). "[P]oetry or jingles can dominate [this] higher level publication," the office proposed (4 Apr. 1968). Exemplifying their elevated design, New York author-agents cut the difference between poem and jingle and submitted a comic ode to the courage of H. Rap Brown, the Black Panther and SNCC veteran famous for finding violence as American as cherry pie. The lowered shades in lines 3 and 4 are an image of a cool pose collapsing into simple imposture. The enjambed "man" in line 7 serves as authenticating syncopation:

> Old Rap Brown
> Came to town
> With his shades
> Hanging down[.]
> He hollored fight
> Take what's right
> Then he flew, man
> In the night. (4 Apr. 1968)[28]

For the second, supposedly unintelligent group of black nationalists, the Manhattan office recommended a pulpy "comic book type publication" (4 Apr. 1968). Taking advantage of suspicions among Nation of Islam members, New York agents mailed out 273 copies of a graphic novelette alleging financial misconduct in a local mosque (8 Apr. 1968). A better-remembered FBI comic picturing the Black Panthers, likely faked by a West Coast field office, ushered the Bureau into the not-so-innocent preserve of children's literature. Over twenty-four pages of captioned line drawings, panoramas of slavery's damage to black masculinity give way to honorific portraits of muscled, rifle-toting Panthers ("Huey P. Newton, Leader of the Black Panther Party, organized the Black brothers to defend their families") ("Black Panther Coloring Book"). Sketches of ghetto resistance, suitable for coloring in red crayon, meet home-made radical slogans ("The only good pig, is a dead pig") and those imported from Panther inspiration Chairman Mao ("Power comes from the barrel of a gun").

"The appeal to children" was a creditable aesthetic concern, the New York office conjectured, given the young folks' habit of growing into "prospective members of [nationalist] groups" (4 Apr. 1968). An entire pseudo-underground newspaper, a magnum opus of FBI-authored black nationalism, synthesized high and low styles of address to encroach on the territory of the *Black Panther*, the party's popular adult weekly. Issues of *Blackboard*, a cutely titled Bureau forgery internally assessed as "a most successful counterintelligence endeavor," were falsely attributed to the Black Student Union at Southern Illinois University (qtd. in Churchill and Vander Wall 116). "[M]ailed anonymously by Special Agents," reported the St. Louis field office, a run of the paper was "sent to virtually every black activist organization and Black Nationalist leader in the [Missouri-Illinois] area" (116). Surviving copies of *Blackboard* have proven impossible to find, but history records that the editorials, cartoons, and poems of the finished product were convincing enough to alarm the *St. Louis American*, a storied and genuine black paper. African American activists on both sides of the Mississippi, an *American* columnist cautioned, should fear cross-contamination from this "absolutely scandalous 'underground' sheet" (116).

Despite the scandal of their inspiration, Bureau authors could express pride in their better reproductions of black voices, lauded by FBI headquarters for feats of "imagination and enthusiasm," compliments seemingly borrowed from the forced cheer of creative writing professors (U.S., Federal, COINTELPRO, 8 Apr. 1968). "Read that language," requested a San Francisco FBI agent emboldened by retirement (Bergman and Weir 48). "Would you think that was written by a bunch of white men? When you listen to them every day for a couple of years you get to know their vocabulary" (48). This agent's overt distance from the subjects of his racial impersonation (the "them") mingles with the self-satisfaction of educated linguistic proximity, evidence of the unstable repertoire of white "panic, anxiety, terror, and pleasure" Eric Lott influentially X-rayed beneath the mask of nineteenth-century blackface minstrelsy (*Love and Theft* 6). As Michael Szalay has it, the burnt cork of blackface returned, in "dematerialized" form, in the 1960s writing of Joan Didion, Norman Mailer, William Styron, and John Updike, the hip literature of a " 'second skin' meant to hold together the straining coalitions of a Democratic Party undergoing decisive change" (*Hip Figures* 4). Political fictions of racial ventriloquism also reemerged on the American right represented by the proud FBI agent, but under deep cover. Even while Black Arts intellectuals demanded minstrelsy's final public burning, or turned its racial tables in Adrienne Kennedy's *Funnyhouse of a Negro* (1964) and other dramas of remedial "whiteface" (McAllister 156–200), this agent and similar COINTELPRO authors retooled the love and theft of blackface in counterintelligent secrecy. In place of the nineteenth century's open promotion of blackface as America's national art, they covertly ministered to the health of a runaway American security state. Instead of pursuing the allegiance of hip-seeking white Democrats, they wooed the credulity of black radicals themselves. COINTELPRO minstrelsy's baseline of success, criminological and artistic, lay in its ability to cross over from crude ritual imitation to the functionally real thing.

Such crossover was a tall order, of course, perhaps minstrelsy's toughest assignment since its conquest of the black image in the northern white mind. Individual author files of the late 1960s and early 1970s indicate that the Bureau pursued the demanding goal of mock authenticity with assistance from a liberal wiretapping of African American voices, a development hinted in the San Francisco agent's comment on "listen[ing] to them every day." Scarce in author dossiers prior to 1965, transcripts and summaries of bugged phone conversations accent the montage modernism of several Black Arts files (Baldwin's file in particular is a type of telephone book). As early as 1936, the FBI devoted a four-page section of its agent training manual to so-called sound equipment; with the pursuit of Martin Luther King and the post-1967 black freedom movement, such training was put to use in the wiretapping of hundreds of African Americans suspected of "subversive activities" (Jeffreys-Jones 125). The Bureau's many accounts of black authors' phone manners are both sobering signs of civil liberties violations and untapped sources for literary history, Afro-America's and the FBI's.[29] They are not, however, proof of waning Bureau interest in the traffic of the printed black word. FBI author files of the Black Power era, set apart by pages of "telephonic advice," also document close reviewing of published African American literature, and redoubled concentration on this literature verbalized in performance. COINTELPRO minstrelsy, in other words, fed on the FBI's fresh awareness of the politicized nexus between written and oral Black Arts literature.

Amiri Baraka's file is a striking example of this awareness, not the bulkiest dossier of the Black Arts period, but the most incendiary and thus the most representative. The file sprang to life in 1957, triggered by an Air Force investigation of the author's possible "Fraud Against the Government" (U.S., Federal, Baraka, 25 Apr. 1958). "Everett L. Jones," a.k.a. "Leroi Jones," a.k.a. "Prof. Everett Leroi Jones," a.k.a. "Second Lieutenant Leroi Jones" even then frustrated squares with his self-improvising "aliases" (28 Jan. 1957). Yet he first attracted Bureau flak for his failure to admit to one early incarnation: the radically curious Air Force sergeant who unconvincingly denied involvement in the rump parties of American Marxism. The FBI decided against prosecution for this misrepresentation in 1958, but only after the young Baraka, now a publisher of Allen Ginsberg and Jack Kerouac, outlasted a pointed agent interview. In the style of Sterling Brown, his teacher of both Shakespeare and Bessie Smith at Howard University, Baraka refused to hand over the names of other party sympathizers and steered his interlocutors through a thoughtful leftist critique of the Soviets' "decadent totalitarianism" (25 Apr. 1958). "You apparently have made quite a study of politics, Communism and democracy," admitted a Bureau questioner (24 Apr. 1958).

Baraka's file swells with the founding of BARTS, the origin of his notoriety at the FBI as well as the canonical birthplace of the Black Arts movement. A series of unsolicited letters to Hoover express astonishment over BARTS's brief receipt of federal antipoverty funds. How could "white tax money" be "used to teach colored children to hate us?" asked one citizen (U.S., Federal, Baraka, 10 Dec. 1965). The aging director replied to the wave of complaints by reiterating that "this Bureau is ever cognizant of its responsibilities," and by passing the buck to the Office of Economic Opportunity, the federal agency where the Great Society cut checks to the BARTS summer school (7 Dec. 1965). The non-butt-covering aspect of the Bureau's response went unmentioned in external correspondence: namely, tightened surveillance of Baraka to rival other candidates for the imaginary post of "Black Messiah" (9 Oct. 1970). Nominated as "the person who will probably emerge as the leader of the Pan-African movement in the United States" (9 Oct. 1970), Baraka impressed Bureau agents as the most contagiously articulate risk on their new "Rabble-Rouser Index," an elite registry of troublemakers able to glamorize racial discord.

Baraka's place on this index was secured by the FBI's systematic acquisition of African American texts, never more ambitious than in the COINTELPRO moment. Recognizing that "[p]rint culture provided an absolutely essential technology of time-space compression" for the national networks of the New Left (Cynthia A. Young 9), the Bureau spent freely on titles liable to shrink distances between black and white radical ghettoes. The New York field office was again a hub of counterliterary action, tasked with purchasing a copy of Baraka's volume *Four Revolutionary Plays* (1969) on the same bookstore run that netted Robert Conquest's *The Great Terror* (1968), an unrelenting, once-controversial history of Stalin's 1930s purges (19 Mar. 1970). These books and others were then "carded and filed" for the flagship FBI library on Pennsylvania Avenue in Washington, D.C., the national police collection with which Hoover was eager to complement the Library of Congress (19 Mar. 1970). Less commercially ambitious Baraka publications, issued by the exploding number of independent black nationalist presses, were acquired by confidential sources able to penetrate racially exclusive gatherings. A Baraka showcase entitled *Black Arts* (probably the anthology of that name edited by Detroiters Ahmed Alhamisi and Harun Kofi Wangara in 1969) was obtained for Washington through an unnamed African American informant of the Houston field office, his or her FBI handler unable to resist the temptation to literary criticism. "The booklet, which contains an ample amount of the usual obscenities," the handler maintained, "is a good example of the trash which is promulgated in the name of 'black art'" (23 Apr. 1970).[30] Full-fledged analyses of Baraka titles were more hedged yet more revealing. *Black Fire* (1968), the milestone Black Arts anthology Baraka edited with Larry Neal, was granted a thorough "Synopsis" and "Book Review" after cataloging in the Bureau library (29 Apr. 1969). "This book presents the militant black man's view of the world and of himself in an anthology of essays, poems, short stories and plays," reported police-reviewer G. C. Moore, an associate Bureau director and administrator of the "Extremist Intelligence Section" whose high position signaled the weight of his task (29 Apr. 1969). Sure of his conclusion that the anthology contained two mentions of the FBI, Moore reversed course to concede the limits of white-on-black measurement, yielding respectfully to the bedrock Black Arts principle of mutually exclusive racial epistemologies: "It obviously was written for the benefit of and was directed to the black man and was not written for the minds of white critics" (29 Apr. 1969).

For the white FBI agents tasked with writing black, the acquisition and reviewing of African American literature was nevertheless an operational windfall. Appraising another text selected for the FBI library, Baraka's ingenious and notorious manifesto-poem "Black Art" (1966), the Bureau learned that this literature more than ever craved the existential authority of "live / words of the hip world" (ll. 9–10). Bureau field offices thus facilitated the labors of COINTELPRO minstrels by recording and disseminating live articulations of the black texts they also amassed in print. Baraka's trip-wired object poems, designed to ignite before vocal black audiences, conspired to "wrestle cops into alleys / and take their weapons from them leaving them dead" (Baraka, "Black Art" ll. 21–22). In turn, the cops of the FBI, primed by their own faith that engaged language did the work of weapons, conspired to infiltrate the scenes of these poems' activation at a safe distance. Guided by a corps of black informers wearing wires, Bureau surveillance spread out to document the spectacles in which Black Arts writing strived to alchemize static representation into dynamic being.

Baraka's file thus includes meticulous FBI performance reviews, of-the-moment accounts of Black Arts writing deployed as a talking book and maneuvering live to align a redeemed lyric voice with revolutionary action. Tracking his exhibition of the New Thing before Middle America, the file provides a roadmap to the seeding of BARTS's kinetic style beyond 125th Street. A handful of performance reports in the collection are satisfied to skim newspaper accounts at second hand. For example, one 1967 dispatch on Baraka's appearance before a Connecticut "Black Anger Arts Festival" quotes at length from the *Hartford Courant*: "The lights in the cafeteria dimmed. Suddenly, JONES and his henchmen burst in, shouting obscenities, gibberish, random phrases such as 'White man, the jig is up!' and 'Git 'em, git 'em, git 'em,' making a row by banging canes on tables, knuckling tambourines, and generally putting on one devil of a good show" (8 Dec. 1967). Most of the file's performance accounts are firsthand, however, and not as cynically amused by Baraka's theater of cruelty. Stopping at the University of Cincinnati in 1968, Baraka inspired the local special agent in charge (or SAC, in Bureau jargon) to enhance his city's reputation for censorship. Baraka's appearance on a Negro History Week program, this SAC boasted to headquarters, had been tape-recorded without the writer's knowledge by "a confidential source whose identity cannot be revealed" (28 Feb. 1968). Classifying the "Negro playwright-poet" as a connoisseur of "obscene words"—"Nobody says *muthafucka* like Amiri Baraka," confirms vernacular theorist Kimberly Benston (189)—the SAC telexed eight copies of a complete transcript to Hoover (28 Feb. 1968). Cover pages of this transcript gasp that "JONES, in a poem, has Negroes going into any business . . . and stealing anything they wanted" (28 Feb. 1968). "What JONES is preaching borders on absolute anarchy," the SAC concludes, recommending "that the Bureau consider furnishing this information directly to President Johnson" (28 Feb. 1968).

The transcript of the preaching that follows the SAC's summary, however, surrounds full texts of "Black People!" (1967) and other Baraka poems with notes and textures curiously partial to Black Arts aesthetics. The sudden, embodied immediacy of Baraka's (delayed) appearance is highlighted by a reproduction of his SNCC host's staccato introduction: "He's alive! He's here! He's our cat Leroi!" (28 Feb. 1968). Stagy directions on the poet's clothing, "entirely in black, with a loose turtle-neck sports shirt" (28 Feb. 1968), underline the theatricalization of Black Arts authorship, the metabolic conversion of poets into performers, "the way James Brown is a performer—loud, gaudy and racy," as Baraka collaborator Larry Neal embroidered it ("And Shine" 655). The dynamics of the audience's active consumption—"Clapping," "Wild Clapping," "Laughter," etc.—are indicated poem by poem and at times stanza by stanza, signaling the public formation of meaning through call, response, and the neglected third dimension, just as vital in African American performance, of the caller's recomposition in process (28 Feb. 1968).

Blow-by-blow Bureau reports on later Baraka performances feature similar contextual cues, from details on the after-party following a reading in Baltimore (21 Mar. 1968) to fascination with the "kissing and licking [of] members of the audience" expected to accompany traveling productions of the ritual drama *A Black Mass* (1966) (7 Feb. 1969). Judging from the Baraka file, FBI ghostreaders concluded that the most authentic-seeming imitations of black writing would emerge from the thickest transcriptions of its recital. Baraka's "sing song manner" of reciting "The Dance of the Toms," a naming and shaming of bankrupt would-be liberators, might have authorized the Bureau's juvenile ode to H. Rap Brown (28 Feb. 1968). Gravitating to the impolite climax of "Black People!" as helplessly as the campus radicals of SDS ("Up against the wall mother / fucker this a stick up!" ll. 10–11), COINTELPRO literature might have arrived at its regular fusion of reductive obscenity and revolutionary expansiveness (28 Feb. 1967). Assuming the accents of Mozart, Jomo Kenyatta, and the Green Lantern in a single performance, the cross-hierarchical shape shifting of the typical Baraka live session might have empowered the high-low mash-ups of the Bureau's comic books. Despite Baraka's versified curse that "J. EDGAR HOOVER WILL / SOON BE DEAD" ("Three Movements" ll. 13–14), Hooverite counterliterature stood to profit from the range of his poetic responses to live black company. Like the academic critics after them, FBI specialists in African American literature were poised to make hay from Black Arts doctrine on the intimacy of speech and script.

Generalizations about the performance-conscious universe of Black Arts files are not easy. As noted earlier, FOIA law sanely stipulates that requests for FBI records on living individuals must be self-generated.[31] Unlike Baraka, who short-circuited possessive Bureau archivism by publicizing his own file, most surviving veterans of the Black Arts movement have not shared the results of any FOIA requests. As a result, assessing the relevant archival field is more challenging than for earlier stages of Bureau counterliterature. Author self-reports on Bureau run-ins provide needed help. Sonia Sanchez, for example, has recounted the interest of FBI agents in her earliest black studies classes (*Conversations* 115–16). Poet and professor Nikki Giovanni has published verse about what she swears was an actual visit from a pair of G-Men. "[I]t would be a patriotic gesture," Giovanni has her F.B. eyes advise, "if you'd quit saying / you love rap brown and if you'd maybe give us some / leads / on what some of your friends are doing" ("I Laughed" ll. 13–16). Ishmael Reed, the iconoclast who pictures J. Edgar Hoover "smiling in hell" while witnessing the self-betrayal of the radical 1960s (*Airing* 94), has cultivated his reputation as one of the Bureau's at-large public enemies. Further guesswork on the game of cops and writers is irresistible: given the service of the Black Arts to Black Power, it is hard to imagine *any* high-profile author of the movement failing to provoke COINTELPRO-related spying. Three less sweeping conclusions, meanwhile, can be drawn with greater certainty: first, that individual FBI files are common though not universal among the ranks of the Black Arts departed (twelve in number, in my count, out of seventeen requested); second, that the great majority of these files currently open to research follow Baraka's in logging novel audio surveillance or intensified Bureau book collecting; and third, that with few exceptions, these accessible files monitor author-audience dynamics, chronicling the literature of Black Power as it vocalized itself at a series of public readings and meetings.

The dossier of Hoyt Fuller, the editor who reintroduced *Negro Digest* as *Black World* (the Bureau subscribed to both), might be mistaken for a professor's file of conference souvenirs. Historians seeking a session-by-session account of Chicago's Congress of Afrikan Peoples meeting should proceed directly to the Fuller papers, where his address on the black media, "Information and Communication for Survival," is encased by ninety pages of conference proceedings and registration forms (U.S., Federal, Fuller, 18 Apr. 1974). The Fuller collection, stretching from 1954 to 1974, also fixes the origins of the FBI's appearance on the black nationalist conference circuit: the July 1967 National Conference on Black Power in Newark, New Jersey. The sponsoring hotel, the Robert Treat, obliged Bureau agents by handing over its registration cards, placing Fuller in attendance along with scores of now-censored names (24 July 1967). Black Arts theorist Larry Neal's file (1965–72) feints in the direction of the intentional fallacy, the New Critical principle that strips interpretive authority from contextual accounts of an author's political allegiances. The savviest agents at the New

York office, now experienced with entertaining radical positions during their COINTELPRO writing assignments, initially underplayed the significance of Neal's commitment to RAM and other vehicles of Black Nationalist politics. The racial militancy coloring his poems and essays, one G-Man speculated, might not be propositional content identical with his own values: "His occupation of being a writer may have motivated his desire to acquire knowledge of the racial movement, without influencing his personal beliefs" (U.S., Federal, Neal, 13 Sept. 1967). Neal's contribution to a 1968 "'black get-together' of unknown origin" erased such educated doubts, however (21 Oct. 1968). "Among the entertainment was a recital of a poem by [Neal] entitled 'Black Power,' " reported a New York agent, "an emotional type of poem with a lot of screaming and which called for negroes [sic] to love each other, stay together, and fight together for killing 'the man'" (21 Oct. 1968). As Neal's file swims on, performance trumps publication as an index of sincerity, and the man rallies by placing the poet's name in double jeopardy: it appears not only on the Security Index, but also on a shorter list of individuals "believed to be covered by the agreement between the FBI and the Secret Service concerning Presidential protection" (n.d.). Assassinating the president, the Bureau decided, might feature within Neal's promise "to deny the patriotic assumptions of the white and Negro establishment" (Neal, "And Shine" 640).

Performance beats publication in poet-editor Dudley Randall's relatively thin file (1966–69). Concern for the printed products of Randall's Broadside Press takes a backseat to his public debut of the anthology *For Malcolm* (1967) at a Friday Night Socialist Forum (U.S., Federal, Randall, 14 Oct. 1969). The heavier FBI compilation on *Black Metropolis* coauthor St. Clair Drake (1961–71), a Black Arts figure by virtue of his counsel to Kwame Nkrumah, highlights a young genre of embodied literary performance: the televised author interview (U.S., Federal, Drake, 27 Feb. 1964). Pauli Murray's file (1966–67) keeps eyes peeled for hints of lesbianism (3 Jan. 1967) while transcribing interviews with the Harper editor who contracted *Proud Shoes* (1956), the story of Murray's freedom-fighting North Carolina family (U.S., Federal, Murray, 11 Jan. 1967). The contents of Addison Gayle Jr.'s file, probably still buried in a legal morass at the National Archives,[32] remain as murky as those of Iceberg Slim (born Robert Beck) and Sherley Anne Williams, destroyed under "disposition schedules" of the FBI Records Retention Plan (Hardy, 24 Oct. 2007; Hardy, 13 Feb. 2009). The file of Carolyn Rodgers, the founder of the Third World Press, has apparently been mistakenly lost rather than systematically deleted. "[P]otentially responsive records were not in their expected location and could not be located after a reasonable search," the Bureau's Record/Information Section has informed me (Hardy, 31 July 2012). Poet Lucille Clifton's file consists in an often-illegible outline of an early check-cashing case, the only purely criminal investigation in the full collection of fifty-one author dossiers.

Quite the opposite, the longest open file of the Black Power era, James Baldwin's, sixteen years (1958–74) and 1,884 pages thick, volunteers lucid commentary on most every subject imaginable. Too self-contained for membership in BARTS but first on a Bureau list of "Independent Black Nationalist Extremists," Baldwin inspired digests of bugged telephone calls following all of his returns to the scene of American racial politics (U.S., Federal, Baldwin, 8 Jan. 1968). Malcolm X, his confidences recorded in several documents, is overheard endorsing the eloquence of "Brother BALDWIN," "very influential among the intellectuals" (28 July 1961). The hip colloquialism of the brother's private speech is an object of special Bureau attraction, one source, possibly, of the COINTELPRO minstrel's over-eager slang: "It is noted that in greeting . . . BALDWIN stated 'Hello, baby, how are you' and in closing the conversation stated that 'It's good to hear from you, baby'" (3 Jan. 1965). Agent-authored reviews welcome Baldwin's books into the national FBI library, from *Another Country* (1962) and *The Fire Next Time* (1963) to *Blues for Mister Charlie* (1964) and *No Name in the Street* (1972). Covert reports on dozens of speaking engagements validate Baldwin's public claim that "there probably was a CIA or FBI agent in the group" when he unloaded his mind (1 Aug. 1968). Bureau informants followed his talks from Mississippi farm fields to a New York dinner of the Emergency Civil Liberties Committee, where Baldwin shared the dais with a certain "Bobby Dyllon" (1 June 1964). (In distinction to Baldwin's address, the folk singer's "was rather one of free association" [1 June 1964].) Along the trail of lectures, Baldwin conducts an unhidden running battle with FBI surveillance, climaxing in the promise that he will publish an anti-FBI book with the power of an "atom bomb" (7 June 1963). *The Blood Counters*, Baldwin's never-completed rejoinder to FBI discrimination, figures in part 5 of this book, a survey of African American "counter-counterliterature" over the long haul. In and beyond this ghost-text, the weird intimacies of COINTELPRO had the unintended consequence of energizing new combinations of Afro-modernist literature. Baldwin's ability "to disrupt the fetishizing machinations of the racial gaze by an eyeballing disposition of his own" (Wallace 141) was trained under the eyes of COINTELPRO counterliterature—an enraging but decipherable policing of formal publication, live performance, and even ostensibly private conversation. As we will see, the minstrel-style mock-up of black expression this policing fostered was not exactly flattering, but still perhaps the most inspirational threat to black creativity the FBI ever invented.

COINTELPRO minstrelsy was in fact the inspiration behind my organizing idea of FBI counterliteratures, dependent counterstatements to African

American writing that convert various currencies of literary capital into changing forms of criminological capital. The Bureau's programmatic effort to imprison Black Power by miming its literary voice provides a dramatically literal-minded instance of this idea in action. Earlier, less flagrant stages of Bureau counterliterature, however, are just as significant in diagramming the FBI's long contest with Afro-modernism, an unsung influence on the Bureau's well-recorded history. In the 1920s, the archival technology of the FBI author file transformed the New Negro into a new criminal genus. In the 1940s, it translated the mounting black internationalism of World War II into directions for mass detention on the home front. In the 1950s, it answered the mainstreaming of black writing on the eve of civil rights with Total Literary Awareness, a cool war to deter cultural assimilation before it occurred. Stage by counterliterary stage, the Bureau's implausible expertise on African American literature helped to magnify the authority of Hooverite antiradicalism inside FBI headquarters. Stage by stage, the Bureau's approximation of inside dope on the mind of black America helped to augment its clout with the executive or legislative branches of the U.S. government, sanctioning a shifting patchwork of federal exceptions to the rule of free expression. By the heyday of COINTELPRO minstrelsy, the Bureau's sparring with black letters had fittingly opened an official zone of indulgence for "black propaganda," the intelligence trade name for damaging expression presented in the style of the enemy. FBI counterliterature had merged with FBI counterintelligence and had done a good deal to merge strategically with Afro-modernism.

The history of FBI counterliterature ended with two bangs—a break-in and a death—soon after its peak in the form of COINTELPRO minstrelsy. The break-in in question was not the opening fiasco of the Watergate scandal, from which the Hooverites' fear of bad publicity and rogue intelligence operators initially insulated the Bureau. (FBI associate director Mark Felt, a Hoover loyalist willing to defend his boss's pursuit of Martin Luther King, indeed turned out be the legendary "Deep Throat" [Felt and O'Connor 193–226].) The lethal burglary was instead the "radical Watergate" undertaken by some of the Bureau's New Left critics, eager to try a black bag job of their own. One night in March 1971, a group styling itself the Citizens' Commission to Investigate the FBI forced its way into a Bureau field office in Media, Pennsylvania, and carted off hundreds of pages of secret case records.[33] File-for-file revenge had finally been taken on the original sin of the FBI library, the raiding of leftist archives. Within weeks, the first public word of COINTELPRO trickled into U.S. newspapers, the program's preventive listing of 100,000 citizen-subversives, many nonwhite, stirring outrage. "Minority groups need never be reminded that such a list exists," sermonized a black weekly in Los Angeles, "[b]ut it has taken a handful of stolen documents to awaken the snug 'Anglos,' who can now simmer and squirm while trying to figure out what's next" (qtd. in Jeffreys-Jones 177). Hoover spent little time squirming before closing the COINTELPRO shop, among his last significant actions as director. Sealing the counterintelligence program's extinction, he died of a heart attack before breakfast on May 2, 1972, awaited by the African American staff critical to his morning routines.

Hoover was thus spared the indignity of 1975, the so-called Year of Intelligence, during which the congressional Church and Pike commissions condemned COINTELPRO and its paraliterature first among the offenses of domestic spying. But he had lived long enough to see an equally astonishing intelligence spectacle: the bureaucratically administered makeover of white-bread G-Men into African American writers. In director Florian Henckel von Donnersmarck's Academy Award–winning film *Das Leben der Anderen*, or *The Lives of Others* (2006), a severe captain of the Stasi, the secret police that pervaded East Germany, is assigned to wiretap a respected playwright flirting with dissidence. So far, so much like an earnest postcommunist documentary: the actual Stasi, the nucleus of "the poster child of informer states" (Hewitt 105), organized a special unit focused on literature; four hundred superliterate informers came to its aid by the 1970s, including twelve of nineteen members of the high-profile East German Writers' Association (114). Somehow, however, von Donnersmarck's Stasi protagonist escapes statistics and solemn social realism and grows to admire and imitate the increasingly nonconforming writer he shadows. At the end of his assignment, tragically botched for reasons of love and conscience, his typewriter is as busy as his bugging equipment, and an aestheticist myth of German reconciliation, East and West writing liberally in common, is born. Akin to von Donnersmarck's hero, FBI spies on the Afro-modernist beat also fell into a gratifying resemblance to their literary targets: *Black Fire* reviewer G. C. Moore was not alone in enjoying aspects of his time in the shoes of the Black Arts enemy. Yet despite the sanction for this makeover at headquarters, G-Men authors never became their targets' comrade-liberators: not a single permanent defection to the Afro-modernist side of the wall has been discovered. Authoring semiappreciative works of literary criticism, the subject of the next part of *F.B. Eyes*, is as close as Hoover's ghostreaders came to the final, uplifting twist of von Donnersmarck's fable of the Stasi convert, lured by the ironic familiarities of literary surveillance into the pursuit of literary freedom.

Part Three/Thesis Three

The FBI Is Perhaps the Most Dedicated and Influential Forgotten Critic of African American Literature

Caught out in a self-lacerating mood, J. Edgar Hoover once returned an FBI memo on the problem of James Baldwin with a handwritten challenge: "Isn't Baldwin a well-known pervert?" (U.S., Federal, Baldwin, 20 July 1964). Despite the career-threatening context, M. A. Jones, an officer of the FBI Crime Records Section, answered Hoover's marginal question by carefully distinguishing between fictional and personal testimonies. "It is not a matter of official record that he is a pervert," Jones stipulated, even though "the theme of homosexuality has figured prominently in two of his three published novels. Baldwin has stated that it is also 'implicit' in his first novel, *Go Tell It on the Mountain*. In the past, he has not disputed the description of 'autobiographical' being attached to the first book" (20 July 1964). "While it is not possible to state that he is pervert," Jones concluded, Baldwin "has expressed a sympathetic viewpoint about homosexuality on several occasions, and a very definite hostility toward the revulsion of the American public regarding it" (20 July 1964). Hoover did not glide gently into agreement with Jones's subtle distinctions among sexual acts, sympathies, and representations, echoes of the New Critical–style fastidiousness that led a New York agent to consider the intentional fallacy in the case of Larry Neal. Less enlightened FBI informants continued to protest higher education's embrace of a Baldwin novel they mistakenly called *Another World*, remarkable for its depiction of "a Negro male making love to a white female" (1 Feb. 1966). (The 1962 novel Baldwin actually titled *Another Country* was somehow reconceived by these informants as a bohemian soap opera.) The Bureau director thus continued to explore ways to ban Baldwin's book under the

Interstate Transportation of Obscene Matter statute—this despite the report of the Justice Department's General Crimes Section that "*Another Country* by James Baldwin has been reviewed . . . and it has been concluded that the book contains literary merit and may be of value to students of psychology and social behavior" (13 Sept. 1963). With rival units in the Justice Department discovering the novel's redeeming social importance, it was left to Hoover and like-minded Bureau sticklers to contemplate *Another Country*'s resemblance to the landmarks of modernist obscenity. "In many aspects it is similar to the *Tropics* books by [Henry] MILLER," wrote Washington, D.C.'s special agent in charge (19 Sept. 1962). For this reason, perhaps, the SAC ostentatiously instructed that his borrowed copy "need not be returned" to his office (19 Sept. 1962).

Blurb-worthy praise is not the norm in the FBI's more than fifty files on Afro-modernist writers: the General Crimes Section looks to be a better source of pull quotes applauding "literary merit" and "value to students of psychology and social behavior." Yet the risky refinement of M. A. Jones's reply to Hoover's leading question, its overspilling of the need to label, discipline, and punish, is emblematic of more than a few Bureau readers' indulgence of writers' prerogatives. Hoover himself, we have learned, possessed an inflated wariness and respect for the authors who doubled as "thought-control relay stations" (qtd. in Robins 50). Authors/relay stations of special prominence, W.E.B. Du Bois included, were at times spared in-person interviews by Bureau agents for fear of their "access to the subversive press," a megaphone whose range the FBI exaggerated (U.S., Federal, W.E.B. Du Bois, 12 Oct. 1960). Total Literary Awareness, COINTELPRO minstrelsy, and other instruments of Bureau counterliterature took the opposition seriously enough to fight on its own literary turf. Moreover, despite all the resources devoted to frustrating black literary communication, Bureau encounters with Afro-modernist writing could not always resist the pleasures of the enemy text.

FBI ghostreaders, the files confide, succumbed to the spell of African American literature in several genres. To begin with a familiar figure, the Philadelphia G-Man sent to paint a true picture of communist influence on Lorraine Hansberry's play *A Raisin in the Sun* discovered a drama worthy of first-rate characterological analysis. The receptive insight of this agent's review—it would receive a noninflated A in many college English classes—flowed from inspiration beyond the call of police duty. With its swelling existential vocabulary, his sketch of Beneatha Younger, an articulately dissatisfied Hansberry character searching for "a means of self-expression and self-identification," doubles as a confession of his own unfulfilled literary need (U.S., Federal, Hansberry, 5 Feb. 1959). A G-Man Gustave Flaubert, this reviewer might as well have admitted of Mademoiselle Younger, *c'est moi*.

In their less-sensitive fashion, the unnamed Bureau authors of a case summary in Chester Himes's file were moved to compose capsule interpretations of every early story he placed in *Esquire* magazine. Ordered to check for treasonous speech during World War II, these authors decide at the outset that none of Himes's "fiction articles" incorporates "material which could be termed seditious" (U.S., Federal, Himes, 8 Jan. 1945). Even so, they gloss seven separate stories in turn, all of their brief rewritings specifying Himes's "descriptive material," philosophical and "sordid" (8 Jan. 1945). Both Larry Neal's file and Amiri Baraka's file contain copies of a frankly titled "Book Review" of *Black Fire*, the agenda-setting Black Arts anthology they coedited in 1968. As part 2 has testified, G. C. Moore, an FBI associate director and designated critic of the collection, acceded to the tenet of racially distinct faculties of aesthetic judgment, the first law of Black Arts criticism. *Black Fire* "obviously was . . . not written for the minds of white critics," he admitted (U.S., Federal, Neal, 29 Apr. 1969). But racial distance could not prevent this stimulated white reviewer from issuing both praise and damnation. Before reproducing Charles Anderson's poem "Prayer to the White Man's God" as a characteristic Black Arts text, Moore quotably describes a "flaming indictment of American prejudice" paired with a "love of all things black—black people, black traditions, black voices, black art, and black futures" (U.S., Federal, Baraka, 29 Apr. 1969). The anthology's "ample servings of filth" and " 'far out' . . . method of presentation," he judges, are balanced by a handful of "works [that] tend to have an energy that succeeds in impressing one with the violence and passion of the author's emotions" (29 Apr. 1969). Moore ends with his finger on the scale, emphasizing *Black Fire*'s general disorder: "the expression never achieves the precision and control which are the hallmarks of successful art" (29 Apr. 1969). Even this censure, however, rests on artistic grounds, not moral or criminological ones. In the end, *Black Fire*'s contributors are cleared of tight-knit plans for urban violence and convicted of emotionally sloppy neo-Romanticism, a noncriminal violation of one remaining aesthetic universal.

Further literary surrenders, identifications, and judgments on the part of FBI readers could be mentioned, but the point has been made: while at least one Bureau agent insisted that "we've never held ourselves out as great book reviewers," the Bureau's many files on Afro-modernists are, among other things, recognizably literary-critical documents (qtd. in Robins 401). Elizabeth Renker's history of the academic profession of American literature distinguishes between a primary archive of formal literary-critical interpretation and a secondary archive of literary-critical bureaucracy, the latter composed of such tedious documents as "course catalogs, hiring records, administrative bulletins, presidents' reports, minutes of departments meetings, [and] curriculum development materials" (Renker 6). In the case of FBI literary criticism, the equivalents of these two archives jostle within the very same files. The mixed genre of the FBI author file thus incorporates more than bureaucratic "judicial text" and identity-fixing "police text," types of Bureau file prose distinguished earlier in *F.B. Eyes*. It also includes literary-critical text, a strain of writing administrative, evaluative, and sometimes appreciative in nature. It is not too much to propose that the FBI's reading-intensive files qualify as works of literary commentary, state-subsidized explications debating informal curricula and obliquely bidding for interpretive dominance. By the same token, it is no exaggeration to claim that the G-Men compelled to supply these files with literary notes and queries qualify as critic-spies.

Recognizing the similarity of the creative writer and the espionage agent has been a minor staple of British literary culture since the (pre-Harlem) English Renaissance. An Elizabethan "dramatist-spy" such as Christopher Marlowe, remarks John Michael Archer, knew that his work on both sides of the hyphen depended on the "necessary lie" and on "observation of men and manners [that] made their manipulation through spectacle possible" (75). A century later, Daniel Defoe, one father of the modern English novel, also helped to parent the British state spy service and, just as significantly, a long line of British intelligence officers who found their mirror image in the fiction maker (Riebling 83). Freed by modernity to embrace the silence, exile, and cunning undergirding the writer-spy allegory (Hollander xviii), John le Carré, Ian Fleming, Graham Greene, T. E. Lawrence, Compton Mackenzie, and Somerset Maugham all walked in Defoe's double footsteps, their stories and novels of the great game of intelligence coloring the imaginations of spy colleagues as well as civilian readers. (The use of "mole" to refer to a penetration agent, for instance, became identifying slang among intelligence officers only after its introduction by le Carré [Riebling 83].) But what of the less-familiar allegory of the *critic* and the spy? What, in particular, of the all-American, file-stuffing figure of the FBI ghostreader, as I call this Hooverite agent of state interpretation? What were the habits, convictions, and effects of the Bureau critic-spies whose observation of texts was enabled by decryption, identity theft, and hermeneutics of suspicion—techniques academic critics often share with intelligence agents—but also by systematic FBI surveillance?

This third part of *F.B. Eyes* looks for answers to these questions down several intersecting paths. Together, its first two sections illuminate the interpretive assumptions of Bureau ghostreading against the backdrop of the best-documented entanglement of American criticism with American espionage: namely, the firsthand stamp of the New Criticism on the counterintelligence branch of the

Central Intelligence Agency (CIA). CIA-endorsed formalism, its high-wire, Yale-rooted history explored in section 1, was eventually integrated into FBI critical practice. As section 2 confirms, however, Bureau ghostreaders cobbled together a distinct mode of FBI reading decades before the CIA's creation, a didactic yet meticulous biohistoricism in sympathy with academic schools of the late 1910s, 1920s, and 1930s. Even the Bureau's postwar assent to aspects of the New Criticism, various FBI files show, did not drown out the siren call of Marxian ideology critique, a forte of Depression-era critical culture that FBI critic-spies retooled to combat the Marxist pole of the Cold War.

Section 3 asks into the background and outlook of the FBI agents tasked with criticizing Afro-modernism. With the exception of M. A. Jones, G. C. Moore, and other Bureau executives authorized to sign commissioned review essays, Hoover's individual ghostreaders tend to disappear behind cloaks of bureaucratic anonymity and later FOIA censorship; the depersonalized, montaged "poetics of the personal file," we noted earlier, perversely fulfills the antibourgeois desire for communal composition (Vatulescu 14). Even so, the literary lives and opinions of two supervising editors at the FBI—Robert Adger Bowen of the Bureau of Translations and William C. Sullivan of the Domestic Intelligence Division—have been detailed on the record and here serve to address the irresistible bourgeois question of whodunit. Finally, section 4 assesses the impact of FBI ghostreading on an interested non-Bureau audience: not, in this case, African American writers themselves, their literary responses to FBI counterliteratures outlined in part 5, but the self-appointed model citizens who turned to Hoover as a literary-critical wise man and potential literary-critical collaborator. Despite the privileged contents of FBI files, a fairly accurate impression of the Bureau's attentiveness to Afro-modernist literature escaped the Washington Beltway, refueling the machinery of ghostreading with correspondence warmly imagining the state apparatus as a community of patriotic bookworms. Employed to analyze the Bureau as a literary-critical institution, the compromised evidence provided in liberated FBI files is again no fast lane to absolute knowledge. Yet enough is revealed to propose the third and thus far most literary of our five theses: *The FBI is perhaps the most dedicated and influential forgotten critic of African American literature.*

Reading Like a CIA Agent

Before Ian Fleming retired to his money-spinning James Bond novels, intrigues pitting the British Secret Intelligence Service (SIS) against the global terrorists of SPECTRE, he labored to capture another vicious clash between enemy espionage outfits: the embryonic war between the FBI and CIA. The pre-Bond Fleming, a British naval commander sent on a nonfictional secret mission to the United States in 1941, reckoned that a world-class foreign intelligence service could not be built by England's Atlantic ally without the voluntary movement of an immovable obstacle, one J. Edgar Hoover. In a private meeting with the Bureau director at FBI headquarters, Fleming and another visiting officer respectfully rehearsed a list of British recommendations for improved wartime espionage (Riebling 10). Last but not least on their list was a proposal for a new office to take charge of overseas spy work while coordinating all branches of American intelligence, the FBI not excepted. The Brits' target of persuasion, Fleming wrote, was "a chunky enigmatic man with slow eyes and a trap of a mouth" who listened with quiet concentration (qtd. in Riebling 10). When Hoover opened his trap in response, he bared what Fleming called "toes covered with corns"—in less thickly metaphorical words, exquisite sensitivity to the threat to FBI sovereignty in the clamor for a U.S. central intelligence agency (qtd. in Riebling 10). Civilly but unmistakably, Hoover pronounced himself unmoved by his callers' wish list; without fanfare, he was already handling U.S. foreign intelligence operations in Latin America (a development pursued in part 4 of *F.B. Eyes*). Fleming thus left FBI headquarters with further ingredients for spy fiction, not the go-ahead for a U.S. counterpart to James Bond's internationally savvy MI6, licensed to kill outside the polite limits of the United Kingdom.

Despite the glamorously hush-hush wartime successes of the Office of Strategic Services (OSS), the CIA's immediate predecessor, Hoover in fact helped to delay the establishment of U.S. central intelligence until the 1947 passage of President Harry Truman's National Security Act. The FBI's Republican allies on Capitol Hill even then insured that the new agency could not access Bureau files, the sanctum of Hoover's charismatic-bureaucratic power, except in cases vital to national security, so declared only in written requests by the CIA director (Riebling 77). Nor could the CIA assume "police, subpoena, law-enforcement powers or internal security functions" when gathering intelligence on U.S. soil ("National Intelligence"). This second limitation, breached too often in practice, was a good thing for American democracy, and a sharp-eyed anticipation of the issues sparking the FBI-CIA rivalry that exceeded trifling motives of ego and turf. Mark Riebling, a scholar of the unyielding wedge between the two intelligence outfits, explains that the CIA's code of "extra-legal virtue" in the world-historical struggle with communism did not suit it for domestic police work (85). More to the point, "this Cold War code grew and operated against the grain of J. Edgar Hoover's basic task, the enforcement of the very laws the CIA would try to break" in the hunt for Soviet game (86). Hoover's legalism, particularly on the counterliterary beat, was not quite as basic as that. All the same, the CIA's gung-ho tackling of covert actions in which the pretense of fair play was consciously abandoned indeed increased the divide between the two agencies, arguably culminating in the series of bungled communications before 9/11.[1]

Easily caricatured cultural differences, too, kept the two pillars of U.S. state intelligence at arm's length. Though transposable media stars, Hoover's dark-suited G-Men were snobbishly dismissed by OSS types as "Irish-Catholic Texans from second-rate law schools," organization men willing to tolerate the FBI dress code and other microtyrannies thanks to formative training in high school football and the Marine Corps (Riebling 8). Focusing further east but hitting just as hard on class, ethnic, and educational differences, CIA wits insisted that the initials FBI really stood for "Fordham Bronx Irish" (Richard Gid Powers, *Broken* 356). FBI agents retaliated by insulting OSS analysts as WASPy "Oh, So Socials" hired straight from Ivy League eating clubs. The typical CIA agent they later pictured combined foppishness and recklessness less appealingly than Fleming's James Bond. Only a preppy adventurer inexperienced with physical violence, they imagined, would court danger like the ironically self-involved "Company" man. CIA higher-ups, meanwhile, did little to discourage the impression of their agency as an exclusive state university run by robust eggheads. CIA headquarters in Langley, Virginia, was nicknamed "the campus," a far cry from the Bureau's Seat of Government, a headquarters handle betraying Hoover's erratically repressed rivalry with the White House. "By the mid-1960s," reports Frances Stonor Saunders, the CIA bragged "that it could staff any college from its analysts, 50 per cent of whom held advanced degrees, 30 per cent doctorates" (236). The FBI's law and accounting graduates, closer to 100 percent of the agent corps, were better prepared to staff an imaginary professional school, an institution far from Berkeley and other Hoover-investigated hotbeds of student radicalism.

Foreign-language expertise was many times more common at the CIA than at the FBI. Yet if the CIA had ever committed to building a conventional university, its most distinguished department would have been English. Even British historians are bound to admit that the anglophone "'man of letters' was, if anything, even more conspicuous a figure in the upper echelons of the American secret service than in MI6" (Wilford 99). There were American creative writers with more or less furtive lives in the CIA—William F. Buckley, John Hunt, Edward S. Hunter, Robie Macauley, Peter Matthiessen, Jack Thompson, and others—though relatively few with the talent of their British cousins. (For quick and dirty illustration of this difference, compare the espionage fiction of (a) MI6 veteran David John Moore Cornwell, better known by his pen name, John le Carré; and (b) CIA "political action specialist" David St. John, better known by his given name, E. Howard Hunt, the unquiet American who authored ten or more pulp thrillers between disasters at the Bay of Pigs and the Watergate Hotel.) Where the CIA school of English plainly excelled MI6 was not in the creation of imaginative literature, but in the dependent arts of literary criticism and patronage; for a long, odd time, the CIA volunteered as an American "Ministry of Culture" (Rogin 16), or perhaps as a sneaky precursor of the National Endowment for the Arts.[2] The Paris-based Congress for Cultural Freedom, unmasked as a CIA front in 1967, fought its cultural Cold War by creating *Encounter*, a distinguished literary monthly originally edited by the Anglo-American odd couple of class-conscious poet Stephen Spender and neoconservative Irving Kristol. *Partisan Review*, founded as a Marxist little magazine in 1934, received cash infusions from the congress after refining an American concoction of high modernism and High Church anti-Stalinism (Wilford 103–5). The CIA may have indirectly paid for classic *Review* contributions by W. H. Auden, Saul Bellow, Elizabeth Bishop, George Orwell, Susan Sontag, and Wallace Stevens. By contrast, the half of T. S. Eliot's *Four Quartets* published in the *Review* in 1940–41 arrived too early for Company sponsorship. Eliot's imprimatur was nonetheless a crucial prize in another successful mission of the CIA school of English: the translation of the New Criticism into a prop of agent training and counterintelligence theory, the practical criticism of modernist poetry assimilated into modern espionage technique. Not for nothing would Allen Ginsberg, decades after accosting Walt Whitman in a California supermarket, fantasize about buttonholing Eliot on the fantail of a boat to Europe, and asking "What did you think of the domination of poetics by the CIA?" (Ginsberg 61).

The Company's domination of poetics, such as it was, was facilitated by an Ivy League bastion older than the United States, a Collegiate Gothic hub where the networks of American academic and state intelligence overlapped almost seamlessly. A statue of patriotic martyr Nathan Hale, "the first American spy," greets employees on their way to work at the CIA's Virginia campus. It is cast from an original on the Old Campus at Yale University, placed there to honor Hale's old school tie (he was an early Yale graduate) and, less officially, the shared coordinates of Langley and modern New Haven (Winks 15). "Somehow," observes Yale historian Robin W. Winks, "the idea of Yale as a place, and of intelligence work as an activity, became linked, if not by Hale, then by the events of World War II" (15). Winks's figures on the migration of Yalies into the World War II spy business reveal his "somehow" to be somewhat disingenuous.

Yale's class of 1943 alone contributed forty-two BAs to the payrolls of U.S. espionage, most going to "the OSS, many to remain on after the war to form the core of the new CIA" (Winks 35).

The lead recruiter of the flood of Yale spies was a tenure-track English instructor trained in New Haven, a Massachusetts Yankee with a tubercular hip named Norman Holmes Pearson. A 1941 Yale PhD whose dissertation annotated Nathaniel Hawthorne's *Italian Notebooks*, Pearson welcomed his American-abroad assignment to London and the "X-2" division of the OSS. Behind its seductively vacant name, X-2 functioned as the counterintelligence division of the OSS, a unit with the recursive duty of countering threats to friendly intelligence operations—to adapt a phrase from part 2, call it the task of spying on the spies likely to spy on you. X-2 played a supporting role in the greatest Allied espionage triumph of the war, the application of broken German codes in an intricate "Double-Cross system" that transformed Nazi spies into deadly double agents.[3] What Pearson cited as the foremost independent accomplishment of X-2 was a bookish, Hooverite one, however, the OSS-FBI rivalry be damned. Applying his research skills beyond the Yale library, Pearson built a comprehensive, Bureau-type card index system on 300,000 Axis intelligence threats. With assistance from this paper weapon, the OSS "contributed to the apprehension of 1,300 enemy agents in military zones alone and was primarily responsible for rendering ineffective German 'stay-behind' networks—intelligence groups left to be overrun as the Allied troops advanced, then to work from behind the Allied lines" (Winks 265).

The X-2 card catalog was nerdy-serious business, the unduplicable contribution of the Yale-OSS "bad-eyes brigade" to the war against real fascism. Its lead author, a collector of Ezra Pound manuscripts and the eventual literary executor of the Imagist poet H.D., saw no reason why such archival work could not also support the innovations in espionage tradecraft suggested by the promodernist New Criticism. Back in New Haven, Pearson's literary-critical practice had been shaping up as a pragmatic bridge between curatorial historicism and its formalist opposite. In his methodological peacemaking, he predicted the anticommunist gentlemen's agreement between "historical descriptions that were resolutely capitalist and untheoretical" and "theoretico-critical descriptions that were formally unhistorical and apolitical"—a tacit alliance of methods beneath the Cold War hegemony of the American New Criticism (Epstein 68). Seen in its own time, Pearson's peacemaking shrewdly cut the difference between his home department's magisterial school of eighteenth-century studies and the modish interest in the new southern formalists, then qualifying for Yale job offers (Cleanth Brooks arrived first in 1947) by publishing *Understanding*

Poetry (1938) and other conquering New Critical textbooks. Pearson himself specialized in books for the classroom. Before OSS, he had coedited a two-volume *Oxford Anthology of American Literature* (1938) with a fellow Yalie, poet William Rose Benét. This field-shaping resource, reprinted into the 1960s, began with prosaic, historically responsible excerpts from settlement chroniclers John Smith and William Bradford. (Pearson's OSS cryptonym was "Puritan," of course.) Yet the editors' introduction still insisted that all contents were chosen for "purely literary" reasons (Benét and Pearson v). Pearson's dedication to the mixing of the old historicism and the new formalism extended from the *Oxford Anthology* to the OSS.[4] To supplement an intelligence brain trust brimming with Yale librarians (e.g., Herman W. Leibert) and textual critics (e.g., W. S. Lewis, the editor of Horace Walpole's many letters), he recruited an entrepreneurial English major whose familiarity with the New Critics surpassed that of his professors. Pearson's student James Jesus Angleton, the Yale man who evolved into one of the most fictionalized spies in American history, received his BA at New Haven in 1941, the same year that John Crowe Ransom published *The New Criticism*, the book that certified the movement's family name. Briefly posted to the Harvard law school, Angleton set sail for the London office of X-2 in 1943.

Angleton, chief of CIA counterintelligence from 1954 to 1975, followed Pearson into the most secret of secretive intelligence specialties and was thus unable to speak unguardedly for decades. Fictional clones have been eager to do his talking for him, however. Gaunt, nearsighted, Angletonian characters addicted to poetry and cigarettes are legion in intellectually invested spy fiction, from Norman Mailer's *Harlot's Ghost* (1991), to William F. Buckley's *Spytime* (2000), to Stieg Larsson's *The Millennium Trilogy* (2005–7).[5] (Two of the Pound-quoting, nicotine-craving Angleton's actual nicknames at the CIA: "the Poet" and "Virginia Slim.") Ironically, Angleton first came to Pearson's attention by creating custom forums for public self-expression. While still an undergraduate, too busy reading and writing modernist verse to attend classes, he worked to raise a pair of little magazines from scratch.[6] The first was *Vif*, French for alive or quick, a plush journal for "those at American Universities who love the French language" (qtd. in Holzman, *James* 12). Angleton assumed the position of *Redacteur en Chef* by plying a background unusually cosmopolitan even among Yale Francophiles. Born in 1917 and raised, like Pound, in Idaho long enough to claim frontier American roots, Angleton had moved to Mussolini's Milan with his businessman father, who shipped him yearly to sub-Etonian English public schools. His mother, Carmen Mercedes Moreno of Mexico, contributed his middle name, Jesus, pronounced with a soft Spanish

"J," along with other reminders of a cross-border ethnicity that Angleton's wife alternately described as "Chicano," "Latino," or "Aztec," a non-WASPy trace her husband concealed at the Company (Holzman, *James* 8–9). (While Hoover may have feared that the head of the FBI was part black, Angleton knew that the chief of CIA counterintelligence was Mexican American. In both cases, expertise in double agency was energized by awkward private allegories of racial doubleness.) For *Vif*, Angleton wrote oracular French-language verse in offset fragments, imitations of "Mélange Adultère de Tout" (1920) and the rest of T. S. Eliot's francophone imitations of French symbolism. There may be a coded reference to interracial mélange in Angleton's overtly erotic poem "Caresse Primordiale" (1939), in which a "Trait de pinceau," or a trace of the paintbrush, reveals the impure fruit of knowledge (l. 1).

The fruit of Angleton's second act of journal raising is better remembered, praised from afar as "the *ne plus ultra* of little mags" (Victor Navasky, qtd. in Whittemore 339). If another American master spy edited a small-batch modernist poetry journal important enough to be reprinted for libraries in the 1970s, the proof is hidden.[7] With assists from poet-classmate Reed Whittemore and a back-page ad from the *Kenyon Review*, Angleton unveiled the first issue of *Furioso* in the summer of 1939. Its intent was to ignore, furiously, the apprentice narcissism of the college literary magazine, and to create instead what Librarian of Congress Archibald MacLeish described without condescension as a "new magazine of Poetry" on *Furioso*'s first-ever page (1). Ezra Pound, e. e. cummings, and William Carlos Williams were inveigled into the inaugural issue, drawn by Angleton's lecture invitations and the chance to offload material such as Pound's "Introductory Text-Book," four barely connected quotations from John Adams, Thomas Jefferson, Abraham Lincoln, and George Washington, a rickety Mount Rushmore pointing to the coin and credit obsessions of *The Cantos*.

Before Angleton decamped to OSS, *Furioso* had printed fully cooked poems by Lawrence Durrell, Charles Henri Ford, Marianne Moore, Dylan Thomas, and Wallace Stevens. The two crucial English influences on the American New Criticism, William Empson and I. A. Richards, became repeat contributors and inspirational touchstones. Both Englishmen are reverently invoked in "A Primer for Modern Poetry," a review of Cleanth Brooks's *Modern Poetry and the Tradition* (1939) that stands as a civil *Furioso* manifesto. "We hear a lot these days about the modern critical revolution," declared Andrews Wanning, Angleton's favorite Yale teacher, yet "the essence of that revolt lies in the discovery that it is possible and proper for a poet to mean two differing, or even opposing things at the same time" (23). The New Critical appetite for ambiguous meaning became the consuming habit of *Furioso*. It bolstered Angleton's close friendship with Empson, the author of *Seven Types of Ambiguity* (1930), a logic-chopping deployment of intensive "verbal analysis" the future CIA officer hoped to re-publish with a New York house (Holzman, *James* 22). Though Angleton had no luck in persuading Empson to report for a Yale professorship during the Battle of Britain, he eventually succeeded in bringing the anatomy of ambiguity home to U.S. counterintelligence.

The utility of New Critical close reading in routine counterintelligence work is not, in truth, all that ambiguous. "Sensitivity to pattern is essential in detecting deception," submits William R. Johnson, one of the few CIA men to venture a signed primer for students of counterintelligence, or "CI," for short (9). This sensitivity is whittled to a fine point, he continues, in those "studying English poetry" (9), the New Criticism's somewhat parochial master genre. "It is no accident," insists Johnson, yet another spy-product of the Yale English department, that several of the best "CI officers in World War II were drafted into that war from positions as critics of English literature. They had been trained to look for multiple meanings, to examine the assumptions hidden in words and phrases, and to grasp the whole structure of a poem or play, not just the superficial plot or statement" (10). As a happy result, "the multiple meanings, the hidden assumptions, and the larger pattern of a CI case were grist for their mill" (10). In the event that "I catch [CIA trainees] studying Brooks and Warren's *Understanding Poetry*," Johnson confesses, "I do not instantly send them off to the firing range. I tell them to go read Cleanth Brooks on the 'language of paradox,' because CI is the act of paradox'" (10). Johnson's commentary, an explicit drafting of New Critical brands and techniques into CIA service, is the sort that makes close reading seem redundant. The same man who led the Saigon CIA station as the final overloaded helicopter escaped the U.S. Embassy here recommends Cleanth Brooks for the Company syllabus, with the proviso that counterintelligence puts paradoxical language into paradoxical action. Postwar English majors, soaked in *Understanding Poetry* but itching to *do* something with their grasp of poetic irony, needed only to apply to Langley.

Johnson's confidence that multiple, contradictory meanings are the common coin of the literary critic and the counterintelligence agent incongruously stemmed from an anxious source. The little magazine boss–turned–espionage chief who recruited Johnson from academia to the CIA—none other than James Jesus Angleton—arrived earlier at the intersection of counterintelligence and New Critical paradox, searching for safe passage as his literary-critical orientation assimilated his anticommunism. Surveying the Soviet threat after World War II, Angleton developed the approach to counterintelligence that provided the basis of Johnson's notion of CI as "the act of paradox." Nearly "in his own language," Angleton called this approach "'the practical criticism of ambiguity,' a phrase derived from the titles of two of the most influential texts of formalist criticism, Richards's *Practical Criticism* and Empson's *Seven Types of Ambiguity*" (Epstein 84). According to William H. Epstein, the sharpest theorist of the secret agency of Cold War English studies, Angleton toiled throughout his CIA career to replicate the successes of the Double-Cross system, only to trip over fresh ambiguities with each practical step. Steering U.S. counterintelligence through the gloom of the Cold War, "he was never sure if he had a superior source, an unpenetrated agency, and a controlled network of double-agents" (85). Lacking these conduits of reliable counterespionage, even the most sanitary U.S. counterintelligence on enemy intelligence could not be ruled out as Soviet counterintelligence (or make that hostile Soviet "counter-counterintelligence," if the matter remains too clear). Cold War CI was therefore less a complex system of palpable double-crosses than a prismatic reflection of self and doubled-self, other and doubled-other, all identities subject to confusion with their opposite numbers. Spying on spies now required unnerving treks though "a wilderness of mirrors": so Angleton liked to put it, stealing a line from T. S. Eliot's poem "Gerontion" (1920), the mini–*Waste Land* and New Critical mainstay later recited at the CIA legend's funeral (Winks 327).

Given the collapse of counterintelligence certainties following the Good War and the Double-Cross system, Angleton's continued recourse to Richards and Empson first among the New Critics was far from arbitrary. Brooks and his southern American comrades tended to celebrate quasi-mystical, last-stand harmonies stabilizing structural tensions within the best-made English poetry. For example, in William R. Johnson's preferred Cleanth Brooks essay, "The Language of Paradox," otherwise known as the first chapter of *The Well Wrought Urn* (1947), the very distinction between scientific and poetic statements is premised on the latter's achievement of nonlogical "fusion," a final, intuitive welding "together [of] the discordant and the contradictory" (18). In distinction, Richards's *Practical Criticism* (1929) admits en route to its reformist pedagogical program that the "omnipresent ambiguity of abstract terms . . . may well appear to present insuperable difficulties for the speculative apprehension of the world" (322). Empson's *Seven Types of Ambiguity* (1930) ends closer to the creeping epistemological crisis where Richards, his Cambridge tutor, begins. The "most ambiguous" variety of ambiguity "that can be conceived," Empson pronounces, is a seventh and ultimate type in which "two opposite meanings defined by the context . . . show a fundamental division in the writer's mind" (192). In Empsonian ambiguity's purest form, the discordant and the contradictory in language remain unsynthesized in the creator as well the beholder.

In Angletonian ambiguity, for its part, Empson and Richards's doubts about self-consistent meaning are amplified by the specter of Soviet infiltration of the sign, heightening the suspicion that ambiguity's empire could overcome the most studious spy-reader. Seen through Angleton's darkening lens, the contradictions of the CI wilderness of mirrors thus often remained insurmountably divided. Norman Pearson's compromise between historical positivism and southern formalism no longer dominated the way from Yale English to the profession of counterintelligence. Now required on the road between New Haven and Langley was a deregionalized New Criticism reattuned to tenacious ambiguity—ambiguity spotted in abstract language, in applied CI, in their many meeting points, in most everything but the unalterable moral difference between U.S. and Soviet camps. Defined anachronistically, CI under Angleton therefore felt its way past Pearson's compromise to a patriotic approximation of deconstructive criticism. Fiercely attached to the foundations of anticommunism yet persuaded of the relentlessness of semiotic difference, the Angleton way of reading pre-echoed aspects of a later formalist Yale School, the Americanized deconstruction of Harold Bloom, Paul de Man, Geoffrey Hartman, and J. Hillis Miller, all fascinated, too, with the restless deferral of unmixed meaning. By the late 1970s, humanist critics of Yale's deconstructive "Four Horsemen" had classified the quartet's accent on the undecidability of texts as a reinvention of Empson's wheel, a derivative eighth type of ambiguity. By the late 1980s, the discovery of de Man's anti-Semitic journalism had inspired defenders of the Yale School to advance desperate cases for deconstruction's inherent resistance to totalitarianism (Lehman 209–43). Whatever the wisdom of these intellectual shifts in Angleton's direction, his Empsonian and antitotalitarian anticipation of Bloom and company underscores the fluid border between New Critical and deconstructive concepts in practice.

The effects of Angletonian ambiguity on the daily operations of CIA counterintelligence are clearer. Angleton's reading of the pervasiveness of Soviet infiltration led to the extremes of the "Great Mole Hunt," a remorseless search for communist traitors inside the CIA. Before his suspicious hermeneutic was deposed, Angleton had accused most CIA Soviet division officers of selling themselves to Moscow; he had discounted the word of every actually existing Soviet defector and Soviet–turned–U.S. double agent. Even the break between Moscow and Beijing had been dismissed as a pseudo-reversal within a Soviet "master plot" (Weiner, *Legacy* 275–76). As judged by an in-house CIA historian, "the Poet" had descended into an unreliable narrator of "loose and disjointed" scenarios, a thinker "whose theories, when applied to matters of public record, were patently unworthy of serious consideration" (qtd. in Weiner, *Legacy* 276). For all this, Angleton succeeded in retaining his position as the mastermind of CIA counterintelligence until the congressional revelations of 1975, the "Year of Intelligence" that J. Edgar Hoover died in time to avoid. The reign of the Poet happened to coincide with a twenty-year stretch in which, as far as we know, the CIA went unpenetrated by a single Soviet spy or U.S. turncoat (Weiner, *Legacy* 277). Even dangerously paranoid readers, it appears, can frustrate real enemies.

Reading Like an FBI Agent

Thanks to the shared seriousness of their anticommunism, James Jesus Angleton eventually became J. Edgar Hoover's best source and liaison at the CIA (Weiner, *Enemies* 177). None of his willingness to work with the FBI could have been predicted in the 1940s, however. While briefly hitting the books at Harvard Law, the young Angleton was visited by a G-Man hungry for enlightenment on the politics of high modernism. An "F.B.I. agent came to my study in Cambridge," the Poet informed e. e. cummings and his wife, Marion, in a manic 1943 letter (Angleton, letter). "Tell me all, [the agent] says," narrated Angleton. "Sir, I replied. Firstly I can rely upon my Constitutional rights and tell you nothing or I can deceive you or I can tell you all; but if I tell you all it will take a long time." "Tell all," the Bureau caller insisted, perhaps familiar with the lengths necessary to illuminate his subject of interest, Ezra Pound, then under investigation for radio diatribes on behalf of fascist Italy. Angleton obliged with a whirlwind tour of the less offensive highlights of the Pound era: "I take him from 1913 through all of Ezra's poetry—through the books of the Cantos explaining and declaiming. He writes in one notebook and then in several. I don't talk of Fascism or Jews—I talk of Jefferson and Social Credit, The New English Weekly, and America I love you. Thank you Mr. Angleton, he says, and looks hopelessly at his notebooks." In the afterglow of the tutorial, Angleton expressed a certain pity for the inferior critic-spy: "I only wanted to give you both sides of the picture, I said." Yet Angleton's recital hits its punch line in the comic inadequacy of the G-Man's response to word of Pound's complexity: "Poets are funny and art's a strange thing he replied and left" (29).

As it happens, the FBI agent's own record of his interview with Angleton has survived, and it is both less oblivious and less deferential to its source than Angleton could predict. According to Michael Holzman, Angleton's Bureau visitor was independently conversant enough to recognize that "the young law student admired Pound's poetry, agreed with his political theories, but found the latter distorted by Pound's prejudices against Jews and International Bankers, thought the radio broadcasts that were the grounds for the treason indictment incoherent, and agreed both to testify and to name names" (*James* 30). Angleton's impression of the G-Man's clueless philistinism anticipates the CIA line on the tribe of "Fordham Bronx Irish." Yet it also manages to ignore all signs of a crafty intelligence behind an overt insensitivity—the possibility of a mask of puzzlement composed to elicit, say, a long, incriminating monologue on the poetic and economic bases of Pound's handcrafted fascism. An intermittently cagey critical intelligence tied to the hypothesis that "Poets are funny and art's a strange thing" is in fact a hallmark of FBI reading, the Bureau's generic alternative to Angleton's practical criticism of ambiguity.

In logical distinction to the New Critical drift of CIA reading, FBI reading shares a fair bit with the most relevant academic criticism of its pre–New Critical origin. And this academic criticism in turn shares its condition of emergence with the FBI's Radical Division, the incubator of *Radicalism and Sedition among the Negroes as Reflected in Their Publications*, the founding rock of Hooverite commentary on African American writing. The American university's study of American literature, Gerald Graff details, owed its start "in large degree to the impetus of . . . superpatriotism" circa 1918–20 (130). Fred Lewis Pattee, the self-described "Penn State Yankee" who may have been the first regularly appointed professor of American literature anywhere, recalled "a kind of educational Monroe Doctrine" emerging during World War I and its antiradical aftermath, a nationalist tropism, both expansionist and inward turning, demanding "for Americans American literature" (qtd. in Graff 130). In the thick of the fight, Pattee's own *Century Readings for a Course in American Literature*, an artifact of the Red Year of 1919, reasoned that

the new insistence upon the teaching of Americanism in our schools and colleges, especially in those that for a time were under government control, has brought the study of American literature into the foreground as never before. More and more clearly is it seen now that the American soul, the American conception of democracy—Americanism—should be made prominent in our school curriculums as a guard against the rising spirit of experimental lawlessness which has followed the great war, and as a guide to the generation now molding for the future. . . . [This textbook] is, if the compiler has done what he considers to be his duty, a handbook in Americanism." ("Introductory Note.")

Hoover's Radical Division library never replaced pilfered anarchist literature with reeducational copies of *Century Readings*. But Pattee's unintended echo of the Hoover library's well-publicized civic commitment—protecting "against the rising spirit of lawlessness which has followed the great war"—confesses an eccentric harmony between early FBI counterliterature and the earliest Americanist faculty. As Pattee suggests, literary-critical schools "under government control" possessed few instincts or resources with which to resist the teaching of Americanism through a foregrounded national literature. On land grant campuses such as Illinois, Michigan, and Pattee's Penn State, quads were refitted as troop training grounds, and required courses were redesigned as studies in war issues. At Berkeley, a dutiful great books class rematerialized as a massive outdoor lecture, "Books on the Great War" (Graff 129). Mobilized for the war effort, the higher literary learning rendered service as a semifederal bureau of patriotic aesthetics, like the FBI proper a state-sanctioned advocate of mental Americanism.

Which is not to suggest that the FBI proper failed to respect the increasingly professionalized, expert-centered habitus of the academic literary critics doing their duty to Americanize. In 1916, three years prior to Pattee's genteel enlistment in the Red Scare, the Modern Language Association (MLA), the leading professional association of U.S. college literature teachers, amended its constitution to emphasize the centrality of specialized "*research* in the Modern languages and their literatures" (qtd. in Graff 121; emphasis mine). The previous formula, emphasizing "study" in the modern languages, was dropped because of its inadequate aura of rigorous scientific investigation. By 1929, the MLA president proclaimed, ex cathedra, that "henceforth, our domain is research" (qtd. in Graff 121). The FBI, its scientific crime laboratory and degreed G-Men proud symbols of a parallel professionalization of U.S. criminology, could only applaud the MLA's shift. Quietly wading into the battle between expert literary scholars and knowingly amateurish "critics," FBI ghostreaders chose the side of literary fact over value, hard-nosed investigation over sensitive appreciation; when in literary-critical uniform, G-Men would be "research men" as well. Choosing sides among the ranks of the conquering scholars, meanwhile, Bureau critic-spies favored the emerging literary historians over the lingering linguistic philologists, the former more likely than the latter to join Pattee and other early Americanists in establishing the pedigree of modern U.S. texts, the Hooverites' major counterliterary target from the Harlem Renaissance through the Black Arts movement. While the philologists' ideal audience remained the multilingual *internationale* of letters, the then-new historians promised to contribute "scientific consciousness and spirit" to the project of assessing American writing's allegiance to the American conception of democracy (Morize 3).

The Bureau handbooks issued to novice G-Men integrated no excerpts from Harvard professor André Morize's *Problems and Methods of Literary History* (1922), the standard manual for would-be professional literary historians between the world wars. Even so, first-wave Bureau ghostreaders give the impression of having memorized the methodological catechism of this "Guide for Graduate Students" (Morize i). "[T]hose who have faith in literary history," Morize began, "ask merely that the critic . . . be sure to criticize established facts, indisputable chronology, correct texts, exact biographies" (2–3). The creative interpretation of modern U.S. texts, valued even by the buttoned-down FBI, was obliged to wait on the accurate assembly of the literary-historical record. The longest memorandum included in the very first FBI file on an Afro-modernist author, Claude McKay's, thus establishes a definite, chronologically organized, heavily annotated bibliography of the subject's oeuvre from the June 1921 article "How Black Sees Green and Red" to the August 1923 poem "May Day—1923" (U.S., Federal, McKay, 26 Jan. 1924). While it fails to compare minute differences in reprintings like a variorum edition, the same memo exactly transcribes four poems first printed in radical magazines: the FBI would unleash its networked counterliterature only against the "correct texts" of the enemy (26 Jan. 1924). Getting a "closing stanza" just right seems no less pressing than reproducing the red meat of a captured letter from the African Blood Brotherhood, Harlem's groundbreaking Black Marxist sect (26 Jan. 1924).

While other habits of the McKay file were abandoned along the way, the effort to fix indisputable chronologies and exact texts remained key to FBI reading throughout the Hoover era. Ralph Ellison's file, for example, offers a fuller bibliography of his apprenticeship as a Marxist author-editor than either he or most of his academic critics have been willing to pursue in the byways of the left press. For Bureau ghostreaders, *Invisible Man* is but one entry in a numerated literary record linking the procommunist Ellison of the Great Depression to the anti-"Brotherhood" Ellison of the Cold War: "2. The 'Champion' of Nov., [*sic*] 1937, page 3, reflects one RALPH ELLISON as a member of the Editorial Board. The 'Daily People's World' of 12/15/54, page 7, reflects one RALPH ELLISON as the writer of an article," and so on (U.S., Federal, Ellison, 29 April 1958). Richard Wright's file and a few dozen others enhance an inclusive list of publications with multiple copies of the most influential. In addition to several separate facsimiles of the essay "I Tried to Be a Communist" (1944), creative nonfiction explaining Wright's break with party discipline, his Bureau dossier takes in the whole issue of the *Atlantic* in which the piece first appeared. The soundness of the many politically freighted restatements of Wright's text could thus be checked against an original kept at the Seat of Government (U.S., Federal, Wright, 5 Aug. 1944). Langston Hughes's file encompasses literary documents of a more collectable sort. Amid a big sea of red tape is the original text and setting of "Song of Spain," a Hughes poem featured in the anonymously published *Harvard Communist*, ten cents a copy in the Depression year of 1937 (U.S., Federal, Hughes, 7 Oct. 1942). On the relatively few occasions when Bureau bibliography goes wobbly, the culprit is often the Cold War push for Total Literary Awareness. Amiri Baraka's file accurately checklists his complicated small-press publication history until an overeager special agent blesses a tip that " 'The Black Bohemians: A Study of the Contemporary Negro Intellectual,' is to be published soon" (U.S., Federal, Baraka, 30 Nov. 1964). Here, the Hoover-mandated craving for forward-leaning literary intelligence undermines the related desire for established literary-historical facts.

When early FBI reading leaps from the compilation of the literary record to the heights of interpretive criticism, it stops short of embracing the author-sidelining doctrine of the intentional fallacy and other features of the CIA–New Critical exchange program. Angletonian spy-reading, a distant influence on the likes of M. A. Jones and the G-Man reviewer of *A Raisin in the Sun*, begins to affect Bureau ghostreaders with the second Red Scare, the era when the CIA began to exceed the FBI in elite anticommunist cachet and the American New Criticism grew from Southern Agrarian credo to national collegiate champion. By contrast, the interpretive dimension of early FBI reading, a method born during the first Red Scare, reflects both the Bureau's place atop a federal intelligence hierarchy free from Ivy League intruders and the biographical imperative of pre–New Critical historicism. Once "indisputable chronology [and] correct texts" were nailed into place, Morize instructed, the professional literary scholar was bound to turn to the building of "exact biographies" (2–3). "[T]he relation between a book and the personality of the author," he explained, "is of necessity so close that a knowledge of the work presupposes complete acquaintance with the antecedents and the life of the writer" (210). Unlike some other Morizean seekers after biographical exactness, FBI readers did not deserve Cleanth Brooks's charge that unreconstructed literary historians favored unironic "investigations of [the] ironic question, 'What porridge had John Keats?' " ("Keats's Sylvan Historicism" 153). But just barely.

The FBI file of Keats admirer Claude McKay, for instance, avoids inquiry into the Jamaican-born poet's inspirational breakfasts but exhibits the brusque, gossip-hungry diligence of biohistoricism, the infatuation with the literary artifact imagined as an exotic confessional. Chosen from dozens of McKay poems, the sonnet "America" (1921) is seen to deserve exacting transcription but is stripped of all rhetorical friction. A straightforward political moral—support your local America-hating alien—is thought clear as day and attributed to McKay the (political) man. Glossing "America," the poem, is thus the information that the poet arrived "at Ellis Island, New York, as a witness in behalf of . . . a British Communist" within months of its publication (26 Jan. 1924)—McKay's verse had failed the test of Americanism necessary for both FBI approval and canonization in Pattee's *Century Readings*. The affected principle of FBI interpretive theory debuts, loudly and explicitly, earlier in the same file. Given that the "[s]ubject is apparently a poet, or at least he has written considerable verse," McKay's "views, beliefs, principles, et cetera may properly be inferred from quotations from his writings" (26 Jan. 1924).

Avoidance of the "biographical fallacy" thus remained a task for CIA tradecraft, and the only thing New Critically ambiguated by the FBI's slant on McKay's sonnet was its author's patriotism. As early Bureau ghostreaders knew them, professional poets, or at least authors of considerable verse, were less rather than more liable than casual writers to avoid declarations of personal judgment. Contra Cleanth Brooks, a serious poem thus operated as a elaborate but candid profession of its author's faith, perhaps the furthest thing imaginable from a dramatic "speech, a consciously riddling paradox, put in the mouth of a particular character, and modified by the [work's] total context" (Brooks, "Keats's Sylvan Historicism" 154). As late in the day as the Larry Neal file, in fact, a poet's work as such—publishing quotable confessions of "views, beliefs, principles, et cetera"—was seen to render him or her especially "useful to the extremist cause in the event of a revolution" (U.S., Federal, Neal, 11 Jan. 1972). Even as Neal's file suggests the sympathy of some G-Men for the New Critical notion of the nonauthorial speaker, other ghostreaders submit the suspect's literary employment as sufficient reason for advanced "Category III" status in the latest version of the Security Index (11 Jan. 1972). When the FBI administered the final political Rorschach, poets would not be allowed to hide behind their dramatic characters.

By the 1950s, the twofold literary-critical language found in the Larry Neal file, both biohistorical and novice New Critical, would not seem exceptional in FBI reading. On the academic side of the fence, Norman Pearson's OSS-shaping compromise between Yale formalists and historicists had been reinvented as the predictable drift of U.S. English departments. Professorial "critics and scholars of the forties and fifties," Gerald Graff narrates, "reached an understanding that reconciled their conflict at a certain level: critics dealt with literary works 'in themselves' in an 'intrinsic' fashion, while historians dealt with their 'extrinsic background.' More precisely, criticism and history were but aspects of a total activity of literary understanding, so that potentially any professor was both critic and scholar, and the sense of the necessary antagonism between these functions began to wane" (183). More and more FBI ghostreaders joined their academic colleagues in serving as switch-hitting critic-scholars: the Bureau agents assigned to produce works of COINTELPRO minstrelsy, for example, employed front-line extrinsic scholarship to author believable literary imitations, perhaps the closest form of close interpretation. Thanks to the nature of the "extrinsic background" postwar FBI ghostreaders researched when pursuing the scholarly side of their dual roles, however, very few would have won tenure prior to the mainstreaming of academic Marxism. With the blessing of FBI headquarters, they calculated quanta of ideology with a precision usually confined to students of Raymond Williams, Terry Eagleton, and Fredric Jameson.

FBI criticism reached its quasi-Marxist height after the Great Depression, the heyday of American literary communism. When self-consciously proletarian contributors to the *Anvil*, *New Masses*, and *Modern Quarterly* were reexamining their commitments in the wake of the 1939 Hitler-Stalin pact, FBI ghostreaders were only getting acquainted with the basics of radical aesthetics. It was not until the 1950s, in fact, that Bureau critics produced their best efforts to measure the politics of literature. Demystifying the political leanings of texts in every genre, FBI criticism then came to mirror that variety of Marxist literary analysis both closest to the concerns of mainline literary historicism (text X echoes political tendency Y) and most likely to devolve into political prescription (text X *should* echo political tendency Y). The pile of Bureau observations on the writing life of Frank Marshall Davis is a graphic case in point. When polishing his weekly fiction-and-opinion columns for the *Honolulu Record*, Davis, a Communist Party member since the 1940s, might have predicted a line-by-line hunt for fidelity to mainland communist policy. He would not have guessed, however, that the critical agency doing the hunting would be the FBI. A summary document by Honolulu special agent Leo S. Brenneisen includes four tight pages comparing lines from Davis's "Frank-ly Speaking" series with the "CP Line" supposedly engraved in the *Daily Worker* and the party's theoretical journal, *Political Affairs*. These file pages are neatly divided into two columns: excerpts from Davis fill the left-hand side with condemnations of white supremacy and nuclear testing in the Pacific, while apposite quotations from the communist press, matched paragraph for paragraph with Davis's arguments, fill the right (U.S., Federal, Davis, 14 May 1956) (see figure 3.1).

HN 100-5082

Excerpts from "Frankly Speaking"	CP Line
"The Southern Negro is shoved down into an inferior position from birth. He is fed the doctrine of White Supremacy with his mother's milk. He learns that Southern culture demands that he live Jim Crow even before he learns his ABC's. He knows that jail or the grave waits for those who dare defy the system. . . .	has had to pay real attention to this powerful international condemnation of Jim Crowism. For it has proved disastrous to Wall Street's pretensions of democracy, pretensions which are indispensable for its program of imperialist aggression . . . "
"There is no doubt in my mind that the demonstrations against her had the blessing of the trustees and many university officials. From press reports, a high proportion of those taking part in the demonstrations had no connection at all with the school. There was token protection for Miss Lucy, sure, but there was obviously no genuine determination by officials to insure full safety and bust up all attempts at hoodlumism.	". . . In this respect the aim of the Washington government is not to abolish Jim-Crow segregation and persecution, but simply to smooth over some of its most scandalous features, so that it will not stand out so obnoxiously and be such an intolerable stench in the nostrils of the democratic forces of the world. . . "
"Gov. James E. Folsom, highest elected state official, sided with the racists by refusing to send National Guardsmen to the campus to maintain order and by issuing a solemn comment on sociology which would have been hooted at as ridiculous even in the Stone Age.	". . . we must explain to the workers and other democratic forces in other countries the very limited character of the government's anti-Jim Crow actions, such as the desegregation order of the armed forces, the Supreme Court's school desegregation order and the like. We must point out strongly the continuing reality of the Jim-Crow system. . ."
"Folsom declared it was the conclusion of himself and several million servicemen who have traveled all over the world that 'it is normal for all races not to be overly fond of each other' and said he considered the demonstrations 'a result of such feelings.'"	(William Z. Foster, "Notes on the Struggle for Negro Rights," Political Affairs, May 1955, pages 32, 37, 39.)
(Issue of February 9, 1956, p 8).	". . . Officials of both South Carolina and Virginia have defied the United States Supreme Court to abolish segregation in their states. And behind a smoke-screen of vicious racism and threats of anti-Negro violence, the Deep South states are holding out for their right to exercise local option on the U. S. Constitution."

- 5 -

FIGURE 3.1: One from column A and one from column B: FBI ghostreaders graphically match the words of Frank Marshall Davis to the Communist Party line. (Courtesy of the FBI.)

Nowhere else is the notion of a writer's plagiarism of the party line presented so symmetrically.

Calvin Hernton's file offers something similar: an FBI informant's bluntly ideological assessment of the early poems "The Lynchers" and "The Poet," an interpretive exercise designed to override Hernton's protective unwillingness to "make any statements verbally which [might be] considered . . . outright revolutionary" (U.S., Federal, Hernton, 30 Aug. 1955). Reproduced line by line, irregular free verse margins included, Hernton's two poems are judged to be "revolutionary" and "somewhat revolutionary and certainly follow[ing] the

Communist Party line," respectively (30 Aug. 1955). Deep in the Cold War, FBI reading could thus resemble an efficiency expert's idea of a Marxist original. The Marxian strain in Bureau criticism was nonetheless capable of acknowledging a lack of communist inspiration. Among the last contributions to George Schuyler's file is a stand-alone review of one of his dismissive articles on the civil rights movement, "Road to Ruin." "The article starts in a provocative and prophetic manner," notes critic-spy F. J. Baumgardner, but ultimately fails to support the Bureau-favored claim that African American invective was "communist-inspired and directed" (U.S., Federal, Schuyler, 26 Sept. 1963). Even here, however, Baumgardner joins the makers of the Hernton and Davis files in assuming that the end of literature is to teach, delight, and convert. In the same postwar era in which FBI ghostreaders drew on New Critical lesson plans, they thus also opened themselves to the charges that New Critics aimed at literary Marxists, among the Bureau's sworn foes. G-Man readers steered free of Keats's porridge but probably earned a share of the blow Cleanth Brooks directed at "the Marxist critics [who] have merely revived and restated the didactic heresy," the sacrilege of reading for message over method (*Modern Poetry* 47).

In the last analysis, however, perhaps the most distinctive trait of FBI criticism had little to do with its catholic acceptance of both Marxist and New Critical prompts. The racial diversity of the modern American texts on which Bureau critic-spies practiced their craft distinguishes FBI reading from Brooks as well as from most of his whipping boys. More important here, this diversity also sets FBI reading apart from CIA reading under Angleton's sway. Thanks to the same black renaissance that the Bureau brought to the attention of federal authorities, occasional courses such as "Literature by Negro Authors" appeared in the catalogs of African American colleges beginning in the mid-1920s (Renker 92). The road to consistent self-study was slow, however. A 1933 survey commissioned by the *Journal of Negro Education* discovered only four black postsecondary schools in which specific courses on the Negro in literature were regularly staffed (92). In ironic contradiction, FBI reading emerged from the patriotic bonfire of 1918–20 eager to tackle African American writing. In this respect, if none other whatsoever, the FBI's various Book Review sections outpaced the language and literature programs of America's historically black universities. The Bureau's commentators on McKay and his New Negro comrades instead followed the lead of the more independent African American critics who advised Harlem's renaissance on its own metropolitan ground. When not seeking this renaissance's demise, FBI ghostreaders walked in the advanced path of Alain Locke and W.E.B. Du Bois, literary intellectuals hounded by the Bureau but as free as their Bureau antagonists from English department squeamishness over non-English pedigrees.

James Jesus Angleton, another English department escapee, brought Pound and Eliot, Richards and Empson, to bear on the CIA's "practical criticism of ambiguity." The FBI sampled both of the American poets above, plus the bulk of the interwar African American canon, when shaping its practical alternative. The result was a studiously political biohistoricism reflecting some of the basics of pre–New Critical academic criticism, yet adaptable enough for pluralistic retraining after World War II. Over the entire lifecycle of FBI reading, Hoover's critic-spies approached black texts with seriousness as well as malicious intent—and this when the many editions of Fred Lewis Pattee's *Century Readings for a Course in American Literature* neglected to include a single work by an African American author,[8] and the vast majority of university critics of all backgrounds failed to dare any different. For all its offenses, the Bureau never misread African American literature as an invitation to relax critical standards. The ham-handed weaknesses and surprising strengths of FBI reading of this literature, an interpretive practice born in the first Red Scare and reborn in the second, were very like the strengths and weaknesses of FBI reading in general.

Critics behind the Bureau Curtain: Meet Robert Adger Bowen and William C. Sullivan

One limitation of FBI reading was its modest public profile. With the possible exception of J. Edgar Hoover, his specifically literary-critical identity to be discussed later on, the Bureau produced no strong alternative to James Jesus Angleton, the master spy whose inscrutability never hid his standing as the master theorist of CIA reading. (William Faulkner's brother Murry, an FBI agent and the author of the biographical study *The Falkners of Mississippi* [1967], qualifies as a challenge to Angleton only for inherited proximity to modernist greatness.) For this reason, among others, the Company's reputation as a keen interpreter of textual difficulty far exceeds the Bureau's. When Don DeLillo's postmodern classic *White Noise* (1985) ushers in a blurry minor character who "reviewed fiction for the CIA, mainly long serious novels with coded structures" (203), the satire of misapplied academic energy can thus count on cynical smiles of recognition. On the contrary, reviewers of fiction for the FBI await their poet and remain spies stranded in the cold. The anonymity promoted by Hoover's insistence on interchangeable, instantly transferable G-Men masked living ghostreaders; the after-the-fact concealment caused by FOIA name removal has reinforced these readers' obscurity after Hoover's death. In the wake of this double burial, reconstructing the literary-critical lives and opinions of the majority of trench-level Bureau readers means indulging in sociological approximation.

But approximate we will. While most G-Men were not, in fact, Bronx-born Irish-Catholics educated at Fordham, it is the case that few arrived at agent training class with advanced degrees from the Yale English department. Unlike Angleton, who never took to law school, the typical Bureau agent of the Hoover era entered the FBI as a successful white male law graduate seeking a patriotic plum job. (Shockingly, Hoover had entered the Bureau with the identical resume.) Between 1924, Hoover's first year as the FBI director, and 1933, the first year of FDR's Bureau-friendly first term, the proportion of special agents with legal training rose from 30 percent to 74 percent (Schmidt 46). Into the 1960s, G-Men with JD degrees, now an even greater share of the force, actually earned more than CIA agents with PhDs (Richard Gid Powers, *Broken* 259). As the social convulsions of the late 1960s isolated "Bureau think" from the higher reaches of American university culture, Hoover's institution was obliged to hire some recruits with undergraduate degrees alone, provided they also had three years (the traditional time en route to the JD) of relevant work experience (259). Even then, however, a BA remained a requirement, which meant that most FBI agents continued to chase literary bad guys with help from at least a smattering of college-level requirements in English and composition. Given this general level of acquaintance with academic literary criticism—better than nodding but short of expert, often flavored by subsequent legal education in statutory interpretation—the inclination of FBI reading to refract the most ordinary science of university English departments makes good sense.

But what were the sources of the attention Bureau critic-spies showered on African American texts, the aspect of FBI reading that breaks most sharply with academic norms? How did the same ghostreaders who impersonated bibliographers before the Cold War and marxisant New Critics after it learn to train their lenses on Afro-modernism during both periods? Fortunately, demographic summary is not the only tool available to help answer these questions. Two of the most influential FBI ghostreaders of the Hoover era, Robert Adger Bowen and William C. Sullivan, broke the rule of anonymity by arranging posthumous but richly self-expressive accounts of their literary attitudes. Bowen's and Sullivan's accounts each challenge facets of Hoover's narrative authority but only intensify the engagement with African American speech and literacy he made Bureau writ. Read in succession, their confessions disclose that FBI reading was molded, early and late, by supervising critics convinced of their intimacy with the grain of the black voice—an intimacy gauged in part by its hoped-for superiority to Hoover's.

Robert Adger Bowen, Hoover's senior by twenty-seven years, was born in 1868 in Charleston, South Carolina, the cultural capital of the recently defeated Confederacy. Practiced in measuring his life by the tape of the director's, he managed to survive his FBI boss by several days, dying in a Greenville, South Carolina, nursing home in May 1972. In his final decade, challenged by the civil rights movement, a still-alert Bowen began donating his papers to the Clemson University Library. There they now sit in the same building as the Strom Thurmond Institute, a public-affairs foundation that aims to "initiate conversation and promote movement on critical issues" without delving too uncomfortably into its namesake's split biography: filibustering arch-segregationist by day, distantly generous father of a black daughter by night ("The Strom Thurmond Institute"). Bowen's commentaries grapple with the contradictions of southern history more readily than the Thurmond Institute. His unpublished poems on the civil rights struggle, for example, insult the Klan while lamenting passive resistance as doomed social climbing ("Sit in: kneel-in: lie-in: butt-in: / Yet he'll never, never get in" ["The Barrier" ll. 1–2]). For their part, several of the outlandish contradictions of Bowen's life history cohere only within the peculiar logic of the FBI's war with Afro-modernism.

The third son of one of the leading white families of South Carolina, its fortune derived from slavery, shipping, and banking, Bowen was raised in old country homes with titles, mythologies, and large black staffs: Rivoli, his parents' plantation; Ashtabula, his grandparents'; and Woodburn, the homestead of other maternal relatives. Among Bowen's keepsakes at Clemson is the original of his father's 1865 contract with Rivoli's liberated slaves, obliging them to remain on the plantation all week, to abstain from liquor, and to keep "strange freedmen" off the place, signed with row upon row of stylized "X"s ("Work Agreement"). The birth of a postemancipation sharecropping "system in which contract was the vehicle of servitude" and ascetic constraints were "inseparable from peonage" could not be clearer (Hartman 126). Despite his attachment to Rivoli and its sister estates, however, Bowen's moment in the literary sun derived from an early decision to enjoy his family's plantations at a distance. Following the near-completion of a BA at the College of Charleston, Bowen attended Washington and Lee in Virginia and then began graduate work in English at Cornell. New York City beckoned after a much-praised thesis, "Nathaniel Hawthorne as Author." (He and his seeming polar opposite, Norman Holmes Pearson, a Yalie, Yankee, and OSS officer, shared this Americanist focus as graduate students, part of their common road to U.S. government work.) Beginning in 1894, Bowen pursued an urbane literary life as a private secretary to critic-architect Russell Sturgis, one of the founders of the Metropolitan Museum of Art. After some success placing stories of the South, he moved on to publishing work at Macmillan and D. Appleton and Company, Bowen the editor most pleased with his role in cultivating Ellen Glasgow, Joel Chandler

Harris, and Horace Traubel's editions of Walt Whitman. (Bowen, who wrote animated, not-for-publication poems on male beauty and kept clipping files on both Whitman and Oscar Wilde, was not alone in addressing turn-of-century homoerotic desire through a private discipline of aesthetic appreciation.)[9] Publishing under his own name, Bowen reviewed occasionally for the *New York Times* and briefly made the best-seller list with *Uncharted Seas* (1912), a novel of southern nostalgia and cosmopolitan opera the *Chicago Post* praised for "hold[ing] all the glamour of romance and the possibility of truthfulness at the same time" (qtd. in Bowen, "Press/Book Reviews").

A follow-up novel successfully balancing truth and romance failed to materialize, and Bowen did not resist when invited to enter federal government service during the First World War—or rather, as he liked to remember the timing, under the influence of "the Espionage and Trading with [the] Enemy Act" (Bowen, "Robert Adger Bowen Anthology" 1). "It is I," Bowen boasted in corrective testimony meant for Clemson, "who named . . . 'The Bureau of Translations and Radical Publications,' " the federal agency that became the FBI's literary-critical outpost in Manhattan in the thick of the Hoover Raids ("Bureau of Translations" 1). There he supervised "some forty-five translators of foreign languages and suspected English language publications," acting as Hoover's New York reader-in-chief, the chairman of a kind of federal literature and language department before the founding of the CIA's national campus (1). And there he prepared the decisive draft of *Radicalism and Sedition among the Negroes as Reflected in Their Publications*, preliminary versions of which he curated for posterity. "To J. Edgar Hoover," Bowen pridefully noted, *Radicalism and Sedition* "remained a 'masterpiece'"—as it should have, reflecting Hoover's observations and prejudices so scrupulously (Marginalia). "The response of the alien and Negro press," Bowen admitted, "was not so flattering" ("The Re-Action" 1).

With the initial transfer of the "Bureau of Translations" from the Post Office to the Justice Department, Bowen was summarily rehired as an FBI executive, "the first, as J. Edgar Hoover used to tell [him], who had ever become so without application" (Bowen, "Bureau of Translations" 1). With the closing of the New York translation office in 1926, Bowen was abruptly reappointed once more, this time as a more typical, nose-to-the-street FBI special agent. The shift made for a poor fit: Bowen had no legal training and little aptitude for hands-on learning as a detective. His new Bureau supervisors complained of his habit of spending hours with the *Daily Worker*—the remnant of a special ghostreading assignment from Hoover—and rated him a below-average agent with no "investigative instinct" apart from "radical press matters" (U.S., Federal, Bowen,

31 Mar. 1928). Bowen thus retired to South Carolina, permanently, in 1928. Though he lived to be more than a hundred, he never forgave Hoover for his unprepared demotion. His personal copy of *The FBI Story*, Don Whitehead's authorized Bureau history, is sprinkled with remedial marginalia and tipped-in typewritten sheets. Bowen's commentary includes the complaint that "I never had one word or hint as to the duties of a Special Agent or way of executing them. I was simply turned loose in New York to do or die" (Marginalia). Critical notes on another FBI publication intimate that Bowen's disappointment with Hoover was partly romantic, perhaps related to the arrival of Clyde Tolson as the director's constant companion circa 1927: "I might add certain personal experiences of my own, VERY personal, but they would only prove that J. Edgar Hoover himself is no God but a very human man" (Bowen, Notes).[10] Bowen nonetheless exploited his reassignment as an ordinary field agent by attempting his own *FBI Story* before Whitehead's. Bowen's "Memoirs of a G-Man," serialized in the *Greenville News* in 1940, suffered from the absence of the snappy, hard-boiled prose of *Persons in Hiding* and other Hoover-signed FBI narratives of the era. "To those whose duty it is to carry out the purposes of the Federal Bureau of Investigation, the FBI of the present-day G-Man," Bowen undramatically began, "there come many experiences that serve as an unexpected fillip to their work, such fillips sometimes proving more agreeable in the retrospect than at the time of happening" ("Memoirs," 12 May 1940). Less absorbing than intended, and never republished in book form, Bowen's G-Man memoirs at least allowed him to pose with a Hoover-style fedora (see figure 3.2) and to break minor professional confidences to recall his side specialty in "negro cases" [*sic*] ("Memoirs," 28 July 1940). Defending his close contact with black sources before a jury of white South Carolina readers, Bowen explained that "the agent goes where the nose of his assignment leads him, and grins and bears what he may not exactly fancy. It is all in the day's work, and there is no room for the welcher" (28 July 1940).

The main event in Bowen's transformation from Palmetto State squire to New York G-Man was his work in the vineyards of turn-of-the-century race literature. Bowen came to the attention of D. Appleton, and thus to the counterliterary Bureau of Translations, because of his accomplishments as a white purveyor of black dialect fiction—as a lesser Joel Chandler Harris, to be exact, the Georgia-born writer whose Uncle Remus tales Bowen the editor helped to retain in the Appleton catalogue. Harris's initial collection for Appleton, *Uncle Remus, His Songs and Sayings* (1880), secured an international reputation for his mock-native informant and encouraged the professionalization of U.S. folklore collecting in the 1880s and 1890s. As Bryan Wagner reports, the new American

FIGURE 3.2: Robert Adger Bowen saved every installment of his 1940 column "Memoirs of a G-Man," with this page from his scrapbook also including a poem he published in the *Greenville News* ornately praising English resistance to Nazi Germany. (Courtesy of the *Greenville News* and the Clemson University Special Collections Library.)

Folklore Society had no doubt that the Uncle Remus stories, harvested on the Turnwold Plantation outside Atlanta, possessed scientific worth as reliable transcriptions of oral literature (116). Like Harris before him, an editor of the *Atlanta Constitution*, Bowen's first dialect tales appeared in the pages of southern newspapers and likewise aimed to enlighten the region through its unheard black bards. Bowen's "Miss Ang'la: A Story," for example, was serialized in the

Birmingham Age-Herald in 1889. From Harris, Bowen borrows the narrative framing device of a wily black raconteur addressing a young white charge: in Bowen's variation, a faithful Mammy, installed in "[t]he drawing-room of an old country mansion in South Carolina," unfolds a midnight yarn to a sleepy schoolgirl ("Miss Ang'la," 20 Oct. 1889, 14). "It's a long sad tale an' I much doubt if I can tell it straight," Bowen's Mammy begins, "what wi' the heaviness o' my heart, an my memory bein' only middlin'" (14). The narrator's memory is far better than that—photographic, in fact—as is Bowen's recall of the nonphonetic indulgences of Harris's version of black speech. Malapropisms are rare, though outbreaks of unscientific Remus-style eye dialect are too many to count (always "wuz" for "was," for instance).

Where Bowen's Mammy breaks from Harris's Uncle is in the political allegory of her recitation. Remus tells animal fables advancing postbellum national reconciliation to a white narratee born from his parents' South-North marriage. Mammy, on the other hand, fluently weeps her way through a grotesque tragedy of white southern inbreeding. The Miss Ang'la of Bowen's title, a pale country heiress with "a wealth o' quaint conceits" (14), fatally marries an uncannily sympathetic young man who just happens to be her long-lost brother. Attempting a Poe-fed gothic minstrelsy, Bowen's nightmare of the incestuous madness of old southern houses resists Harris's advocacy of the New South, a regional ideal culturally distinct but socially interconnected with the rest of a rapidly industrializing nation. Bowen's structurally similar 1892 fiction "Miss Em'ly: A Story in Dialect" again sidesteps Harris's New South boosterism while seconding Harris's speculations on the African retentions in African American English. "For the sake of intelligibility to those not 'to the manner born,'" runs Bowen's opening note, "it has been necessary greatly to emancipate the African element from the language of the following story" (Bowen, "Miss Em'ly" 8). Bowen's text proceeds to upend Harris's promotion of interregional marriage, sealed in the Remus stories through the blessings of an avuncular black minister. Miss Em'ly, the darling of another "old country mansion in South Carolina" (8), is mistakenly shot through the throat and killed by a Master Echard, a jealous young lover who stems from a related planter family, "j[o]ined too, yuh see, on ole Missis's side" (10). Or so says another Bowen Auntie who has placed her boss in a listening attitude "on dish yere sofa" and lightly Africanized the voice silenced in Ang'la's prime (8). Once more in a Bowen dialect story, a masterful African American narrator is the sole productive issue of an inbred South Carolina plantocracy, a people of refinement prone to erotic fratricide. Bowen's meek have inherited the memory of the southern past and the language of the southern future, though not the ownership of the southern earth.

By the time of his last major dialect story, "A Case of Conjur," published in the New York–based *Appleton's Booklover's Magazine* in 1905, Bowen's African American speakers are inheriting their own small plots, but losing their right to the last word. The story's title advertises a change of rivals: Bowen now directs his intertextual animus at Charles W. Chesnutt, the African American stenographer-turned-author whose first book, *The Conjure Woman* (1899), employed dialect literature to comment bitingly on Harris-built legends of interracial understanding. Bowen draws not only on Chesnutt's interest in conjure, the syncretic African American folk magic otherwise known as hoodoo, but also on his inversion of Harris's narrative framework. In "A Case of Conjur," as in the seven stories of *The Conjure Woman*, the frame narrator is a white speaker of Standard English. In Bowen's revision, this narrator is not a cousin of Chesnutt's clueless midwestern carpetbagger, but a manor-born southerner comfortable with the ways of plantation folk. Two kernels in the first sentence establish the narrator's conversance: his ironically familiar explanation of unfamiliarity, and his reference to Bowen's ancestral home. "Scarcely more than a name to most, a name to conjure with," Bowen punningly begins, "you might have lived on Rivoli a lifetime and never have seen her, unless you had gone to her cabin" (Bowen, "A Case" 468). The "her" in question is Aunt Lithy, a confidence woman whose inability to set foot outside her cabin and toil in the fields is revealed to be the product of common laziness, not incapacitating hoodoo. "Don' talk tuh me 'bout her cunjur," concludes Lithy's rival among the field hands (469). "I al'ays did 'spec' it wuz jes' pure cussed lazy" (469). Chesnutt's couching of conjure as a pretext for everyday resistance is here played for laughs, with even Lithy getting the joke. By the end of her case study, she has learned to work diligently to preserve a cabin of her own, investing a combination of sweat equity and demonstrative Christianity similar to the home-loving heroine of Zora Neale Hurston's later story "Sweat" (1926). Bowen looks with some cynicism at Lithy's final "religious ecstasy" (475) yet is willing to place the folkloric substance of his challenge to Chesnutt in her mouth. Retraining herself to love labor, Lithy sings "Little David play on yo' harp" and "I'se troubled wid 'flictions jes' like Job" (471), quoting directly from two African American spirituals the young Bowen had phonetically rendered in a song-catching chapbook now preserved at Clemson. The FBI administrator proud to have drafted *Radicalism and Sedition* thus prepared to specialize in black dialect literature—and to monitor the New Negro press—by writing up "Negro Songs as [S]ung at Protracted Revival Meetings in South Carolina near the Rivoli Plantation," a manuscript record of twenty-four hymns and spirituals learned at the vernacular taproot. His ear to the same ground cultivated by his father's sharecroppers, Bowen collected black folksongs like a Dixiefied John Lomax—like a Lomax, that is, whose ethnography could accommodate revision as a tool of state surveillance.

If "A Case of Conjur" begins with a rejection of Joel Chandler Harris's narrative framing, it returns to Remus's turf in this reliance on African American art harvested at first hand. It is one of the less authentic incidents in "Conjur," however, that clinches its selective alliance with Harris: Bowen has an ex-slave call without reluctance for the intervention of the white police. At a height of frustration, Aunt Lithy asks her master to sic "de sherrif" on her skeptical rival (474). Like Remus before her, Bowen's black mouthpiece blesses the state's claim to a monopoly on punishment; her master's authority has become a means to access the clout of the sheriff, and with him, the higher power of state law. As Bryan Wagner notes, Harris's original Uncle Remus sketches, published in the *Atlanta Constitution*, "treated many of the same topics as the crime reporting that appeared in adjacent columns" (154). The *Constitution's* early, urban Remus "was not merely contiguous to the newspaper's campaign for the police—he was part of it," endorsing the argument, akin to Bowen's "Case of Conjur," that "modern policing was compatible with white supremacy" and crucial to a rationally governed post-Reconstruction South (154, 145).

Harris's mature, rural-set Remus sketches recast his storytelling uncle as "a mouthpiece not for the newspaper, but for the black tradition" (Wagner 159). In one important sense, however, this change is less than meets the eye, since these best-loved tales of Uncle Remus also seek to sell the legitimacy of state authority to a national market including southern citadels of local control. "By superannuating the trickster tradition," or situating Remus's animal allegories of slavery in a past accessible only through his gaudy imagination, Harris's best-selling books reaffirmed his support for the police power (168). The temporal distance of the Br'ers and brutes depicted by the rural Remus, actors on a supposedly premodern/African stage of development abandoned in the moment of telling, "reinforced an old mythology about the origin of modern government by threading it through a new idea about black culture" (168). "Demonstrating the [black folk] tradition's obsolescence became a means to explain not only" this culture, Wagner concludes, "but also why it was sensible to have a state with enough muscle to keep the peace"—a well-policed modern state supplanting the rough justice of Remus's captivating yet brutal state of nature (168).

As abstruse as it may seem, Wagner's counterintuitive analysis of Remus's collaboration with modern law enforcement can help to clarify Bowen's reception of New Negro writing at the FBI's Bureau of Translations. When Bowen marveled at the "marked ability" of Claude McKay and other New Negro authors while preparing his crucial draft of *Radicalism and Sedition*, he confronted his own obsolescence in the bargain ("Radicalism" 1). The FBI's initial black literary targets loomed as gravediggers of his vocation as an imaginative writer, honed within a dialect school in which quasi-learned impressions of plantation "bombast and nonsense," the New Negroes' linguistic nemesis, were the coin of the realm (1). As Wagner reminds us, Bowen also had reason to marvel over the New Negroes' breach of the alliance between black dialect writing and white police power—an alliance Bowen had endorsed in his late dialect work, and had lived out, as literally as possible, in his career transition from a purveyor of the African element in American speech to a counterliterary executive of the FBI. When the literature of McKay and similar New Negroes invoked the sheriff only to defy his insults to black manhood, they broke faith with a politics of dialect that Bowen had made into a personal playbook. Bowen the author-cop, like Hoover the cadet-detective, thus battled the New Negro with a heat that reflected insufficient distance. Hoover had drilled like a New Negro and worried that he might have genetic reasons to become one. Bowen had written as an Old Negro and feared that his disobedient New Negro heirs might be too articulate to resist. Among his papers destined for Clemson, Bowen indeed kept a hand-typed copy of McKay's poem "The Tropics in New York" (1920), a Harlem migrant's restatement of Bowen's fate as a South Carolina–born Manhattanite (Typescript copy of "The Tropics").

Another virtual heir of Bowen, William C. Sullivan, the overseeing Bureau critic-spy of the Black Power era, was less a New Negro than an imaginary inheritor of New England abolitionism. Though unfamiliar with Fordham and the Bronx, Sullivan was born Irish Catholic in small-town Bolton, Massachusetts, in 1912. He never forgot his immigrant parents' dairy farm, unlike Bowen's Rivoli, a place claimed by its owners' own hard labor. At the FBI, this rural start made Sullivan the rare agent who could tell Sam Noisette, Hoover's doorman and amateur landscape painter, the direction real cattle grazed while on a hill (Sullivan, *The Bureau* 124). Sullivan's upbringing also left him the single Hoover deputy who openly declared himself a liberal Democrat and an admirer of Hoover's hated Kennedys. Friends and enemies at the Seat of Government saw him as a gifted hothead able to move up while standing out, an exception to Hoover's rule of rewarding agents who looked the part. Mark Felt of "Deep Throat" fame, the Watergate hero who vied with Sullivan as a possible Hoover successor, described him as surprisingly "short, barely over the minimum height of 5 feet 7," a "pale and drawn" character who dressed professorially in rumpled jackets (102) (see figure 3.3).

Sullivan's professorial eloquence was also exceptional and drew from his pre-Bureau stint as a Bolton public school English teacher. "He was extremely intelligent and well read," admitted Felt (Sullivan, *The Bureau* 101). "An excellent conversationalist," Felt affirmed, the unconventional Sullivan did not absentmindedly neglect to ingratiate "when it served his purposes. He had expansive writing talent and cultivated Hoover shamelessly with flattering letters and unusual gifts from his travels" (101). When Bureau executives needed book recommendations—or, in FBI White House liaison Deke DeLoach's case, an entire unread library to decorate the shelves of a new home—they turned to Sullivan first (Sullivan, *The Bureau* 63). By the bitter end of his FBI career, kept from restructuring the Bureau after Hoover's death, Sullivan regretted that he had failed to keep to his early academic path. "My only ambition was to join the faculty of a small New England College," he recalled in his posthumous memoir, *The Bureau: My Thirty Years in Hoover's FBI* (1979), a book polished by journalist Bill Brown, and calculated, like Bowen's papers, to set the preferred record straight (15). Sullivan took the Internal Revenue Service job that brought him to the attention of Hoover, this memoir confesses, mainly because of its location in Boston, a university-rich city that "gave me the opportunity to take courses toward my graduate degree" (15). Improving on his low honors BA from American University, he excelled in wide-ranging masters coursework at Boston College (receiving a solid A in "Communism—A World Revolution," for example) but then quit a graduate program in education short of finishing his thesis (U.S., Federal, Sullivan, 9 May 1941). Again like Bowen, Sullivan was a professor manqué, a graduate student tempted by world war and practical ambition to apply his overgrown literacy to the business of federal intelligence. Like ABDs before and since, he reinvented himself as the most professorial type in a nonprofessorial bureaucracy, an advocate for what he called "incisive, independent, free, probing, original, creative thinking," a value of the modern liberal arts downplayed in FBI agent training class (Sullivan, *The Bureau* 243).

Hired away from Boston by the FBI in 1941, Sullivan was asked to lead six different field offices in three years, an ordeal visited only on Hoover's elect, before winning an invitation to national headquarters in 1944. He was shuffled from job to job in Washington as well, finally landing at Domestic Intelligence. Amid the many reassignments, Hoover persisted in tapping Sullivan's literary ability. If Bowen was the most significant inside-the-Bureau ghostwriter of the Hoover Raids, Sullivan became the presiding ghost of Hooverism's Cold War pinnacle. As Sullivan portrays it, *Masters of Deceit* (1958), the two-million-seller officially "written by the Master of Deceit who never even read it," was his idea "in the first place" (*The Bureau* 90, 89). Better documented is Sullivan's place on the six-person Bureau team that did the book's basic research and composition, producing what was, in Sullivan's

FIGURE 3.3: William C. Sullivan (*right*), a G-Man with a literary attitude, chats with Yale University president Kingman Brewster Jr. (*left*) before addressing a convention of editors and publishers in 1970. (Courtesy of and copyright © Bettmann/Corbis.)

estimation, "a serious study of communism" in its initial drafts (91). Unhappy that *Masters* was "watered down and jazzed up prior to publication" under Hoover's name, Sullivan proposed a more substantial academic follow-up (91). *A Study of Communism*, employed as a high school textbook from its publication in 1962, was something closer to an exclusive Sullivan effort, underlining in tight-knit, logical prose the party's recruitment of "the youth of our nation," also recruited to read the book in social studies class (Hoover, *A Study* 169). Sullivan was happier with the results of this second try, and initially willing to hide his light under Hoover's signature. His misgivings over Hoover's dependence on ghostwriting boiled over, however, in an internal Bureau memo reproduced in Sullivan's memoirs. The dispatching of two experienced FBI "espionage specialists" to New York to complete *A Study*'s glossary, he protested, gave even the most politically ambitious literature too much credit (*The Bureau* 92). Sullivan did not refuse Hoover's $250 bonus in lieu of royalties after *A Study of Communism* followed *Masters of Deceit* onto the best-sellers lists. But the FBI's campaigns to hype both books with planted reviews and bulk purchases struck him as unseemly echoes of communist propaganda.

Thanks to the techniques of lit.-cop federalism, the "FBI could make a best-seller out of a calculus textbook" (91).

Sullivan's sometimes-uncomfortable ability as a ghostwriter was put to good use in his involvement in FBI counterintelligence; as with James Jesus Angleton, "CI" was a natural home for his suggestible literary intellect. Next to Hoover, Sullivan was the Bureau executive most responsible for the FBI's fiction-filled counterintelligence programs, or COINTELPROs, against "white hate," "black hate," and the New Left. Named supervisor of the Domestic Intelligence Division in 1961, Sullivan hung on to his job by showing the COINTELPRO manager's paramount skill: "he could orchestrate these campaigns without getting caught" (Richard Gid Powers, *Secrecy* 424). Had Sullivan had his way in the Nixon years, however, he would have come closer to exposure. Keeping pace with the Plumbers, Nixon's off-the-books secret service, he reearned his nickname of "Crazy Billy" by forcing Hoover, no life partner of the ACLU, to thwart Sullivan's plans for illegal surveillance. Sullivan hoped to investigate every single college student in the SDS, 100,000 strong in 1968, until Hoover confined matters to the Weathermen (those who cannot teach, spy, perhaps) (Richard Gid Powers, *Secrecy* 461). Despite its name, the notorious "Huston Plan" of 1970, an abandoned Nixon administration end-run around FBI and CIA autonomy, was principally drafted by Sullivan and proudly reprinted in his memoirs, another item on an imposing CV of covert writing (453). In the case of the Huston Plan, it again came down to Hoover to override Crazy Billy's advocacy of bugging, mail opening, and burglary. "Use of this [last] technique," Sullivan conceded, "is clearly illegal," but it "is also the most fruitful tool and can produce the type of intelligence which cannot be obtained in any other fashion" (qtd. in Sullivan, *The Bureau* 255–56). Where his approach to counterintelligence was concerned, the FBI's outstanding liberal Democrat hustled to overtake Hoover on his right.

Nonetheless, Sullivan's memoirs paint his stewardship of the FBI's postcommunist COINTELPROs as the instinct of a passionate antiracist. *The Bureau* launches its account of Sullivan's COINTELPRO career with the investigation of "white hate." Disturbed by the FBI's tendency to watch and wait over scenes of violence against civil rights protestors, Sullivan reached for one of his favorite weapons—interoffice correspondence—and "wrote a strong memo to Hoover recommending that the responsibility for investigating the Klan be shifted to my division, Domestic Intelligence" (126–27). Hoover was persuaded by Sullivan's vigorous prose, but it was Sullivan alone, *The Bureau* asserts, who made the decision to redirect counterintelligence techniques originally perfected against the Communist Party "toward investigating the Klan" (128).

"'Let's destroy these fellows, just utterly destroy them,'" Sullivan instructed the Bureau's Mississippi office (129). The Catholic Sullivan understood the Klan's horror at first hand, he insisted. "I first encountered the Klan when I was a boy in Bolton," his memoir testifies, "and I can still vividly recall the fiery coffins the local anti-Catholic Klansmen burned as a show of strength in our town" (127).

Sullivan's identification with persecuted African Americans is not confined to his tale of the anti-Klan COINTELPRO and becomes one of his memoir's organizing motifs and ethical alibis. The Hoover Bureau's sorry number of full-time black employees, Sullivan pronounces, is "one of the most shameful chapters in the history of the FBI," and a special hindrance to his Domestic Intelligence unit (*The Bureau* 269). Pressed by a lack of black special agents when investigating "black hate," Sullivan is forced to do their job himself. Camouflaged in torn clothes and dark stubble, he claims, he infiltrated the 1968 Poor Peoples' encampment in Washington. Spotting Stokely Carmichael while disguised as a once-again-poor person, Sullivan approached him directly "and asked how he thought things would work out" (133). Carmichael, "well composed" and, in contrast to Sullivan, "neatly dressed," answered without hesitation, none the wiser about sharing attitudes with the FBI man charged to do him in (133). Sullivan's enjoyment of the game of almost-black-like-me also affected his jarringly flexible evaluation of Martin Luther King. "I personally believed that . . . King could be the leader his people needed," *The Bureau* attests (135). "I was one hundred percent for King" at the start of the 1960s, Sullivan continues, "because I saw him rising as an effective and badly needed leader for the black people in their desire for civil rights" (135). For all practical purposes, however, Sullivan's opinion of King followed Hoover's into the gutter. By 1964, Sullivan had declared King a compromised and expendable figurehead, while still assuming the intimacy required to nominate a replacement. "I suggested to Hoover that we recommend to the NAACP that another man be chosen as successor to King," Sullivan's memoir notes (144). "Dr. Samuel Riley Pierce, a black educator with a fine reputation" whom Sullivan had recommended "to lecture in my place when I could not accept an offer," was his ideal King-in-waiting (144). Pierce, a lifelong Republican, eventually served as President Ronald Reagan's only African American cabinet member. But it was Sullivan who most coveted the role of Negro spokesperson, and most relished the chance to lecture in King's place. He did not envy King's violent death, of course, which Hoover detailed him to investigate. Sullivan too, however, was fatally shot, killed in an eerie 1977 hunting accident before he could present scheduled testimony to the House Select Committee on Assassinations. Bulletins from TASS, the official Soviet press agency, blamed an FBI-CIA plot against a man who knew too much (Bill Brown 10).[11]

Sullivan lectured King from a position inside the civil rights movement in his lasting contribution to U.S. race-writing, the letter anonymously mailed to King's home in 1964. Though the only extant copy of this letter was discovered in Sullivan's locked office files, and he admitted his possible involvement under oath before Senate investigators, his memoir declines to confirm his authorship.[12] "I did not know about the unsigned note until it surfaced in the press," he improbably pleads (*The Bureau* 142). Sullivan's memoir nonetheless reveals the King letter as a typical Sullivanism, a recognizable product of the rhetoric produced where the COINTELPRO hard line met Sullivan's pretentions to blackness. When the letter informs King that "you know you are a complete fraud and a great liability to all us Negroes," it employs much the same register as the memoirist who self-assuredly chooses a second King for the NAACP (Sullivan, letter to Martin Luther King Jr.). As we saw earlier, Sullivan's willingness to tell a King he was a discredit to their common race became common procedure among FBI authors of COINTELPRO minstrelsy, imposters who began writing in numbers in 1967. Sullivan would personally approve some of the racial counterfeits drawn up in various field offices, the Bureau's master "COINTELPRO—Black Hate" file thus vacuuming up documents addressed to Sullivan when not meant for Hoover.[13]

Looking back from the suicide letter into the deeper Bureau past, Sullivan's possessive investment in blackness seems like an endorsement of Robert Adger Bowen's, and like evidence of a tendency of FBI master critics to stalk black expression with jealous intensity. In distinction to James Jesus Angleton, the Anglophilic Mexican American "Poet" who ruled CIA counterintelligence, both Bowen and Sullivan considered themselves the most articulate of white American Negroes. Graduate students and literary hopefuls–turned–Bureau men of letters, both wrote in Afro-America's guise as well as Hoover's. Bowen's papers and Sullivan's memoirs are somewhat less accessible than the evidence of Angleton's poetry habit. But these collections manage to reveal that FBI literary criticism was steered at its start and finish by Hoover ghosts attracted in similar measure to the literary life and the life of black America. Bowen's staff at the Bureau of Translations and Radical Publications had solid, career-building reasons to know of his interest in the New and Old Negro. So did Sullivan's subordinates in the field offices expected to produce the literature of the "black hate" COINTELPRO. Both of these Bureau master critics knew enough to please and challenge Hoover with news of the latest extremes of Afro-modernism. Considered through the working lives of Bowen and Sullivan, FBI literary criticism emerges as a competitive field of local professional incentives as well as a dialogue with parallel academic trends—a field of career contention among G-Men, to be precise, that rewarded the study of African American writing.

Ask Dr. Hoover: Model Citizen Criticism and the FBI's Interpretive Oracle

While Robert Adger Bowen and William C. Sullivan, winners on the field of FBI criticism, were practically unknown outside the Bureau, news of the FBI's knowledge of African American literature still trickled out from the file cabinets on Pennsylvania Avenue. Members of Congress including George H. W. Bush, another Yalie bound for the CIA, somehow knew and relied on the authority of Bureau ghostreading. Beyond the Beltway, more than a few Americans conceived of J. Edgar Hoover in particular as an arbiter of Afro-modernism—no match for James Jesus Angleton, perhaps, as a sentry at the border of espionage and high modernism, but all the same a dependable federal explicator. Critical inquiries could not be settled by the masters of deceit deployed as radical authors, Hoover's fans believed, but could be directed to the oracle at FBI headquarters.

Witness Langston Hughes's FBI file, five hundred pages and counting, and by World War II an archive documenting the interest of ordinary Americans in questions at the bloody crossroads of literature and politics. The principal of Bridgeport, Connecticut's, Central High School set the tone in 1944, writing to Hoover "to obtain from your organization, if it is available, information or an opinion regarding the Negro poet, Mr. Langston Hughes," scheduled to read his verse before "a typical student body that is not concerned with the Negro problem" (U.S., Federal, Hughes, 26 Oct. 1944). Answering the principal within a week, Hoover explains that while he appreciates "your interest in making this request," he cannot meet it helpfully thanks to the meddling of Attorney General Francis Biddle, his adversary at the wartime Justice Department, who "has ruled that information in the possession of this Bureau is confidential and cannot be released except upon his express authorization" (1 Nov. 1944). Hoover's Bureau had a good deal of relevant information on hand, in fact. A 1943 security investigation had uncovered the danger of "Chant for May Day," "Ballads of Lenin," and other Hughes poems of the Red Decade (28 Aug. 1943). "All of these poems make reference to the injustices of the wage earner's lot," Hoover advised the New York field office, "and in most of them there is also a reference to the workers taking over the Park Avenue section or in short, all the desirable aspects of the living of the well-to-do" (28 Aug. 1943). Hoover's desire to share

his line on Hughes's poetry—he was wrong on the number of references to Park
Avenue, but right about their metonymic character—could not be much clearer
if spelled out in his signature blue ink. Yet the director suppressed himself, as he
did in the similar case of the Richmond, Virginia, American Legion officer who
asked for "all information you [have] on this negro [*sic*] Langston Hughes," the
author of "the lyrics to a suggestive musical show called 'Street Scene' which is
now playing on Broadway" (27 Feb. 1947).

By December 1947, the month in which Soviet-backed communists assumed
control of Romania, an emboldened Hoover had shifted his tack to legally protected oversharing. Answering a query into "the noted Negro Poet" from the
black businesspeople of the Springfield, Illinois, Urban League (23 Dec. 1947),
Hoover again stipulates that "information contained in the files of this Bureau
is confidential" (31 Dec. 1947). This time, however, he also encloses one of his
latest nonclassified publications, a pamphlet titled "Secularism—Breeder of
Crime" commenting on the poem "Goodbye Christ" (1932), a swipe at religious duplicity Hughes wrote while traveling in the atheistic Soviet Union (31
Dec. 1947). Based on a Hoover lecture to a conference of Methodist ministers,
"Secularism" begins by rallying the denomination's "eight and one-half million
members" to confront a like-sized population less eager to serve as "an irresistible force for good": the "seven and one-half million . . . men and women, boys
and girls who have been arrested for an offense sufficiently serious to warrant
their fingerprints being taken and forwarded to the FBI" (Hoover, "Secularism" 1).[14] In Hoover's war between the Christian good and the biometrically
documented evil, the devil's party receives inspiration from Hughes, a genius
of "blasphemous utterances" (6). The first four stanzas of "Goodbye Christ"
become Exhibit A:

> Listen, Christ,
> You did all right in your day, I reckon—
> But that day's gone now.
> They ghosted you up a swell story too,
> Called it Bible—
> But it's dead now (ll. 1–6)

Hoover had private reasons to object to the poem's ridicule of ghostwritten infallibility, but his public objections parry Hughes's challenge to ideas of
the classlessness, racelessness, and general validity of Christianity. In a nutshell, "Secularism" interprets "Goodbye Christ" as an even more particular
and self-interested argument, partisan Sovietism in free verse hiding behind

a pseudo-egalitarian black vernacular. The poem's pretentions to the common African American touch are "a cover to conceal" communism's "real aims of undermining democracy" and true religion (7). Hughes's speaker and his political stablemates may "claim to stand for equal rights, for better working conditions, for the abatement of poverty, for the equitable division of the products of industry and for the rights of racial groups and political minorities" (7). Beneath the brave words, however, they are agents of a narrow "conspiracy against Christianity and democracy—and they know it" (7). "Goodbye Christ" is poetic confirmation that "Communism is secularism on the march," and thus the "mortal foe" of God and the Constitution, neither of which, Hoover forgets, much mentions the FBI (6). Hoover's hasty interpretation of Hughes's poem, possibly "ghosted . . . up" like Hughes's Bible, says nothing of the double-edged humor in a "[p]easant" narrator commanding "Christ Jesus Lord God Jehova" to "[b]eat it on away from here now" (l. 22, 18, 19). Anticipating the politically inverted Marxism of Bureau criticism in the 1950s, Hoover identifies the poem's radical speaker with Hughes, and Hughes with the poem alone, pigeonholing him as the lyric confessor of communism at its most sacrilegious. The crude efficiency of Hoover's reading would trouble Hughes for more than a decade, dogging him into the glare of an appearance before Senator Joseph McCarthy's Permanent Sub-Committee on Investigations in 1953, a trial during which McCarthy placed "Goodbye Christ" into the record (Rampersad 218). Thanks in part to the shadow of "Secularism—Breeder of Crime," the Cold War American right knew Hughes best as the author of an infamous blasphemy.

For a year or more, Hoover mailed "Secularism" to anyone who contacted FBI headquarters seeking insight into Hughes. The FBI director's critical opinions were thus planted across the country at taxpayer expense, reaching corners unpenetrated by the little modernist magazines. A copy of "Secularism" was sent to Springfield to answer a telegram concerning "LANGSTON HUGHES COLORED POET" (24 Jan. 1948). Another was addressed to Tempe, Arizona, bound for a correspondent who wondered if Hughes was "a poet spreading Communistic propaganda" or a legitimate artist deserving the State College's "highest degree of freedom of speech" (20 Mar. 1948). One more copy arrived in Grass Valley, California, where a homemaker had explicitly requested tips on "Goodbye Christ" (23 Apr. 1948). The boldest (and most naively appreciative) readers of "Secularism" challenged Hoover to defend his interpretive methods. An intellectually adventurous Methodist minister from Illinois, bolstered by Hughes's self-defense and the strictures of the New Criticism, argued that the text of "Goodbye Christ" was "itself . . . not evidence" of its author's opinions (20 Feb. 1948). If the intentional fallacy applied at all, he supposed, it would apply to the limit case of godless Bolshevism in the confessional mode. "Though written in the first person (as poets so often do)," the minister maintained, Hughes's poem "does not [necessarily] express his own conviction but is a representation of what those on the extreme left are thinking. I myself greatly dislike the poem but if the interpretation is what he claims it to be, then it is not evidence that he is a Communist" (20 Feb. 1948).

Hoover's controlled reply failed to question why the minister presumed an absence of speakerly irony in Hughes's self-interpreting claims. It failed to engage with the substance of the minister's arguments much at all, in fact, and instead wheeled out the kind of contextual artillery made available by FBI archivism: "You will observe that Mr. Hughes is referred to as a member of the American section of Moscow's 'International Union of Revolutionary Writers'" (26 Feb. 1948). Debate with the Bureau's critic-in-chief, this episode demonstrated, would not resemble the finicky postpublication disputes at the back of academic journals. Into the 1950s, however, private citizens suspected that "Mr. J. Edgar Hoover, Chief of the F.B.I.," possessed authenticating knowledge of African American poetry: "I was told this was written by a Negro Communist. Can you tell me if this is true?" (8 July 1954). (Hughes's "Youth" was the mystery poem in question.) Other correspondents, positively inviting government censorship, saw the director as a qualified judge of the English curriculum: "The faculty of the State Street School, Hackensack, New Jersey, is considering the adoption of a textbook published by the Iroquois Publishing Company which contains a poem by the negro [sic] poet, Langdon [sic] Hughes. . . . Would you please send to me a summary of Mr. Hughes' status as you know it . . . ?" (12 Jan. 1953). Tackling the 1960s, U.S. congressmen recruited Hoover to soothe their constituents' literary anxieties. G. Robert Watkins, Republican of Pennsylvania, wrote Hoover with the news that "I am enclosing herewith a letter from [name removed] of Newtown Square, Pennsylvania, wherein she expresses concern about a Mr. Langston Hughes" (1 Mar. 1965). George H. W. Bush, Republican of Texas, expected Hoover's help in placating a resident of his Houston district confused by the state of black theater. "I would appreciate any assistance you could give [name also removed] in obtaining the additional information he requests," the future president informed the eternal director (17 July 1970). In his own letter to Hoover, Bush's constituent described his curiosity about the "writings and connections Langston Hughes had with communists," and about something less concrete: "I seem to remember that [A Raisin in the Sun] was a highly controversial production written by a Leroi [sic] Jones and that Jones is something of a professional trouble maker and rabble rouser. If you cannot furnish information pertaining to this play and its author please advise where I might obtain such details" (8 July 1970). *A Raisin* was no rabble-rousing *Dutchman*, but Bush and his constituent rightly supposed that Hoover's Bureau possessed the tools to know differently.

"Secularism—Breeder of Crime" effectively publicized J. Edgar Hoover as a grim-faced expert on Langston Hughes. As the Bush correspondence in Hughes's file hints, however, the FBI director was consulted on a wide range of issues in African American letters, expected by some to perform the office later filled by *The Oxford Companion to African American Literature* or the *Encyclopedia Africana*. For the whole of his Bureau directorship, Hoover fed excessive respect for his knowledge by broadcasting occasional literary-critical opinions. A 1926 newspaper feature, for instance, found him intelligently speculating on the balance of romance and realism in the mystery genre, then advertised as his favorite pleasure reading.[15] "It is not necessary in fact," he assured his interviewer, "for a mystery story to stick entirely within the realities of everyday experience to be entertaining. A good one must satisfy one's sense of reasonableness and probability, of course, just as a well-constructed mystery story in the end should lead to an unexpected solution" (Britt). With less thought and greater seriousness, a 1964 law review article found Hoover flinging stock charges of obscenity at literary modernism, in some truth an "-ism" devoted to "the centrality of so-called dirty words" (Glass 209). The social pollution of pornography, Hoover declared, was worsened by "[t]he shameful contest raging among those authors of contemporary 'literature' who appear bent on determining how many suggestive passages and four-letter words can be crowded onto the bookshelves of our Nation" ("Combating" 470). Encouraged by these pronouncements as well as by Hoover's air of righteous omniscience, citizens for and against literary mystery frequently wrote him seeking interpretive pointers. The collective result of their correspondence is a critical genre we can term "model citizen criticism." In model citizen criticism, patriotic common readers—black and white—hail the repressive state apparatus that had first hailed them and expect to ignite sympathetic literary-critical action from the national police. The prospect of informed and humanized state censorship, the genre reveals, kindled dynamic readings of African American literature at the conservative grassroots. Thick deposits of model citizen criticism accordingly run through at least five major Afro-modernist files opened after Hughes's.

Quotable highlights of model citizen criticism are many, but any account of the genre's development should include the following examples. July 1944: A Mrs. Something, named redacted in FOIA processing, contacts Hoover on Liberty Bell Stationary to demand scrutiny of "Dr. Walter White," who speaks and writes "for 'The Advancement of the Colored People,'" but "is advancing them the wrong way if I can read between the lines" (U.S., Federal, White, 21 July 1944). Proof of White's negative influence is discovered in the changed behavior of the author's maid, "the sweetest darkie in the world until recently" (21 July 1944). June 1945: A self-identified colored person writing from Los Angeles urges Hoover to "get a copy of [Richard Wright's] books and go through them" (U.S., Federal, Wright, 18 June 1945). *Native Son* was damaging to the national will, the Californian warns, but "if people in Germany should get a hold of Black boy I'm awfull afraid Uncle Sam's face is going to be red for you cant rule a German if you cant rule America" (18 July 1945). This summoning of Hoover's power figures the transatlantic traffic of African American literature as a threat to national authority and possible U.S. empire. Against the grain of most scholarship on the Black Atlantic, however, the radical mobility of Wright's 1945 memoir is dreaded, not celebrated, by the letter's purportedly black author. "We colored people," Hoover's correspondent is certain, "want Richard Wright's books baned [sic]" since they "sure don't do America any good in the foreigner's eye sight" (18 July 1945). September 1945: A second disgusted reader of *Black Boy*, likely a nonblack native of Dallas, reports to Hoover that he has "looked over the book . . . supposedly written by a negro [sic] named Richard Wright," and found it "to be very racially inflammatory" (27 Sept. 1945). "[I]t is my opinion," the citizen-critic announces, "that all the publicity given to the book is being financed—either by some person or organization—for propaganda purposes: to fan the flames of dissension and seditious discontent. How Hitler (if he is yet alive) must laugh, and laugh" (27 Sept. 1945). Wright's memoir is once again deemed an objective ally of Nazi Germany—on the evidence of his self-critical essay "How Bigger Was Born" (1940), a reading Wright himself half expected years before. And Hoover's FBI is once more respectfully urged to step up its counterliterary game and better represent a warring people's desire for discerning state censorship: "Am offering this suspicion, in case you should deem it advisable to investigate the book and the financing of its extensive publicity" (27 Sept. 1945).

Cut to November 1952, and the mounting pressure of the long Cold War. A correspondent who had previously sought "employment as an [FBI] investigator or in any capacity he might serve with or without compensation" (U.S., Federal, Schuyler, 8 Dec. 1952) writes Hoover in the wake of reading the "November 30, 1952, edition of the Pittsburgh Courier, a negro [sic] newspaper (and a very honest and excellent newspaper in spite of some of its feature writers)" (29 Nov. 1952). An article by George Schuyler, the letter-writer relates, has swayed him that the *Courier* columnist is a "man of dubious loyalty and integrity in spite of his sometime anti-Communist writings" (29 Nov. 1952).

Hoover does not reply with the information that the Bureau's opinion of Schuyler is the same—Schuyler's Custodial Detention listing remains a state secret—but he does take the letter writer's advice to decline honorary membership in football star Fritz Pollard's new Negro Hall of Fame (8 Dec. 1952). May 1962: A "Southern Negro" asks for Hoover's collaboration on "a Venture" to repatriate the foremost international voice of literary Afro-modernism (U.S., Federal, W.E.B. Du Bois, 10 May 1962). W.E.B. Du Bois and Booker T. Washington were once the "most read Negroes in Africa," this correspondent explains (10 May 1962). "[S]ince Washington has passed on," the correspondent reasons, "Du-Boise [sic] is surely the Most read living Negro on the old Continent" (10 May 1962). Much as Carl Jung "took the leadership" and expanded the popular influence of psychoanalysis after Sigmund Freud's death, Du Bois has built on Washington's foundation to become the one writer capable "of directing the course of Africa" (10 May 1962). Why not, then, devise a joint "strategy to re Americanize [sic]" the potent Du Bois, and by this means to re-Americanize Africa? (10 May 1962). "Consideration was given to try this project as an individual," the writer concludes, "but considering its scope, I feel that help and direction will be needed" (10 May 1962). Hoover again proves a reserved reading partner, responding with a fistful of anticommunist pamphlets ("Shall It Be Law or Tyranny?," etc.) and the bare recognition that "[t]he motives prompting your writing me are appreciated" (22 May 1962). As the next part of *F.B. Eyes* confirms, however, Hoover's Bureau in fact cooked up its own projects to reorganize the Afro-modernist diaspora.

Cut, finally, to the beginning of the Black Power era, and the emergence of James Baldwin as one of its vocal explainers. January 1965: A troubled member of a Baptist church in Fort Worth, Texas, implores Hoover to read and ban Baldwin's *Another Country*, a novel containing "every filthy word, compound word and phrasing that could be used to portray . . . Drug addiction and Sex perversion at its vilest. Unless or/and until one has read this Book of degradation, any attempt the writer makes to describe the contents will fall short of the degenerate nature of the Book" (U.S., Federal, Baldwin, 22 Jan. 1965). The churchgoer confesses inadequacy to the tasks of plot summary and linguistic analysis but expects the Bureau to purchase and analyze copies of its own: "Many Book stores and Drug [stores] in Fort Worth . . . have it in stock, with a price of 76 cents for paper bind" (22 Jan. 1965) (see figure 3.4).

Direct acquaintance with Baldwin's froth of filthy and compound words will overpower First Amendment scruples, the writer believes: "Mr. Hoover, is there any Federal law which would prohibit the publication or the sale of this degrading Book?" (22 Jan. 1965). Hoover indeed kept on the lookout for such a law,

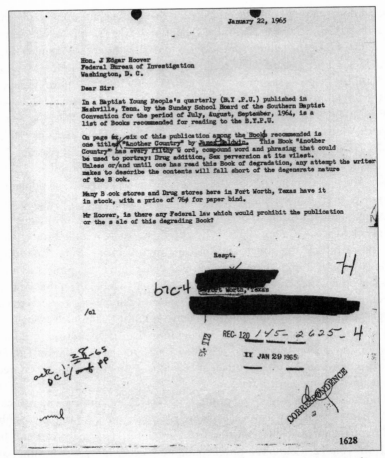

FIGURE 3.4: Model-citizen criticism calling on Hoover: A Texan requests the banning of James Baldwin's novel *Another Country* while informing the FBI where it can be purchased in Fort Worth. (Courtesy of the FBI.)

heartened, perhaps, by spontaneous donations to the FBI library. April 1965: A female civilian from Olive Branch, Mississippi, mails Hoover "one copy each of two books by the writer, James Baldwin. They are entitled 'Blues for Mr. Charlie' and 'Another Country'" (22 Apr. 1965). "Mr. Hoover," this correspondent asks in a cover letter, "will you please examine these books and advise me?" (22 Apr. 1965). Both books are prepared for easy sampling: "Due to previous references some of the pages have been turned down or marked in ink. You might use that for quick check" (22 Apr. 1965). The Mississippian's modest fantasy of Hoover personally leafing through her copies of Baldwin restates a public assumption as a private desire. A swath of common American readers imagined the Bureau director as an appropriate one-to-one audience for their thoughts and queries on African American writing. And very few of these readers conceded that Hoover might be too busy with weightier matters to reply. Defying the CIA's reputation as the mind and campus of America, citizen critics approached Hoover as an upstanding alternative to tenured experts. The FBI's Public Hero, they trusted, was capable of translating literary reception into patriotic action.

In this way, the authors of model citizen criticism pictured a responsive contact at the Seat of Government. Yet how should Hoover's correspondents be pictured by twenty-first-century critics of "reading acts," a growing population interested in the nuances of common readings? Leon Jackson, a shrewd historian of American print culture, laments the "mutual disinterest" of African American studies and that element within "the history of the book" that charts the history of reading (255). "Until recently," Jackson observes, scholarship on African American reading acts has wrestled with abstractions of readership, "what one academic hopefully called 'Probable Readers' of 'Possible Stories'" (282). Reverting to extrapolated "constructs such as the implied reader, postulated reader, or ideal reader, . . . this body of scholarship, although interesting, is more akin to rhetorical analysis than reading history" (282). State-of-the-art reading history proper, Jackson specifies, works to recover real rather than rhetorically posited readers in action. At its nitty-gritty best, it bypasses the possible readers conjured up by the authors of primary texts to concentrate on the traces left by actual readers of these texts. Challenging but not impossible to find, such traces have been recovered "[b]y looking at reading diaries, annotations, and other marks left in books; conducting interviews; exploiting amazon.com feedback; and doing fieldwork with participants in reading groups and combining the results with the theoretical insights of reception theory" (282).

FBI author files and amazon.com customer reviews would not be mistaken for each other in a police lineup. But the files just discussed are buried treasures of reader feedback that invite African American studies and materialist reading history to scrap what remains of their mutual indifference.[16] The Baldwin file and other Bureau collections of model citizen criticism contain rare direct accounts of the reactions of non-elite readers to African American texts. These accounts shed light on the historically and politically situated responses of racial conservatives—not all of them nonblack—to Afro-modernist literature. They uncover a pointed interest in this literature's image and effect in the world beyond the States; Bureau-friendly common readers, they demonstrate, noticed the far reaches of the Black Atlantic before most of their academic contemporaries. They illustrate the use of African American texts as occasions for embodied exchange with a personification of U.S. national security. For some Hoover correspondents, it seems, black literature offered a prosthetic means to reach out and touch the state, the governmental power that may favor sovereign compulsion over national fraternity, but which still profits like the nation from the imaginary communion of citizens. Most crucially, these accounts of the real readers of Afro-modernism are notable for their conviction that Hoover's FBI was an invitingly real reader as well. They envision a reading public for African American literature that includes the Bureau in its official capacity, and thus accepts the underlying object of Bureau literary federalism, the carving out of space for the state police within the print public sphere. If common readers with more liberal politics joined the midcentury Book-of-the-Month Club to display their "support for the rule of knowledge, information, and expertise" (Radway 297), then the common readers who wrote Hoover declared their preference for a well-policed state that reflected their image of mental order.

These readers, the authors of model citizen criticism, did not know that Hoover's ghostreaders read the lessons of Marxism, New Criticism, and old-line bibliographic historicism into African American texts, overseen by Robert Adger Bowen and William C. Sullivan. But Hoover's public statements and the air of interest all this interpretive activity generated inspired them to formalize responses to African American literature in progress. Under cover of the CIA's high cultural reputation, the FBI led U.S. intelligence in attracting attention to Afro-modernism—outside the federal government as well as within it. To politically attuned readers in Fort Worth and Olive Branch, the FBI's uneasy dedication to black letters was thus an open secret.

Part Four/Thesis Four

The FBI Helped to Define the Twentieth-Century Black Atlantic, Both Blocking and Forcing Its Flows

If dreams and histories of African Americans in Paris cohere into an expressive genre, that genre is a modernist indictment of racial antiquity, a moveable feast exposing the past-frozen provincialism of American apartheid. And if that genre mandates a mise-en-scène, it is the French café–turned–ecumenical black church, the Parisian quarter refuge crossed with the black diasporan contact zone. In Tyler Stovall's exemplary book *Paris Noir: African Americans in the City of Light* (1996), the social architecture of the café grounds as well as symbolizes the freedom enjoyed by "the veritable black colony" that settled the Left Bank after World War II (Fabre, *From Harlem to Paris* 5). Assimilating the everyday life of their French hosts more gamely than the earlier expatriate generation of Gertrude Stein and her Imagist pupils, these escapees from U.S. racism went native to choose carefully among terraces and proprietors, settling on the Café Tournon outside the Luxembourg gardens and, as a lesser alternative, the Café Monaco on the rue Monsieur-le-Prince, the same street on which Richard Wright, the best-connected black émigré in the city, discovered his most comfortable Paris apartment. Once dug in, the literary wing of black Paris employed its preferred cafés as both workplaces and social clubs, tending to coffee, page counts, alcohol, serious conversation, and sexual pursuit. In their double occupation of café space, transplanted African American writers proved their receptiveness to several strains and moments of Parisian café culture. Looking backward into French history, they paid their respects to the working-class cafés of the nineteenth century, humming "people's parliaments" where the realms of work and leisure overlapped in public living rooms larger than the average Paris studio (Haine 3). Looking sideways at their French contemporaries, they cemented their likeness to the postoccupation existentialist network of Simone de Beauvoir and Jean-Paul Sartre, so identified with punctual writing hours and assignations at the Café de Flore and the Deux Magots that the latter spot advertised itself as the "rendez-vous de l'élite intellectuelle."[1] No less vital for Stovall than his subjects' Francophilic adoption of café sociability, however, is their distinctive use of café space to nurture a race-proud but desegregated urbanity. "Black Americans of all descriptions, from tourists to GIs on weekend passes to students, soon learned that one could go to certain cafes and meet well-known figures," he reports (Stovall 189). Greeting Wright at work on a manuscript or on the Tournon's pinball machine, black newcomers to Paris were invited to enter what Stovall labels "a new type of black community, one based on positive affinities and experiences rather than the negative limitations of segregation, one that included a wide variety of individuals yet at the same time celebrated black culture" (xv).

So rests Stovall's self-declared "tale of romance and freedom," a candid articulation of the penchant to volunteer black Paris as a lesson to a primitive U.S. home front, a "vision of complete human liberation," as Stovall has it, "bequeathed . . . across the sea" (xvi). Yet it remains the case that the openness of Stovall's novel community, founded on the accessible pluralism of the Tournon and the Monaco, exposed it to a specter that arrived along with the modern Parisian café in the revolutionary upheaval of 1789: the political spy. With the speedup of the Cold War in the late 1950s, the black precinct or "*Rive noire*" of the city Brent Hayes Edwards honors as "a special space for black transnational interaction, exchange, and dialogue" became a space jeopardized by partition, information hoarding, and denunciation (*The Practice* 5). "Everybody thought everybody else was informing on someone or other for somebody," confessed an eyewitness of the Tournon scene, once a spot where postnationals drank off American racial masks, now a magnet for anxiety over American state sleuthing (qtd. in James Campbell, *Exiled* 91). Agnes E. Schneider, a consul at the U.S. Embassy in Paris, was said to employ fifty plainclothes informants who haunted cafés popular with American expatriates, trawling for excuses to deny passport renewals (Rowley 452). Spy stories inspired by "Spider Schneider" and more shadowy predators bounced around the Tournon's walls and stained most everyone inside. Regulars disagreed on who betrayed whom for which intelligence agency but agreed that black café intellectuals had begun to resemble the generic café waiter in *Being and Nothingness* (1943), Sartre's then-famous personification of bad faith's self-enslaving impostures.

Chester Himes, lured to Paris by Wright in 1953, rehearsed his Harlem detective fiction by investigating if William Gardner Smith, a Philadelphia-raised novelist at Agence France-Presse, received payments from the CIA. Both charged essayist and "Bootsie" cartoonist Ollie Harrington—Wright favorite, café lothario, and easygoing hard-core leftist—with treasonous undercover work. Wright expressed doubts about the loyalties of younger Smith ally Richard Gibson, another black Philadelphian on the Agence payroll, and only slightly less concern about everyone else with whom he spoke or slept. For his trouble, Wright was suspected of operating as either a diplomatic mole or a G-Man turncoat. "There is a story, a rumor about you that is going about," warned Kay Boyle, a habitué of Stein's Paris salon writing all the way from Connecticut (Boyle). The rumor had it that Wright was "working with the State Department, or the FBI, I don't know which, and that you give information about other Americans in order to keep your passport and be able to travel" (Boyle). Beneath its highly personal surface, this piece of transatlantic gossip voiced the fear that African American mobility could not be purchased without collaboration and betrayal.

The buzz Boyle communicated about Wright was half true where the State Department was concerned, though the information he bartered concerned Africans rather than African Americans. Troubled by the attraction of Soviet models in newly independent Ghana, the postcommunist Wright had submitted a confidential four-page analysis to the department advising that Kwame Nkrumah slept beneath a portrait of Lenin and awoke to apply Marxist precepts to African conditions (Rowley 437). Less confidentially, Wright defensively bragged to fellow expatriates that he "had the State Department in my pocket—they call me in for conferences, the fools" (U.S., Federal, Wright, 11 Feb. 1960). Unlike his pas de deux with the State Department, Wright threw no bones of antagonistic cooperation to Hoover's FBI, an organization he rightly assumed had tailed him since 1942. The Bureau's New York field office considered conscripting Wright as an informant after he published "I Tried to Be a Communist" in 1944, his "Dear John" letter to the party (28 July 1944). Yet Hoover warned from on high that Wright's renunciation may have come from a political position to the party's left, a fringe of the radical fringe where organized communism was not "revolutionary enough at the present time with respect to the advancement of the Negro" (4 Aug. 1944). New York agents seem to have taken Hoover's caution to heart, and Wright seems to have avoided tricksterish maneuvers to convince them otherwise: his FBI file contains no evidence of a warm personal interview or mutually beneficial exchange of texts. Even after his good-bye to the party, Wright thus kept his place on the Custodial Detention index. His relocation to France was assumed to rescind his wised-up anticommunism and to reconfirm the worst of his "past activities" (19 Feb.

1947). With the rest of the Tournon all-stars—Himes, Smith, Harrington, and James Baldwin, all fellow Custodial Detention listees—the Wright who chose exile thus remained a nominee for summary arrest and indefinite confinement. Hoover's police archives arranged to meddle in African American literary history even when that history arranged to slip U.S. national bonds.

The tangle of suspicion and surveillance at the Tournon grew into the centerpiece of black Paris with what Wright christened "*l'affaire Gibson*," or the Gibson Affair, a high-stakes game of ghostwriting under Harrington's signature. Much remains mysteriously contradictory about the affair, but Richard Gibson has confessed to its precipitating falsehood, the forging of Harrington's name on a 1957 letter to *Life* magazine condemning French rule in Algeria.[2] "Any American who thinks that France, of her own will, will grant Algeria, if not independence, at least some liberal status where seven million Algerians will not be crushed economically and militarily by a million Europeans is mad," the letter bluntly concluded (Letter to the Editor). That Gibson's deception was also an accurate disclosure of Harrington's anticolonial convictions bought little forgiveness within black Paris. Scandal centered on the forger's malicious local politics, his inviting of attention to Harrington's illegal residence in Paris (the letter was signed from the French capital), and his heightening of the guilty contradiction between black expatriate sympathy for Algerian independence and black expatriate reluctance to risk expulsion from metropolitan France. In the aftermath of the counterfeit letter, Wright drew even closer to Harrington, supposing himself a secondary victim indirectly accused of surrender to American intelligence. Fighting spy rumors with amateur counterespionage, Wright embraced the role of the film noir detective, a tarnished but ethical American antihero fittingly adopted by the French. He began assembling homemade investigative files and drafting an interrogation of thirty-one leading questions, seizing on the theory that the Gibson Affair should have been named after William Gardner Smith. "Why were Ollie [Harrington] and I linked as targets of Smith?" Wright planned to quiz Gibson and other prime suspects, "Ollie as an alleged Red and I as an alleged FBI man?" (qtd. in James Campbell, *Exiled* 202).

Harrington was not alone in mocking his friend's case of spies on the brain. But Wright's film noir/*Rive noire* posing, we will see, was catching among his literary peers, propelling a wave of author-as-detective texts within the Tournon circle. Wright's posing lost all traces of comedy after his abrupt death inside a Paris clinic in 1960, a disaster which Harrington was the first to credit, probably too creatively, to FBI agents and/or the CIA. Assassination theories aside, American intelligence was guilty of coconspiracy in convincing the residents of *Paris noir* that U.S. intelligence had penetrated their refuge. Imported

American-made "cloak-and-dagger terrorism," all Tournon factions agreed, "was poisoning the climate around the expatriate Paris community" (Harrington 23). *Native Son*'s ex-native creator, the Paris-lover who once discovered more freedom in one square block of the city than in the whole of the United States, thus lived his final French years demanding the seemingly inalienable "right to exercise my conscience and intelligence to the extent of refusing to 'inform' and 'spy' on my neighbor because he holds political convictions different from mine" (Wright, "I Choose" 2). As Wright came to see it, the residents of the Parisian hub of black transnational dialogue were pressured to snitch away the foundations of their dissenting community.

This fourth part of *F.B. Eyes* marshals the largely uncompiled evidence of FBI author files to suggest that the worst suspicions about the stakeout of Paris noir were basically correct—that Wright was not too wrong, it follows, when he darkly joked that any African American "who is not paranoid is in serious shape," at least if he or she sought literary license outside the United States during the Hoover era (qtd. in Rowley 491). Two decades before American involvement in World War II opened the floodgates of black Paris, the FBI began to influence the movements of expatriate Afro-modernists—this even as it manipulated lit.-cop federalism to nationalize itself in the mind of white America. In the French capital of black transnationalism, and satellites beyond, FBI agents and informers kept tabs on a network of black literary travelers they hoped to link by the vulnerabilities of statelessness alone. Thus this book's fourth thesis: *The FBI helped to define the twentieth-century Black Atlantic, both blocking and forcing its flows.*

The first two sections of part 4 show that this thesis bears on matters broader than the sanity of Wright's paranoia. Section 1 begins by outlining some classic and novel ideas of the state in relation to the nation, the police, and transnational literature. The state's own adventures in transnationalism, this section proposes, point up the need to better integrate the dynamics of state security and state symbolism into U.S. literary history—even and especially following this history's "transnational turn." Section 2 pursues the ship of state throughout transnational African American literary history in particular. Since the appearance of Paul Gilroy's paradigm-shifting book *The Black Atlantic: Modernity and Double Consciousness* (1993), attention to transatlantic pathways has clarified the ties of black American writing to anti-imperialist Pan-Africanism, to less radical black cosmopolitanisms, and to the print-cultural practice of black diaspora. Yet the history of FBI counterliterature advises that the revision Gilroy sparked should not discount the state power lurking on the right side of the "nation-state" hyphen—a power itself capable of thinking, feeling, and intruding beyond the nation.

Section 3 documents the first of two main means by which Hoover's state police acted on the transnational flows of the Black Atlantic: the translation of foreign language communications and the ransacking of U.S. passport applications to track or immobilize literary travelers. FBI files remind us that for a most-wanted set of the diaspora-minded, internationalism meant the prospect of global surveillance or national house arrest. Section 4 clarifies a second, complementary means by which the Bureau acted against traveling black authors: the roundabout weapon I label "state-sponsored transnationalism." When not kept from drifting, black moderns could be pushed to drift: FBI author files also contain signs of government "stop notices," orders that encouraged wandering and echoed the forced dislocation of the Middle Passage. Finally, section 5 briefly weighs the FBI's interference in transnational black literature against the CIA and the State Department's better-known international sponsorship of African American music. As the Cold War state arranged to export what it heard as the democratic abstraction of jazz, it also fought to manage the travels of black writing's social text.

The collected sections of part 4 do not succeed in exposing the Black Atlantic idea as an upbeat error. Nor do they intend to. In ironic tune with the Cold War state's selective embrace of African American art, the aim of the whole is more modest and ambivalent. In sum, part 4 highlights the rocky and fiercely resisted course of Black Atlantic modernism, the fact that the literary practice of the twentieth-century black diaspora sought liberties around an ocean tossed by state repression. As we will see, even Hoover's publicly xenophobic FBI privately conceded that this literary practice might overcome the ethnocentrism of the homeland-nation. Only rarely, however, could Afro-modernism escape the FBI's transatlantic dragnet untouched, and evade the retaliation of a traveling state police. Throughout its surprisingly wide sphere of influence, Hoover's patriotic Bureau confessed its own impatience with national limits, flashing its capacity to alter cultural worlds over and above national laws.

The State in the Nation-State; the State of the Transnational Turn

What, beyond a flag and a prayer, binds the nation-state together? When its boundaries are broken, just what is escaped? For those now driving the transnational turn in U.S. literary scholarship—foes of American exceptionalism and friends of the hemispheric, the diasporan, and the cosmopolitan; the transatlantic, the transpacific, and the archipelagic; the species-wide, the planetary, and the "deep-temporal"—the answers to both questions have usually been keyed to the nation alone.[3] The national imaginary is the cement of the nation-state, the new transnationlists generally hold. Nationhood, nationalism's concretization, is the blinding wall that Americanist scholarship must climb to perceive itself accurately as a subset, one guide of many to a postimperial World Republic of Letters. Against the grain, the view through F.B. eyes holds that these answers may be mistaken, since the nation is not always the nation-state's decisive underwriter and border enforcer. In their eagerness to flee the territory of the American Century, transnational Americanists have tended to erase the hyphen in the nation-state form, either ignoring the factor on the right side of the compound, the state, or predicting its withering with every blow directed at the factor on the left, the nation.[4] The up-armored U.S. state of the twenty-first century, however, is intent on surviving waves of economic globalization and other challenges to exceptionalist strains of U.S. nationalism; if this state has any say in the matter, postnational Americanism will not celebrate a poststate society anytime soon. Just as critical to the study of American literature is the state's interference in transnational dreams located in the deeper past: throughout most of the twentieth century, U.S. state security helped to shape the direction of U.S. literature abroad.

But what, to begin with, characterizes the state sector of the nation-state? And what does this sector contribute to the literary business of imagining communities of the familiar and the foreign? Though nationalism-weary literary scholars have not always been careful to recognize the state's relative autonomy from the nation,[5] Montserrat Guibernau expresses a consensus among political theorists when distinguishing between the state as an institution that "claims the *monopoly of the legitimate use of physical force* within a given territory" and the nation as a human group "conscious of forming a community, sharing a common culture, attached to a clearly demarcated territory, having a common past and a common project for the future and claiming the right to rule itself" (13–14; emphasis in original). States, then, manage territory by brandishing and administering the threat of authorized violence, otherwise known as exercising "sovereignty." Nations, in distinction, may or may not control the territory they collectively imagine that culture, history, and the shedding of shared blood make theirs. (Instructively, the etymological roots of "nation" reach into the Latin word *natus*, or birth, but into no word for domination [Hart and Hansen 505]. In the dictionaries of the Royal Spanish Academy, *nación* was not specifically tied to *gobierno*, the Spanish word for government, until 1884 [Hobsbawm 15].) With this difference between the state and the nation in mind, we can quickly locate examples of self-conscious nations that are not sovereign states (e.g., the Basque Country jutting across France and Spain), and vice versa, states that are not nations (e.g., Sudan before the 2011 separation of the Islamic North and Christian South).

Myth-busting theorists of nationalism have enjoyed collecting evidence that culturally integrated nations generally postdate states.[6] Most nations are modern miscellanies of invented traditions, the record shows, not human government *au naturel* or the state's primitive reason for being. No heroic excavation is required, E. J. Hobsbawm notes, to demonstrate "the actual multinationality or multilinguality or multiethnicity of the oldest and most unquestioned" European states, France, Spain, and Britain (33). It was only in the revolutionary upheaval of the late eighteenth century, in fact, that state and nation became ordinarily attached in the nation-state, with the United States, Brazil, and the rest of the postcolonial, "creole" nation-states of the New World bidding to lead the way.[7] Under the hyphenated sign of the nation-state, a national group enjoys the patent on rightful violence within a secured territory yet also expects to unify its population through "cultural homogenization" (Guibernau 14). Repurposing Étienne Balibar, we can thus say that the modern territorial nation-state fastens together a cultural "*ethnos*," a people understood as a "community of membership and filiation," and a political "*demos*," a people understood as the subject of "decision making and rights" (76).

While the native language of the state, sovereignty, and the native language of the nation, culture, may harmonize when preaching unity to the population of a nation-state, these languages remain analytically and practically distinct in many accounts. As Guibernau sees it, for example, "nation, state, and nationalism," the last the nation-focused "sentiment of belonging to a community whose members identify with a set of symbols, beliefs and ways of life," compose "a triad characterized by constant tension" (14). Appropriate to the state, Guibernau assumes, is a border-sealing pedagogy of violence best described by sociologist Max Weber, who quotably classified the state as a "compulsory association" that "has been successful in seeking to monopolize the legitimate use of physical force as a means of domination within a territory" ("Politics" 82–83). Appropriate to the nation and its sentiment of nationalism, Guibernau assumes, is a comparatively voluntary, psychologically unifying pedagogy of emotion and imagination best defined by Marxist historian Benedict Anderson. According to Anderson's well-known formula, a nation is "an imagined political community" (6). By "imagined," Anderson does not mean hallucinated. Given the nation's usual size, he reasons, a political community of face-to-face intimacy is impossible, requiring national populations to be schooled in fellow feeling through the fictions of the novel and the newspaper. To the delight of literary historians of many nationalities, Anderson touts these two products of "print capitalism" as the main training grounds of homogeneous national time, or the idea of an abstract but sturdy national community "moving steadily down (or up) history" (26).

Marxist philosopher Louis Althusser, a more orthodox revisionist than Anderson, is for some good reasons mainly absent from state-of-the-art discussions of imagined nations and transnational literatures. All the same, Althusser provides timely insight into the state violence–versus–national imagination divide—call it the Weber-Anderson gap—just outlined. Althusser's "Ideology and Ideological State Apparatuses" (1969), best remembered today for its vivid sketch of ideological "interpellation," is as much an imaginative theory of the state as a refined theory of ideology. Althusser here begins by blessing the classical Marxist idea that the state is first and foremost a class-warfare operation, a system of agencies of "repressive execution and intervention 'in the interests of the ruling classes'" (137). These agencies include "the police, the courts, the prisons; but also the army, which . . . intervenes directly as a supplementary repressive force in the last instance, when the police and its specialized auxiliary corps are 'outrun by events'; and above this ensemble, the head of State, the government and the administration" (137). Althusser's final reference to "the administration" confesses his light debt to Weber's theories of bureaucratic officialdom. More thoroughly Weberian is his emphasis on the state's debt to repressive violence in both the first and the last instances. Althusser is also not unique in giving the police first place in the inventory of the state's repressive forces—a place that Hoover's police moved heaven and Washington, D.C., to retain.

Most creative in Althusser's reconsideration of the state is the police presence within his famous illustration of the process of ideological interpellation or hailing, an illustration given second life in the performative gender theory of Judith Butler.[8] "There are individuals walking along," Althusser memorably narrates, and they are transformed into political subjects of ideology when "[s]omewhere, usually behind them," the "most common everyday police (or other) hailing" rings out: "Hey, you there!" (174). Loudmouth street cops, Althusser suggests, enforce the dominance of the ruling classes through the promise of violence but do so with the connivance of ideological allies. What Althusser baptizes as the repressive side of the state machinery, the "Repressive State Apparatus" or the "RSA"—specifically, the police in league with "the Government, the Administration, the Army, . . . the Courts, the Prisons, etc."—thus has a supportive complement, the "Ideological State Apparatus" or the "ISA" (142–43). Among the specific agencies of the ISA are education, or "the system of the different public and private 'Schools,'" and—most important for this discussion—the "cultural ISA (Literature, the Arts, sports, etc.)" (143). The RSA and ISA combine physical and intellectual muscle to guarantee that state power remains where Marxist theory says it should: in the hands of the ruling classes until the end of class history.

Following his anecdote of police interpellation, Althusser does not move to dismantle the difference between the RSA and the ISA even in the last instance. The RSA "functions massively and predominantly *by repression* (including physical repression), while functioning secondarily by ideology," he stipulates, whereas the balance of repression and ideology in the ISA is the mirror opposite (145; emphasis in original). Yet it remains the case that Althusser's police, leading symbols of the RSA, also lead the ideological shouting. "Hey, you there!" is the everyday greeting of cops, not priests or artists. And it remains the case that Althusser admits that "[t]here is no such thing as a purely repressive apparatus," quite obviously in the instance of the police, who, like the army, "also function by ideology both to ensure their own cohesion and reproduction, and in the 'values' they propound externally" (145). The police, then, seem to qualify as both the most representatively repressive and the most plainly ideological agency within the RSA. A pair of American acronyms, CIA and FBI, testifies that the prospect of a jointly repressive and ideological agency of state policing is not a purely academic one. More relevant in the present context, however, is the fact that Althusser situates both the repressive and the ideological work of the police on the ground of the state. All the agencies of the predominantly repressive RSA and the predominantly ideological ISA share an "S" at their core; all are more or less instrumental expressions of state interests. One thing Althusser's model of the state avoids, in other words, is confining the ideological and imaginative aspects of modern government solely to the nation and its nationalisms.[9]

Even while Althusser stops short of dismantling the RSA-ISA opposition, then, he points a way beyond the state violence–versus–national imagination divide and helps us to begin bridging the Weber-Anderson gap.[10] For all his hard-line anachronism, he anticipates recent directions in cultural anthropology that suggest that it is "possible to speak of states, and not only nations," as imagined communities (Ferguson and Gupta 981). States, too, Althusser suspected, are "entities that are conceptualized and made socially effective through particular imaginative and symbolic devices," and entities that seek social effectiveness by conceiving imaginative and symbolic devices in turn (Ferguson and Gupta 981). States, this is to suggest, pay their police both to repress threats by means of force and to forestall threats by means of imagination; they live not by violence alone, but by backing Leviathan's "publique Sword" with the symbol (Hobbes 231). Always a monopolist of the legitimate use of violence, the imagined, imagining, and symbol-wielding state therefore threatens the nation's monopoly on legitimate ideas of the literary. Even when this state plays the real to the nation's imaginary, it reserves the right to reimagine the agencies of the latter, and to violate national borders in the process. Most modern nations seek the secure borders of statehood, but some of the most powerful modern states stray beyond the imaginative containers of nationality—the "deterritorialized" empire of the twentieth-century United States perhaps most of all.[11]

Regardless of the lessons of Althusser, the transnational reach of an imagined and imagining U.S. state is seldom considered by the transnational turn in U.S. literary scholarship. This turn is often indifferent to the state's ideological work even within the compass of the nation-state; in recent postnational Americanism, the idea of the ISA has given way to something like faith in an "INA," an exclusively formative Ideological Nation Apparatus.[12] As a consequence, even some of the most adventurous transnational Americanism preemptively restrains its dizzying expansion of U.S. literary networks. Space permits reflection on just one example of this self-restriction, but it is a dazzling one: Wai Chee Dimock's *Through Other Continents: American Literature across Deep Time* (2006), a bold argument that transcending the spatial axis of the nation means exceeding the minutiae of nation-time.

The introduction of *Through Other Continents* opens with the specter of U.S. Marines quickly taking Baghdad in the first chapter of the Iraq War, but just as quickly surrendering the contents of the Iraqi national and Islamic libraries to looters, a culture crime of 2003 that reminds Dimock of the sacking of the Iraqi capital by a grandson of Genghis Khan 745 years earlier. The introduction nears its close with approving nods to Fernand Braudel, a French historian, and Immanuel Wallerstein, an American sociologist, whose thick descriptions of maritime worlds and global commodity chains might themselves fill libraries.[13] The state-relatedness of Dimock's bookending soldiers and scholars goes unnoticed, with each group instead allegorized to highlight "the glaring inadequacy of a nation-based model of world politics [and] literary studies" (2). Characteristic of a good deal of transnational Americanism, what by rights is a nation-state-based enemy here contracts into a national target alone.

For Dimock, the ignorance of the invading U.S. Marines demonstrates not the ironic parochialism of the far-reaching imperial state, but rather the woefully "short chronology of a young nation" (2). Stranded in the shallows of the mechanical clock, immature America is unequipped to comprehend the long history of "many parts of the non-Western world," the native soil of "a very different ontology of time," not to say a fantasy of temporal primitivism (2). As a result, America's adolescent army misses the boat on Dimock's vision of "deep time," the nonshrunken, nonserial, and nonstandardized temporality she hopes that transnational Americanism will inherit on the far side of national space. In contrast, Dimock's mature scholars, Braudel and Wallerstein, are praised for going deep first. The forecast of deep time in Braudel's concept of the *longue durée*, a chronology measured in the slow-paced, everyday rhythms of centuries, is recommended as an antidote to the thin temporal slices of U.S. national becoming. In the meantime, Wallerstein's world-systems theory is praised for demonstrating how the *longue durée* reveals "the folly of shoehorning large-scale developments into the chronology of a single nation" (5). Only a transnational "world-system," Dimock agrees, "can bear the explanatory weight of [the] deep structural transformations" beneath the foundations of U.S. development (5).

Missing from Dimock's recruitment of Braudel and Wallerstein is their similar reluctance to dispense with the state when surpassing the tape of the nation. Braudel's crowning historical trilogy, *Civilization and Capitalism* (1967–79), devotes a climactic section of its second volume to the imposition of the "all-pervasive state" and its challenge to his *Annales*-school signature of lower-strata epochal continuity (515). Wallerstein, for his part, explicitly instructs that statehood precedes and underpins nationhood, "and not the other way around, despite a widespread myth to the contrary" ("The Construction" 304).[14] Both of Dimock's theoretical inspirations therefore advise that beneath the fine crust of nation-time lies the time of the state, a temporal gauge antedating not only national literatures but also the global hegemony of the short-sighted West. There are grounds to hope that transnational Americanism will soon abandon the figment of deep time, a token of literary immortality warding off a new century of instant textual obsolescence. Even now, there are reasons to see that the state belongs with world religions and the morphology of language on Dimock's honor roll of transnational phenomena that majestically "unfold against long durations" (5). If there is an international idiom of deep time, a kind of lingua franca of the *longue durée*, the state has spoken it fluently for ages. The national vernacular, by comparison, ranks only as the state's second, acquired language.

The State of Black Transnationalism; the State in the Black Atlantic

Past the time of its introduction, Wai Chee Dimock's *Through Other Continents* contains the hint that nation-focused critics of African American writing have more in common with the Marines who neglected Iraqi libraries than with fellow scholars Braudel and Wallerstein. These critics would be better off guarding their subject's wealth by widening their field of vision, she indicates, since "African-American literature is infinitely richer when it is seen not as nation-based, self-contained within the United States, but as a diasporic formation, a literature of the two Americas with arcs reaching back to Africa" (163). What seals the cohesion of the black literatures of North and South America, and allows their mutual reconnection to the African continent, Dimock argues, is not their makers' similar "pigment of the skin," nor their comparable heritage of oppression and resistance, nor even their intertextual signifying on each other's tropes of color and history (142). Instead, the international link is the "creolized" or combined and synthesized "linguistic force" these literatures commonly unleash, a composite of European and African syntaxes and nonverbal signals concentrated in their renderings of vernacular black languages (142). On the hunt for vernacular distinctions, African American literature ironically becomes "an exemplary paradigm" for writing everywhere across the globe (142); its comfortably transnational stylistics makes it an ideal case of world literature's necessary employment of impure, belatedly national languages (142). And its safe delivery of a substratum of African speech "through standard English into the black vernacular" shows that literary language is fundamentally deep-temporal, the fruit of the "durational existence" of linguistic intermixture or *créolité*, a "long-standing, ongoing, and never-ending synthesis" interweaving Old and New World tongues (146). To Dimock, the root transnationality of African American writing derives from its status as a long-durational creole literature, a linguistic force that can be summoned wherever and whenever Black Atlantic expression taps the synthesis of African and European languages. Its transatlantic combinations are ancient, ever present, and—to this point—everlasting.

As most every nonliterary scholar of the African diaspora sees it, however, the transnationality of African American writing cannot be concurrent with itself and will not be found within a uniformly deep time. Within the historical and sociological branches of African diaspora studies, black transnationality of many kinds is conceived as longstanding but nondurational, a condition with a definite beginning and a profoundly split secular history. To this way of thinking, the dispersal of African peoples throughout Europe, the Caribbean, and the two Americas indeed opens the possibility of creatively creolized language—but only because of the equal breadth of the transatlantic trade in African captives that flourished from 1450 until the end of the nineteenth century. Joseph E. Harris, a pioneer in the application of the diaspora concept to African history, canonically distinguishes between a first, centuries-long "involuntary" diaspora capped by the colonial partition of Africa at the Berlin Conference of 1884–85, and a second, self-consciously "mobilized" diaspora, a liberation movement of an optimistically imagined long twentieth century (15). Harris's first, involuntary diaspora is the precondition for African colonization but also the immediate result of the African slave trade, the trigger that first "made the African presence essentially global," transporting somewhere between twelve and twenty-five million survivors of the transatlantic Middle Passage to the American hemisphere alone (9). Harris's second, mobilized diaspora—an elective journey of black communities real and imagined—is the result of "an effective international network" of resistance composed of "descendant Africans with a consciousness of the identity of their roots, occupational and communication skills, social and economic status, and access to decision-making bodies in their host country" (15). In the space between the first and second African diasporas, the "forced migration" of the enslaved painfully blooms into the voluntary remigration of the emancipated (Inikori 13).

Fatefully, the transition from the first to the second African diasporas involved the evolution of "racialization," the imposition of European racial thinking on African bodies, into an elective mobilization of black communities around signs of race. Not the least product of this racial self-mobilizing, notes literary historian Brent Hayes Edwards, is the discourse of "African diaspora" itself, a concept-metaphor "that becomes necessary in the same period that the 'mobilized diaspora' is taking shape" ("The Uses" 56). Edwards endorses as well as historicizes the mid-twentieth-century turn to diaspora, a trope of black transnationalism derived from the New Testament Greek word διασπορά, a synonym for scattering or dispersion initially applied to the Babylonian exile of the Jews (an exile creatively misread, to great historical effect, as a typology of black captivity and deliverance in African American Christianity). In particular, Edwards approves of the diaspora trope's departure from "Pan-Africa" and "Pan-Africanism," terms wedded to the specific politics of the Pan-African Congress, a movement assembled at W.E.B. Du Bois's several world conventions of black leaders, the first held in Paris in 1919 (not by pure chance, in a world capital of black transnationalism in the same Red Year as the FBI's *Radicalism and Sedition*). Unlike "Pan-Africa," "diaspora" is a signifier that "allows for an account of black transnational formations that attends to their constitutive differences," the many "political stakes of the organization of the 'African abroad'" (54). The "accepted risk," concedes Edwards, "is that the term's analytic focus 'fluctuates'" (54). On the flip side, however, the signal opportunity is that the term issues an invitation to transvalue imposed removal as freedom of movement.

This invitation is accepted in Paul Gilroy's *The Black Atlantic: Modernity and Double Consciousness* (1993), a book that launched a thousand paper ships, and the single provocation most responsible for "re-worlding" African American literary studies following the nation-first canon and theory wars of the late 1980s. Gilroy's sworn enemy is cultural nationalism in black or white, all such nationalism resting on "overintegrated conceptions of culture which present immutable, ethnic differences as an absolute break in the histories and experiences" of human populations (*Black* 2). Gilroy's alternative curriculum thus dovetails with Dimock's in favoring international continuities over national separations, and traveling cultures over fixed and self-consistent ones. He splits from her, however, in steadily shaming nationalism's debt to racism. The final undoing of the nation, he supposes, will not be its twilight struggle with the *longue durée*, but instead its corrupt birth "as an ethnically homogenous object" (2). Postracist intellectuals, an inevitably postnationalist group, must then theorize the unhomogenous stuff of Dimock's linguistic force: *créolité, métissage, mestizaje,* and the rest of the international vocabulary of cultural border crossing. Seen from Gilroy's personal wheelhouse, the black British intellectual's outstanding postracist assignment is to theorize "one small area in the grand consequence of this historical conjunction" of hybridities (3). This area is the Black Atlantic, an oceanic zone "based on the structure of the African diaspora [in] the Western hemisphere" (15). Grasped as a "single, complex unit of analysis," the Black Atlantic is both undersized (in comparison to a whole world of intercultural mixtures) and outsized (in comparison to national cultural topographies) (15). Within it, the cargo of the African American intellectual legacy resurfaces as a common black possession.

Above all, Gilroy's Black Atlantic model has succeeded as a reprojected classroom map, a heady but instantly recognizable charting of the transnationality of black "structures of feeling, producing, communicating, and remembering" (3). All at once, however, this model is a polemical contribution to the specialized history of the black diaspora concept. Edwards worries that Gilroy's adaptation of the Atlantic as a heuristic unit substitutes indistinct impressions of transnational cultural circuits for "specific ground-level histories of culture in port cities and on ships around the world" ("The Uses" 63). Despite its reliance on established diasporan routes, one disadvantage of Gilroy's terminological shift is thus its simultaneous fuzzing and narrowing of the diasporan horizon, its confinement of the African diaspora within a single liquid field "without even replacing it with a contextualized history of transnational cultures in the Western hemisphere" (63). What is more, Gilroy's change of terms risks rewriting the idea of a two-stage African diaspora as a melodrama of material defeat avenged by symbolic victory. With its investment in open transnational lines of "feeling, producing, communicating, and remembering," the Black Atlantic model effectively redefines the second, mobilized African diaspora as a *mentally mobile diaspora*; the recipe for meaningful black diasporan "movement" is reduced from one part expanded intellectual traffic plus one part organized racial resistance to the former ingredient alone. In Gilroy's condensed formula for self-made black transnationalism, Harris's pride in "descendant Africans" with "access to decision-making bodies" is thus retrained on the pleasures of black thinkers merely circulating.

To Gilroy's mind, of course, the Black Atlantic world is not simply a spawning ground of liberating intellectual exchanges. He never forgets that the first, involuntary African diaspora was formed in the bloody channels of the Atlantic slave trade. Even those who know *The Black Atlantic* only by citation know that its central "chronotope" or crystallizing time/space optic is the sailing ship, a seagoing symbol selected in part for its capacity to "refer us back to the middle passage, to the half-remembered micro-politics of the slave trade" and the uncanny music of the "slave sublime" (17, 37). Yet in practice, in the chosen and compensatory ocean voyages *The Black Atlantic* spends many of its pages diagramming, half-memories of slavery dim and the supervised black travels of the twentieth century are forgotten. It is racist folly, Gilroy submits, to assign "uncoerced or recreational travel experiences only to whites while viewing black people's experiences of displacement and relocation exclusively through the very different types of traveling undergone by refugees, migrants, and slaves" (133). The intellectual products of the uncoerced or recreational second African diaspora indeed "evoke and affirm a condition in which the negative meanings given to the enforced movements of blacks are somehow transposed. What was initially felt to be a curse—the curse of homelessness or the curse of enforced exile—gets repossessed" (111). A criminal hex is broken and recast as a superior way of seeing and knowing, "a privileged standpoint from which certain useful and critical perceptions about the modern world become more likely" (111).

Richard Wright's expatriation to France—often dismissed or regretted prior to *The Black Atlantic*—exemplifies the power of this privileged standpoint, suggests Gilroy. An anthology of Paris-based travel experiences, Wright's post-1947 life in motion "bears witness to the value of critical perceptions that could only have been gained through the restlessness, even homelessness, that he sometimes manages to make into an analytical opportunity" (150). But sometimes, as Gilroy himself allows, the Paris-based Wright could not manage to convert his perceptions of homelessness into analytical advantages. Sometimes, through no fault of his own, the comparable restlessness of U.S. state security stood in his way—a source of continued interference in the second, voluntary African diaspora that *The Black Atlantic* is poorly positioned to recognize. The term "nation-state" earns three mentions in Gilroy's index; in the chapters before it, however, this dual institution virtually dissolves into the nation alone, much as in Dimock's diminished attack on "the glaring inadequacy of a nation-based model" (2). "The statist modalities of Marxist analysis" are prominently mentioned in Gilroy's introduction, but only (and unfairly) as artifacts of nationalist illusion and sources of the misapprehension that "modes of material production and political domination [are] exclusively *national* entities" (4; emphasis in original). Thus assimilated into the very nationalism the Black Atlantic model exists to overcome, state analysis logically fails to shape Gilroy's perception of a second, uncoerced African diaspora specially equipped to view modernity in the raw.

Certainly, the absence of the state considered as a *trans*national entity makes systematic sense within the context of *The Black Atlantic*'s intellectual biography. As Gilroy reads the intellectual history of the European left, attending more closely to Raymond Williams than Louis Althusser, Marxism's alleged "statist modalities" are morbidly attached to the ethnocentric "white Englishness" of British labor history and early Birmingham School cultural studies, the baseline academic others of his own Black British antinationalism.[15] Yet thanks to the wide distribution of *The Black Atlantic* outside Black Britain, Gilroy's antistatism has gone viral, and in other, North American hands, becomes significantly less motivated. Despite all the differences of location and stance, in fact, a misprizing of the state and of state-level transnational analysis links a number of the most powerful diasporic revisions of African American literary history produced in wake of *The Black Atlantic*.[16]

Brent Hayes Edwards's *The Practice of Diaspora: Literature, Translation, and the Rise of Black Internationalism* (2003) would seem to be an exception to this rule, in part because it has little in common with *The Black Atlantic* other than its transatlantic span and deservedly broad influence; as discussed above, Edwards has criticized Gilroy for the equal constriction and abstraction of his Black Atlantic paradigm. Countering Gilroy's abstraction, *The Practice* concentrates on specific episodes of print-cultural exchange between two particular Black Atlantic ports, New York and Paris, in the definite period between the world wars. Edwards thus details the dense bilingualism of black periodicals in the interwar era: the French pages featured in New York's Garveyite *Negro World*, among others, and the English-language poems by

Countee Cullen and Langston Hughes reprinted in the Parisian journal *Les Continents*. Countering the constriction of Gilroy's Black Atlantic paradigm, *The Practice* elaborates an exportable, potentially transoceanic theory of diaspora as a dynamic Babel of translations. The discourses of black diaspora must themselves *"travel"* among the various European languages of decolonizing black populations, Edwards stresses (*The Practice* 7; emphasis in original). As a result, these discourses "allow new and unforeseen alliances and interventions on a global stage" by exploiting, not erasing, the "unavoidable misapprehensions" of cross-lingual paraphrase (5). Where there is black diaspora, Edwards holds, there must also be the cross talk of "blindnesses and solipsisms, self-defeating and abortive collaborations, [and] a failure to translate even a basic grammar of blackness" (5).

Edwards therefore pictures a second, voluntary African diaspora obliged to practice a mode of translation unable to guarantee insight—unlike Gilroy, he offers no assurances that "homelessness" often compounds analytical profit. All things considered, however, he recuperates the inescapable failure of intraracial translation as the only path to diasporan movement. "My contention, finally," Edwards announces, "is that articulations of diaspora demand to be approached" through the aptly untranslatable notion of "*décalage*," the French word for a gap in time or space (*The Practice* 15). "For paradoxically," he concludes, "it is exactly such a haunting gap or discrepancy that allows the diaspora to 'step' or 'move' in various articulations"; in the human body, as in the second, voluntary African diaspora, "it is only *difference*—the separation between bones or members—that allows movement" (15). Through Edwards's half-francophone, half-deconstructive lens, the Black Atlantic's "single, complex unit of analysis" appears to disclose the antithetical dependence of international racial movement on racial self-division.

Quite unlike Gilroy, *The Practice of Diaspora* admits state surveillance into its discrepant analysis of diasporan writing. To reconstruct the literary Black Atlantic as a divided archive, rather than a peripatetic abstraction, is to come to terms with "a great variety of texts," Edwards maintains (7). "[F]iction, poetry, journalism, criticism, position papers, circulars, manifestoes, anthologies, correspondence, [and] surveillance reports" must all be considered as interpenetrating diasporan genres (7). Specimens of this last genre— documents of espionage—make several passing appearances in *The Practice* as Edwards inspects the francophone side of black internationalism. Spy-texts are dangled, for example, in his sketch of François Coty, a Parisian fascist whose articles *contre le communisme* "relied on information gathered by the spies of the French Ministère des Colonies" (259). They are central to his case that French intelligence invidiously misread the moderate Afro-Parisian newspaper *La Dépêche africaine* as "a disguised communist enterprise" (284). But Edwards's treatments of the counterparts of Coty and *La Dépêche africaine* within the anglophone Harlem Renaissance discuss no form of state surveillance, this despite the facts that the FBI outdid French intelligence in detecting communism in the most circumspect New Negro journals, and that Edwards's list of traveling writers associated with Harlem is in most respects a tacit list of victims of Bureau espionage. Claude McKay, Walter White, Gwendolyn Bennett, Langston Hughes, Alain Locke, and J. A. Rogers all "spent time abroad and especially in Paris in the 1920s," as Edwards remarks (*The Practice* 4). They all also earned notice from the FBI as they looked beyond U.S. territory, provoking a police bureaucracy that documented their print-cultural diaspora in an archive of its own.

Neither French nor American state surveillance affects the inner workings of décalage, Edwards's "model of what resists or escapes translation" but ultimately permits progress across the African diaspora (15). In her book *Black Empire: The Masculine Global Imaginary of Caribbean Intellectuals in the United States, 1914–1962* (2005), Michelle Ann Stephens protests that Edwards's notion of décalage illuminates, but "without articulating as such, the *political* stakes of difference in the black internationalisms of the [interwar] period" (4; emphasis in original). To claim that the unifying language of the second, voluntary African diaspora was structured by differences is for Stephens a mere "starting point" (5). What begs for attention, she believes, is the underlying politics of those differences. Stephens identifies the nation as the encompassing political arrangement "that not only haunted but effectively created differentiated and heterogeneous understandings of blackness" (5). "Blackness," she declares, "as much as any radicalized consciousness during this period," was an imaginary measure forged in the nation and "burdened by the national" (5). In her view, the production of transnational blackness through deconstructive décalage inevitably answered linguistic differences exaggerated by national authorities. Reconceived in line with its political history, décalage thus mandates a theory of the second, voluntary African diaspora "more materialist" than Edwards's, and more cognizant of "the politics and cultures of metropolitan nationalism" standing in its way (5).

Both French and American state surveillance records divulge metropolitan plans to hinder black internationalism. However, records from both sides of the Atlantic also document the efforts of state police forces to haze this internationalism along routes leading beyond the national metropolis. The American FBI, for one, plunged directly into the transnational black print culture that Edwards casts as the "ground of a nascent discourse of black internationalism" (*The Practice* 265). The majority of the U.S.-based periodicals that Edwards reads as "the 'means toward' a Black International" (265) were secretly infiltrated or widely "retranslated" (as in *Radicalism and Sedition among the Negroes*) by the FBI. Robert Adger Bowen and other early Bureau ghostreaders operated near the ground level of the cosmopolitan black press to intensify the "blindnesses and solipsisms, [the] self-defeating and abortive collaborations," that accompanied the struggle of black internationalists "to translate even a basic grammar of blackness" (5). Impressed despite themselves with the quality of New Negro writing, these ghostreaders nonetheless threw wrenches into self-managed New Negro décalage.

Concerned with the national encumbrances on diasporic translation, Stephens's *Black Empire* is also notable for its attention to the state's part in the second-wave, voluntary Black Atlantic. "[U]nderstanding empire," the state's extension of sovereignty beyond national limits, "has been the Caribbean intellectual's special experience of and contribution to the twentieth-century global imaginary," she contends (11). When Caribbean-born Afro-modernists such as McKay, Marcus Garvey, and C.L.R. James attempted "to imagine a transnational form of black nationality," they thus envisioned a black sovereignty able to "transcend nationalism and reimagine the state itself" (4). Stephens's stake in ideas of the state is characteristic of one strong line within the black transnational criticism that has followed on Edwards—an anti-imperialist line that has crested in such theoretically ambitious studies as Nicole A. Waligora-Davis's *Sanctuary: African Americans and Empire* (2011). Waligora-Davis tailors Giorgio Agamben, a pervasive theoretical touchstone of the post-9/11 academic left, to explain the enduring statelessness of African Americans as a defining ploy of the U.S. state. This state's self-denying domestic imperialism, she argues, has spared no outrage to ensure that African Americans continue to occupy an Agambenian "state of exception—an anomalous legal zone where law is suspended"—long after Emancipation (xii). *Sanctuary* and similar anti-imperialist approaches are prone to hyperbolize what Waligora-Davis fashions as the denationalizing "liminality of the modern black subject in the United States" (xiii). Yet their attention to the overhang and reinvention of race-baiting imperial statism in the twentieth century reminds us that not every form of statelessness is a liberating good, and that neither Edwards-style décalage nor Gilroy-style mental homelessness can squelch all evidence of coercion in the second, mobilized African diaspora. What is left to explore here are the specifics of the FBI's practice of diasporic coercion—specifics with definitional consequences when we classify either the Black Atlantic or the U.S. national-security state as a meaningfully literary organism.

Checking Diasporan ID: Hostile Translation and the Passport Office

The FBI file of Langston Hughes, opened the year that his poetry first announced that "I, too, sing America" ("I, Too" l. 1), repeatedly quotes his claim that "Negroes are growing in international consciousness" (U.S., Federal, Hughes, 3 June 1947). Hughes's file and many others also confirm that the Bureau concluded it should grow in the same way. Part 1 of *F.B. Eyes* suggested that the Bureau's earliest appointments with African American writing were premised on the New Negro's emergence as a national (not just southern) actor; they were partly dedicated, we have seen, to solidifying the Bureau's status as a player in nation-building U.S. print culture. But the open comfort of the Harlem Renaissance with the simultaneously national and transnational implications of New Negro modernity dictated a comparable range in Hoover's first ghostreaders. Not only the revolutionary black voices quoted in *Radicalism and Sedition* strived to narrow the miles between Harlem and Africa, and the tensions between black American nationalism and diasporic Pan-Africanism. Alain Locke's peacemaking *New Negro* (1925) anthology, its introduction bent on assuring sympathetic whites that its titular hero was "a social protestant rather than a genuine radical" (11–12), praised Harlem's emergence as a global "race capital" as well as its yearning for "nothing but American wants" (7). Hughes's file and the rest of the earliest relevant FBI paperwork consequently recognize New Negro targets as subjects in communication with international movements ("the Negroes are growing in international consciousness") as well as subjects of American patriotism ("I, too, sing America"). While the Bureau's anxieties over black internationalism spiked during World War II, the Hooverites' intent to entrap New Negro authors within "a whole mass of documents" grasped the need to reinforce disciplines of "enclosed, segmented space" as early as 1922 (Foucault, *Discipline* 197). In advance of Brent Hayes Edwards's worldly revision of Harlem's renaissance, the FBI thus widened the net of counterliterary inquiry to reflect the evidence that the American "'New Negro' movement is at the same time a 'new' black internationalism" (Edwards, *The Practice* 2).

The FBI indeed rushed to internationalize its oversight of Afro-modernist writing through an Edwardsian tool: a rough and ready practice of diasporic translation. As noted earlier, the Bureau actively recruited U.S. diplomats to translate Claude McKay's Russian-language contributions to the Soviet press, themselves first translated out of McKay's transnational English. In particular, F.W.B. Coleman, President Warren Harding's minister to the newly independent Baltic States, was persuaded to forward to Washington renditions of McKay's two appearances in *Izvestia*, a Bolshevik paper of record founded in 1917 (U.S., Federal, McKay, 11 Dec. 1922). (Coleman's prefatory text clarifies that "Comrade MacKay [sic]" was a journalist and poet with specialties in "agriculture" and in denouncing "the 'Back to Africa' movement, headed by Marcus Garvey" [11 Dec. 1922].) Translations from the Russian of McKay's 1922 "The Race Question in America" and "The Race Question in the United States" thus enter the first FBI file on an Afro-modernist writer and multiply the complexities of décalage at a distance by Anglicizing McKay's Marxist alternative to Garveyite Pan-Africanism. Items in Richard Wright's file reveal that the Bureau's attention to black transnationalism in translation endured the shift to the Cold War. One 1947 FBI memorandum addressed directly to Hoover fastens on an interview with the expatriated Wright "that appeared recently in *Die Weltwoche* [the *World Week*]," a German-language journal out of Zurich, Switzerland (U.S., Federal, Wright, 19 Feb. 1947). In a lucky, cost-cutting break, a trustworthy English version could be found in the U.S.-published journal the *New Leader*, the memo notes (19 Feb. 1947). Two decades later, James Baldwin's file absorbed a less easily fulfilled translation request from Bureau headquarters.[17] FBI correspondence confirms that Hoover's office prompted Turkish experts in New York to prepare an English transcription of a 1966 Baldwin interview in Istanbul's *Yeni Gazette* (U.S., Federal, Baldwin, 6 Dec. 1966). (Multiple copies of this Baldwin interview were demanded, specified right down to the paper type: one "bond, three thins, and one yellow" [6 Dec. 1966].) The resulting Turkish-to-English translation of the article "Looking at New York from Istanbul" opens with Baldwin's conflicted suggestion, spoken from a "large green garden" overlooking the Bosphorus, that first-rate writing on Harlem had become too costly to produce in Black Manhattan (20 Dec. 1966). The "noise and tumult" of racially fraught New York was poisonous to literary concentration, he explains, yet so would be permanent removal from "the black-white conflicts in my country" (20 Dec. 1966). Baldwin's exile in a Turkish Eden had increased his fluency but did not cancel his obligation to "contribute my share by returning to America" (20 Dec. 1966). His FBI file bears witness that New York (in the shape of its police translators) could not quit him either,[18] and that U.S. law enforcement was primed for his return. It also goes to show the Bureau's understanding that the course of black transnationalism followed the facts of linguistic difference. Aggravating the ambiguities of communication within the black diaspora and its chosen political allies, Hoover's ghostreaders added the strain of hostile retranslations circulated across state channels to worsen "the haunting gap or discrepancy" involved in any articulation of international blackness (Edwards, *The Practice* 15).

But how did the FBI, a de facto national police force formed to investigate federal crimes within the United States, involve itself in language translation? Wasn't the CIA created to complement the Bureau's domestic focus with an international intelligence operation? Replies to both of these questions can begin with the Special Intelligence Service (SIS), the short-lived branch of Hoover's FBI acknowledged by the CIA as "the first foreign-intelligence bureaucracy in U.S. history" (Webb 4). Worried by Axis intrigue in Latin America, but not yet able to rely on the OSS, President Franklin D. Roosevelt directed the FBI to begin collecting intelligence throughout the Western Hemisphere in June 1940. Hoover answered Roosevelt's order by establishing a new FBI division, the SIS, and announcing that he was looking for new agents with linguistic ability (Jeffreys-Jones 114). In 1941, one of these new agents, Joseph E. Santoiana Jr., was commissioned to launch an FBI Spanish-language school. Santoiana's academy would outlast the SIS—it operated for several decades, while the Bureau's almost six hundred agents in Latin America were withdrawn in 1946. Its postwar survival reflected Hoover's reluctance to cede an inch to the CIA, the OSS's successor, even in its foreign element. Wooing Congress as it weighed the creation of a central intelligence agency, Hoover had in fact promised that the FBI would do a dirty job better and cheaper. The Bureau could offer "worldwide intelligence coverage" for $45 million less per year than the CIA, he wrote, and this without pampering the "dreams of visionary but impractical empire builders" (qtd. in Weiner, *Enemies* 152). Hoover's practical bid to dominate international espionage lost the day, but the Bureau never surrendered its insistence on placing legal attaché agents, otherwise known as FBI "legats," in important foreign capitals. By 1953, legats provided the Bureau with diplomatically immune eyes and ears in London, Madrid, and Paris, together with the hemispheric centers of Havana, Rio de Janeiro, and Mexico City. Supplying the legal advice referenced in their job title did not keep these FBI visitors from sampling local cultures of radicalism. Legats served as "responsible American official[s] with regard to clandestine intelligence matters, particularly in the field of subversive activities," as one self-produced FBI history phrased it (qtd. in Weiner, *Enemies* 117). The expatriates of Tournon-era black Paris thus had reason to sense that G-Men were still too close for comfort.

Communications to and from European legats can be found throughout the Wright and Baldwin files, and they identify one vital source of FBI foreign intelligence after World War II. (News of Wright's death was first conveyed to Hoover by the FBI's legat in Paris, for example [U.S., Federal, Wright, 7 Dec. 1960].) Yet the international breadth of the surveillance in Claude McKay's file, closed in the year the SIS was launched, requires other explanations. Even before the SIS, the Bureau was deeply involved in the control of passports, an emblematically modern state business that boomed as the FBI's Radical Division was created.[19] The passport historian John Torpey maintains that the "guns of August 1914" destroyed a tranquil fin-de-siècle in which western European "governments viewed foreigners without 'suspicion and mistrust'" and allowed them "to traverse borders relatively unmolested" (111). On the American side of the Atlantic, the era of international laissez-faire began with the Fourteenth Amendment of 1866, opening American citizenship to "all persons born or naturalized in the United States" (Robertson 148). Breaking with the early nineteenth-century practice of denying U.S. passports to free persons of color (Wong 243), the amendment ushered in a post–Civil War interregnum in which passports were rarely required for black or white American travelers. This relatively enlightened era, the counterpart of Radical Reconstruction in the history of U.S. national identification, was first threatened a year after the assassination of Archduke Franz Ferdinand. President Woodrow Wilson's Executive Order 2285, drafted as Europe militarized shifting borders in 1915, required all persons, native-born Americans included, to display "passports of the Governments of which they are citizens" prior to leaving the United States ("Executive Order 2285"). "Each applicant for a passport must inform the Department of State at which point he intends to depart, on what date, and by what ship if he sails from an American port," the order directed, ensuring the document's utility in international policing ("Executive Order 2285"). The good old days of free travel collapsed completely with the Congressional Passport Control Act of 1918 and a 1919 act extending travel restrictions beyond the exceptional state of war. Seeking the whereabouts of McKay and other expatriate black radicals in December 1922, FBI headquarters thus logically thought first to ask "whether or not passports have been issued to these subjects" (U.S., Federal, McKay, 12 Dec. 1922).

In the wake of World War I, the American state sealed what Torpey, nodding to Max Weber, labels the "monopolization of the legitimate 'means of movement'" to and from its territory (4). Crucially for this discussion, it chose to administer these means through the FBI. The Bureau was commissioned to investigate many U.S. passport applications for the State Department in 1918.

Two years later, FBI agents were routing 292,000 pre-passport name checks through Hoover's central file system and conducting approximately 10,000 field inspections of foreign visa requests (Schmidt 175). As Bureau historian Regin Schmidt confirms, the FBI regularly tested the politics of would-be travelers, with the Chicago field office, for example, browsing through its own files to determine if a hopeful tourist was "of radical tendencies or a member of any radical society" (qtd. in Schmidt 176). The intent of such political research is clarified by the case of two American officers of Marcus Garvey's Universal Negro Improvement Association (UNIA) who requested documents for travel to Africa, an arena of practical UNIA organizing as well as this movement's spiritual home. FBI sleuths informed the State Department that Garveyism "is the cause of the greater part of the negro [sic] agitation in this country," and that national security would be jeopardized "should these passports be granted" (qtd. in Schmidt 176). The UNIA officials were denied passports and permission to depart the United States, an outcome that reveals another source of the symbolic potency of Garvey's free-sailing "Black Star Line." In and beyond this case of frustrated Garveyism, the traveling cultures of the second, voluntary black diaspora were destined to mature in the very moment that the United States joined European countries in challenging internationalism through the culture of state paperwork. "Black intellectuals and activists were especially eager to participate in the institutional discourses of internationalism that developed in the West after World War I," Brent Edwards remarks, yet these Western inspirations were themselves required to contend with the stiffened state discourse of the passport ("Three Ways" 288).

Despite its formally diminished role in the rationing of passports after 1922, Hoover's Bureau continued to involve itself in the vetting of citizens seeking their share of the means of movement. (Conveniently feeding this involvement was the fact that Ruth Shipley, the head of the State Department's Passport Office for nearly three decades beginning in the 1920s, was the sister of an early FBI executive [Robertson 200].) In 1938, Hoover surprised his New Deal ally at the White House with a grandiose plan to expand the FBI by another 5,000 agents, the better to oversee the granting of passports on its own (Weiner, *Enemies* 80). President Roosevelt refused most of this particular enhancement of Bureau authority, but a fairly straight line may still be drawn between the FBI's capacity to thwart Garveyite travel and its determining role, played thirty years later, in the two most publicized passport denial cases of the Cold War, both involving African American artists. The Cold War state's sharp eye on the international activities of such artists is increasingly well detailed by historians of the long civil rights movement. Mary L. Dudziak's revisionist survey of

Cold War civil rights, among others, describes the U.S. government's efforts to manage the travels of African Americans at a time when communism and Americanism wrestled for ideological advantage in Europe and in the emerging postcolonial states of Asia and Africa. African Americans willing to say the right, anticommunist thing about U.S. race relations "could find their travel and international contacts facilitated, directly or indirectly, by the state department," Dudziak demonstrates (61). On the contrary, African American critics of racism unwilling to praise the "Free World" and condemn the Soviet bloc could find themselves unable to leave the United States under any state's sponsorship. With world-class irony, W.E.B. Du Bois, known even at the FBI as the "father of 'Pan-Africanism'" (U.S., Federal, W.E.B. Du Bois, 17 Nov. 1961), was stripped of his right to travel throughout the diaspora in 1952, the very year his transnational romance *Dark Princess* (1929) had set the final freedom of "the Dark World" (296). Singer-actor Paul Robeson, perhaps the most internationally successful black performer of midcentury, met the same penalty a year earlier after informing a Paris audience that African Americans would abstain from any war against the Soviet Union. Du Bois and Robeson's cancelled U.S. passports now rank as quintessential documents of both anticommunist excess and the defensive Cold War renationalizing of "black antiracist theory and practice" (Singh 164). Their status as emblems of the FBI's long-term interference in black diasporan travel is, by contrast, hardly recognized.

Orders to confiscate Paul Robeson's passport were first issued by Hoover in July 1949, beating State Department officials to the punch by more than a year (Robeson 212). The subsequent withdrawal of W.E.B. Du Bois's passport was closer to a collaborative project, with both the Bureau and the State Department pressing to immobilize the century's representative black diasporan intellectual. One of the earliest documents in Du Bois's FBI file, created in 1942, inadvertently predicts the storm to come over his internationalism: it mistakenly casts its subject as a member of the "International Association for Colored People" rather than the (national) NAACP (U.S., Federal, W.E.B. Du Bois, 13 Feb. 1943). Nearer to accuracy is the Bureau's opening description of "a great negro [*sic*] educator, author, lecturer, and publisher," a decorated artist best known for "'Souls of Black Folk' and the 'Quest of the Silver Fleese [*sic*],'" and a supercilious Harvard man "very studious and not inclined to be a social mixer" (13 Feb. 1943). A 1949 letter from an anonymous Bureau agent conveys the kind of foreign news that dominates the remainder of Du Bois's file: here was one "United States negro [*sic*] scientist" prized enough in the communist world to receive column inches in the Polish press and a major speaking part at the Moscow Peace Conference (20 Sept. 1949). By 1951, the State Department was stirring up shades of the McKay file, summoning the FBI "to ascertain [the] dates Dr. DUBOIS entered and left the United States during the last two years" (7 Apr. 1951). Thirteen photographs of Du Bois's passport were couriered to the Bureau for this purpose, with the State Department suggesting "that the Bureau have the visas and visa control stamps translated in order to determine where DUBOIS visited and on what dates" (7 Apr. 1951). Bypassing its own dedicated "translation unit" (7 Apr. 1951), the State Department revealed its good opinion of the Bureau's ability to decode foreign languages. On the linguistic front, Hoover's FBI at times rivaled the CIA as a provider of basic international intelligence.

In Du Bois's case, the FBI's return as the State Department's passport enforcer meant a rapid evaporation of freedom of movement. Before Du Bois heard the news in 1952, the State Department had telegrammed the FBI to confirm that a "REFUSAL NOTICE IS ON FILE IN [the] PASSPORT DIVISION," the predestined result of calling on Hoover's investigators in the early Cold War (U.S., Federal, W.E.B. Du Bois, 29 Nov. 1951). The octogenarian who had arguably invented Pan-Africanism was therefore barred from joining C.L.R. James, Martin Luther King, and other diasporan dignitaries at independence celebrations in Ghana, the first sub-Saharan African nation to shake off European rule. Pried free with help from the Supreme Court, Du Bois's U.S. passport was eventually returned, but the FBI's hackles were locked in place, its international contacts plaguing his travels for the rest of his life. Du Bois's Bureau file shows that when he and his wife, Shirley Graham, first cashed in their released passports by sailing for France in August 1958, an FBI informer loitered near the gangplank (19 Aug. 1958). Another Bureau source revealed that the couple's complete trip "would take them half way around the world," their "itinerary call[ing] for visits to Czechoslovakia, the Soviet Union, China and Ghana, Africa" (22 Sept. 1958). Echoing the Bureau's absorption in McKay's shipping schedule, FBI spies fanned out to plot Du Bois's international movements before the fact. Others chronicled the content and ambiance of his speeches when abroad, such as an informer in the Netherlands who witnessed Du Bois "look up from his notes" and spontaneously mourn the many years "when [he] could not travel" (29 Sept. 1958).

Preparing for Du Bois's delayed journey to decolonizing Africa, the FBI broadcast his application for a passport to attend "the inauguration of the new government of Ghana" in 1960 (25 May 1960). The need for travel details was great, a later Bureau memo suggested, since Kwame Nkrumah, Ghana's young prime minister, had appointed Du Bois to edit an "Encyclopedia Africana, a study of Africa's peoples and history and culture, the plan of which was originally conceived by him in 1909" (17 Nov. 1961). With rare deference, the Bureau cast the *Encyclopedia* as the life's work of a pioneering scholar, not simply as a token of Accra's self-positioning as the knowledge capital of liberated Africa. Given its fixed interest in his coordinates, the FBI's final investigation of Du Bois naturally involved another search through the Passport Office. This time, the responsible Bureau agent could confirm that Du Bois's U.S. passport was once again voided; following the author's enrollment in the Communist Party and his naturalization as a Ghanaian citizen, the agent relates, "any further use of same might subject him to prosecution" (21 Mar. 1963). In a telling turn of phrase, Du Bois's expatriation is then reset as the U.S. government's doing: "It is noted that the subject has now been officially expatriated by the Department of State" (21 Mar. 1963). A tidbit in Shirley Graham's file hints that the FBI may have forced the passport cancellation to begin with: a party infiltrator had overheard talk that Graham had joined her husband as "a citizen of Ghana," information that spurred the Washington field office to consult with the State Department to determine if she had followed the letter of the law and "given up her U.S. citizenship" (U.S., Federal, Shirley Graham Du Bois, 24 Sept. 1963). In any event, the once-secret record shows that the FBI joined the State Department in favoring a second restriction of Du Bois's freedom of movement. If U.S. intelligence had its say, liberated Ghana, a haven for African American internationalists, would become a narrowing vise. Thanks to divisive rumors of assassination attempts and CIA penetration of Accra's expatriate colony—a kind of second coming of the paranoid fragmentation of Paris noir—waves of popular anti-Americanism indeed began to sweep Du Bois's final home (James T. Campbell 347). In 1966, three years after the Bureau clipped Du Bois's obituary from the *Daily Worker* (U.S., Federal, W.E.B. Du Bois, 1 Sept. 1963), a U.S.-supported coup toppled Nkrumah and doomed the *Encyclopedia*. Shirley Graham Du Bois, still deprived of her U.S. passport, was deported from Ghana to England carrying only the clothes on her back, her husband's Africana library forcibly retained (Gaines 232).

The story of the seizing of Du Bois's passport is thus also a cautionary tale illustrating the FBI's power to twist the cultural history of the Black Atlantic and the second, mobilized African diaspora. Without the Bureau's services to the Cold War state, Du Bois might have visited Ghana in 1957, the Pan-African nation's year zero, and assumed the editorship of the *Encyclopedia Africana* free from the greatest provocation to trade in American citizenship. Shirley Graham, for her part, would have had years more time to prepare the debut of Ghana State Television, a stepping-stone to African self-representation. The counterfactuals invited by the first five years of Du Bois's immobility are even more baroque.[20] Would his final long works of imaginative literature, the three historical novels jointly known as *The Black Flame* (1957–61), have been so apocalyptic (and so underread) without his U.S. house arrest? Would he still have publicly joined the Communist Party in defiance in 1961, and would the entire ideological matrix of African independence have been subtly different if he had not? What can be known with confidence is the Bureau's wish to reproduce Du Bois's altered prospects across the full range of African American authorship. Numerous other FBI author files suggest that the now-you-see-it, now-you-don't game played with Du Bois's passport was half punitive spectacle and half disciplinary business as usual.

Richard Wright's FBI file underlines the Bureau's hawkish attention to the passport status of Cold War black Paris, or make that attention to "possible subversives among U.S. personnel in France" (U.S., Federal, Wright, 11 Feb. 1960). Less predictably, it also exposes the Bureau's involvement in frustrating Wright's early effort to visit the Soviet Union. An FBI ghostreader records that on September 27, 1940, years ahead of the Cold War, Wright was informed "by letter . . . that there was no imperative necessity for his journey to the Soviet Union" (13 Feb. 1958). Wright's intent to study "national minority problems" and consult with the Soviet Writers' Union would never be realized, with both the literary and political trajectories of the Black Atlantic swerving slightly as a result (13 Feb. 1958). The FBI lobbied harder to confiscate Ollie Harrington's travel papers. If the "opportunity presented itself," a 1952 bulletin counseled, the passport of Wright's closest Paris companion "should be picked up and validated only for return to the United States, in view of [his] affiliation with the Communist movement" (U.S., Federal, Harrington, 21 Oct. 1952). As it turned out, these strictures meant that Harrington would reexpatriate to East Berlin, but never return to his native country. William Gardner Smith's impact on black Paris and Harrington's reputation was influenced by a two-year passport withdrawal instigated by the FBI.[21] A highly classified "Security Information" report in Smith's FBI dossier states that "a refusal notice appears in his passport file . . . under date of December 4, 1951, and is based upon information furnished by the Bureau" (U.S., Federal, Smith, 1 Nov. 1952). Harold Cruse was made to surrender his passport in 1952, the initial year of Du Bois's detention, following the transmission of an FBI "name check" to the State Department (U.S., Federal, Cruse, 5 Feb. 1953). Bureau interviewers, courting Cruse as an informer with limited success, were not content until he admitted the justice of this punishment. Eventually, waxing Orwellian, they certified that a reeducated Cruse had accepted state truth, and "realized now that the State Department had every reason to believe he had an ulterior motive in requesting a passport in view of his previous actions" (15 Sept. 1955).

Willard Motley's file advises that the "previous actions" justifying a reduction of mobility might be sexual as well as literary-political. His FBI dossier includes pungent documents of popular anticommunism: an unsolicited letter to Hoover, for instance, tattling on a seditious oath supposedly shouted over a hotel dinner near Motley's home in Cuernavaca, Mexico. "I heard Willard Motley, a negro [sic] writer and eight of his black and white friends toast the Communists and cry 'down with the United States,'" the letter recounted (U.S., Federal, Motley, 29 Sept. 1951). Yet Motley's 1952 request for permission to reenter the United States was refused not for party membership but as "a result of the extreme derogatory information developed against the subject's moral character that reflects that MOTLEY was a homosexual" (18 Mar. 1954). The legal trigger cited was Section 12 (a) of the McCarran-Walter Act, passed earlier in the same year, which denied visas to gays and lesbians along with political subversives (18 Mar. 1954). Whatever its authors' intentions, McCarran-Walter created a more flexible pretext for arresting radical motion. Nineteen fifty-two, probably the worst year of the century to volunteer as an African American internationalist, also stands as the year when the FBI learned that charges of homosexuality could restrain unwanted travels.

Like W.E.B. Du Bois, many African American authors were first separated from their traveling shoes during the second Red Scare. The Cold War harbors of black Paris, black-and-white Mexico, and black-led Ghana were prime targets of Bureau passport sweeps. Even so, the passport status of Claude McKay and Richard Wright attracted FBI snooping prior to 1945, and the list of Afro-modernists whose passports were not revoked but combed for scraps of criminal behavior and "derogatory information" is long, geographically dispersed, and politically varied (U.S., Federal, Hansberry, 30 Mar. 1953). The passport records of James Baldwin, Alice Childress, Katherine Dunham, Lorraine Hansberry, Chester Himes, Langston Hughes, John O. Killens, Julian Mayfield, Louise Thompson Paterson, Dudley Randall, George Schuyler, and Walter White were all studied by the Bureau, with Childress's checked twice after New York agents discovered her ties to a "Committee to Restore Paul Robeson's Passport" (U.S., Federal, Childress, 20 Mar. 1958). Kevin K. Gaines's study of modern African American expatriation suggests that the fairly wide ideological spectrum of these targets, communist and black nationalist and NAACP-style integrationist, was precisely the point. In spite of their "adherence to color-blind ideals," Gaines argues, "U.S. officialdom and its media auxiliaries arrogated to themselves the role of prescribing normative Negro American civic identities, seeking to delegitimize and discourage" most forms of transnational solidarity felt by African Americans (25). Much the same idea is put more colorfully in Ralph Ellison's novel *Three Days Before the Shooting . . .* , the unfinished follow-up to *Invisible Man,* when a white southern reporter insists that the federal government could not "overlook the political implications of a nigra eating too much Chinese or Japanese or Jewish food. Call the FBI if you catch him buying French wines, German beer, or drinks like Aquavit [a Scandinavian liqueur] or Pernod [a French one]" (57). The files of the nonfictional FBI make good on Ellison's riff and Gaines's argument, while also revealing the Bureau's extraordinary involvement in delegitimizing and discouraging black literary transnationalisms in particular. One measure to deter Afro-modernist writers from creating "new and unforeseen alliances and interventions on a global stage," the Bureau knew, was to borrow the means of cross-diasporic translation (Edwards, *The Practice* 5). Another was to deny these writers access to "Passportese," the official state language required for international exploration from World War I forward. Pragmatically mixing and matching the two measures, the FBI became a persistent enemy of those hoping to chart their own course through the black West considered as a "single, complex unit of analysis" (Gilroy, *The Black Atlantic* 15). When counterintelligence agents at the Soviet KGB forged a letter insinuating that the Passport Office bent to Hoover's will, it had a fair share of genuine Black Atlantic history to exploit (Andrew and Mitrokhin 235). And on the morning after African American novelist Lloyd Brown celebrated the return of Paul Robeson's passport with a drunken toast of his own—"that Negro got away, he got away"—it would not have shocked him to learn that a Bureau spy had been there to hear (U.S., Federal, Lloyd Brown, 4 Sept. 1958).

State-Sponsored Transnationalism: The Stop Notice and the Travel Bureau

FBI folklore tells us that J. Edgar Hoover once scrawled the command "Watch the borders!" on an errant Bureau memo. Teams of special agents were hurried to the Mexican and Canadian borders in response, legend has it, before Hoover's readers realized he was alarmed by the memo's inadequate space for marginal commentary: the borders he wanted watched were the typewritten kind (Kessler, *The Bureau* 83). The humor of this FBI story (such as it is) cuts several ways. It tweaks Hoover's picky despotism, and his subordinates' blinding rush to satisfy it. It pokes fun at the gap between strenuous Bureau manhunting in the provinces and fussy print consciousness at the Seat of Government. Less obviously, the story also encodes a suppressed truth about FBI counterliterature in action. Literary boundary breaking, it turns out, really could send FBI agents running to scrutinize geopolitical frontiers. The unintended slippage between print and state limits at the heart of the "Watch the borders!" story became intentional policy, or close to it, on the Afro-modernist beat, where federal literary criticism was sometimes translated into federal border policing. African American authors learned that writing beyond the nation-state required them to breach doubly hardened state borders—borders patrolled not only from the inside out, with authors sometimes denied the ability to travel internationally, but from the outside in, with the FBI scrambling to deny or taint the homecoming of black expatriates. Reinforcing the country's front lines at harbors and airports, the Bureau aspired to stage-manage the practice of black diaspora when it failed to prevent it.

While passports were the main instruments of the FBI's strategy to preempt black diasporan travel, "stop notices" defined its effort to oversee this travel in progress. Much as W.E.B. Du Bois headed up the list of besieged passport applicants, Claude McKay led the roll of Afro-modernist writers threatened by these "stops," instructions to advise and defer to the Bureau if a suspect tried to pass through a designated point of entry. The chapter of McKay's FBI file dealing with his pilgrimage to the Soviet Union resonates around a Bureau-requested stop notice to hold the poet for "appropriate attention" if he attempted to reenter any part of the United States (U.S., Federal, McKay, 12 Dec. 1922). In early 1923, the federal priority of obstructing McKay's return was made known to every reasonably sized U.S. port city. Immigration and customs officers readied themselves to conduct "surveillance" and to confine man, "baggage," and "documents" in New York and Los Angeles, Seattle and Portland, Charleston and Wilmington, New Orleans and Baltimore (1 Apr. 1923; 23 Jan. 1923). Bureau agents in this last city paraded their seriousness in a bulletin sent straight to Hoover, boasting of a clued-in "Local Police Department" on the "lookout" for one "Claude McKay (colored)" (23 Mar. 1923). Milwaukee's special agent in charge compensated for the fugitive's unlikely return via Lake Michigan by digging up "a copy of the magazine called 'Soviet Russia Pictorial,'" and discovering an identifying "photograph of Claude McKay" in Moscow (17 Mar. 1923). Within shouting distance of the Harlem Renaissance, Bureau vigilance made McKay a young writer to watch in more places than literary New York, a welcoming locale he could not reenter at will. Few other writers of American consequence have been subject to so thorough a police dragnet, or so quickly made to follow a movement-building debut— *Harlem Shadows* (1922), the renaissance's first poetry collection—with such challenged freedom of movement.

McKay was well aware of his status as a most wanted man. He insisted to Max Eastman, his most sympathetic American editor, that he was afflicted by government spies, not "persecution mania," and that he knew that U.S. authorities would not "let me in with my Russian record without special intervention" (letter to Max Eastman, [?] Apr. 1933). Eventually, after more than a decade of separation, the belief that McKay's talent was of irreplaceable value to the international reputation of African American letters enabled his return to the States: veteran Harlem Renaissance entrepreneurs James Weldon Johnson and Walter White (a cagey Hoover friend) intervened with the State Department on McKay's behalf, allowing his reentry in 1934. McKay's earlier partings from the country may have been scheduled with Bureau assistance. He shipped off from New York to London in the fall of 1919, in the nick of time to avoid the December deportation of Emma Goldman and fellow "enemy aliens" aboard the "Soviet Ark" arranged by Hoover. The eleven-year excursion throughout western Europe and North Africa that began just after McKay's Soviet hajj was both a chosen bohemian adventure and a compulsory Black Atlanticism, mandated if not defined by stop notices and similar directives of the British and French governments. In a frank letter from a contact at Her Majesty's Office of Works, McKay learned that the British Foreign Office retained "a full record of [his] political and other activities" and would bar his admission to Jamaica, his native island, and other "British Colonial and Protectorate Territories" (Postgate). French intelligence, the same letter testified, kept abreast in caution: it "had reason" to oppose his "presence on French Protectorate soil" (Postgate). More than freely elected cosmopolitanism thus fueled what Alain Locke denounced as McKay's "chronic and perverse truancy" (82), and what McKay alternatively glossed as the flight of his "vagabond soul" (letter to Harold Jackman). When writing the novel *Home to Harlem* (1928), the first black best seller of the Harlem Renaissance, McKay could not confidently go home to Harlem. He imagined his protagonist's pleasure-soaked return in place of his own.

As with the seizure of Du Bois's passport, the FBI's wielding of stop notices against McKay encouraged the general application of an effective strategy. A good number of later author files feature stops, and the deceptively colorless language used to deploy them. William Gardner Smith's file, for example, contains a document asking "that the Washington Field Office place stop notices with the U.S. Bureau of Customs for the return to the United States of the captioned subject" (U.S., Federal, Smith, 8 Oct. 1952). Reminiscent of the all-points/all-ports bulletin issued to frustrate McKay's arrival from the Soviet Union, this document requests "that stops be placed with all east coast ports" (8 Oct. 1952) (see figure 4.1).

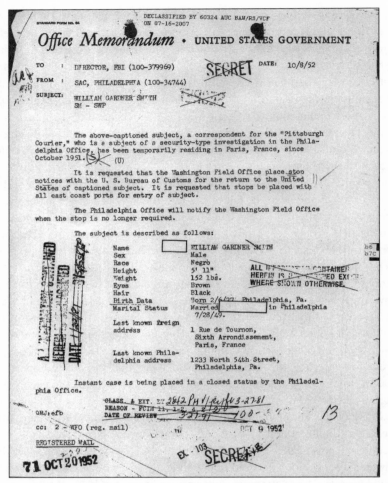

FIGURE 4.1: A once-secret FBI request to place "stop notices" at "all east coast ports of entry" to guard against the re-Americanization of William Gardner Smith. (Courtesy of the FBI.)

Stop notices pursued Smith throughout his expatriate career. In 1968, the FBI's concern over his French writing on American race riots led to further "stops with United States Customs"—stops requested, that is, after Bureau agents heard of Smith's interest in visiting home when questioning his proud mother in the comfort of her American "residence, 1330 South 20th Street, Philadelphia, Pa [*sic*]" (19 Feb. 1968; 13 May 1968). The Chicago home of Willard Motley's mother also received a call from local special agents, who learned that her son "always flies by commercial airlines when returning home," preferring the direct route from Mexico City (U.S., Federal, Motley, 20 Aug. 1954). With an accidental assist from Mrs. Mary Motley, the FBI thus gathered that the novelist's "port of entry into the United States" would be "Chicago, Illinois," and proceeded to place a targeted stop there "for information concerning the subject if he should return" (20 Aug. 1954). Louise Thompson Patterson's plans for a China trip led to a blanket U.S. stop notice (U.S., Federal, Patterson, 11 Oct. 1960), as did W.E.B. Du Bois's growing ties to Nkrumah's Ghana (U.S., Federal, W.E.B. Du Bois, 24 Apr. 1963). When Du Bois finally outran his first passport cancellation, he thus ran into the Bureau's remedy for those who succeeded in crossing the Black Atlantic. Du Bois, Smith, and Motley were not unique, in fact, in facing both a potential inability to escape the United States and a potential inability to return to it. At the FBI, chasing a seized passport with a stop notice was accustomed procedure.

After the assassination of Martin Luther King, a distraught James Baldwin described himself as "the only mobile black American left" and thus a leading candidate for the vacant position of America's most wanted (qtd. in James Campbell, *Syncopations* 98). G-Men listened in on his every transatlantic phone call, Baldwin insisted to a Turkish friend, and seemed equipped to make trouble anywhere in the world (96). In Sedat Pakay's documentary film *From Another Country* (1973), Baldwin can be seen coming across a (planted?) copy of *The FBI Story* at an Istanbul *sahaflar*, a sidewalk seller of used books. After glancing at a nearby (also planted?) edition of *Kara Yabanci*, or *Dark Stranger*, the Turkish translation of his 1962 novel *Another Country*, he chooses the Hoover-approved history to hold close to the camera, accenting the Bureau's projection of literary competition a civilization away from Pennsylvania Avenue (Zaborowska 36). The Turkish Baldwin captured by Pakay was prone to exaggerate his high place in FBI demonology; by the time he encountered *The FBI Story* in Istanbul, Hoover's ghostreaders had lowered their sights to his abandoned script for a Malcolm X biopic. Yet what Baldwin self-diagnosed as his "superbly paranoiac intelligence" was on the mark in perceiving that the Bureau distrusted the international mobility of African American authors and texts (qtd. in James Campbell, *Syncopations* 83). Baldwin's "friendly file," as he liked to call it, dramatizes the lengths to which stop notices were combined with passport checks to unfriend African American authors with global reach (*The Devil* 547).

According to the Baldwin file, the writer's retreats to southern France did not prevent the FBI's legal attaché in Paris from providing Bureau headquarters with rapid access to his passport history. The Seat of Government in

Washington was thus able to share the basics of Baldwin's travel plans with the CIA and the State Department, relative novices apprised that the "[s]ubject is a Negro male" who has authored "several books and has been active in the Civil Rights movement" (1 Nov. 1966; 2 Nov. 1966). It took the Bureau's documentation of copious stop notices, however, to produce a nearly real-time file record of Baldwin's international movements. Over one two-year slice of the late 1960s, FBI correspondence on these stops records (1) the Bureau-bound telephone call of a U.S. immigration agent in Montreal, reporting before takeoff on Baldwin's seat "aboard Air Canada flight #572 to New York, N.Y." (6 Sept. 1967); (2) an alert from Bureau headquarters to New York's Kennedy airport warning that Baldwin would likely return from London "during the month of January 1968" (5 Jan. 1968); (3) a later dispatch confirming that Baldwin had returned on "7/11/68 aboard Pan Am Flight #101 from Paris" and had been questioned about "his birthdate, 2/2/24," on his arrival (11 July 1968); and (4) a letter to Hoover relating that the "noted author . . . had arrived at Los Angeles International Airport from Mexico City at 11:50 a.m." on April 9, 1969, "and is scheduled to be in Los Angeles for approximately three days" (28 Apr. 1969). More permanent coordinates were requested at customs, with Baldwin asked to supply his personal and business addresses in Harlem (28 Apr. 1969).

Stop notices did not detain Baldwin for long once he reached New York or Los Angeles; considered as appliances of border policing, they were usually less literal than their name suggests. Yet stops had the power to pinpoint their target's border crossings to the minute, sometimes before that minute arrived, and occasionally down to the airplane seat number. They provided various state agencies with a pretext to interview suspects on arrival, and to spread a common climate of suspicion across departmental lines. Most valuable of all was the stop's unwritten service as a government travel advisory: if you had appreciated territories beyond the ideological orbit of the U.S., stop notices instructed, you should continue to do so, and stay away. Baldwin's stops were not altogether like McKay's, since only the latter writer fully expected to be turned back at U.S. checkpoints. But Baldwin, too, trusted that stop orders warned of mortal harm. As he conceived it, Hoover's accomplices at the border ensured that the same state-composed document that pronounced him "a free citizen of a free country" in Europe "underwent a sea change" when displayed "on the other side of the ocean" (James Baldwin, *No Name* 378). Reinterpreted at the checkpoints of white America, Baldwin's U.S. passport advised him "that I was not an African prince, but a domestic nigger and that no foreign government would be offended if my corpse were to be found clogging up the sewers" (378). No welcoming light—just the opposite—was signaled by this passport's green binding. In 1976, with Hoover's shadow lifted, Baldwin could suggest that the Bureau's threats had taught him a valuable lesson: his literary vocation and his love for the United States "might, never, in my life, be reconciled" (*The Devil* 549). FBI agents had not marched him aboard his first boat to France in 1948 but had done their part to keep him sailing back in search of reconciled work and community.

From time to time, Hoover's G-Men camouflaged themselves as commercial travel agents. In September 1968, for example, a special agent telephoned the New York apartment of Harold Cruse—now known and feared for *The Crisis of the Negro Intellectual* (1967)—and pretended to be an employee "of a travel agency" hoping to book his next international trip (U.S., Federal, Cruse, 30 Sept. 1968). More often than not, however, Hoover and his agents used stop notices to expedite the travel of Afro-modernists already outside the country. The FBI revered national laws, national symbols, and national literary publicity, but in this respect claimed the authority to define citizenship beyond national borders. Here, as in its many trials-by-passport, the FBI assumed the right to prescribe suitable "civic identities" to black subjects (Gaines 25). In the case of the stop notice, however, state police power was harnessed to promote black statelessness rather than homebound Negro Americanism. On the reverse of the renationalizing passport seizure was a Bureau weapon we can call "state-sponsored transnationalism," a denationalizing administered from without.

In the end, the FBI files that document state-sponsored transnationalism also expose imperfections in Paul Gilroy's winning model of black internationalism. Not ten years after the publication of *The Black Atlantic*, Sandra Gunning observed that Gilroy's nautical world "of African diasporic hybridity enriched by cultural crossovers" had sparked a love affair with "diaspora identification" among scholars of African American culture (33). A "romanticizing [of] the revolutionary and subversive power of this identification," she cautioned, threatened to obscure "the very real impact of color, status, region, and gendered experience as sites of intra-racial difference within the context of the black diaspora" (33). Under Gilroy's spell, she concluded, the great advantage of the diaspora concept, its tolerance for variety and friction, was placed at risk. The Bureau's countersubversive surveillance of black diasporan travel reinforces Gunning's early warning against romanticizing the subversive politics of diasporan identity. At the same time, however, this surveillance demands the inclusion of national origin alongside color, status, region, and gender on her list of unsung scenes of diasporan difference. The threat of passport cancellation, perfected against the U.S.-born Du Bois, could trouble almost any Afro-modernist brave enough to travel outside the United States. In distinction, the discipline of the stop notice was pioneered and sharpened into deportation actions against an honor roll of black migrants from the Caribbean, writers and activists whose willful revisions of the Middle Passage brought unwilled transatlantic returns. Think not only of McKay, informally extradited from his adopted Manhattan, but of fellow Jamaican Marcus Garvey, forced to reemigrate from Harlem to Kingston after his Bureau-spearheaded conviction for mail fraud. Think too of the deportation of Trinidad-born critic/theorist/novelist/Trotskyist faction leader C.L.R. James, who filled his days awaiting expulsion on Ellis Island by taking stock of *Moby-Dick* and untimely anticapitalism. ("If Captain Ahab were to express [his] opinions today," James vented in *Mariners, Renegades, and Castaways: The Story of Herman Melville and the World We Live In* (1953), "he would not only be blackballed by every employer in the country, but he would be rigorously investigated by the FBI" [12].) James's Trinidadian countrywoman, editor-organizer Claudia Jones, was likewise ejected from the United States to England for sins of communism. According to Carole Boyce Davies, her intellectual biographer, Jones's FBI file alone proves the need to integrate deportation, "the other side of immigration," into twenty-first-century conceptions of the mobilized African diaspora (137). Jones's predecessor Claude McKay appears just once in Gilroy's *Black Atlantic*, in relation to his involvement with ships, perhaps "the most important conduit of Pan-African communication before the appearance of the long-playing record" (Peter Linebaugh qtd. in Gilroy, *The Black Atlantic* 13). Had this literary immigrant also entered the book for his involvement with the Bureau, we might now have a richer, more nationally differentiated sense of the state-sponsored transnationalism, "stopped" and deported, that helped to mold the second, iconically voluntary stage of black diasporan travel. If it had been up to McKay's pursuers at the Bureau, in fact, the FBI would have supplanted both the ship and the LP as a medium of Pan-African messaging.

Jazz Ambassadors versus Literary Escapees

When the bebop bandleader Dizzy Gillespie half-seriously ran for president in 1964, he half-seriously nominated Miles Davis, a famously muted jazz voice who then favored Company-like Ivy League tailoring, to head up the CIA (Gillespie 457). Artists in the literary wing of African American modernism were somewhat less free to crack wise about the consonance of black art and U.S. intelligence. The State Department might send Gillespie, Louis Armstrong, and lesser trumpet virtuosos on goodwill tours of Europe, Africa, and the Middle East, convinced that international news of racial discrimination was America's

Achilles' heel in the global battle with communism, and that jazz swung with the corrective sounds of interracial democracy (Von Eschen 1–26). The CIA might fight its cultural Cold War by prying open European roles for soprano Leontyne Price and other African American opera divas, reasoning that the living presence of transcendent black voices would prevent "all criticisms to the effect that we . . . wouldn't let our own 'out'" (qtd. in Saunders 119). The FBI, by contrast, aspired to keep African American writers on the lam when not down on the farm, reflecting those interests in the federal bureaucracy comfortable with the Cold War state's reluctance to enforce racial equality on the home front. The addition of FBI author files to the civil rights archive reveals a dialectic of Cold War recruitment of African American art stretched between Hoover's suspicious ghostreaders and the eager listeners of the Company and the diplomatic corps, between the strategic export of black music's democratic abstraction and the managed travels of Afro-modernist literature's social text.[22]

To be trailed or propelled by the Bureau was not to be remade by it entirely. FBI files on African American authors capture Hoover's critic-spies making like G-Men Dr. Bledsoes, devising secret letters and scheming to keep those writers running. Their efforts produced victories in Paris noir, Cuernavaca, and Accra but never installed an intelligence network sharp enough to dictate all routes within a vast transatlantic territory. In the last analysis, however, the repercussions of Hoover's early interest in cartography should not be ignored by Black Atlantic theory. His FBI strived to outmap a navy of literary voyagers and succeeded in penetrating the time and space of the twentieth-century Black Atlantic system. The non-synchronous present of this system, indebted to the barbarous modernity of the transatlantic slave trade, was punctuated by echoes of a past of forced transportation courtesy of FBI stop notices.[23] Its sprawling diasporic geography was split internally not only by energizing linguistic differences, but also by the renationalizing atomization of passport seizures. In both respects, a chiefly repressive state police force influenced the making of a resistant black transnationalism, thus arguing that the state powers most opposed to discourses of adversarial internationalism may still do their part to translate them into action.

In particular, the FBI did its part to tinge the modern, mobilized black diaspora with old bitterness. *Galut* (גלות in Hebrew) is a synonym for "exile" in the Jewish Hellenistic tradition, signifying "anguish, forced homelessness, and the sense of things being not as they should be" (Wettstein 2). African diaspora scholarship, Brent Hayes Edwards suggests, has been too inclined to overlook this term and its eschatological resonances, mistakenly assuming that the Greek word "diaspora" was employed "to translate a relatively wide number of Hebrew words . . . relating both to scattering and exile" ("Diaspora" 82). In truth, "diaspora" was most often used in the Septuagint, the Jewish Torah rendered into Koine Greek, to indicate "a state of dispersal resulting from voluntary migration" (82). It is never used to translate *galut*, a Hebrew keyword for exile, and the term of choice for ideas of uprooting "laced with a sense of violence, suffering, and punishment" (82). Edwards contends that accounts of black transnationalism could improve their accuracy by recognizing this etymological distinction. They would also do well to reflect the state intrusion that made the twentieth-century Black Atlantic a confluence of both diaspora *and* galut, an arena of transnational home making etched by a battle with forced homelessness.

Part Five/Thesis Five

Consciousness of FBI Ghostreading Fills a Deep and Characteristic Vein of African American Literature

Try to imagine a world in which a national police force collects and dissects African American literature; a strange world in which the repressive state apparatus moonlights as a racially expressive apparatus, not only shadowing the leading lights of black criticism, but also commissioning its own variety. Richard Wright could imagine such a world, since he suspected he was living in one beginning in 1942. Late in that tense wartime year, J. Edgar Hoover, agitated by Wright's photo-history *Twelve Million Black Voices* (1941), ordered the Bureau's New York field office to review all of the author's publications for signs of subversion. "If your inquiry develops information of an affirmative nature," Hoover directed, "you should of course cause an investigation to be undertaken as to the subject's background, inclinations, and current activities" (U.S., Federal, Wright, 8 Dec. 1942). Inevitably, information of an affirmative nature was developed, and an investigation undertaken, leaving Wright wary of the G-Men who seemed to track his literary and romantic itineraries all over greater New York.[1] Wright's flight to France, launched in 1947 with unspoken encouragement from his Bureau pursuers, initially delivered on the promises of expatriation. Even before the Gibson Affair divided black Paris and brought his mistrust to a boil, however, Wright grew troubled by the sense that G-Men lurked around foreign corners.

Consider Wright's voyage to Buenos Aires aboard the S.S. *Uruguay* in 1949. A snapshot taken below deck captures a healthy forty-year-old adopting the Ernest Hemingway brand of office casual, working bare-chested on a punching bag to slim down enough to play his most vivid character, the teenaged Bigger

Thomas, in the film version of *Native Son*. Yet this willfully anti-intellectual Wright interrupted his rejuvenation in international waters long enough to compose a poem whose satire of U.S. espionage incompletely masked its anxiety. In "The FB Eye Blues" (1949), the inspiration for this book's title, Wright turned the tables on Bureau note taking, worrying classic blues lines with wry digs at spy-sight:

> That old FB eye
> Tied a bell to my bed stall
> Said old FB eye
> Tied a bell to my bed stall
> Each time I love my baby, gover'ment knows it all.

> Woke up this morning
> FB eye under my bed
> Said I woke up this morning
> FB eye under my bed
> Told me all I dreamed last night, every word I said.

> Everywhere I look, Lord
> I see FB eyes
> Said every place I look, Lord
> I find FB eyes
> I'm getting sick and tired of gover'ment spies. (ll. 1–15)

"The FB Eye Blues," nine cut-up A-A-B blues stanzas in all, owes most of its title to an old, inside-the-Bureau term for FBI special agents, "F.B. Eyes." Its drama of the indiscreet spy and the riled victim dips deep into blues history—something Wright supposedly knew nothing about—to revisit Bessie Smith's recording of "Eavesdropper's Blues," a song written for this queen of the music by J. C. Johnson in 1924:

> I heard the folks were talkin' here yesterday
> As I listened by the door;
> But eavesdroppers, they never hear no good, they say,
> And I think that I be sore! (J. C. Johnson, ll. 1–4)

As the final stanzas of Wright's poem confirm, his blues vamps on Johnson and Smith's by recasting their first-person female perpetrator as a male mark of the state: the mannish speaker of "The FB Eye Blues" is the party eavesdropped on—and possibly bugged in bed—by a government listener able to recite "every word [he] said." Here, as in thousands of pages of Bureau files, the interaction between the FBI and the African American writer is imagined as action between men. Maybe as a result, Wright's male speaker is less confident than Johnson and Smith's spied-on "folks" of his righteous difference from the snoops who leave him sick and tired. Living under Bureau scrutiny, Wright suggests, comes awkwardly close to sleeping and cowriting with the brother-enemy. The eye of the Bureau seems to share his speaker's experience of lovemaking ("Each time I love my baby, gover'ment knows it all" [l. 5]) and to inhabit his verbal unconscious along with him ("Told me all I dreamed last night, every word I said" [l. 10].) In several respects, then, Wright's FBI—an eye that hears even better than it sees—refuses to skulk on the side of the door Johnson and Smith reserve for eavesdroppers only. The seer and the seen, the overheard and the listener with perfect recall, share the same bed stall.[2]

Wright's need to box with the Bureau's shadow even while steaming beyond the nation-state may reveal his suspicion that the F.B. eye was just as able as he to board a master symbol of Black Atlantic mobility. More certainly, this need reveals one of the defining impulses in the black literary modernism born in 1919 with the Harlem Renaissance and the FBI's Radical Division. Wright's wrestling with the FBI is characteristic of a longer literary line forced to reckon with its image in the Bureau's spyglass. The unsung poem "The FB Eye Blues" indeed ranks as a textbook piece of Afro-modernist writing, in some respects as emblematic as the canonical prose of *Native Son*.[3] A bit paradoxically, it is the extraordinary openness of the poem's rendezvous with the FBI that underlies its representativeness. Like the nine volumes of Laurence Sterne's *Tristram Shandy* (1759–67), an exceptionally meandering heap of self-conscious narration that just may qualify as "the most typical novel in world literature" (Shklovsky 170), the nine stanzas of "The FB Eye Blues" flaunt a generic trait generally more restrained elsewhere.[4] The "I"-versus-spy clash of Wright's poem, this is to say, is a pronounced case of a tacitly common drama—a drama at least as typical of Afro-modernism as Sterne's self-reflexive tale-telling is of the world novel. For as quiet as it's kept, the leading edge of Afro-modernism regularly sharpened itself against the specter of FBI surveillance.

The specifically literary effects of FBI surveillance might be measured in slippery but provocative metrics of silencing: the number of novels abandoned or banned from bookstores and libraries; the number of early radical poems unreprinted or apologized for; the number of whole literary careers shortened or never started. Proof of book killing, stop-the-presses FBI censorship of Afro-modernist literature is lacking, however. Unlike the censorship applied by South Africa's apartheid regime, the Bureau's response to black books was not "essentially prohibitive" (McDonald 12). As we saw earlier, the Total Literary Awareness campaign of the Cold War, the closest thing to classic prepublication censorship in the annals of Bureau counterliterature, thwarted Max Lowenthal's FBI history much better than Lorraine Hansberry's play *A Raisin in the Sun*. But what about the consequences of more subtle methods of FBI suppression, the damage done when the aura or potential of state censorship promotes self-censorship? When the Bureau flexed its power to discourage expatriate Afro-modernists from returning to write in the United States, did it inspire them to abandon other artistic liberties on their own? Isn't the complete history of Bureau counterliterature, the failed preemption of Hansberry's play included, the history of a fluid strategy to make heavy-handed state censorship redundant?

Poet and journalist Natalie Robins, the author of the most comprehensive survey of the "FBI's war on freedom of expression," concludes that the Bureau's stifling influence on American writing as a whole was oblique but profound (Robins 1). Through a string of leading questions, she contends that FBI censorship worked best when least direct, worming its way into literary fashion and literary self-consciousness through Bureau-fueled angst:

> How many writers were censored, even in vague, dimly perceived ways, by nervous editors, publishers, teachers, or administrators who may have received visits or questions from FBI agents, or simply had heard of the writer's reputation as a "radical"? And how many, knowing that relatives, friends, neighbors, acquaintances, or colleagues were being interviewed by the FBI, engaged in some form of self-censorship? . . . Will we ever know whether a particular character, scene, locale, or plot direction was a result of either conscious or unconscious self-censorship? Or that a book or play or article was aborted by fear? Or that an entire generation of writers and a genre of writing became suddenly "unfashionable" because of the tales of suspicion borne by the FBI to a society that had grown fearful and wary of ideas? (398–99)

We will never know precisely how many writers and works were lost to these "vague, dimly perceived ways" of censorship, in fact—the rules of vague, dim, and absent evidence prevent it. But we have no reason to doubt that testimony of possible losses is plentiful in the records of the FBI's culture war on African American letters. Not every editorial in the *Negro Digest* and the *Chicago*

Defender, we have learned, defied the underlying message of frequent FBI agent visits during World War II. FBI files of the 1950s suggest that expatriate novelists Willard Motley and William Gardner Smith heard straight from maternal sources that G-Men were paying house calls to their relatives in the United States. According to biographer James Campbell, the many reports of wiretapping in James Baldwin's FBI file pinpoint the main cause of his shrunken productivity after 1963, the year of John F. Kennedy's slaying and Baldwin's outraged discovery of Bureau surveillance of civil rights protestors in Selma. "It is hard to write between assassinations," Baldwin mordantly explained, and even tougher, adds Campbell, "when everyone—or so it seems—is listening to the writer's private conversation with himself" (*Syncopations* 100). Everyone, that is, except the distracted, Bureau-tapped writer in question.

Amiri Baraka, who would not rule out the possibility that the FBI assassinated Richard Wright,[5] theorized that Bureau persecution first pointed Wright toward Euro-quietism, another kind of writer's block. Alienated in the Parisian orbit of "Gertrude Stein and Jean-Paul Sartre" in the years after *Native Son*, Wright's Bureau-seared "consciousness goes through a real weird shift," Baraka judged, and "he no longer is the same kind of very relentless revolutionary voice of the early days" (qtd. in Robins 287). Baraka's account of Wright's change of mind seconds the gist of Robins's proposal that FBI antagonism, filtered through a frightened literary public, may have neutered "an entire generation of writers and a genre of writing": specifically, Wright and other U.S. writers raised on leftist social realism in the 1930s and early 1940s (398–99). If Robins's fears are justified, then the Bureau cunningly arranged to supplant an entire crop of plain-speaking progressive authors with cryptic, deskbound modernists. Hoover's ghostreaders, she submits, accelerated the political devolution of twentieth-century literary style.[6]

The idea of an FBI-prompted turn to an allegedly disinterested, objectively reactionary literary modernism rhymes with more familiar accounts of the CIA's championing of abstract expressionism over social realism in the visual arts. It fails to fit, however, with many of the known details of the FBI's literary Kulturkampf. Unlike the eggheads at the CIA-funded Congress for Cultural Freedom, FBI ghostreaders showed no favoritism to U.S.-bred high modernism, however effectively marketed in opinion-leading European capitals. G-Men did not mistakenly associate London-bound Ezra Pound, the Bureau's first individual writer-target, with proletarian fiction. They neglected to advance the careers of Wright's Paris acquaintance Gertrude Stein, briefly investigated by the Bureau in the late 1930s, and T. S. Eliot, the mind of Europe whose two-page FBI file collects communist objections to his anti-Semitism (Robins 207–9, 424).

In any event, the transatlantic high modernism these poets instigated preceded and informed the Depression-era turn to radical social realism. Outside of U.S. English departments, then embracing an Eliotic-Angletonian New Criticism, this modernism was a spent or secondary influence (an imprisoned influence, in Pound's case) for many live American writers by the late 1940s, the time the FBI is supposed to have embarrassed a literary generation in its direction. In imaginative literature, unlike the visual arts, even the ironically past-conscious avant-gardism of "late modernism" was by then a contested force linked with modernism's snowballing institutionalization.[7] Put more directly, to suggest that the Cold War Bureau shrewdly moved the mountain from left-realism to right-modernism is not only to credit the Hooverites with super-supple powers they did not possess; it is also, in significant ways, to get American literary history backward.

The course of African American literary history in particular is reversed by the mountain-moving scenario, but not mainly because it places the realist cart before the modernist horse. As it happens, the idea of high modernism deposing social realism during the Cold War maps smoothly onto one outmoded narrative of African American literary development, the narrowly Oedipal tale in which Baldwin and Ralph Ellison belatedly pioneer black modernism after thunderous breaks with Wright's proletarian aesthetics and Marxist politics. The most glaring problem with the mountain-moving scenario when applied to African American literature is this instead, in a nutshell: Wright marked his expatriation to a postwar world including Stein and Sartre with "The FB Eye Blues." The Cold War year of 1949 found Wright jousting with the Bureau by name rather than renouncing his "revolutionary voice" under Hoover's thumb—and not for the last time, given the counter-FBI speeches and spy plots of his final book-length fiction, *Island of Hallucination* (1959). Furthermore, despite Baldwin's filleting of the sentimental didacticism of everybody's protest novel, *Native Son*, he followed in Wright's footsteps to protest Bureau spying, passionately threatening federal "Blood Counters" with an exposé meant to pin Hoover "to the wall" (U.S., Federal, Baldwin, 7 June 1963). Ellison much more politely called out Hoover and the Bureau, devoting a draft section of *Invisible Man* (1952), the Great American Negro Novel of the Cold War, to the G-Man's role in the dream life of the Great Migration. Ellison's disaffection with Richard Wright's blues, mounting with every year of labor on this novel, thus exempted "The FB Eye Blues," a work of both special frankness and stealthy influence.

None of these relatively obscure or unfinished texts addressing the FBI came to dominate their author's reputations or royalty checks. But their family resemblance indicates a key pitfall in breaking modern African American literary history into succeeding camps of brave realists and Bureau-browbeaten modernists. Even on the far side of the Cold War dividing line, perhaps the three most prominent African American authors of the mid-twentieth century wrote to answer the literary incursions of Hoover's police. And they were not alone. One of the common features of what I have loosely called Afro-modernism—the diverse body of audacious and self-consciously modern black American writing produced between 1919 and 1972—is an impulse to dramatize the problem of FBI ghostreading. Beyond Baraka's chastened Wright and Campbell's unproductive Baldwin and all the other hazy data of indirect Bureau censorship lies the collected works of a modernism that overtly addresses Hoover's Bureau across various styles, genres, and generations. The page production of many years of Afro-modernist literature, in other words, is proof that African American authors often declined to suffer ghostreading in silence. Hunting for submerged traces of what Bureau-threatened writers purged from their work is thus not the only means of measuring the FBI's footprint in African American writing. Descriptive, close-to-the-surface reading will also do the trick, since buried evidence of self-silencing is balanced by evidence highlighted on the exterior of modern black texts. John A. Williams, the novelist and anticensorship campaigner, might insist in this connection that African American texts have *never* had the luxury of reticence in the face of censorship. As he sees it, "blackballing," a spectrum of racially divisive literary restrictions akin to political blacklisting, has plainly molded African American writing since its emergence in the middle of the eighteenth century, not accidentally the era of the first slave laws proscribing black literacy ("Blackballing" 11–12).[8] Williams's literary history is true enough, of course, yet his fiction is its own, differently weighted argument. As we will see, *The Man Who Cried I Am* (1967), Williams's most successful novel, condenses the lengthy history of blackballing in the figure of the black-baiting federal intelligence bureaucracy—a figure that crystallizes the historically persistent threat of racialized censorship and that appears elsewhere, in several shapes, over the long haul of Afro-modernism.

Here is a truth of twentieth-century literature not universally recognized: the long haul of Afro-modernism was steered by literary intellectuals, Williams included, who were convinced that nonfictional government intelligence agents watched them like hawks. Author memoirs and FBI file records verify that many of these literary intellectuals were questioned by live FBI agents who flashed their badges and pledged their allegiance to Hoover: this underpublicized most-wanted list includes James Baldwin, Amiri Baraka, Gwendolyn Bennett, Lloyd Brown, Sterling Brown, Harold Cruse, Frank Marshall Davis, Ray Durem, E. Franklin Frazier, Nikki Giovanni, Calvin Hernton, Charles S. Johnson,

Georgia Douglas Johnson, Audre Lorde, Pauli Murray, Larry Neal, Louise Thompson Patterson, William Pickens, J. Saunders Redding, Sonia Sanchez, William Gardner Smith, Walter White, and Richard Wright.[9] A larger pool of African American writers and critics, other records suggest, assumed that they were FBI suspects without the confirmation of agent questioning, among them Johari Amini (Jewel Lattimore), Gwendolyn Brooks, Frank London Brown, Alice Childress, St. Clair Drake, Shirley Graham Du Bois, W.E.B. Du Bois, Ralph Ellison, Hoyt Fuller, Sam Greenlee, Lorraine Hansberry, Ollie Harrington, Chester Himes, Langston Hughes, Lance Jeffers, James Weldon Johnson, Bob Kaufman, John O. Killens, Paule Marshall, Julian Mayfield, Claude McKay, Willard Motley, Gloria Naylor, Dudley Randall, Ishmael Reed, George S. Schuyler, A. B. Spellman, and Theodore Ward.[10]

Obviously, there are pivotal contributors to Afro-modernism missing from these two lists. Jessie Fauset, Zora Neale Hurston, Nella Larsen, Ann Petry, and Jean Toomer are absent, none of whom, the Bureau's FOIA office informs me, was ever monitored through a file at FBI national headquarters (the Hoover Bureau's preoccupation with the case of G-Men v. black men may have spared most from the F.B. eye). All the same, the sheer number and stature and corroborating interconnection of the African American authors convinced of FBI surveillance suggests a peculiar feature of the literature they created together: from the Harlem Renaissance through the Black Arts movement, this literature had every reason to recognize that FBI agents ranked with its most reliable and formidable readers. Much as the U.S. Communist Party taught its members to anticipate Bureau surveillance, and as elected politicians in Washington learned to assume that their private conversations were bugged by Hoover, Afro-modernists passed down word of the Bureau's reading habits and generally came to expect FBI attention. Chester Himes, for example, informed his younger admirer John A. Williams "that the FBI had a dossier on me going back to my childhood" (Himes, qtd. in Williams, "My Man Himes" 86). For this and other reasons, Williams assumed the same was true for him. Like other groups mistrusted at FBI headquarters, the Afro-modernists (several of whom were also communists or politicos familiar with the ways of D.C.) honed aspects of their craft in reaction. African American authors were not privy to the classified theories of FBI literary criticism identified in part 3 of this book, but they appreciated that the terms of their writing might help to set them.

This fifth and last part of *F.B. Eyes* thus argues that Afro-modernist literature "pre-responded" to FBI inspection, internalizing the likelihood of Bureau ghostreading and publicizing its implications with growing bluntness and embellishment over the years from 1919 to 1972 and beyond. Thus the fifth and last of the book's five theses, and the one that finally involves closer encounters with black poems, stories, essays, and novels than with their silhouettes in FBI files: *Consciousness of FBI ghostreading fills a deep and characteristic vein of African American literature.* A shaping consciousness of the national-security state is not unique to Afro-modernist writing, to be sure. The epistemological skepticism of much U.S. postmodernism, notes Timothy Melley, was fostered by its creators' wariness of a pervasive "covert sphere" penetrated and epitomized by the cynical discourse of the CIA (5). Thanks to post-1945 novelists such as William Burroughs, Don DeLillo, Joan Didion, E. L. Doctorow, William Gibson, Norman Mailer, and Thomas Pynchon, the covert sphere's half-public, half-privileged domain of fantasy about "the clandestine dimensions of the state" has incited high-status literary experiments alongside countless spy thrillers and science fictions (5). Afro-modernist writers rivaled the generic range and frequent seriousness of Melley's mostly white postmodernists when concentrating on the intersecting domains of state secrecy and state literacy.[11] And as with Melley's postmodernists, the majority of the most active Afro-modern respondents to government ghostreading were men, a circumstance that partly reflects the gendering of U.S. intelligence history and that ironically begins to fade only with the masculinist Black Arts movement. In crucial distinction to Melley's writers, however, the Afro-modernists accepted the inspiration of the national-security state decades before the "post-" met the modern, or epistemological uncertainty became a required sign of literary contemporaneity, or the CIA became the exemplary face of U.S. state security. Homing in on the Bureau that documented its invention, Afro-modernism confidently represented the ploys and tastes of state intelligence as early as the Harlem Renaissance.

Section 1 of this part of *F.B. Eyes* thus examines decisive responses to FBI surveillance in both the early journalism and the foundational poetry of the Harlem movement. Just as James Weldon Johnson and other columnist-midwives of the renaissance publicly greeted *Radicalism and Sedition among the Negroes*, the Bureau's original rejoinder to New Negro writing, Claude McKay refined the opening statements of renaissance verse with an eye to his vocal state readership. McKay's once-scandalous preference for the Shakespearian sonnet, this section suggests, purposefully echoed the censor-burdened poetry of early modern England, a prior expression of cultural renaissance saddled and energized by state interference.

Following McKay's combatively evasive sonnets and an unusual moment of quiet during the Great Depression, most Afro-modernist replies to Bureau ghostreading opted for greater transparency. Full treatment of the conversation of "post-Harlem" writing with the FBI would fill another book, so further sections of part 5 spotlight a handful of major authors and episodes. A second section ranging from George Schuyler's pulp fiction to Langston Hughes's "Simple" stories to Ralph Ellison's drafts of *Invisible Man* charts the FBI's migrant status in Afro-modernism from the mid-1930s through the early Cold War. The third and fourth sections explore later, historically distinct combinations. In the third, the focus is the expatriate trio of Richard Wright, William Gardner Smith, and Chester Himes, and their interlocking fictions of Paris noir in the late 1950s and early 1960s. In the fourth, the focus is wider, owing to the profusion of black Bureau writing in the late 1960s and early 1970s. Briefly taking the stage are the novelists John A. Williams, James Baldwin, Chester Himes (once more), Sam Greenlee, Melvin Van Peebles, and Ishmael Reed. Also featured are the poets Amiri Baraka, Nikki Giovanni, and Sonia Sanchez, an argumentative collective joined in conversation over Hoover's place in the demonology of the Black Arts movement. A fifth and last section of part five sketches African American literature's less heated skirmish with the FBI after Hoover's death—a skirmish now led by black women including Ai, Audre Lorde, Danzy Senna, and Gloria Naylor.

Each of these sections reveals an Afro-modernism mindful of at least some of the FBI's hostile maneuvers as a would-be censor and border guard; the effective disappearance of a number of important African American texts criticizing the Bureau (e.g., Baldwin's exposé *The Blood Counters*) may signal this mindfulness as well as more common writer's blocks. Yet each section also reveals a literature eager to reemploy the burden of FBI reading as a spur to aesthetic research, a provocation for fresh narrative stances or new literary subgenres from the novelistic "antifile" to the anti-elegiac "Hoover Poem," both described below. This creative reception of Bureau ghostreading did not transform FBI surveillance into a good thing for African American literature, full stop; the business of this book's first four parts, from stop orders to Custodial Detention listings, has illustrated why it was not such a thing, in some detail. But the literary record shows that knowledge of FBI ghostreading acted like a historically "normal" dose of threatened state censorship, fueling a split experience of alarming vulnerability and enhanced cultural confidence among its targets. This experience in turn nurtured a historically recurring style of inverse logic through which the persecuted writer anticipates winning by losing, or securing final spiritual victory by spinning political abjection into artistic gold.[12]

The "most ancient and insoluble predicament" of artistic censorship, remarks Annabel Patterson, is that "controls against freedom of expression are as likely to increase resistance as to weaken it, and to increase the value of works that if disregarded by the authorities would become insignificant to their audience also" (907). Tacitus, the ancient Roman historian, thus boasted in his *Annals* that "genius chastised grows in authority" (152). For better and worse, the Afro-modernism chastised by the Bureau grew in the knowledge that it was good enough—or BaddDDD enough[13]—to keep the state up at night, turning its pages. This knowledge was a matter of self-definition as well as self-respect. Kenneth Warren, the risk-taking, black bourgeois–shocking literary critic, mistakes a historical part for a historical whole in his thesis that African American literature, in its entirety, lived, died, and cohered in opposition to "the social world defined by Jim Crow," the legally segregated U.S. scene of the 1890s to the 1960s (*What Was* 1). Closer to the truth is the claim that the Afro-modernist chapter of this literature, 1919 to 1972, took shape in opposition to the wider world defined by the FBI. Warren's generic African American author is an especially literate version of W.E.B. Du Bois's socially black person, one whose racial identity is performatively sealed as he or she roams beneath the Mason-Dixon line and is required to "ride 'Jim Crow' in Georgia" (W.E.B. Du Bois, *Dusk* 666). The deliberately modern and cosmopolitan African American author conjured up by many Afro-modernists, by contrast, was such a person now bound to ride the whip of the FBI most everywhere. More than a casual trickle of Afro-modernist texts suggest that the victorious race-writer of their era would outwrite the long arm reaching from Georgia to New York to Paris, from the South to the North to the eastern shore of the Black Atlantic. Afro-modernism, they proposed, was a literature best created in worldly defiance of the F.B. eye.

Reading Ghostreading in the Harlem Renaissance: New Negro Journalists and Claude McKay

Earlier pages of *F.B. Eyes* have shown that inside the Bureau, the 1919 report *Radicalism and Sedition among the Negroes as Reflected in Their Publications* cemented J. Edgar Hoover's newly minted anticommunism to the FBI's established New Negrophobia. It enriched the reputation of Robert Adger Bowen, the report's primary ghostwriter, who basked in Hoover's opinion that his effort made a masterpiece. Outside the Bureau, *Radicalism and Sedition* raised many of the alarms that Bowen and Hoover had intended. Extracted in the *New York Times*, quoted in the *Congressional Record* and compliant local newspapers, it prominently annotated early Harlem Renaissance poetry as a siren song of treason and assured the conservative public "that the Bureau of Investigation has been making a most exhaustive study of all radical activities along this line" ("Radicalism among Negroes Growing"). Meanwhile, for the smaller public of New Negro literary intellectuals, *Radicalism and Sedition* proved that the Bureau was watching and reading them intently, and would continue to do so as long as they considered racial inequality "cause for the utterance of inflammatory statement" (U.S., Senate, *Radicalism* 161–62). What Hoover and Bowen's exercise in state literary criticism failed to realize, however, was its hope that New Negro publications would thereafter stop reflecting literate radicalism among the Negroes. The magazines censured in *Radicalism and Sedition* instead responded to Bureau interpretation with unawed counterinterpretations of their own; even as the Justice Department touted the intimidating effects when "persons of revolutionary design [know] that the Government is watching them very closely" (qtd. in Schmidt 171), New Negro journalists read their state readers out publicly. In the process, the periodical instigators of Harlem's renaissance announced that lit.-cop federalism, the Hoover Bureau's investment in the print public sphere, would be publicized and answered as such.

Over the course of November 1919, just weeks after *Radicalism and Sedition*'s appearance, the *Negro World*, the Garvey movement's multilingual weekly, published several reactions to its image in the F.B. eye. One was a livid letter to the editor suggesting that the militancy of the new black writing was simply the fault of white injustice. Two others signed by the Reverend William H. Ferris, the *Negro World*'s Harvard-trained literary editor, were flattering around their sharp edges. In the first, Ferris acknowledged that *Radicalism and Sedition* was "the most thoughtful study of Negro radicalism that we have seen for some time" ("The Rise").[14] He did not know that this thoughtful study's lead author, Robert Bowen, ensconced in the Bureau's department of Translations and Radical Publications, would return the compliment by secretly transcribing his words for safekeeping, noting that "[e]vidently The Negro World is pleased to be taken seriously" (Bowen, "The Re-Action" 2). A second Ferris response also made it into Bowen's analysis of "The Re-Action to Date of the Negro Press," an early salvo in the war of mirrors, G-Man reflecting Afro-modernist and vice versa, that Bureau ghostreading triggered. In his "Thanksgiving Sermon" for 1919, Ferris brashly gave thanks that *Radicalism and Sedition* "shows that the Negro's aspirations are now being taken seriously" ("Thanksgiving"). The federal government "does not regard black men as monkeys but as men," he deduced, "[a]nd we ought to be thankful that we are now being considered as human beings" ("Thanksgiving"). For Ferris, state-chastised black expression was grateful to grow in authority, even if that authority was condemned to accept the state's degraded standard. His Thanksgiving homily celebrated the instrumental success of New Negro writing—at long last, it seemed to have proven black humanity—while regretting the low bar it was obliged to clear.

The Marxist-nationalist editors of the *Crusader*, another Harlem journal quoted in *Radicalism and Sedition*, complemented Ferris in welcoming Bureau ghostreading as a fortunate fall. The Bureau's report "confirms what we have suspected and hoped for," wrote the *Crusader*'s editors in December 1919; as a matter of fact, "the United States Government is closely scrutinizing month after month the contents of *The Crusader* . . . and other 'radical Negro publications' " ("The Government and the Negro"). A month after Thanksgiving, the *Crusader* thus reworked the *Negro World*'s holiday conceit to declare itself "grateful indeed to have the ear of the United States government" ("The Government and the Negro"). The typically less militant *New York Age* opened its review of *Radicalism and Sedition* with purer scorn. Contributing editor James Weldon Johnson, a veteran of the FBI-creating Teddy Roosevelt administration as well as an industrious promoter of the Harlem Renaissance, began by insisting that the Bureau's case against New Negro expression was not worth the government paper it was printed on. "If any jury of fair-minded persons can find in [these] twenty-seven pages devoted to the Negro anything which justifies those pages being made a part of a report against 'persons advising anarchy, sedition, and the forcible overthrow of the Government,' " Johnson swore, "the writer will agree to eat a bundle of these reports without taking water" ("Report"). But Johnson then proceeded to dwell on the report's more appetizing status as backhanded praise. As psychologized by the author of *The Autobiography of an Ex-Colored Man* (1912), an unprolific but major black novelist, *Radicalism and Sedition*'s institutional author is a critic-spy impressed beyond comprehension—and beyond racial convention—by the self-knowledge and articulateness of the New Negro. "He is a man who has evidently, like many others, been asleep on the Negro," Johnson specifies; "he has been thinking of the Negro in terms of twenty or thirty years ago; all at once he is called on to read a number of Negro publications, and he is amazed, overwhelmed, dumbfounded, to find that the Negro knows what he wants" ("Report"). What astonishes the man most, Johnson decides, is the fact that offending poems and essays "are written by Negroes who know how to use the English language," and do so "in a clear, intelligent, and forcible way" ("Report"). Seen in the light of Johnson's G-Man, the Harlem Renaissance was no racialist revival, but instead a black invasion, ex nihilo, of lucid Standard English. Despite his bewilderment, Johnson's representative Bureau ghostreader thus feels his way toward Johnson's own conclusion that black literary rebirth would first defy distorted black dialect.

In his response to the collective reaction of the New Negro press, Robert Adger Bowen retyped Johnson's editorial line by line and construed the whole as unusually "ugly" ("Re-Action" 3). In truth, however, Johnson's contribution to the genre was unusual only in its nuanced personification of *Radicalism and Sedition*'s implied author—a personification that hit Bowen, once a promising novelist himself, where it hurt. Like Johnson, Ferris, and the staff of the *Crusader*, the editors of the anti-Garveyite *Messenger* magazine openly entertained the fact of Bureau reading ("A. Mitchell Palmer"). W.E.B. Du Bois, then the editor of the *Crisis*, the organ of the renaissance-funding NAACP, met Bureau interest with the jibe that "[w]e black folk have for some years been trying to get the United States Department of Justice to look into several matters that touch us" ("Causes" 5). With rare consistency across ideological divisions, the architects of the black-run, Harlem-based periodical culture of the young renaissance thus spread the news (not all bad) that the Bureau was poring over their stuff. Year one of the rebirth, 1919, was known throughout this culture as the year of the Red Summer and of Claude McKay's "If We Must Die"—and likewise as the year of *Radicalism and Sedition*'s inspection of both.

Along with other dynamic stretches of Anglo-American modernism, the greater New Negro era was a magazine era.[15] As a result, the near-uniform interest of Harlem journals in the influx of Bureau ghostreading was no small, subliterary wrinkle. The Harlem Renaissance answered the massive social changes of World War I and the Great Migration, of course, but also "the emergence of a whole new matrix of magazines centered in New York City," the initial publishers of almost every writer associated with Harlem's vogue (Hutchinson 126). In Harlem, as in Paris, the most accessible and enthusiastic channels of black transnational communication between the world wars were found "at the stratum of periodical culture" (Edwards, *The Practice* 8). One of the first consistent messages that Harlem periodicals beamed to their peers across the Atlantic concerned the reading habits of the U.S. federal police, an interpretive community who somehow grasped the stakes of literary self-modernization, and would be tuning in as the diaspora spoke for itself.

Claude McKay, the earliest Afro-modernist author to impress his way into his own FBI file, appeared in almost every Harlem journal that answered *Radicalism and Sedition* in kind—one of the reasons his file was created in the first place. Though McKay dismissed what he saw as Garvey's posturing utopianism, he contributed to the *Negro World* throughout 1919; he overlooked his intense dislike of Du Bois while selling the *Crisis* articles on the Soviet Union. The *Messenger* and the *Crusader* competed to reprint (and reprint again) his sonnet "If We Must Die," the cornerstone of *Radicalism and Sedition*'s poetry criticism. McKay likely learned of Attorney General A. Mitchell Palmer's claim that most subscribers to these journals were known to the Justice Department. "I have here mailing lists of these radical papers showing who is reading this stuff mostly," Palmer assured an open session of Congress (qtd. in Schmidt 171). All this to say that McKay's intimacy with Harlem Renaissance periodical culture stood to acquaint him with the intimacy of Bureau reading—a probability that approaches a certainty given his later comments on impermeable government intelligence at the U.S. border (letter to Max Eastman, [?] Apr. 1933). Beginning in late 1919, the inaugural poet of the Harlem Renaissance surely wrote with knowledge of his FBI audience.

McKay's poem "If We Must Die," conceived before late 1919, is probably the only Shakespearian sonnet to command similar attention in the Attica Prison uprising, *The Norton Anthology of African American Literature*, and FBI spy-criticism. But Bureau ghostreaders were equally impressed by later McKay poems. Robert Adger Bowen, we have seen, kept a copy of "The Tropics in New York" (1920) for his private enjoyment. Before it came to represent McKay in dozens of collections, the sonnet "America" (1921) was introduced in full into his FBI file:

> Although she feeds me bread of bitterness,
> And sinks into my throat her tiger's tooth,
> Stealing my breath of life, I will confess
> I love this cultured hell that tests my youth!
> Her vigor flows like tides into my blood,
> Giving me strength erect against her hate.
> Her bigness sweeps my being like a flood.
> Yet as a rebel fronts a king in state,
> I stand within her walls with not a shred
> Of terror, malice, not a word of jeer.
> Darkly I gaze into the days ahead,
> And see her might and granite wonders there,
> Beneath the touch of Time's unerring hand,
> Like priceless treasures sinking in the sand.

Beginning with line 8 of "America," the first line of the sonnet's inverting second half, McKay's speaker is reenvisioned as a courtly renegade ("a rebel") with unchallenged access to a sovereign ("a king in state"). Courtly political intrigue, rather than courtly love, has become the reigning enterprise. Like the narrator's grandfather in Ralph Ellison's FBI-conscious *Invisible Man*, a kindred "spy in the enemy's country" made to "give up [the] gun back in the Recon-struction" (16), McKay's rebel selects weapons of indirection, verbal cunning, and the silent collection of intelligence. Through a mysterious channel of in-side information, this secret agent knows of the violent future to be dealt by "Time's unerring hand"—through a whimper of fate, or perhaps a bang from a well-placed explosive. As part 1 detailed, U.S. politicians and industrialists were in fact sent mail bombs for May Day in 1919, and Attorney General Palmer's home was attacked soon after, events leading straight to the Hoover Raids and, by extension, to *Radicalism and Sedition*. McKay's thick layers of allusion and anachronism would appear to disallow references to these actual acts of sabo-tage, but his revival of Elizabethan court discourse, at least, does not mask his desire to exploit a modern fear of Red mutiny. Many of the English Renais-sance sonnets on which McKay draws were products of a court culture of royal surveillance and rebellious countersurveillance, a milieu in which aristocratic author-soldiers, Sir Philip Sidney among them, propelled early modern intel-ligence and the rise and fall of great powers (Archer 3). When the noble lover of McKay's first seven lines gazes darkly into the mirror of the second seven, he or she thus glimpses a dangerous but majestic reflection, a secret agent of political reprisal who threatens presently (Palmer's house or the White House?) while speaking with historical dignity (in the cadence of Elizabeth's courtly writer-spies, as well as Petrarch and Percy Shelley, whose 1818 sonnet on the ruined colossus of Ozymandias informs McKay's lines on the sinking of America's "granite wonders").

"America," along with the rest of McKay's so-called violent sonnets, has been praised for propelling dignified expressions of rage, revenge, and active resis-tance into the main current of African American poetry. For Addison Gayle Jr. and other Black Arts critics of the 1960s and 1970s, these poems qualified McKay as the twentieth century's model "Black poet at war," the modern elder in whose path all "Black poets who direct their art towards Black people . . . are sojourners" (Gayle, *Claude McKay* 40). The FBI ghostreaders who fastened onto "America" and like-minded McKay sonnets are notable for predicting this contribution before most of the non-Harlem public. And McKay's work is notable for giving them biting clues to do so. The second half of "America" flaunts the specter of Bolshevik saboteurs, just as the first revels in contact with Miss Liberty as well as Shakespeare's Dark Lady. Along with its clever argu-mentative turns, its learned redeployment of sonnet history, and its respectably classical moral on the fall of the mighty, McKay's sonnet thus offered Bureau spy-critics reason for nightmares over race and radicalism. The trained com-munist, J. Edgar Hoover once wrote, "is one on whom the party depends to commit espionage, derail a speeding train, and organize riots. If asked, gun in hand, to assault the Capitol of the United States, he will be expected to obey"

(*Masters* 59). McKay encouraged Bureau ghostreaders to discover such a disciplined militant near the fallen capitol of "America," its sinking granite cursed by a rebel spy. Other McKay sonnets written in the wake of *Radicalism and Sedition* invite the same response, from a poem threatening a citadel named in its title, "The White House" (1922), to one titled "Enslaved" (1921), which begs that "the white man's world of wonders utterly / . . . be swallowed up in the earth's vast womb" (ll. 10–11). In these seemingly candid first-person lyrics, both poems captured in his FBI file, McKay indulges his Bureau reputation as an evasive radical provocateur.

When it came to McKay's famous mix of radical content and seemingly conservative form, the F.B. eye presented stricter inspiration. McKay's lofty calls for insurrection bait his government readership with a taste of revolutionary confession but also accept this readership's advice for staying clear of outright censorship. Not coincidentally, the text of the wartime Sedition Act that invigorated the early Bureau also resembles an instruction manual for the classic McKay poem. This act prohibited "disloyal, profane, scurrilous, or abusive" language about the U.S. government, military, and flag ("Sedition Act of 1918"); so do McKay's better sonnets, but only through graceful verbal substitution at the verge of law breaking. The vicious "foe" of "If We Must Die" is thus threatened with death but is never specified (l. 9), while an "avenging angel" is beckoned to consume the "white man's world" in "Enslaved" (ll. 10–11), replacing the avenging "New Soldier and Worker" McKay felt able to summon in the London-based *Workers' Dreadnought* ("Song").

There are several reasons why McKay's sonnets sidestepped the formal revolution of high modernism, from his early Jamaican training in the Elizabethans and Romantics, to his conviction that the Poundian theater of modernist rebellion was nothing *but* formal, mere "bourgeois attitudinizing of the social revolutionary ferment" (McKay to Max Eastman, 25 Apr. 1932). One neglected reason why these sonnets retained an uncolloquial, sometimes archaic diction, however, was the need to elevate and obfuscate "anti-American" speech—thus ensuring that this speech would remain free. "America" and the like lured Bureau attention with their whispers of direct action, but their backward-looking anti-Imagism, their *in*direct treatment of the mutinous thing, frustrated prosecution by observing the letter of U.S. sedition law (never quite overturned within Hoover's FBI). In this sense, early Bureau counterliterature, taking shape as a crusade against profane or unreservedly critical political writing, helped to invigorate McKay's brightly torn brand of Afro-modernism, one in which speaking as a rebel but without "a word of jeer" is the highest prize ("America" l. 10). Fluency with the exalted but double-jointed language of the Shakespearian sonnet, McKay discovered, was of serious modern use when state reading once more intersected with literary renaissance, and aspiring censors again demanded that poets master the cover of linguistic refinement. In McKay's renaissance, as in Shakespeare's, the elevated language of the fourteen-line formula offered shelter for unruly sentiments.

Invisible G-Men En Route to the Cold War: George Schuyler, Langston Hughes, and Ralph Ellison

Claude McKay produced his American sonnets from a position strikingly close to the public exchanges between FBI ghostreading and New Negro journalism. While less eager to needle Bureau spy-critics, many of the other writers of the Harlem Renaissance also had practical reasons to retain the fact of Bureau spy-criticism: like the author of "America," their work appeared in the same Harlem publications that pursued the story of Hoover's literary detectives. Before the 1920s were through, for example, the *Messenger* alone ran sixteen poems each by FBI "filees" Langston Hughes and Georgia Douglas Johnson, as well as smaller batches by Arna Bontemps, Countee Cullen, Helene Johnson, Richard Bruce Nugent, and Wallace Thurman. Zora Neale Hurston, Eric Walrond, and Dorothy West all placed stories there, while George S. Schuyler was hired in 1923 as the *Messenger's* "full-time all-duty man," paid just ten dollars a week but granted a monthly satirical column, Shafts and Darts (Kornweibel, *No Crystal Stair* 53). Those *Messenger* contributors determined to overlook nearby items sparring with the Bureau presumably found it harder to ignore the editors' complaints that a Justice Department provocateur was feeding rumors of the journal's bankruptcy (53). The federal government's three-year-long denial of the *Messenger's* second-class mailing permit pounded the lesson home: its contents were studied and disfavored by a state police devoted to proactive reading.

Messenger columnist George S. Schuyler's political fiction of the 1930s indicates that at least one reluctant New Negro aged out of Harlem periodical culture without forgetting its response to FBI surveillance. His linked novels *The Black Internationale* and *Black Empire*, published serially and pseudonymously in the *Pittsburgh Courier* between 1936 and 1938, introduce cyclotrons, electric rays, and other science fiction standbys of the period into plots of white-supremacist espionage and black-supremacist counterintelligence. Both of Schuyler's transatlantic pulp fictions pit the dashing and ruthless anticolonial conspiracy of Dr. Henry Belsidus against a secretly feeble enemy: the massed power of the entire Euro-American world. By the end of his two-stage, two-book campaign, Belsidus has liberated Africa and its diaspora through a quasi-fascist regimen of health food and gas chambers. On the way to victory, Schuyler settles local scores with intelligence techniques associated with the Bureau. The Black Internationale's shockingly pale security chief, Martha Gaskin, takes investigative cues from Hoover. Parroting the Bureau director, then synonymous with scientific fingerprinting, she orders her black-masked lieutenants to "[p]lace the fingers of your right hand on the inked surface," or else (Schuyler, *Black Empire* 186). Yet even Hoover would have been startled by the categorical finality of Gaskin's fingerprint test, which instantly exposes a European-controlled double agent to torture by a "very corrosive acid" (189). A graphic scene earlier in *The Black Internationale* confirms that Schuyler here takes gruesome revenge on the racial wiles of state security. Belsidus's first item of business at the first meeting of his revolutionary "Delegates of Black Nations" is the histrionic liquidation of race-betraying police informers. "Gentlemen," he announces, "before we begin we must rid ourselves of spies" (29). Three black delegates are then dragged painfully to their deaths, as Belsidus coolly explains that every white imperial power "has a certain number of colored or Negro police agents to spy on such gatherings and conferences to find out what our people are doing or plan to do" (31).

Schuyler's good-bad doctor explicitly condemns the sold-out black spies of the London-based British Colonial Office and the Paris-based Sûreté Générale, the closest French relation to the FBI. All the same, the negative inspiration of the Bureau's earliest black informers, drawn in numbers to the offices of the *Messenger*, is not hard to see. Members of Schuyler's Black Internationale refer to their organization as the "B.I.," assuming the familiar acronym for Hoover's Bureau before the "F"-for-federal was added in 1935. Like John A. Williams's *The Man Who Cried I Am*, Schuyler's fiction thus confronts the (F)BI with a racially reversed concentration of its own medicine, imagining Gaskin and other white informers loyal to a Pan-African spy network both indebted and poisonous to federal intelligence. Williams's foreword to a 1991 reprinting of *Black Empire* indeed admits the similarities between several of his chimerical political novels and Schuyler's tributes to Dr. Belsidus. Schuyler's political tune would change in aversion to the civil rights movement, Williams hastens to add, implying that the older author may have "supplied information to the FBI on domestic African-American 'radicals' through the 1960s and 1970s" (Foreword ix), decades in which Schuyler definitely placed himself in the ideological corner of "J. Edgar Hoover, director of the FBI" (Schuyler, *Black and Conservative* 280). In the mid-1930s, however, Schuyler could imagine enlisting as a Hooverite (F)BI man only through fictions of emulative opposition. Like McKay's use of a self-preserving poetic diction, Schuyler's imposition of a pseudonym between himself and *Black Empire* was thus well advised.

If other Afro-modernists active in the 1930s planned fictional exchanges with the Bureau, the evidence is hidden. The Great Depression, a profitable slump for the FBI, witnessed an unusual cooling of Bureau interest in African American writing and an equally unusual pause in this writing's notice of the FBI. Complementing the absence of fresh files on black authors until 1939, Afro-modernists seem to have accepted the Bureau's olive branch and refused Schuyler's lead toward a Depression literature of retaliatory counterintelligence. However, by the start of the 1940s and World War II, the FBI's counterliterary attention to Afro-modernism had returned with a vengeance, pushing Schuyler and a minimum of ten other African American writers onto Hoover's Custodial Detention list. Whether or not they guessed their fate, several of these projected federal prisoners (Langston Hughes, Richard Wright, and Chester Himes among them) wrote the Bureau onto their own lists, publishing reckonings with the FBI more explicit than Schuyler's, let alone Claude McKay's.

Take the case of Langston Hughes, no aficionado of the English sonnet but then otherwise known by the title "Shakespeare in Harlem." In 1943, the year that FBI agents began sneaking into his poetry readings, he published "What Shall We Do about the South?," an essay dragging the Bureau into debates over southern American exceptionalism. Here, Hughes adapts a stock device of modern African American narrative—the progressively revealing railway journey into the heart of Jim Crow—to recommend "an immediate and intensive federally directed program of prodemocratic education, to be put into all the schools of the South from the first grade to the universities" ("What Shall We Do" 222). If the embattled Spanish Loyalist government could arrange "trench schools for its soldiers and night schools for civilians even in Madrid under siege," reasons a southbound Hughes, a U.S. government unshaken by Nazi bombers could do something similar in Dixie (222). Hoover's FBI, Hughes specifies, would need to reeducate itself to get this educational job done. Black teachers of American democracy could enlighten the region only if spared the fate of "Hugh Gloster, professor of English at Morehouse College," who "was illegally ejected from a train" in Mississippi, and then "beaten, arrested, and fined because, being in an overcrowded Jim Crow coach, he asked for a seat in an adjacent car which contained only two white passengers" (221). "Legally," Hughes reminds his reader, "the Jim Crow laws do not apply to interstate travel but the FBI has not yet got around to enforcing that Supreme Court ruling" (221). Inch-thick FBI files were opened for less pointed criticism of Bureau inaction. In Hughes's case, however, the file was already filling. His anticipation of the arguments of the antisegregationist Freedom Riders, survivors of a brutal interstate bus trip in 1961, went unnoticed by FBI investigators, otherwise occupied by Hughes's draft status and possible sympathy for Japan's dark-skinned empire.

Bitter-comic commentary on the FBI's practical alliance with Jim Crow ranges into Hughes's "Simple" stories of the early 1950s, fictions originally written for the *Chicago Defender* and its nationwide black audience that showcased the post-folk wisdom of Jesse B. Simple, the Virginia-born, Harlem-made everyman who became Hughes's most beloved character. In a number of Simple tales, the Bureau figures as a politically neutral plaything of Harlem sexual signifying. At the close of "It's Okay to Be Reserved" (1951), for example, an uninterested woman who captures Simple's eye wittily responds to his flirtatious questions by asking "Are you the FBI?" (6). "I am only Drinks-I-Buy," replies a rejected but still rhyming Simple (6). In contrast, in "Something to Lean On," a *Defender* sketch included in *Simple Speaks His Mind* (1950), the first of four Simple books, the signifying blisters as well as appropriates the Bureau. Hughes's talkative hero here bellies up to the neighborhood bar, his favorite place to lean "[b]ecause everything else I lean on falls down . . . including my peoples, my wife, my boss, and me" (133). When a skeptical foil accuses Simple of using "that old color argument as an excuse again," he replies that the whole U.S. Constitution has fallen down around him, much "like it fell down on that poor Negro lynched last month," none of whose killers was jailed (134). "But just kidnap some small innocent white baby and take it across the street, and you will do twenty years," Simple protests (134). "The F.B.I. will spread its dragnet and drag in forty suspections"—Simple-speak for the compound of "suspects" and "inspections"—"before morning" (134). Like Hughes's earlier essay "What Shall We Do about the South?," this not-so-simple story accuses the FBI of color-coded threat assessment and inadequate reverence for federal law, the latter charge built to penetrate the heart of the least racially liberal G-Man. As Hughes's mouthpiece tells it, the Bureau's fierce pursuit of the Lindbergh kidnappers—a famous case of the 1930s still profiled on the Bureau's website—would remain an exceptional success until officers of the Constitution quit leaning on the color bar.

Hughes kept this drumbeat playing throughout his harshest trials of the Cold War, from his testimony before HUAC to J. Edgar Hoover's mass-mailed flaying of "Goodbye Christ." Contrary to the theory that his psychological dependence on the good opinion of ordinary African Americans intensified a new "determination to avoid the left" and the ostracism that befell W.E.B. Du Bois (Rampersad 190), Hughes's contributions to the black press in particular continued to hammer FBI anticommunism. A *Chicago Defender* column from 1956, for example, lambastes the Bureau in tandem with William Faulkner's pledge "that he would take up public arms against his own government in case worse came to worse down South" (Hughes, "Concerning" 91). Hughes wonders if the punishment visited by the FBI on Paul Robeson—national house arrest—will also be applied to the "great Mississippi writer" for saying something sincerely treasonous: "Will Mr. Faulkner get a passport?" (91). With ironies dripping and multiplying, Hughes hopes that Faulkner will indeed get one, since he also hopes that the bearer will remain equipped to "get away from us Negroes who upset him so badly" (91). Before launching into such white flight, however, Faulkner would benefit from changing his spots and sampling the racially distinct wages of subversive speech. Stepping into the imaginary shoes of Dilsey Gibson, Lucas Beauchamp, and dozens of other rounded black characters was one thing, Hughes hints; stepping outside of Faulkner's home laboratory of Yoknapatawpha County and publicly speaking as a black militant was another. "If he gets that upset over being white, what would happen to him if he were black—especially after making such statements? I know what would happen. He would be in jail," or else "surveyed by the FBI" and lesser anticommunist watchdogs (92).

Hughes did not know that Faulkner's brother Murry, a long-serving G-Man, protected his famous sibling's eighteen-page Bureau file from the worst of Hooverism. But Hughes realized that the Mississippi modernist stood on the right side of the Bureau's racially uneven tolerance for provocative literary statement. Hughes's protest of discriminatory FBI "surveying," its alternating excess and fatal thinness when applied to African Americans, endured into the mid-1960s. "Concernment," a story in the final Simple collection, *Simple's Uncle Sam* (1965), finds Hughes's vernacular spokesman daydreaming of adequate federal protection for "the first Negro engineer on a New York–to–Jackson [Mississippi] train": "every coach would have to have soldiers in the vestibules and the FBI in the smoking rooms" (254). For Simple and his creator, the Bureau stood as a custodian of African American mobility, a regular denier of passports but, at the same time, a potential guarantor of interstate travel and the Great Migration's hard-earned liberties (Mississippi to New York/New York to Mississippi is the recurrently imagined circuit). In 1965, as in 1943, Hughes's hope is that the FBI will transform its national jurisdiction into a force for nationwide racial equality.

On the road to *Invisible Man*, Ralph Ellison's Cold War daydreaming about the FBI involved larger amounts of faith and desire. Like Hughes's, Ellison's vision of the Bureau was first stamped by the culture of the Depression-era

Harlem left, not the warmest audience for *G-Men Magazine* and other New Deal broadcasters of the Hoover legend. Hughes had personally introduced Ellison to Richard Wright and the rest of this left after bumping into the Tuskegee dropout in the foyer of the Harlem YMCA in 1936. Nonetheless, by the late 1940s, Ellison's relationship to the communism that preoccupied Harlem radicals was rockier than Hughes's, and the seven-year struggle to complete *Invisible Man* (1952), his first and only published novel, thus overlapped with the task of unwriting his radical past. Literary historian Barbara Foley has scrupulously documented the deletion of Ellison's early leftism from successive drafts of *Invisible Man*, emphasizing his trading of procommunist characters and incidents for stances more palatable to the "substantial anticommunist readership" of 1952, already primed for accounts of the black and the ex-Red by Chester Himes's novel *Lonely Crusade* (1947) and Richard Wright's essay "I Tried to Be a Communist" (1944) (Foley, *Wrestling* 9). A trying job of literary revision that Ellison described as a wrestling match with Proteus, the shape-changing Greek god of the sea, is thus rechristened by Foley as a concrete "process of anticommunist-ization" (8). In the instance of *Invisible Man*'s wrestling with the FBI, however, Ellison engaged in a process of anti-anticommunist-ization as well: he cut away a vital scene of G-Man shape-shifting that borrowed freely from Cold War narratives awarded Hoover's seal of approval. In Ellison's discarded fiction of the FBI, Hughes's association between the Bureau and African American mobility is thus repeated, but with an intricate political difference.

The FBI, an absent presence in the published text of *Invisible Man*, makes numerous overt appearances in the drafts of the novel sifted by Foley. In one preliminary version, New York G-Men are suspected of sabotaging a racially inclusive Popular Front–style poster campaign. Hustling to organize Harlem for Ellison's lite-communist "Brotherhood," the Invisible Man plasters uptown with posters of a multicultural "Rainbow of America's Future." These uplifting images disappear as soon as they are mounted, leading Brotherhood organizers to accuse the FBI of street-level censorship. Eventually, however, the Invisible Man spots a lifted copy of the poster in the apartment of black communist sympathizers. "At least four of my friends got them on their walls," admits a guilty Harlem housewife (qtd. in Foley, *Wrestling* 273). Foley casts this outwardly trifling episode as a display of "Popular Front propaganda at its most effective, as well as the genuine appeal for Harlemites of the Left's multiracial approach to the fight against racism" (*Wrestling* 273). But the remounted posters are more than signs of communism's real Harlem success deceitfully obscured in Ellison's final draft. The odd practical sympathy between the interests of the FBI (the removal of a communist poster) and the preferences of progressive Harlemites (the private enjoyment of that poster) is foreshadowed by an earlier draft episode in which the Invisible Man volunteers to do the Bureau's bidding.

Chapter 7 of the published, 1952 version of *Invisible Man* finds the titular hero rebuked and scorned by Dr. Bledsoe, a PhD in educational hypocrisy, and maneuvered aboard a bus from his Tuskegee-like southern college to a hand-to-mouth life in New York City. Not until the bus reaches "the Jersey countryside" do the narrator's "spirits begin to raise" and his "old confidence and optimism" reappear as desirable qualities (Ellison, *Invisible* 156). Awake but with his "eyes gazing blankly upon the landscape" (157), he daydreams of urbane self-improvement in the Big Apple: attending prestigious public lectures; learning "the platform tricks of the leading speakers"; meeting affluent white businessmen with his "most polished tones" at the ready; keeping his hair dressed, his nails clean, and his "armpits well deodorized" (157). In this wish-fragment of the Great Migration, the Invisible Man's reverie of deodorized and deracialized sophistication causes him to ignore the decisive moment of transition from extended South to emblematic North. An impatient New York baggage handler is forced to stir him from his daydream—"Buddy, are you getting off here?" (157)—after he misses the welcoming vista of the Hudson River and the Manhattan skyscrapers beyond it. Here, again, the Invisible Man has symbolic vision trouble.

Alternatively, in the original draft from which chapter 7 derives, Ellison allows the Invisible Man to absorb his passage into the city of dreams. In this prior rendition, the protagonist briefly rouses as his bus enters "the Holland Tunnel" beneath the Hudson (Ellison, "Writings" 185). The tunnel's "long rows of bright lights" illuminate the bus's way through the underworld, and the none-too-subtle birth canal of the Invisible Man's infant northern self (Ellison, "Writings" 185). These lights also give birth to another waking fantasy, a second, wilder daydream to counterpoint his restrained thirst for lectures and antiperspirants: "I dreamed the round spots of brightness were the portholes of a tremendous ship such as I had seen in the movies in which I was about to take a long and pleasurable voyage at the end of which I would complete an important mission" (186). His bus now a Hollywood vessel, his projected New York calling swings from urbane reeducation to secret employment as "an important undercover man, smart, intelligent and very clever, assigned important work because, being black, I was unsuspected" (186). His imaginary white supervisor is no longer one of Bledsoe's businessman contacts, but instead "a master FBI man" (186). Like the historical Hoover, this FBI boss is functionally dependent on black service; he too proves what Ellison elsewhere called "the white American's inescapable Negro-ness" ("Homage" 676). Unlike Sam Noisette and other actual Hoover special agents/domestics, however, the Invisible Man's self-preserving playacting of the part of the help is known and approved by his FBI superior. Ellison's mini-Hoover, in other words, is in on the masquerade of black subservience.

We are "surrounded," recites Ellison's dream narrator, setting the movielike action, "and I, disguised as a porter," receive "secret papers" from the master FBI man "just before the enemy breaks into the stateroom" ("Writings" 186). Hand-guns flash, "and the FBI man falls" (186). Against instinct, the Invisible Man must smother his urge to return fire: "I want to shoot back, but I musn't give myself away" (186). Instead, he digs further undercover as a movie-made racial stereotype. "I pretend cotton-eyed fear, like Mantan Moreland," the comic actor then known for the role of Birmingham Brown, detective Charlie Chan's eye-rolling black chauffer (186).[16] The quick-trigger enemy turns to the Invisible Man "as they ramshack [sic] the cabin in vain" and reveal stereotypical shades of their own: "'Vere are zey, Sambo?' they bark" (186). Despite these shouted threats channeling the Klan through ideologically promiscuous Nazi-Soviet accents, the Invisible Man denies everything. "Boss, Ah don't know nothing about no papers," he whines, barely reworking Butterfly McQueen's notorious plea about "birthin' babies" in Gone with the Wind (1939). "Sambo is stupid," the rival spies conclude (186), at once confirming his value as an invisible G-Man, an FBI undercover agent with a disguise rooted deep in the eyes of the white beholder. Finally able to remove his Sambo mask in the absence of enemy observation, Ellison's protagonist "stand[s] looking at the dead FBI man, my fists clinched in anger. I rush to the door and look out, the alleyway is empty. I return and raise up the FBI man's head. His eyes flicker, he is not quite dead. He motions me to take his automatic and his badge and papers. He is sinking fast" (186). With his last breath, the master FBI man haltingly asks the invisible G-Man to "[make] my ... report ... to J. Edgar ... Hoo ..." (187). "Sure," replies his black partner, summoning "heroic despair and determination" (187). Just after the invisible G-Man accepts this appointment with J. Edgar You-Know-Who, the baggage carrier also found in the published version of the novel star-tles him with the news that "[t]his is New York" (187). In Ellison's preliminary typescript, however, the Invisible Man is more inclined to shoot the messenger: "I whirl, my gun ready, and open my eyes" (187). Like Hughes's pioneering train engineer, but this time with government weapons of his own, Ellison's protagonist takes the South-North road in sympathy with the FBI.

Barbara Foley's interpretation of this FBI dream scene keeps faith with her thesis that Ellison's revisions sacrifice leftist insight to the convenience of Cold War anticommunism. "While in his fantasy the invisible man [sic] is incorporated into rather than targeted by the state's surveillance apparatus," she observes, "the surfacing of the FBI from his political unconscious suggests an awareness of governmental authority that would be utterly implausible in the protagonist of the 1952 text" (*Wrestling* 191). Foley's reading is not incredible, as far as it goes, but it bypasses what is most germane and dramatic in the Invisible Man's FBI fantasy: the fact that his awareness of governmental authority is an excited and approving one, and that his political unconscious entertains incorporation into the state's surveillance apparatus in an act of self-aggrandizing wish fulfillment, not realistic accommodation.[17] Moreover, this wish fulfillment loots consensus-building Hollywood movies rather than communist tracts or proletarian novels for plotting and atmosphere. Mantan Moreland and Butterfly McQueen's major-studio vehicles enter the patchwork, but so do the fighting G-Man pictures of the 1930s and *I Was a Communist for the FBI* (1951), the touchstone pro-informer film of the early Cold War. (Ellison's deleted scene of secret Bureau service might indeed be titled *I Was a Sambo for the FBI*.) The Invisible Man's dream montage of these popular movies thus could not have been edited out of the final draft because of its challenge to the published novel's anticommunism. Just the opposite, in fact: his dreaming of northern liberation in the vocabulary of FBI undercover work threatens to give the ideological game away, to expose the heart of the published novel as a not unsympathetic report to J. Edgar. In his vision of junior partnership with a master FBI man, Ellison's narrator displays some of the naiveté that informs his early hopes of pleasing white captains of industry. Yet his agreement to bring news to Hoover also anticipates the full-grown wisdom of the published novel's famous last line. With his mission to communicate with the foremost enforcer of U.S. anticommunism, Ellison's African American hero telegraphs his conclusion that "on the lower frequencies, I speak for you"—the "you" in question a more-than-southern national audience in training to accept the integrated wisdom of Cold War liberalism, the knowledge that with racial diversity, "you'll have no tyrant states" (Ellison, *Invisible* 581, 577). The most likely scenario, then, is that Ellison removed his FBI sequence because it too patently and prematurely courted the "substantial anticommunist readership" of 1952 (Foley, *Wrestling* 9).

Had the published text of the most-studied African American novel preserved its message to Hoover, there might be no reason for the present argument: like many other signifying chains traced through *Invisible Man*, proof of Afro-modernism's tradition-unifying revisions of Ellison's FBI scene would already have been found in bulk. What remains of the FBI scene in the published text of Ellison's novel is significant enough, however, a palimpsest that underwrites the novel's primal mystery. In the second paragraph of chapter 1, the Invisible Man plants the clue of his grandfather's last words, never before "mentioned outside the family circle" (Ellison, *Invisible* 16). "After I'm gone," instructs the dying grandfather, "I want you to keep up the good fight. I never told you, but our life is a war and I have been a traitor all my born days, a spy in the enemy's country ever since I gave up my gun back in the Reconstruction. Live with your head in the lion's mouth. I want you to overcome 'em with yeses, undermine them 'em with grins, agree 'em to death and destruction, let 'em swoller you till they vomit or bust wide open" (16). The Invisible Man's surviving kin warns him "to forget what [the old man] had said," but his grandfather's deathbed advice survives, taunting and intriguing him into the epilogue (16). He is cautioned that he takes after the "odd old guy" (16), and with reason: his dream of secret service in the FBI epitomizes his grandfather's advice nearly line by line. Onboard the tremendous ship he summons beneath the Hudson River, the invisible G-Man agrees to "keep up the good fight" after the passing of a Bureau elder, another whisperer of another deathbed confidence. Much like the grandfather, a traitorous resident of a conquered country (the restored post-Reconstruction South), the master FBI man is a spy in a stateroom (a room in the ship of state) taken by the enemy. For his part, the invisible G-Man follows the speaker of McKay's "America" as a spy-inheritor also forced to give up the gun; this second time, arms are holstered in the interest of safeguarding state secrets sought by the Nazi/Soviet enemy. With his convincing pretense of "cotton-eyed fear" and servile ignorance (Ellison, "Writings" 186), the invisible G-Man cleverly escapes "the lion's mouth," overcoming his spy-rivals "with yeses," agreeing "'em to death and destruction" (*Invisible* 16). In their unaffected ignorance, the twin-totalitarian bad guys "vomit" him free along with a mouthful of "Sambos" (16), enabling him to carry papers to Hoover, a virtual *Invisible Man* at the top of the pile. Hundreds of pages before the epilogue considers the national code behind the grandfather's advice, Ellison's FBI dream scene thus contemplates the value of this advice to a black operative of the U.S. national police.

The patriotic redefinition of the grandfather's words in the epilogue of the published novel has been promoted by many guides to *Invisible Man*, and protested by a few. In the latter camp is Foley, who attacks the epilogue's affirmation of "the principle on which the country was built" as a liberal-pluralist distortion of American communism (Ellison, *Invisible* 574). Donald Gibson, one of Foley's critical inspirations, joins this camp as well, objecting that the grandfather, while publicly draped in red, white, and blue, recommends a "war so private and subjective that the enemy does not even recognize that he is at war" (66). Had Gibson been allowed access to the preliminary drafts seen by

Foley, however, he might have been reminded that the kind of publicly deniable psychological war advocated by the grandfather, a self-declared spy, is just the kind of war waged by intelligence agents. In his daydream of the FBI, Ellison's narrator answers his grandfather's prompting by fancifully enlisting in J. Edgar Hoover's confidential army of spooks, a federal ghost-militia mindful that black American life, too, is a shadow war. Both the Hoover of the Cold War and Ellison's invisible enlistee thus agree on this much: that spying can be a patriotic American pursuit despite the squeamishness of a proudly open society, and that African American spies in particular may confirm their indispensable Americanness in the practice of their craft. Behind *Invisible Man*'s performance of the idea that the black "mask was an inseparable part of the national iconography" thus lies a thesis on national espionage buried when the FBI scene hit the cutting-room floor (Ellison, "Change" 103). The black mask, the novel once proposed, also complemented the loyal-American disguise of the Bureau secret agent.

Access to Ellison's abandoned fiction of the FBI thus allows us new access to the stakes of his influential revision of tropes of black duality. His invisible G-Man keeps a respectful distance from Paul Laurence Dunbar's shaded plantation eyes—no longer laughing, as in "We Wear the Mask" (1896), to conceal "torn and bleeding hearts" (Dunbar l. 4), but instead collecting vanguard intelligence while rolling with stereotype. Accentuating voluntary, ideologically motivated self-splitting, the invisible G-Man removes Du Boisian double consciousness from the region of given racial fate, disowning any state in which African Americans are imagined to be born self-divided, half Negro and half American, by virtue of direct, organic inheritance. (The fact that Ellison's hero inherits the wisdom of spying from his grandfather and his unrelated FBI superior, not from his mother or nebulous father, is here to the point.) When the Invisible Man operates as a Sambo for the FBI, double consciousness indeed mushrooms into a form of double agency, a means to spy on Cold War America's totalitarian enemies while wearing an American costume these enemies hoped to exploit. In his shipboard fantasy, the invisible G-Man's Sambo guise is reborn as a weapon against communism rather than fruit for communist propaganda in the decolonizing world. Given all that rides on the dormant scene of the Invisible Man's imaginary enlistment in the FBI, it is not too surprising that Ellison recapped it deep in the weeds of his never-finished second novel. There, a conked hustler in the mold of Rinehart, the Invisible Man's many-sided double, impersonates *"both a root doctor and an undercover man for J. Edgar Hoover,"* savoring each role while hedging folkways with stateways, *"voodoo mystery with civil authority"* (*Three Days* 551; emphasis in original). The life of the post-*Invisible* Ellison, a prize-winning public man, may have replayed the dormant scene as well. By enlisting in the CIA-backed Congress for Cultural Freedom in 1956, he joined his most celebrated character as a cosmopolitan agent of national racial brotherhood.

Mysteries and Antifiles of Black Paris: Richard Wright, William Gardner Smith, and Chester Himes

In the court of literary history, Ralph Ellison's *Invisible Man* is the novel most responsible for deposing Richard Wright's *Native Son* and the accompanying "triumph of naturalism" from the heights of African American letters (Bell 150). But *Invisible Man* is at the same time often cited to explain the postnaturalist experiments of *The Outsider* (1953), the novel Wright published less than a year after Ellison's, both books aiming to chip away at *Native Son*'s outsized reputation. Wright himself might have been quizzed about *The Outsider*'s connections to *Invisible Man* had he embarked on the 1953 tour of literary New York his publishers recommended. He declined to make the trip from Paris, however, concerned that his tormentors in the U.S. government would prevent his return to home and café on the Left Bank. Any American book tour, Wright informed his literary agent, awaited improbable signs that the newly elected Eisenhower administration would disinfect federal strongholds of anticommunism "and make things so that a man can get his passport without being too scared" (qtd. in Fabre, *The Unfinished Quest* 375).

The text of *The Outsider*, by contrast, was unafraid to pique the interest of the Feds. As in the drafts of *Invisible Man*, the FBI makes a revealing cameo appearance, this time as a stalker of Wright's criminal antihero, Cross Damon, as murderously divine/demonic as his clunky name. In "Decision," *The Outsider*'s final book, Ely Houston, a hunchbacked district attorney and symbol of the wounded law, describes how he reeled in Damon through a kind of existentialist detective work. This studious federal investigator boasts of knowing "your Heidegger, your Husserl, your Kierkegaard" just as well as his philosophy-reading suspect, who obligingly leaves copies of these pre-Sartrean clues lying around his abandoned room (Wright, *The Outsider* 560). Houston nonetheless relies on the pre-existentialist criminology of the FBI's famous fingerprint lab, one of Schuyler's inspirations in the 1930s, to solve the mystery of Damon's second self, assumed after a false report of his death. "We got your fingerprints out of [a victim's] apartment," expounds Houston, "and the FBI has at last identified you" (508). What the FBI knows scientifically, Houston leaps to ponder and narrate. Analogously, the full text of

The Outsider leaps to make philosophical narrative out of its author's fear of FBI exposure.

Jeffrey Clapp notes that *The Outsider* is not unique in Wright's work in its preoccupation "with the most intensive and widely distributed form of state power, the police" (1). Almost all of Wright's novels address the U.S. state's policing of racial discrimination, crystallized in jarring scenes of inquisition and confession. *Native Son* stages extravagantly racist interrogations by a white district attorney far cruder than Ely Houston. *Savage Holiday* (1954), the closest successor to *The Outsider*, suggests that confessing to the police is something that even the most culpable white criminals cannot do, at least structurally, while *The Long Dream* (1959) upends *Savage Holiday* to dissect a young black southerner's refusal to admit guilt despite a year of jail time (Clapp 1–2). "For Wright's protagonists," Clapp argues, "the police are always the state that can be seen" (1), and what these protagonists typically see of the state through the bloody prism of police racism is the violation of "constitutional principle" (1), the very thing *Invisible Man* concludes that spylike black Americans are built to safeguard.

Seeing the state everywhere the mind can travel, Wright's shipboard poem "The FB Eye Blues," introduced above, resituates the police-state dynamics of his novels in introspective territory, the traditional ground of lyric verse. When the self-reflexive voice of this written blues finds Hooverite eyes looking back from his desires and sentences, he confronts an enemy within as much as a public enemy of the Constitution. Police power is thus indulged and internalized by the speaker of Wright's FBI poem, but not necessarily as a token of the Bureau's controlling creative authority. As Ellison elegantly suggested before his break with the older author, Wright's work transliterates a blues music impulse that struggles "to keep the painful details and episodes of a brutal experience alive in one's aching consciousness, to finger its jagged grain, and to transcend it . . . by squeezing from it a near-tragic, near-comic lyricism" ("Richard Wright's Blues" 129). Wright's final completed novel, *Island of Hallucination*, indeed revisits his "FB Eye Blues" to squeeze more transcendent good than ill from the experience of Bureau surveillance—for 517 typescript pages, it strives to reboot Wright's overfamiliarity with police spies as a tragicomic resource. Akin to Wright's private investigation of the Gibson Affair, the black Paris scandal outlined in part 4 that triggered worries about the Bureau's international antennae, *Island of Hallucination* undertakes to out-investigate the FBI, to outplot the file-keeping, mind-reading government agents who seemed to memorize everything that Wright "dreamed last night, every word [he] said" (Wright, "The FB Eye Blues" l. 10). Wright's last literary reckoning with the FBI—for him the most intellectually invasive as well as the most widely distributed sign of U.S. state power—thus took the form of citizen policing.

Finished in 1959, *Island of Hallucination* remains an appropriately semise-cret text, opened to readers at Yale's Beinecke Library only in 1996, and still un-published in 2014. Wright's sole fiction of black life in France, *Island* assimilates the known unknowns of the historical Gibson Affair, the generic requirements of the score-settling novel with a key, and the violent pulp modernism of the postwar detective narrative to picture Paris noir as a worldly house of spies. The Paris beloved by black refugees from McCarthyism, Wright's novel submits, is ironically a capital of the Cold War erected on the foundation of a capital of modernity. Trafficked by all parties to the U.S.-Soviet conflict, the City of Light has become the world headquarters of cultural jousting between official capitalism and certified communism and the many cells and forces probing for a third way beyond them. *Island's* typical black exile, whether American, Ca-ribbean, or West African, enters this headquarters as a secret agent of one side or several—"a fake Stalinist or Trotskyist by day," perhaps "a G-man at night" (Wright, *Island* 243)—and retrains homegrown double vision on international intelligence work. Somewhere in "the secret councils" of Paris, Wright's narra-tor deduces, "a decision had been made releasing swarms of Uncle Toms from their customary subservience and sicking them as spies upon white and black alike" (240). The novel's discourses of black internationalism thus prolifer-ate not only through bilingual scenes of cross-diasporic translation, but also through shadowy, sometimes impenetrable plots of literary impersonation and interracial counterintelligence peddling.

In the process, *Island of Hallucination* suggests that the "post-Gibson" tale of Paris noir must begin to signify more than an inspiring cancelation of Ameri-can racism. On Wright's spyland in the Seine, African American cosmopoli-tans lose the liberal bargaining chip of the French idyll but gain a place in the cockpit of Cold War history. What might be called Wright's "wish image" of black Paris here complements a crowded field of texts employing the French capital as a token of separation from all deemed antique in black life (Braddock and Eburne, Introduction 4). Yet lush dreams of postracial Paris are themselves wished into the past in Wright's dream work, couched as late-model detritus to be escaped in the city's ongoing contemporaneity. The coded advice to black diaspora studies contained within Wright's spy-text thus entails both satiric ne-gation and imaginative optimism: *Island of Hallucination* is a guidebook to a transnational black metropolis inescapably molded by state surveillance and thereby forced toward self-renovation. The same Parisian disenchantments that left a bitter author demanding the right not to "'inform' and 'spy' on my neighbor" (Wright, "I Choose" 2) sparked Wright to consider the existential compensations of a new Afro-modern type, an expatriate spy figure that Dashiell Hammett, an innovator of the hard-boiled detective novel, might have christened the "Transcontinental Op."

Island's opening chapters, set in the air between two continents, reintroduce readers to the Fifth Amendment hero of Wright's previous novel. The Mississippi-born black teenager Rex "Fishbelly" Tucker, tough enough to resist false confession in *The Long Dream*, enters *Island*'s French circle in flight from his father's destiny, state execution at the hands of a white police chief. He carries baggage borrowed from Wright's Paris brother Chester Himes— black bourgeois upbringing, incisive intelligence deflected into premature hustling and prison time—and arrives in Paris on a plane packed with U.S. national terrors. Fishbelly's American seatmates comprise a gallery of lynchers in button-downs. "That nigger's being spoilt as sure as God made green apples and when he gets back home he'll be fit for only tar and feathers," hisses one typical passenger (Wright, *Island* 2). Fishbelly's first French acquaintances reveal themselves as classic American confidence men who happen to have been born under the Eiffel Tower. Preying on his desire for cheap rent and instant repatriation, the husband-and-wife grifters Jacques and Nicole quickly relieve Fishbelly of two thousand dollars, their weapons cognac, jukebox jazz, and Nicole's seductive grasp of segregation's sexual politics. "He had, of course, heard of the confidence game," Fishbelly reflects in the aftermath, "but he had never heard of its being used against black men with sex as the bait, with racial balm as the lure, and sympathy as the come-on" (46).

Interested sympathy is also the weapon of Fishbelly's first African American acquaintance in Paris, a night-crawling café intellectual nicknamed Mechanical who grows into the novel's most absorbing and least credible case history. With "[m]echanized laughter and windshield wiper hand" (53), Mechanical steers the new arrival to a Pigalle prostitute with paraffin breasts and a missing navel, a fellow automaton too deadened to have been born to Charles Baudelaire's diseased sources of "light and life" (Baudelaire l. 15). The sexual transaction is roughly consummated beneath "a faded painting of a French soldier," the alliance between declining Parisian erotic and imperial authorities staring Fishbelly and the reader in the face (Wright, *Island* 56). The political initiation of Wright's protagonist, meanwhile, is consummated in one of the few episodes of *Island of Hallucination* to have seen print.[18] Zoot-suited for a Sunday promenade, his glad rags topped by a "dark gray felt hat" with a "speckled orange and black band" (76), Fishbelly stumbles across a mob of French student radicals protesting the Paris visit of U.S. general Matthew Ridgway, a historical figure tenuously linked to germ warfare in North Korea and violently protested by the actual French left in May 1951. The distinctions between Fishbelly's and Ridgway's decorated Yankee headgear are easily overlooked; without warning, the student demonstrators adjust their chant from "RIDGEWAY [sic], GO HOME!" to "QUEL CHAPEAU AMERICAN!" (77–78). Reframing the earlier polemical tableau of the French soldier and prostitute, Wright ironically dramatizes the equation of U.S. military and cultural imperialisms through a French modernist intertext. Fishbelly learns that even imported African American style is associated with U.S. hyperpower by reprising the role of Flaubert's young Charles Bovary, similarly schooled by French pupils in *charivari*, or ritualized anarchy, for the sin of a gaudy "[c]omposite" hat divided by a "red band" (Flaubert 4). The bitter-comic project behind all these early incidents in *Island* is to shred the blacks-in-Paris romance, nearly as familiar a modern fiction, Wright implies, as Flaubert's *Madame Bovary*. Every set piece of this romance is shaken, from the progressive de-Americanization of the journey to the formal sympathy of the Parisian public, from the emotional rescue of flesh-and-blood interracialism to the prefabricated association of black Americans with the anticolonial left. The reigning mode of the novel's first and second books, named "Ghosts" and "False Faces," respectively, is thus satirical. And the primary hallucination these books puncture is that of Paris the dream city, a paradise island isolated from American phantoms and tricksters and their dishonest French relatives.

The pleasures of Paris that survive Wright's omniscient narrator gradually surface as book 2 flows into book 3, titled "Time Bombs." The French capital hints at its sophisticated earthiness; its lifting of the social death sentence, if not all racist supervision, from the backs of transplanted black southerners; and its promise as an everyday Bandung Conference of mingled "Africans, Chinese, Indonesians" (Wright, *Island* 75). With this change in urban lenses, the governing mode of the novel shifts from broad literary satire to pointed roman à clef, a development that may explain *Island*'s continued lack of publication. The relatively few prior analyses of the novel essentially second Wright's finally misleading claim that "the book is true" (qtd. in James Campbell, "The Island"); the cast of characters, they note, could be lifted from a Café Tournon seating chart.[19] *Island*'s Bill Hart, a leftist agent provocateur taking cover as a fascist, is modeled on possible intelligence agent Richard Gibson, or so says Gibson himself in an often-convincing academic essay first published in 2005 ("Richard Wright's" 906). Wright's character Cato, an imposing and idiosyncratic Trotskyist theorist "smooth black of skin, graying at the temples, big boned, stooped of shoulders" (Wright, *Island* 359), is C.L.R. James, called Nello by close comrades. Nell*ie*, Cato's disciplined lieutenant and the only female character in the novel to escape the part of pneumatic national icon, is derived from Pamela Oline, a white expatriate red-baited while a U.S. diplomat in Mexico (Gibson 910). The Café Tournon makes a recognizable appearance as itself, its yellow awning sheltering what Mechanical describes as the "headquarters where we talk politics. Man, everything happens here between men and women except marriage, but even that has been known to take place" (Wright, *Island* 100).

In truth, the most meaningful couplings to occur under the café's influence involve male characters and scramble the novel's otherwise efficient key matching literary and historical figures. Ned Harrison, Fishbelly's "brown, slightly gray, rotund," and impossibly wise tutor (111), conflates features of Ollie Harrington with those of the mature Richard Wright, like Ned an African American expatriate accused by other black Parisians of working as a "government spy" or undercover G-Man (409). Mechanical, formally known as Charles Oxford Brown, blends the imagined worst of Richard Gibson and William Gardner Smith (also triple-named) with that of disloyal Wright mentee James Baldwin. Appropriating the triggering felony of this last author's autobiographical essay "Equal in Paris" (1955), Mechanical treats a stolen hotel bed sheet as the madeleine of his Paris education. If any veteran of Paris noir deserved to charge *Island of Hallucination* with libel, it is thus Baldwin, not Gibson, as usually supposed. Baldwin's nervous mechanical caricature, addicted to an Aunt Jemima–style pancake mix, can satisfy his shamefaced homosexuality only through opportunistic masochism. "[T]his bastard loved to be punished," discovers Fishbelly, resolving "that it was impossible to deal with such a man" (182).

Wright does not flinch from charging his abject Baldwin with authorship of the Gibson Affair: Mechanical is the Tournon spy who ghostwrites a revolutionary letter to the editor of *Life* magazine, thus menacing Ned Harrison with deportation. "Ned's cooked," enthuses Mechanical over his typewriter, his "robot's straggling eyes glow[ing] with ecstasy" (386). Wright's revenge on Baldwin is just as crudely ecstatic, an overdetermined blend of pre–*Soul on Ice* (1968) homophobia and deferred combat with the Oedipal brilliance of Baldwin's Wright-bashing essays "Everybody's Protest Novel" (1949) and "Many Thousands Gone" (1951). Considered solely as a structuring element of *Island*'s revisionist architecture, however, Wright's revenge is complexly ingenious. At one malicious swoop, Wright's involvement of Baldwin in the Gibson Affair analogizes literary infidelity with political treason, likening Baldwin's parasitical war on Wright's prose style with cloak-and-dagger double agency. More overtly, this involvement traces the spy plot of black Paris back to the immediate postwar era, the scene of Baldwin's noisy break with Wright's social realism, not to mention the time of the bona fide anti-Ridgway demonstration. In the heart of *Island*'s books 2 and 3, faith in a golden, "pre-Gibson" age of Paris noir is therefore among the hallucinations under fire.

The sensational interest of the novel's final movement, spread between book 3 and the concluding book, titled "Kinship," springs from another of Wright's changes to the historical record. The subject of Mechanical's deviant ghost-writing is not the Algerian War, as in the real Gibson Affair, but instead the Cold War, which envelops and warps its significance. For the secretly Trotsky-ist Mechanical, the Cold War clash between first and second worlds pits two unworthy evils: "the formless, predatory, naïve American capitalist system" and Soviet communism as "shamed and perverted" by Stalin (Wright, *Island* 391). Despite his curse on both these houses, Mechanical joins the rest of Wright's Tournon crew in thinking that the Cold War crosscurrents of his adopted city make it an inspiring hub of world history. "Paris is the center of the Cold War," the crew trusts (209). "UNESCO's here. . . . NATO's here. Paris is a crossroad of the world in thought, art, politics, pleasure" (209). With this superimposi-tion of city and transnational maps, Wright's novel verges on Frances Stonor Saunders's influential history *The Cultural Cold War* (1999), an account of the Paris-based Congress for Cultural Freedom, the CIA front group dedicated to abstract expressions of U.S. propaganda around the Free World. Wright, like El-lison a beneficiary of Congress funding,[20] was well positioned to forecast Saun-ders's exposure of Parisian machinations "to nudge the intelligentsia of western Europe away from its lingering fascination with Marxism and Communism towards a view more accommodating of 'the American way' " (Saunders 1). In *Island*'s early telling of the tale, however, the intelligentsia of black Paris ranks as a major agent and stealthy rival of this European operation, an instrument of cultural warfare capable of out-intriguing both superpowers in the interest of non-European revolution.

Seen from the perspective of Wright's world-making Left Bank, the Cold War intensifies the modern commodification of intelligence and creates a seller's market, lucrative and literary, for its black procurers. "Information is needed about everything, everybody, everywhere," contends Mechanical, for once channeling Wright's own insight, and "you can get fifty dollars just for going into any of the little offices scattered all over Paris and writing all you know on a given subject" (Wright, *Island* 157). African American expatriates, Wright's logic continues, are exceptional producers of such wordy espionage, groomed in the advantages of twofold vision by "bitter race wars" at home and encouraged when abroad to loiter "around a café all day and night," among the best of occupations for literary intelligence gathering (214, 210). Paid not only by the FBI and CIA but also by the French Sûreté Générale, black spies born in the United States hone their skills against the Parisian maestros of the trade and at times outdo their Old World professors. "You're prejudiced in favor of American Negroes," observes Fishbelly to one slippery French radical (295). "That being the case, wouldn't we make the best spies?" (295).

The thick spaghetti of espionage plots intersecting in the pages of *Island of Hallucination* is intended to answer this question in the affirmative, with Wright the author proving himself the master spy of his many master spies. Metafictional self-congratulation aside, the question is also positively answered by narrative events at the close of the novel, infused in its last book and a half with a Gothic brand of noir. Mechanical, running scared from his cell of anti-colonial Trotskyists pretending to be colorblind Stalinists pretending to work for American capitalists, achieves an operatic end by hanging himself from a gargoyle on the Notre Dame cathedral, a crowd of white Parisians howling below. His self-lynching caps a series of reflections on the soul-threatening excesses of undercover work and rivals the "QUEL CHAPEAU!" incident in its intertextual transparency. Bookending the novel with another deep bow to the French canon, Mechanical's suicide replays the climax of *Notre-Dame de Paris* (1831), in which Victor Hugo's sexually grotesque Frollo plummets from cathedral to pavement. Yet the secondhand spectacle of Mechanical's death retains the power to shock Fishbelly into self-authorship, jolting him from small-time pimping to existentialist accountability. "When you can accept responsibility for what you do," Ned praises Wright's young protagonist, "then you are starting to grow up, to be free" (514). The political complement of Fishbelly's freedom, Wright suggests, will negate and reinvent Mechanical's dizzying taste for spying on spies, taking independent black responsibility for Cold War intrigue and its transcendence. The future of liberated Paris will belong to "Bebop sleuths with a Louis Armstrong cover!" (241), hipper children of Ellison's G-Man with a Sambo cover who will scout the road beyond two clumsy "historical giants, American and Russia" (392).

Despite the affective landscape of Wright's last years in France, plagued by resident spies and the transatlantic reach of the FBI, the ultimate thrust of his Paris novel is *anti*-paranoid. According to Dorothy Padmore, a close family friend, Wright went to his death convinced he was "the victim of a plot, evidence of which he had gathered, and which implicated the French security, the American FBI (and perhaps CIA) and ex-Trotskyists" (qtd. in James Campbell, *Exiled* 243). *Island of Hallucination* knits all these malign forces into an intricate counterplot within Wright's control, an exhaustive investigation of the scene of the Gibson Affair, its city and its world. In Inspector Wright's novelized case file, both of his incarnations—Fishbelly, the Wright who fled to Paris, and Ned

Harrison, the Wright who aged there—go free, as does greater Paris noir, vividly cleared by Mechanical's self-punishment for the crime of spying for others. Wright's final novel under F.B. eyes thus sketches, before the fact, his favored alternative to his mysteriously premature death. It answers the nagging claim that expatriation severed his connection to timely racial subject matter with a case for Cold War Paris as an incubator of new black selves of international significance. And it gives evidence, more abstractly, of the value of integrating histories of state surveillance not only into Black Atlantic theory, the subject of part 4, but also into the narrower field of African American literary history, the subject of this one. Wright's *Island* cannot be mapped without clarifying its wrangle with Bureau ghostreading, accentuated on practically every page, and converted into practically a whole novel's rhyme and reason.

Wright's formula for converting ghostreading into novel-writing did not reach many readers in the home of the FBI, however: *Island of Hallucination* failed to impress editors at Doubleday, then Wright's U.S. publisher, and their hesitation to contract the book led him to shift to other final projects. But within black Paris, the gist of Wright's inspections of the Gibson Affair, literary and otherwise, were common knowledge. Word of Wright's detective work sparked in-jokes about a black boy–turned–Sherlock Holmes. It also quickly fueled a serious species of African American expatriate writing, a novel pastiche of spy fiction, radical political confession, and (most revealingly) the FBI case file commandeered as a tip sheet for novelistic structure. In this sense, Wright's stint as Holmes's darker brother prompted a wave of black Watsons, faithful assistants in a French-based revival and expansion of the African American detective tradition. Just coincidentally, perhaps, this tradition had been launched over fifty years prior by Pauline Hopkins's *Hagar's Daughter* (1901–2), serial fiction pitting Venus Johnson, a black servant/sleuth, against the white chief of a U.S. government "secret service" headquartered on Pennsylvania Avenue (Hopkins 186). From the get-go, African American detective literature seemed to prepare itself for professional competition with Hoover's Bureau.

William Gardner Smith, accused by Wright of hatching the Gibson Affair, forgave this suspicious black Holmes in *The Stone Face*, a novel published by the high-end New York firm of Farrar, Straus in 1963. Like Wright's probe of Cold War Paris noir in *Island of Hallucination*, Smith's book reanimates several of the strongest personalities in the Tournon entourage. His stand-in for Wright, the self-exiled African American writer James Benson, resembles James Baldwin in name only and is more appreciatively drawn than any of *Island*'s renderings of Smith. Looking like Wright's Ned Harrison, and pushing "forty-five, a handsome man with graying temples and an ironic expression in his pale brown eyes," Smith's Benson is mildly rebuked for writing too little rather than for supervising schemes of literary forgery (William Gardner Smith, *The Stone Face* 31). The one-eyed painter Simeon Brown, Smith's own look-alike, praises Benson's novels as "[v]ery strong, very bitter" (31), and protests the vow that there "[a]in't gonna be no more [of them]. I ain't got nothing more to say to them people" (31). The relative kindness of Smith's roman à clef mirrors his relatively healthy management of debt to Wright, a mentor whose getaway to France had inspired him to consider his own transatlantic move. Were the food and water safe in Paris? the twenty-four-year-old Smith had innocently asked Wright before taking the boat in 1951. More crucially, could U.S.-made record albums play on French gramophones? (Fabre, *From Harlem to Paris* 240). Smith thus did not go Baldwin's route in reckoning with the aging of Wright's influence, even though Wright grafted Smith, Gibson, and Baldwin's features into a single ugly Frankenspy in his *Island of Hallucination*.

As a result, *The Stone Face* has no truck with the rumor that Wright was Paris noir's most devious espionage agent, a tool of the FBI or the State Department who traded information on other expatriates to retain his threatened U.S. passport. The Smith character who carries the germ of state surveillance in Wright's stead is the outwardly timid Doug, a minor African American official at the U.S. Embassy in Paris whom the rest of Smith's Tournon regulars warily tease as a "*government* man. A government *agent*" (William Gardner Smith, *The Stone Face* 32; emphasis in original). Doug denies that his embassy job disguises his true calling as a G-Man "legat" or legal attaché. He consumes most of his small share of the plot by vacillating between two potential wives, one a white American heiress who's "father's a high State Department man" and the other a "sweet little French girl" (136), each representing a political alliance that Simeon learns to shun while falling for a beautiful Polish Holocaust survivor. Doug's "mouselike, gloomy" aspect nonetheless flits through multiple scenes of black expatriate laughter and conversation, his "enormous, indignant eyes and huge ears" suggesting Uncle Sam's voracious interest in the secrets of black Paris (32). No sensitive artist himself, Doug is still equipped to capture the emerging expression of the Browns and the Bensons. Like the genuine FBI critic-spies of the Cold War, he positions himself to preread black art in the making. Smith's rendering of Doug's quick but inconclusive powers of attention thus predicts both the unstoppable eagerness and the exploitable indecision of state ghostreading of his own novel.

Smith's solution to the crime of the state's roving eye is not Wright's. In *The Stone Face*, "Bebop sleuths" fail to inherit the cream of Parisian intelligence history and the high ground of the Left Bank. Simeon, Smith's single-eyed, far-seeing double, instead resolves to sail back to the United States and do his painting and sleuthing in another belly of the beast. He buys his return ticket free from nostalgia for those whom Babe, a pleasure-seeking Tournon buddy, denounces as "them crackers and phoney liberals and neurotics and McCarthys," an American citizenry sick and dying to inform from right to left (212). But the French—people and state—hold no greater appeal, condemned by their support of a Paris *préfecture de police* that trains "clubs and submachine guns" on Algerian immigrants when not surveilling their ghettoes in the grimy north of the city (201). In lieu of *Island of Hallucination*'s adaptation of the anti-Ridgway riot, Smith offers a groundbreaking depiction of the October 1961 attack of the Paris police on unarmed Algerian demonstrators, perhaps "the bloodiest act of state repression of street protest" in modern Western European history, a massacre of a hundred or more marchers thrown into the Seine and mostly buried in official French memory prior to the twenty-first century (House and MacMaster 1). Witnessing and resisting this police riot, and absorbing its lessons in comparative racialization, Simeon begins to call fellow African Americans "America's Algerians" (William Gardner Smith, *The Stone Face* 210). He resolves to join the black American civil rights workers struggling at least as bravely as the Algerian guerillas fighting in their own colonized country. Simeon will answer the "enormous, indignant" eyes of the state, now seen as French as well as American, by returning the look of those imperial eyes he knows best.

Antiracial theorist Paul Gilroy has pounced on Simeon's decision to return from Paris, panning what he considers a "capitulation to the demands of a narrow version of cultural kinship that Smith's universalizing argument appeared to have transcended" (*Against Race* 323–24). Closer to the nuances of the case, Michael Rothberg instead proposes that Smith's hero has learned to travel and identify "multidirectionally," to recognize the U.S. civil rights movement and the Algerian War of Independence as both distinct actions and related "vehicles of remembrance for each other" (229). The modern Gorgon of the "Stone Face," Smith's master icon of racism everywhere, must be resisted in a specific, familiar somewhere, Simeon concludes; yet Simeon reaches this conclusion only after recalling his special responsibility to black America through unforgettably bloody witness of its Algerian analog. His renewed "cultural kinship" is not so much a narrowing of Smith's universalizing case as a demonstration of its feasible value, its soundest application beyond gauzy one-worldism. Following his repatriation, Simeon will remember his chosen people as "America's Algerians" even while embracing them on their own terms.

In "The Brother," the third and final book of *The Stone Face*, Simeon's multidirectional discovery of his racial duty also reveals Smith's verdict on the Gibson

Affair and the fall of Paris noir it encapsulated, the latter captured in the novel by a dismal catalog of pleasure-quarantined American expatriates and brutalized Algerian protestors: "Doug made love to his State Department girl, Babe belched after a gigantic meal and joked off a feeling of guilt, Benson lay drunk and bitter in bed with his mistress, and Ahmed lay dead, his head battered to a pulp by police clubs, on the corner of the rue du Bac and the Boulevard Saint-Germain" (William Gardner Smith, *The Stone Face* 202). A better Paris noir might have survived, Smith implies, had Richard Gibson's pro-Algerian letter to *Life* carried dozens of signatures. Everyone at the Tournon should have claimed the anticolonialism of this true forgery, Smith suggests, not only to preserve the expatriate community's local harmony but also to retain the best in African American internationalism. The Gibson Affair whodunit chased in Wright's *Island* is here replaced by pursuit of a greater "whatdunit"; not even Doug, Smith's State Department–loving G-Man, is investigated for an individual crime. For *The Stone Face*, the guilty party is rather a many-authored transnationalism that confines itself to a handful of Left Bank cafés and falsely imagines that Doug, Babe, Benson, and company are "America's Frenchmen." Any black worldliness forced to discount Algeria, the front lines of the U.S. civil rights movement, and the more distant reverberations of the Holocaust, the novel judges, deserves a merely alienated exile.

Inevitably, Smith's nonfictional returns from Paris exile, actively tracked by Hoover's Bureau, were less satisfying than the one foreseen by Simeon. Written up in *Return to Black America*, a 1970 memoir, Smith's brief homecomings in the riot-torn summers of 1967 and 1968 reminded him that he could no longer "pretend to speak in the name of the black people of America" (5). It did not take a permanent native, however, to learn that the Black Power revolt, unbowed by pervasive "F.B.I. spies," threatened "the U.S. with its gravest internal challenge since the Civil War" (10, 177–78). Back in Paris noir, one of Smith's most talented Tournon colleagues, Chester Himes, was less certain of the gravity of "that Black Power shit," as his own novel of Black Power pronounced it (*Plan B* 10). But Himes agreed with Smith's estimate of the chances for an expatriate's reimmersion in black America. Following his 1953 relocation to Europe aboard the S.S. *Ile de France*, Himes too returned most comfortably through the agency of fiction. Writing his Harlem-set detective novels in Paris offered him a chance to indulge Afro-American memories without disenchanting the pleasures of "pure homesickness" (Himes, qtd. in John A. Williams, "My Man Himes" 50). Beginning with the Coffin Ed Johnson and Grave Digger Jones thriller *La Reine des Pommes* (1957), awarded the *Grand Prix de la Littérature Policière* at a televised Paris cocktail party, Himes sailed home without physically leaving France: "I went back, I was very happy, I was living there. . . . I began creating also all the black scenes of my memory and my actual knowledge" (50).

The best-loved tale of the origin of Himes's detective writing turns on a thousand-dollar proposition from Marcel Duhamel, the editor of *La Série Noire*, a prestigious line of hard-boiled titles that included French translations of Hammett and Raymond Chandler. After accepting Duhamel's offer to add black cops to his "Black Series," Himes would insist that he began working in the genre for bread alone. The truth of the matter is somewhat less hard-boiled, however, since Himes had been experimenting with lower-paid, artsier detective fiction prior to Duhamel's proposal. With the outbreak of the Gibson Affair, in fact, Himes made like Richard Wright and William Gardner Smith in testing the outer reaches of detective literature as a solution to the mystery of Paris noir. In 1956, a year before the publication of *La Reine des Pommes*, he fired off *A Case of Rape*, translated from "the American" and initially published under the French title *Une Affaire de Viol* in 1963. This skeletal but thoroughly imagined novel ensured that Himes's first three-dimensional black detective character was a volunteer writer-citizen rather than a badge-wearing Grave Digger or Coffin Ed, a private investigator based on the Parisian Richard Wright rather than any Sam Spade from the *Série Noire*.

"Based on" the Parisian Richard Wright may actually be too weak a formulation. Himes's Left Bank sleuth Roger Garrison rhymes with Wright's Ned Harrison, the self-created Wright twin who later appeared in *Island of Hallucination*. More significantly, Garrison matches the biographical Wright in every relevant particular. In a concentrated profile titled "The Investigator," *A Case of Rape* introduces an amateur detective and professional novelist who is born the son of "poverty stricken Negro sharecroppers" but raised under the intellectual wing of the U.S. Communist Party, which praises his first literary efforts in its own self-interest (*A Case* 31). "[P]rodded by both the communists and his publishers," Garrison then writes a *Black Boy*–like autobiography "hailed as a major work of art; he [is] heralded as a genius and catapulted to fame" (31). Still impatient "for both personal and creative freedom, for a culture free of racial bias in which to develop his talent," Garrison flees from fame to Paris (31). Like the historical Wright in the years after "I Tried to Be a Communist," the expatriated Garrison cancels his party card and denounces communism "with the furious emotionalism that can only be experienced by a former convert" (32). As a result of this political change of heart, Garrison is discarded by the pro-Soviet U.S. left and "hailed by the rightist press and literary circles in France as the great genius of his race" (32). "It was not until he had been dropped" by the

Parisian cognoscenti as well, observes Himes's exacting third-person narrator, "that he fully understood his position as a political figure" and recognized the limits of French *égalité* (32). Once more with feeling, Garrison renounces a recent conversion. Seeking revenge against his second country, he launches an investigation of French racism under the pretext of a reinvestigation of a case of rape. In Himes's novel of politicized detection, the Gibson Affair that Wright inspected even before *Island of Hallucination* is thus recoded as a racially over-loaded sexual scandal.

At the tragic epicenter of this scandal is a dead white American woman, Elizabeth Hancock Brissaud, an emerging novelist and sometime employee of the American Hospital in Paris. According to the testimony of the Paris police, she has been raped and slain by a quartet of Tournon clones including a Smith-type, a Baldwin-type, an Ollie Harrington-type, and (most gruesomely) an uncomplimentary type of Himes himself. Garrison, Himes's unmistakable Wright-type, feels duty-bound to reinvestigate this awful crime, driven by "a personal stake"—he "could identify with the defendants"—and by an imported ideological agenda (30). The Paris court that convicts four black men of rape and murder should itself be placed on trial, Garrison assumes, seeking to rerun the radical plot of *Native Son* on French soil (30). The court's guilty verdict "did not in reality constitute a conviction," Garrison supposes, but instead "a political conclusion by the French Republic, identical to that prevailing in the American South, that all Negro men were potential rapists" (30). In other words, Himes's Inspector Wright presumes along with the narrator of Smith's *The Stone Face* that he is investigating a case of imperial "whatdunit," a crime of the state linking systematic French and American racisms.

Himes's meta–detective novel discovers that Wright (and by ahistorical extension, Smith) is a mostly bad detective. A late section titled "The Missing Evidence" reveals that no gang rape has taken place, just as Garrison suspects, but that one of the Tournon gang had indeed slipped Brissaud a fatal overdose of the aphrodisiac Spanish fly, in Himes's hands a symbol of the erotic hyperbole too open to manipulation by black men in white France. The justice dealing of the French Republic, then, is not wholly in the pocket "of an international conspiracy to maintain white supremacy" (104). Garrison himself, moreover, is informally convicted of assault on Brissaud's budding literary career. Himes's all-knowing narrator provides proof that Garrison has secretly written a poison-pen letter to Brissaud's publisher, career-threatening correspondence comparable to Richard Gibson's misattributed letter to *Life*. Himes's readers, too, are not let off scot-free. All of us, his final page declares, are accountable for the unforgiven crime of the twentieth century, "man's inhumanity to man" (105).

Insofar as Garrison's actions metacritically investigate Wright's amateur investigation of the Gibson Affair, they thus disclose two dire failings in the inspector general of the Tournon: an anti-deductive prejudice that dooms Wright's stint as a second Sherlock Holmes, and a moral responsibility for Gibson's confessed offense that exposes Wright as the lead author of the Gibson Affair. Insofar as *A Case of Rape* anachronistically investigates the specifically fictional detection of Wright's book *Island of Hallucination*, it advises that efforts to extract a classic historical novel as well as a detective mystery–cum–roman à clef from the wreckage of the affair must not miss new couplings of race and gender—these among the advances, Himes suggests, that made Paris noir a miniature of contemporary world history. Nodding openly to Simone de Beauvoir's *The Second Sex* (1949), a feminist classic written in some of the same Paris cafés, Himes's novel describes Brissaud's flight "from all the despair and indignities of life, where women were the second sex" and "pride in race" may be the pivotal fallacy on which patriarchy rests (Himes, *A Case* 85). Himes, uncharacteristically temping as a second-wave feminist, thus parts from Wright in discovering that a white woman who challenges imperial hypocrisy to fraternize with black expatriates is "as much a casualty of racism" as her African American companions (83).[21] In Himes's historical novelization of black Paris, the generically authorized illustration of how private crises "coincide and interweave within the determining context of an historical crisis" (Lukács 41) thus entwines a false case of rape with a larger Cold War emergency that includes both gender and race.

When he learned that Himes had written an ambitious detective novel schooling his own detective work, Wright assumed that U.S. intelligence was his old friend's uncredited coauthor. *A Case of Rape* took all its "information from undercover agents of the American CIA," Wright informed his Dutch translator (qtd. in James Campbell, *Exiled* 243). Unsurprisingly, no independent support for Wright's accusation has been found, yet he was not completely off the mark, in fact, in supposing that Himes accepted literary inspiration from an American spy service. While it never explicitly mentions the FBI or its G-Men, thus separating itself from Wright's *Island* and Smith's *The Stone Face*, the formal design of *A Case of Rape* resembles nothing so much as a Hoover Bureau case file. Over the course of 105 pages, the length of a substantial FBI dossier as well as an atypically brief novel, Himes advances libelously sharp judgments by way of unflappable, unconditional prose. "It is to be noted that Roger [Garrison] made a number of appalling errors in both outlook and execution of his investigation," reads a representative sentence (Himes, *A Case* 3). Himes divides larger units of this serenely cruel officialese into numbered, memorandum-type sections rather than full-fledged chapters. Section 1, "The Charge," thus leads into fourteen terse segments including "The Verdict" (only one sentence long), "The Fourth Estate" (a collection of virtual press clippings familiar to readers of Hoover-era FBI files), and "Roger's Errors" (a damning inventory of the flaws in Wright's detective work).

Himes's eccentrically spare design is not a polished "synopsis" of an unwritten longer novel (Sallis v): it summarizes no overarching plot as such. Neither is it a supereconomical but common sort of police procedural: its eagle eye anatomizes not one but a competing pair of criminal investigations, the first involving state-sanctioned cops (the Paris police) and the second involving an amateur detective known to contemplate a future as a detective novelist (Roger Garrison, Himes's inept Inspector Wright). Borrowing the FBI's executive authority and narrative command, Himes's case history thus empowers itself to inspect the operations of both state police power and its most literate citizen challengers. And it flavors its inspection with the kind of informed yet resentful conjecture on left-wing intellectual affiliations that ordinary police tended to leave to the Hoover boys. One of Himes's Tournon suspects, for instance, is knowledgably smeared for his dual membership in "the leftist international writer-artist-refugee set" and in "the French communist party, connected with the superintellectual cell that held shop on rue Pierre Curie" (52). Damning associations established, Himes's contemptuous narrator then puts the boot in: in the suspect's scruffy but effete part of Paris, these memberships alone "qualified him as an indispensable authority on the world situation" (52).

Himes's recourse to FBI file rhetoric does not prove *A Case of Rape* an open-and-shut case of sympathetic Hooverism, of course. For starters, the novel's dictum that all modern readers—ghostreaders presumably included—are guilty of "man's inhumanity to man" involves a most un-Hooverite spreading of criminal responsibility (105). What Himes's file style instead lays bare is the generic innovation that joins his Tournon novel to Wright's and Smith's. Despite their irritable differences, *A Case of Rape*, *Island of Hallucination*, and *The Stone Face* are all examples of African American detective fiction stretched in the direction of the "antifile," my coinage for a type of novelized counterinvestigation that represents and recodes known forms of state surveillance. All three of these antifiles were written by black expatriates convinced of the FBI's practically simultaneous close reading. All thematize Afro-modernist artists as author-spies bid to outwrite critic-spies. All place the acknowledged stuff of FBI files—styles of belligerent fact-finding, political labeling, and/or hard-nosed analytical speech—at odds with these files' usual government ghostreaders. All adopt the antifile to narrativize the heady fact/fiction confusions surrounding the Gibson Affair, and to synthesize two factual/fictional literary forms—the roman à clef and the greater historical novel—under the shelter of the detective tradition. Finally, all three document the FBI's transatlantic reach while realizing its promise as an unsettling source of formal inspiration. In the case of the antifile, the FBI's ghostreading of Afro-modernism spurred innovations in form as well as content, hitting this literary double for the first time since Claude McKay's Harlem Renaissance.

Black Arts Antifiles and the "Hoover Poem": John A. Williams, James Baldwin, Sam Greenlee, Melvin Van Peebles, Ishmael Reed, Amiri Baraka, Nikki Giovanni, and Sonia Sanchez

John A. Williams's *The Man Who Cried I Am* (1967), the iconic historical novel of the Black Arts 1960s, is an antifile about an antifile. Williams's long, jet-setting, and temporally jumbled narrative, opening in a Tournon-like Amsterdam café and touching down in Paris, Leiden, Lagos, New York, and Washington, D.C., makes dramatic characters of all three Tournon antifilers. In particular, haggling at the emotional axis of the novel, a Chester Himes understudy named Max Reddick serves as Williams's cancer-ridden writer-protagonist, while a Richard Wright surrogate named Harry Ames serves as this protagonist's profane writer-father. Like the Paris antifiles of Himes and Wright, *The Man Who Cried I Am* fuses roman à clef payback, historical novel-scaled ambition, and a coordinating expatriate detective mystery to measure the power of U.S. state surveillance to shape (but not break) African American literary history. In Williams's addition to this Bureau-nourished form, however, the structural matrix of the antifile also becomes an overt plot device: *The Man's* protagonist inherits a file of photostats edited by Harry/Wright that exposes the shocking plan of the FBI and other U.S. government agencies to imprison and murder "all 22 million members of the [U.S. black] Minority" (Williams, *The Man* 372). Williams's decision to accept the legacy of the antifile proves the genre's imaginative interest a decade after the Gibson Affair, still tempting authors to ruminate on the power of U.S. state surveillance to cross the Black Atlantic. Yet Williams's decision to up the ante, to sensationalize the genre as a potentially race-saving revelation, also reflects the extraordinary intensity and blatancy of FBI ghostreading in the Black Arts era, the phase of African American literary history in which dam breaks, and incriminating representations of the Bureau flow from every corner, from black women as well as men.

Heightened FBI ghostreading haunted the Black Arts movement from the start, thanks in part to a much-threatened, never-delivered anti-Bureau book by James Baldwin. *The Blood Counters*, supposedly titled after "the negroes' [*sic*] nickname for the FBI," was the talk of Bureau critic-spies in 1963 and 1964 (U.S., Federal, Baldwin, 17 July 1964). Baldwin's lawyer Clarence Jones was captured on an FBI wiretap promising that his client's book would "BE LIKE AN ATOM BOMB WHEN IT IS DROPPED" (6 June 1963). Despite Jones's overheard confidence, Baldwin's FBI manuscript never reached waiting arms at the Dial Press—in any case, a firm where one of the Bureau's "contacts in the publishing field" stood ready to "secure the proofs" and forward them to FBI headquarters, the spirit of preemptive Total Literary Awareness policy surviving the 1950s (5 Aug. 1964).[22] By 1965, more obvious informers waited on other explosive manuscripts as the Black Arts movement built itself in Harlem. As we saw earlier, the BARTS Theatre/School, the prototypical Black Arts institution, knew in its first and only summer of operation that FBI agents attended its readings and classes. Driven by the "Black Hate" counterintelligence program created in 1967, the investigative tracks of the Bureau grew even clearer as the Black Arts movement propagated beyond black Manhattan. *Black Fire* (1968), the movement's thickest national anthology, thus featured an essay warning that inflexible black rebels "will be quickly disposed of by the FBI and other agencies" (Hernton 103). The home of the Watts Writers Workshop, the movement's best-publicized West Coast outlet, was burned to the ground by an admitted FBI infiltrator in 1973, as good a public marker as any for the beginning of the movement's end (Widener 113).

From start to finish, then, writers associated with the Black Arts were educated that the FBI sought to kill—not merely to oversee—what John A. Williams praised as their "Renaissance II" ("The Harlem Renaissance" 17). While the twentieth century's first African American literary rebirth, the Harlem-based "Renaissance I," opened in proximity to excited reports of a high-placed Hooverite readership, the second opened and closed alongside dark tales of a final showdown with the FBI. Not only the Black Panthers, trusted the Black Artists, were high on the Bureau's hit list. "ATTENTION!!!! / ALL KNOWN OBVIOUSLYBLACKS MUST BE KEPT / UNDER STRICT SURVEILLANCE," wrote poet Johari Amini (a.k.a. Jewel Lattimore), imagining the response of state policemen to those "carrying literature saying / be very black . . . live love / disseminate black" (ll. 47–49, ll. 8–10). The stylized paranoia of Williams's *The Man Who Cried I Am*, a novel that situates a plot to exterminate Afro-America at the vanishing point of Afro-modernism, thus stemmed from sensible fears of literary disappearance as well as credulous Holocaust analogies.

By far the most famous pages of *The Man* describe the fictional "King Alfred Plan," a genocidal work of the FBI, the CIA, and other U.S. security services named for the earliest English monarch to describe himself in quasi-racial, Anglo-Saxon terms. Williams relishes the chance that the King Alfred papers, first disclosed in Harry's special edition, permit him to interpolate pseudodocuments composed in file style. The 400-page antifile that is Williams's novel accordingly climaxes in the five "found" pages of Harry's shorter antifile that simulate uncut government prose. A joint memo signed by the Bureau, the CIA, and the Department of Justice allows Williams to explain the weaponization of prurient personal files (a routine tactic of Hoover's FBI) in the most revealingly vanilla state English: "There are 12 major Minority organizations and all are familiar to the 12 million. Dossiers have been compiled on the leaders of the organizations, and can be studied in Washington. The material contained in many of the dossiers, and our threat to reveal the material, has considerably held in check the activities of some of the leaders" (Williams, *The Man* 373). Dossiers filled with embarrassing personal scandals are not the most banally evil weapons conjured up in Williams's King Alfred papers. The specter of Nazi poison-gas canisters and less traceable instruments of mass death enters a "Committee Report" euphemistically describing "9,000,000 objects, or 1,500,000 each year. Production could not dispose of the containers, which proved a bottleneck. . . . We suggest that vaporization techniques be employed to overcome the Production problems inherent in KING ALFRED" (376).

Williams did his best to expose the King Alfred Plan as both *The Man*'s publicity engine and as a type of public antifile meant to avert actual black genocide, successfully inspiring an opportunistic blurb from New York City mayor John Lindsay that served each purpose equally. "If this book is to remain fiction," Lindsay counseled, "it must be read" (qtd. in Williams, Afterword 411). Williams had New York City subway cars plastered with details of the plan around the novel's release date, and later allowed rap music progenitor Gil Scott-Heron to record a tribute transparently titled "King Alfred Plan" (John L. Jackson 111). "[W]hite paranoia is here to stay," sang Scott-Heron in 1972, so concentration camps for blacks "are being prepared night and day, night and day" (l. 2). For Scott-Heron's jazz rant, as for Williams's antifile, the fate of Europe's Jews is a relevant cautionary tale. So is J. Edgar Hoover's Custodial Detention program, a roundup in fact planned for more than half of the "filed" African American authors discussed in *F.B. Eyes*. Federal bad guys with ugly orders were "[a]ll ready in D.C. to preventatively detain you and me" (l. 5), warned Scott-Heron. More than twenty years after *The Man* entered "the unofficial canon of books most commonly used to ground racial-conspiracy theories within the African American community" (John L. Jackson 114), Williams was more prepared than ever to cite FBI wrongdoing as King Alfred's historical anchor. In a 2004 republication of the novel, he suggested that Kenneth O'Reilly's revelations in *"Racial Matters": The FBI's Secret File on Black America, 1960–1972* (1989) provided a persuasive after-the-fact explanation of why "so many readers said they believed the King Alfred Plan was real" (Afterword 411).

In his own right, Williams believed that King Alfred was real insofar as it revealed the undercover truth of modern African American authorship. A rarely discussed feature of Williams's plan is its service as a sign of the high stakes of black male literary inheritance: in *The Man*, the King Alfred Plan both decodes and symbolizes the risky international espionage mission senior Afro-modernists were serially fated to will to their writer-sons. Harry/Wright inherits the bulk of the King Alfred antifile from an African diplomat who dies in Ghana on the same night as W.E.B. Du Bois, the African American literary giant and FBI scapegoat whose lifespan nearly linked black Renaissances I and II. Harry then passes the decolonized, Du Bois–instilled antifile down to Max/Himes through a safe house (and shared female lover) in the Netherlands, but not before meeting his own end at the hands of Alfonse Edwards, a Richard Gibson–styled black American who has "quit Uncle Sam's foreign service to write a novel about it," and who carries the mystery of the Gibson Affair and of Wright's death in Paris with him wherever he skulks (Williams, *The Man* 370).[23] Max then places a long-distance call to New York and bravely conveys every sentence of the antifile to Minister Q, a Malcolm X clone who warns Max that anything said to him over the telephone is also said to U.S. intelligence. The government agents phone tapping the Minister then activate a Europe-based CIA death squad composed of Edwards and Roger Wilkinson, the latter a William Gardner Smith replica with a transparent cover as "one of those [black expatriate] writers who, whenever race riots broke out back home, was summoned hastily by the local magazine or newspaper editors to explain what was going on" (26). In *The Man*'s final chapter, Edwards/Gibson again proves the more lethal government agent. Wielding a syringe of morphine, he executes a remanned, pistol-packing Max, now trading fire with his pursuers and recouping what had been a slow, unheroic death from a highly symbolic case of rectal cancer. The next delivery of the antifile, and with it, the perpetuation of Afro-modern literary paternity, thus lies with Williams's undrugged, unpenetrated, and now totally unblind Minister Q, last seen walking off to a political gathering in Harlem under threat from black agents of federal intelligence. Though clouded by the 1965 assassination of Malcolm X, Williams's conclusion realizes a repeated dream of the Black Arts moment, imaginatively proving black writing a fearless helpmeet to black nationalist politics.

Among other, less appealing things, the King Alfred Plan's cementing of Williams's hetero-only literary patriarchy stages the idea that to write well in Du Bois's wake is to enlist in a black secret service. A bit like the revolutionary spies of George Schuyler's B.I., or Black Internationale (a group Williams acknowledged in a 1991 Schuyler reprint), the bookish members of Williams's anti-FBI or counter-CIA expose the ominous plans of U.S. intelligence. They recognize that such exposure will be punished by a prying state and a squad of minor black writer-informers but agree to risk death to correct the racial balance of world-altering change. As Max/Himes phrases it pages before his final sacrifice, "the secret to converting *their* change to *your* change was *letting them know that you knew*" (386; emphasis in original). Creating transformative antifiles that let U.S. state intelligence know that you knew of its intrigues, and damning the torpedoes that had subsequently followed Du Bois to Africa and Wright to France: this is how Williams's representative Black Arts man declares his existential "I Am," and how Williams's restrictive vision of the male line of Afro-modernism approximates the chain of FBI-conscious black authors traced in this part of *F.B. Eyes*.

Imaginary martyrdom was the high price of admission to Williams's virile Afro-modernist canon. In *The Man Who Cried I Am*, the King Alfred papers that bind this canon together are also a prevue of the deadly film cartridge in David Foster Wallace's *Infinite Jest* (1996), another post-1945 meganovel wrapped around a top-secret intertext that dooms every character that receives it. But there was in fact no shortage of authors willing to pick up the pieces of King Alfred and the self-endangering antifile form in the years immediately after *The Man*. In the late 1960s, the "how-to" novel of black radical counterintelligence became a strategic Black Arts subgenre—and a Bureau-monitored suggestion box for black revolution. Chester Himes, the main model for *The Man*'s Max Reddick, paid Williams's novel the critical tribute of *Plan B* (1993), an unhinged thriller sketching an African American conspiracy to engineer a reverse King Alfred and massacre American whites. Begun in 1968, and finally published after Himes's death, this self-designated sequel to Williams's King Alfred Plan (read "Plan A") kills off Coffin Ed and Grave Digger, Himes's popular Harlem detectives, in order to ease the birth of a harder black plainclothes agent. Tomsson Black, *Plan B*'s bloodthirsty arch-spy, outduels the CIA as well as the FBI, the latter terrified to reveal that Black's troops possess large "caches of arms and ammunition, explosives, and drugs of a kind known as 'Truth Serums'" (Himes, *Plan B* 134): in other words, the weapons of Schuyler's Black Internationale rediscovered for the Black Arts epoch. Sam Greenlee's *The Spook*

Who Sat by the Door (1969), wrongly advertised as the first Black Nationalist novel, may have been the first to track a conversion from affirmative-action baby to guerilla mastermind. Like *The Man* and *Plan B*, Greenlee's antifile mixes attacks on the FBI with blows against the CIA, the latter increasingly framed by Black Artists as the Bureau's partner in crime. Greenlee's spy-hero is proud of his place in the inaugural class of black CIA recruits: "You know how they call CIA agents spooks? First time we'll ever get paid for that title" (Greenlee 13). He is much prouder, however, of his elaborate scheme to hijack government intelligence training for the benefit of the secretive "Black Freedom Fighters," another descendant of Schuyler's Black Internationale. Greenlee, for his part, was gratified to hear the story (probably apocryphal) that *The Spook* "became required reading in the FBI academy" ("Sam Greenlee").

Close to the same vein, but far more subtly, Melvin Van Peebles's pre-blacksploitation novel *A Bear for the FBI* (1968) dramatizes the undercover potential of even the meekest black literary hopeful. The inspirational antagonism of the Bureau needs no mention beyond Van Peebles's title, borrowed from a now-forgotten joke about the white-bread censorship of the *Reader's Digest*, its editors always receptive to a defanged Hooverism. (The *Digest's* ideal article, went the joke, would be accepted under the title "I Screwed a Bear for the FBI and Found God," but run under the title "The Most Memorable Animal I Ever Met" [Van Peebles 7].) Finally, at the end of this road sits Ishmael Reed's *Mumbo Jumbo* (1972), an esoteric deconstruction of the believable revolutionary antifile and of Black Arts prose in general, published in the year of Hoover's death. Amid its device-baring diagrams, photographs, and "partial bibliography," *Mumbo Jumbo* casts the wicked "Wallflower Order," the investigative and censorship arm of white backlash, in the structurally unfunky mold of Hoover's FBI. In Reed's self-reflexive hands, the centuries-old war between the Africanized god Osiris and the Europeanized god Set erupts in a lopsided battle of detective agencies, Wallflowers versus hoodoo adepts, beneath the monuments of the Harlem Renaissance. Condemned to the losing side of this literary-historical and world-historical clash, the Bureau-like Wallflowers come to respect the mystic readings of Reed's hoodoo ringleader PaPa LaBas, "a 'so-called' astrodetective they have under surveillance" (Reed, *Mumbo Jumbo* 64). In the early going, however, the Hoover Raids are cited to typify the white detectives' ham-fisted methods—"*5000 'Reds' are routed from their beds, imprisoned or deported*" (48; emphasis in original)—and to underline the need for a spiritually elevated black response that transcends the terms of federal espionage.

From its own early going in the mid-1960s, Black Arts poetry anticipated *Mumbo Jumbo* in refusing to fight the FBI with the mirroring fire of a black

Bureau of Investigation. Rather than drawing up plans for a retaliatory Afro-modernist spy service, the poets of the movement answered the reckless eye-balling of the Bureau with blasts of less derivative personal insult. In the typical Black Arts Bureau poem, oppositional rhetoric thus remains the rule, but the corrupt myth and person of the FBI director receives the beating rather than the Bureau's files and detention plans. Paradoxically, this insulting habit of Black Arts poetry stemmed in part from its affection for the reverential per-sonal elegy. When not testing free verse and variable lineation as signs of social freedom, or exploding the differences between the performed and the printed, Black Arts poets often wrote traditionally elegiac lyrics of loss, mourning, and replenishment—the polar opposite, in other words, of the passionately disre-spectful "Hoover Poem," a mouthpiece for cheering the imminent death of the Hoover Bureau and its supporting players.

As Black Aesthetician Carolyn Gerald explained in 1969, it was "the work of [our] poets to give us back our heroes" as well as "to provide us with new ones" (28). Above all, Black Arts poets worked to restore the heroism of ex–Nation of Islam leader Malcolm X and "sheets of sound" free jazz saxophonist John Col-trane, two figures of uncompromising cultural promise dead, like the subjects of classic pastoral elegies by Milton and Shelley, before their time. In the after-life, these two African American heroes joined hands at the crossroads of what Howard Rambsy II calls the "Malcolm-Coltrane express," a long line of Black Arts elegies employing "the two men as vehicles for transmitting ideas about the movement's commitment to radical politics and creativity" (103). Oppos-ing and elucidating this line is a mode of Black Arts poetry less talked about, a string of anti-elegies—several by the same poets who mourned Malcolm and Coltrane—that unmourn Hoover and employ his FBI as a vehicle to ridicule Black Power's most ruthless enemies. The Malcolm-Coltrane express, this is to say, was complemented and fueled by the Hoover Poem, a means to com-memorate black heroism elsewhere.[24]

One of the initial recipes for the Hoover Poem, Amiri Baraka's "Three Move-ments and a Coda" (1963–65), migrated into some of the Black Arts' most influ-ential gatherings, from the *Black Fire* anthology, to Baraka's own *Black Magic: Collected Poetry, 1961–1967* (1969), to Stephen Henderson's *Understanding the New Black Poetry: Black Speech and Black Music as Poetic References* (1973). The hulking capitalization of Baraka's second movement packs Hoover inside a parade of white idols of home, state, and media, all condemned by black-ness, the ascending "QUALITY OF NIGHT," to a depthless, "BLACK HOLE" grave (Baraka, "Three Movements" l. 1, l. 3). "THE LONE RANGER / IS DEAD. / THE SHADOW / IS DEAD. / ALL YOUR HEROES ARE DYING," intones Baraka's speaker, a graveside priest offering anything but consolation (ll. 9–13). Most painful of all, the speaker continues, "J. EDGAR HOOVER WILL / SOON BE DEAD. YOUR MOTHER WILL DIE," followed by the white Father-in-Chief, President "LYNDON JOHN-SON" (ll. 13–14). Hoover's location between the bygone supermen of 1930s and 1940s radio—the Lone Ranger and the Shadow—and the dimming political star of LBJ reflects his status as a liaison between the federal government and the national media. His place right before the dearest heroine of all—"YOUR MOTHER"—shows his high target value in Baraka's variation on the dozens. No differently from the rest of Baraka's expiring white heroes, however, Hoover is treated to a defiantly unmournful preburial. The second of Baraka's "Three Movements" gestures toward elegiac style in its incantatory refrains, but his broken chorus repeats the uncomforting tenses "DIE," "DYING," and "DEAD," in uppercase like one of Robert Indiana's pop art memento mori. The whole poem abstains from elegiac apotheosis, with Hoover's passing explicitly dismissed as one of the merely "natural / things. No one is / threatening anybody / that's just the way life / is, / boss" (ll. 15–20). The jig is simply and naturally up for the boss of the white security state, and a new crew of black "lovers," "dancers," and "dynamite singers," vernacular artists brave enough to defy white law, has become the deserving subject of future memorials (ll. 33, 34). In sharp distinction to the Black Arts "Coltrane Poem" dissected by critic Kimberly Benston, the dead and nearly gone of the Hoover Poem stay that way. If the latter Black Arts genre matches the former in transforming loss "into an instrument of the living imagination," it is only because this loss is imaginatively celebrated (Benston 146). Unlike "[t]he stilling of Coltrane's horn," treated in the Coltrane Poem as "a representative assault on the black voice," the stilling of Hoover's voice speeds the liberation of black speech (145).

The parenthetical subtitle of Nikki Giovanni's full-grown Hoover Poem of 1968, "A Short Essay of Affirmation Explaining Why (With Apologies to the Federal Bureau of Investigation)," politely tips its hat to its expected Bureau readership. The apologies end there, however: what follows expresses no repentance whatever to "Miss Hoover" (l. 48) and the unmanly G-Men who conspire to plant "That little microphone / In our teeth / Between our thighs / Or any-place" (ll. 10–13). Giovanni's poetic essay is written in answer to the question of why black folks strike white ones as paranoid and prone to talk "to themselves" (l. 4). Unnamed "recent events" involving Hoover's FBI "have shown / We know who we're talking / to" (ll. 7–9); vocal black paranoia, the poem explains, does not mean that no one in Washington is after black America. Giovanni's speaker is not too shy to suggest that the FBI has been after black Americans for sexual satisfaction, and her denunciation exploits Hoover's queerness to metaphorize the Bureau's surveillance bugs as "a mechanical dick / . . . lightening the way / for whitey" (l. 31, ll. 33–34). Despite the confession of assault, the final agenda is affirmative, as advertised. Giovanni's poem concludes with a pledge that FBI buggery has ended with pre-black history:

> They ain't getting
> Inside
> My bang
> or
> My brain
> I'm into my Black Thing
> And it's filling all
> My empty spots. (ll. 39–46)

"Sorry 'bout that, / Miss Hoover," read the final lines, a couplet killing off the remains of Hoover's allure, and unmourning the sexualized intimacy of Bureau surveillance (both physical ["My bang"] and intellectual ["My brain"]) previously exposed in Richard Wright's poem "The FB Eye Blues." When the '68-model Hoover pulls down his britches, Giovanni suggests, black targets with a healthy Black Thing see only the "change uh life" (Hurston 94). And like Joe Starks, Zora Neale Hurston's menopausal patriarch in *Their Eyes Were Watching God* (1937), Giovanni's withered, impotent Hoover is not expected to survive the exposure. Beyond these possibly accidental echoes of prior Afro-modernism, Giovanni actively shapes her Hoover Poem according to an emerging Black Arts pattern, a gay-baiting symbolism in which state intelligence is an effeminate queer rapist, and effective black resistance to invasive surveillance is the resurrection of "the impenetrable body of the normatively sexed man," a preferred trope of national integrity in Cold War containment culture at large (Carlston, *Double Agents* 8). Notwithstanding first impressions, the speaker who fills her "empty spots" with blackness instead of with Miss Hoover's phallus is a close relative of John A. Williams's Max Reddick, the titular *Man Who Cried I Am*, who heals his rectal wound with his own gun and his disembodied service to the prince of the Black Thing, Minister Q. As poet-critic Cheryl Clarke observes, Giovanni was not the only woman writer associated with the Black Arts who supposed that the "theory of redemptive/compensatory manhood absorbed the 'race' as a whole in the United States" (53).

Sonia Sanchez's earlier Hoover Poem, the never-republished "A Modern Song of the F.B.I." (1966), has a title that could have been used for practically every piece of literature discussed in this part of *F.B. Eyes*. Distinctively, however, Sanchez's ballad of the Bureau allows Hoover to sing his own tune of institutional death and helpless nostalgia: in this case, the anti-elegy for the Hoover Bureau is voiced by the head G-Man. "O bring back the good old days" (l. 1), the poem generically begins, gradually revealing the Bureau identity of the speaker (a southern-born, Hooverian royal "we" arrives in line 18) and his special longing for the years before the civil rights movement stole the FBI's mojo. "O bring back the good old days" (l. 38), the poem recites,

> before americans discovered that
> negroes were living or rather
> more dying or maybe to be
> a little more specific being
> killed in the south and
> nothing was being done about
> it, not even by that high-
> powered-always-get-your-man-
> organization. (ll. 39–47)

The FBI's self-described offense against murdered Negroes in not merely a sin of omission. "[M]y god, we always / do get our man," adds Sanchez's Hoover, "but no one / told us it was now / unlawful to kill them" (ll. 48–51). The Hoover Bureau's rumored involvement in the assassination of Malcolm X and other black leaders is thus confirmed in the horse's mouth, but couched as a thing of the lawless past. A quartet of apostrophes, the rhetorical figure traditionally used to address an absent object of desire, then accentuates the distance from the FBI's gang- and Commie-busting prime. "O, O, O, O, bring back the good old days" (l. 51), begs Sanchez's Hoover, doing his best *Waste Land* impression ("O O O O / That Shakespeherian Rag" ll. 128–29) to highlight the mock-grandeur of premodern times:

> [the days] before unrest
> when banks were robbed and little
> kids kidnapped and we carried our
> party cards and quiet reigned
> over the land (save for a few
> communistic-inspired-black-outbursts). (ll. 53–58)

With its Eliotic apostrophes, e. e. cummings–style lowercase, and liberally en-jambed free verse, Sanchez's modern song of the FBI embraces some of the most recognizable formal signatures of American poetic modernism. The content of this same song insists that the era of the racially modern, finally realized by black unrest, is curtains for Hoover, however. New black days are dispatching a once high-powered legend and institution, and all songs of the FBI, whatever their form, are now mournful in practice.

Intriguingly, in her life after "A Modern Song" and her time with BARTS, Sanchez has suggested that the FBI's dying gift to Afro-modernism included more than the Hoover Poem. In a 1999 interview, she recalls her part in founding the black studies department at San Francisco State University in the late 1960s, and the surprising academic lesson then taught by home-invading G-Men. Unlike Nikki Giovanni's comical "fuck you" (l. 17) to a pair of FBI callers in another Black Arts text, "I Laughed When I Wrote It" (1972), Sanchez the classroom teacher expresses serious thanks for the agents' intrusion:

> One day two FBI agents came to my house and told my landlord that they should put me out. One of the FBI men put his hand in my face and said I was one of those radicals up on the campus and that the landlord should put me out. He said, "You're teaching 'Du Bois'" (pronounces it the French way). . . . So I responded, "But I'm just teaching literature." And it hit me. I was teaching sociology, economics, the culture of a people. See, they understood that better than I did. . . . And I thank those two FBI men for showing me how. (Sanchez, *Conversations* 115–16)

The Hoover Poem may have done its part to finish off the Hoover Bureau. As Sanchez sees it, however, the academic interdiscipline of black studies, the Black Arts' most durable institutional achievement, owed something to the Hoover boys' inability to detach African American literature from black culture and power. Perhaps for this reason, some African American authors wrote up the FBI even after Hoover was buried in the Congressional Cemetery, and even after the Black Arts movement, undermined by COINTELPRO infiltration, was mostly retired to the officially integrated American university.

Bureau Writing after Hoover: Dudley Randall, Ai, Audre Lorde, Danzy Senna, and Gloria Naylor

The Hoover Poem was not the only strain of Black Arts poetry eager to taunt FBI ghostreaders. Dudley Randall, the Detroit poet and publisher of the Broadside Press, committed himself to disseminating what we can call the "Informer Poem," minor verse that let the Bureau "know that you knew" by exposing the pathology of the agents and infiltrators paid to rat on Afro-America.[25] One of the least familiar writers Randall selected for his sweeping anthology *The Black Poets* (1971) was Ray Durem, a veteran of the Spanish Civil War and the U.S. Communist Party represented by his posthumous poem "Award (A Gold Watch to the FBI Man who has followed me for 25 years)" (1964), the equivalent of an anti-elegy delivered at an obscure G-Man's retirement dinner: "Well, old spy / looks like I / led you down some pretty blind alleys" (ll. 1–3). In *For Malcolm* (1969), a thinner anthology of memorial verse, Randall featured Umbra Workshop organizer David Henderson's poem "They Are Killing All the Young Men," a long meditation on the eternal (elegized) spirit of El-Hajj Malik El-Shabazz and the ephemeral (anti-elegized) ambition of Raymond A. Wood, a genuine black police spy of the mid-1960s: "why did not ALL the infiltrators go to their bosses / with news of the plot / Why did not J. Edgar Hoover / issue a statement that Malcolm X's life /was indeed in danger?" (ll. 154–58). Meanwhile, in his own collection *More to Remember: Poems of Four Decades* (1971), Randall incorporated a trio of curt and acidly funny Informer Poems, titled "Informer," "F.B.I. Memo," and "Abu," respectively. "Informer" reads this way, in its entirety:

> He shouted
> "Black Power!"
> so loudly
> we never heard
> his whispers
> to the F.
> B.
> I. (ll. 1–8)

Similar to the Bureau-faked Black Arts literature of COINTELPRO minstrelsy, Randall's ideal black informer was distinguishable from the ideal black militant only in the volume of his nationalist overstatement. Skeptically eying the blow-dried Africanisms of Black Power fashion, Randall's "F.B.I. Memo" puts the point slightly differently:

> The perfect spy
> for the F.B.I.
> must have:
> Afro
> tiki

dashiki
Swahili
and cry
Kill the honkies!" (ll. 1–9)

It was the simultaneously deprecating and revealing landscape of the Hoover Poem, however, that seems to have made the deepest impression on African American poets of the generation after the Black Arts. In her 1993 collection *Greed*, for example, the black Irish Choctaw Japanese poet Ai (born Florence Anthony) presents two raw riffs on the genre's allegorical connection between Bureau history and Hoover's body: the autobiographically indexed poem "Hoover, J. Edgar" ("I'm the man behind the man / behind the man" [ll. 1–2]) and "Hoover Trismegistus." In this latter work of melodramatic monologue, Hoover speaks in the manner of Sonia Sanchez's "A Modern Song of the F.B.I." In "Hoover Trismegistus," however, Ai's ventriloquism places words deeper in the mouth of Hoover's unconscious. Her Hoover's cross-dressing, gender-troubling desire for Clyde Tolson, his longtime second-in-command, is no painful stretch. Majestically comfortable with either sex, Ai's FBI deity is a state-sanctioned descendant of Hermes Trismegistus, the syncretic Greek-Egyptian god of alchemy and creative translation. In contrast, her Hoover's suspicion that Tolson spotted his tinge of black ancestry (the Egyptian in the Greek?) is impossible for him to stomach:

I could be both [man and woman], couldn't I?
That part was easy,
but what I couldn't endure
was the face in the bathroom mirror.
Was I a throwback to some buck
Who sat hunched over in the hull
of a ship,
while the whip lashed his back?
"Do I look colored to you?" I ask Clyde,
who always, always turns aside my question. . . . (ll. 4–13)

Several elements in Ai's update of the Hoover Poem are typical of the black Bureau literature—more sporadic and less defining than in the years of Afro-modernism—that followed Hoover's passing. Ai draws on both chilling FOIA revelations and the backlog of humanizing sexual gossip released by Hoover's death, especially the flimsy tales of transvestism popularized by Anthony

Summer's titillating biography *Official and Confidential* (1993). She publicly broaches the possibility of Hoover's black ancestry, and the implications for African American and U.S. national identity should his FBI be revealed as the stronghold of a closeted part-black man—implications also explored in part 1 of this book. Finally, she observes Hoover's supposed desire to be both man and woman from the perspective of a woman writing as a man. Widening the opening created by Sonia Sanchez, Nikki Giovanni, and other poets of the Black Arts movement, she thus carves out fresh black feminist approaches to Hoover and the Hooverites, amending the dominant Afro-modernist plot of fraternal rivalry.

For a number of reasons, postmodern play and plausible deniability included, the landmarks of self-consciously post-Hoover prose by African American women take the form of confessional fiction or symbolically heightened memoir.[26] Published ten years after Hoover's state funeral was Audre Lorde's *Zami: A New Spelling of My Name* (1982), a "biomythography" of the self-described "black feminist lesbian mother poet" that efficiently demythologizes the FBI's institutional biography (Lorde, *The Cancer Journals* 17). In *Zami*'s expressionistic account of Lorde's Harlem childhood, her older sisters cement her attraction to fiction by retelling episodes of radio series including *The FBI in Peace and War*. By "the height of the McCarthy era," however, Lorde's adolescent avatar, now a proud "menace to the status quo," decides that she will not allow a team of FBI investigators "past my door" (Lorde, *Zami* 121). Unlike Sanchez's pair of Bureau visitors, these two G-Men hold no knowledge worth having, and are not menacing on their face: "They stood outside, stupid and male and proper and blonde and only a little bit threatening in their buttoned-downed shirts and striped ties" (121). At least according to the FBI, which failed to locate a Lorde file after my 2006 FOIA request, neither Lorde's closed door nor *Zami*'s blasé put-down resulted in retaliatory FBI counterliterature.

By way of contrast, Danzy Senna's Clinton-era best seller *Caucasia* (1998) projects a post-Hoover Bureau that remains more than a bit threatening to those born when white radicalism courted Black Power. In this autobiographical fiction of racial limbo and the long-term costs of COINTELPRO, the lives of a pair of biracial sisters, Cole and Birdie, are painfully split in 1975 when the FBI comes looking for their movement-veteran parents. The dark-skinned Cole escapes to Brazil with Deck, her theory-driven black professor father. The lighter-skinned Birdie goes underground in New Hampshire with Sandy, her wellborn white activist mother, who combs the newspapers each morning for her photo "under the word 'WANTED'" (Senna 127). When Sandy's name fails to appear on any of the Bureau's Most Wanted lists, she insists that truly dangerous threats to the system are instead smothered by the silent treatment. "Cointelpro is clearly in cahoots with the media," she assures her puzzled daughter (127). Despite the ironic humor of Sandy's unsatisfied desire for Bureau notoriety, Senna's novel pivots on the tragic consequences of FBI "reracialization," the organization's proficiency in tearing radical integration apart limb from limb and sister from sister. FBI harassment continues to alienate and constrain part-black lives, *Caucasia* argues, and thus to inspire plots of politicized self-division in a moment of multicultural feminism.

Akin to *Caucasia*, Gloria Naylor's *1996* (2005) is a self-described "fictionalized memoir" that pictures the post-Hoover security state with disgust and respect. The parallels stop here, however, given the acknowledged eccentricity of *1996*, a post-9/11 adjustment of black Bureau literature that Naylor admits she did not want to write. Following deeper in the footsteps of George Orwell's *1984* (1948) than her own *The Women of Brewster Place* (1983), Naylor details how the island retreat of a respected black woman writer becomes a haunted house of surveillance and self-doubt. The writer-protagonist's quarrel with a Jewish cat lady next door at first seems petty, but Naylor's neighbor reveals herself as the sister of the deputy director of the National Security Agency (NSA), and the stakes of the disagreement escalate wildly. The NSA official accepts the challenge of knowing his sister's enemy and quickly rediscovers the value of the racialized literary surveillance first systematized by Hoover's FBI:

> He types in the name Gloria Naylor, and a list of roughly 50 names is scrolled in front of him. Only one is in blue, on the Watch List. He clicks on that name and there she is—a photo, a social security number, and a synopsis. Every black, Latino, and Asian writer who has had any press coverage is on the NSA's watch list. This list was allegedly disbanded back in the '70s, so now it is a list that doesn't exist inside of the NSA. . . . By the end of the day at least half a dozen people will be put to work. All of [Naylor's] books are assigned to readers for a detailed synopsis of each one. Every newspaper article, every book review, is to be read and analyzed. . . . Files from the FBI and CIA are ordered. And just to be thorough, a background check going to her college days. Yes, by the end of the day, Gloria Naylor's life will become, no pun intended, an open book. (Naylor 33)

Naylor's *1996* can be said to embody paranoia rather than represent it: nearly a quarter of the book's pages are consumed by addenda that reprint conspiratorial lawsuits and pseudoscientific papers on mind control. The obsessional mistrust pervading the book's anti-Semitism is hard to miss or exaggerate. Naylor has her Jewish deputy director of the NSA reach out to the Anti-Defamation League, which then taps a local temple to do the dirty work of twenty-four-hour surveillance, the ancient Jewish conspiracy finally perfected on a South Carolina barrier island in the mid-1990s. By this point in our journey up from 1919, however, it is also hard to miss just how much Naylor's fictionalized NSA shares with the historical FBI.

There are untrivial differences between Naylor's NSA and this book's Bureau, of course. Her federal security agency employs twenty-first-century data mining and a vast computerized archive, relying on old-school Bureau paperwork only for deep background. (Dramatic leaks in 2013 exposing the NSA's digital reading of millions of Americans' private communications make Naylor seem a prescient realist, in this respect at any rate.) Her watch list indexes a wide range of U.S. minority authors, while her illustrative black literary target is a postmodern woman rather than an Afro-modernist man. But there is much in common between her ghostreading bureaucracy and Hoover's. Her literary enemies list echoes the Bureau's author-filled Custodial Detention listings. Her government ghostreaders acquire collected works and produce detailed synopses of African American fiction in the dogged style of Hoover's various book review sections. Her spy-critics build their book reports on criminal background checks much as the mixed genre of the counterliterary FBI file layered literary-critical analyses on police procedurals. Like Naylor's well-published NSA victim, her life an open book to a readerly state, the national loyalty of the fifty-one African American writers filed by Hoover's FBI was indeed tested through literary evidence. In the case of Naylor's novelized memoir, paranoia thus makes for bad neighbors and, despite itself, for penetrating literary history.

The ghostreaders returned to life in *1996* prompt a final speculation on the FBI readership that shaped the production of Afro-modernism, a readership whose undigested legacy continues to touch African American writing today. Terence Whalen sensibly observes that "writers necessarily have some notion of audience which, above and beyond post-publication feedback, guides them in the production of texts" (10). The large and impressive company of Afro-modernists reviewed by the FBI were shadowed by what Whalen calls the "Capital Reader," the personification of the logic of literature as commodity who "pre-reads" any text produced for a capitalist marketplace (10). As much discussion of African American writing appreciates, these modernists were also preread by a racially divided general audience which carved out distinct interpretive paths before the first page was printed. Writers from Claude McKay to Gloria Naylor commonly supposed, I conclude, that the next most powerful prereader of African American letters was the "Capitol Reader," accent on the "o," the ghostly school of Hoover embedded in the Washington headquarters of the U.S. national-security state. In the case of McKay's and Naylor's poems and novels—and those of many in between, convinced of the FBI's hot and literate pursuit—the Capitol Reader inspired decisive prerevisions, not all regrettable, even when the tune wandered far from "The FB Eye Blues."

Appendix

FOIA Requests for FBI Files on African American Authors Active from 1919 to 1972

Author	FOIA Request Officially Received by FBI or Fulfilled by Another Party	Results	Number of Pages in File/Dates of File, If Any
1. Attaway, William	Nov. 20, 2006	paper sent, Mar. 16, 2007	pages: 30/dates: 1945–50 (not correct "Wild Bill" Attaway, however)
2. Baldwin, James	June 9, 2003	CD-rom sent, June 11; now also available via FBI website	pages: 1,884/dates: 1958–74
3. Bambara, Toni Cade	Sept. 25, 2006	no records, Oct. 5	
4. Baraka, Amiri (LeRoi Jones)	Jan. 30, 2014	incomplete file self-deposited in Baraka papers at Moorland-Spingarn Collection, Howard University; full file requested after Baraka's death in Jan. 2014	pages: approx. 700–800/dates: 1957–71 (incomplete file)
5. Beck, Robert (Iceberg Slim)	May 7, 2007	searching files notice, Aug. 2; accessioned to National Archives notice and records destroyed notice, Oct. 24; specific case files—concerning "white slave traffic"—not among NARA holdings, Feb. 27, 2008 (interagency miscommunication)	file acknowledged but destroyed and/or missing
6. Bennett, Gwendolyn	Nov. 20, 2006	paper sent, May 4, 2007	pages: 107 released (115 reviewed)/dates: 1941–59
7. Bonner, Marita	Nov. 20, 2006	no records, Nov. 30	
8. Bontemps, Arna	Sept. 25, 2006	no records, Dec. 14	
9. Braithwaite, William S.	May 7, 2007	no records, June 25	
10. Brawley, Benjamin	May 7, 2007	no records, June 25	
11. Brooks, Gwendolyn	Apr. 10, 2007	no records, Apr. 16; appealed May 8; appeal received and in backlog, May 30; appeal denied, Sept. 3	

Author	FOIA Request Officially Received by FBI or Fulfilled by Another Party	Results	Number of Pages in File/Dates of File, If Any
12. Brown, Frank London	Apr. 10, 2007	under analyst review, July 12; still under analyst review, Oct. 12; still under analyst review, Jan. 14, '08; still under analyst review, Apr. 15; paper sent July 28	pages: 90 released (111 reviewed)/ dates: 1955–57
13. Brown, Lloyd	paper sent by Mary Helen Washington, 2006		pages: 382/dates: 1940–70
14. Brown, Sterling	Sept. 25, 2006	paper sent, Jan. 15, 2007	pages: 104 released (105 reviewed)/ dates: 1941–53
15. Butler, Octavia	Apr. 4, 2012	no records, Apr. 20	
16. Cayton, Horace	Feb. 27, 2008	no records (same date)	
17. Childress, Alice	paper sent by Mary Helen Washington, 2006		pages: 27/dates: 1951–57
18. Clifton, Lucille	Apr. 2, 2012	paper sent, July 19	pages: 55/dates: 1958–59
19. Cruse, Harold	Apr. 17, 2008	paper sent (same date)	pages: 76/dates: 1950–69
20. Cullen, Countee	Oct. 4, 2006	no records, Oct. 19	
21. Cuney, William Waring	Feb. 8, 2007	no records, Feb. 21	
22. Davis, Frank Marshall	Nov. 20, 2006	paper sent, May 25, 2007	pages: 601 released (698 reviewed)/ dates: 1944–63
23. Dodson, Owen	Mar. 23, 2007	no records, Apr. 5	
24. Drake, St. Clair	Feb. 19, 2008	paper sent, Dec. 11	pages: 324 released (335 reviewed), plus 4-page supp. from U.S. Office of Personnel Management, sent Jan. 2009; plus 3-page supp. from U.S. State Dept.; plus further 1-page supp. from U.S. Office of Personnel Management, sent May 1, 2009/dates: 1961–71

Author	FOIA Request Officially Received by FBI or Fulfilled by Another Party	Results	Number of Pages in File/Dates of File, If Any
25. Du Bois, Shirley Graham	Feb. 8, 2007	records found and being duplicated, Apr. 17; paper sent, May 16	pages: 1,068/dates: 1950–75
26. Du Bois, W.E.B.	paper sent by Claire Culleton, 2006; now also available via FBI website		pages: 756/dates: 1942–63
27. Dumas, Henry	Apr. 10, 2007	no records, Apr. 16	
28. Dunham, Katherine	Feb. 4, 2008	paper sent (same date)	pages: 229/dates: 1944–68
29. Durem, Ray [Ramón]	Apr. 3, 2012	CD-rom sent by NARA, Sept. 28	pages: 312/dates: 1940–67
30. Elder, Lonne, III	Apr. 10, 2007	under analyst review, July 10; paper sent, Aug. 27	pages: 9/dates: 1954
31. Ellison, Ralph	May 22, 2003	paper sent, 2005	pages: 8 (plus 43 further pages sent by Barbara Foley, 2008)/dates: 1950–64
32. Fauset, Jessie	Nov. 21, 2006	no records (same date)	
33. Fisher, Rudolph	Oct. 4, 2006	no records, Oct. 19	
34. Forrest, Leon	Dec. 15, 2008	no records, Dec. 18	
35. Frazier, E. Franklin	Nov. 7, 2007	paper sent, Dec. 18	pages: 388/dates: 1953–61
36. Fuller, Hoyt	Sept. 25, 2006	no records, Oct. 27; appealed, Dec. 2; appeal granted, May 23, 2007; request noted by FBI, Oct. 24; under analyst review, Jan. 22, 2008; paper sent Mar. 18, 2008	pages: 157/dates: 1954–74
37. Gayle, Addison, Jr.	Oct. 4, 2006	no records, Oct. 19; appealed, Dec. 2; appeal granted, Apr. 2, 2007; resumed search noted, Apr. 23; in backlog, May 10; likely accession to National Archives reported, July 17; received at NARA notice, Aug. 9; NARA finds no Gayle-specific materials, Sept. 10	probable file acknowledged but missing

Author	FOIA Request Officially Received by FBI or Fulfilled by Another Party	Results	Number of Pages in File/Dates of File, If Any
38. Goines, Donald	Feb. 11, 2008	no records (same date)	
39. Grimke, Angelina Weld	Oct. 4, 2006	no records, Oct. 19	
40. Grimke, Archibald	Nov. 21, 2007	no records, Dec. 3	
41. Haley, Alex	Apr. 10, 2007	no records, Apr. 16; appealed, May 8; appeal received and in backlog, May 30; appeal denied, Sept. 3	
42. Hansberry, Lorraine	paper sent by Kathlene McDonald, 2006		pages: 1,020/dates: 1952–65
43. Harrington, Ollie	paper sent by Brian Dolinar, 2006		pages: 167 released (205 reviewed)/ dates: 1951–2002
44. Hayden, Robert	Sept. 25, 2006	no records, Dec. 27	
45. Hemphill, Essex	Apr. 2, 2012	no records, Apr. 24	
46. Henderson, George Wylie	May 7, 2007	no records, May 31	
47. Hernton, Calvin	Feb. 6, 2007	in backlog, May 9; under analyst review, Aug. 10; paper sent, Nov. 5	pages: 41/dates: 1955–69
48. Himes, Chester	paper sent by Brian Dolinar, 2006		pages: 95/dates: 1944–64
49. Hughes, Langston	June 9, 2003	CD-rom sent, June 11; paper sent by Brian Dolinar, 2004	pages: 553/dates: 1925–70
50. Hurston, Zora Neale	Sept. 25, 2006	no records, Nov. 6	
51. Jackman, Harold	Mar. 23, 2007	no records, Mar. 28	
52. Jeffers, Lance	Feb. 15, 2008	in "perfected backlog," May 15; under analyst review, Sept. 8; paper sent, Oct. 28	pages: 187/dates: 1949–66
53. Joans, Ted	Apr. 10, 2007	no records, Apr. 16	
54. Johnson, Charles S.	Mar. 23, 2007	in "perfected backlog," June 21; under analyst review, Oct. 1; paper sent, Nov. 21	pages: 348 released (442 reviewed)/ dates: 1952–56; plus one additional document sent by State Dept., Feb. 21, 2008

Author	FOIA Request Officially Received by FBI or Fulfilled by Another Party	Results	Number of Pages in File/Dates of File, If Any
55. Johnson, Fenton	Apr. 10, 2007	no records, Apr. 16	
56. Johnson, Georgia Douglas	Nov. 21, 2006	paper sent, Feb. 21, 2007	pages: 6/dates: 1945
57. Johnson, Helene	Apr. 10, 2007	no records, Apr. 30	
58. Johnson, James Weldon	Sept. 25, 2006	no records, Oct. 4	
59. Jordan, June	Apr. 10, 2007	no records, May 21	
60. Kaufman, Bob	Nov. 20, 2006	paper sent, Apr. 13, 2007	pages: 42 released (47 reviewed)/dates: 1950–70
61. Killens, John O.	Feb. 6, 2007	paper sent, Apr. 26	pages: 194/dates: 1941–73
62. Knight, Etheridge	Sept. 25, 2006	no records, Oct. 4	
63. Larsen, Nella	Nov. 21, 2006	no records, Nov. 29	
64. Lewis, Theophilus	Apr. 10, 2007	no records, Apr. 16	
65. Locke, Alain	Oct. 4, 2006	records destroyed notice, Oct. 19; appealed, Nov. 15; transferred to National Archives (NARA) notice, Feb. 20, 2007; received at NARA notice, Mar. 15; NARA can't find records because of FBI's retention of "central name index," Feb. 27, 2008	file acknowledged but destroyed or missing
66. Lorde, Audre	Sept. 25, 2006	no records, Oct. 4	
67. Mayfield, Julian	Feb. 6, 2007	records found, Apr. 25; in backlog, May 9; under analyst review, Aug. 10; still under analyst review, Nov. 9; paper sent, Sept. 5, 2008	pages: 412 released (445 reviewed), plus 2-page supp. from State Dept., sent Oct. 2008/ dates: 1954–74; plus denial of associated CIA records, sent June 26, 2009
68. McKay, Claude	May 27, 1997	paper sent 1998; now also available via FBI website	pages: 193/dates: 1921–40
69. Micheaux, Oscar	Feb. 12, 2008	no records (same date)	

Author	FOIA Request Officially Received by FBI or Fulfilled by Another Party	Results	Number of Pages in File/Dates of File, If Any
70. Motley, Willard	Apr. 10, 2007	paper sent (same date)	pages: 144/dates: 1951–67
71. Murray, Pauli	May 17, 2007	paper sent (same date)	pages: 288/dates: 1966–67
72. Neal, Larry P.	Sept. 25, 2006	paper sent, Jan. 22, 2007	pages: 129 released (138 reviewed), plus 1-page supp. from National Security Div., Dept. of Justice, sent Aug. 29, 2007/dates: 1966–72
73. Nugent, Richard Bruce	Nov. 20, 2006	no records, Nov. 27	
74. Offord, Carl Ruthven	Feb. 6, 2007	no records, Feb. 21	
75. Ottley, Roi	Apr. 10, 2007	no records (same date)	
76. Parks, Gordon	Apr. 10, 2007	no records (same date)	
77. Patterson, Louise Thompson	Oct. 10, 2006	paper sent, Nov. 28	pages: 921/dates: 1941–74
78. Petry, Ann	Sept. 22, 2006	no records, Sept. 22	
79. Pickens, William	Feb. 15, 2008	paper sent, July 7	pages: 247/dates: 1947–64
80. Poston, Ted	Feb. 11, 2008	no records (same date)	
81. Randall, Dudley	Feb. 6, 2007	in backlog, May 9; under analyst review, Aug. 28; still under analyst review, Feb. 4, 2008; paper sent, Mar. 14, 2008	pages: 46/dates: 1966–69
82. Razaf, Andy	May 27, 1997	paper sent, 1998	pages: 3/dates: 1949
83. Redding, J. Saunders	May 7, 2007	searching files notice August 2; under analyst review, Nov. 1; still under analyst review, Feb. 11, 2008; paper sent, Apr. 2008	pages: 105 released (136 reviewed), plus 1959 Civil Service Commission supp., sent Oct 2008/dates: 1953–68
84. Richardson, Willis	May 7, 2007	no records, May 31	

Author	FOIA Request Officially Received by FBI or Fulfilled by Another Party	Results	Number of Pages in File/Dates of File, If Any
85. Rodgers, Carolyn M.	Apr. 3, 2012	"potentially responsive" records "not in their expected location and could not be located after a reasonable search for these records"; after a second unsuccessful search, request is closed "administratively," July 31.	probable file acknowledged but missing
86. Rogers, J. A.	Mar. 23, 2007	paper sent (same date)	pages: 12/dates: 1942–67
87. Schomburg, Arthur A.	Mar. 23, 2007	no records, Mar. 28	
88. Schuyler, George S.	Sept. 22, 2006	paper sent, Dec. 6; Defense Dept. review reported, Dec. 18; CIA review reported, with material classified and withheld, May 25, 2007	pages: 169 released (181 reviewed), plus 7 from Defense Dept.)/dates: 1942–67
89. Smith, William Gardner	Oct. 11, 2006	in backlog, May 9, 2007; under analyst review, Aug. 10; still under analyst review, Nov. 5; paper sent, Feb. 21, 2008	pages: 169 released (224 reviewed), plus 1 telegram reviewed and cleared by State Dept., and 1-page supp. of confidential source document declassified in 2009, sent Oct. 29, 2009/ dates: 1951–74
90. Spencer, Anne	Nov. 21, 2006	no records, Nov. 29	
91. Thomas, Lorenzo	Sept. 22, 2006	no records, Oct. 4	
92. Thurman, Wallace	Oct. 4, 2006	no records, Oct. 19	
93. Tolson, Melvin B.	Nov. 20, 2006	no records, Nov. 27	
94. Toomer, Jean	Nov. 22, 2006	no records, Nov. 29	
95. Turpin, Waters Edward	Apr. 10, 2007	no records, Apr. 16	
96. Walker, Margaret	Sept. 22, 2006	records destroyed notice, Nov. 14; appealed, Dec. 2; appeal granted re. Miami Field Office only, Feb. 15, 2007; Miami request noted, Mar. 20; Miami confirms records destroyed, May 16	file acknowledged but destroyed

Author	FOIA Request Officially Received by FBI or Fulfilled by Another Party	Results	Number of Pages in File/Dates of File, If Any
97. Walrond, Eric	Nov. 21, 2006	no records, Nov. 29	
98. Ward, Theodore	Mar. 26, 2007	searching for/ evaluating "files that may be responsive to [my] request," June 21; under analyst review, Sept. 25; still under analyst review, Mar. 25, 2008; still under analyst review, June 25; paper sent, Oct. 24	pages: 289/dates: 1944–66
99. Wells-Barnett, Ida B.	Feb. 12, 2008	no records (same date)	
100. West, Dorothy	Sept. 22, 2006	no records, Sept. 29	
101. White, Walter	Apr. 5, 2007	searching for/ evaluating "files that may be responsive to [my] request," July 9; paper sent, Aug. 9	pages: 83/dates: 1943–57
102. Williams, Sherley Anne	Dec. 15, 2008	records destroyed notice, Feb. 13, 2009; appealed Feb. 19; appeal noted, Mar. 11; appeal denied, Mar. 30	file acknowledged but destroyed
103. Wilson, August	May 7, 2007	no records, May 31	
104. Woodson, Carter	Feb. 12, 2008	no records (same date)	
105. Wright, Richard	paper sent by Claire Culleton, 2004; now also available via FBI website		pages: 244/dates: 1942–63
106. Yerby, Frank	Feb. 6, 2007	no records, Feb. 21	

Notes

Introduction

1. My account of the origin and reception of Sullivan's infamous letter to King is drawn from Richard Gid Powers's *Broken: The Troubled Past and Uncertain Future of the FBI* (2004), the institutional history that John J. Fox Jr., the Bureau's resident historian, recommended to me as the best of its kind; see in particular pages 245–47. In 2013, the garbled references to Sullivan's dirty trick in an episode of *Drunk History*, the Comedy Central television series, suggested that his letter had become a bitter chestnut of U.S. national memory.

2. Rhodri Jeffreys-Jones, the leading British expert on American intelligence, identifies race as a dominant theme in FBI history in his post-9/11 synthesis *The FBI: A History* (2007). His confidence about the significance of the Bureau's antiblack racism, "deeper than that of the nation at large" (1), is bolstered by a wave of FOIA-assisted studies that first rose in the 1980s. At the crest of this wave is Kenneth O'Reilly's influential *"Racial Matters": The FBI's Secret File on Black America, 1960–1972* (1989) and his documentary collection *Black Americans: The FBI Files* (1994), assembled with editorial help from David Gallen. Among an ever-growing array of print and electronic sources on relevant individual cases is volume 2 of Robert A. Hill's edition of *The Marcus Garvey and Universal Negro Improvement Association Papers* (1983); Clayborne Carson's *Malcolm X: The FBI File* (1991), also edited by David Gallen; Michael Friedly's *Martin Luther King, Jr.: The FBI File* (1993), yet another Gallen-assisted compilation; and David Garrow's measured account in *The FBI and Martin Luther King, Jr.: From "Solo" to Memphis* (1981). The publication of Dale Anderson's photo-packed, large-type history for young readers, *The FBI and Civil Rights* (2010), testifies to the strength of the historiographical shift.

3. The long history of FBI stalking of African American protest in fact outlived King's assassination, with lethal results in the case of the Black Panther Party. To believe John Potash, the author of *The FBI War on Tupac Shakur and Black Leaders* (2007), a radical press publication blurbed by Kathleen Cleaver and Mumia Abu-Jamal, the stalking continued into the 1990s. Contrary to Potash, however, the West Coast rapper Tupac does not qualify as a black leader on par with the Bureau-harassed King and Malcolm X, and the claim that black musicians Bob Marley, Jimi Hendrix, and Jam Master Jay also suffered political murders is disqualifying. Potash's case for the survival of deadly FBI counterintelligence programs nonetheless makes eerie hay from the Bureau's documented targeting of several Black Panthers in Tupac's immediate family.

4. Some in Sullivan's initial audience may have taken this reading a step further, and come to suspect that his letter had predicted Martin Luther King's assassination. Ralph Abernathy was not the only SCLC insider to wonder, three-and-a-half years later in Memphis, if a gunman acting under Hoover's influence had martyred "the king God didn't save" (John A. Williams, *The King* 5). In 1979, a congressional inquiry credibly

disproved rumors of the FBI's involvement in King's murder. Word of Sullivan's lead role in the Bureau's hunt for assassin James Earl Ray, however, could not have reassured skeptics close to the original scene. Sullivan provocatively discusses his role in the Ray investigation in the posthumous memoir *The Bureau: My Thirty Years in Hoover's FBI* (1979), a remarkably frank yet puzzling text explored in part 3. After securing Ray's arrest thanks to heavy lifting by the Royal Canadian Mounted Police, Sullivan concluded that the Bureau had gotten only one of its men: "I was convinced that James Earl Ray killed Martin Luther King, but I doubt if he acted alone. Ray was so stupid that I don't think he could have robbed a five- and ten-cent store" (145). Sullivan thus denies one theory of a second gunman—he explicitly attacks the idea that "the FBI itself had a hand in King's murder" (145)—and feeds another.

5. Since the turn of the millennium, signs of the Bureau's interest and influence have been found all over twentieth-century U.S. media culture. On the common presence of pop artist Andy Warhol and rhythm and blues "race musicians" in a spacious FBI "Obscene File," see Douglas M. Charles's *The FBI's Obscene File: J. Edgar Hoover and the Bureau's Crusade against Smut* (2012). On Ronald Reagan's alliance with the FBI as a Hollywood actor as well as a Berkeley-bashing California governor, see Seth Rosenfeld's controversial best seller *Subversives: The FBI's War on Student Radicals, and Reagan's Rise to Power* (2012). On Reagan's part in Hollywood's once-powerful "countersubversive network," see John Sbardellati's more academic *J. Edgar Hoover Goes to the Movies: The FBI and the Origins of Hollywood's Cold War* (2012). On the slow legal extraction of Hoover's Beatle-related correspondence and the rest of John Lennon's FBI files, the records of "a kind of rock 'n' roll Watergate" (9), see Jon Wiener's *Gimme Some Truth: The John Lennon FBI Files* (1999).

6. Regarding "some black writers," Natalie Robins's *Alien Ink: The FBI's War on Freedom of Expression* (1992) employs Amiri Baraka as a talkative "formal witness" and rewardingly delves into the files of James Baldwin, Langston Hughes, and Richard Wright as well. These four famous names represent no more than 2.7 percent of the total Robins considers, however. Herbert Mitgang's *Dangerous Dossiers: Exposing the Secret War against America's Greatest Authors* (1988) profiles no African American authors at all but does quote Allen Ginsberg's pointed observation on the cross-referencing of his Bureau file and Amiri Baraka's: "Most people don't realize what he and other black literati have been through, assuming that all past injustices have been redressed or somehow disappeared out of mind" (Mitgang 204).

7. Two important books published just before this book went to press suggest that the ironic "conspiracy" or understanding between modern literature and state surveillance may be an international—even definitional—one. Eva Horn's *The Secret War: Treason, Espionage, and Modern Fiction* (2013), translated from a German original first published in 2007, employs evidence from Rudyard Kipling to Steven Spielberg to argue that fiction "is the most lucid way of shedding light onto the structure of the modern political secret" (25). Defining the modern so as to include the European Renaissance, David Rosen and Aaron Santesso's *The Watchman in Pieces: Surveillance, Literature, and Liberal Personhood* (2013) investigates "how the theory and practice of surveillance have developed in close coordination with literary culture over the past three and a half centuries; if surveillance is, on some level, all about reading and authorship, so literature has been deeply engaged with, and transformed by, changing ideas about observation and control" (13).

8. The introduction to my edition of Claude McKay's *Complete Poems* (2004) includes a more nuanced account of the Bureau's pursuit of the poet around the Black Atlantic

and the Black Sea. Analysis of the whole of McKay's trailblazing FBI file can be found in my 2003 essay "F.B. Eyes: The Bureau Reads Claude McKay," a first crack at the mystery of FBI ghostreading.

9. Less systematically, I also set out to learn how many major African American theaters, literary journals, literary workshops, and related institutions had FBI files of their own. The results of my FOIA requests showed files for the Black Arts Repertory Theatre/ School, *Ebony*, *Negro Digest* (later *Black World*), and the *Black Scholar* (its file shows that the Bureau took out no fewer than four subscriptions). I quote from and otherwise employ these institutional files at various points in *F.B. Eyes* and plan to make copies available to all comers at this book's website, to be found at http://digital.wustl.edu/fbeyes. The list of those literary institutions without dedicated FBI files (according to the FBI, that is) is longer and represents a far higher "miss rate" than in the case of my requests for files on individual authors. No files were found for the American Negro Theater, the Broadside Press, the *CLA Journal*, the Harlem Writers Guild, the *Journal of Negro History*, the National Negro Theater, *Negro American Literature Forum* (later *Black American Literature Forum* and *African American Review*), the Negro Ensemble Company, the South Side Writers Group, and the Third World Press. In the arena of Afro-modernism, the FBI thus seems to have kept its eye peeled for isolable threats.

10. The scholars who saved me time and postage by sharing their own FOIA-accessed FBI files are acknowledged individually at appropriate moments throughout *F.B. Eyes*. They also deserve collective recognition here. I thank you (and J. Edgar Hoover thanks you), Claire Culleton, Brian Dolinar, Barbara Foley, Kathlene McDonald, and Mary Helen Washington.

11. For a more rounded picture of this file-stalking of white American writers, see in particular Herbert Mitgang's *Dangerous Dossiers* (1988), Natalie Robins's *Alien Ink* (1992), and Claire A. Culleton's *Joyce and the G-Men: J. Edgar Hoover's Manipulation of Modernism* (2004).

12. Lively examples and semischolarly variants of the FBI-scholar-as-detective narrative can be found in James Campbell's *Syncopations: Beats, New Yorkers, and Writers in the Dark* (2008), Claire A. Culleton's *Joyce and the G-Men* (2004), Seth Rosenfeld's *Subversives: The FBI's War on Student Radicals, and Reagan's Rise to Power* (2012), Athan G. Theoharis's "The Freedom of Information Act versus the FBI" (1998), and Jon Wiener's *Gimme Some Truth* (1999). Not coincidentally, all of these texts also publicize genuine revelations from FBI documents—often the fruit of hard-fought lawsuits against FOIA roadblocks.

13. According to FBI correspondence, the African American authors whose files I was the first to request are the following: Gwendolyn Bennett, Frank London Brown, Sterling Brown, Lucille Clifton, Harold Cruse, Frank Marshall Davis, St. Clair Drake, Ray Durem, Lonne Elder III, Hoyt Fuller, Calvin Hernton, Lance Jeffers, Charles S. Johnson, Georgia Douglas Johnson, Bob Kaufman, Julian Mayfield, Larry Neal, Dudley Randall, Andy Razaf, J. Saunders Redding, George S. Schuyler, William Gardner Smith, Theodore Ward, and Walter White.

14. My thanks to essayist and novelist Caleb Crain, who helped disentangle the FBI "Records Retention" process by tapping his contacts at both the National Archives and the National Security Archive.

15. For a cogent introduction to national security excisions and other common trials faced by FOIA researchers working with the FBI archive, see Athan G. Theoharis's "The Freedom of Information Act versus the FBI" (1998). While my own experience was

reassuring, other FOIA users have been less impressed with the promised openness of federal agencies under the Obama administration. John Hudson's 2012 story "Obama Administration Distorted Its Transparency Record: Ex-DOJ Official" tells why.

16. Relatedly, Vatulescu responds to Walter Benjamin's famous warning about the aestheticization of politics by observing that Soviet-era secret police files "had been 'aestheticized' long before [she] got to see them. When tracing previous readings of the files," Vatulescu "was struck by a widespread tendency to describe police records in literary terms" (16). In certain respects closer to home is Peter D. McDonald's conclusion that many of the files produced by South African censors under the apartheid regime "read more like exercises in literary criticism than legalistic judgments" (17).

17. In his most influential work of the late 1970s, Michel Foucault parried the "repressive model" of power associated with the vision of an absolutely powerful state. Two centuries after the French Revolution, historians had still "not cut off the head of the king," this Foucault complained (*The History of Sexuality* 188). In *The Covert Sphere: Secrecy, Fiction, and the National Security State* (2012), literary critic Timothy Melley similarly cites Foucault and rebuts the post-Foucauldian assumption that reexamining state security means resuscitating the king or sovereign and the repressive model built around him. "My argument is not that power is *primarily* 'repressive,'" he specifies, "but that state secrecy is a crucial part of a larger ideological system for managing the contradictions of U.S. empire" (13; emphasis in original).

18. Here sandwiched between two accepted period terms—the Harlem Renaissance and the Black Arts movement—is the "Indignant Generation," Lawrence P. Jackson's candidate to typify African American literature in the relatively neglected era from the 1930s to the 1960s; for the implications of his term, see his comprehensive and impeccably researched book *The Indignant Generation: A Narrative History of African American Writers and Critics, 1934–1960* (2011). Like me, Jackson accents a number of rhymes between Harlem Renaissance and midcentury black literatures, suggesting that indignant writers and critics punctured New Negro presumptions by reinventing renaissance habits for midcentury, arming these habits to survive the Great Depression, New Deal and newer liberalisms, and the growth of grittier black cultural capitals. In distinction to Jackson, however, I emphasize the connection-making endurance of FBI ghostreading, an ironic vehicle of intergenerational bonding among African American writers in the years between the Harlem Renaissance and the self-conscious revival of black renaissancism in the 1960s—years I imagine as collectively "Afro-modernist."

19. The notion of counterliterature also crystallizes a revealing difference between Hoover's ghostreaders and the Progressive criminologists studied by Khalil Gibran Muhammad, a leading historian of the origins of the present-day U.S. "prison-industrial complex" and the notion of inherent black criminality that feeds it. Like Muhammad's early twentieth-century police reformers, the early Bureau adopted the Progressive mantle of unbiased, scientific law enforcement while still effectively incriminating black culture. Parting from Muhammad's more faithful Progressives, however, the Hooverites would not remain true believers in "black inferiority or black pathology despite a shift in the social scientific discourse on the origins of race and crime" (Muhammad 9). They instead challenged themselves to incriminate black culture with black literature's involuntary assistance—simulating the hip urbanism and even the enjambed lines of Black Arts poetry, for instance, in misinformation meant to implicate Black Power. For Bureau ghostreaders of the 1920s and after, black culture in written practice was less irreversibly

pathological than treacherously logical, and therefore a set of texts and cues suitable for creative incorporation. Inside Bureau history, then, is a practice of internalizing black writing that provides a distinctive lens on the criminological prehistory of today's crisis of black incarceration, the "New Jim Crow" denounced by Michelle Alexander. Black culture could be forcefully criminalized, the view through this lens suggests, without being cast as an untouchably morbid world apart.

20. For a speculative primer on the current groundswell of academic "surface reading," including its tendency to segregate enthusiastic/popular and suspicious/professorial modes of interpretation, see Stephen Best and Sharon Marcus's "Surface Reading: An Introduction" (2009).

21. Brent Hayes Edwards's elegant study *The Practice of Diaspora: Literature, Translation, and the Rise of Black Internationalism* (2003), the most influential work of black transnational scholarship since Paul Gilroy's *The Black Atlantic*, highlights both the problem and the opportunity of mistranslation through its core concept of "*décalage*," a customized French word for "what resists or escapes translation" but ultimately permits progress across the African diaspora (15).

22. "BaddDDD," that is, meaning dangerously good, as in Sonia Sanchez's *We a BaddDDD People* (1970), a Black Arts collection written by a poet who knew there were FBI ghostreaders at the door.

Part One/Thesis One
The Birth of the Bureau, Coupled with the Birth of J. Edgar Hoover, Ensured the FBI's Attention to African American Literature

1. Recent Hollywood portraits of Hoover blur this split picture of youth and age. In Michael Mann's stylized cops-and-gangsters film *Public Enemies* (2009), actor Billy Crudup presents a hidebound but still vigorous FBI director, conquering Depression challenges at a midpoint between Jazz Age slickness and Cold War stolidity. Leonardo DiCaprio's impersonation in Clint Eastwood's *J. Edgar* (2011) slips dizzyingly between a twenty-four-year-old and seventy-year-old Hoover, with latex prosthetics the consistent co-star.

2. My account of *Birth of a Nation*'s kid-gloves treatment of the "Bureau of Military Justice" is indebted to Rhodri Jeffreys-Jones's *The FBI: A History* (2007), a deft, abundantly researched, and groundbreakingly sensible academic history of the FBI in the context of American race relations. I have learned much from Jeffreys-Jones in this connection and others, yet his organizing story line nevertheless seems based on a wish-fulfilling logical fallacy. To support the proposition that the Bureau "lost its character" after holding high the flame of racial liberty (16), he relabels the actions of distinctly unrelated units of federal law enforcement as early actions of the FBI. Jeffreys-Jones's Bureau thus falls from a grace borrowed from the U.S. Marshals and Secret Service. Tim Weiner's *Enemies: A History of the FBI* (2012), another brilliantly researched history of the Bureau, begins more conventionally with J. Edgar Hoover's first day of work at the Justice Department, followed by a flashback to President Teddy Roosevelt's 1908 call for federal "investigative personnel" (10). Weiner's purifying focus on the FBI "as a secret intelligence service" (xv), rather than as a hybrid intelligence service/national police force, leads to a problem of scale opposed to Jeffreys-Jones's exaggerated prehistory.

Racial matters enter Weiner's narrative in earnest only with the COINTELPRO counter-intelligence actions of the 1950s, and thus too long after the Bureau's conception.

3. Michael Newton's unforgiving *The FBI and the KKK: A Critical History* (2005) convincingly bats down happy-talk about Hoover's role in the 1922 Morehouse Parish case against seventeen Louisiana Klan komrades. A scene drawn from the case in the Hollywood film *The FBI Story* (1959), Newton notes, is perfectly right to show Klansmen stunned by the heroic antiracism of their G-Men pursuers—the Klansmen appear to know that "no such [thing] ever happened" in fact (25). Even Newton acknowledges Hoover's personal distance from the white terrorist group, however, emphasizing claims of organizational parallelism and cooperation that extend beyond Hoover's service. Both the Bureau and the Klan, Newton contends, "have traditionally championed right-wing causes that include persistent strains of xenophobia, racial and religious bigotry, sexism, homophobia, and vigilante 'justice.' While theoretically at odds since 1922, the two organizations have secretly collaborated in pursuit of common goals and enemies" (1).

4. The status of Hoover and Tolson's longtime bond as a "spousal relationship" is established in Richard Gid Powers's unequaled biography *Secrecy and Power: The Life of J. Edgar Hoover* (1987) and assumed in Clint Eastwood's biographical movie *J. Edgar* (2011). Though cast as an institutional skeleton in the closet in Ronald Kessler's book *The Secrets of the FBI* (2011), this relationship was the most open of secrets in official Washington, D.C., which granted Tolson the widow's seat at Hoover's state funeral. Debates within the queer public sphere over the value of the partnership as a prototype of gay marriage are introduced in Hank Hyena's column "J. Edgar Hoover: Gay Marriage Role Model?" (2000). In *J. Edgar Hoover, Sex, and Crime: An Historical Antidote* (1995), a book-length rebuttal of Anthony Summers's sensational biography *Official and Confidential: The Secret Life of J. Edgar Hoover* (1993), prolific FBI historian Athan Theoharis, no friend of the Hoover effect on American democracy, persuasively disproves Summers's hearsay on Hoover's transvestism, supposedly a target of Mafia blackmail. Gay studies scholar David K. Johnson concurs with Theoharis, viewing Summers's portrayal of Hoover's sexuality as itself something of an anticommunist cliché. In *The Lavender Scare: The Cold War Prosecution of Gays and Lesbians in the Federal Government* (2004), Johnson insists that the tale of Hoover's eroticized cross-dressing "is more a reflection of Cold War political culture than an examination of it. It utilizes the kind of tactics Hoover and the security program he oversaw perfected—guilt by association, rumor, and unverified gossip" (11). Less convincing is the thick-witted attack on Summers in *Hoover's FBI: The Inside Story by Hoover's Trusted Lieutenant* (1995), the memoir of Cartha "Deke" DeLoach, Hoover's third-in-command from 1965 to 1970: "Contrary to what Summers would have you believe, neither Hoover nor Tolson was the least bit effeminate. Both were tough and manly. Hoover was a bull dog. Tolson was a strapping, healthy fellow in his youth. He played first base on the FBI's champion baseball team, and there wasn't the slightest sign of weakness or 'prettiness' in his face. He was certainly more of a man than Mr. Summers, and I've seen both at close quarters" (63). Presenting an insightful, agenda-broadening response to both Summers and Theoharis, Claire Bond Potter's "Queer Hoover: Sex, Lies, and Political History" (2006) contends that the facts of Hoover's sexuality are less revealing than the cultural narratives and "political structure that sheltered and used" them (359–60). Whatever its truth-value, gossip about Hoover's preferences in love and fashion provides "crucial historical evidence

about the tension between public political culture and private citizenship," opening the way to "a queer method for integrating the histories of state, sex, and citizen" (360, 361).

5. As folklorist Patricia A. Turner details in *I Heard It through the Grapevine: Rumor in African-American Culture* (1993), tales of the FBI's involvement in the assassination of Martin Luther King Jr. have been prevalent and persistent among African Americans. Dozens of her black informants, interviewed in the early 1990s, attributed King's death to a Hoover-thickened plot—almost as many as those who blamed the Ku Klux Klan. Given the Bureau's documented attempt to drive King to suicide, Turner argues, rumors of FBI malevolence are entirely reasonable to blacks "from a variety of occupational and social backgrounds," chiming with revisionist historical scholarship and, more crucially, with the "black history to which [black citizens] have been privy" (120). Quoting Tamotsu Shibutani, Turner concludes that vernacular narratives of deadly FBI hostility to King are not "pathological," but instead traces of "the efforts of men to come to terms with the exigencies of life" (120). From this perspective, Big Daddy's elaborate variation on the assassination rumor comes to terms with the exigencies of suppressed interracialism by recreating King as an agent of aggressive counterintelligence.

6. On the comparatively humble function of intelligence services as intragovernmental newspapers—"global news service[s], delivering daily bulletins"—see Tim Weiner's discussion of President Harry Truman's plans for the CIA (*Legacy* 3). On the coalition of print capitalism, the public sphere, and national identity in the uniting of the United States, see Michael Warner's seminal *The Letters of the Republic: Publication and the Public Sphere in Eighteenth-Century America* (1990), and its later, disuniting challenges in Trish Loughran's *The Republic in Print: Print Culture in the Age of U.S. Nation Building, 1770–1870* (2007) and Leonard Tennenhouse's *The Importance of Feeling English: American Literature and the British Diaspora, 1750–1850* (2007).

7. Worthwhile studies tracing the FBI's heavy hand in (nonliterary) U.S. mass culture include Richard Gid Powers's landmark *G-Men: Hoover's FBI in American Popular Culture* (1983), condensed yet chronologically extended in his essay "The FBI in American Popular Culture" (2000); Claire Bond Potter's revision of both Powers and theories of the evolution of the American state in *War on Crime: Bandits, G-Men, and the Politics of Mass Culture* (1998); William Beverly's creative analysis (bordering on invention) of the genre of the fugitive in *On the Lam: Narratives of Flight in J. Edgar Hoover's America* (2003), its thoughts on the Hoover men and cartography addressed elsewhere in part 1; Michael Kackman's investigation of prime-time secret agents in *Citizen Spy: Television, Espionage, and Cold War Culture* (2005); Bob Herzberg's breezy, largely descriptive *The FBI and the Movies: A History of the Bureau on Screen and behind the Scenes in Hollywood* (2007); John Sbardellati's scholarly *J. Edgar Hoover Goes to the Movies* (2012), a rounded account of the "countersubversive tradition" and FBI operations against Hollywood prior to the 1950s; and Mary Elizabeth Strunk's *Wanted Women: An American Obsession in the Reign of J. Edgar Hoover* (2010), a kind of scholarly most-wanted list examining the presence of ten female outlaws in film, advertising, and popular literature as well as in Hoover's criminological imagination. Intriguing, sometimes eccentric, and more tightly focused are Douglas M. Charles's documentation of the popular film and music swallowed up in *The FBI's Obscene File: J. Edgar Hoover and the Bureau's Crusade against Smut* (2012); Daniel Leab's *I Was a Communist for the FBI: The Unhappy Life and Times of Matt Cvetic* (2000), the story of a psychologically wounded FBI informer whose undercover life inspired both a successful radio show and a well-reviewed

Warner Brothers film; Jon Wiener's *Gimme Some Truth: The John Lennon FBI Files* (1999), the record of a serious history professor's long struggle, culminating in a successful Supreme Court case, to unseal the Bureau's dossier on the ex-Beatle; and Tim Coates's self-published, self-explanatory edition of *Marilyn Monroe: The FBI Files* (2003). For an example of the Bureau's embrace of visual culture in the telling of its own history, see *The Story of the FBI: The Official Picture History of the Federal Bureau of Investigation* (1954), introduced by Hoover and attributed to the editors of *Look* magazine.

8. Better late than never. "I seriously doubt whether the communists were responsible for the placing of those bombs," Hoover eventually admitted to Congress in 1930 (United States, House, *Investigation* 32). "I have always viewed them as being more the work of individual anarchists" (32).

9. The Cold War eminence of this 1920 document is highlighted by *J. Edgar Hoover Speaks concerning Communism* (1970), a quotable tool for anticommunists compiled by James D. Bales. "Hoover's prophetic and chilling brief on the Communist Party delivered in 1920" is hailed on the dust jacket and enshrined in a chapter of its own.

10. The rivalry between FBI archivism and left-leaning librarianship persisted throughout the twentieth century and peaked in congressional hearings over the Bureau's "Library Awareness Program" of the 1980s. See Herbert N. Foerstel's *Surveillance in the Stacks* (1991) for a partisan history of the "heavily publicized confrontation between the FBI and the library profession" (ix). Foerstel writes with pride of the willingness of the "the nation's most 'wimpish' profession" to box with its "most awesome law-enforcement agency" (ix). By this late date, bad blood will probably not be cooled by knowledge of the G-Men's early debt to the librarians.

11. The main line of French theoretical revision runs from Michel Foucault to Jacques Derrida. In *The Archaeology of Knowledge* (1969), a philosophical introduction to his early, discursive method, Foucault redefines the archive as less a dusty storehouse than an engendering "first law of what can be said" (129). In the less systematic deconstructive workout of *Archive Fever* (1995), Derrida's reflections on e-mail traffic and Freud's final resting place flavor the observation that the archive "produces as much as it records the event" (17).

12. Richard Gid Powers uncharacteristically makes this misattribution error in *Secrecy and Power: The Life of J. Edgar Hoover* (1987), describing *Radicalism and Sedition* as "the first of [Hoover's] many 'exposes' of radical influence within the black community" (128). Notes and drafts of *Radicalism and Sedition* in Clemson's Robert Adger Bowen papers (more on this Hoover subordinate in part 3) establish his central contribution. See in particular box 10, folder 86, of the Bowen papers in the Special Collections Library, Clemson University Libraries, Clemson, South Carolina. David Levering Lewis's claim for Loving's involvement rests on softer interpretive ground: namely, similarities "in analytical power and scope of detail" between *Radicalism* and an earlier Loving report to the director of military intelligence (*W.E.B. Du Bois* 7). Loving also figures in Alfred W. McCoy's *Policing America's Empire: The United States, the Philippines, and the Rise of the Surveillance State* (2009), a weighty postcolonial history of the migration of counterinsurgency techniques from the occupied Philippines to the U.S. metropole. McCoy's case for the application of imperial racism to a suspect African American population suffers from his reliance on Loving, a military policeman in the Philippines who did indeed return to the United States to investigate "Negro subversion" for the Military Intelligence Division (MID) during World War I, but who then urged the court martial

of a bigoted white commander, advocated the commissioning of black officers, and led the MID to seek a "square deal for the negro [*sic*]" in and outside the army (McCoy 309). Despite his background in policing the Philippine resistance, Loving's activities in the United States do not neatly indicate that "African Americans were another source of the MID's ethnic anxieties" (308)—anxieties that motivated Hoover's Radical Division far more directly.

13. This stunned and nervous praise of the paper quality of New Negro magazines echoes that of Congressman James F. Byrnes of South Carolina, who in 1919 declared the *Messenger*'s stock too fine to be unfinanced by the IWW (Schmidt 184). In these outbursts, the history of racial paranoia crosses tragicomically with the history of print culture.

14. Bryan Burrough is one such shrewd FBI historian, and probably among the most financially comfortable. His popular history *Public Enemies: America's Greatest Crime Wave and the Birth of the FBI* (2005), indebted to Claire Bond Potter's academic study *War on Crime: Bandits, G-Men, and the Politics of Mass Culture* (1998), was transformed into a visually elegant Hollywood crime drama in 2009. Directed by Michael Mann and starring Johnny Depp, the cinematic *Public Enemies* dabbles in Burrough's theme of the FBI's maturation under fire when not ranking styles of masculine cool in digital close-up.

Part Two/Thesis Two
The FBI's Aggressive Filing and Long Study of African American Writers Was Tightly Bound to the Agency's Successful Evolution under Hoover

1. Accounts of the Bureau's "war on words"—a vivid phrase of poet-journalist Natalie Robins's that unintentionally snubs the Bureau's war *of* words—can be found in her indispensable book *Alien Ink: The FBI's War on Freedom of Expression* (1992), as well as in Herbert Mitgang's *Dangerous Dossiers* (1988); in Claire A. Culleton's *Joyce and the G-Men* (2004); and in the Claire A. Culleton and Karen Leick-edited anthology *Modernism on File: Writers, Artists, and the FBI, 1920–1950* (2008), which explores the FBI's prying into Continental European film and painting as well as Anglo-American literature. Erin G. Carlston includes an illuminating review of this last title, complete with reflections on the nascent academic genre of "the criticism of FBI files" (617), in "Modernism under Surveillance: American Writers, State Espionage, and the Cultural Cold War" (2010). On the somewhat better-studied topic of the Bureau's "secret file on black America"—a phrase of intelligence historian Kenneth O'Reilly—see his pioneering history *"Racial Matters": The FBI's Secret File on Black America, 1960–1972* (1989) and the other titles mentioned in the second endnote to the introduction. Synthesizing "war on words" and "secret file on black America" approaches to FBI history is a basic purpose of this book.

2. Hoover secured Garvey's arrest in January 1922. Convicted of mail fraud in 1923, the UNIA head may have suffered even more when the Bureau leaked word of his secret summit with the Ku Klux Klan. President Calvin Coolidge commuted Garvey's five-year prison sentence four years later, but only in return for his deportation, a punishment treated in relationship to theories of the Black Atlantic in part 4. For the instructive tale of Hoover's successful operation against a "notorious Negro agitator," see Colin Grant's stylish biography *Negro with a Hat: The Rise and Fall of Marcus Garvey* (2008).

294 | NOTES TO PART TWO/THESIS TWO

3. The Claude McKay file, now prepackaged for rapid FOIA examination, has been treated as several sorts of picture window in recent scholarship. Gary Holcomb's *Claude McKay, Code Name Sasha: Queer Black Marxism and the Harlem Renaissance* (2007) borrows its dashing title from the file. Holcomb quotes from a Bureau communication admitting that "confusion has been caused by various ways of spelling" McKay's Russian alias, alternately "rendered Sasha, Sayesh, and Sascha" (23). Such problems of transliteration strike Holcomb as emblems of the Bureau's indecision among "Communists, Negroes, and homosexuals" when searching for categories of supreme degeneracy (24). Josh Gosciak's "Most Wanted: Claude McKay and the 'Black Specter' of African American Poetry in the 1920s" (2008) examines the file's counterpoetic securing of American borders "in anticipation of [McKay's] powerful metaphors breaking through" (91). My own earliest (and lengthiest) take on the meaning of the McKay file can be found in "F.B. Eyes: The Bureau Reads Claude McKay" (2003).

4. My hunt for a copy of Alain Locke's FBI file, now likely lost somewhere in the National Archives thanks to the FBI Records Retention Plan, led to a midlife reading of *The Trial*. The whole bureaucratic story is recounted in the introduction. For a broader, less bitter account of the counterhistoricism of the Records Retention Plan (the ironic result of a 1980 court case brought to ban wholesale file purging), see Alex Heard's "The Department of Forgetting" (2008).

5. Sean McCann's *A Pinnacle of Feeling: American Literature and Presidential Government* (2008) suggests that Wilson's assumption of awesome power was accompanied by a literary rhetoric perhaps "learned from Lincoln himself," an expressive vocabulary articulating "a theory of democratic legitimacy that, although it fit only awkwardly with the existing constitutional design of American government, would go on to become a significant, tacit justification for the rise of presidential power" (xii–xiii). In McCann's transformative understanding, the political history of U.S. presidential sovereignty is "matched by a comparable literary history" beginning with Whitman and intensifying during the twentieth century, Gertrude Stein's progressivism and Philip Roth's *The Plot against America* unexpected steps along the way (x). My study differs from McCann's in focus and direction, emphasizing the relocation of specific sovereign powers from the White House to the FBI's Seat of Government, and the counterliterary upshot of this relocation in the Bureau's interference with African American literary history (an imposition which in turn imposed itself on FBI history). Yet we share a fundamental concern with the relations among American literature, U.S. state power, and democratic potential brought to the fore by the living history of the early twenty-first century.

6. To Hoover's way of thinking, modernist authors, notoriously keen on arcane knowledge, were nevertheless ripe targets for official propaganda. Here, the director's opinion overlaps the counterintuitive propaganda theory of Jacques Ellul, excavated for the new modernist studies by Mark Wollaeger. "[S]ince information actually generates the problems that propaganda exploits and for which it pretends to offer solutions," Ellul contended in 1973, information-hoarding "intellectuals are most easily reached by propaganda, particularly if it employs ambiguity" (114, 113).

7. While the escalation of other forms of official secrecy under the Obama administration has troubled civil (and uncivil) libertarians, FOIA backlogs were reduced by 40 percent across the federal government in 2009, the first year of the administration's first term ("Secrecy Report Card" 1). Admittedly, this figure says nothing in particular about the relative success of FOIA requests at the FBI, and overall FOIA release rates may well

have changed for the worse since 2009; see John Hudson's 2012 piece "Obama Adminis-tration Distorted Its Transparency Record: Ex-DOJ Official."

8. Bygone post–Civil War "Black Codes" also criminalized rebellious expression by freedmen. Mississippi's code, for example, passed in defiance of the Thirteenth Amend-ment in 1865, proscribed "seditious speeches" along with jury service, vagrancy, and bowie knives (Ash 227).

9. Citing the Bureau's many counterliterary files on nonblack voices of the 1930s, Rhodri Jeffreys-Jones maintains that "[t]he FBI's hostility to creative writers stored up trouble for the future and meant it was out of step with New Deal policy. Through the Federal Writers' Project and similar programs for theater, music, and art launched in 1935, the Roosevelt administration had shown a tolerant and friendly face to potential rebels, if with a view to cooptation. In contrast, the FBI turned a philistine countenance on those who dared to differ" (130). Beyond the high file count, however, the face the Bureau turned to New Deal literature was in no way smugly indifferent or simply hostile. As discussed later in part two, Hoover published his own first book in 1938 thanks to his fame as a New Deal avenger. And he seeded the work of fellow authors through his makeover of the FBI as an alternative federal writers' bureau.

10. Richard Gid Powers is not isolated in recommending that FDR's reputation be ad-justed to "bear the final responsibility for removing all effective restraints from Hoover's surveillance of the American political scene" (Secrecy 233). Frank J. Donner likewise underlines the soaring costs of Roosevelt's issuance of what became a "hunting license for all seasons" (68). Yet Donner also emphasizes the intelligence system's twisting of the arm of the presidency "to force a permanent grant of authority to engage in subversive activities intelligence" (67). Former special agent Raymond J. Batvinis, reconsidering FDR's promotion of Hoover's investigative latitude in The Origins of FBI Counterintel-ligence (2007), notes the firestorm of antagonism generated within the Postal Service, Secret Service, Internal Revenue, Customs, and other rival agencies (58–59). All these historians draw to varying degrees on the comprehensive Church Committee report of 1976, the multivolume record of a damning post-Watergate (and post-Hoover) Senate investigation into federal intelligence excesses. (Formally, the complete published report is known as the Final Report of the Select Committee to Study Government Operations with Respect to Intelligence Activities; Senator Frank Church, Democrat of Idaho, served as the committee's chair.) Braced by thick footnotes and citations, the Final Report cen-sures the mutual decision of FDR, the FBI, and the larger Justice Department "not to seek legislative authorization for the expanding domestic intelligence program" (United States, Senate, Select Committee, Intelligence Activities 28).

11. The version of RACON I quote from was collated from a number of declassified archival copies by historian Robert A. Hill; see his meticulous book The FBI's RACON: Racial Conditions in the United States during World War II (1995). Hill's introduction, 218 footnotes strong, is alone worth the admission price—not least for his relatively speculative claim on the straight line from RACON to the Bureau's "Ghetto Informant Program," one of several FBI efforts of the 1960s to surveil black communities (49).

12. Frederick Collins's status as the Courtney Ryley Cooper of the early 1940s—in other words, Hoover's pet enlistee in the Bureau's federal writers' project—shines through in The FBI in Peace and War (1943), Collins's faithful updating of Hoover's Persons in Hiding's case-file narrative. In a wartime expansion of a Depression structure, chapters cataloging "The Robbers" and "The Kidnappers" are followed by portraits of

"The Nazi Spies," "The Jap Spies," and "The Enemy Within." (The "Austrian paper hanger," Hoover remarked in an contemporaneous speech, was as much a gangland "product of his times" as "Capone, Buchalter, Karpis, Dillinger, Touhy, and a host of other gangsters who almost seized control of whole communities" [qtd. in Powers, *Secrecy* 258].) Restaffing the Hoover-Cooper school of logrolling, Hoover's introduction praises Collins's pick-me-up for the home front: "Not only is it a story that should be told and Mr. Collins qualified to tell it authoritatively, but—coming as it does in wartime—it ought to bring a message of good cheer, to all who read it" (vii). The Hoover-Collins collaboration cooled when the latter attempted to resell *The FBI in Peace and War* as a radio serial without the director's authorization. "Hoover was furious," notes Richard Gid Powers, "and countered with a show of his own" (*Broken* 189). Membership in Hoover writers' project required greater fealty than membership in Henry Alsberg's—in part because the Bureau director was a jealous author.

13. In *Black Is a Country: Race and the Unfinished Struggle for Democracy* (2004), a revisionist internationalizing of the "long civil rights era," Nikhil Pal Singh casts Charles Johnson's *To Stem the Tide* as a herald of the worldly racial logic of U.S. liberal nationalism after World War II. "[P]rogress on issues of racial equality at home," Singh writes, "were [*sic*] the litmus test of America's claims to global leadership" (139–40). In this respect, Johnson's pamphlet comes considerably closer to Gunnar Myrdal's *An American Dilemma* (1944) than to the FBI's *RACON* (1943, ed. R. Hill).

14. "At least" this number, that is, because I did not request the FBI files of all African American authors active during World War II; because the Bureau, however accommodating, "knowingly uses a search process," revolving around a central database of electronic names, that sometimes "doesn't find relevant records" ("2009 Rosemary Award"); and because several files of the period have been misplaced or shredded. As the introduction notes, for example, Margaret Walker's national headquarters file was in all probability "destroyed on November 12, 2003" under provisions of the joint FBI–National Archives Records Retention Plan (Hardy, 14. Nov. 2006). Other FBI paperwork on Walker, once kept by the Bureau's Miami field office, was "destroyed [in] September of 1990" (Hardy, 16 May 2007). More rarely, Bureau records policy would do well to err on the side of increased repression. My FOIA request for the file of William Attaway, the author of the migration novel *Blood on the Forge* (1941), mistakenly outed the thirty-page file of "Wild Bill" Attaway, a volunteer Bureau informant and "American Republican Revolutionist" (United States, Federal, Attaway, 13 June 1950). In any case, this book's appendix offers a full list of the author files I sought through the Freedom of Information Act, with the introduction providing a sketch of my principles of selection.

15. Thanks are due to fellow Illini Brian Dolinar for providing me with copies of the Himes, Ollie Harrington, and Langston Hughes files. Claire Culleton, a friend of this project from the start, passed along convenient copies of W.E.B. Du Bois's and Richard Wright's Bureau paperwork. Fewer thanks go out to Accuracy in Media (AIM), the still red-hunting outfit that publicized Barack Obama's imaginary "Communist Party connection through [Frank Marshall] Davis" during the 2008 election cycle (Kincaid). To its small credit, AIM's fear mongering briefly thrust *Politico*-style relevance on such painstaking scholarship as James Smethurst's *The New Red Negro: The Literary Left and African American Poetry, 1930–1946* (1999) and John Edgar Tidwell's edition of Frank Marshall Davis's *Black Moods: Collected Poems* (2002).

16. Sterling Brown's FBI file muddles through another decade, closing with reports of a 1953 Bureau re-interview in which the subject "[a]dvised he has never been a Communist, has never had any affiliation with or sympathy for the Communist Party and has never adhered to its principles such as the advocacy of the use of force and violence to overthrow the government" (United States, Federal, Sterling Brown, 18 May 1953). While misrepresenting his onetime compassion for the party, Brown's responses had the virtue of averting another Hatch Act case.

17. Hoover's commitment to preventive detention lists reentered the news in 2007, when newly declassified documents revealed his plans "to suspend habeas corpus and imprison some 12,000 Americans he suspected of disloyalty" in the wake of the Korean War (Weiner, "Hoover"). As reported by intelligence historian Tim Weiner in the *New York Times*, "Hoover wanted President Harry S. Truman to proclaim mass arrests necessary to 'protect the country against treason, espionage and sabotage.' The F.B.I. would 'apprehend all individuals potentially dangerous' to national security, Hoover's proposal said. The arrests would be carried out under 'a master warrant attached to a list of names' provided by the bureau" ("Hoover"). Weiner mentions the legal shield given Hoover's proposal by the Internal Security or McCarran Act, authorization for the detention of "dangerous radicals" passed by Congress in 1950 and noted elsewhere in part 2. Though Truman, alarmed by China's entrance into the war, declared a national emergency that December, the act was passed only over his veto and was never tapped to activate Hoover's Korean War–era mass detention proposal, one in a dreadfully long series. McCarran has nonetheless achieved notoriety within "racial paranoia's canonical texts," perceptively discussed by anthropologist John L. Jackson (111). One of these texts, Samuel F. Yette's *The Choice: The Issue of Black Survival in America*, a 1971 manifesto condemning government measures favoring "Black genocide," views the McCarran Act as an effort to legitimize, before the fact, concentration camps filled with African Americans (301).

18. Alternatively, in their introduction to *Modernism on File: Writers, Artists, and the FBI, 1920–1950* (2008), Claire A. Culleton and Karen Leick decry Hoover's move to consign "many of the twentieth century's most original and imposing writers and artists" to the Custodial Detention list (8). Yet the essays that follow cite the listing of just one non–African American author, Henry Roth, who appeared on the Security Index from 1951 to 1955, years after World War II (Kellman 40). Culleton's own history of "Hoover's manipulation of modernism," *Joyce and the G-Men* (2004), discusses planned detention only in the case of Langston Hughes, while Herbert Mitgang's earlier study of much the same topic, *Dangerous Dossiers* (1988), notes evidence of this severe measure in the files of four of the thirty-five American authors he treats (by name, these four are Nelson Algren, Lillian Hellman, Dorothy Parker, and Elmer Rice). Alexander Stephan's *"Communazis": FBI Surveillance of German Emigré Writers* (2000), comments on the indexing of several literary immigrants suspected of an anti-American double whammy but also records their preference for continued German-language writing once settled in Hollywood and other American landscapes. (The major works of German literature thus produced in the United States include Thomas Mann's *Doctor Faustus*, Bertolt Brecht's *The Caucasian Chalk Circle*, and Franz Werfel's *The Song of Bernadette* [ix].) With apologies to Werner Sollors's vision of a multilingual U.S. canon, I do not count the émigrés as nonblack makers of American literature.

Meanwhile, for an unusually revealing firsthand record of what a Custodial Detention listing meant for the genre of the FBI author file, see the Lloyd Brown dossier. Documents within this dossier itemize the features of Custodial Detention/Security Index cards (9 Dec. 1941) and reveal standard forms and procedures for their alteration (22 Mar. 1950; 7 Sept. 1961). The file also includes a copy of Biddle's directive firmly but ineffectively canceling the initial Custodial Detention program (16 July 1943). Most fascinating, however, is the unrelated recounting of a farcically obtuse Bureau effort to recruit Brown as a Communist Party informant. "[E]fforts were made to bring BROWN around to discussing himself and the communist conspiracy, and, to neutralize by reason, his apparent obsession with lack of freedom because he was negro [sic]," narrated a New York agent in 1962 (21 Feb. 1962). To this recruiter's dismay, Brown "ignored all these efforts and continued ranting in an irrational manner. . . . In view of BROWN's hostile attitude coupled with his expressed obsession with negro [sic] inequality, no recontact is contemplated at this time" (21 Feb. 1962). The same file bears witness that Brown's acquaintances outside the FBI were more eager to stay in touch. "Subject has left many good friends in the various places in which he worked," notes a 1941 report, since "it is rumored he can 'shake a mean hoof' on the dance floor, [and he] lays claim to be a shark at shooting pool, a claim hotly disputed in many and diverse quarters" (6 Dec. 1941). Someone willing to talk to the Bureau knew how to signify. A hat tip to Mary Helen Washington for providing me with a copy of Brown's file, freeing me from the need to increase (yet again) the Bureau's FOIA workload. My copy of the Alice Childress file comes from the same source.

19. In an afterword to a 2004 reprinting of *The Man Who Cried I Am*, John A. Williams invoked the Bureau harassment documented in Kenneth O'Reilly's "*Racial Matters*" (1989) to help account for the "great heft" of his novel's higher, predictive realism (412). O'Reilly's "book, and several others," he submits, "remains a sobering record of those fragile and dangerous times, when government was not (nor is it now) what most of us would wish or need it to be" (J. Williams, Afterword 412). Williams's afterword is again discussed briefly in part 5 of *F.B. Eyes*.

20. Details on the care and feeding of the FBI faction in Congress can be found in Curt Gentry's aggressively investigated biography *J. Edgar Hoover: The Man and the Secrets* (1991), also a vital source for understanding the Bureau's "Total Literary Awareness" push of the 1950s. Hoover's congressional A-team at midcentury, Gentry concludes, was not composed of loyal cheerleaders quick to feed Bureau press releases into the *Congressional Record*. Instead, it featured quieter, more powerful "majority and minority leaders, Speakers, and the chairmen of the key committees," Washington hands, like Hoover, "long on seniority" and bureaucratically shrewd enough to keep the dollars flowing (e.g., Everett Dirksen, John McLellan, and John Stennis) (407).

21. Jon Wiener considered the not-just-archival significance of Culleton's discovery in a 2008 *Nation* column, "J. Edgar Hoover, Author." "Today," Wiener observes, "Henry Holt publishes many writers on the left, including Noam Chomsky, Barbara Ehrenreich, Mike Davis and Chalmers Johnson—all of them bestsellers. Almost nothing like their work was published, by Holt or any other mainstream publisher, in the era of *Masters of Deceit*. The book business has changed for the worse in many ways since the 1950s, but this broadening of debate is clearly a change for the better" ("J. Edgar Hoover"). The live value of Culleton's findings nevertheless cannot support her hyperbolic suggestion that Hoover "used his power to micromanage

intellectual life in the United States by working effectively with publishing companies" ("Extorting" 249).

22. I am obliged to the generosity of Kathlene McDonald, the Hansberry specialist at the City College of New York, who shared her copy of the playwright's giant file.

23. In an astute prereading of the Hansberry file, Cheryl Higashida also comments on the Bureau reviewer's lopsided attention to the Nigerian Joseph Asagai. The intense interest in this African character, "despite the fact that he appears in far fewer scenes than Ruth, Walter, and Beneatha Younger, suggests how much [his] vision meant to the state" (903).

24. Barbara Foley charitably supplemented the eight pages of Ellison file I originally received with dozens more—another proof that different FOIA requests for the same Bureau materials can yield very different documents.

25. Colin A. Beckles's sociological article "Black Bookstores, Black Power, and the F.B.I.: The Case of Drum and Spear" (1996) discusses the Bureau's haunting of one prominent Pan-African bookseller in Washington, D.C., perhaps the country's leading supplier of textbooks to groundbreaking black studies departments until 1972. According to Drum and Spear's owners, the store was conspicuously visited and revisited by FBI agents, much as Bureau teams plagued black newspapers during World War II. Times had changed enough, however, for the Bureau to pay for the privilege, the better to stock its library of black radicalism: "They [FBI agents] would come in and you always knew that's who they were; they had those funny suits and the little ties and stuff and they were one of the few white people who would come in the store. . . . [T]hey would spend lots of money on the books and they would walk out with them" (qtd. in Beckles 68).

26. The left-on-left controversy sparked by Seth Rosenfeld's cannily publicized book *Subversives: The FBI's War on Student Radicals, and Reagan's Rise to Power* (2012) has been settled, I believe, by his online publication of Richard Aoki's FBI file. Despite some typical Bureau inaccuracies, this document verifies that "Aoki was secretly providing information to agents during the period he gave the Black Panthers guns and firearms training" (Rosenfeld, "FBI Files"). *Subversives* critic Donna Jean Murch, one of a rising generation of revisionist Black Panther scholars, is persuasive, however, when noting that had Rosenfeld "delved more carefully into the spate of recent books, dissertations, and edited collections on black radicalism, it would have been much harder to attribute the use of armed self-defense solely to his Svengali-like Aoki, who appears in [*Subversives*] replete with sunglasses at night, 'slicked back hair,' 'ghetto Patois,' and a menacing 'swagger.' At the very least, pinning so much on Aoki is a big leap" ("Countering Subversion").

27. The extent to which Maulana Karenga's US organization knowingly tolerated the FBI's campaign against the Panthers remains an open question. The matter will not be settled by conservative polemicist Ann Coulter's column "Kwanzaa: Holiday from the FBI" (2008), in which surprising criticism of the FBI's "ultimately . . . foolish" plan to split Black Power nationalism is topped by abuse of a Pan-African holiday created by "proto-fascists, walking around in dashikis, blowing away Black Panthers and adopting 'African' names" (Coulter). On the subject of FBI "snitch-jacketing," see Huey Newton's well-researched PhD dissertation–cum–autoethnography, *War against the Panthers*, produced to satisfy the requirements of the History of Consciousness Program (naturally) at the University of California, Santa Cruz, in 1980. Defending his name against

charges of police collaboration informs this doctoral candidate's atypical scholarly agenda (70–107).

28. A similarly crude FBI-authored poem of radical character assassination can be located in the James Baldwin file. Attempting to alienate the largely white Socialist Workers Party (SWP) from supporters of black self-defense advocate Robert F. Williams in Monroe, North Carolina, the FBI anonymously distributed copies of a ditty slurring an SWP member as a frightened thief:

> Georgie-Porgie, down in Monroe,
> Found himself alone with the dough,
> Called the cops, and what did he say?
> "Bad guys came and took it away." (United States, Federal, James Baldwin
>   file, 10 Apr. 1964)

29. One example of the specifically literary-historical lessons to be learned from FBI wiretapping can be found in the James Baldwin file. There, transcripts of the Baldwin camp's disputes with the Actors Studio illuminate the racially fraught production history of *Blues for Mister Charlie* (1964). Baldwin's lawyer admits that the studio "will do as little as they can and let the 'nigger' do all the work" but advises that his client should ignore the prospect of an underfunded production and "spend all his time polishing scenes for the opening" (United States, Federal, Baldwin, 6 May 1964).

30. Further evidence of the FBI's ironic capitalization of the alternative economy of black nationalist publishing can be located in its 1970–76 dossier on the *Black Scholar*, the influential "journal of black studies and research" published by the Black World Foundation in Oakland beginning in 1969. Hoover's office in Washington instructed the San Francisco station to take out no fewer than four subscriptions. It was otherwise "difficult for the field to obtain an unlimited number of copies," the Seat of Government reasoned, an ample supply needed to "insure it is properly reviewed and necessary dissemination made of pertinent articles" (United States, Federal, *Black Scholar* 30 Dec. 1970). For additional illumination of the Bureau's faith in the power of "discreet" subscriptions, see its 1942–75 file on *Negro Digest/Black World* (internal case file no. 100–71654).

31. The FBI's website explains the strict protocol for requests for information on a living person other than the FOIA requester: "[Y]ou *must* submit his/her notarized authorization, or you may use [a] 'Privacy Waiver and Certification of Identity Form,'" a document through which that living party relinquishes his or her right to privacy under penalty of perjury ("FOIA Request Instructions"; emphasis in original).

32. The FBI acknowledged the existence of a personal file on Addison Gayle Jr. in July 2007, following the success of an appeal I initiated in December 2006. Quickly enough, however, the Bureau passed the buck to the National Archives, describing this collection as the file's probable home after an accession swap. Contrary to the Bureau's suggestion, the National Archives reported it could not locate Gayle's file on its premises.

33. The identity of five of the eight Media burglars, and something like the full story of their discovery of COINTELPRO, was finally revealed in January 2014 in journalist Betty Medsger's methodically researched book *The Burglary: The Discovery of J. Edgar Hoover's Secret FBI*.

Part Three/Thesis Three
The FBI Is Perhaps the Most Dedicated and Influential
Forgotten Critic of African American Literature

1. Mark Riebling's *Wedge: The Secret War between the FBI and the CIA* (1994), the book that inspired my account of Ian Fleming's secret mission to Hoover, is the best-researched and most readable history of the (nonliterary) rivalry between the two intelligence empires. Republished as *Wedge: From Pearl Harbor to 9/11* in 2002, the book's second coming is indicative of Al Qaeda's boost to intelligence history, the genre's fortunes having sagged with the fall of Soviet communism. In Riebling's judgment, further books on future chapters of the FBI-CIA rivalry will be necessary. Beginning with "the restoration of formal liaison in 1972," the year of Hoover's death, "the existence of FBI-CIA problems has typically been denied by the parties in power, while the sins of the past are acknowledged readily" (453).

2. The most influential reconstruction of the CIA's career as a secret impresario of high culture is Frances Stonor Saunders's *The Cultural Cold War: The CIA and the World of Arts and Letters* (2000). David Caute's *The Dancer Defects: The Struggle for Cultural Supremacy during the Cold War* (2003), the encyclopedic work of a veteran historian, ranges beyond Saunders's focus on the Congress for Cultural Freedom, the CIA's elite cultural front group, to concentrate on Soviet artistic weapons as well. It also takes snobbish aim at Saunders's background in film production, describing "a young English writer . . . with a television crew" who "set out to nail CIA clandestine involvement in a range of cold war cultural activities and to establish its role as the mover and shaker responsible for promoting American abstract expressionist art abroad" (540). According to Caute, the truth about the CIA's Kulturkampf is less scandalous than meets the eye. "While this relatively young agency did certainly involve itself in clandestinely promoting literary magazines, music festivals, and orchestral tours, along with much else within the United States, the financing of American art exhibits abroad was largely the work of the Rockefellers, the Whitneys, and the Guggenheims" (540). Caute expresses greater sympathy for art historian Serge Guilbaut's *How New York Stole the Idea of Modern Art* (1983), which describes the cooptation of abstract expressionist painting by Cold War liberalism rather than a singularly potent CIA; more recently, Guilbaut's book has been slammed as the inspiration for a simple-minded school of left-wing musicology in Charles Rosen's "Music and the Cold War" (2011). Hugh Wilford's *The Mighty Wurlitzer: How the CIA Played America* (2008) assesses the conclusions of both the Saunders/"revisionist" and Caute/"post-revisionist" positions. The former is essentially correct in arguing that the CIA's tastes in literature and the visual arts "were predominantly highbrow and modernist," Wilford finds (106). But the latter hits pay dirt in "the realm of music," where the claim for "the CIA's aesthetic preference for modernism" has been overstated (108). More importantly, the postrevisionists have the better argument on the baseline question "of the Agency's cultural influence" (113).

3. The classic history of the "Double-Cross system" just happens to be written by the Oxford professor of modern history who once ran the system for British intelligence; see J. C. Masterman's *The Double-Cross System in the War of 1939 to 1945* (1972). Norman Holmes Pearson not only vouched for Masterman's credibility in the book's foreword ("I can endorse [its] authenticity, having been aware of many of the

cases in connection with my own war work" [ix]) but opened doors at the Yale University Press, the book's savior, after the British government denied domestic publication for almost a decade. The tale of Pearson's campaign to help Masterman evade Britain's Official Secrets act is told in Robin W. Winks's plummy and gripping *Cloak and Gown: Scholars in the Secret War, 1939–1961* (1987; 1996), the Yaliest possible account of the Yale-OSS-CIA conveyer belt (291–96). More might be said about the publication of Masterman's book as the fruit of mutual recognition between Yale/CIA and Oxford/MI5, two similarly tight networks of regnant academia and national counterintelligence. James Smith's *British Writers and MI5 Surveillance, 1930–1960* (2013) has recently said a good deal about MI5's FBI-style monitoring of George Orwell, W. H. Auden, and other British writers on the left.

4. Pearson's dedication to the blending of historical and formal analysis also informed his later work administering Yale's interdisciplinary program in American studies. Contrary to academic rumors, this pacesetting program was founded in 1948 by other Yale scholars with less intriguing ties to the OSS/CIA. Michael Holzman's article "The Ideological Origins of American Studies at Yale" (1999) combs Pearson's papers in the Beinecke Library to cast the making of "American studies as something beyond the study of American literature and history, as an enterprise that would be, among other things, an instrument for ideological struggle in what some . . . termed the American crusade in the cold war" (71).

5. Norman Holmes Pearson, the Yale-OSS elder whom Angleton nicknamed "Hi Ho Silver Tongue" in honor of his articulate intelligence briefings (Winks 349), inspired fewer literary doubles. He was thus delighted to find himself a character in John Hollander's *Reflections on Espionage: The Question of Cupcake* (1976), a book-length sequence of ninety-eight poetic "transmissions" inspired by J. C. Masterman's *The Double-Cross System*. In the guise of "Puritan," a name borrowed from his OSS cryptonym, Pearson appears as a favorite of "Kilo," a spitting image of Ezra Pound. As a poetic aide-de-camp "no longer / In the [spy] service, yet . . . / . . . involved with the work still, and always" (5/9 ll. 22–24), Puritan embodies Hollander's exploration of the far reaches of the spy-writer allegory. In his introduction to a 1999 reprinting of the poem, Hollander observed that "[s]pies are actors in improvised scenarios, and case agents are their author-directors. *Actor* and *agent* have a common Latin ancestry, and secret agency—in the most general sense—invokes many aspects of poetic identity" (xviii).

6. The Michael Holzman of "The Ideological Origins of American Studies at Yale," discussed above in note 4, is the very same Michael Holzman who produced *James Jesus Angleton, the CIA, and the Craft of Intelligence* (2008), the intellectual biography containing the most serious analysis of Angleton's editing and literary self-education at Yale. I draw a good deal from this biography, especially its treatment of Angleton's correspondence and its rousing effort "to establish the study of secret intelligence as a realm of the history of ideas" (xi). Meanwhile, the portrait of Angleton penned by Robin Winks, a diplomatic rather than a literary historian, revealingly delves into "the Poet's" theory of Empsonian ambiguity but also emphasizes his atypical refusal to abandon counterintelligence work in favor of "the cozier networking of [the] faculty club" after World War II (372).

7. A full run of *Furioso*, eight volumes originally issued between 1939 and 1953, was republished in facsimile by the Kraus Reprint Company in 1972. Angleton's little

college magazine thus reentered big college libraries as a licensed monument of late modernism.

8. To be fair, the fourth, 1932 edition of Pattee's *Century Readings* sampled the literature of an all-white "anti-slavery movement," including bits of John Greenleaf Whittier, Harriet Beecher Stowe, Abraham Lincoln, and "songs and ballads of the Civil War."

9. "The Devoté," an undated, unpublished poem by Bowen, places its male hero on an erotic natural pedestal: "About his feet the purple clover breathed / Perfumes more sweet than on an altar rise, / His knees the luscious grasses inter-wreathed, / Kissing the rounded beauty of his thighs" (Bowen, "The Devoté" ll. 9–12). The antique iambic meter, superior pagan altar, and beautifully rounded thighs could be taken from one of Claude McKay's free-love poems in *Harlem Shadows* (1922).

10. Bowen glued several different photo-portraits of Hoover into his copy of Don Whitehead's *The FBI Story*. In a tipped-in sheet in the same volume, he informed posterity that "[i]t will be noted from the letters pasted in this book and certain written matter that my personal relations with J. Edgar Hoover, the Director, were very friendly. At once upon my being demoted from Special Employee [at the Bureau of Translations] to Special Agent these relations ceased abruptly" (Bowen, Marginalia). "[O]nce meeting on the street in Washington the Director failed even to see me," Bowen lamented (Marginalia). "It was better so, I suppose, than not stopping to speak" (Marginalia). In the unpublished typescript poem "The Giver," kept a few boxes away at Clemson and written in the era of *The FBI Story*, Bowen treats the loss of a male lover who had once "held the jewel out" (l. 1), but who lately "passed me on the street, nor glanced at me / He who once held my heart within his hand. / Did he, perchance, recall how we had planned / To go life's way in mutual constancy?" (ll. 5–8). Two central stanzas addressing this hardened lover were whited out by either Bowen or his heirs. It is possible that Bowen intended users of his Clemson archive to fill in the blanks with Hoover's name. For what it's worth, Bowen's FBI employee file, accessed through my FOIA request in 2013, contains a Bowen letter begging "My dear Mr. Hoover" to ignore "gossip" suggesting "that I have resigned my position under you, and have gone South to live—or die" (United States, Federal, Bowen, 7 Mar. 1925).

11. Despite his investigation of the Soviet response and his professional interest in drumming up scandal around Sullivan's death, Bill Brown, the reporter who completed and published Sullivan's memoir, concluded that his killing was not a political assassination. "I flew up to Bill's home for the funeral and spoke with the local authorities as well as his family," he recounts (10). "I was convinced, as were they, that his tragic death was indeed accidental," and that both the Soviets and the remnants of Hooverism were innocent (10).

12. Richard Gid Powers, by contrast, ratifies Sullivan's authorship of the King letter in his benchmark biography of Hoover, *Secrecy and Power* (1987); see in particular footnote 59 on page 579. My own copy of the letter was reproduced from the copy now kept in Hoover's Official and Confidential files at the U.S. National Archives.

13. For a taste of Sullivan's presence in the FBI's collective COINTELPRO—Black Hate file, see the 13 October 1967 memorandum sent him by the Philadelphia field office. This memo seeks his approval for "A Time of Challenge," an FBI-ghostwritten pamphlet pretending to be the work of black Vietnam veterans, but in fact "prepared as a counterintelligence tactic to oppose the influence of extremists of the

right and left in riots and civil disorders" (United States, Federal, COINTELPRO, 13 Oct. 1967).

14. Hoover touted the FBI's enormous fingerprint collection and onetime state-of-the-art fingerprint identification laboratory in almost every story of the Bureau he signed or approved. For a few lively examples, see Hoover's gangster-versus-G-Man book *Persons in Hiding* (1938) and its defense of a national fingerprint depository (86–97); Frederick L. Collins's *The FBI in Peace and War* (1943), which predicts that the fingerprints of "substantially every adult person in the United States will be represented in the Bureau's files" (ix); and Don Whitehead's *The FBI Story* (1956), prepared to argue that the FBI fingerprint Identification Division was "in an astonishing volume of cases . . . a protector of civil rights" (137). Like many U.S. salesmen of the fingerprint system, Whitehead cannot think of the advantages of the method without also thinking of the epidermic metaphysics of American race relations. He thus alludes to the "natal autograph" proving racial belonging in "Twain's story of 'Puddn'nhead Wilson' [*sic*]" (132) and the apparent civil rights victory of the "Will West incident." In this nonfictional criminal case of 1903, the facial similarity of two separate African American suspects named Will West discredited the Bertillon bodily measurement system used to identify criminals since the 1880s. As Whitehead reports, the case freed the innocent half of the two Wests and "spurred agitation in the United States for use of the fingerprint as the infallible means of criminal identification" (133). Compulsory fingerprinting might treat all citizens as potential lawbreakers, concentrating biopower in the state. To Whitehead's mind, however, it allowed the police to see beyond the racist error that "they all look alike." Whitehead and other literary Hooverites expended so much energy dramatizing the achievements of FBI fingerprinting that the national fingerprint library at Bureau headquarters (a regular stop on guided tours) became confused with its acres of investigative files in general. "Fingerprint File" (1974), the Watergate-era protest number that may be the Rolling Stones' worst-ever single, thus indicts "some little jerk in the FBI / A-keepin' papers on me six feet high."

15. Later journalism recorded Hoover's affection for Mark Twain, "whose framed autograph hung on the wall of a hallway" in his Washington, D.C., home, and his swapping of cowboy Western novels with President Dwight Eisenhower (Robins 50). Natalie Robins notes that at the time of his death, Hoover's personal library included such humbling how-to titles as *Modern Sex Life, Eat and Stay Well, Health in the Later Years*, and *How to Overcome Nervous Stomach Trouble* (50). His enjoyment of the doggerel of Robert Service, perhaps the most commercially successful English-language poet of the twentieth century, is briefly considered in part 1.

16. Other invitations to reconsider the mutual indifference of African American studies and materialist reading history have been issued and answered over the last decade or so, from Elizabeth McHenry's prize-winning institutional history *Forgotten Readers: Recovering the Lost History of African-American Literary Societies* (2002); to Ronald J. Zboray and Mary Saracino Zboray's study of the reading diaries of Charlotte Forten Grimké and James Healy, among others, in *Everyday Ideas: Socioliterary Experience among Antebellum New Englanders* (2006); to Karla F. C. Holloway's memoiristic but wide-ranging *Bookmarks: Reading in Black and White* (2006); to a number of the discussions of late nineteenth- and twentieth-century African American print culture in the essay collection *Publishing Blackness: Textual Constructions of Race since 1850* (2013), edited by George Hutchinson and John K. Young.

Part Four/Thesis Four
The FBI Helped to Define the Twentieth-Century Black Atlantic, Both
Blocking and Forcing Its Flows

1. Returning the favor by looking back at the African American expatriates of the
1950s, the upscale twenty-first-century Café Tournon advertises itself as the legendary rendezvous "des écrivains afro-américains ex-patriés et des artistes, comme James
Baldwin, Chester Himes, Richard Wright, William Gardner Smith, le peintre Beauford
Delaney et le sculpteur Howard Cousins" ("L'Historique").

2. Richard Gibson's most elaborate account of the affair that bears his name is also
his most recent, a convincingly professorial 2005 contribution to the journal *Modern
Fiction Studies*, later republished in Jeremy Braddock and Jonathan P. Eburne's collection *Paris, Capital of the Black Atlantic* (2013). Neither "a confession nor an apology,"
Gibson's perceptive and densely footnoted essay denies his responsibility for destroying
"a certain cozy easiness of life in Paris for African Americans" and instead pins blame on
the global crisis of the Algerian War of Independence ("Richard Wright's" 896). Fending
off the factual errors of unconspiratorial historians—Michel Fabre and Tyler Stovall in
particular—and fingering Richard Wright's chief suspect, William Gardner Smith, for
the original idea of "a letter-writing ring" (911), Gibson nonetheless admits that Smith
"did not write the letter to *Life* magazine. I did" (912).

3. The "new transnationalist" elaboration of these extranational tropes can be gathered
from the following: on the hemispheric, see Caroline F. Levander and Robert S. Levine's
collection *Hemispheric American Studies* (2008); on the diasporan, see Dalia Kandiyoti's
Migrant Sites: America, Place, and Diaspora Literatures (2009); on the cosmopolitan, see
Tom Lutz, *Cosmopolitan Vistas: American Regionalism and Literary Value* (2004); on the
transatlantic, see Susan Manning and Andrew Taylor's *Transatlantic Literary Studies: A
Reader* (2007); on the transpacific, see Yunte Huang's *Transpacific Imaginations: History,
Literature, Counterpoetics* (2008); on the archipelagic, see Brian Russell Roberts's "(Ex)
Isles in the Harlem Renaissance: The Insular and Archipelagic Topographies of Wallace
Thurman's *The Blacker the Berry*" (2011); and on the species-wide, the planetary, and the
"deep-temporal," see Wai Chee Dimock's *Through Other Continents: American Literature
across Deep Time* (2006) and her and Lawrence Buell's anthology *Shades of the Planet:
American Literature as World Literature* (2007).

4. There are substantial and influential exceptions to the rule of the forgotten or diminished state in transnational Americanism, however. These include the best part of
the work of Donald Pease (see in particular his "Re-Thinking 'American Studies' after
US Exceptionalism" [2009]), Eric Lott (e.g., "National Treasure, Global Value, and
American Literary Studies" [2008]), and Anna Brickhouse (e.g., "Scholarship and the
State: Robert Greenhow and Transnational American Studies, 1848/2008" [2008]). As
the title of the Brickhouse essay hints, the state-consciousness of U.S. literary scholars
rises in proximity to American studies, an interdiscipline with an obtrusive history of
state sponsorship.

5. The point on the state's relative autonomy from the nation is made more positively
in Matt Hart and Jim Hansen's introduction to a special issue of *Contemporary Literature*
entitled "Contemporary Literature and the State"—a far-ranging piece which also makes
a case for reconciling the "apparently rooted and territorial" concept of the state "with
new approaches to transnational and world literature" (502).

6. In the Anglo-American context, perhaps the most influential of these myth-busting scholars of nationalism have been Ernest Gellner (nationalism as a necessary identity under modernization), Anthony Giddens (nationalism as a psychological Romanticism), Eric Hobsbawm (nationalism as an artifact of modern social engineering), and Benedict Anderson (nationalism as an imaginary relationship to the explosive interaction of capitalism, print, and linguistic diversity). Gendered and sexed myths of the nation untouched by these four theorists are addressed by the feminist scholars assembled in Tamar Meyer's *Gender Ironies of Nationalism* (2000).

7. From the perspective of U.S. literary history, Benedict Anderson has made the most potent argument for the nationalist prescience of the new American states of the late eighteenth and early nineteenth centuries. See his chapter "Creole Pioneers" in *Imagined Communities* (47–65).

8. Judith Butler's academically famous retooling of Althusserian interpellation appears in the chapter "Gender Is Burning" in *Bodies that Matter* (1993), headed by an epigraph from Althusser's "Ideology and Ideological State Apparatuses" (Butler 81–98).

9. Like Michel Foucault's now prominent idea of "bio-power," Althusser's twofold state map provides a recipe for unsettling the binary antagonism between an essentially repressive sovereign state and an essentially ideological citizen-subject. Emphatically unlike Foucault, however, Althusser denies that "[t]he State is superstructural in relation to a whole series of power networks that invest the body, sexuality, the family, kinship, knowledge, technology, and so forth" (Foucault, "Truth" 122). For Althusser, such primarily nonrepressive networks continue to be threaded through the bedrock of the state—and only incidentally through the basis of the nation.

10. Corrections of the divide between state violence and national imagination might be discovered in other classic sources, of course. To name one, Ernest Gellner's *Nations and Nationalism* (1983) ties the progress of the state to its imposition of cultural standardization. Put in Althusserian terms, Gellner assumes that the state will fail if the ISAs fail to have their way.

11. I allude here to Michael Hardt and Antonio Negri's peak-neoliberal-era reclassification of the United States as an imperial rather than imperialist power, a distinctly constitutional empire projecting "a *decentered* and *deterritorializing* apparatus of rule that progressively incorporates the entire global realm within its open, expanding frontiers" (xii; emphasis in original).

12. The further the transnational turn roams from its early debts to postcolonial thought, the less likely it may be to entertain the state's ability to draw and erase national lines and to conceive and "hail" transnational subjects. For a snapshot of some of the transnational turn's founding engagements with postcolonial theory and history, see Amy Kaplan and Donald Pease's anthology *Cultures of United States Imperialism* (1994). Like several of her contributors, Kaplan protests both the absence of international "empire from the study of American culture" and the "absence of the United States from the postcolonial study of imperialism" (11). Her later monograph, *The Anarchy of Empire in the Making of U.S. Culture* (2002), extends the theme in a manner roughly parallel with my own interest in the transnational state's shaping of national cultures, exploring how "[t]he idea of the nation as home . . . is inextricable from the political, economic, and cultural movements of empire" (1). While stemming from comparative rather than American literary studies, Emily Apter's book *Against World Literature*

(2013) demonstrates how a postcolonial perspective concentrates attention on the state checkpoints that challenge the "soft, hospitable border that [has] made its way most frequently into literary cartography" (104).

13. The footnotes of Dimock's *Through Other Continents* suggest that we should meet Fernand Braudel's corpus through his short essay "History and the Social Sciences: The *Longue Durée*" (1958). The same notes recommend all three volumes of Immanuel Wallerstein's most influential work of "world-systems analysis," *The Modern World System* (1974–89). In confidence, however, less ambitious readers can begin with *The Essential Wallerstein* (2000), a compilation Wallerstein chose and introduced himself.

14. Preceding and underpinning Wallerstein is the firsthand opinion of Colonel Józef Piłsudski, the liberator of Poland, who declared that "the state . . . makes the nation and not the nation the state" (qtd. in Hobsbawm 44–45).

15. Gilroy's objections to the "ethnocentric bias" of first-wave British cultural studies are lodged at length in *"There Ain't No Black in the Union Jack": The Cultural Politics of Race and Nation* (1987), a book produced in the wings of the new-model, Stuart Hall–directed Birmingham School.

16. See, for example, Ifeoma Nwankwo's *Black Cosmopolitanism: Racial Consciousness and Transnational Identity in the Nineteenth-Century Americas* (2005), which examines "the Atlantic power structures' obsession with preventing the blossoming" of black cosmopolitanism but divorces those structures from the state (10); and Anita Patterson's *Race, American Literature, and Transnational Modernism* (2008), which closely reads the opposition of black modernist poetics to a "racial nationalism" cordoned off from racial statism (239).

17. The 1,884-page James Baldwin file now freely available through the FBI was first extracted by literary journalist James Campbell, the plaintiff in the landmark FOIA case *James Campbell v. U.S. Department of Justice*. My debt to Campbell runs deeper than this file and this case, however, and also involves his moving account of Baldwin's war with the FBI in *Syncopations: Beats, New Yorkers, and Writers in the Dark* (2008).

18. These New York police translators kept the faith at least until 1969. In October of that year, a language specialist at the Manhattan FBI office rendered another Baldwin interview from Turkish into English, this one a piece in *Milliyet*, an Istanbul daily, commenting on Baldwin's feast-or-famine work habits: "There are times when he writes continuously for 24 hours without food and drink. Under such circumstances, he does not even notice if you shout at him or hit him on the shoulder. Afterwards, he lies down and sleeps. Moreover, he is in a sound sleep for 48 hours. If you are able to awaken him, how fortunate you are" (United States, Federal, Baldwin, 23 Dec. 1969).

19. FBI author files remind us that with or without access to passport records and the SIS, the Bureau's domestic resources sometimes circulated foreign tales. The dossier of black Beat Bob Kaufman, for example, a member of the merchant marine before becoming "*Rimbaud Noir*" to the French, reflects the treachery of several U.S.-based informants "of known reliability" with knowledge of his seagoing life (United States, Federal, Kaufman, 16 Jan. 1950). Political speech uttered beyond U.S. territory was thus recorded in the Bureau's national archive. The U.S.-based papers of the Merchant Marine were raked over to produce a detailed "Sea Service Record" for Kaufman, an index of twenty cruises taken from 1942 to 1948 showing the consistent designation of "Foreign" under a column marked "Nature of Voyage" (31 Jan. 1951).

20. Counterfactual speculation has also surrounded the passport troubles of Linus Pauling, the Nobel Prize–winning chemist prevented from attending a 1952 London conference organized to honor his work. Historian Kathryn S. Olmstead remarks on the possibility that had Pauling "been allowed to attend the conference, he might have seen the X-ray images of DNA taken by British scientists, and he, rather than the Cambridge University team of James Watson and Francis Crick, might have solved the riddle of the double helix" (84). Pauling's immobility in 1952, the annus horribilis of the Bureau's passport crackdown, highlights the fact that passport denials were employed also to punish and miseducate non–African American intellectuals.

21. The question of exactly which two years found William Gardner Smith without a U.S. passport remains unsettled. The evidence of his FBI file includes a 1951 refusal notice but is otherwise ambiguous. Literary biographer Leroy S. Hodges Jr. insists on a two-year length but quotes a 1964 Smith letter protesting that "they took my passport away from me once, and they might do it again if I returned [to the United States]" (qtd. in Hodges 109). Given the documented renewal of Smith's passport in September 1953 (Hodges 109), 1951–53 seems the likeliest solution to the mystery.

22. With his self-involved liaison with the State Department and his inclusion in Richard Crossman's *The God That Failed* (1949), the CIA's preferred anticommunist anthology, Richard Wright may seem an exceptional literary presence on the musical/state-exported side of this Cold War dialectic. Yet as Frances Stonor Saunders notes, the CIA-funded anticommunist culture lobby quickly distrusted Wright. According to philosopher Sidney Hook, Wright became a personal, subpolitical anti-Stalinist, an unreliable enemy of the Soviet enemy "flattered by the use which Sartre makes of him as a kind of club against American culture analogous to the use which the Communists make of Robeson" (qtd. in Saunders 69). Wright was "the only member of *The God That Failed* group to lose his membership [in] that group of apostles" and to be monitored by the CIA as well as the FBI (69). On balance, he belongs on the literary/state-badgered side of the fence.

23. Michael Hanchard's crisp distinction between "state memory," vertically organized and nationally engrossed, and "black memory," its horizontal "archaeological deposits strewn across several time zones and territories," is thus a candidate for historical deconstruction (46).

Part Five/Thesis Five
Consciousness of FBI Ghostreading Fills a Deep and Characteristic Vein of African American Literature

1. According to a well-sourced section of Hazel Rowley's biography, Richard Wright "was conscious of being followed by the FBI" soon after the creation of his FBI file (276). Rowley notes that Naomi Replansky, one of Wright's extramarital lovers in Brooklyn, was interviewed during the course of their 1943–44 affair by FBI agents eager to learn if she too was married. This voyeuristic snooping incensed Wright, and probably helped to inspire his poem "The FB Eye Blues." Replansky went on to publish an anxious verse tribute to Wright titled "Even the Walls Have Ears," this short-lived couple reunited in their joint composition of Bureau love poetry (276).

2. An odd remake of "The FB Eye Blues" arrived with Blossom Dearie's 1973 recording of "I'm Shadowing You," a song the pip-squeak jazz singer–pianist cowrote with

"Moon River" lyricist Johnny Mercer. "Happy as can be, / Just you, J. Edgar Hoover, and me," went the tag line of one verse, Wright's bizarre love triangle (speaker, "baby," and FBI) twisted for smiles. It is just possible that Wright heard Dearie sing other songs in Paris twenty years earlier, and that Dearie there absorbed some of the spy stories of the Café Tournon. A white bebopper born in upstate New York, she performed with several African American musicians in the French capital from 1952 to 1956.

3. The poem is unsung in part because it has not been easy to locate. The most accessible version can be found in the *Richard Wright Reader* (edited by Ellen Wright and Michel Fabre, 1978), which claims the text as a Wright original and attributes its initial printing to a shadowy bootlegged pamphlet: "'The FB Eye Blues' originally was published as an unauthorized leaflet in New York, ca. 1949" (242). Thanks to the outer reaches of the Internet, I acquired what appears to be an equally unauthorized reprinting of the 1949 original: a single-sided sheet (22 x 28 centimeters) folded twice to create a four-page booklet, and anonymously published in 1969. The publication history of "The FB Eye Blues" thus seems to have been calculated to evade the F.B. eye.

4. Viktor Shklovsky, the author of the famous quip about *Tristram Shandy* as "the most typical novel in world literature," had secret police blues of his own. In her book *Police Aesthetics: Literature, Film, and the Secret Police in Soviet Times* (2010), Cristina Vatulescu observes that this Russian Formalist "had firsthand knowledge of the methods of the Soviet secret police, having undergone a number of interrogations" (162). Shklovsky's foundational concept of aesthetic estrangement, or *ostranenie*, she argues, came to reflect the political estrangement practiced by the Cheka, the Bolshevik state security force (161–86).

5. Baraka is quoted to this suspicious effect in Natalie Robins's book *Alien Ink*: "Addison Gayle, who's a black literary critic, stopped short of saying that the FBI had actually murdered Wright. But I don't see any reason to rule that out" (287).

6. It is worth noting that Robins derives her account of the FBI's preference for modernism above social realism from a number of the agency's literary victims. Howard Fast, the blacklisted author of *Spartacus* (1951), is quoted in Robins's *Alien Ink* insisting that "[t]he terrible thing the FBI did was to destroy social writing in America. . . . The whole great American tradition of social commentary that produced all of our great writers, right up to World War II and the few years after World War II, this is over" (399). On this narrow score, however, FBI deputy director and Hoover loyalist Cartha De-Loach, also quoted by Robins, has the better part of the argument: "I think it's absolutely false to say that the FBI destroyed social writing in America. . . . Because you do have social writing today. You have many individuals who are responsible for social writing" (399). Fast and Robins's thesis is essentially restated by Claire Culleton in *Joyce and the G-Men: J. Edgar Hoover's Manipulation of Modernism* (2004).

7. See, for substantiating example, Tyrus Miller's *Late Modernism: Politics, Fiction, and the Arts between the World Wars* (1999), which depicts an unseasonably age-conscious Anglo-American late modernism flourishing in the late 1920s and 1930s, but visibly fading in the 1940s.

8. In *The War on Words: Slavery, Race, and Free Speech in American Literature* (2010), Michael T. Gilmore takes Williams's notion of blackballing and runs. Nineteenth-century American race writing, Gilmore argues, was touched by "the perseverance of the censor's presence" on either side of the black-white divide and of the historical fracture of the Civil War (1).

9. If not otherwise mentioned here, the basis of my claim that these writers were questioned by self-identified Bureau agents can be located in their personal FBI files. The other writers listed speak of FBI grilling in public statements of their own. James Baldwin portrays interrogation (and virtual rape) at the hands of racist G-Men in *The Devil Finds Work* (1976). Nikki Giovanni describes a knock on the door from "one white agent [and] one black" (l. 2) in "I Laughed When I Wrote It (Don't You Think It's Funny?)" (1972), a poem she claims is both comical and true. Audre Lorde depicts a similar home visit in her autobiographical text *Zami* (1982), while Sonia Sanchez has spoken about the educational benefits of an FBI interview in several forums (see in particular pages 115–16 of the collection *Conversations with Sonia Sanchez*). All three of these women's literary responses to FBI attention are addressed in part 5.

10. Again, if not otherwise mentioned here, the basis of my claim that these writers assumed they were FBI suspects can be located in their personal Bureau files. For the rest, a 1967 poem by Johari Amini (Jewel Lattimore), "Upon Being Black One Friday in July," dramatizes her consciousness of "STRICT SURVEILLANCE" by several echelons of the state police (l. 49); Gwendolyn Brooks's authorized biographer George E. Kent suggests that she learned of her naming in privileged FBI investigations through her Chicago coworker Margaret Burroughs (also an FBI "filee") (Kent 55); Sam Greenlee has boasted about his supposed notoriety at the FBI training academy ("Sam Greenlee"); James Weldon Johnson wrote of his reflection (and that of many of his New Negro friends) in the early spy-criticism of the FBI ("Report"); Paule Marshall, Ishmael Reed, and A. B. Spellman received word of their place on FBI enemies lists through Natalie Robins's *Alien Ink*, if not before; and Gloria Naylor casts the FBI as a personal enemy and devious NSA collaborator in *1996*.

11. Timothy Melley's book (an inspiring influence on this one) indeed places Ishmael Reed and John A. Williams on an initial roll call of "influential literary figures" for whom "the covert state has become a central object of reflection and . . . a major stimulus of postmodern epistemological skepticism" (10). Neither African American skeptic is discussed further for more than a sentence, however, and Afro-modernism's previous interest in a covert sphere centered on the FBI goes unmentioned.

12. For this riff on a persecuted writer's "winning by losing," I rely on sociologist Pierre Bourdieu's essay "The Field of Cultural Production, or: The Economic World Reversed" (1983): "[A]t least in the most perfectly autonomous sector of the field of cultural production, . . . the economy of practices is based, as in a generalized game of 'loser wins,' on a systematic inversion of the fundamental principles of all ordinary economies," including "that of power (it condemns honours and temporal greatness)" (39). In the Afro-modernist sector of the cultural field, the ordinary economy of power was partly steered by the honor seekers of the FBI.

13. On the goodness of "BaddDDD"-ness, a reference to Melvin Van Peebles's independent film *Sweet Sweetback's Baadasssss Song* (1971) and especially to Sonia Sanchez's ghostread poetry in *We a BaddDDD People* (1970), see endnote 22 to the introduction.

14. My account of this and two other November 1919 pieces in the *Negro World* is beholden to Robert Adger Bowen's careful surveillance of black radical journalism. The *Negro World* is known to have been published between August 1918 and October 1933, but microfilm versions of the journal begin with issues of the 1920s, and even the archive of Robert A. Hill's Marcus Garvey and Universal Negro Improvement Association Papers Project does not hold the relevant 1919 copies. (My thanks to Professor Hill and

to UCLA graduate researcher Danny Franken for their investigations in this archive on my behalf.) I thus rely on Bowen's reproduction of *Negro World* items in "The Re-Action to Date of the Negro Press to the Attorney General's Report" (1919), a seven-page document now held in the Bowen papers at Clemson University. The accuracy of Bowen's quotations elsewhere in his love-hate battle with the New Negro press gives me confidence in this case—and my need of Bowen's help to reconstruct the writings of his Garveyite suspects highlights, once again, the strangely interdependent histories of early Bureau ghostreading and early Harlem Renaissance journalism.

15. A black magazine era preceded a black "program era," in fact, but with the latter not quite the sort memorably appreciated by literary historian Mark McGurl. The growth of university creative writing programs was not, I suspect, the central transformation affecting postwar African American literature—a literature that McGurl freshly approaches in several individual cases, from his discovery of the proudly fictional "meta–slave narrative" to his discussion of the ambivalent politics of education in Toni Morrison's *Beloved* (1987). This is not to say that recent African American texts are exotically innocent of the influence of mass higher education, or that studying this influence will not illuminate many of them. It is instead to suggest that the advent of black studies, rather the arrival of the creative writing program, has served as the key innovation focalizing postwar African American literature's relation to the U.S. university.

16. As Barbara Foley notes, "Ellison scribbled 'Mantan Moreland' in place of 'Stepin-fetchit,'" thus preferring an African American film actor more closely tied to detective pictures (*Wrestling* 391).

17. Foley's interpretation makes greater sense in the context of her discovery that Ellison may have published an anti-FBI letter in the Communist Party–affiliated *People's Daily World* two years after *Invisible Man* (1952). Warning workers against Bureau agents, this letter to the editor insists that "[t]hese rattlesnakes are like Anyface. . . . Unless you're prepared to stool on your Union, your friends, or anyone else they decide you shall finger, they're deadly enough to spit out their fangs at your kids" (qtd. in Foley, *Wrestling* 67). Foley is an excellent literary historian, but I suspect that the letter, "noted only in [Ellison's] FBI file," is a slippery counterliterary forgery or a simple FBI attribution error (67). Its rhetoric is radically overheated in a high-Depression style the Ellison of the 1950s had worked hard to bury.

18. Ellen Wright, Wright's second wife and literary agent, liked this "Quel Chapeau" incident in *Island of Hallucination* well enough to approve its posthumous publication in Herbert Hill's anthology *Soon, One Morning: New Writing by American Negroes, 1940–1962* (1963).

19. The best of these prior analyses of *Island of Hallucination* are by James Campbell ("The Island Affair"), Rebecca Ruquist, and Richard Gibson, the aging VIP of the Gibson Affair ("Richard Wright's").

20. Wright was a relatively uncooperative and short-lived beneficiary of Congress for Cultural Freedom funding, however; see note 22 to part 4.

21. With just a little irony, Himes's citation of Simone de Beauvoir in correction of Inspector Wright overlooks her citation of Wright in *The Second Sex* (1949). During her long consideration of "lived experience," Beauvoir briefly wheels in *Black Boy* to evoke the similar existential difficulties of presumably white women and "the blacks who came to France from Africa" (736–37). In other words, Beauvoir uses Wright to make much the same intersectional point that Himes uses Beauvoir to charge Wright with ignoring.

22. Baldwin's later writing on the FBI hints that *The Blood Counters* might really have been the explosive device Clarence Jones promised. In *The Devil Finds Work* (1976), a long essay on black film going and Hollywood's racial imagination, Baldwin describes his first encounter with the Bureau outside a movie theater showing G-Man pictures. A requisite two-agent team interviewed him in Woodstock, New York, in 1945, he narrates, their interest then leaving him without "the remotest notion as to why they had come looking for me" (547). "Much later in my life," he continues, "I knew very well what I had done to attract their attention, and intended, simply, to keep on keeping on. In any case, once you *have* come to the attention of the FBI, they keep a friendly file on you, and your family, and your friends" (547; emphasis in original). The G-Men's attention was hardly friendly in 1945, however: "They conveyed, very vividly, what they would do to me if I did not tell the truth—what they would do to smart niggers like me. (I was a smart nigger because I worked, part-time, as an artist's model, and lived in an artist's colony, and had a typewriter in my shack.) My ass would be in a sling—this was among the gentler warnings. They frightened me, and they humiliated me—it was like being spat on, or pissed on, or gang-raped—but they made me hate them, too, with a hatred like hot ice, and all I knew, simply, was that, if I could figure what they wanted, nothing could induce me to give it to them" (547). With eloquent intemperance, Baldwin recounts his FBI trial in terms commonly used in Black Arts anti-Hoover poems. The Bureau's practical white rape is countered by black hate and repaired through a pledge to out-write rather than inform.

23. Richard Gibson in fact wrote a poorly reviewed race novel called *A Mirror for Magistrates* (1958), its London place of publication and allusive Tudor-revival title the only clear ties to foreign service.

24. R. Clifton Spargo's contribution to *The Oxford Handbook of the Elegy* (2010) suggests that the roots of the Hoover Poem may be historically deep as well as politically local: "Anti-elegy designates not so much a new form of poetry or a break with the tradition of elegy as a tendency within elegiac poetry to resist consolation by setting a contemporary mourner against past cultural and poetical conventions—a tendency that becomes fully pronounced by the middle of the twentieth century, extending thereafter into the late twentieth and now into the early twenty-first century" (415).

25. Gerald Early, my guide and colleague at Washington University, points out that the black Informer Poem is informed by the contemporaneous genre of the black Informer Film. Highlights of this genre begin with Jules Dassin's *Up Tight!* (1968), an all-black remake of John Ford's *The Informer* (1935) transferring the action from Dublin to Cleveland; and *The Lost Man* (1968), a Sidney Poitier vehicle remaking the James Mason film *Odd Man Out* (1947). Blaxploitation films with at least a subtheme of informing include Gordon Parks's iconic *Super Fly* (1972) and the foundational independent feature *Sweet Sweetback's Baadasssss Song* (1971) directed by Melvin Van Peebles, also the author of *A Bear for the FBI* (1968). Along related lines, Early notes that "[i]n the original Broadway cast production of *Jesus Christ Superstar*, Ben Vereen played the role of Judas. When he became ill, Carl Anderson, also black, played the role of the most infamous informer in history. Blacks at the time, as I remember, noted this. Also, the role, in subsequent productions, has tended to go to blacks. Interesting. The show opened on Broadway in 1971, during the very era of which you write" (Early).

26. For their part, African American men producing self-consciously post-Hoover prose—and there have been several—have tended to cluster in the subgenre of political

crime fiction. See, for example, Walter Mosley's Easy Rawlings mystery *A Red Death* (1991), in which a black detective of the 1950s is invited to become an FBI informer; and Jake Lamar's self-advertised " 'militant' mystery" *If 6 Were 9* (2001), in which a black revolutionary–turned–conservative college professor is haunted by a lover's murder and the bloodstained ghosts of COINTELPRO.

Works Cited

"18 USC § 2385—Advocating Overthrow of Government." [U.S. Alien Registration Act of 1940.] *Onecle*. Web. 29 Dec. 2013. http://law.onecle.com/uscode/18/2385.html.

"2009 Rosemary Award for Worst FOIA Performance Goes to FBI." *National Security Archive*. 13 Mar. 2009. Web. 27 Apr. 2014. http://www.gwu/~nsarchiv/news/20090313 /index. htm.

Ackerman, Kenneth D. "Five Myths about J. Edgar Hoover." *Washington Post* 7 Nov. 2011. Web. 27 Apr. 2014. www.washingtonpost/opinions/five-myths-about-j-edgar -hoover/2011/11/07.

——. *Young J. Edgar: Hoover, the Red Scare, and the Assault on Civil Liberties*. New York: Carroll and Graf, 2007.

Adler, Bill, ed. *Kids' Letters to the F.B.I.* Illus. Arnold Roth. Englewood Cliffs, NJ: Prentice-Hall, 1966.

Agamben, Giorgio. *State of Exception*. 2003. Trans. Kevin Attell. Chicago: U of Chicago P, 2005.

Ai. *The Collected Poems of Ai*. Intro. Yusef Komunyakaa. New York: Norton, 2013.

——. "Hoover, J. Edgar." 1993. *The Collected Poems of Ai*. 190–93.

——. "Hoover Trismegistus." 1993. *The Collected Poems of Ai*. 193–96.

Alexander, Jack. "The Director—I." *New Yorker* 25 Sept. 1937: 20–25.

——. "The Director—II." *New Yorker* 2 Oct. 1937: 21–26.

——. "The Director—III." *New Yorker* 9 Oct. 1937: 22–27.

Alexander, Michelle. *The New Jim Crow: Mass Incarceration in the Age of Colorblindness*. New York: New Press, 2010.

Alhamisi, Ahmed, and Harun Kofi Wangara, eds. *Black Arts: An Anthology of Black Creations*. Detroit: Black Arts Publications, 1969.

Althusser, Louis. "Ideology and Ideological State Apparatuses (Notes towards an Investigation)." 1969. *Lenin and Philosophy and Other Essays*. Trans. Ben Brewster. New York: Monthly Review, 1971.

Amini, Johari (Jewel Lattimore). "Upon Being Black One Friday in July." 1967. *Understanding the New Black Poetry: Black Speech and Black Music as Poetic References*. Ed. Stephen Henderson. New York: William Morrow, 1973. 354–55.

"A. Mitchell Palmer." *Messenger* 2.7 (Aug. 1920): 75.

Anderson, Benedict. *Imagined Communities: Reflections on the Origin and Spread of Nationalism*. 1983. New York: Verso, 1991.

Anderson, Dale. *The FBI and Civil Rights*. Broomall, PA: Mason Crest, 2010.

Andrew, Christopher, and Vasili Mitrokhin. *The Sword and the Shield: The Mitrokhin Archive and the Secret History of the KGB*. New York: Basic Books, 1999.

Angleton, James Jesus. "Caresse Primordiale." 1939. Holzman, *James Jesus Angleton* 7–8.

——. Letter to e. e. and Marion Cummings. 1943. Holzman, *James Jesus Angleton* 29.

Apter, Emily. *Against World Literature: On the Politics of Untranslatability*. New York: Verso, 2013.

Archer, John Michael. *Sovereignty and Intelligence: Spying and Court Culture in the English Renaissance*. Stanford: Stanford UP, 1993.

Ash, Stephen V. *A Year in the South: Four Lives in 1865*. New York: Macmillan, 2002.

" 'Attempt to Terrorize Has Failed,' Says Palmer." *Washington Post* 4 June 1919: 1.

"Auxiliary Unit Provides Flag Codes." *Palm Beach Post* 4 July 1964: 4.

Baldwin, James. *The Devil Finds Work*. 1976. *James Baldwin: Collected Essays*. New York: Library of America, 1998. 477–572.

———. *No Name in the Street*. 1972. *James Baldwin: Collected Essays*. New York: Library of America, 1998. 349–475.

———. "An Open Letter to My Sister, Angela Y. Davis." *If They Come in the Morning: Voices of Resistance*. Ed. Angela Y. Davis and Bettina Aptheker. New York: Signet, 1971. 19–23.

Baldwin, Roger N. Memo on the Bureau of Investigation. 1924. Cunningham, *There's Something Happening Here* 20.

Balibar, Étienne. "World Borders, Political Borders." Trans. Erin M. Williams. *PMLA* 117.1 (Jan. 2002): 1–78.

Baraka, Amiri. *The Autobiography of LeRoi Jones/Amiri Baraka*. 1984. Chicago: Lawrence Hill, 1997.

———. "Black Art." 1966. *Black Magic: Collected Poetry, 1961–1967*. 116–17.

———. "The Black Arts Movement." 1994. *The LeRoi Jones/Amiri Baraka Reader*. Ed. William J. Harris. New York: Basic Books, 1999. 495–505.

———. *Black Magic: Collected Poetry, 1961–1967*. New York: Bobbs Merrill, 1969.

———. "Black People!" 1967. *Black Magic: Collected Poetry, 1961–1967*. 225.

———. "Three Movements and a Coda." 1963–65. *Black Magic: Collected Poetry, 1961–1967*. 103–4.

———. "The Wailer." Larry Neal, *Visions of a Liberated Future: Black Arts Movement Writings*. Ed. Michael Schwartz. New York: Thunder's Mouth, 1989. ix–xix.

Batvinis, Raymond J. *The Origins of FBI Counterintelligence*. Lawrence: UP of Kansas, 2007.

Baudelaire, Charles. "Le Crépuscule du Soir." 1857. Trans. David Paul. *Flowers of Evil: A Selection*. Ed. Marthiel and Jackson Matthews. New York: New Directions, 1958. 97–99.

Beauvoir, Simone de. *The Second Sex*. 1949. Trans. Constance Borde and Sheila Malovany-Chevallier. New York: Vintage, 2011.

Beckles, Colin A. "Black Bookstores, Black Power, and the F.B.I.: The Case of Drum and Spear." *Western Journal of Black Studies* 20.2 (1996): 63–71.

Bell, Bernard W. *The Afro-American Novel and Its Tradition*. Amherst: U of Massachusetts P, 1987.

Benét, William Rose, and Norman Holmes Pearson. Preface. *The Oxford Anthology of American Literature*. Ed. Benét and Pearson. Vol. 1. New York: Oxford UP, 1938. v–vi.

Benston, Kimberly W. *Performing Blackness: Enactments of African-American Modernism*. New York: Routledge, 2000.

Bergman, Lowell, and David Weir. "Revolution on Ice: How the Black Panthers Lost the FBI's War of Dirty Tricks." *Rolling Stone* 9 Sept. 1976: 41–49.

Best, Stephen, and Sharon Marcus. "Surface Reading: An Introduction." *Representations* 108.1 (fall 2009): 1–21.

Beverly, William. *On the Lam: Narratives of Flight in J. Edgar Hoover's America.* Jackson: UP of Mississippi, 2003.

"Black Panther Coloring Book." 1969. Archive.org. Web. 18 Apr. 2014. https://archive .org/details/BlackPantherColoringBook.

Bloom, Joshua, and Waldo E. Martin Jr. *Black against Empire: The History and Politics of the Black Panther Party.* Berkeley: U of California P, 2013.

Booker, Simeon. "The Negro in the FBI—J. Edgar Hoover." *Ebony* Sept. 1962: 29–34.

Bourdieu, Pierre. "The Field of Cultural Production, or: The Economic World Reversed." 1983. Trans. Richard Nice. *The Field of Cultural Production: Essays on Art and Literature.* Ed. Randal Johnson. New York: Columbia UP, 1993. 29–73.

Bowen, Robert Adger. "The Barrier." N.d. Robert Adger Bowen Papers, Box 4, Folder 52.

———. "Bureau of Translations and Radical Publications." 1961. Robert Adger Bowen Papers, Box 10, Folder 87.

———. "A Case of Conjur." *Appleton's Booklover's Magazine* 6 (Oct. 1905): 468–76.

———. "The Devoté." N.d. [circa 1950–65]. Robert Adger Bowen Papers, Box 3, Folder 28.

———. "The Giver." N.d. [circa 1950–65]. Robert Adger Bowen Papers, Box 3, Folder 28.

———. Marginalia on personal copy of Don Whitehead, *The FBI Story* (New York: Random House, 1956). Robert Adger Bowen Papers, Box 10a.

———. "Memoirs of a G-Man." *Greenville News* (Greenville, South Carolina). Serialized weekly 12 May to 21 July 1940. Robert Adger Bowen Papers, Box 1, Folder 9.

———. "Miss Ang'la: A Story." *Age-Herald* (Birmingham, Alabama). Serialized weekly 20 Oct. to 10 Nov. 1889. Robert Adger Bowen Papers, Box 2, Folder 18.

———. "Miss Em'ly: A Story in Dialect." *Cornell Magazine* 5 (Oct. 1892): 8–18.

———. "Negro Songs as Sung at Protracted Revival Meetings in South Carolina near the Rivoli Plantation." Robert Adger Bowen Papers, Box 1, Folder 9.

———. Notes on an undated newspaper article, "Federal Bureau of Investigation also Subject to Political Pressures." Robert Adger Bowen Papers, Box 10, Folder 80.

———. "Press/Book Reviews of *Uncharted Seas*, circa 1913." Robert Adger Bowen Papers, Box 12, Folder 104.

———. "The Radical Press in New York City." Robert Adger Bowen Papers, Box 10, Folder 80.

———. "Radicalism and Sedition among the Negroes as Reflected in Their Publications." Draft of 2 July 1919. Robert Adger Bowen Papers, Box 10, Folder 86.

———. "The Re-Action to Date of the Negro Press to the Attorney General's Report." 1919. Robert Adger Bowen Papers, Box 10, Folder 86.

———. "Robert Adger Bowen Anthology." N.d. Robert Adger Bowen Papers, Box 9, Folder 73.

———. Robert Adger Bowen Papers (MS 119). Special Collections Library, Clemson University Libraries, Clemson, SC.

———. Typescript copy of "The Tropics in New York" by Claude McKay. Robert Adger Bowen Papers, Box 9, Folder 79.

Boyle, Kay. Letter to Richard Wright. 5 Oct. 1956. Richard Wright Papers. James Weldon Johnson Manuscripts, Yale Collection of American Literature, Beinecke Rare Book and Manuscript Library, Yale University, New Haven, CT.

Braddock, Jeremy, and Jonathan P. Eburne. Introduction. Braddock and Eburne, *Paris, Capital of the Black Atlantic: Literature, Modernity, and Diaspora* 1–14.

Braddock, Jeremy, and Jonathan P. Eburne, eds. *Paris, Capital of the Black Atlantic: Literature, Modernity, and Diaspora.* Baltimore: Johns Hopkins UP, 2013.

Braudel, Fernand. *Civilization and Capitalism, 15th–18th Century.* Vol. 2. *The Wheels of Commerce.* 1979. Trans. Sian Reynolds. New York: Harper and Row, 1982.

———. "History and the Social Sciences: The *Longue Durée.*" 1958. Trans. Sarah Matthews. *On History.* Chicago: U of Chicago P, 1980. 25–54.

Brickhouse, Anna. "Scholarship and the State: Robert Greenhow and Transnational American Studies, 1848/2008." *American Literary History* 20.4 (winter 2008): 695–722.

Britt, George. Interview with J. Edgar Hoover. *Akron Free Press* 24 Mar. 1926. Records of the Federal Bureau of Investigation (RG 65), Director's Office Records and Memorabilia, J. Edgar Hoover's Scrapbooks, Box 1, Apr. to Dec. 1920 folder. U.S. National Archives and Records Administration, College Park, MD.

Brooks, Cleanth. "Keats's Sylvan Historicism." *The Well Wrought Urn.* 151–66.

———. "The Language of Paradox." *The Well Wrought Urn.* 3–21.

———. *Modern Poetry and the Tradition.* Chapel Hill: U of North Carolina P, 1939.

———. *The Well Wrought Urn: Studies in the Structure of Poetry.* New York: Harcourt, Brace, and World, 1947.

Brown, Bill. Introduction. William C. Sullivan, with Bill Brown. *The Bureau: My Thirty Years in Hoover's FBI.* New York: W. W. Norton, 1979. 9–10.

Brown, Julia Clarice. *I Testify: My Years as an F.B.I. Undercover Agent.* Boston: Western Islands, 1966.

"The Bully Bolsheviki." Circa 1920. Records of the Federal Bureau of Investigation (RG 65), Director's Office Records and Memorabilia, J. Edgar Hoover's Scrapbooks, Box 1, Apr. to Dec. 1920 folder. U.S. National Archives and Records Administration, College Park, MD.

Burrough, Bryan. *Public Enemies: America's Greatest Crime Wave and the Birth of the FBI, 1933–34.* New York: Penguin, 2005.

Butler, Judith. *Bodies That Matter: On the Discursive Limits of "Sex."* 1993. New York: Routledge, 2011.

Campbell, James. *Exiled in Paris: Richard Wright, James Baldwin, Samuel Beckett, and Others on the Left Bank.* 1995. Berkeley: U of California P, 2003.

———. "The Island Affair." *Guardian* 7 Jan. 2006. guardian.co.uk. Web. 24 June 2008. http://books.guardian.co.uk/departments/classics/story/0,1680833,00.html.

———. *Syncopations: Beats, New Yorkers, and Writers in the Dark.* Berkeley: U of California P, 2008.

Campbell, James T. *Middle Passages: African American Journeys to Africa, 1787–2005.* New York: Penguin, 2006.

Carlston, Erin G. *Double Agents: Espionage, Literature, and Liminal Citizens.* New York: Columbia UP, 2013.

———. "Modern Literature under Surveillance: American Writers, State Espionage, and the Cultural Cold War." *American Literary History* 22.3 (fall 2010): 615–25.

Carson, Clayborne. *Malcolm X: The FBI File.* Ed. David Gallen. New York: Carroll and Graf, 1991.

Caute, David. *The Dancer Defects: The Struggle for Cultural Supremacy during the Cold War.* New York: Oxford UP, 2003.

──. *The Great Fear: The Anti-Communist Purge under Truman and Eisenhower*. New York: Simon and Schuster, 1978.

Chafee, Zechariah, Jr. *Free Speech in the United States*. Cambridge: Harvard UP, 1941.

Charles, Douglas M. *The FBI's Obscene File: J. Edgar Hoover and the Bureau's Crusade against Smut*. Lawrence: UP of Kansas, 2012.

Churchill, Ward, and Jim Vander Wall. *The COINTELPRO Papers: Documents from the FBI's Secret Wars against Dissent in the United States*. 1990. Cambridge: South End, 2002.

Clapp, Jeffrey. "Richard Wright and the Police." *Post45* 12 Sept. 2011: 1–17. Web. 30 Nov. 2012. https://post45.research.yale.edu/archives/926.

Clarke, Cheryl. *"After Mecca": Women Poets and the Black Arts Movement*. New Brunswick: Rutgers UP, 2005.

Coates, Tim, ed. *Marilyn Monroe: The FBI Files*. N.p.: Tim Coates Books, 2003.

Collins, Frederick L. *The FBI in Peace and War*. New York: G. P. Putnam's Sons, 1943.

Comfort, Mildred Houghton. *J. Edgar Hoover: Modern Knight Errant*. Minneapolis: T. S. Denison, 1959.

Cook, Fred J. *The FBI Nobody Knows*. New York: Macmillan, 1964.

Coulter, Ann. "Kwanzaa: Holiday from the FBI." Human Events.com 2 Jan. 2008. Web. 26 May 2009. http://www.humanevents.com/article.php?id=24253.

Crossman, Richard, ed. *The God That Failed*. New York: Harper and Brothers, 1949.

Cruse, Harold. *The Crisis of the Negro Intellectual*. New York: William Morrow, 1967.

Culleton, Claire A. "Extorting Henry Holt and Co.: J. Edgar Hoover and the Publishing Industry." Culleton and Leick, *Modernism* 237–52.

──. *Joyce and the G-Men: J. Edgar Hoover's Manipulation of Modernism*. New York: Palgrave Macmillan, 2004.

Culleton, Claire A., and Karen Leick. "Introduction: Silence, Acquiescence, and Dread." Culleton and Leick, *Modernism* 2–19.

──. eds. *Modernism on File: Writers, Artists, and the FBI, 1920–1950*. New York: Palgrave, 2008.

Cunningham, David. *There's Something Happening Here: The New Left, the Klan, and FBI Counterintelligence*. Berkeley: U of California P, 2004.

Davies, Carole Boyce. *Left of Karl Marx: The Political Life of Black Communist Claudia Jones*. Durham: Duke UP, 2007.

Davis, Frank Marshall. *Black Moods: Collected Poems*. Ed. John Edgar Tidwell. Urbana: U of Illinois P, 2002.

Dearie, Blossom. "I'm Shadowing You." By Blossom Dearie and Johnny Mercer. *Blossom Dearie Sings*. Daffodil, 1973. LP.

DeLillo, Don. *White Noise*. 1985. New York: Penguin, 1999.

DeLoach, Cartha D. ["Deke"]. *Hoover's FBI: The Inside Story by Hoover's Trusted Lieutenant*. Washington, DC: Regnery, 1995.

"Deportation." *Messenger* 2.3 (Mar. 1920): 5.

Derrida, Jacques. *Archive Fever: A Freudian Impression*. 1995. Trans. Eric Prenowitz. Chicago: U of Chicago P, 1998.

Diffee, Christopher. "Sex and the City: The White Slavery Scare and Social Governance in the Progressive Era." *American Quarterly* 57.2 (June 2005): 411–37.

Dimock, Wai Chee. *Through Other Continents: American Literature across Deep Time*. Princeton: Princeton UP, 2006.

Dimock, Wai Chee, and Lawrence Buell, ed. *Shades of the Planet: American Literature as World Literature*. Princeton: Princeton UP, 2007.

Dittmer, John. *Local People: The Struggle for Civil Rights in Mississippi*. Urbana: U of Illinois P, 1994.

Donner, Frank J. *The Age of Surveillance: The Aims and Methods of America's Political Intelligence System*. New York: Vintage, 1981.

Du Bois, W.E.B. *Black Reconstruction in America, 1860–1880*. 1935. New York: Atheneum, 1992.

———. "Causes of Discontent." *New York Sun* 12 Oct. 1919: 5, 7.

———. *Dark Princess*. 1929. Jackson: UP of Mississippi, 1995.

———. *Dusk of Dawn: An Essay toward an Autobiography of a Race Concept*. 1940. *W.E.B. Du Bois: Writings*. New York: Library of America, 1986. 549–802.

———. "Returning Soldiers." *Crisis* 18 (May 1919): 13.

Dudziak, Mary L. *Cold War Civil Rights: Race and the Image of American Democracy*. Princeton: Princeton UP, 2000.

Dulles, Allen. *The Craft of Intelligence*. New York: Harper and Row, 1963.

Dumm, Thomas L. "The Trial of J. Edgar Hoover." *Secret Agents: The Rosenberg Case, McCarthyism, and Fifties America*. Ed. Marjorie Garber and Rebecca L. Walkowitz. New York: Routledge, 1995. 77–92.

Dunbar, Paul Laurence. "We Wear the Mask." 1896. *The Collected Poetry of Paul Laurence Dunbar*. Ed. Joanne M. Braxton. Charlottesville: UP of Virginia, 1993.

Durem, Ray. "Award." 1964. *The Black Poets*. Ed. Dudley Randall. New York: Bantam, 1971. 164.

Early, Gerald. "Re: Informer Films." Message to William J. Maxwell. 17 Apr. 2011. E-mail.

Editors of *Look*. *The Story of the FBI: The Official Picture History of the Federal Bureau of Investigation*. New York: E. P. Dutton, 1954.

Edwards, Brent Hayes. "Diaspora." *Keywords for American Cultural Studies*. Ed. Bruce Burgett and Glenn Hendler. New York: New York UP, 2007. 81–84.

———. *The Practice of Diaspora: Literature, Translation, and the Rise of Black Internationalism*. Cambridge: Harvard UP, 2003.

———. "Three Ways to Translate the Harlem Renaissance." *Temples for Tomorrow: Looking Back at the Harlem Renaissance*. Ed. Geneviève Fabre and Michel Feith. Bloomington: Indiana UP, 2001. 288–313.

———. "The Uses of Diaspora." *Social Text* 19.1 (spring 2001): 45–73.

Eliot, T. S. *The Waste Land*. 1922. *The Complete Poems and Plays, 1909–1950*. New York: Harcourt Brace, 1971. 37–55.

Ellison, Ralph. "Change the Joke and Slip the Yoke." 1958. *The Collected Essays of Ralph Ellison*. 100–12.

———. *The Collected Essays of Ralph Ellison*. Ed. John F. Callahan. New York: Modern Library, 1995.

———. "Editorial." *Negro Quarterly* 1.4 (winter 1943): 300–301.

———. "Homage to Duke Ellington on His Birthday." 1969. *The Collected Essays of Ralph Ellison*. 676–83.

———. *Invisible Man*. 1952. New York: Vintage, 1989.

———. "Richard Wright's Blues." 1945. *The Collected Essays of Ralph Ellison*. 128–44.

——. *Three Days before the Shooting* . . . . Ed. John F. Callahan and Adam Bradley. New York: Modern Library, 2010.

——. "Writings File." Ralph Ellison Papers, Box 145, Folder 13. Manuscript Collection, Library of Congress, Washington, DC.

Ellul, Jacques. *Propaganda: The Formation of Men's Attitudes*. Trans. Konrad Kellen. New York: Vintage, 1973.

Empson, William. *Seven Types of Ambiguity*. 1930. New York: New Directions, 1966.

"Enter the New Negro, a Distinctive Type Recently Created by the Coloured Cabaret Belt in New York." *Vanity Fair* Dec. 1924: 61–62.

Epstein, William H. "Counter-Intelligence: Cold-War Criticism and Eighteenth-Century Studies." *ELH* 57.1 (spring 1990): 63–99.

"Executive Order 2285." [Order requiring American citizens traveling abroad to procure passports, issued 15 Dec. 1915.] *The American Presidency Project*. Web. 21 Apr. 2014. http://www.presidency.ucsb.edu/ws/?pid=75392.

Fabre, Michel. *From Harlem to Paris: Black American Writers in France, 1840–1980*. Urbana: U of Illinois P, 1991.

——. *The Unfinished Quest of Richard Wright*. 2nd ed. Trans. Isabel Barzun. Urbana: U of Illinois P, 1993.

FBI.gov. 2013. Federal Bureau of Investigation. Web. 18 July 2013. http://www.fbi.gov/.

"The FBI Reviews a Book." *Nation* 27 Jan. 1951: 86.

"Federal Flashes." *G-Men* Nov. 1935: 122.

Felt, Mark, and John O'Connor. *A G-Man's Life: The FBI, Being "Deep Throat," and the Struggle for Honor in Washington*. New York: Public Affairs, 2006.

Ferguson, James, and Akhil Gupta. "Spatializing States: Toward an Ethnography of Neoliberal Governmentality." *American Ethnologist* 29.4 (2002): 981–1002.

Ferris, William H. "The Rise and Significance of the Radical Movement in Negro Thought." 1919. Bowen, "The Re-Action to Date of the Negro Press to the Attorney General's Report" 2.

——. "Thanksgiving Sermon." 1919. Bowen, "The Re-Action to Date of the Negro Press to the Attorney General's Report" 2.

Flaubert, Gustave. *Madame Bovary*. 1857. Trans. Geoffrey Wall. New York: Penguin, 2003.

Foerstel, Herbert N. *Surveillance in the Stacks: The FBI's Library Awareness Program*. Contribs. in Political Science 266. New York: Greenwood, 1991.

"FOIA Request Instructions." FBI.gov. Federal Bureau of Investigation. Web. 6 Aug. 2009. http://foia.fbi.gov/foia_instruc.htm.

Foley, Barbara. *Spectres of 1919: Class and Nation in the Making of the New Negro*. Urbana: U of Illinois P, 2003.

——. *Wrestling with the Left: The Making of Ralph Ellison's Invisible Man*. Durham: Duke UP, 2010.

Foucault, Michel. *The Archaeology of Knowledge* and *The Discourse on Language*. 1969, 1971. Trans. A. M. Sheridan Smith. New York: Vintage, 1982.

——. *Discipline and Punish: The Birth of the Prison*. 1975. Trans. Alan Sheridan. New York: Vintage, 1979.

——. *The History of Sexuality. Vol. 1. An Introduction*. Trans. Robert Hurley. New York: Vintage, 1978.

Foley, Barbara. "Truth and Power." 1977. *Power/Knowledge: Selected Interviews and Other Writings, 1972–1977.* Ed. Colin Gordon. Trans. Colin Gordon et al. New York: Pantheon, 1980. 109–33.

Fox, John F., Jr. [Historian, Federal Bureau of Investigation.] Personal interview. 6 Aug. 2012.

"Freedom of Negro Press." *Chicago Defender* 20 Dec. 1941: n.p.

Friedly, Michael, with David Gallen. *Martin Luther King, Jr.: The FBI File.* New York: Carroll and Graf, 1993.

Furioso. 1939–53. Vols. 1–8. New York: Kaus Reprint, 1972.

Gaines, Kevin K. *African Americans in Ghana: Black Expatriates and the Civil Rights Era.* Chapel Hill: U of North Carolina P, 2006.

Garrow, David J. *Bearing the Cross: Martin Luther King, Jr., and the Southern Christian Leadership Conference.* New York: Vintage, 1986.

———. *The FBI and Martin Luther King, Jr.: From "Solo" to Memphis.* New York: W. W. Norton, 1981.

Gates, Henry Louis, Jr., and Nellie Y. McKay, eds. *The Norton Anthology of African American Literature.* 2nd ed. New York: W. W. Norton, 2004.

Gayle, Addison, Jr. *Claude McKay: The Black Poet at War.* Broadside Critics Series 2. Detroit: Broadside, 1972.

———. Introduction. *The Black Aesthetic.* 1971. Ed. Addison Gayle Jr. Garden City, NY: Anchor-Doubleday, 1972. xv–xxiv.

Gellner, Ernest. *Nations and Nationalism.* Ithaca: Cornell UP, 1983.

Gentry, Curt. *J. Edgar Hoover: The Man and the Secrets.* New York: Norton, 1991.

Gerald, Carolyn. Contribution to symposium "The Measure and Meaning of the Sixties: What Lies Ahead for Black Americans?" *Negro Digest* 19.11 (Nov. 1969): 24–29.

Gibson, Donald. *The Politics of Literary Expression: A Study of Major Black Writers.* Westport, CT: Greenwood, 1981.

Gibson, Richard. *A Mirror for Magistrates.* London: Anthony Blond, 1958.

———. "Richard Wright's 'Island of Hallucination' and the 'Gibson Affair.'" *Modern Fiction Studies* 51.4 (winter 2005): 896–920.

Giddens, Anthony. *The Nation-State and Violence.* Berkeley: U of California P, 1985.

Gillespie, Dizzy, with Al Fraser. *To Be, or Not . . . to Bop: Memoirs.* Garden City, NY: Doubleday, 1979.

Gilmore, Michael T. *The War on Words: Slavery, Race, and Free Speech in American Literature.* Chicago: U of Chicago P, 2010.

Gilroy, Paul. *Against Race: Imagining Political Culture beyond the Color Line.* Cambridge: Belknap–Harvard UP, 2000.

———. *The Black Atlantic: Modernity and Double Consciousness.* Cambridge: Harvard UP, 1993.

———. *"There Ain't No Black in the Union Jack": The Cultural Politics of Race and Nation.* 1987. Chicago: U of Chicago P, 1991.

Ginsberg, Allen. "T. S. Eliot Entered My Dreams." *City Lights Journal* 4 (1978): 61–65.

Giovanni, Nikki. *The Collected Poetry of Nikki Giovanni, 1968–1998.* New York: Harper Perennial, 2003.

———. "I Laughed When I Wrote It (Don't You Think It's Funny?)." 1972. *The Collected Poetry of Nikki Giovanni, 1968–1998.* 185–86.

———. "A Short Essay of Affirmation Explaining Why (With Apologies to the Federal Bureau of Investigation)." 1968. *The Collected Poetry of Nikki Giovanni, 1968–1998.* 21–22.

Glass, Loren. "#$%^&*!?: Modernism and Dirty Words." *Modernism/Modernity* 14.2 (2007): 209–23.

Goodrum, Charles A., and Helen W. Dalrymple. *The Library of Congress.* Boulder: Westview Press, 1982.

Gosciak, Josh. "Most Wanted: McKay and the 'Black Specter' of African American Poetry in the 1920s." Culleton and Leick, *Modernism* 73–103.

"The Government and the Negro." *Crusader* 2.4 (Dec. 1919): 5.

Graff, Gerald. *Professing Literature: An Institutional History.* Chicago: U of Chicago P, 1987.

Grant, Colin. *Negro with a Hat: The Rise and Fall of Marcus Garvey.* New York: Oxford UP, 2008.

Green, Constance McLaughlin. *The Secret City: A History of Race Relations in the Nation's Capital.* Princeton: Princeton UP, 1967.

Greenlee, Sam. *The Spook Who Sat by the Door.* 1969. New York: Bantam, 1970.

Guibernau, Montserrat. *Nations without States: Political Communities in a Global Age.* Cambridge: Polity, 1999.

Guilbaut, Serge. *How New York Stole the Idea of Modern Art.* Trans. Arthur Goldhammer. Chicago: U of Chicago P, 1983.

Gunning, Sandra. "Nancy Prince and the Politics of Mobility, Home, and Diasporic (Mis)Identification." *American Quarterly* 53.1 (Mar. 2001): 32–69.

Haine, W. Scott. *The World of the Paris Café: Sociability among the French Working Class, 1789–1914.* Baltimore: Johns Hopkins UP, 1996.

Hanchard, Michael. "Black Memory versus State Memory: Notes toward a Method." *Small Axe* 26 (June 2008): 45–62.

Hardt, Michael, and Antonio Negri. *Empire.* Cambridge: Harvard UP, 2000.

Hardy, David M. [Section Chief, Record/Information Dissemination Section, Federal Bureau of Investigation.] Letter to the author. 19 Oct. 2006.

———. Letter to the author. 14 Nov. 2006.

———. Letter to the author. 16 May 2007.

———. Letter to the author. 24 Oct. 2007.

———. Letter to the author. 13 Feb. 2009.

———. Letter to the author. 25 May 2012.

———. Letter to the author. 31 July 2012.

Harrington, Oliver W. *Why I Left America and Other Essays.* Ed. M. Thomas Inge. Jackson: UP of Mississippi, 1993.

Harris, Joseph E. "The Dynamics of the Global African Diaspora." *The African Diaspora.* Ed. Alusine Jalloh and Stephen E. Maizlish. Arlington: Texas A&M UP, 1996. 7–21.

Harris, Trudier. "Lance Jeffers." *The Oxford Companion to African American Literature.* Ed. William L. Andrews, Frances Smith Foster, and Trudier Harris. New York: Oxford UP, 1997. 397–98.

Hart, Matthew, and Jim Hansen. "Introduction: Contemporary Literature and the State." *Contemporary Literature* 49.4 (winter 2008): 491–513.

Hartman, Saidiya V. *Scenes of Subjection: Terror, Slavery, and Self-Making in Nineteenth-Century America*. New York: Oxford UP, 1997.

"Hatch Act." [5 U.S.C. §7321–26.] *U.S. Office of Special Counsel*. 22 June 2012. Web. http://www.osc.gov/haFederalStatute.htm.

Hawkes, Terence. "William Empson's Influence on the CIA." *TLS* 10 June 2009. Web. 15 June 2010. http://entertainment.timesonline.co.uk/tol/arts_and_entertainment /the_tls/article6469054.ece.

Heard, Alex. "The Department of Forgetting: How an Obscure FBI Rule Is Ensuring the Destruction of Irreplaceable Historical Records." *Slate* 24 June 2008. Web. 11 Dec. 2008. http://www.slate.com/id/2191902.

Henderson, David. "They Are Killing All the Young Men." 1964. *For Malcolm: Poems on the Life and Death of Malcolm X*. Ed. Dudley Randall and Margaret G. Burroughs. Detroit: Broadside, 1969. 46–54.

Hernton, Calvin C. "Dynamite Growing out of Their Skulls." *Black Fire: An Anthology of Afro-American Writing*. Ed. LeRoi Jones and Larry Neal. New York: William Morrow, 1968. 78–104.

Herzberg, Bob. *The FBI and the Movies: A History of the Bureau on Screen and behind the Scenes in Hollywood*. Jefferson, NC: McFarland, 2007.

Herzog, Todd. "Crime Stories: Criminal, Society, and the Modernist Case History." *Representations* 80 (fall 2002): 34–61.

Hewitt, Steve. *Snitch! A History of the Modern Intelligence Informer*. New York: Continuum, 2010.

Higashida, Cheryl. "To Be(come) Young, Gay, and Black: Lorraine Hansberry's Existentialist Routes to Anticolonialism." *American Quarterly* 60.4 (Dec. 2008): 899–924.

Hill, Herbert, ed. *Soon, One Morning: New Writing by American Negroes, 1940–1962*. New York: Knopf, 1963.

Hill, Robert A., ed. *The FBI's RACON: Racial Conditions in the United States during World War II*. 1943. Boston: Northeastern UP, 1995.

———. *The Marcus Garvey and Universal Negro Improvement Association Papers*. Vol. 2. Berkeley: U of California P, 1983.

Himes, Chester. *A Case of Rape*. 1963. New York: Carroll and Graf, 1994.

———. *Plan B*. Ed. Michel Fabre and Robert E. Skinner. Jackson: UP of Mississippi, 1993.

Hobbes, Thomas. *Leviathan*. 1651. Harmondsworth: Penguin, 1968.

Hobsbawm, E. J. *Nations and Nationalism since 1780: Programme, Myth, Reality*. New York: Cambridge UP, 1990.

Hodges, LeRoy S., Jr. *Portrait of an Expatriate: William Gardner Smith, Writer*. Westport, CT: Greenwood, 1985.

Holcomb, Gary Edward. *Claude McKay, Code Name Sasha: Queer Black Marxism and the Harlem Renaissance*. Gainesville: UP of Florida, 2007.

Hollander, John. *Reflections on Espionage: The Question of Cupcake*. 1976. New Haven: Yale UP, 1999.

Holloway, Karla F. C. *Bookmarks: Reading in Black and White*. New Brunswick: Rutgers UP, 2006.

Holzman, Michael. "The Ideological Origins of American Studies at Yale." *American Studies* 40.2 (summer 1999): 71–99.

———. *James Jesus Angleton, the CIA, and the Craft of Counterintelligence*. Amherst: U of Massachusetts P, 2008.

Hoover, J. Edgar. "The Bully Bolsheviki." Hoover, Scrapbooks.

———. "Combating the Merchants of Filth: The Role of the FBI." *University of Pittsburgh Law Review* 25.3 (Mar. 1964): 469–78.

———. Directive to FBI field offices on Custodial Detention policy. 6 Dec. 1939. U.S., Senate, Select Committee, *Hearings*. Exhibit 23. 409–11.

———. "How U.S. Reds Use 'Pseudo Liberals' as a Front." *U.S. News and World Report* 13 Apr. 1956: 138–39.

———. *J. Edgar Hoover on Communism*. New York: Random House, 1969.

———. *J. Edgar Hoover Speaks concerning Communism*. Ed. James D. Bales. Washington, DC: Capitol Hill, 1971.

———. Letter to J. A. Dowd. 1926. Schmidt, *Red Scare: FBI and the Origins of Anticommunism in the United States* 329.

———. *Masters of Deceit: The Story of Communism in America and How to Fight It*. New York: Henry Holt, 1958.

———. "Patriotism and the War against Crime." 1936. Richard Gid Powers, *Broken: The Troubled Past and Uncertain Future of the FBI* 166.

———. *Persons in Hiding*. Boston: Little, Brown, 1938.

———. Scrapbooks. Records of the Federal Bureau of Investigation (RG 65), Director's Office Records and Memorabilia, J. Edgar Hoover's Scrapbooks, Box 1, July 1921 to Dec. 1924 folder. U.S. National Archives and Records Administration, College Park, MD.

———. "Secularism—Breeder of Crime." 1947. Manuscript Archives, Special Collections, J. Willard Marriott Library, University of Utah, Salt Lake City.

———. *A Study of Communism*. New York: Holt, Rinehart, and Winston, 1962.

———. "The Weekly Review." 1906. Richard Gid Powers, *Secrecy and Power: The Life of J. Edgar Hoover* 20–21.

Hoover, J. Edgar, and Frederick L. Collins. "Slickers in Slacks." *Collier's* 16 Oct. 1943: 24, 76–77.

Hopkins, Pauline. *Hagar's Daughter: A Story of Southern Caste Prejudice*. 1901–2. *The Magazine Novels of Pauline Hopkins*. Ed. Hazel V. Carby. New York: Oxford UP, 1988. 1–284.

Horn, Eva. *The Secret War: Treason, Espionage, and Modern Fiction*. 2007. Trans. Geoffrey Winthrop-Young. Evanston, IL: Northwestern UP, 2013.

Horton, Lois E. "The Days of Jubilee: Black Migration during the Civil War and Reconstruction." *Urban Odyssey: A Multicultural History of Washington, D.C.* Ed. Francine Curro Cary. Washington, DC: Smithsonian, 1996. 65–78.

House, Jim, and Neil MacMaster. *Paris 1961: Algerians, State Terror, and Memory*. Oxford: Oxford UP, 2006.

Huang, Yunte. *Transpacific Imaginations: History, Literature, Counterpoetics*. Cambridge: Harvard UP, 2008.

Hudson, John. "Obama Administration Distorted Its Transparency Record: Ex-DOJ Official." *Atlantic Wire*. Atlantic Monthly Group. 9 Mar. 2012. Web. 13 Aug. 2013. http://www.theatlanticwire.com/politics.

Huggins, Nathan Irvin, ed. *Voices from the Harlem Renaissance*. New York: Oxford UP, 1976.

Hughes, Langston. "Concerning a Great Mississippi Writer and the Southern Negro." 1956. *Langston Hughes and the* Chicago Defender: *Essays on Race, Politics, and Culture, 1942–1962*. Ed. Christopher C. De Santis. Urbana: U of Illinois P, 1995. 91–92.

———. "Concernment." *Simple's Uncle Sam*. 1965. *The Collected Works of Langston Hughes*. Vol. 8. *The Later Simple Stories*. Ed. Donna Akiba Sullivan Harper. Columbia: U of Missouri P, 2002. 253–57.

———. "I, Too." 1925. *The Collected Poems of Langston Hughes*. Ed. Arnold Rampersad and David Roessel. New York: Alfred A. Knopf, 1994. 46.

———. "It's Okay to Be Reserved, Says Simple, But Not at My Expense." *Chicago Defender* 8 Sept. 1951: 6.

———. "Something to Lean On." *Simple Speaks His Mind*. 1950. *The Collected Works of Langston Hughes*. Vol. 7. *The Early Simple Stories*. Ed. Donna Akiba Sullivan Harper. Columbia: U of Missouri P, 2002. 133–34.

———. "What Shall We Do about the South?" 1943. *The Collected Works of Langston Hughes*. Vol. 9. *Essays on Art, Race, Politics, and World Affairs*. Ed. Christopher C. De Santis. Columbia: U of Missouri P, 2002. 219–24.

Hurston, Zora Neale. *Their Eyes Were Watching God*. 1937. New York: Harper Perennial, 2006.

Hutchinson, George. *The Harlem Renaissance in Black and White*. Cambridge: Belknap–Harvard UP, 1995.

Hutchinson, George, and John K. Young, eds. *Publishing Blackness: Textual Constructions of Race since 1850*. Ann Arbor: U of Michigan P, 2013.

Hyena, Hank. "J. Edgar Hoover: Gay Marriage Role Model?" *Salon* 5 Jan. 2000. Web. 7 Oct. 2008. http://www.slon.com/health/sex/urge/world/2000/01/05/hoover.

Inikori, J. E. Introduction. *Forced Migration: The Impact of the Export Slave Trade on African Societies*. London: Hutchinson University Library, 1982. 13–60.

I Was a Communist for the FBI. Dir. Gordon Douglas. Perf. Frank Lovejoy. Warner Brothers, 1951. Film.

Jackson, John L. *Racial Paranoia: The Unintended Consequences of Political Correctness*. New York: Basic Civitas, 2008.

Jackson, Lawrence P. *The Indignant Generation: A Narrative History of African American Writers and Critics, 1934–1960*. Princeton: Princeton UP, 2011.

Jackson, Leon. "The Talking Book and the Talking Book Historian: African American Cultures of Print—The State of the Discipline." *Book History* 13 (2010): 251–308.

James, C.L.R. *Mariners, Renegades, and Castaways: The Story of Herman Melville and the World We Live In*. 1953. New York: Allison and Busby, 1985.

J. Edgar. Dir. Clint Eastwood. Perf. Leonardo DiCaprio. Warner Brothers, 2011. Film.

Jeffreys-Jones, Rhodri. *The FBI: A History*. New Haven: Yale UP, 2007.

Jesus Christ Superstar. By Andrew Lloyd Webber and Tim Rice. Dir. Tom O'Horgan. Perf. Ben Vereen and Carl Anderson. Mark Hellinger Theatre, New York. 1971–73. Performance.

Johnson, David K. *The Lavender Scare: The Cold War Persecution of Gays and Lesbians in the Federal Government*. Chicago: U of Chicago P, 2004.

Johnson, J. C. "Eavesdropper's Blues." 1924. Lyrics reprinted in Angela Y. Davis, *Blues Legacies and Black Feminism: Gertrude "Ma" Rainey, Bessie Smith, and Billie Holiday*. New York: Pantheon, 1998. 276–77.

Johnson, James Weldon. "Report of the Department of Justice on Sedition among Negroes." *New York Age* 12 Dec. 1919: n. pag.

Johnson, William R. *Thwarting Enemies at Home and Abroad: How to Be a Counterintelligence Officer*. 1987. Washington, DC: Georgetown UP, 2009.

Joseph, Peniel E. *Waiting 'til the Midnight Hour: A Narrative History of Black Power in America*. New York: Henry Holt, 2006.

Kackman, Michael. *Citizen Spy: Television, Espionage, and Cold War Culture*. Minneapolis: U of Minnesota P, 2005.

Kandiyoti, Dalia. *Migrant Sites: America, Place, and Diaspora Literatures*. Hanover, NH: Dartmouth College / U of New England P, 2009.

Kaplan, Amy. *The Anarchy of Empire in the Making of U.S. Culture*. Cambridge: Harvard UP, 2002.

Kaplan, Amy, and Donald E. Pease, eds. *Cultures of United States Imperialism*. Durham: Duke UP, 1994.

Kellman, Steven G. "Raising Muscovite Ducks and Government Suspicions: Henry Roth and the FBI." Culleton and Leick, *Modernism* 39–52.

Kelso, John M., Jr. [Section Chief, Freedom of Information–Privacy Acts Section, Federal Bureau of Investigation.] Letter to the author. 24 Sept. 1999.

Kent, George E. *A Life of Gwendolyn Brooks*. Lexington: UP of Kentucky, 1990.

Kerr, Audrey Elisa. *The Paper Bag Principle: Class, Colorism, and Rumor and the Case of Black Washington, D.C.*: Knoxville: U of Tennessee P, 2006.

Kessler, Ronald. *The Bureau: The Secret History of the FBI*. New York: St. Martin's, 2002.

———. *The Secrets of the FBI*. New York: Crown, 2011.

Kincaid, Cliff. "Obama's Communist Mentor." *Accuracy in Media* 18 Feb. 2008. Web. 26 May 2009. http://www.aim.org/aim-column/obamas-communist-mentor.

Kornweibel, Theodore, Jr. *No Crystal Stair: Black Life and the Messenger, 1917–1928*. Westport, CT: Greenwood, 1975.

———. *"Seeing Red": Federal Campaigns against Black Militancy, 1919–1925*. Bloomington: Indiana UP, 1998.

LaMontagne, Leo E. *American Library Classification: With Special Reference to the Library of Congress*. Hamden, CT: Shoe String Press, 1961.

Leab, Daniel J. *I Was a Communist for the FBI: The Unhappy Life and Times of Matt Cvetic*. University Park: Pennsylvania State UP, 2000.

Lehman, David. *Signs of the Times: Deconstruction and the Fall of Paul de Man*. New York: Poseidon, 1991.

Letter to the Editor. [Signed by Ollie Harrington, likely written by Richard Gibson.] *Life* 43.17 (21 Oct. 1957): 10.

Levander, Caroline F., and Robert S. Levine, ed. *Hemispheric American Studies*. New Brunswick: Rutgers UP, 2008.

Lewis, David Levering, ed. *The Portable Harlem Renaissance Reader*. New York: Viking, 1994.

———. *W.E.B. Du Bois: The Fight for Equality and the American Century, 1919–1963*. New York: Henry Holt, 2000.

"L'Historique du Café Tournon." *Café Tournon*. Café Tournon. Web. 13 June 2012. http://www.cafetournon.com/accueil.html.

"Lines Sharply Drawn." *Washington Post* 3 Aug. 1902: 1.

The Lives of Others [Das Leben der Anderen]. Dir. Florian Henckel von Donnersmarck. Sony Pictures Classics, 2006. Film.

Locke, Alain. "The New Negro." 1925. *The New Negro*. Ed. Alain Locke. New York: Atheneum, 1992. 3–16.

London, Jack. "Smile of Negro in Evidence." *Galveston Daily News* 5 July 1910: 1, 4.

Lorde, Audre. *The Cancer Journals*. 1980. London: Sheba, 1985.

———. *Zami: A New Spelling of My Name*. 1982. Freedom, CA: Crossing Press, 1997.

The Lost Man. Dir. Robert Alan Authur. Perf. Sidney Poitier. Universal Studios, 1968. Film.

Lott, Eric. *Love and Theft: Blackface Minstrelsy and the American Working Class*. New York: Oxford UP, 1993.

———. "National Treasure, Global Value, and American Literary Studies." *American Literary History* 20.1–2 (spring/summer 2008): 108–23.

Loughran, Trish. *The Republic in Print: Print Culture in the Age of U.S. Nation Building, 1770–1870*. New York: Columbia UP, 2007.

Lowenthal, Max. *The Federal Bureau of Investigation*. New York: William Sloane, 1950.

Lukács, Georg. *The Historical Novel*. 1937. Trans. Hannah and Stanley Mitchell. London: Merlin, 1962.

Lutz, Tom. *Cosmopolitan Vistas: American Regionalism and Literary Value*. Ithaca: Cornell UP, 2004.

MacKay, Cliff. *Atlanta Daily World* column of 1 July 1942. Washburn, *A Question of Sedition* 83.

MacLeish, Archibald. "My [D]ear Mr. Angleton." *Furioso* 1.1 (summer 1939): 1–2.

Mann, James. Address on the Mann Act. 45 *Cong. Rec.* 1040 (1910): 70.

Manning, Susan, and Andrew Taylor, ed. *Transatlantic Literary Studies: A Reader*. Baltimore: Johns Hopkins UP, 2007.

Marable, Manning. *Race, Reform, and Rebellion: The Second Reconstruction and Beyond in Black America, 1945–2006*. 3rd ed. Jackson: UP of Mississippi, 2007.

Marcantonio, Vito. "The 'Index Card Menace to American Liberty.'" 1940. *I Vote My Conscience: The Debates, Speeches, and Writings of Congressman Vito Marcantonio*. Ed. Annette T. Rubinstein. Web. 21 June 2012. http://vitomarcantonio.org/chapter_3.php-97.9k.

Marx, Anthony W. "Race-Making and the Nation State." *World Politics* 48.2 (1996): 180–208.

Masterman, J. C. *The Double-Cross System in the War of 1939 to 1945*. New Haven: Yale UP, 1972.

Mathis, James R. [Archivist, Special Access and FOIA Staff, National Archives and Records Administration.] Letter to the author. 27 Feb. 2008.

Maxwell, William J. "F.B. Eyes: The Bureau Reads Claude McKay." *Left of the Color Line: Race, Radicalism, and Twentieth-Century Literature of the United States*. Ed. Bill V. Mullen and James Smethurst. Chapel Hill: U of North Carolina P, 2003. 39–65.

McAllister, Marvin. *Whiting Up: Whiteface Minstrels and Stage Europeans in African American Performance*. Chapel Hill: U of North Carolina P, 2011.

McCann, Sean. *A Pinnacle of Feeling: American Literature and Presidential Government.* Princeton: Princeton UP, 2008.

McCann, Sean, and Michael Szalay. "Do You Believe in Magic?: Literary Thinking after the New Left." *Yale Journal of Criticism* 18.2 (2005): 435–68.

McCoy, Alfred W. *Policing America's Empire: The United States, the Philippines, and the Rise of the Surveillance State.* Madison: U of Wisconsin P, 2009.

McDonald, Peter D. *The Literature Police: Apartheid Censorship and Its Cultural Consequences.* New York: Oxford UP, 2009.

McGhee, Millie L. *Secrets Uncovered: J. Edgar Hoover—Passing for White?* Rancho Cucamonga, CA: Allen-Morris, 2000.

McGurl, Mark. *The Program Era: Postwar Fiction and the Rise of Creative Writing.* Cambridge: Harvard UP, 2009.

McHenry, Elizabeth. *Forgotten Readers: Recovering the Lost History of African-American Literary Societies.* Durham: Duke UP, 2002.

McKay, Claude. "America." *Liberator* 4 (Dec. 1921): 1921. Reprinted in U.S., Federal, Claude McKay file, 26 Jan. 1924.

——. *Complete Poems.* Ed. William J. Maxwell. Urbana: U of Illinois P, 2004.

——. "Enslaved." *Liberator* 4 (July 1921): 6.

——. "If We Must Die." *Liberator* 2 (July 1919): 21.

——. Letter to Max Eastman, 25 Apr. 1932. Claude McKay Manuscripts, Lilly Library, Indiana University, Bloomington.

——. Letter to Max Eastman, [?] Apr. 1933. Claude McKay Manuscripts, Lilly Library, Indiana University, Bloomington.

——. Letter to Harold Jackman. 10 Mar. 1928. Claude McKay Collection. James Weldon Johnson Manuscripts, Yale Collection of American Literature, Beinecke Rare Book and Manuscript Library, Yale University, New Haven, CT.

——. "Song of the New Soldier and Worker." *Workers' Dreadnought* (2 Apr. 1920): 4.

McLeod, Janice Gahl [Associate Director, U.S. Department of Justice, Office of Information and Privacy.] Letter to the author. 20 Feb. 2007.

Medsger, Betty. *The Burglary: The Discovery of J. Edgar Hoover's Secret FBI.* New York: Knopf, 2014.

Melley, Timothy. *The Covert Sphere: Secrecy, Fiction, and the National Security State.* Ithaca: Cornell UP, 2012.

Meyer, Tamar, ed. *Gender Ironies of Nationalism: Sexing the Nation.* New York: Routledge, 2000.

Miller, Tyrus. *Late Modernism: Politics, Fiction, and the Arts between the World Wars.* Berkeley: U of California P, 1999.

Mitgang, Herbert. *Dangerous Dossiers: Exposing the Secret War against America's Greatest Authors.* 1988. New York: Ballantine, 1989.

Morize, André. *Problems and Methods of Literary History.* Boston: Ginn, 1922.

Morrison, Toni. *Playing in the Dark: Whiteness and the Literary Imagination.* New York: Vintage, 1993.

Muhammad, Khalil Gibran. *The Condemnation of Blackness: Race, Crime, and the Making of Urban America.* Cambridge: Harvard UP, 2010.

Murch, Donna Jean. "Countering Subversion: Black Panther Scholarship, Popular History, and the Richard Aoki Controversy." *Perspectives Online* 50.7 (Oct. 2012):

n. pag. Web. 9 May 2013. http://www.historians.org/Perspectives/issues/2012/1210/Perspectives-on Books_Countering-Subversion.cfm.

Myrdal, Gunnar. *An American Dilemma: The Negro Problem and Modern Democracy.* New York: Harper and Brothers, 1944.

Nadel, Alan. *Containment Culture: American Narratives, Postmodernism, and the Atomic Age.* Durham: Duke UP, 1995.

"National Intelligence Act of 1947." [PL 80–235, 26 July 1947.] 6 July 2010. intelligence .senate.gov/nsaact1947.pdf. PDF file.

Naylor, Gloria. *1996.* Chicago: Third World, 2005.

Neal, Larry. "And Shine Swam On." *Black Fire: An Anthology of Afro-American Writing.* Ed. LeRoi Jones and Larry Neal. New York: William Morrow, 1968. 638–56.

———. "The Black Arts Movement." 1968. *Visions of a Liberated Future: Black Arts Movement Writings.* Ed. Michael Schwartz. New York: Thunder's Mouth, 1989. 62–78.

"Negro FBI Agents in Action." *Ebony* 11.12 (Oct. 1947): 9–13.

Nelson, Dolores M. [Information and Privacy Coordinator, Central Intelligence Agency.] Letter to author. 26 June 2009.

Newton, Huey P. *War against the Panthers: A Study of Repression in America.* Diss. U of California at Santa Cruz, 1980. Ann Arbor: UMI, 1980. ATT 8108338.

Newton, Michael. *The FBI and the KKK: A Critical History.* Jefferson, NC: McFarland, 2005.

———. *The FBI Encyclopedia.* Jefferson, NC: McFarland, 2003.

Nwankwo, Ifeoma Kiddoe. *Black Cosmopolitanism: Racial Consciousness and Transnational Identity in the Nineteenth-Century Americas.* Philadelphia: U of Pennsylvania P, 2005.

Olmstead, Kathryn S. *Real Enemies: Conspiracy Theories and American Democracy, World War I to 9/11.* New York: Oxford UP, 2009.

O'Reilly, Kenneth. *Black Americans: The FBI Files.* Ed. David Gallen. New York: Carroll and Graf, 1994.

———. *"Racial Matters": The FBI's Secret File on Black America, 1960–1972.* New York: Free Press, 1989.

Pattee, Fred Lewis, ed. *Century Readings for a Course in American Literature.* 4th ed. New York: Appleton-Century-Crofts, 1932.

———. "Introductory Note." *Century Readings for a Course in American Literature.* v.

Patterson, Anita. *Race, American Literature, and Transnational Modernism.* Cambridge: Cambridge UP, 2008.

Patterson, Annabel. "Censorship." *Encyclopedia of Literature and Criticism.* Ed. Martin Coyle et al. London: Routledge, 1990. 901–14.

Pearson, Norman Holmes. Foreword. *The Double-Cross System in the War of 1939 to 1945.* By J. C. Masterman. New Haven: Yale UP, 1972. ix–xvi.

Pease, Donald. "Re-Thinking 'American Studies' after US Exceptionalism." *American Literary History* 21.1 (spring 2009): 19–27.

Post, Louis F. *The Deportations Delirium of Nineteen-Twenty.* 1923. New York: Da Capo, 1970.

Postgate, Daisy. [Her Majesty's Office of Works.] Letter to Claude McKay. 18 Dec. 1930. Claude McKay Collection. Yale Collection of American Literature, Beinecke Rare Book and Manuscript Library, Yale University, New Haven, CT.

Postnikov, Alexey V. "Maps for Ordinary Consumers versus Maps for the Military: Double Standards of Map Accuracy in Soviet Cartography, 1917–1991." *Cartography and Geographic Information Science* 29.3 (July 2002): 243–60.

Potash, John. *The FBI War on Tupac Shakur and Black Leaders*. 2007. Baltimore: Progressive Left, 2009.

Potter, Claire Bond. "Queer Hoover: Sex, Lies, and Political History." *Journal of the History of Sexuality* 15.3 (2006): 355–81.

———. *War on Crime: Bandits, G-Men, and the Politics of Mass Culture*. New Brunswick: Rutgers UP, 1998.

Pound, Ezra. "Introductory Text-Book." *Furioso* 1.1 (summer 1939): 28.

Powers, Richard Gid. *Broken: The Troubled Past and Uncertain Future of the FBI*. New York: Free Press, 2004.

———. "The FBI in American Popular Culture." Theoharis, *The FBI: A Comprehensive Reference* 261–307.

———. *G-Men: Hoover's FBI in American Popular Culture*. Carbondale: Southern Illinois UP, 1983.

———. *Not without Honor: The History of American Anticommunism*. 1995. New Haven: Yale UP, 1998.

———. *Secrecy and Power: The Life of J. Edgar Hoover*. New York: Free Press, 1987.

Powers, Tyrone. *Eyes to My Soul: The Rise or Decline of a Black FBI Agent*. Dover, MA: Majority, 1996.

Preston, William, Jr. *Aliens and Dissenters: Federal Suppression of Radicals, 1903–1933*. Cambridge: Harvard UP, 1963.

Public Enemies. Dir. Michael Mann. Perf. Johnny Depp. Universal Pictures, 2009. Film.

Purvis, Melvin. *American Agent*. Garden City, NY: Doubleday, Doran, 1936.

"Radicalism among Negroes Growing, U.S. Record Shows." *World* 17 Nov. 1919: n. pag.

Radway, Janice A. *A Feeling for Books: The Book-of-the-Month Club, Literary Taste, and Middle-Class Desire*. Chapel Hill: U of North Carolina P, 1997.

Rambsy, Howard, II. *The Black Arts Enterprise and the Production of African American Poetry*. Ann Arbor: U of Michigan P, 2011.

Rampersad, Arnold. *The Life of Langston Hughes*. Vol. 2. *1941–1967: I Dream a World*. New York: Oxford UP, 1988.

Randall, Dudley. "Abu." *More to Remember: Poems of Four Decades*. 73.

———. "F.B.I. Memo." *More to Remember: Poems of Four Decades*. 72.

———. "Informer." *More to Remember: Poems of Four Decades*. 71.

———. *More to Remember: Poems of Four Decades*. Chicago: Third World, 1971.

Randolph, A. Philip, and Chandler Owen. "The New Negro—What Is He?" *Messenger* 2.4–5 (Apr.–May 1920): 73–74.

Reed, Ishmael. *Airing Dirty Laundry*. New York: Addison-Wesley, 1994.

———. *Mumbo Jumbo*. New York: Atheneum, 1972.

Renker, Elizabeth. *The Origins of American Literature Studies: An Institutional History*. New York: Cambridge UP, 2007.

Richards, I. A. *Practical Criticism: A Study of Literary Judgment*. 1929. New York: Harcourt, Brace, and World, 1969.

Riebling, Mark. *Wedge: The Secret War between the FBI and the CIA*. New York: Alfred A. Knopf, 1994.

Roberts, Brian Russell. "(Ex)Isles in the Harlem Renaissance: The Insular and Archipe-lagic Topographies of Wallace Thurman's *The Blacker the Berry*." *Arizona Quarterly* 67.3 (autumn 2011): 91–118.

Robertson, Craig. *The Passport in America: The History of a Document*. New York: Oxford UP, 2010.

Robeson, Paul, Jr. *The Undiscovered Paul Robeson: Quest for Freedom, 1939–1976*. Hoboken, NJ: John Wiley, 2010.

Robins, Natalie. *Alien Ink: The FBI's War on Freedom of Expression*. New York: William Morrow, 1992.

Rogin, Michael. "When the CIA Was the NEA." *Nation* 12 June 2000: 16+.

Rolling Stones. "Fingerprint File." *It's Only Rock 'n Roll*. By Mick Jagger and Keith Richards. Rolling Stones, 1974. CD.

Roosevelt, Franklin Delano. "Formal Statement." 1939. Donner, *The Age of Surveillance: The Aims and Methods of America's Political Intelligence System* 58.

Rosen, Charles. "Music and the Cold War." *New York Review of Books*. 7 Apr. 2011: 40–42.

Rosen, David, and Aaron Santesso. *The Watchman in Pieces: Surveillance, Literature, and Liberal Personhood*. New Haven: Yale UP, 2013.

Rosenfeld, Seth. "FBI Files Reveal New Details about Informant Who Armed Black Panthers." *Center for Investigative Reporting* 7 Sept. 2012. Web. 9 May 2013. http://ciron-line.org/reports/fbi-files-reveal-new-details-about-informant-who-armed -black-panthers-3833.

———. *Subversives: The FBI's War on Student Radicals, and Reagan's Rise to Power*. New York: Farrar, Straus and Giroux, 2012.

Rothberg, Michael. *Multidirectional Memory: Remembering the Holocaust in the Age of Decolonization*. Stanford: Stanford UP, 2009.

Rowley, Hazel. *Richard Wright: The Life and Times*. New York: Henry Holt, 2001.

Ruble, Blair A. *Washington's U Street: A Biography*. Washington, DC: Woodrow Wilson Center–Johns Hopkins UP, 2010.

Ruquist, Rebecca. "'*Non, Nous ne Jouons Pas la Trompette*': Richard Wright in Paris." *Contemporary French and Francophone Studies* 8.3 (2004): 285–303.

Sackler, Howard. *The Great White Hope: A Drama in Three Acts*. New York: Samuel French, 1968.

Sallis, James. Introduction. *A Case of Rape*. By Chester Himes. 1963. New York: Carroll and Graf, 1994. v–ix.

"Sam Greenlee." *Contemporary Black Biography*. Gale Group. 2006. Answers.com. 22 Mar. 2013. http://www.answers.com/topic/sam-greenlee.

Sanchez, Sonia. *Conversations with Sonia Sanchez*. Ed. Joyce A. Joyce. Jackson: UP of Mississippi, 2007.

———. "A Modern Song of the F.B.I." 1966. *Afro-Arts Anthology*. Ed. Yusef Iman et al. Newark, NJ: Jihad, 1969. 5–6.

———. *We a BaddDDD People*. Detroit: Broadside, 1970.

Saunders, Frances Stonor. *The Cultural Cold War: The CIA and the World of Arts and Letters*. 1999. New York: New Press, 2000.

Sbardellati, John. *J. Edgar Hoover Goes to the Movies: The FBI and the Origins of Hollywood's Cold War*. Ithaca: Cornell UP, 2012.

Schmidt, Regin. *Red Scare: FBI and the Origins of Anticommunism in the United States*. Copenhagen: Museum Tusculanum Press, 2000.

Schott, Joseph L. *No Left Turns*. New York: Praeger, 1975.

Schrecker, Ellen. *Many Are the Crimes: McCarthyism in America*. Princeton: Princeton UP, 1998.

Schultz, Bud, and Ruth Schultz. *It Did Happen Here: Recollections of Political Repression in America*. Berkeley: U of California P, 1989.

Schuyler, George S. *Black and Conservative: The Autobiography of George S. Schuyler*. New Rochelle, NY: Arlington House, 1966.

———. *Black Empire*. 1936–38. Ed. Robert A. Hill and R. Kent Rasmussen. Boston: Northeastern UP, 1991.

Scott-Heron, Gil. "King Alfred Plan." *Free Will*. Flying Dutchman, 1972. LP.

"Secrecy Report Card, 2010: Indicators of Secrecy in the Federal Government." Open TheGovernment.Org. OpenTheGovernment.Org: Americans for Less Secrecy, More Democracy. 7 Sept. 2010. Web. 16 Sept. 2010. openthegovernment.org/.

"Sedition Act of 1918." [United States Statutes at Large. Vol. 40. 65th Cong. 2nd sess. Chap. 75.] *Wikisource*. 5 May 2013. Web. 23 Apr. 2014. http://en.wikisource.org/wiki/United_States_Statutes_at_Large/Volume_40/65th_Congress/2nd_Session/Chapter_75.

Senna, Danzy. *Caucasia*. New York: Riverhead, 1998.

Service, Robert. "Grin." 1907. *Collected Poems of Robert Service*. New York: Dodd, Mead, 1972. 27–28.

Shakespeare, William. *Measure for Measure*. 1623. New York: Washington Square–Folger Shakespeare Library, 2005.

Shklovsky, Viktor. *Theory of Prose*. 1925. Trans. Benjamin Sher. Elmwood Park, IL: Dalkey Archive, 1990.

Singh, Nikhil Pal. *Black Is a Country: Race and the Unfinished Struggle for Democracy*. Cambridge: Harvard UP, 2004.

Smethurst, James Edward. *The Black Arts Movement: Literary Nationalism in the 1960s and 1970s*. Chapel Hill: U of North Carolina P, 2005.

———. *The New Red Negro: The Literary Left and African American Poetry, 1930–1946*. New York: Oxford UP, 1999.

Smith, James. *British Writers and MI5 Surveillance, 1930–1960*. New York: Cambridge UP, 2013.

Smith, Walter I. Address on the Formation of the Bureau of Investigation. 43 *Cong. Rec.* 3132 (1908): 672.

Smith, William Gardner. *Return to Black America*. Englewood Cliffs, NJ: Prentice-Hall, 1970.

———. *The Stone Face*. 1963. Chatham, NJ: Chatham Bookseller, 1975.

Sollors, Werner, ed. *Multilingual America: Transnationalism, Ethnicity, and the Languages of American Literature*. New York: New York UP, 1998.

Spannaus, Edward. "The Mysterious Origins of J. Edgar Hoover." *American Almanac* Aug. 2000. Web. 28 Sept. 2007. http://american_almanac.tripod.com/hoover.htm.

Spargo, R. Clifton. "The Contemporary Anti-Elegy." *The Oxford Handbook of the Elegy*. Ed. Karen Weisman. New York: Oxford UP, 2010. 413–29.

Stephan, Alexander. *"Communazis": FBI Surveillance of German Emigré Writers*. 1995. Trans. Jan van Heurck. New Haven: Yale UP, 2000.

Stephens, Michelle Ann. *Black Empire: The Masculine Global Imaginary of Caribbean Intellectuals in the United States, 1914–1962*. Durham: Duke UP, 2005.

Stovall, Tyler. *Paris Noir: African Americans in the City of Light.* Boston: Houghton, 1996.

"The Strom Thurmond Institute of Public Affairs." 30 Jan. 2011. Web. http://www. strom .clemson.edu/.

Strunk, Mary Elizabeth. *Wanted Women: An American Obsession in the Reign of J. Edgar Hoover.* Lawrence: UP of Kansas, 2010.

Sullivan, William C., with Bill Brown. *The Bureau: My Thirty Years in Hoover's FBI.* New York: W. W. Norton, 1979.

———. Letter to Martin Luther King Jr. 20 Nov. 1964. Records of the Federal Bureau of Investigation (RG 65), J. Edgar Hoover Official and Confidential files, Box 12, File 24. U.S. National Archives and Records Administration, College Park, MD.

Summers, Anthony. *Official and Confidential: The Secret Life of J. Edgar Hoover.* New York: Putnam, 1993.

Super Fly. Dir. Gordon Parks Jr. Perf. Ron O'Neal. Warner Brothers, 1972. Film.

Sweet Sweetback's Baadasssss Song. Dir. Melvin Van Peebles. Perf. Melvin Van Peebles. Cinemation Industries, 1971. Film.

Szalay, Michael. *Hip Figures: A Literary History of the Democratic Party.* Stanford: Stanford UP, 2012.

———. *New Deal Modernism: American Literature and the Invention of the Welfare State.* Durham: Duke UP, 2000.

Tacitus, Publius (or Gaius) Cornelius. *Annales I–VI, IX–XVI.* Ed. C. D. Fisher. Oxford: Oxford UP, 1922.

Tennenhouse, Leonard. *The Importance of Feeling English: American Literature and the British Diaspora, 1750–1850.* Princeton: Princeton UP, 2007.

Theoharis, Athan G. "Appendix: FBI Field Offices." Theoharis, *The FBI: A Comprehensive Reference* 244–47.

———. "A Brief History of the FBI's Role and Powers." Theoharis, *The FBI: A Comprehensive Reference* 1–43.

———. ed. *The FBI: A Comprehensive Reference Guide.* With Tony G. Poveda, Susan Rosenfeld, and Richard Gid Powers. New York: Checkmark Books–Facts on File, 2000.

———. *The FBI and American Democracy: A Brief Critical History.* Lawrence: UP of Kansas, 2004.

———. "The Freedom of Information Act versus the FBI." *A Culture of Secrecy: The Government versus the People's Right to Know.* Ed. Athan G. Theoharis. Lawrence: UP of Kansas, 1998. 16–36.

———. *J. Edgar Hoover, Sex, and Crime: An Historical Antidote.* Chicago: Ivan R. Dee, 1995.

Toomer, Jean. *Cane.* 1923. New York: Liveright, 1975.

Torpey, John. *The Invention of the Passport: Surveillance, Citizenship, and the State.* New York: Cambridge UP, 2000.

Tucker, Ray. "Hist! Who's That?" *Collier's* 19 Aug. 1933: 158–59.

Turner, Patricia A. *I Heard It through the Grapevine: Rumor in African-American Culture.* Berkeley: U of California P, 1993.

United States [U.S.]. Dept. of Justice. *Annual Report of the Attorney General of the United States for the Fiscal Year 1919.* Washington, DC: GPO, 1919.

————. *Annual Report of the Attorney General of the United States for the Fiscal Year 1920.* Washington, DC: GPO, 1920.

————. *Annual Report of the Attorney General of the United States for the Fiscal Year 1921.* Washington, DC: GPO, 1921.

United States [U.S.]. Federal Bureau of Investigation. William ("Wild Bill") Attaway file obtained under provisions of the Freedom of Information Act. Assorted documents dated 6 June 1945 to 5 July 1950. Internal case file no. 14–34720.

————. James Baldwin file obtained under provisions of the Freedom of Information Act. Assorted documents dated [?] Oct. 1958 to 20 Feb. 1974. Internal case file no. 62–108763.

————. Amiri Baraka file self-deposited in the Amiri Baraka Papers, Moorland-Spingarn Research Center, Howard University, Washington, DC. Assorted documents dated 28 Jan. 1957 to 3 Mar. 1971. Internal case file no. 100–425307.

————. Gwendolyn Bennett file obtained under provisions of the Freedom of Information Act. Assorted documents dated 24 June 1941 to 15 Jan. 1959. Internal case file no. 100–293468.

————. Black Arts Repertory Theatre/School file obtained under provisions of the Freedom of Information Act. Assorted documents dated 26 May 1965 to 18 Aug. 1968. Internal case file no. 105–141216.

————. Black Nationalist Movement, New York Division file obtained under provisions of the Freedom of Information Act. Assorted documents dated from 8 Feb. 1968. Internal case file no. 157–8415–34.

————. *Black Scholar* file obtained under provisions of the Freedom of Information Act. Assorted documents dated 30 Dec. 1970 to 26 Mar. 1976. Internal case file no. 157–20214.

————. Robert Adger Bowen file obtained under provisions of the Freedom of Information Act. Assorted documents dated 1 July 1919 to 12 July 1971. Internal case file no. 67–681.

————. Frank London Brown file obtained under provisions of the Freedom of Information Act. Assorted documents dated 19 Dec. 1955 to 27 Dec. 1957. Internal case file no. 100–30890.

————. Lloyd L. Brown file obtained under provisions of the Freedom of Information Act. Assorted documents dated 20 Feb. 1941 to 16 July 1977. Internal case file no. 100–57876.

————. Sterling A. Brown file obtained under provisions of the Freedom of Information Act. Assorted documents dated 14 Aug. 1941 to 9 June 1953. Internal case file no. 100–43964.

————. Alice Childress file obtained under provisions of the Freedom of Information Act. Assorted documents dated 11 Apr. 1951 to [?] 1957. Internal case file no. 100–379156.

————. Lucille Clifton file obtained under provisions of the Freedom of Information Act. Assorted documents dated 25 Feb. 1958 to 29 July 1959. Internal case file no. 29–22627.

————. COINTELPRO Black Nationalist—Hate Groups file obtained under provisions of the Freedom of Information Act. Assorted documents (6,106 in total) dated 25 Aug. 1967 to 5 Mar. 1971. Internal case file no. 100–448006.

United States [U.S.]. Dept. of Justice. Harold Cruse file obtained under provisions of the Freedom of Information Act. Assorted documents dated 7 Aug. 1950 to 9 Jan. 1969. Internal case file no. 100–370842.

——. Frank Marshall Davis file obtained under provisions of the Freedom of Information Act. Assorted documents dated 5 July 1944 to 9 Sept. 1963. Internal case file no. 100–328955.

——. St. Clair Drake file obtained under provisions of the Freedom of Information Act. Assorted documents dated 11 Sept. 1961 to 28 June 1971. Internal case file no. 97–4852.

——. Shirley Graham Du Bois file obtained under provisions of the Freedom of Information Act. Assorted documents dated 8 Aug. 1950 to 28 July 1975. Internal case file no. 100–370965.

——. W.E.B. Du Bois file obtained under provisions of the Freedom of Information Act. Assorted documents dated 1 May 1942 to 27 Dec. 1963. Internal case file no. 100–99729.

——. Katherine Dunham file obtained under provisions of the Freedom of Information Act. Assorted documents dated 23 Oct. 1944 to 3 Dec. 1968. Internal case file no. 100–334795.

——. Ramon [Ray] Durem file obtained under provisions of the Freedom of Information Act. Assorted documents dated 10 Feb. 1940 to 20 Feb. 1967. Internal case file no. 100–18549.

——. Lonne Elder III [Lonnie Williams] file obtained under provisions of the Freedom of Information Act. Document dated 3 Sept. 1954. Internal case file no. 100–116777.

——. Ralph Ellison file obtained under provisions of the Freedom of Information Act. Assorted documents dated 19 Apr. 1950 to 10 Dec. 1964. Internal case file no. 100–428862.

——. E. Franklin Frazier file obtained under provisions of the Freedom of Information Act. Assorted documents dated 25 June 1953 to 13 July 1961. Internal case file no. 138–825.

——. Hoyt Fuller file obtained under provisions of the Freedom of Information Act. Assorted documents dated 27 Apr. 1954 to 25 Mar. 1974. Internal case file no. 157–16554.

——. Marcus Garvey file obtained under provisions of the Freedom of Information Act. Assorted documents dated 11 Oct. 1919 to [?] 1965. Internal case file no. 190–1781–6.

——. Lorraine Hansberry file obtained under provisions of the Freedom of Information Act. Assorted documents dated 21 July 1952 to 22 Jan. 1965. Internal case file no. 100–107297.

——. Ollie Harrington file obtained under provisions of the Freedom of Information Act. Assorted documents dated 4 May 1951 to 22 June 2002. Internal case file no. 100–379980.

——. Calvin Hernton file obtained under provisions of the Freedom of Information Act. Assorted documents dated 14 Mar. 1955 to 29 Aug. 1969. Internal case file no. 100–417598.

——. Chester Himes file obtained under provisions of the Freedom of Information Act. Assorted documents dated 13 June 1944 to 18 Nov. 1964. Internal case file no. 105–2502.

——. Langston Hughes file obtained under provisions of the Freedom of Information Act. Assorted documents dated [?] 1925 to 8 July 1970. Internal case file no. 100–15139.

——. Lance Jeffers file obtained under provisions of the Freedom of Information Act. Assorted documents dated 8 Feb. 1949 to 15 July 1966. Internal case file no. 100–359726.

——. Charles S. Johnson file obtained under provisions of the Freedom of Information Act. Assorted documents dated 21 Feb. 1952 to 1 Oct. 1956. Internal case file no. 138–3218.

——. Georgia Douglas Johnson file obtained under provisions of the Freedom of Information Act. Document dated 15 Mar. 1945. Internal case file no. 19–1120.

——. Bob Kaufman file obtained under provisions of the Freedom of Information Act. Assorted documents dated 31 Jan. 1950 to 18 Aug. 1970. Internal case file no. 100–366937.

——. John O. Killens file obtained under provisions of the Freedom of Information Act. Assorted documents dated 15 Nov. 1941 to 28 Feb. 1973. Internal case file no. 105–37137.

——. Julian Mayfield file obtained under provisions of the Freedom of Information Act. Assorted documents dated 16 Aug. 1954 to 6 Sept. 1974. Internal case file no. 100–412872.

——. Claude McKay file obtained under provisions of the Freedom of Information Act. Assorted documents dated 16 Dec. 1921 to 31 May 1940. Internal case file no. 61–3497.

——. Willard Motley file obtained under provisions of the Freedom of Information Act. Assorted documents dated 16 July 1951 to 12 Oct. 1972. Internal case file no. 100–382070.

——. Pauli Murray file obtained under provisions of the Freedom of Information Act. Assorted documents dated 14 Dec. 1966 to 12 June 1967. Internal case file no. 140–33958.

——. Larry Neal file obtained under provisions of the Freedom of Information Act. Assorted documents dated 29 Apr. 1965 to 13 Apr. 1967. Internal case file no. 100–443802.

——. *Negro Digest/Black World* file obtained under provisions of the Freedom of Information Act. Assorted documents dated 29 Jan. 1942 to 15 July 1975. Internal case file no. 100–71654.

——. Louise Thompson Patterson file obtained under provisions of the Freedom of Information Act. Assorted documents dated 17 Feb. 1941 to 11 July 1974. Internal case file no. 100–407934.

——. William Pickens file obtained under provisions of the Freedom of Information Act. Assorted documents dated 22 Oct. 1947 to 12 May 1964. Internal case file no. 121–4978.

United States [U.S.]. Dept. of Justice. Dudley Randall file obtained under provisions of the Freedom of Information Act. Assorted documents dated 13 Sept 1966 to 14 Oct. 1969. Internal case file no. 105–157679.

———. Andy Razaf [Andrea Razafkeriefo] file obtained under provisions of the Freedom of Information Act. Assorted documents dated 3 May 1949 to 19 May 1949. Internal case file no. 100–361384.

———. J. Saunders Redding file obtained under provisions of the Freedom of Information Act. Assorted documents dated 13 Feb. 1953 to 15 Aug. 1968. Internal case file no. 123–14868.

———. J. A. Rogers file obtained under provisions of the Freedom of Information Act. Assorted documents dated 14 Apr. 1942 to 2 Feb. 1967. Internal case file no. 100–94297.

———. George S. Schuyler file obtained under provisions of the Freedom of Information Act. Assorted documents dated 16 May 1942 to 30 Oct. 1967. Internal case file no. 100–82799.

———. William Gardner Smith file obtained under provisions of the Freedom of Information Act. Assorted documents dated 5 May 1951 to 7 Nov. 1974. Internal case file no. 100–379969.

———. William C. Sullivan file obtained under provisions of the Freedom of Information Act. Assorted documents dated 1 May 1941 to 13 Feb. 1974. Internal case file nos. 67–205182, 116–472026, and others.

———. Theodore Ward file obtained under provisions of the Freedom of Information Act. Assorted documents dated 3 June 1944 to 17 Nov. 1966. Internal case file no. 100–316008.

———. Walter White file obtained under provisions of the Freedom of Information Act. Assorted documents dated 23 Sept. 1943 to 21 May 1957. Internal case file no. 100–328241.

———. Richard Wright file obtained under provisions of the Freedom of Information Act. Assorted documents dated 9 Dec. 1942 to 9 May 1963. Internal case file no. 100–157464.

United States [U.S.]. House of Representatives. *Attorney General A. Mitchell Palmer on Charges Made against Department of Justice by Louis F. Post and Others: Hearings before the Committee on Rules.* 66th Cong., 2nd sess. Part 1. Washington, DC: GPO, 1920.

———. *Investigation of Communist Propaganda: Hearings before a Special Committee to Investigate Communist Activities in the United States of the House of Representatives.* 71st Cong., 2nd sess. Part 2. Vol. 1. Washington, DC: GPO, 1930.

United States [U.S.]. Senate. *Radicalism and Sedition among the Negroes as Reflected in Their Publications.* Exhibit 10. *Investigation Activities of the Department of Justice.* 66th Cong., 1st sess. Doc. 153. Washington, DC: GPO, 1919.

———. Select Committee to Study Governmental Operations with Respect to Intelligence Activities. *Hearings before the Select Committee to Study Governmental Operations with Respect to Intelligence Activities of the United States Senate.* Vol. 6. 94th Cong., 1st sess. Washington, DC: GPO, 1976.

———. Select Committee to Study Governmental Operations with Respect to Intelligence Activities. *Intelligence Activities and the Rights of Americans: Final Report.* Book 2. 94th Cong., 2nd sess. Report 94–755. Washington, DC: GPO, 1976.

————. Select Committee to Study Governmental Operations with Respect to Intelligence Activities. *Supplementary Detailed Staff Reports on Intelligence Activities and the Rights of Americans: Final Report.* Book 3. 94th Cong., 2nd sess. Report 94–755. Washington, DC: GPO, 1976.

Up Tight! Dir. Jules Dassin. Perf. Raymond St. Jacques and Ruby Dee. Paramount Pictures, 1968. Film.

Vaile, William. Statement in the *Congressional Record*, 5 Jan. 1920, quoted in Hoover, Scrapooks.

Van Peebles, Melvin. *A Bear for the FBI.* New York: Trident, 1968.

Vatulescu, Cristina. *Police Aesthetics: Literature, Film, and the Secret Police in Soviet Times.* Stanford: Stanford UP, 2010.

Vault.fbi.gov. Federal Bureau of Investigation. Web. 18 July 2013. http://www.vault.fbi .gov/.

Von Eschen, Penny M. *Satchmo Blows Up the World: Jazz Ambassadors Play the Cold War.* Cambridge: Harvard UP, 2004.

Wagner, Bryan. *Disturbing the Peace: Black Culture and the Police Power after Slavery.* Cambridge: Harvard UP, 2009.

Wald, Alan M. *American Night: The Literary Left in the Era of the Cold War.* Chapel Hill: U of North Carolina P, 2012.

Waligora-Davis, Nicole A. *Sanctuary: African Americans and Empire.* New York: Oxford UP, 2011.

Wallace, Maurice O. *Constructing the Black Masculine: Identity and Ideality in African American Men's Literature and Culture, 1775–1995.* Durham: Duke UP, 2002.

Wallerstein, Immanuel. "The Construction of Peoplehood: Racism, Nationalism, Ethnicity." 1987. *The Essential Wallerstein.* 293–309.

————. *The Essential Wallerstein.* New York: New Press, 2000.

————. *The Modern World-System*, 3 vols. New York: Academic Press, 1974–89.

Wanning, Andrews. "A Primer for Modern Poetry." Rev. of *Modern Poetry and the Tradition*, by Cleanth Brooks. *Furioso* 1.2 (1940): 23–26.

Ward, Geoffrey C. *Unforgivable Blackness: The Rise and Fall of Jack Johnson.* New York: Alfred A. Knopf, 2004.

Warner, Michael. *The Letters of the Republic: Publication and the Public Sphere in Eighteenth-Century America.* Cambridge: Harvard UP, 1990.

Warren, Kenneth W. *So Black and Blue: Ralph Ellison and the Occasion of Criticism.* Chicago: U of Chicago P, 2003.

————. *What Was African American Literature?* Cambridge: Harvard UP, 2011.

Washburn, Patrick S. *A Question of Sedition: The Federal Government's Investigation of the Black Press during World War II.* New York: Oxford UP, 1986.

Washington, Booker T. Letter to Oswald Garrison Villard. 1913. *The Booker T. Washington Papers.* Ed. Louis R. Harlan and Raymond W. Smock. Vol. 12. Urbana: U of Illinois P, 1982. 248–49.

Washington, Mary Helen. *The Other Blacklist: The African American Literary and Cultural Left of the 1950s.* New York: Columbia UP, 2014.

Webb, G. Gregg. "Intelligence Liaison between the FBI and State, 1940–44: Effective Interagency Collaboration." Cia.gov. Central Intelligence Agency. 12 Apr. 2012. Web. https://www.cia.gov/library/center-for-the-study-of-intelligence/csi-publicatiuons /csi-studies/studies/vol49no3/html_files/FBI_State_3.htm. 1–13.

Weber, Max. *Economy and Society*. 1922. *From Max Weber: Essays in Sociology*. 159–264.

———. *From Max Weber: Essays in Sociology*. Trans. H. H. Gerth and C. Wright Mills. New York: Oxford UP, 1958.

———. "Politics as a Vocation." 1921. *From Max Weber: Essays in Sociology*. 77–128.

Weiner, Tim. *Enemies: A History of the FBI*. New York: Random House, 2012.

———. "Hoover Planned Mass Jailing in 1950." *New York Times* 23 Dec. 2007. Web. 17 Nov. 2008. http://www.nytimes.com/2007/12/23/washington/23habeas.html? scp=1 &sq=Tim+Weiner+Hoover&st=nyt.

———. *Legacy of Ashes: The History of the CIA*. New York: Doubleday, 2007.

Wettstein, Howard. Introduction. *Diasporas and Exiles: Varieties of Jewish Identity*. Ed. Howard Wettstein. Berkeley: U of California P, 2002. 1–17.

Whalen, Terence. *Edgar Allan Poe and the Masses: The Political Economy of Literature in Antebellum America*. Princeton: Princeton UP, 1999.

"What Is the National Archives?" Archives.gov. National Archives. Web. 24 July 2013. http://www.archives.gov/about/.

Whitehead, Don. *The FBI Story: A Report to the People*. New York: Random House, 1956.

Whittemore, Reed. *Against the Grain: The Literary Life of a Poet*. Washington, DC: Dryad–U of Alaska P, 2007.

Widener, Daniel. *Black Arts West: Culture and Struggle in Postwar Los Angeles*. Durham: Duke UP, 2010.

Wiener, Jon. *Gimme Some Truth: The John Lennon FBI Files*. Berkeley: U of California P, 1999.

———. "J. Edgar Hoover, Author." *Nation* 22 May 2008. Web. 17 Feb. 2009. http:// 74.125.95.132/search?q=cache:Skca06rrlgQJ:www.thenation.com/doc/20080609 /wiener+%22modernism+on+file%22&hl=en&ct=clnk&cd=36&gl=us.

Wilford, Hugh. *The Mighty Wurlitzer: How the CIA Played America*. Cambridge: Harvard UP, 2008.

Williams, David. "The Bureau of Investigation and Its Critics, 1919–1921: The Origins of Federal Political Surveillance." *Journal of American History* 68.3 (Dec. 1981): 560–79.

Williams, John A. Afterword. *The Man Who Cried I Am*. 1967. New York: Overlook, 2004. 405–12.

———. "Blackballing." *Censored Books: Critical Viewpoints*. Ed. Nicholas J. Karolides, Lee Burress, and John M. Kean. Metuchen, NJ: Scarecrow, 1993. 11–18.

———. Foreword. *Black Empire*. By George S. Schuyler. Ed. Robert A. Hill and R. Kent Rasmussen. Boston, Northeastern UP, 1991. ix–xv.

———. "The Harlem Renaissance: Its Artists, Its Impact, Its Meaning." *Black World* 20 (Nov. 1970): 17–18.

———. *The King God Didn't Save*. New York: Coward-McCann, 1970.

———. *The Man Who Cried I Am*. 1967. New York: Overlook, 2004.

———. "My Man Himes: An Interview with Chester Himes." *Amistad 1*. Ed. John A. Williams and Charles F. Harris. New York: Vintage, 1970. 25–93.

Winks, Robin W. *Cloak and Gown: Scholars in the Secret War, 1939–1961*. 1987. 2nd ed. New Haven: Yale UP, 1996.

Wollaeger, Mark. *Modernism, Media, and Propaganda: British Narrative from 1900 to 1945.* Princeton: Princeton UP, 2006.

Wong, Edlie L. *Neither Fugitive nor Free: Atlantic Slavery, Freedom Suits, and the Legal Cultures of Travel.* New York: New York UP, 2009.

"Work Agreement." [July 1865 sharecropping contract between O. A. Bowen and his former slaves.] Robert Adger Bowen Papers (MS 119), oversize box. Special Collections Library, Clemson University Libraries, Clemson, SC.

Wright, Richard. "The FB Eye Blues." 1949. *Richard Wright Reader.* Ed. Ellen Wright and Michel Fabre. New York: Harper and Row, 1978. 249–50.

———. "I Choose Exile." Undated manuscript. Richard Wright Papers. James Weldon Johnson Manuscripts, Yale Collection of American Literature, Beinecke Rare Book and Manuscript Library, Yale University, New Haven, CT.

———. *Island of Hallucination.* Ts. Box 34. Folder 472. Richard Wright Papers. James Weldon Johnson Manuscripts, Yale Collection of American Literature, Beinecke Rare Book and Manuscript Library, Yale University, New Haven, CT.

———. *The Outsider.* 1953. New York: Harper Perennial, 1993.

———. *Richard Wright Reader.* Ed. Ellen Wright and Michel Fabre. New York: Harper and Row, 1978.

———. *Twelve Million Black Voices.* Photo direction Edward Rosskam. 1941. New York: Thunder's Mouth, 2002.

Yellin, Eric S. *Racism in the Nation's Service: Government Workers and the Color Line in Woodrow Wilson's America.* Chapel Hill: U of North Carolina P, 2013.

Yette, Samuel F. *The Choice: The Issue of Black Survival in America.* 1971. New York: Berkley Medallion, 1972.

Yoo, John C., and Robert J. Delahunty. "Authority for Use of Military Force to Combat Terrorist Activities within the United States." [23 Oct. 2001 memo to Alberto R. Gonzalez, Counsel to the President, and William J. Haynes II, General Counsel, Department of Defense. Department of Justice, Office of Legal Counsel.] Web. 9 Apr. 2009. www.usdoj.gov/opa/documents/memomilitaryforcecombatus1023200.

Young, Cynthia A. *Soul Power: Culture, Radicalism, and the Making of a U.S. Third World Left.* Durham: Duke UP, 2006.

Young, John K. *Black Writers, White Publishers: Marketplace Politics in Twentieth-Century African American Literature.* Jackson: UP of Mississippi, 2006.

Zaborowska, Magdalena J. *James Baldwin's Turkish Decade: Erotics of Exile.* Durham: Duke UP, 2009.

Zboray, Ronald J., and Mary Saracino Zboray. *Everyday Ideas: Socioliterary Experience among Antebellum New Englanders.* Knoxville: U of Tennessee P, 2006.

Index

Abbott, Robert, 34
Abernathy, Ralph, 2, 285n4
abstract expressionism, 219, 301n2
Accuracy in Media (AIM), 296n15
Adams, John, 137
Adler, Bill, *Kids' Letters to the F.B.I.* 99
Administrative Index, 93
Africa, 187–88, 200
African American studies, 173, 304n16
African Blood Brotherhood, 55, 63, 64, 67, 144
African colonization, 188
African slave trade, 188. *See also* slavery
Agamben, Giorgio, 69, 70, 194
Agitator Index, 93
Ai (Florence Anthony), 23, 224, 271–72; *Greed*, 271; "Hoover, J. Edgar," 271; "Hoover Trismegistus," 271
Alexander, Michelle, 288–89n19
Algeria, 178, 253, 254
Algerian War of Independence, 249, 253
Algren, Nelson, 297n18
Alhamisi, Ahmed, 118
Alien Act (1918), 47. *See also* Smith Act (Alien Registration Act)
alien allegiance, 93
Alien Registration Act (Smith Act). *See* Smith Act (Alien Registration Act)
aliens, 53; and counterintelligence against Klan, 110; and Garvey, 64; Hoover as expert on, 48; McKay as, 66, 207; registration of, 70. *See also* Alien Act (1918); Smith Act (Alien Registration Act)
Allen, Clarence (Big Daddy), 39, 41, 291n5
Allen, Emily, 40
Al Qaeda, 46
Alsberg, Henry, 76
Althusser, Louis, 191, 306nn8, 9, 10; "Ideology and Ideological State Apparatuses," 183–85
ambiguity, 137–38, 139–40, 150
American Civil Liberties Union (ACLU), 67–68

American Folklore Society, 154–55
American Magazine, 78
American Negro Theater, 287n9
American Peace Mobilization, 89
Amini, Johari (Jewel Lattimore), 222, 260; "Upon Being Black One Friday in July," 310n10
Amos, James E., 95, 97, 109
anarchists, 31, 46, 47, 48–49
Anderson, Benedict, 182–83, 184, 306nn6, 7
Anderson, Carl, 312n25
Anderson, Charles, "Prayer to the White Man's God," 129
Anderson, Dale, 285n2
Anderson, Sherwood, 68
Angelou, Maya, 60; *I Know Why the Caged Bird Sings*, 108
Angleton, James Jesus, 136–39, 140–41, 149, 150, 151, 162, 164, 302n6; "Caresse Primordiale," 137; and FBI interpretive criticism, 145; FBI interview of, 141–42; and Hoover, 141, 165
Annales school, 186
Anti-Defamation League, 274
anti-elegies, 224, 265
antifiles, 7, 15, 23, 224, 258–59, 261, 262, 263, 264
anti-Garveyites, 228
anti-Semitism, 23, 274. *See also* Jews
antitrust violations, 33
Anvil, 147
Aoki, Richard, 111, 299n26
Archer, John Michael, 130
Armstrong, Louis, 212
Asagai, Joseph, 299n23
Atlanta Constitution, 155, 158
Atlanta Daily World, 83
Attaway, William, *Blood on the Forge*, 296n14
Attica Prison uprising, 229
Auden, W. H., 134, 301–2n3
Ayler, Albert, 108

Bailey, William A., 41

Baldwin, James, 74, 178, 224, 286n6, 307n18; and abandoned script for Malcolm X biopic, 209; and BARTS, 123; and Café Tournon, 178; and Campbell, 307n17; and CIA, 210; and Civil Rights movement, 210; FBI-authored poem in file of, 300n28; FBI disdained by, 22; FBI in writings of, 6; FBI questioning of, 221, 310n9, 312n22; FBI reading of, 123, 127–28; FBI wiretapping of, 209, 219, 300n29; file on, 7, 59, 106, 116, 123, 196, 209–11, 307n17; in France, 209–10; in Himes novel, 256; and Hoover, 127–28; and King assassination, 209; lectures by, 123; and legats, 198; and model citizen criticism, 171–73; and passport, 20, 21, 204, 209, 210 –11; and political murder, 112; in protest against Bureau spying, 220; and Security Index, 94; and sexuality, 64, 127; and W. G. Smith, 251; and social realism vs. modernism, 220; and stop notices, 21, 209, 210–11; and translation, 196, 307n18; in Turkey, 196; unproductiveness of, 219, 221; and Wright, 220, 248, 252; WORKS: *Another Country*, 123, 127–28, 171, 172, 209; *The Blood Counters*, 22, 123, 220, 224, 260, 312n22; *Blues for Mister Charlie*, 123, 172, 300n29; *The Devil Finds Work*, 209, 211, 310n9, 312n22; "Equal in Paris," 248; "Everybody's Protest Novel," 248; and *The FBI Story*, 209; *The Fire Next Time*, 123; *Go Tell It on the Mountain*, 127; interview in "Looking at New York from Istanbul," 196; interview in *Yeni Gazette*, 196; *Kara Yabanci, or Dark Stranger*, 209; "Many Thousands Gone," 248; *No Name in the Street*, 21, 123, 210; "An Open Letter to My Sister, Miss Angela Davis," 112

Bales, James D., *J. Edgar Hoover Speaks concerning Communism*, 292n9

Balibar, Étienne, 182

Baltic States, 196

Baraka, Amiri (LeRoi Jones), 6, 74, 107–8, 112, 168, 224, 286n6, 309n5; and African American informers, 97; Air Force investigation of, 117; and BARTS, 108; at "Black Anger Arts Festival," 119; FBI book review of, 129; FBI interview with, 117; FBI literary criticism of, 118; FBI performance reviews of, 119–20; FBI

questioning of, 221; file on, 59, 60, 106, 117–21, 145; and Hoover Poems, 23; and Moorland-Spingarn Research Center, 60; on Negro History Week program, 119–20; and Rabble-Rouser Index, 117–18; and Security Index, 94; and Wright, 219, 221; WORKS: *The Autobiography*, 107, 108; "Black Art," 118–19; *Black Arts*, 118; and "The Black Bohemians," 145; *Black Fire*, 118, 125, 129, 260, 265; *Black Magic*, 265; *A Black Mass*, 120; "Black People!", 120; "The Dance of the Toms," 120; *Dutchman*, 19, 169; *Four Revolutionary Plays*, 118; "Three Movements and a Coda," 23, 120, 265–66; "The Wailer," 108

Barker, Ma, 76

Barker gang, 79

Barnes, George Francis, Jr. (Machine Gun Kelly), 49

Barrow, Clyde, 58

Batvinis, Raymond J., 295n10

Baudelaire, Charles, 246

Baumgardner, F. J., 149

Beauvoir, Simone de, 176; *The Second Sex*, 257, 311n21

Beckles, Colin A., 299n25

Bee, 27

Bellow, Saul, 134

Benét, William Rose, *Oxford Anthology of American Literature*, 136

Benjamin, Walter, 288n16

Bennett, Gwendolyn, 287n13; and "Custodial Detention" list, 17–18, 92; and Edwards, 193; FBI questioning of, 221; file on, 9, 59, 67, 88–89; and RACON, 86; and Security Index, 93

Benston, Kimberly, 119, 266

Bentham, Jeremy, 72

Beverly, William, 44

Biddle, Francis, 82, 86, 91, 92, 165, 297–98n18

biographical fallacy, 146

biohistoricism, 131, 145–46, 150

biomythography, 272

Birmingham Age-Herald, 156

Birth of a Nation (1915), 34, 289n2

Bishop, Elizabeth, 134

Black Aesthetic, 10

Black Arts movement, 16, 17, 18, 86, 113, 143, 222, 260, 264–65, 271, 288n18; and aesthetics, 120, 129; and Ai, 272; and author-audience dynamics, 119–20, 121; and Baraka's FBI file, 117; and *Black Fire*, 118; Bureau poems of, 265; and counterintelligence, 60; FBI files on, 116, 121; FBI investigation of, 59, 108–9; and FBI performance reviews, 119–20; and C. Himes, 263; Hoover in demonology of, 23, 224; as masculinist, 223; and McKay, 230; performative verse of, 5–6; and Reed, 264; and Sanchez, 269; theaters of, 108; and J. Williams, 259, 262, 263

Black Arts Repertory Theatre/School (BARTS), 260; and Baldwin, 123; and Baraka's FBI file, 117; FBI file on, 287n9; FBI investigation of, 108–9; and FBI performance reviews, 119; and federal antipoverty funds, 117; and Sanchez, 269

Black Arts West (San Francisco), 108

Black Atlantic, 16, 20–22, 67, 170, 186–95, 202, 203, 217, 251; and Edwards, 191–94; and Gilroy, 189–91, 192; and McKay, 207; and J. Williams, 259. *See also* diaspora; internationalism; transnationality/transnationalism

blackballing, 221, 309n8. *See also* Security Index

Blackboard, 115

Black Cabinet, 36

Black Codes, 295n8. *See also* slave codes

Black Marxists, 144

black nationalism, 23, 93, 121, 195, 300n30; and Baraka, 108, 118; and Black Arts movement, 108; and FBI counterliterary authorship, 114, 115; and FBI informers, 111; and Greenlee, 264; and Neal, 122; and passports, 204; and political murder, 112; and J. Williams, 262

Black Nationalist Photograph Album, 111

Black Panther, 115

Black Panthers, 61, 111–12, 114, 115, 260, 285n3, 299nn26, 27

Black Power, 18, 61, 66, 112–13; and BARTS, 108; and COINTELPRO minstrelsy, 124; and counterliterature, 63; and Hansberry, 102; and C. Himes, 254; and model citizen criticism, 171; and Randall, 270; and W. G. Smith, 254

Black Power manifestoes, 113–14

Black Rep (St. Louis), 108

Black Scholar, 287n9, 300n30

Black Star Line, 199

Black World. See Negro Digest (Black World)

Black World Foundation, 300n30

Blaxploitation films, 312n25

BLKARTSOUTH (New Orleans), 108

Bloom, Harold, 140

blues, 6, 216, 244

Bolsheviks, 46, 47, 52, 54, 55, 230. *See also* communism; Soviet Union

Bonaparte, Charles, 29–30, 33, 99

Bonner, Marita, 8

Bontemps, Arna, 232

Booker, Simeon, "The Negro in the FBI—J. Edgar Hoover," 109

Book of the Month Club, 80

bookstores, 22, 100, 110–11, 217, 299n25. *See also* publishers

Boulin, Herbert, 41

Bourdieu, Pierre, 310n12

Bowen, Robert Adger, 131, 151–59, 164, 165, 174, 194, 310–11n14; background and education of, 151–52; and black dialect, 19, 159; black dialect tales of, 154, 155–57; and black folksongs, 157–58; and Bureau of Translations, 53; and Ferris, 226; and Hoover, 159, 225; and Johnson, 227–28; papers of, 152, 160; as reader, 19; WORKS: "The Barrier," 152; "A Case of Conjur," 157, 158; "The Devoté," 303n9; "The Giver," 303n10; "Memoirs of a G-Man," 154; "Miss Ang'la," 155–56; "Miss Em'ly," 156; "Nathaniel Hawthorne as Author," 152; "Negro Songs," 157–58; "The Re-Action to Date of the Negro Press," 226; *Uncharted Seas*, 153. See also *Radicalism and Sedition among the Negroes as Reflected in Their Publications* (Bowen et al.)

Boyle, Kay, 177

Bradford, William, 136

Braudel, Fernand, 185, 307n13; *Civilization and Capitalism*, 186

Brecht, Bertolt, *The Caucasian Chalk Circle*, 297n18

Brenneisen, Leo S., 147

Briggs, Cyril, 55

British Foreign Office, 207

British state spy service. *See* MI6

Broadside Press, 122, 269, 287n9

Brooks, Cleanth, 146; "Keats's Sylvan Historicism," 145, 146; "The Language of Paradox,"

Brooks, Cleanth (cont)
138, 139; *Modern Poetry and the Tradition*, 137, 149; *Understanding Poetry*, 135–36, 138; *The Well Wrought Urn*, 139
Brooks, Gwendolyn, 222, 310n10
Brown, Bill, 160, 303n11
Brown, Frank London, 59, 94, 106, 222, 287n13
Brown, H. Rap, 114
Brown, Julia Clarice, *I Testify*, 96–97
Brown, Lloyd, 59, 86, 93, 205, 221, 297–98n18
Brown, Sterling, 117, 221; file on, 59, 67, 86, 89–90, 287n13, 297n16; *The Negro Caravan*, 89
Brown, Sterling Nelson, 36
Buckley, William F., 133; *Spytime*, 136
Bulletin of Radical Activities, 52
"Bully Bolsheviki, The," 58
Bureau of Engraving and Printing, 36, 37
Bureau of Investigation. *See under* Federal Bureau of Investigation
Burns, William J., 31, 43, 47, 65, 66–67; *The Masked War*, 31
Burrough, Bryan, 293n14
Burroughs, Margaret, 310n10
Burroughs, William, 223
Bush, George H. W., 165, 168, 169
Bush, George W., 11, 69, 74
Butler, Judith, 183, 306n8
Byrnes, James F., 293n13

Café Monaco, 175, 176
Café Tournon, 197, 305n1; and Baldwin, 178; as gathering place, 175, 178, 179; and Gibson Affair, 178; and Harrington, 178; and C. Himes, 178, 256, 258; and W. G. Smith, 178, 251, 254; and Stovall, 176; and J. Williams, 259; and Wright, 176, 178, 247, 248, 249
Cagney, James, 76
Cain, James M., 78
Caldwell, Erskine, 68
Campbell, James, 219, 221, 307n17
Capital Reader, 274
Capitol Reader, 275
Carlston, Erin, 24
Carmichael, Stokely, 114, 163
Carson, Clayborne, 285n2
Cather, Willa, 4
Caute, David, 301n2

Cayton, Horace, *Black Metropolis*, 84, 122
censorship, 22, 43, 217–18, 224–25; of FBI files, 11; and ghostreading, 6; and McKay, 231; of McKay's FBI file, 66; and model citizen criticism, 169, 170; of national press, 81–82; racialized, 221; and Reed, 264; and Van Peebles, 264
Central Intelligence Agency (CIA), 131–41, 150, 173, 223; and abstract expressionism vs. social realism, 219; and Althusser, 184; and ambiguity, 140; and Baldwin, 210; and Congress for Cultural Freedom, 243, 249; creative writers in, 133–34; and educational background of agents, 133; and FBI, 5, 52, 97, 132–33, 146, 149, 150, 197, 201, 301n1; and FBI's image, 133, 142; and Gillespie, 212; and goodwill tours of musicians, 213; and Greenlee, 264; and C. Himes, 257, 263; and Hoover, 132–33; and literary criticism and patronage, 134; and Mayfield, 105; music sponsorship by, 180; and National Security Act, 132; and New Criticism, 19, 131, 134, 138–39, 142, 145; search for communist traitors inside, 140; and translation, 197; and Truman, 97; and J. Williams, 260–61, 262, 263; and Wright, 250, 257; and Yale University, 134–36, 137, 138, 140
Cerf, Bennett, 101
Chafee, Zechariah, 70
Chandler, Raymond, 255
Chaney, James, 109
charismatic leader, 70–71, 72, 73. *See also under* Hoover, J. Edgar
Chesnutt, Charles W., *The Conjure Woman*, 157
Chicago Defender, 34, 83, 85, 218–19, 235, 236
Childress, Alice, 9, 21, 59, 65, 94, 104, 204, 222
Chomsky, Noam, 298n21
Church Committee report (1976), 295n10
Citizens' Commission to Investigate the FBI, 124, 300n33
Civil Rights Act, 111
Civil Rights Commission, *To Secure These Rights*, 95
civil rights movement, 14, 18, 109, 124, 219; and Bowen, 152; and Hoover, 39; and passports, 199–200; and Schuyler, 149, 233; in Smith, 253, 254; and Sullivan, 1, 162

CLA Journal, 287n9

Clapp, Jeffrey, 244

Clarke, Cheryl, 267

Cleaver, Eldridge, 74, 113; *Soul on Ice*, 248

Clemenceau, Georges, 30

Clifton, Lucille, 60, 122–23, 287n13

Clinton, Bill, 272

Cohn, Roy, 100

COINTELPRO, 289–90n2; anticommunist, 111, 162; and Sullivan, 162–65

COINTELPRO—Black Nationalist/Hate Groups, 15, 109–25, 260, 303–4n13; and Black Panthers, 111–12; congressional condemnation of, 125; and counter-literature, 112–25, 128, 147, 164, 270; organization of, 109–11; public disclosure of, 124–25; and Senna, 272, 273

COINTELPRO—White Heat, 38. *See also* Ku Klux Klan

Cold War, 81, 97, 170, 196, 201, 203, 218, 221; and African Americans in Paris, 176; and American right, 167; and Angleton, 139; and antiradical indexes, 93; and CIA, 132, 134; and civil rights, 200; and Ellison, 144, 236, 237; and FBI anticommunism, 48, 49, 72; and FBI reading, 149; and Hansberry, 18; and C. Himes, 257; and Hoover, 25; and Hughes, 235; investigations of African Americans during, 59, 60; and New Criticism, 135; and passports, 200; and Security Index, 94; and social realism vs. modernism, 220; and Total Literary Awareness, 100, 106, 107, 145; and Wright, 220, 245, 249, 250, 251

Cold War liberalism, 95, 240, 301n2

Cold War state, 180, 199, 202, 213

Coleman, F.W.B., 196

Collier, Rex, 77

Collier's, 84

Collins, Carita Owens, "This Must Not Be!", 55–56

Collins, Frederick L.: *The FBI in Peace and War*, 295–96n12, 304n14; "Slickers in Slacks," 84

Coltrane, John, 23, 265

Coltrane Poems, 23, 266

Comfort, Mildred Houghton, *J. Edgar Hoover, Modern Knight Errant*, 35

comic strips/books, 76, 115

Committee to Restore Paul Robeson's Passport, 21, 204

communism, 3, 8, 106; American literary, 68; and Angleton, 138, 140; and Baraka, 117; and CIA, 132; and COINTELPRO, 111, 162; and communal authorship in FBI files, 65–66; and Congress for Cultural Freedom, 249; and Coty, 192–93; and Ellison, 144, 237, 239–40, 241; and Federal Writers' Project, 76; and Garvey, 55; and good government, 98; and goodwill tours of jazz musicians, 213; and Hansberry, 103, 128; and Harlem radicals, 237; and Harrington, 203; and Hernton, 104; in Himes, 255; and Hoover, 25, 26, 30, 41, 48, 61, 225, 292n8; and Hoover in public esteem, 99; and Hoover Raids, 48; and Hoover's charismatic power, 71; and Hoover's racism, 54; and Hughes, 167, 168, 236, 237; and Jones, 212; and McKay, 63, 64, 65; and modernist authors, 73; and morality, 33; and Motley, 204; outlawing of American, 95; and passports, 204; F. Roosevelt's authorization of investigations of, 80; and Schuyler, 91, 149; strictures against noncriminal investigations of, 68; and Sullivan, 161; and travel control, 200; and White, 87; and Wright, 177, 243, 245, 249. *See also* Bolsheviks; Marxism; Soviet Union

Communist Index, 93

Communist Party, 222, 270; and arrests of 1919 and 1920, 48; and Bennett, 88, 89; and L. Brown, 297–98n18; and S. Brown, 89, 90, 297n16; counterintelligence program against, 110; and Cruse, 106; and Cummings, 96; and Davis, 147–48; and W.E.B. Du Bois, 202, 203; FBI penetration of, 72; and Hansberry, 102; and Hernton, 149; and C. Himes, 255; Hoover's brief against, 49; informers in, 96; and McKay, 63; and Smith Act trials, 95–96; and Sullivan, 162; white chauvinism in, 96

Compromise of 1877, 34, 35

Congress: Church and Pike commissions of, 125; and CIA vs. FBI, 197; and COINTELPRO, 110, 113, 125; corruption in, 33; and exceptional laws, 69; and FBI budget, 46, 77, 98; and FBI counterintelligence programs, 110; and Hoover, 3, 53, 98, 197, 298n20; and Lowenthal, 100;

Congress (cont)
and magazines, 229; and misgivings about Special Agent Force, 29, 99; and Passport Control Act of 1918, 198; and *Radicalism and Sedition*, 53; and Smith Act of 1940, 81; and Truman, 98. *See also* House of Representatives; Senate

Congress for Cultural Freedom, 134, 219, 243, 249, 301n2, 311n20

Congressional Record, 17, 225

Congress of Afrikan Peoples, 121

Congress of Racial Equality (CORE), 3

Conquest, Robert, *The Great Terror*, 118

conscientious objectors, 82

Continents, Les, 192

Cook, Fred, *The FBI Nobody Knows*, 101

Coolidge, Calvin, 293n2

Cooper, Courtney Ryley, 77; *Ten Thousand Public Enemies*, 78, 97

Corey, Herbert, *Farewell, Mr. Gangster!*, 77

Cortez, Jayne, 60

cosmopolitanism, 20, 105, 179, 180, 245

Coty, François, 192–93

Coulter, Ann, 299n27

counter-counterliterature, 123

counterintelligence, 18, 59–60, 61, 289–90n2; and American Africanism, 4; and Angleton, 140; against Communist Party, 110; defined, 62; and Double-Cross system, 62, 135, 139, 301n3; against Ku Klux Klan, 109, 110; and New Critical close reading, 138–39; and Sullivan, 1, 62, 162; in Wright, 245. *See also* COINTELPRO; espionage/spies

counterliterary exception, state of, 69–70, 72, 75, 80, 81, 82, 98. *See also* exception, state of

counterliterature, 73, 76–85, 107, 179, 218, 288–89n19; and African American writing, 80; and Afro-modernist writing, 61; authorship of, 112–17, 118–19; and Baldwin, 123; and COINTELPRO, 112–25, 128, 147, 164, 270; and Cold War, 106; defined, 18, 62; and FBI theory of reading, 144; and Harlem Renaissance, 75; and internationalism, 94; and Lowenthal, 99; during McCarthy period, 63; and McKay file, 63–67; and Roosevelt, 70; and Total Literary Awareness, 100; violence encouraged through, 112–15; and World War II, 63, 85–93

countersubversion, 47, 48, 54, 81

countersurveillance, 230

counterterrorism, 69

Craig, Arthur Ulysses, 41

Crawford, James, 41–42

Crick, Francis, 308n20

crime fiction, 312–13n26

crime rates, 78

crime reporters, 77

criminology, 78, 79

Crisis, 27, 228

Cromer, Kirk, 14

Crossman, Richard, 308n22

Crudup, Billy, 289n1

Crusader, 55, 56, 227, 228

Cruse, Harold, 20, 59, 94, 203–4, 221, 287n13; *The Crisis of the Negro Intellectual*, 106, 108, 211

Cullen, Countee, 192, 232

Culleton, Claire A., 9, 100, 297n18, 298–99n21, 309n6

cummings, e. e., 137, 141, 268

Cummings, Marion Morehouse, 141

Cummings, William, 96

Cunningham, David, 110

Custodial Detention, 91–93, 94, 171, 177–78, 224, 297–98n18. *See also* Security Index

Daily Worker, 91, 101, 147, 153, 202

D. Appleton and Company, 152, 154

Dassin, Jules, 312n25

Davies, Carole Boyce, 24, 212

Davis, Frank Marshall, 8, 59, 86, 93, 147–48, 149, 221, 287n13; "Frank-ly Speaking," 147

Davis, Mike, 298n21

Davis, Miles, 212

Dearie, Blossom, "I'm Shadowing You," 308–9n2

décalage, 192, 193, 194, 196

deconstructive criticism, 140

Deep Throat, 124

deep time, 185–86

Defoe, Daniel, 130

DeLillo, Don, 23, 223; *White Noise*, 150

DeLoach, Cartha "Deke," 160, 290n4, 309n6

de Man, Paul, 140

Democratic New Deal, 98

Democratic Party, 4, 94, 116. *See also* southern Democrats

Dennis v. United States, 95

Department of Homeland Security, 47

Department of Justice, 31, 46, 81, 165, 226; *Annual Report of the Attorney General*, 49; and Bowen, 153; Enemy Alien Registration unit, 47, 48; and Flynn, 31; General Crimes Section, 128; hearings on contributions of to Red Scare, 67; Hoover as employee of, 28; and magazines, 228–29; and *Messenger*, 232; Office of Information and Privacy, 10; Office of Legal Counsel, 69; and records destruction, 67; revisionism and Red Raids, 68; Special Agent Force, 29–30, 99; strictures against noncriminal investigations by, 68; and J. Williams, 261
Department of State, 202
Dépêche Africaine, La, 193
Depp, Johnny, 293n14
Derrida, Jacques, *Archive Fever*, 292n11
detective literature, 245, 246, 251, 254, 257, 258–59. *See also* mystery genre
detention, preventive, 297n17. *See also* Custodial Detention; Security Index
Dewey decimal system, 45
Dial Press, 260
diaspora, 187–88, 193, 194, 202, 213–14; communication within, 197; and deportation, 212; FBI attempts to manage, 206; and Gilroy, 189, 190, 191; and hybridity, 211; multilingual, 21; and print culture, 20; and translation, 192; transoceanic theory of, 192; in Wright, 245. *See also* Black Atlantic
DiCaprio, Leonardo, 289n1
Didion, Joan, 23, 116, 223
Dillinger, John, 58, 79
Dimock, Wai Chee, 189, 191, 307n13; *Through Other Continents*, 185–87
Dirksen, Everett, 298n20
Dixon, Thomas: *Birth of a Nation*, 36–37; *The Klansman*, 34
Doctorow, E. L., 223
Donner, Frank J., 47, 77, 78, 295n10
Double-Cross system. *See* counterintelligence
Doubleday, 251
Double V campaign, 82
Douglas Johnson, Georgia, 59, 67, 86
Douglass, Frederick, 14
Doyle, Sir Arthur Conan, 10, 31
Drake, St. Clair, 60, 222, 287n13; *Black Metropolis*, 84, 122
Dreiser, Theodore, 93
Drum and Spear, 299n25

Du Bois, Shirley Graham, 20, 59, 94, 106, 201, 202, 222
Du Bois, W.E.B., 6, 64, 149, 222, 228; and African American informers, 97; and Communist Party, 202, 203; and Cruse, 203; and Custodial Detention, 93; and double consciousness, 242; and Ellison, 242; and FBI interviews, 128; FBI surveillance of, 201–2; file on, 59, 67, 86, 200–202; and Ghana, 201, 202; and Hughes, 235; and "International Association for Colored People," 200; and internationalism, 200; and McKay, 228; and model citizen criticism, 171; and NAACP, 200; obituary in *Daily Worker*, 202; and Pan-African Congress, 188; passport of, 20, 200–203, 204, 206, 207, 209, 211; and *Radicalism and Sedition*, 55; and socially black person, 225; and stop notices, 21, 209; and J. Williams, 262, 263; WORKS: *The Black Flame*, 203; *Black Reconstruction in America*, 34; *Dark Princess*, 200; *Dusk of Dawn*, 225; *Encyclopedia Africana*, 169; "Quest of the Silver Fleece," 200; "Returning Soldiers," 27–28; *The Souls of Black Folk*, 200
Dudziak, Mary L., 199–200
Duhamel, Marcel, 255
Dumas, Henry, 8
Dumm, Thomas, 39
Dunbar, Paul Laurence, "We Wear the Mask," 242
Dunbar High, 37
Dunham, Katherine, 20, 59, 86–87, 204
Dunham School of Dance, 86–87
Durem, Ray, 59, 86, 93, 221, 287n13; "Award (A Gold Watch to the FBI Man who has followed me for 25 years)", 270
Durrell, Lawrence, 137
Dylan, Bob, 123

Eagleton, Terry, 147
Early, Gerald, 312n25
East German Writers' Association, 125
Eastman, Max, 65, 207
Eastwood, Clint, 45, 289n1, 290n4
"Eavesdropper's Blues" (song), 216–17
Ebony, 97, 109, 287n9; "Negro FBI Agents in Action," 95, 109
Edwards, Brent Hayes, 24, 176, 188, 199, 213–14; *The Practice of Diaspora*, 191–94, 195, 197, 289n21

Ehrenreich, Barbara, 298n21
Eisenhower, Dwight, 304n15
Eisenhower administration, 103, 243
Elder, Lonne, III, 59, 106, 287n13
Eliot, T. S., 150, 219, 220; *Four Quartets*, 134; "Gerontion," 139; "Mélange Adultère de Tout," 137; *The Waste Land*, 139, 268
Ellington, Duke, 37
Ellison, Ralph, 40–41, 311nn16, 17; and American Academy in Rome, 106; assumes himself FBI suspect, 222; and Congress for Cultural Freedom, 243, 249; drafts of *Invisible Man*, 6, 23, 97, 106, 220, 224, 237–42, 243; file on, 7, 8, 59, 106, 144; and Hughes, 236, 237, 239; *Invisible Man*, 84, 97, 144, 205, 229, 236–43, 244; and McKay, 241; in reaction to Bureau attention, 220; and social realism vs. modernism, 220; *Three Days Before the Shooting...*, 205, 242; White House visits of, 106; and Wright, 220, 237, 243, 244, 250; "Writings File," 23
Ellul, Jacques, 294n6
Emergency Civil Liberties Committee, 123
Empson, William, 137, 140, 150, 302n6; *Seven Types of Ambiguity*, 138, 139–40
Encounter, 134
Encyclopedia Africana, 201–2
English Renaissance, 130, 230
Epstein, William H., 43, 139
Eskridge, Chauncey, 2
Espionage Act (1917), 47, 69
espionage/spies, 97; and aesthetics, 15; and creative writing, 130; and Double-Cross system, 62; in Wright, 245–46, 247, 248–50. *See also* counterintelligence
exception, state of, 69–70, 194. *See also* counterliterary exception, state of
Executive Order 2285, 198
expatriates. *See* Black Atlantic
Exposure of the Land Swindlers, The (1913), 31

Fabre, Michel, 305n2
Falkner, Murry, 236; *The Falkners of Mississippi*, 150
Fast, Howard, 309n6
Faulkner, William, 79, 150, 236; *Go Down, Moses*, 40
Fauset, Jessie, 222
"FBI in Peace and War, The" (radio series), 272

FBI Story, The (1959), 290n3
Federal Bureau of Investigation, 266; archive of, 58; Book Review Section, 54; budget of, 46, 77, 98; as Bureau of Investigation, 30, 46, 47; Bureau of Translations, 53, 131, 154, 158; Bureau of Translations and Radical Publications, 51, 153, 164; and CIA, 5, 52, 97, 132–33, 146, 149, 150, 197, 201, 301n1; CIA's image of, 133, 142; crime laboratory of, 143; Crime Records Division, 95; Domestic Intelligence Division, 1, 46, 131, 160, 162, 163; establishment of, 16, 29–30, 99; Extremist Intelligence Section, 118; file system of, 7, 10–11, 45–46, 51–52, 65, 71, 80, 81, 199; fingerprint collection of, 304n14; General Intelligence Division, 46, 81; growth in years after 9/11, 7–8; before Hoover, 29–35; Hoover's hiring by, 16, 25, 29; and Hughes, 235–36; and Huston Plan, 162; informers for, 41, 95–97, 98, 101, 110, 111, 118, 119, 233; Internal Security Division, 83; Library Awareness Program, 292n10; library of, 58, 68, 80, 96, 118, 143; and Library of Congress classification, 45–46; Media, Pennsylvania office of, 124, 300n33; as national detective agency, 30; and national land survey, 44; Obscene File, 286n5; and Office of Strategic Services, 135; as paramilitarized, 26; Publication Section (1920), 31; Publications Section (1935), 76, 77; Radical Division, 3, 7, 25, 26, 46–47, 48, 49, 50, 51, 52, 53, 54–58, 63, 67, 74–75, 81, 142, 143, 198, 217; Radical Division library, 71; Radical Publications Section, 51; Record/Information Dissemination Section, 8, 14, 66; and "Records Retention Plan and Disposition Schedule," 10, 60, 122, 294n4, 296n14; Responsibilities Program, 98; Seat of Government, 14, 38, 83, 93, 99, 111, 133, 159, 173, 209–10, 294n5, 300n30; and Secret Service, 47; self-nationalization by, 35, 52, 54, 57; Spanish-language school, 197; as Special Agent Force, 29–30, 99; Special Intelligence Service (SIS), 197, 198; and State Department, 80; *Survey of Racial Conditions in the United States* (RACON), 83–86, 87, 296n13; transfer of early records to National Archives by, 67;

Translations and Radical Publications, 226; Translations department, 54

Federal Bureau of Investigation agents: African Americans as, 38, 40, 41–42, 95, 109, 163, 239; background and outlook of, 131; as commercial travel agents, 211; as critic-spies, 130; educational background of, 5, 19, 133, 143, 151; and employee discipline, 72; as fact-finding investigators, 49; growth in number of, 77; as legal attaché agents (legats), 197–98, 209–10; literary reviews of, 123

Federal Bureau of Investigation author files, 7–14, 83, 86, 124; absence of new between 1925 and 1939, 68; composition of, 65–66, 131; as genre, 17, 67, 251, 257–58; as literary-critical documents, 127–74; theory and practice of reading in, 18–19, 141–50. *See also* Bowen, Robert Adger; model citizen criticism; Sullivan, William C.

Federal Loyalty Board, 96

Federal Security Agency, 89

Federal Theatre Project, 86

Federal Writers' Project (FWP), 76, 77, 80, 88, 295n9

Feds, 76

Felt, Mark, 124, 159

feminism, 102, 257, 272

Ferris, William H., 228; "Thanksgiving Sermon," 226

Fields, Annie, 42

Finch, Stanley W., 30, 31, 32, 45

fingerprints, 166, 304n14

Fire!!, 88

First Amendment, 62, 69, 70

Fitzgerald, F. Scott, *The Great Gatsby*, 25

Flaubert, Gustave, *Madame Bovary*, 247

Fleming, Ian, 130, 131–32, 133

Floyd, Pretty Boy, 76, 79

Flynn, William J., 30–31, 43, 47, 48

Flynn's Weekly, 31

Foerstel, Herbert N., 292n10

Foley, Barbara, 24, 75, 237, 239–40, 311nn16, 17

Ford, Charles Henri, 137

Ford, John, 312n25

Fortune, 101

Foucault, Michel, 15, 65, 66, 75, 306n9; *The Archaeology of Knowledge*, 292n11; *Discipline and Punish*, 45; *The History of

Sexuality*, 288n17

Fourteenth Amendment, 34–35, 198

Fourth Congress of the Communist International (Comintern), 66–67

Fox, John F., Jr., 14

France, 253, 256; Ministère des Colonies, 193; Sûreté Générale, 233, 249

Franklin, Benjamin, 44; *Autobiography*, 42

Franz Ferdinand, 198

Frazier, E. Franklin, 59, 106, 221

Freedom, 104

Freedom of Information Act (FOIA), 11, 59, 65, 66, 98, 120, 131, 150, 294–95n7

Freedom of Information Act (FOIA) requests, 7, 8–14, 60, 74, 272, 300n31

Freedom Riders, 235

Freedom Summer, 109

French intelligence, 207

Friday Night Socialist Forum, 122

Friedly, Michael, 285n2

From Another Country (1973), 209

Fuller, Hoyt, 59, 106, 121, 222, 287n13; "Information and Communication for Survival," 121

Furioso, 137–38, 302–3n7

Gable, Clark, 38

Gaines, Kevin K., 204–5

Gallen, David, 285n2

galut, 213, 214

Gandy, Helen, 45

gangsters, 49, 58, 68, 76

gang warfare, 110

Garrow, David, 14, 285n2

Garvey, Marcus, 3, 64, 191, 196, 199; and Amos, 95; arrest and deportation of, 293n2; and Bolshevik propaganda, 55; and mail fraud conviction, 212; and Mann Act, 33; and McKay, 228; and transnationalism, 194

Garveyism, 199

Garvey movement, 226

Gates, Henry Louis, Jr., *The Norton Anthology of African American Literature*, 8, 9, 60, 74, 229

Gayle, Addison, Jr., 10, 60, 107, 122, 230, 300n32

Gellner, Ernest, 306n6, 306n10

genocide, 259, 260–63

Gentry, Curt, 100, 298n20

George Washington University, 37–38
Gerald, Carolyn, 265
Ghana, 177, 201–2, 204, 209
"Ghetto Listening Posts," 110
Gibson, Donald, 241–42
Gibson, Richard, 177, 247, 305n2; letter to
  Life, 178, 256, 257; *A Mirror for Magis-*
  trates, 312n23; and W. G. Smith, 254; and
  J. Williams, 262; and Wright, 248, 252
Gibson, William, 223
Gibson Affair, 178, 215, 244, 245, 249, 250,
  259; and C. Himes, 255, 256, 257; and W.
  G. Smith, 178, 253–54; and J. Williams,
  259, 262; and Wright, 251, 256, 257
Giddens, Anthony, 306n6
Gillespie, Dizzy, 212
Gilmore, Michael T., 309n8
Gilroy, Paul, 20, 194, 253, 307n15; *The Black*
  Atlantic, 179, 189–91, 192, 205, 211, 212,
  289n21
Ginsberg, Allen, 117, 134, 286n6
Giovanni, Nikki, 6, 23, 221, 224, 272; "I
  Laughed When I Wrote It (Don't You
  Think It's Funny?)", 121, 269, 310n9; "A
  Short Essay of Affirmation Explaining
  Why (With Apologies to the Federal
  Bureau of Investigation)", 266–67
Glasgow, Ellen, 152
Gloster, Hugh, 234
G-Men (1935), 76
G-Men Magazine, 76, 237
Goldman, Emma, 48–49, 207; "Patriotism: A
  Menace to Liberty," 49
Gone with the Wind (1939), 239
Goodman, Andrew, 109
Gosciak, Josh, 294n3
Government Man (G-Man), 68, 76–78
Graff, Gerald, 142, 146–47
Great Depression, 17, 76, 144, 145, 147, 223;
  and Afro-modernism, 79; decreased FBI
  investigations of African American writers
  during, 234; and New Negroes, 59; and
  radical social realism, 220
Great Migration, 34, 35, 84, 236, 238
Great Society, 111, 117
Greene, Graham, 130
Green Lantern, 120
Greenlee, Sam, 23, 222, 224, 310n10; *The*
  Spook Who Sat by the Door, 263–64
Griffith, D. W., 34

Grimké, Archibald, "Her Thirteen Black
  Soldiers," 56
Guibernau, Montserrat, 181, 182
Guilbaut, Serge, 301n2
Gunning, Sandra, 211

Hale, Nathan, 134
Hammett, Dashiell, 78, 246, 255
Hampton, Fred, 112
Hanchard, Michael, 308n23
Hansberry, Lorraine: *Andromeda the Thief*,
  102; assumes herself FBI suspect, 222;
  and Black Power, 102; and Childress,
  104; contributions to small labor papers,
  101; death of, 101; FBI investigation of,
  101–3, 107; FBI literary interpretation
  of, 102–3, 128; file on, 9, 59, 299n23; and
  lesbian feminism, 102; and Montivedeo
  peace conference, 101; passport of, 20,
  204; *A Raisin in the Sun*, 9, 18, 19, 102–3,
  107, 128, 145, 168, 169, 218; and Security
  Index, 94, 102
Hansen, Jim, 305n5
hard-boiled style, 78, 79
Harding, Warren, 196
Hardt, Michael, 306n11
Harlem: and communism, 237; cultural rebirth of, 29; as global race capital, 195; and
  McKay, 64; riots of August 1943 in, 85; and
  Washington, D.C., 35
Harlem Renaissance, 16, 41, 102, 143, 195,
  207, 259, 262, 288n18; anthologists of,
  74–75; and Black Arts movement, 108,
  260; and counterliterature, 62, 75, 94; and
  Edwards, 193; FBI files on, 67; FBI investigation of, 3, 59, 60, 217, 222; and *Fire!!*,
  88; and Hoover, 29; and Hoover Raids,
  74–75; and G. Johnson, 88; journalism of,
  5; journals of, 35, 55; and Locke, 10; and
  magazines, 228; and McKay, 8; and New
  Crowd Negroes, 27; possible missing files
  on, 67; racial radicalism of, 62; and *Radi-*
  calism and Sedition, 17, 52–53, 54, 225;
  and Reed, 264; reply to FBI ghostreading
  in, 22; and Washington, D.C., 37
Harlem Writers Group, 108
Harlem Writers Guild, 86, 287n9
Harrington, Ollie, 20, 94, 106, 177, 178, 203,
  222, 248, 256
Harris, Joel Chandler, 152–53; *Uncle Remus*,

His Songs and Sayings, 154–55, 156, 158
Harris, Joseph E., 187–88, 190
Harris, Trudier, 104
Hart, Matt, 305n5
Hartford Courant, 119
Hartman, Geoffrey, 140
Harvard Communist, 145
Hatch Act, 89, 90, 297n16
Hawthorne, Nathaniel, *Italian Notebooks*, 135
H.D. (Hilda Doolittle), 135
Hellman, Lillian, 297n18
Hemingway, Ernest, 68, 215
Hemmings, Sally, 40
Henckel von Donnersmarck, Florian, 125
Henderson, David, "They Are Killing All the Young Men," 270
Henderson, George Wylie, 8
Henderson, Stephen, *Understanding the New Black Poetry*, 265
Hendrix, Jimi, 285n3
Henry, Sir Edward, 49
Henry Holt, 100–101, 298n21
Hermes Trismegistus, 271
Herndon, Calvin, 59, 221, 287n13; "The Lynchers," 148–49; "The Poet," 148–49; *The Recognition of Man*, 104
Higashida, Cheryl, 299n23
Hill, Milt, 101
Hill, Robert A., 285n2, 295n11
Himes, Chester, 10, 20, 176–77, 178, 224, 254–59, 311n21; assumes himself FBI suspect, 222; *A Case of Rape (Une Affaire de Viol)*, 255–59; and Custodial Detention, 93, 234; FBI interpretations of, 129; file on, 59, 86; *Lonely Crusade*, 237; and Paris, 23, 254–55, 257, 258; passport records of, 204; *Plan B*, 254, 263, 264; *La Reine des Pommes*, 254, 255; and J. Williams, 259, 262, 263; and Wright, 246, 255–58; writings about FBI, 6
Himes, Ron, 108
historical novels, 6, 259
Hitler-Stalin pact, 147
Hobsbawm, E. J., 182, 306n6
Hodges, Leroy S., Jr., 308n21
Holcomb, Gary, 24, 294n3
Hollander, John, 302n5
Holmes, Lola Belle, 96
Holocaust, 254
Holzman, Michael, 24, 141–42, 302n4, 302n6

homelessness, 190, 191, 192, 194
homosexuality, 272; and Ai, 271; and Baldwin, 127; and Bowen, 153; and Hoover, 39, 127, 290–91n4; and McKay, 64, 66; and Motley, 105–6, 204; in Wright, 248. *See also* lesbianism; sexuality
Honolulu Record, 147
Hook, Sidney, 308n22
Hoover, Celia, 40
Hoover, Christian, 40
Hoover, Dickerson, Jr., 37, 38, 44
Hoover, Dickerson Naylor, Sr., 37, 44, 49
Hoover, J. Edgar, 43, 141; and Angleton, 141, 165; appearance of, 25, 26, 38, 39; autograph of, 43; and Biddle, 81, 82; birth certificate of, 38; birth of, 16, 35; and Bowen, 151–52, 153, 154, 159, 225; and Central High cadet corps, 25–26, 36, 37, 54; character of, 25–26, 77, 205; charismatic leadership and bureaucracy of, 30, 62, 70–71, 72, 73, 77, 99, 132; childhood memories of, 35; and communism, 25, 26, 30, 41, 48, 54, 61, 71, 99, 225, 292n8; and Congress, 3, 53, 98, 197, 298n20; and James Crawford, 42; death of, 17, 23, 42, 60, 71, 98, 125, 224, 264, 271, 272; education of, 25–26, 35, 37–38, 47; family of, 35, 37, 38, 44, 49; FBI before, 16, 29–35; and FBI file system, 45–46; FBI hiring of, 16, 25, 29; and FBI library, 49–52, 118, 143; and Fields, 42; and Fleming, 132; at George Washington University, 37–38, 47; and Goldman, 49; House testimony in 1930 of, 73; HUAC testimony of, 97–98; and Hull, 80; and Japanese internment, 93; and Kappa Alpha Order, 38; and Library of Congress, 16, 45–46, 47, 49, 50, 51; as Library of Congress messenger, 44–45; and McCarthy, 99; and "Negro FBI Agents in Action," 109; and "The Negro in the FBI," 109; and Noisette, 38, 41–42, 95, 97, 109, 159, 238–39; and Old First Presbyterian Church, 37; racial heritage of, 38–42, 54, 137, 271, 272; racism of, 14, 15, 35, 54; and *Radicalism and Sedition*, 53; and F. Roosevelt, 76, 77, 80–82, 83, 97, 199; and R. Service, 57; and sexuality, 39, 64, 127, 266–67, 271–72, 290–91n4; and Sullivan, 1, 160, 162, 163; as Sunday school teacher, 37; and Tolson, 39, 71, 154, 271, 290–91n4;

Hoover, J. Edgar (cont)
and transvestism, 39, 271–72, 290n4;
and Truman, 97–98; upbringing of, 44;
and Walter White, 21, 41, 87; and White
House, 133; and Wilson, 36; as young
militant, 28–29; youth of, 25; WORKS:
address of 1959, 35; *Bulletin of Radical
Activities*, 52; and "The Bully Bolsheviki,"
58; "How U.S. Reds Use 'Pseudo Liberals'
as a Front," 97; *J. Edgar Hoover on Communism*, 25; *Masters of Deceit*, 25, 31, 61, 100,
160–61; "Patriotism and the War against
Crime"(1936 address), 78; *Persons in
Hiding*, 7, 78–79, 97, 154, 295n12, 304n14;
"Secularism—Breeder of Crime," 166–68,
169, 235; "Shall It Be Law or Tyranny?",
171; "Slickers in Slacks," 84; *A Study of
Communism*, 161; "The Weekly Review,"
42, 44, 52
Hoover, John T., 40
Hoover, William, 40
Hoover Poems, 15, 224, 312n24; and
Ai, 271–72; and Baraka, 265–66; and
Giovanni, 266–67; and Randall, 271; and
Sanchez, 267–69
Hoover Raids, 47–49, 50, 51, 52, 68, 85, 98,
153, 160, 230; and ACLU, 67; and charis-
matic power, 71; and communism, 61; and
Custodial Detention program, 92; defined,
48; and Harlem Renaissance, 74–75; and
immigrants, 64; and Reed, 264
Hopkins, Pauline, *Hagar's Daughter*, 251
Horn, Eva, 286n7
House of Representatives, 69, 70, 73; House
Appropriations Committee, 81; House
Select Committee on Assassinations, 163;
House Un-American Activities Committee
(HUAC), 96, 97–98, 99, 100, 235 . *See also*
Congress; McCarthy, Joseph
Howard University, 36, 37, 89, 90
Huggins, Nathan Irvin, *Voices of the Harlem
Renaissance*, 74, 75
Hughes, Langston, 19, 63, 74, 88, 192, 286n6,
297n18; assumes himself FBI suspect,
222; and Black Arts movement, 108; and
communism, 237; as criminal, 75; and
Custodial Detention, 17–18, 93, 234; and
Edwards, 193; and Ellison, 236, 237, 239;
FBI in works of, 234–36; file on, 7, 8, 59,
67, 68, 145, 165–69, 195, 234–35; Hoover
on, 165–69; HUAC testimony of, 235; and
international consciousness, 20; and inter-
national movements, 195; passport records
of, 20, 204; and Wright, 237; WORKS:
"Ballads of Lenin," 165; "Chant for May
Day," 165; "Concerning a Great Mississippi Writer and the Southern Negro," 236;
"Concernment," 236; "Goodbye Christ,"
166–68, 235; "I, Too," 195; "It's Okay to Be
Reserved," 235; "The Negro Artist and the
Racial Mountain," 53; poems in *Messen-
ger*, 232; "Shakespeare in Harlem," 234;
"Simple" stories, 22–23, 224, 235; *Simple
Speaks His Mind*, 235; *Simple's Uncle Sam*,
236; "Something to Lean On," 235; "Song
of Spain," 145; "What Shall We Do about
the South?", 234, 235; "Youth," 168
Hugo, Victor, *Notre-Dame de Paris*, 250
Hull, Cordell, 80
Hunt, E. Howard (David St. John), 134
Hunt, John, 133
Hunter, Edward S., 133
Hurston, Zora Neale, 222, 232; "Characteris-
tics of Negro Expression," 53; "Sweat," 157;
Their Eyes Were Watching God, 267
Hyena, Hank, 290n4

Iceberg Slim (Robert Beck), 60, 122
Ideological Nation Apparatus (INA), 185
Ideological State Apparatus (ISA), 183–84
Imagism, 175, 231
Immigration and Nationality Act, 105
imperialism, 185, 194, 247, 253, 256, 257
"I'm Shadowing You" (song), 308–9n2
Independent Black Nationalist Extremists
list, 123
Indiana, Robert, 266
Indignant Generation, 16, 288n18
Informer, The (1935), 312n25
Informer Film genre, 312n25
Informer Poem genre, 269–71, 312n25
informers, African Americans as, 41, 95–97,
110, 111, 119, 233, 270. *See also* snitch
jackets
intentional fallacy, 121, 127, 145, 167–68
Internal Security Act (McCarran Act), 98,
297n17
internationalism, 16, 124, 180; and Afro-
modernists, 21; and counterliterature,
94; and W.E.B. Du Bois's passport, 200;

and FBI, 20; FBI concern about, 17, 195; francophone side of, 192–93; and Ghana, 202; and Hansberry, 103; and Hughes's file, 195; and New Negro, 195; racialist, 75; in Smith, 254; and state paperwork, 199; state surveillance of, 193–94; in Wright, 245, 251. *See also* Black Atlantic

International Workers of the World (IWW), 63–64, 293n13

interpellation, 183, 184, 306n8

Interstate Transportation of Obscene Matter statute, 128

Iraq War, 185

I Was a Communist for the FBI (1951), 97, 240

Izvestia, 196

Jackson, George, 113

Jackson, John L., 297n17

Jackson, Lawrence P., 24, 288n18

Jackson, Leon, 173

James, C. L. R., 194, 201, 247; *Mariners, Renegades, and Castaways*, 212

James Campbell v. U.S. Department of Justice, 307n17

Jameson, Fredric, 147

Jam Master Jay, 285n3

Japan, 83, 235

Japanese internment, 92, 93

jazz, 23, 212–113

J. Edgar (2011), 45, 289n1, 290n4

J. Edgar Hoover Building, 14, 71

Jeffers, Lance, 59, 65, 94, 104, 222, 287n13

Jefferson, Thomas, 40, 137

Jeffreys-Jones, Rhodri, 32, 285n2, 289n2, 295n9

Jesus Christ Superstar, 312n25

Jews, 141, 142, 261, 273–74. *See also* anti-Semitism

Jim Crow, 83, 225, 234, 235

John Birch Society, 96

Johnson, Chalmers, 298n21

Johnson, Charles S., 59, 106, 221, 287n13; *To Stem the Tide*, 84, 296n13

Johnson, David K., 290n4

Johnson, Georgia Douglas, 9, 37, 87–88, 222, 232, 287n13

Johnson, Helene, 232

Johnson, Jack, 25, 26, 32–34, 35

Johnson, James Weldon, 6, 21, 22, 57, 207, 222, 223, 227–28, 310n10; *The*

Autobiography of an Ex-Colored Man, 227; *Book of American Negro Poetry*, 55, 56

Johnson, J. C., "Eavesdropper's Blues," 216–17

Johnson, John H., 83

Johnson, Lyndon, 109, 119, 266

Johnson, Manning, 96

Johnson, William R., 138, 139

Jones, Clarence, 260, 312n22

Jones, Claudia, 212

Jones, James Wormley, 41

Jones, M. A., 127, 128, 131, 145

Joseph, Peniel, 102

Journal-Courier, 102

journalism, 5, 17, 82, 85–86, 223, 310–11n14. *See also* magazines; newspapers

Journal of Negro Education, 149

Journal of Negro History, 287n9

journals, 35, 54–58. *See also* media

judicial texts, 66, 89, 90, 130

Junior G-Men Club, 77

Kafka, Franz, 11

Kaplan, Amy, 306–7n12

Kappa Alpha Order, 38

Karenga, Maulana (Ron), 111, 299n27

Kaross, Sonia, 50

Kaufman, Bob, 59, 94, 106, 222, 287n13, 307n19

Keats, John, 145

Kennedy, Adrienne, *Funnyhouse of a Negro*, 116

Kennedy, John F., 219

Kennedy family, 159

Kent, George E., 310n10

Kenyatta, Jomo, 120

Kenyon Review, 137

Kerouac, Jack, 117

Kessler, Ronald, 290n4

Key Activist Index, 93. *See also* Custodial Detention; Security Index

KGB, 44, 205. *See also* NKVD

Khrushchev, Nikita, 97

Killens, John O., 20, 59, 65, 86, 94, 204, 222; '*Sippi*, 86; *Youngblood*, 86

King, Coretta Scott, 2

King, Martin Luther, Jr., 109; assassination of, 41, 163, 209, 285n3, 285–86n4, 291n5; depression of, 2; extramarital affairs of, 2; FBI vendetta against, 3; and Felt, 124; file on, 74, 83; harassment of, 46; and Hoover,

King, Martin Luther, Jr. (cont)
1, 2, 3, 39, 41; and independence celebrations in Ghana, 201; and knowledge of FBI
surveillance, 6; and Nobel Peace Prize, 1,
2; Sullivan's evaluation of, 163; Sullivan's
letter to, 1–5, 18, 54, 61–62, 113, 164,
303n12; and wiretapping, 2, 116
Knight, Etheridge, 113
Korean War, 98, 297n17
Krasnov, N. N., *The Hidden Russia*, 101
Kristol, Irving, 134
Ku Klux Klan, 290n3, 291n5; and Bowen, 152;
counterintelligence program against, 38,
109, 110; and Ellison, 239; and Garvey,
293n2; and Griffith, 34; and Hoover's racism, 14; and Kappa Alpha Order, 38; and
Sullivan, 162–63

Lamar, Jake, *If 6 Were 9*, 312–13n26
Larsen, Nella, 222
Larsson, Stieg, *The Millennium Trilogy*, 136
Latin America, 132, 197
Lavender Scare, 64
Lawrence, T. E., 130
Leben der Anderen, Das (The Lives of Others)
(2006), 125
le Carré, John (David John Moore Cornwell),
130, 134
Leibert, Herman W., 136
Leick, Karen, 297n18
lesbianism, 102, 122, 204, 272. *See also*
homosexuality
Lewis, David Levering, 53, 292–93n12; *The
Portable Harlem Renaissance Reader*, 74,
75
Lewis, John, 109
Lewis, W. S., 136
Liberator, 63, 65
libraries, 22, 100, 217
Library of Congress, 16, 44–46, 47, 49, 50, 51,
52, 80, 118
Life, 101
Lightfoot, Claude, 96
Lincoln, Abraham, 69, 137, 294n5
Lindbergh kidnappers, 235
Lindsay, John, 261
lit.-cop federalism, 63, 67, 68, 76, 82, 179; de-
velopment of, 43–58; and FBI card index,
52; and Lowenthal, 99; and print public
sphere, 16–17, 29, 43, 58, 79, 174, 226. *See
also* media

literacy, 113, 151, 221
Little, Brown, 78
Locke, Alain, 37, 88, 149; and Edwards, 193;
file on, 10–11, 59, 67; and McKay, 207;
New Negro, 10, 195; and *Survey Graphic*,
55, 56
Lomax, John, 158
London, Jack, 32
London Metropolitan Police, 49
Look, 101
Lorde, Audre, 23, 222, 224; *The Cancer Jour-
nals*, 272; *Zami*, 272, 310n9
Lost Man, The (1968), 312n25
Lott, Eric, 116
Loughran, Trish, 291n6
Louisville Courier-Journal, 47
Loving, Arthur, 53, 292–93n12
Lowenthal, Max, 101, 106, 218; *The Federal
Bureau of Investigation*, 99–100
Lowery, Joseph, 2
Lucas, William E., 41
lynching, 3, 34, 35, 41, 55

Macauley, Robie, 133
MacKay, Cliff, 83
Mackenzie, Compton, 130
MacLeish, Archibald, 137
Macmillan, 152
Madhubuti, Haki, 60
magazines, 121, 225–29, 311n15. *See also*
journalism; media; periodicals
Mailer, Norman, 4, 116, 223; *Harlot's Ghost*,
136
Malcolm X (El-Hajj Malik El-Shabazz), 74,
123, 265, 270, 285n3; assassination of, 107,
268; and Baraka, 112; and FBI counterlit-
erary authorship, 113, 114; FBI investiga-
tion of, 3; and J. Williams, 262
Malcolm X Society, 111
Mann, James, 32
Mann, Michael, 289n1, 293n14
Mann, Thomas, *Doctor Faustus*, 297n18
Mann Act. *See* White Slave Traffic Act (Mann
Act)
Mao Zedong, 115
Marable, Manning, 87, 95
Marcantonio, Vito, 81
March on Washington movement, 3
Marley, Bob, 285n3
Marlowe, Christopher, 130
marriage laws, 33, 69

Marshall, Paule, 60, 222, 310n10
Marxism, 174, 220; and Althusser, 183, 184; and Baraka, 117; and Congress for Cultural Freedom, 249; and critique of ideology, 131; and *Crusader*, 227; and Gilroy, 191; and Hoover, 167; and internationalism, 47, 75; and literary analysis, 147–49; and McKay, 66; and New Critics, 151; and *Radicalism and Sedition*, 17. *See also* communism
Marxist-Leninist canon, 96
Mason, James, 312n25
Masses, 31
Masterman, J. C., 301–2n3, 302n5
Matthiessen, Peter, 133
Maugham, Somerset, 130
May Day bombing campaign of 1919, 46
Mayfield, Julian, 20, 59, 94, 104–5, 204, 222, 287n13; *The Grand Parade*, 105; *The Hit*, 105; *The Long Night*, 105
McCann, Sean, 24, 294n5
McCarran Act (Internal Security Act), 98, 297n17
McCarran-Walter Act, 204
McCarthy, Joseph, 64, 96, 97, 98–99, 101, 167
McCarthy era, 106; counterliterature during, 63; and Lorde, 272
McCarthyism, 86, 95; and black art, 108; and S. Brown, 89, 90; FBI's technical assistance to, 98; in Wright's *Island of Hallucination*, 245
McCarthyite Republicanism, 81
McCoy, Alfred W., 29212
McDonald, Peter D., 288n16
McGhee, Ivory, 39, 40
McGhee, Millie L., *Secrets Uncovered*, 39–41, 42
McGhee family, 39–40, 41
McGurl, Mark, 311n15
McKay, Claude, 259, 274–75, 286–87n8; assumes himself FBI suspect, 222, 229; as aware of wanted status, 207; Bowen's reception of, 158–59; as criminal, 75; and Edwards, 193; and Elizabethan court discourse, 230; and Ellison, 241; FBI as audience of, 229; FBI commentators on, 149; FBI file on, 7, 8, 59, 63–67, 74, 87, 144, 145–46, 201, 206–7, 228, 231, 294n3; and FBI interpretive theory, 146; FBI's collected writing on, 62; FBI translation of Soviet press articles on, 65; FBI translation of Soviet press contributions of, 66; and Jamaica, 207; and magazines, 228–29; nationality of, 64; passport of, 20, 198, 204; reply to FBI ghostreading in, 22; and Schuyler, 233; and Shakespearian sonnet, 22, 223, 231–32; and Soviet Union, 64, 65, 66–67, 196, 206, 207; State Department letters on, 65; and stop notices, 21, 206–7, 210, 212; and transnationalism, 194; travels of, 8, 66–67; WORKS: "America," 146, 229–31, 232, 241; *Complete Poems*, 8; "Enslaved," 231; foreign political speeches of, 65; *Harlem Shadows*, 64, 206, 303n9; *Home to Harlem*, 21, 207; "How Black Sees Green and Red," 144; "If We Must Die," 55, 57, 63, 228, 229, 231; letters purloined from, 66; letter to Harold Jackman, 207; letter to Max Eastman, 25 Apr. 1932, 231; letter to Max Eastman, [?] April 1933, 21, 207; "May Day—1923," 144; "The Race Question in America," 196; "The Race Question in the United States," 196; "Song of the New Soldier and Worker," 231; sonnets of, 22, 56, 65, 223, 231–32; Soviet press contributions of, 66, 196; "The Tropics in New York," 159, 229; "The White House," 231
McKay, Nellie Y., *The Norton Anthology of African American Literature*, 8, 9, 60, 74, 229
McLellan, John, 298n20
McQueen, Butterfly, 239, 240
media, 266, 286n5; and CIA and FBI, 133; and COINTELPRO, 113, 273; and early FBI, 31; and FBI, 5; and FBI's desire for publicity, 43, 77–78, 95; and Hoover and McCarthy, 99; and HUAC, 99; and lit.-cop federalism, 16–17, 29, 43, 58, 79, 174, 226; and roundup of radicals in 1919 and 1920, 48–49. *See also* journals; lit.-cop federalism; magazines; newspapers; propaganda; publicity; publishers; radio shows; *specific publications*
Media, Pennsylvania FBI office, 124, 300n33
Medsger, Betty, 300n33
Melley, Timothy, 24, 223, 288n17, 310n11
Melville, Herman, 4; *Moby-Dick*, 212
Mercer, Johnny, 308–9n2
Messenger, 48, 53, 55, 228, 232, 233, 293n13
Mexico, 204
Meyer, Tamar, 306n6
MI6, 130, 132, 133, 134

Miller, Arthur, 68
Miller, Henry, 128
Miller, J. Hillis, 140
Miller, Tyrus, 309n7
Milton, John, 265
minstrelsy, 4, 116. *See also* counterliterature
Mitgang, Herbert, 9, 286n6, 297n18
model citizen criticism, 169–74
modernism, 47, 294n6; and Angleton, 141, 165; and "Communist thought-control relay stations," 73; and counterliterature, 75; and detective narrative, 245; and Harlem Renaissance, 74–75; and Hoover, 169; and McKay, 64, 231; montage, 51, 65, 116; New Deal, 79; and obscenity, 128; and Pan-Africanism, 20; and Pound, 31; and Pound and Reed, 32; and practical criticism, 134; and radical propaganda, 73–74; and realism, 219–21, 309n6; and Sanchez, 269; and socialism, 31; and Wright, 217
Modern Language Association (MLA), 143
Modern Quarterly, 147
montage, 51, 65, 68, 116
Moore, G. C., 118, 125, 129, 131
Moore, Marianne, 137
Morehouse Parish case, 290n3
Moreland, Mantan, 239, 240
Moreno, Carmen Mercedes, 136
Morize, André, 145; *Problems and Methods of Literary History*, 144
Morrison, Toni, 4; *Beloved*, 311n15
Moscow Peace Conference, 200
Mosley, Walter, *A Red Death*, 312–13n26
Mother Earth, 49
Motley, Mary, 208–9
Motley, Willard: assumes himself FBI suspect, 222; and black lists, 94; file on, 59; and homosexuality, 64, 105–6, 204, 219; *Knock on Any Door*, 105; *Let No Man Write My Epitaph*, 105; passport of, 20; and stop notices, 21, 208–9; *We Fished All Night* (cited in FBI file as *They Fished All Night*), 105
Mozart, Wolfgang Amadeus, 120
Muhammad, Elijah, 3
Muhammad, Khalil Gibran, 288n19
Murch, Donna Jean, 299n26
Murray, Pauli, 60, 64, 222; *Proud Shoes*, 122
Myrdal, Gunnar, *An American Dilemma*, 84, 296n13

mystery genre, 169. *See also* detective literature

NAACP, 67, 163, 164, 228; and W.E.B. Du Bois's passport, 200; FBI investigation of, 3; and passports, 204; and Sullivan's letter, 3; in Washington, D.C., 37; and White, 41, 87
Nash, Diane, 109
nation, 181–83, 185, 186, 191; definition of, 181–82. *See also* state
National Archives and Records Administration (NARA), 10, 11, 300n32
National Conference on Black Power, 121
National Endowment for the Arts, 134
National Equal Rights League, 3
nationalism, 182, 306nn6, 7; and academic criticism, 142; black sovereignty able to transcend, 194; and *Crusader*, 227; debt to racism of, 189; and Gilroy, 189
national land survey, 44
National Negro Theater, 287n9
National Security Act, 132
National Security Agency (NSA), 23, 61, 100, 273–74
national-security state, 23–24, 223
Nation, "The FBI Reviews a Book," 100
Nation of Islam, 3, 111, 115
nation-state, 180–86, 182, 191
nation-time, 186
Native Son (1951), 216
Naylor, Gloria, 222, 224, 274–75; *1996*, 23, 24, 273–74, 310n10; *The Women of Brewster Place*, 273
Nazi Germany, 170
Nazis, 64
Nazi-Soviet pact of 1939, 90
Neal, Larry, 60, 222, 287n13; "And Shine Swam On," 120, 122; and Baraka, 107–8; and Black Arts movement, 108, 121; *Black Fire*, 118, 125, 129, 260, 265; "Black Power," 122; FBI file on, 146; FBI reading of, 121–22, 127, 129; and intentional fallacy, 121, 127; and Security Index, 94
Negri, Antonio, 306n11
Negro American Literature Forum (Black American Literature Forum; African American Review), 287n9
Negro Digest (Black World), 83, 121, 218–19, 287n9, 300n30
Negro Ensemble Company, 287n9

Negro Playwrights Company, 89
Negro World, 55–56, 57, 191, 226, 227, 228, 310–11n14
New Criticism, 19, 127, 130, 137–38, 151, 167, 174, 220; and ambiguity, 140; and CIA, 134, 138–39, 142, 145; and FBI, 131, 146; and FBI ghostreaders, 149; and intentional fallacy, 121, 127; and Marxists, 149; and Pearson, 135–36; and U.S. English departments, 146–47
New Crowd Negroes, 27
New Deal, 63, 76, 77, 78, 79, 81, 88, 89
New Haven Register, 102
New Leader, 196
New Masses, 86, 147
newspapers, 299n25; and Anderson, 182–83; and Baraka, 118; FBI harassment of black, 112; FBI infiltration and retranslation of black, 194; FBI subscriptions to black, 121; and Harlem Renaissance, 5; Hughes's contributions to black, 235–36; images of New Negroes in, 27. *See also* media; periodicals
Newton, Huey, 111, 299–300n27
Newton, Michael, 290n3
New York Age, 57, 227
New Yorker, 16–17, 78
New York Public Library, Billy Rose Theatre Collection, 104
New York Times, 17, 31, 53, 225
Nichols, Louis, 99, 101
9/11 attacks, 7–8, 14, 46, 69
Nixon, Richard, 111
Nixon administration, 162
Nkrumah, Kwame, 105, 122, 177, 201–2, 209
NKVD, 44. *See also* KGB
Noisette, Sam, 38, 41–42, 95, 97, 109, 159, 238
Norfolk Journal, 85
Nowell, William O., 96
Nugent, Richard Bruce, 232
Nwankwo, Ifeoma, 307n16

Obama, Barack, 8, 69, 86
Obama administration, 11, 74, 294–95n7
obscenity, 128
Odd Man Out (1947), 312n25
Odets, Clifford, 79
Office of Economic Opportunity, 117
Office of Strategic Services (OSS), 132, 133, 135, 136, 137, 197
Oklahoma City Black Dispatch, 82

Old First Presbyterian Church, Washington, D.C., 37
Oline, Pamela, 248
Olmstead, Kathryn S., 308n20
O'Neal, William, 112
O'Reilly, Kenneth, *"Racial Matters,"* 96, 111, 112, 262, 285n2, 293n1, 298n19
Organization of Afro-American Unity (OAAU), 3
Oriental Gardens (Washington, D.C.), 37
Orwell, George, 11, 134, 301–2n3; *1984*, 273
Ott, George, 40
Overman Act (1918), 69
Oxford Companion to African American Literature, The, 169

Padmore, Dorothy, 250
Pakay, Sedat, 209
Palmer, A. Mitchell, 73, 82, 228–29; bombing of house of, 46, 230; and FBI library of radical literature, 50; and FBI Radical Division, 47; and McKay, 230; and *Radicalism and Sedition*, 53; and *Red Radical Movement*, 52; and roundup of radicals, 48; and Stone, 68
Palmer Raids, 48. *See also* Hoover Raids
Pan-African Congress, 188
Pan-Africanism, 20, 103, 179, 188, 195, 196, 200, 201
Paris, 178–79, 197, 213, 224; African Americans in, 20, 175–79, 202, 203, 204, 244; and C. Himes, 23, 254–55, 257, 258; Johnson in, 33; and magazines, 228; in Smith, 254; and Wright, 23, 175, 176–79, 190–91, 243, 245, 247, 248–49, 250–51
Parker, Bonnie, 58
Parker, Dorothy, 297n18
Parkin, Harry, 33
Parks, Gordon, 312n25
Partisan Review, 134
Passport Control Act of 1918, 198
passports, 15, 20–21, 69, 198–205, 213, 308nn20, 21; and Baldwin, 20, 21, 204, 209, 210–11; and S. Du Bois, 20, 201, 202; and W.E.B. Du Bois, 20, 200–203, 204, 206,207, 209, 211; and Executive Order 2285, 198; and Hansberry, 20, 101, 204; and C. Himes, 204; and Hughes, 20, 204; and McKay, 20, 198, 204; and Motley, 20; and Randall, 204; and Schuyler, 20, 204;

passports (cont)
and W. G. Smith, 203; and White, 20, 204; and Wright, 21, 203, 204. *See also* stop notices
Paterson, Louise Thompson, 20, 204
Patriot Act of 2001, 7
Pattee, Fred Lewis, *Century Readings*, 142–43, 146, 150, 303n8
Patterson, Anita, 307n16
Patterson, Annabel, 224–25
Patterson, Louise Thompson, 59, 67, 86, 93, 102, 209, 222
Pauling, Linus, 308n20
Pearl Harbor, attack on, 81, 89
Pearson, Norman Holmes, 135–36, 140, 146, 152, 301–2n3, 302nn4, 5; *Oxford Anthology of American Literature*, 136
Pease, Donald, 306n12
Peebles, Melvin Van, 310n13; *A Bear for the FBI*, 312n25
periodicals: audience for black, 82; bilingualism of in interwar era, 191–92; and Edwards, 194; FBI acquisition and reading of black, 50, 54, 80, 228; FBI endorsement of, 76; and Schuyler, 232. *See also* magazines; newspapers; *specific periodicals*
Petrarch, Francis, 230
Petry, Ann, 222
Philbrick, Hubert, *I Led Three Lives*, 97
Pickens, William, 59, 106, 222
Pierce, Samuel Riley, 163
Piłsudski, Józef, 307n14
Pinkerton, Allan, 31, 47; *The Molly Maguires and the Detectives*, 30
Pinkerton Agency, 30
Pinkertons, 47
Pittsburgh Chronicle, 85
Pittsburgh Courier, 82, 83, 170, 232
Plessy v. Ferguson, 34
Poe, Edgar Allan, 4, 156
Poitier, Sidney, 312n25
police text, 65, 66, 75, 87, 130
Political Affairs, 147
Pollard, Fritz, 171
Poor Peoples' encampment, 163
Popular Front, 68, 80
Post, Louis, 51–52, 58
post-9/11 period, 69, 194, 273
postmodernism, 24, 223
Potash, John, 285n3

Potter, Claire Bond, 290–91n4, 293n14
Pound, Ezra, 135, 136, 150, 219, 220, 302n5; and Angleton, 141–42; *The Cantos*, 137; file on, 31–32, 64; "Introductory Text-Book," 137; and McKay, 231; radio broadcasts of, 141, 142
Powers, Richard Gid, 31, 33, 71, 77, 290n4, 292n12, 295n10, 295–96n12, 303n12
Powers, Tyrone, 3
Price, Leontyne, 213
print public sphere, 16–17, 29, 43, 58, 79, 101, 174, 226. *See also* media
Prism system, 100
prison conversion narrative, 113
professionals, 36
Progressives, 30, 32, 34, 36, 71
proletarian aesthetics, 220
proletarian literature, 79
proletarian realism, 90
propaganda: African Americans as receptive to, 73, 85; by COINTELPRO, 124; and Congress for Cultural Freedom, 249; criminalizing of, 70; and Custodial Detention program, 92; and Ellison, 237, 242; and Ellul, 294n6; FBI apparatus for, 77; FBI as investigating, 49, 81; and FBI report on Hansberry, 103; and Garvey, 49; and Hughes, 167; as menace, 72; modernist literature as, 73–74; recriminalization of radical, 70; and Sullivan, 161–62; and Wright, 170. *See also* media
Public Enemies, 77, 78
Public Enemies (2009), 289n1, 293n14
public enemy plot, 97
Public Hero Number One, 76
publicity, 6, 29, 43, 58, 211, 261; and agent discipline, 72; and civil rights activism, 109; and Hoover and McCarthy, 98, 99; and Hoover's charismatic power, 71, 77–78; and Johnson, 33, 35; and Media break-in, 109; and model citizen criticism, 170; and race, 95; and Weber, 71. *See also* media
publishers, 100–101, 298–99n21
Purvis, Melvin, *American Agent*, 79
Putnam, Herbert, 45, 49, 50, 51, 52
Pynchon, Thomas, 223

Rabble-Rouser Index, 93, 117–18. *See also* Custodial Detention; Security Index

race, 107; and aesthetic judgment, 129; and
African diaspora, 188; and Angleton,
136–37; and FBI, 2, 17, 52, 285n2; in
Himes, 256; and Hoover, 14, 15, 26, 37–38,
54, 137; and Johnson, 32–34; and Mann
Act, 32, 33; and McKay, 230; and Old First
Presbyterian Church, 37; and R. Service,
57; in Washington, D.C., 35–37, 38
race riots, 3, 53–54
racial discrimination, 73; and goodwill tours
of jazz musicians, 212–13; and Wilson, 36;
in Wright, 244
racialist internationalism, 75
racialization, 188
racial parity, 73
racial primitivism, 41
racial segregation, 82; and Civil Rights Commission, 95; and FBI, 41; literary threats to,
18; and U.S. military, 95, 109; and Washington, D.C., 35, 36, 37, 38, 40, 41, 54; and
Wilson, 36; and Wright, 246
racism: of FBI, 3; and C. Himes, 256, 257; and
Hoover, 35, 54; McGhee on, 41; nationalism's debt to, 189; in Smith, 253; and travel
control, 200; in Washington, D.C., 39; and
Wilson, 36–37; in Wright, 244, 245. See
also white supremacy
RACON. See under FBI, Survey of Racial
Conditions in the United States
radicalism: and academic criticism, 142;
counterintelligence programs against, 110;
and McKay, 64, 230; and Schuyler, 91; and
White, 87
Radicalism and Sedition among the Negroes
as Reflected in Their Publications (Bowen
et al.), 19, 52–58, 195, 292–93n12; African
American responses to, 22, 223, 225–28;
contents of, 17; deterence and education
through, 6; drafting of, 153, 157, 158–59,
188; and McKay, 63, 223, 228–29, 230, 231;
and modernism, 75, 85, 142; and periodicals, 194; and Red Summer, 73
radical literature, 50–51, 217, 251; FBI
subscriptions to publications featuring, 80;
and Hoover, 49–50, 79; and modernism,
73–74
Radical Reconstruction, 34, 198
radicals, 46; deportation of, 48, 49; discontinued collection of data on, 68; FBI library
of writings by, 49–52; and Hoover's filing

system, 46; roundup in 1919 and 1920 of,
47–49, 50
radio, 43, 141, 142. See also media
Radio Gangbusters, 76
radio shows, 76, 266, 272, 295n12. See also
media
Rambsy, Howard, II, 265
Randall, Dudley, 20, 60, 222, 269–71, 287n13;
"Abu," 270; The Black Poets, 270; "F.B.I.
Memo," 270–71; For Malcolm, 122, 270;
"Informer," 270; More to Remember, 270;
passport records of, 204
Randolph, A. Philip, 3, 55
Random House, 101
Rand School, Meyer London Library, 51
Ransom, John Crowe, The New Criticism, 136
Ray, James Earl, 285–86n4
Razaf, Andy, 7, 106, 287n13; "Don't Tread on
Me," 56, 58; "(What Did I Do to Be So)
Black and Blue," 7
Reader's Digest, 101, 264
Reagan, Ronald, 163, 286n5
realism, 219–21. See also social realism
Reconstruction, 30, 34
Red Decade, 165
Redding, J. Saunders, 59, 222, 287n13; To Make
a Poet Black, 105; Stranger and Alone, 105
Red Radical Movement, The (pamphlet), 52
Red Raids, 68, 96. See also Hoover Raids;
Palmer Raids
Red Scare (first), 82, 93, 292n8; and African
American FBI informants, 41; and Alien
Registration Act, 70; hearings on Justice
Department's contributions to, 67; and
Hoover, 16, 29, 48; and interpretive read-
ing, 145, 150; and New Negro art, 75; and
Pattee, 143; and Red Raids, 68
Red Scare (second): and interpretive reading,
145, 150; and passports, 204. See also Mc-
Carthy, Joseph; McCarthyism
Red Summer, 28, 60, 85, 228; and African
American readership, 73; and African
Americans, 74–75; initiation of, 46; and
McKay, 56, 62; race riots of, 3; and Radical-
ism and Sedition, 53, 56, 73
Reed, Ishmael, 6, 23, 60, 222, 224, 310nn10,
11; Airing Dirty Laundry, 121; Mumbo
Jumbo, 264
Reed, John, 31–32, 64; Ten Days That Shook
the World, 31, 51

Renker, Elizabeth, 129–30
Replansky, Naomi, "Even the Walls Have Ears," 308n1
Repressive State Apparatus (RSA), 169, 183–84, 215
Republican Party, 34, 36, 98, 132, 163, 168
Reserve Index, 93. *See also* Custodial Detention; Security Index
revolution, 48, 49, 51, 226; and Alien Registration Act, 70; and Baraka, 119; and Black Atlantic, 211; and S. Brown, 297n16; and COINTELPRO, 110, 111, 114, 120; and Custodial Detention program, 92; and Hatch Act, 89; and Hernton, 148–49; and C. Himes, 263; and McKay, 63, 66, 231; and nation-state, 182; and Neal, 146; and *Radicalism and Sedition*, 227; and Randolph, 55; and Red Summer, 46; and I. Reed, 264; and Schuyler, 233; and sexuality, 64; and Smith Act trials, 95; and J. Williams, 263; and Wright, 219, 220, 248. *See also* sedition; treason
Revolutionary Action Movement (RAM), 111, 122
rhythm and blues, 286n5
Rice, Elmer, 297n18
Richards, I. A., 137, 140, 150; *Practical Criticism*, 139
Ridgway, Matthew, 246–47, 248
Riebling, Mark, 132, 301n1
Robert Treat Hotel, 121
Robeson, Paul, 104, 200, 205, 236, 308n22
Robins, Natalie, 9, 68, 93, 218, 219, 286n6, 309nn5, 6, 310n10; *Alien Ink*, 74
Rodgers, Carolyn, 10, 122
Rogers, Ginger, 77
Rogers, J. A., 59, 67, 86, 93, 193
roman à clef, 93, 247, 251–52, 257, 259
Romania, 12, 65
Roosevelt, Franklin D., 69, 70; and African American press, 86; as authorizing Hoover's investigations, 80–81, 295n10; and censorship, 81–82; and Custodial Detention program, 92; death of, 94; and FBI Special Intelligence Service, 197; and Hoover, 76, 77, 80–82, 83, 97, 199; and limited state of emergency, 81, 92; Twelve Point Crime Program, 77
Roosevelt, Theodore, 29–30, 34, 99, 227
Roosevelt (Franklin) administration, 295n9

Rosen, Charles, 301n2
Rosen, David, 286n7
Rosenfeld, Seth, 111, 299n26
Roth, Henry, 297n18
Roth, Philip, *The Plot against America*, 294n5
Rothberg, Michael, 253
Rowley, Hazel, 308n1
Russian People's House, 50
Russian Revolution, 31, 47

Sackler, Howard, *The Great White Hope*, 34
Sanchez, Sonia, 6, 23, 60, 107–8, 222, 224, 272, 310n9; *Conversations with Sonia Sanchez*, 121, 269; "A Modern Song of the F.B.I.", 267–69, 271; *We a BaddDDD People*, 289n22, 310n13
Santesso, Aaron, 286n7
Santoiana, Joseph E., Jr., 197
Sarkozy, Nicolas, 30
Sartre, Jean-Paul, 219, 220, 308n22; *Being and Nothingness*, 176
Saturday Nighters Club, 37
Saunders, Frances Stonor, 133, 301n2, 308n22; *The Cultural Cold War*, 249
Schmidt, Regin, 199
Schneider, Agnes E., 176
Schrecker, Ellen, 72, 95–96, 98
Schreiber, Belle, 33
Schuyler, George S., 222, 287n13; *Black and Conservative*, 91, 233; *Black Empire*, 232–34; *The Black Internationale*, 232–33, 263, 264; *Black No More*, 91; and Custodial Detention, 17–18, 93, 171; file on, 59, 67, 86, 90–92, 149; and model citizen criticism, 170–71; passport of, 20, 204; *Pittsburgh Courier* column of, 91, 92; "Propaganda and Its Effects," 91; pulp fiction of, 22, 224, 232; "Road to Ruin," 149; and Rogers, 93; Shafts and Darts column of, 232
Schwerner, Michael, 109
Scotland Yard, 49
Scott-Heron, Gil, "King Alfred Plan," 261
Seale, Bobby, 111
Secret Agent X-9 (comic strip), 76
Secret Service, 31, 47, 122, 289n2
Security Index, 92, 93, 102, 146, 297n18. *See also* Custodial Detention
sedition, 73, 82. *See also* revolution; treason
Sedition Act (1918), 47, 69, 70, 231
self-censorship, 22, 218, 221

Senate, 53, 69, 164; and COINTELPRO, 110, 113, 114; *Investigation Activities of the Department of Justice*, 53; Permanent Sub-Committee on Investigations, 98–99, 167

Senna, Danzy, 23, 224; *Caucasia*, 272–73

Série Noire, La, 255

Service, Robert, 304n15; "Grin," 57

sexuality: and Ai, 271–72; and Baldwin, 64, 127; and Bowen, 153; and Garvey, 33; and Giovanni, 266–67; in Himes, 256; and Hoover, 39, 64, 127, 290–91n4; and Johnson, 32–33; and McKay, 64, 66; and Motley, 64, 105–6, 204; and Murray, 64; and revolution, 64; and Sullivan's letter, 2, 4; in Washington, D.C., 39; and Wright, 217, 246, 248

Shakespeare, William, 117, 230; *Measure for Measure*, 55

Shakespearian sonnet, 22

Shakur, Tupac, 285n3

Shelley, Percy Bysshe, 265; "Ozymandias," 230

Shibutani, Tamotsu, 291n5

Shipley, Ruth, 199

Shklovsky, Viktor, 309n4

Show Them No Mercy, 76

Sidney, Sir Philip, 230

Singh, Nikhil Pal, 296n13

slave codes, 75. *See also* Black Codes

slavery, 152, 158, 188, 190

Sloane, William, 99

Smethurst, James, 24

Smith, Bessie, 117; "Eavesdropper's Blues," 216–17

Smith, James, 301–2n3

Smith, John, 136

Smith, William Gardner, 224, 287n13, 305n2, 308n21; FBI file of, 59; FBI questioning of, 222; FBI visit to relative of, 219; and Gibson Affair, 178, 253–54; and C. Himes, 176–77, 255, 256; *The Last of the Conquerors*, 106; and Paris, 23; passport of, 20, 203, 209; *Return to Black America*, 254; and Security Index, 94; *The Stone Face*, 251–54, 256, 257, 258; and stop notices, 21, 207–8, 209; and J. Williams, 262; and Wright, 248, 252

Smith, Worthington, 41–42

Smith Act (Alien Registration Act), 70, 81, 98. *See also* Alien Act (1918)

Smith Act trials, 95–96, 97

snitch jackets, 111, 113. *See also* informers, African Americans as

Snowden, Edward, 24

Sobonya, David, 13

socialism, 3, 31

Socialist Workers Party (SWP), 106, 300n28

social realism, 219, 220, 309n6. *See also* realism

social security, 77

sociology, 45, 84, 85

soldiers, 56, 91

Sollors, Werner, 297n18

Sontag, Susan, 134

South, 3, 34, 36, 156, 158, 234, 235, 256, 268

South Africa, 218, 288n16

Southern Christian Leadership Conference (SCLC), 2, 285n4

southern Democrats, 30, 95. *See also* Democratic Party

Southern Illinois University, Black Student Union, 115

South Side Writers Group, 287n9

Soviet Ark. *See* U.S.S. *Buford*

Soviet Union, 83; and African Blood Brotherhood, 55; and Angleton, 138, 140; and Baraka, 117; deportation of radicals to, 49; emergence of as threat, 48; and Hughes, 166–67; intelligence service of, 44, 139; and McKay, 64, 65, 66–67, 196, 206, 207; and modernism, 51; police files of, 7, 12, 15, 65; spying by, 97; and Truman, 94; and Wright, 203, 249, 308n22. *See also* Bolsheviks; communism

Soviet Writers' Union, 203

Spanish Civil War, 68, 86, 270

Spargo, R. Clifton, 312n24

Special Agent Force. *See* Department of Justice

Spellman, A. B., 60, 222, 310n10

Spender, Stephen, 134

spy fiction, 93, 134, 251

Stanciu, Cristina, 8

Stasi, 125

state, 43, 179; and Althusser, 183–85, 306n9; black sovereignty as reimagining, 194; and Braudel, 186; and civil society, 43; Cold War, 180, 199, 202, 213; definition of, 181–82; and Dimock, 185; and Gilroy, 191; in Himes, 256; interventionist, 77; and monopoly on force, 181; national-security,

state (cont)
23–24, 223; in nation-state, 180–86; and post-9/11 growth in intelligence, 7–8; security, 40; and Stephens, 194; time of, 186; and violence, 181, 182, 183, 184–85, 306n10; and Wallerstein, 186; in Wright, 244. *See also* nation
State Department: and Baldwin, 210; bowdlerization of libraries of, 100; and Cruse, 203–4; and Du Bois's passport, 200–201; and FBI investigations, 80; and goodwill tours of jazz musicians, 212–13; and international sponsorship of African American music, 180; and McKay, 65, 207; Passport Office, 199; and Robeson's passport, 200; and Wright, 177
state exceptionalism, 69–70
state-sponsored transnationalism, 180, 211
state surveillance: and antifile, 258; of black internationalism, 193–94; and Edwards, 192–93; modern literature and, 286n7; and J. Williams, 259; in Wright, 245, 251
Stein, Gertrude, 175, 177, 219, 220, 294n5
Steinbeck, John, 68
Stennis, John, 298n20
Stephan, Alexander, 297n18
Stephens, Michelle Ann, 24; *Black Empire*, 193, 194
Sterne, Laurence, *Tristram Shandy*, 217
Stevens, Wallace, 134, 137
St. Louis American, 115
Stone, Harlan, 67–68, 80
stop notices, 21, 180, 206–11, 212, 213, 224. *See also* passports
Stovall, Tyler, 305n2; *Paris Noir*, 175, 176
Student Nonviolent Coordinating Committee (SNCC), 3, 111, 114
Students for a Democratic Society (SDS), 114, 120, 162
Sturgis, Russell, 152
Styron, William, 4, 116
Subversive Reference, 93
Sullivan, William C., 131, 151, 159–65, 174, 303n11, 303–4n13; background of, 159; and black authorship, 4–5; *The Bureau*, 160, 162, 285–86n4; and counterintelligence, 15; death of, 163–64; education of, 160; and Hoover, 160, 162, 163; at Internal Revenue Service, 160; and King assassination, 285–86n4; letter to King, 1–5, 18,

61–62, 113, 164, 303n12; literary artifice of, 1–2, 3–4; and *Masters of Deceit*, 160–61; persona of, 3–4; as reader, 19; and *A Study of Communism*, 161
Summer, Anthony, *Official and Confidential*, 271–72
Summers, Anthony, 290n4
Sun Ra Arkestra, 108
Super Fly (1972), 312n25
Supreme Court, 34, 67–68, 95
Surine, Don, 98–99
Survey Graphic, 55
Suydam, Henry, 77
Swearingen, Wesley, 38
Sweet Sweetback's Baadasssss Song (1971), 312n25
Szalay, Michael, 24, 76, 79, 116

Tacitus, *Annals*, 225
Taft, William Howard, 36
Tennenhouse, Leonard, 291n6
terrorism, 11, 46, 47, 49–50
Theoharis, Athan, 290n4
Third World Press, 10, 122, 287n9
This Is Your F.B.I., 76
Thomas, Dylan, 137
Thompson, Jack, 133
Thurman, Wallace, 232
Thurmond, Strom, 152
Thurmond Institute, 152
Time, 101
Titus, Earl E., 55
Tolson, Clyde, 39, 71, 154, 271, 290–91n4
Toomer, Jean, 88, 222; *Cane*, 37
Torpey, John, 198
To Secure These Rights. See Civil Rights Commission
Total Information Awareness (TIA), 100
Total Literary Awareness (TLA), 100–107, 110, 124, 128, 145, 218, 260
Tougaloo College, 111
translation, 20, 51, 180, 195–97, 201, 289n21; and African diaspora, 192; and Baldwin, 196, 307n18; and black transnationalism, 196–97; and Bowen, 153; and CIA, 197; failure of intraracial, 192; and McKay, 65, 66, 196; and Wright, 196, 245
transnational Americanism, 185, 186
transnationality/transnationalism, 8, 43, 179, 180–81, 183, 185, 305nn3, 4, 306n12;

black, 67, 186–95, 196–97, 205, 213; and Gilroy, 189, 190; and Pan-African Congress, 188; in Smith, 254; state-sponsored, 21, 180, 211, 212; and translation, 196–97; in Wright, 245. *See also* Black Atlantic
trash covers, 81
Traubel, Horace, 153
treason, 85, 100, 236, 248; and civil rights movement, 109; and C. Himes, 129; and McKay, 66; and Pound, 31, 142; and *Radicalism and Sedition*, 225; and Reed, 31. *See also* revolution; sedition
Trotter, William Monroe, 3
True Detective Mysteries, 31
Truman, Harry, 94–95, 297n17; and CIA, 97; and Congress, 98; desegregation of military by, 95, 109; FBI secret file on, 98; Hoover's break with, 97–98; and Lowenthal, 99; and National Security Act, 132
Turner, Patricia A., 291n5
Twain, Mark, 304nn14, 15
Twelve Point Crime Program, 77

Umbra, 104
Umbra Workshop, 270
unionists, 106
United Nations Educational, Scientific and Cultural Organization (UNESCO), 106
Universal Negro Improvement Association (UNIA), 3, 199, 293n2
University of California, Berkeley, 143
University of California, Los Angeles, 111
Updike, John, 116
Up Tight! (1968), 312n25
Uptown Writers, 108
Urban League of Springfield, Illinois, 166
U.S. Coastal and Geodetic Survey (USCGS), 37, 44, 52
U.S. Marshals, 289n2
U.S. military, 95, 109
U.S. Post Office, 153
U.S. Saving Bonds program, 106
U.S.S. *Buford*, 49, 64, 94

Valentino, Rudolph, 38
Vanity Fair, 27
Van Peebles, Melvin, 224; *A Bear for the FBI*, 264
Van Vechten, Carl, 75
Vatulescu, Cristina, 7, 11–12, 14, 15, 65, 288n16, 309n4

Vereen, Ben, 312n25
veterans, 27–28
Vidal, Gore, 38, 39
Vif, 136, 137
V-J Day, 94
Voting Rights Act, 111

Wagner, Bryan, 154–55, 158, 159
Wald, Alan, 24
Waligora-Davis, Nicole A., *Sanctuary*, 194
Walker, Margaret, 11, 60, 296n14; *Jubilee*, 10
Wallace, David Foster, *Infinite Jest*, 263
Wallace, George, 97
Wallerstein, Immanuel, 185, 307nn13, 14; "The Construction of Peoplehood," 186
Walpole, Horace, 136
Walrond, Eric, 8, 232
Wangara, Harun Kofi, 118
Wanning, Andrews, "A Primer for Modern Poetry," 137
Ward, Theodore, 59, 93, 222, 287n13; *Big White Fog*, 86, 89
Warhol, Andy, 286n5
Warner, Michael, 291n6
War on Crime (comic strip), 76
Warren, Kenneth, 24, 225
Warren, Robert Penn, *Understanding Poetry*, 138
Washburn, Patrick S., 82
Washington, Booker T., 171; letter to Oswald Garrison Villard, 37; *A New Negro for a New Century*, 36
Washington, D.C.: black southern migrants in, 36; and race riots of 1919, 53–54; racism in, 39; and segregation, 35, 36, 37, 38, 40, 41, 54; Seventh Street, 37; sexual mores in, 39; and South, 36
Washington, George, 137
Washington, Mary Helen, 24
Washington Committee for Democratic Action, 89
Washington Post, 36, 46
Washington Times-Herald, 81
Watergate, 60, 124, 159
Watkins, G. Robert, 168
Watson, James, 308n20
Watts Writers Workshop, 260
Weathermen, 162
Weber, Max, 182, 183, 184, 198; *Economy and Society*, 70–71

Weiner, Tim, 289–90n2, 291n6, 297n17
Wells-Barnett, Ida B., 3
Werfel, Franz, *The Song of Bernadette*, 297n18
West, Dorothy, 232
Whalen, Terence, 274
White, Walter, 21, 169–70, 207, 222, 287n13;
    and Edwards, 193; file on, 59, 67, 86, 87;
    The Fire in the Flint, 87; and Hoover, 21,
    41, 87; and NAACP, 41, 87; and passport,
    20, 204; *The Rising Wind*, 87; *Rope and
    Faggot*, 87
white hate groups, 109, 110. *See also* Ku Klux
    Klan
Whitehead, Don, *The FBI Story*, 21, 48, 100,
    101, 154, 209, 303n10, 304n14
White Slave Traffic Act (Mann Act), 32–33, 54
white supremacy, 32, 33, 91, 95, 147, 158, 256.
    See also racism
Whitman, Walt, 134, 153, 294n5
Whittemore, Reed, 137
Wiener, Jon, 298n21
Wilde, Oscar, 153
Wilford, Hugh, 301n2
Wilkins, Roy, 2, 3
Williams, John A., 7, 23, 222, 224, 309n8,
    310n11; *The Man Who Cried I Am*, 6,
    93–94, 221, 233, 259, 260–63, 264, 267,
    298n19
Williams, Raymond, 147, 191
Williams, Robert F., 300n28
Williams, Sherley Anne, 11, 60, 122; *Dessa
    Rose*, 10
Williams, William Carlos, 137
Will West incident, 304n14
Wilson, Woodrow, 36–37, 69, 72, 198, 294n5
Winchell, Walter, 86–87, 100
Winks, Robin W., 134–35, 301–2n3, 302n6
wiretapping, 81, 116, 125, 219, 260, 300n29
Wollaeger, Mark, 294n6
women, 9, 49, 76
Wood, Raymond A., 270
Workers' Dreadnought, 231
Works Progress Administration (WPA), 76,
    88, 89
World Sunday School Convention, 37
World War I, 27–28, 47, 52, 70; and academic
    literary criticism, 142, 143; and Bowen,
    153; and passports, 198; and propaganda,
    72; and Schuyler, 92; state exceptional-
    ism following, 69–70; whitening of U.S.

citizenship after, 64
World War II, 59, 68, 94, 139, 179; America's
    entrance into, 80; and Angleton, 138; and
    black internationalism, 17, 124; Double-
    Cross system in, 62; end of, 94; European
    outbreak of, 80–81; and FBI files, 67; in-
    vestigations during, 86; journalism during,
    82–83, 85–86; treasonous speech during,
    129; and Yale and CIA, 134–35; and zoot
    suits, 84
Wright, Ellen, 311n18
Wright, Richard, 74, 112, 224, 263, 286n6,
    305n2, 308n22; and Africans, 177; as
    aware of FBI surveillance of, 308n1; and
    Baldwin, 220, 248, 252; and Baraka, 219,
    221; and Beauvoir, 311n21; and Bennett,
    89; and black transnationalism, 196; Bue-
    nos Aires voyage of, 215; and concerns of
    about return from abroad, 243; and Con-
    gress for Cultural Freedom, 249, 311n20;
    and Custodial Detention, 93, 177–78,
    234; death of, 178, 198, 262; and Ellison,
    220, 237, 243, 244, 250; FBI as suspected
    of assassinating, 219; FBI file on, 7, 8, 59,
    80, 86, 144–45, 196, 203; FBI questioning
    of, 222; as film noir detective, 178; flight
    to France, 215; and Gilroy, 190–91; and
    Harrington, 177; and C. Himes, 176, 246,
    255–58; and Hughes, 237; and legats, 198;
    and Paris, 23, 175, 176–79, 190–91, 243,
    245, 247, 248–49, 250–51; passport of, 21,
    203, 204; persecution of, 219; in Smith,
    251–52; and social realism vs. modern-
    ism, 220; and Soviet Union, 203; and
    State Department, 177; and as suspected
    of spying, 177; and J. Williams, 93–94,
    259, 262; WORKS: *Black Boy*, 170, 255,
    311n21; "Blueprint for Negro Writing,"
    53; "The FB Eye Blues," 5, 6, 216–17, 220,
    244, 267, 308n1, 308–9n2, 309n3; "How
    Bigger Was Born," 170; "I Choose Exile,"
    179, 245–46; *Island of Hallucination*, 220,
    244–51, 252, 253, 254, 255, 256, 257, 258,
    311nn18, 19; "I Tried to Be a Commu-
    nist," 144, 177, 237, 255; *The Long Dream*,
    244, 246; *Native Son*, 79, 80, 170, 179, 216,
    217, 219, 220, 243, 244, 256; *The Outsider*,
    243–44; *Savage Holiday*, 244; *Twelve Mil-
    lion Black Voices*, 79, 215; *Die Weltwoche*
    interview with, 196

Yale University, 19, 131, 134–36, 137, 138, 140, 301–2n3, 302n4
Year of Intelligence, 125, 141
Yellin, Eric S., 36
Yeni Gazette, 196
Yette, Samuel F., *The Choice*, 297n17

Young, Andrew, 2
Young, John K., 107
Young, P. B., Sr., 82–83, 85–86

Zoot Suit Riots, 85
zoot suits, 84